Personal Financial Planning

Kwok Ho
Chris Robinson
York University

Captus Press

PERSONAL FINANCIAL PLANNING, SECOND EDITION

Captus Press Inc.
York University Campus, 4700 Keele Street,
North York, Ontario M3J 1P3 Canada
Telephone: (416) 736–5537   Fax: (416) 736–5793
Email: info@captus.com   Internet: http://www.captus.com

Canadian Cataloguing in Publication Data

Ho, Kwok, 1948–
    Personal financial planning

2nd ed.
Includes index.
ISBN 1–896691–18–8

1. Finance, Personal – Canada.   I. Robinson,
Chris, 1950–   .   II. Title.

HG179.5.H6 1997   332.024'00971   C96–932426–X

Note to Readers
Readers wishing further information on data provided through the
co-operation of Statistics Canada may obtain copies of related publications by mail from: Publications Sales, Statistics Canada,
Ottawa, Ontario, K1A 0T6, by calling (613) 951–7277 or toll free
800–267–6677. Readers may also facsimile their orders by dialing
(613) 951–1584.

Super Rep™ is a trademark of PlanPlus Inc. All other brand and
product names are trademarks or registered trademarks of their re-
spective companies.

0 9 8 7 6 5 4 3 2
Printed in Canada

To my wife, Frances Chung
— Kwok Ho

To my parents, Fred and Fran Robinson
— Chris Robinson

Table of Contents

About the authors

Preface

We wrote this book to provide a thorough coverage of personal finance grounded in finance theory. No such work is widely available for use in universities and colleges, but financial institutions need people who have proper training to work with their clientele. In addition, students need to learn how to manage their own finances in an orderly way.

We have taught part-time and full-time undergraduate students at York University using some of the material in this textbook, including many of the problems. They find it both personally relevant, and useful in their work. We hope you will enjoy it too.

In the second edition we have added two new chapters. Chapter 18 teaches how to integrate all the different pieces of a problem into a comprehensive plan. Chapter 19, co-authored with Moshe Arye Milevsky of York University, contains the first professional version of probabilistic financial planning, based on several years of academic research.

Farshad Adlgostar helped us create problems and solutions. Syed Ahmed, Bob Barney, John Benson, Shawn Brayman, Trevor Chamberlain, John Churchill, Coleen Clark, Esther Deutsch, Ken Hopper, Franck Lerman, Simeon Ling, Jane Londerville, Maureen MacDonald, Joanne Magee, Bernice Miedzinski, Moshe Arye Milevsky, Fred and Fran Robinson and David West provided helpful comments on various sections. Nora Campbell typed and edited about half of the manuscript. We would like to acknowledge also the support and patience of the students on whom we have practised the ideas contained in this book. Ron Edwards' editing provided many lessons in how to write correctly and clearly.

Chris Robinson previously wrote a private textbook in personal finance for the Institute of Canadian Bankers, in 1986–87. For the knowledge and skills that he gained from that experience, he thanks: Gilles Bernier of Laval University, his co-author; Rosaire Couturier, Director of the Institute of Canadian Bankers; and Jerome Camus, Pierre Goulet and Mark Webb, who worked for the Institute at the time.

Last, but not least, we are grateful to the staff at Captus Press who endured the various birthing pains of this book without reproach — Randy Hoffman, Wai Wo Lai, Drew Ellis and Marva Palmer.

Kwok Ho
Chris Robinson
Toronto, Ontario
December 1996

chapter 1

Introduction

OBJECTIVES OF THE BOOK

Personal finance has exploded into popular consciousness in the last decade. Every bookstore carries a wide variety of publications, from those dealing with very simple budgeting and planning to those covering complex income taxation issues that were once found only on the bookshelves of accountants and lawyers. Television programmes on personal finance and consumer issues draw large ratings, and there is even one aimed specifically at teenagers and their financial concerns. Local radio stations feature financial advisers with daily tips or hotline phone-in programmes. Financial institutions offer solutions to your financial planning problems, often at the touch of a computer button. Financial planning has become a rapidly-expanding (and little-regulated) new 'profession.'

What can we offer with this book that hasn't been written or said already? The advice that you receive from these popular sources is often valuable and very timely. For example, if you want to know more about Registered Retirement Savings Plans, you can be sure that the rules, issues and investment choices will be discussed endlessly in every newspaper in the two months before the annual February deposit deadline. The same holds true for Canada Savings Bonds and the November 1 purchase deadline. And so on.

The weakness of this popular advice is that it is fragmented and relates to the specific financial product or issue in isolation. Our book builds upon a coherent and consistent framework of basic finance principles to allow you to develop a complete plan or response to a personal financial situation. It requires more work and attention than does the popular 'Make Your Money Grow,' or, 'How to be a Millionaire and Retire Early,' but the foundation it provides leads to sound planning.

We cannot make you rich or secure with this book. We cannot even ensure that you don't starve. Only you can do these things. What we can do is give you the means to manage whatever money you have and can save in a rational manner, so that you have the best chance possible to realize your goals in life. All of this financial planning occurs within the context of a family unit, though the unit can be a single person or parents with four dependent children.

At the same time, you can use this foundation to help others manage their personal finances. Financial institutions are recognizing that they must offer much more service to their individual or retail customers, and personal financial planning is one way to do it. If you are a student interested in working for a bank, trust company, insurance company, independent financial planning company or investment dealer, personal financial planning is a valuable part of your education.

We introduce each chapter with the specific learning objectives for the material to be covered. These learning objectives are the pieces building towards the two objectives of the book:

1. Learn to manage your own family's personal finances using sound principles to help you achieve your goals in life; and,
2. Learn the foundations of personal financial planning as the first step in providing financial counselling to others.

In the rest of this chapter we present a simple model of the *financial planning process*. We describe the contents of the book by showing how the different elements of financial planning fit into this simple model. We then go beyond the book with advice on how to keep up to date in financial planning, and where to go for further help in designing and implementing your plan.

A SIMPLE MODEL OF FINANCIAL PLANNING

Money won't make you happy, as many poets and singers have told us, but its absence can lead to a lot of unhappiness. Personally, we don't believe that accumulating great wealth is a sure route to a happy life. However, human society uses money as a medium of exchange and so we have to learn to manage it if we are to survive. The goals that we strive for using personal financial management are therefore financial ones, though they are simply means towards non-financial ends, like having enough to eat, a place to live, entertainment etc.

Think of the financial planning process as a series of decisions on how much money you need at some future time in order to meet your goals, and how you will get that money. Goals must be in monetary terms, and have some date attached to them, in order to plan for them. To reach the goal, you have two sources of money. You have some money now, which earns more money as you invest it over time. You earn money by working and you consume some of that money as well, with the net amount being your savings. The saved money goes into the investment pot with the previous savings and earns investment income too. If you are to meet your goals, you must arrange your affairs so that the following equation is true:

Financial goal (at time n)

= Existing savings + investment income for n years on the existing savings

  + (Earnings − consumption each year)

  + investment income on the annual savings, n.[1]

---

[1] We model this process more formally in Chapter 3.

Reprinted with permission — The Toronto Star Syndicate. © 1994 GREG HOWARD distributed by King Features Syndicate.

THE CONTENTS OF THE BOOK

Every chapter in the book relates to some part of this equation. Chapters 2–6 present the fundamental tools or mechanics of personal financial management. The student must understand these techniques thoroughly and be able to apply the calculations throughout the rest of the book. Chapters 7–15 contain the elements that we combine to form the financial plan. Chapters 16–17 discuss retirement planning, which incorporates all the fundamentals and elements, directed towards the specific goal of a comfortable retirement. Chapter 18 draws it all together to show you how to prepare a comprehensive plan. Chapter 19 introduces a new theoretical model in the personal finance field — probabilistic financial planning.

Chapter 2, **Time Value of Money**, covers the basic arithmetic of finance that allows us to compare amounts of money received or paid at different times.

Chapter 3, **Setting Goals**, discusses how to set realistic financial goals and how to adjust your goal when it isn't realistic.

Chapter 4, **Budgeting**, shows you how to determine your present financial position and plan for future saving. The techniques are simple financial accounting applied to personal, instead of corporate, affairs.

Chapter 5, **Family Life Cycle and Financial Intermediation**, puts personal finance into its context in the entire economic system. We explain how different aspects of personal finance are more important at different stages in the family life cycle. The system of financial intermediation and institutions that we use to implement our plans has evolved in our economy to meet those needs.

Chapters 6 and 7, **Personal Income Tax**, and **Income Tax Planning**, provide a basic introduction to this extremely complex topic, which plays a major role in determining both the rate of return on your investments and the amount of money you save. Chapter 6 explains the basic structure of the personal tax system, focusing on the personal income tax return. Chapter 7 shows how these rules affect financial decisions, and how you must use your knowledge to minimize your taxes. Most people will find that these two chapters explain what they need to know for most situations they will encounter. What we have left out, however, is a huge field, and in some cases, the effect can be very large.

Chapter 8, **Risk Management**, is the theoretical basis for insurance, but you will see in later chapters that there are other ways to control risk as well.

Chapters 9 and 10, **Life, Health and Disability Insurance**, and **Property, Casualty and Liability Insurance**, are the principal means of financing risks that you cannot control by other means. We go into some detail on how to calculate your requirements, and the characteristics of insurance policies that you need to know to choose the right ones for your specific risk management needs.

Most families will encounter periods early in the life cycle when they need to borrow money. As well, most people use credit or charge cards as a matter of convenience. Chapter 11, **Debt and Credit Management**, provides advice on these subjects.

In the long run, we all hope that we will have positive savings, and we then have to decide how to invest them, which is the subject of Chapters 12–15. Chapter 12, **Your Personal Residence**, discusses the problem of whether to rent or buy, and develops a framework for deciding which house to buy and how to go about it. Chapter 13, **Investment Management Principles**, discusses in intuitive terms a topic that has generated a huge and very technical research literature in finance. Your investment decisions will determine how high your rate of return is and how risky. The factors that bear upon this decision require some study.

Theory is a necessary foundation for investment management, but you must invest your money in the real world. Chapters 14 and 15, **Investment Vehicles**, and **Mutual Funds**, describe the different choices available to you and what sort of values and variations in rates of return you might expect from each. Financial market institutions are constantly inventing new instruments; so some of the basic characteristics described in Chapters 13 and 14 are important in order to understand how to assess innovations.

Chapter 16, **Retirement Planning**, takes us back to square one as we try to determine how much we need to live in retirement and how much our current savings pattern will provide. Thus, our goal of wealth available for retirement must equal the *present value* of all the consumption during retirement. Once we determine the desired standard of living and what it entails in wealth at retirement, we can plan how we will achieve the required savings, and how we will invest our savings.

Chapter 17, **Maturation of the Retirement Plan**, builds a risk management framework for the decision on how to organize the retirement savings and their withdrawal from the preretirement investment instruments. We provide an introduction to estate planning.

Chapter 18, **Comprehensive Planning**, shows how to integrate all the previous chapters in a complete financial plan for a family. Most of the chapter is devoted to solving a comprehensive case study.

Chapter 19, **Probabilistic Financial Planning**, is unique in the personal finance literature. In this chapter we explain how to use models we have developed that do not assume certain, fixed rates of return and certain dates of death. Instead, we treat the rate of return as a stochastic or probabilistic variable with mean and standard deviation drawn from historic experience in capital markets. The date of death is distributed according to the standard Canadian mortality tables. We use these models to plan under uncertainty and to estimate the probability of success of our plans.

GOING BEYOND THIS BOOK

Keeping Up to Date

Warning! By the time you finish reading this book, some of the details may be obsolete! The environment of personal finance changes rapidly, and some of the structural factors like tax rules and financial instruments may have changed making some of what we say incorrect or irrelevant. That is why we concentrate on fundamental finance principles, since they do not change quickly and provide a long-term basis for financial planning.

Even though the principles stay the same, the environment in which you make your decisions is changing. The level of interest rates and inflation, trends in consumer spending and expectations about future incomes, all affect personal financial planning. Only a few years before we wrote this book, protection against inflation was a major concern. The developed western economies enjoyed a long period of booming incomes and low inflation (1–3%) from about 1953 through the mid-1960s. Inflation started rising in 1968, and throughout the 1970s and '80s it was the biggest single worry for financial planners, sometimes hitting double digits.

In 1993–96 we found ourselves back in a world of 1–2% inflation. Now, however, incomes are falling, unemployment is widespread and seemingly permanent for a growing number of people. Consumer spending is declining, especially on consumer durables — refrigerators, cars, furniture — the engine of the post-War boom economy. People who thought they had secure and rising incomes for life — civil servants, teachers, doctors, auto workers, municipal workers, pulpwood cutters — have found their incomes frozen or their jobs eliminated altogether. In this scary world, security has taken on new importance, and planning for it is much different than it was in a world where inflation was higher, but everyone believed that they could outrun it.

Your financial plan requires constant attention in this turbulent and risky environment. Even if your personal circumstances don't seem to have changed, you are at greater financial risk than at any time since the depression of the 1930s. The principles and analytical techniques in this book should remain useful, but what you put into the analysis keeps changing.

The first source is a familiar one. The major daily newspapers record the important economic events and provide valuable statistics in their business pages. You can track returns on your investments and changes in mortgage rates daily if you need to. If unemployment in your occupation is high, you know to make doubly sure of your safety nets just in case you, too, lose your job.

The dailies usually feature some personal finance articles in the business sections. For this more directed material, we think that the specialist business newspapers are the best source:

The Globe and Mail, Report on Business section. The daily newspaper (Monday to Saturday) contains specific articles on issues like income tax, investments and insurance. A regular question and answer column provides sophisticated advice on a wide variety of problems. The monthly *ROB Magazine* has longer articles and sometimes case studies of real families.

The Financial Post. The daily newspaper (Tuesday to Saturday) and the monthly magazine are devoted to business, and contain many personal finance articles, cases and columns similar to the Globe's. The income tax coverage is particularly good.

There are many other sources of financial planning advice. Investment dealers, mutual funds, banks, trust companies, insurers, credit unions and caisses populaires are all in the financial intermediation business. One way for them to get your business is to publish newsletters and brochures providing personal finance tips. These publications vary widely in quality, since their primary purpose is to get you to buy the particular institution's offerings. The best of them are quite good, however, because these institutions have the resources to hire the best professional advisers, and the incentive to give good advice to maintain their reputation. Most of these publications are free, but you have to search a bit to find them. Their industry associations publish general interest personal finance tracts as well.

Professional accountants do a lot of personal finance work, especially on income tax. The largest public practice firms of chartered accountants (CA) and certified general accountants (CGA) publish newsletters and specific issue pamphlets that are free upon request. If you want to know how a provincial or federal budget may affect you, their postbudget analyses are useful. *CA Magazine* (monthly) has a personal finance column. The provincial and federal associations of the CAs, CGAs and the certified management accountants (CMA) also have some publications, mostly dealing with income taxes.

Professional and occupational associations provide useful financial information for their members through their regular magazines and special bulletins. This information can be particularly valuable since it will reflect issues specific to a given occupation. Taxes and insurance are the topics most often seen in these sources. We have seen very good material for teachers, university professors and medical professionals, for example.

We do not recommend relying on television or radio for anything but the most general reminders about personal finance. The nature of the broadcast media does not lend itself to the careful analysis necessary for important financial decisions.

Getting Expert Help

Choosing an Adviser
Before we get into details, let us express our own preference for the type of advisers you should seek. Aside from the obvious requirement for technical competence, we look for honesty and a commitment to serve our personal finance needs as thoroughly as possible. The institution or adviser that wants to help us first, before selling us the most profitable product or service, is the one we want. We trust those who do not make extravagant claims about tax savings waiting to be seized or huge profits from _____ (fill in the latest advertised scam). If we are looking to establish a long-run relationship, say banking or an insurance policy, we want someone who has our long-run interests in mind, too.

Implementing the Plan
No matter how good this book is and how skilled you become at personal financial planning, you will need expert help to implement many aspects of your plan. If you want to invest in the stock market, you need a registered representative licensed to execute trades on your behalf. You need banks and insurance companies and their employees for the services they provide. You may be able to write a simple will and buy a house without a lawyer,[2] but you need their help with more complex transactions.

---

[2] Your local library or business book store has detailed guides on how to write a will, transfer property and write and execute other basic contracts. We do not advise you either to choose or to avoid this way of saving legal fees, but we ourselves pay lawyers to do this kind of work, and stick to what we know best.

The key to dealing with these people effectively and enlisting their best services on your behalf is to know what you need. You must have a financial plan before you start buying insurance, investing in penny mines, *etc*. Use this book as a reference in specific areas. For example, you should determine whether you really need life insurance, how much you need and what special characteristics should be attached to the policy *before* you visit an insurance agent. Chapter 9 shows you how to do this. Then, it is an easy matter for the agent to provide you with one or more policies meeting your requirements. The agent gets a good commission without much work, and you get what you need. If you wander into his office with only a vague idea of what you need, the easiest course of action for the agent to follow is to sell you the policy paying the largest agent's commission. Even the most experienced and honest agent may have a hard time selling you the right insurance if you don't have a financial plan.

Financial Planners

We classify them into four categories based on the way in which they are paid. 'He who pays the piper calls the tune' is the old saying, and the quality of the financial plan they play for you is affected by who pays them. You should ask any financial planner how she is remunerated before you commit yourself. Disclosure requirements vary by jurisdiction.

Salaried employees of institutions such as banks or trust companies, are sometimes designated as financial planners and provide advice to their customers free of charge, or for a nominal fee. The advice often consists of a computer printout from a generalized computer package, based upon inputs from the customer. The only reason for this service is to sell you the particular products and services of the institution; so the advice you get is very limited in value. Sometimes, these institutions have professionally-trained advisers working in private banking units where their job is to smooth the lives of the wealthiest customers. Sometimes the goodwill of these customers is worth so much to the bank that something approaching expert independent advice is rendered, but this service is not offered to everyone.

Commission planners receive their compensation in the form of fees and commissions from the sellers of services and products that they recommend. They may be employed directly by the institution (but paid by commission, not salary), act as exclusive or general agents or simply search all opportunities in the market without allegiance to any institutions. These planners may have a little more independence, but the incentive is to steer you into the products that pay the best commissions. The commission dollars come from someone, and that someone is you. For example, whole life insurance provides the best commissions, but costs more than individual or group term insurance.

Fee-based planners receive their compensation partly in the form of a fee, usually hourly, that you pay them, and partly from commissions from the institutions. These planners are almost always independent of specific institutions, but still have incentives to choose the highest commissions. The conflict of interest is reduced, but not eliminated.

Fee-only or *fee-for-service planners* charge the client directly on an hourly basis for the time spent doing the planning. These planners earn all their income from their clients and take no commissions. The hourly fee ranges from $50 to $250.

How do you decide which one you need? In our opinion, if you want proper financial counselling and you have enough assets and difficult issues to justify the cost, the fee-only planner is the best bet. The cost of poor advice given to generate commissions or justify an employee's salary is less obvious than the independent planner's service fees, but you could lose a great deal more. If your needs are simple and don't justify the hourly fees, then the other planners will probably do a good enough job. Just as with implementation of the plan, your best bet is always to do as much of the planning yourself as you can. The cost of this book and the time spent to understand it is far less than the loss you could suffer from underinsurance or an ill-advised investment.

How do you know who is qualified to be a planner? There are few regulations governing financial planners in Canada[3] and almost anyone can hang out a shingle. Financial planners are bound by the same statutes and common law that apply to anyone selling services. They must perform their work with due care, and they cannot misrepresent their work or their qualifications. We cannot offer any sure-fire guide as to which planners will do the best work, though. There are two national groups that are independent of the financial institutions:

The *Canadian Association of Financial Planners* (CAFP) requires its applicants be sponsored by three members and submit a sample financial plan for consideration by a committee. An applicant who passes this hurdle must write a six-hour comprehensive examination and then practise as an associate for a year before being granted the *Registered Financial Planner* (RFP) designation. The Association's members are governed by a code of ethics and a set of rules and regulations to enforce the code. The CAFP does not offer courses.

The *Canadian Institute of Financial Planning* offers six correspondence courses leading to the designation of *Chartered Financial Planner*. In the future, it will offer a programme that leads to the designation Certified Financial Planner (CFP).

The **Canadian Securities Institute** (CSI) offers a variety of investments courses and some more general courses related to personal finance. Its primary focus is education of employees of securities dealers and portfolio managers. The **Life Underwriters Association of Canada** (LUAC) traditionally concentrated on education in the life, health and disability insurance field but its personal finance programme now leads to the CFP designation. The **Institute of Canadian Bankers** (ICB) offers programmes in personal finance both directly and through community colleges.

Many other professionals have also entered this field to some extent. The most notable ones are professional accountants. Although the course of study and codes of ethics of the CA, CGA and CMA associations are not intended to deal with personal finance, the substantial expertise these professionals acquire in income tax and budgeting, and in analysis of financial problems generally, has allowed them to enter the field. Some of them practise solely in the personal finance field, and others make it an important part of their work. These are usually sole practitioners. Some of the large firms have established separate groups that deal with personal financial planning (often as part of their income tax departments). Accountants are most qualified to deal with difficult tax

---

[3] Financial planners fall under provincial jurisdiction, and so the rules vary.

issues. Although they are quite capable of becoming expert in other areas, the formal course of study does not lead them into areas like insurance and investment theory in any depth. Professional accountants charge fees at the upper end of the scale. One of the benefits of dealing with them is that their rigorous courses of study and high qualification standards provide some assurance of good-quality work. Their long-established existence within the framework of self-regulating associations with well-developed codes of ethics reduces the probability of negligence and professional misconduct.

Lawyers are frequently involved in the execution of specific parts of financial plans, like estate planning and income taxation. Few lawyers have the financial training to suit them to giving broad-based financial counselling. Other finance professionals that provide financial planning services include insurance agents, investment dealers, mutual fund salespersons, credit union advisers and trust officers.

The **Financial Planners Standards Council of Canada** (FPSCC) is a new umbrella group that has a mandate to provide a uniform set of educational and practice standards for personal financial planning in Canada. It was established in November of 1995, and has eight member organizations: LUAC, CSI, CIFP, CAFP, Canadian Institute of Chartered Accountants, Society of Management Accountants of Canada, Certified General Accountants Association of Canada and the Credit Union Institute of Canada. The FPSCC now has the power to approve educational programmes leading to the designation of Certified Financial Planner (CFP). So far, it has approved programmes offered by LUAC, CSI and CIFP. The only significant organization in the financial planning field that has not joined the FPSCC is the ICB. Only not-for-profit organizations may belong, but these nine organizations represent the majority of people working in personal financial planning and education.

The Council has developed a code of ethics for financial planners that includes both principles and specific rules to make the principles operational. The regulatory situation does not give the Council any formal power, but with the voluntary support of so many of the players, it may well bring about a more organized and stable playing field in financial planning, which will benefit consumers.

COMPUTER SOFTWARE

There are many computer software packages in personal finance, including Super Rep, Asset Architect, Quicken and Microsoft Money. Most personal finance software programs run on DOS or Windows and are user-friendly. They can handle many of the elements of personal finance that we discuss in this book. For example, you can use them to solve problems in the time value of money, mortgages, personal financial statements, cash budgets, tax return preparation, investment record-keeping and retirement planning.

They can be very useful tools in the hands of a user who understands the principles of personal finance. However, they are nothing more than tools and cannot replace a sound understanding of the theory and concepts of personal finance. As the saying goes, "garbage in, garbage out." Inappropriate or uniformed use of these packages can generate only useless or even misleading financial plans. You must learn personal finance, and how computers can help, before you use them.

We have coded a number of the problems and sections with a diskette, as appears in the margin to the left of this paragraph. Students can solve these problems with the aid of Super Rep for Students, an abridged version of the Super Rep package used by professional planners. An appendix in Chapter 2 shows how to use Super Rep to solve some problems that are also demonstrated using a calculator. If you have not purchased this software with the book, you may buy it directly from Captus Press or your bookstore.

SUMMARY

The objective of this book is to teach you how to plan your own or other families' personal finances using sound principles of finance. Personal financial planning is a series of decisions on how to accumulate and protect the money you need to meet specified future goals. The topics you must learn to do this planning include: time value of money, budgeting, goal-setting, risk management, income taxation, insurance, debt management, investment principles and practice, and retirement planning. We also suggest sources for updating your knowledge, and how you can get further help from experts if this book is not enough for your needs.

KEY TERMINOLOGY

computer software / getting help / how to choose an adviser / keeping up to date / personal financial planning process / professional planners / different types / know what you need

DISCUSSION QUESTIONS

1. Explain the significance of the entries under **Key Terminology**.
2. What are the objectives of studying personal financial management? Why study principles, when all you really need to know is how to do it?
3. Name and describe briefly the elements of a financial plan. You should refer to the section on the contents of the book.
4. How would you go about selecting a personal financial adviser? The chapter offers some advice, but you should be able to say more.
5. Financial planners are largely unregulated. If they were to be regulated, it would be a provincial matter. Find out what regulations, if any, govern financial planners in your province. The best starting point in your search is probably the government ministry handling consumer affairs.
6. Should financial planners be:
    (a) unregulated;
    (b) regulated by a government department, using statutory regulations; or
    (c) required to form a self-regulating association whose power derives from a law, but which decides by vote of its members what ethical conduct and standards of performance must be followed?
7. Will this book (or any popular book on personal finance or personal investments) provide you with the clue to become rich and secure?

chapter 2

Time Value of Money

LEARNING OBJECTIVES

This chapter teaches the most important single technique in personal financial planning — how to compare monetary amounts that you pay or receive at different times. This technique is called the **time value of money** or **interest rate mathematics**. It is the arithmetic of personal financial management, and you must become as comfortable with it as you are with basic arithmetic.

Underlying the time value of money is the concept of a rate of return. We use the rate of return to compare different investments and loans, and so we need to understand the assumptions underlying the calculations. The advertisements you see in newspapers and flyers claiming high rates of return or low interest rate charges are often misleading if you don't realize the different ways in which they can be calculated. Understanding rate of return is an essential preparation for debt and credit management and investment management.

Once you have mastered the mechanics of time value, we continue the topic of rates of return with **holding period returns** and multiple period rates of return. We discuss the problem of the **reinvestment assumption** that is inherent in any multi-period rate of return. We then extend our discussion to the sources of differences in rates of return: **risk**, **inflation** and **income taxes**.

In later chapters we show you how to apply the techniques in many different problems, including bond valuation, residential mortgages and consumer loans. The traditional method uses tables of values, but we operate using a financial calculator. Such calculators are now cheaply available and everyone who wants to solve personal finance problems should own one. Separate sections will show step-by-step solutions to some problems using one specific calculator: the Texas Instruments BA-35.

In the Appendix to this chapter, we include step-by-step solutions to the same problems, but using Super Rep for Students instead. You will need to learn how to use Super Rep for Students before you attempt to replicate the answers you got with a calculator. Henceforth, we will refer to this software as Super Rep for convenience, but you should remember that the abridged student version does not include all of the regular package's capabilities.

Our learning objectives are:

1.   To master completely the mechanics of the time value of money;
2.   To understand the concept of rate of return over one and many periods, and the different factors affecting the rate of return.

RATE OF RETURN — Single Period

Suppose you can invest in a **discount bond** for $909.09 today. In one year's time you will receive $1,000. A discount bond is an investment that pays no interest during its life; therefore, the interest you receive on it is part of the final payment. What rate of return do you earn on this bond?

First, we note that the amount you earn is $1,000 − $909.09 = $90.91. You invest $909.09 to get $90.91; so your rate of return is $90.91 ÷ $909.09 = .1000 or 10.00%. In general, if we call the rate of return k, and the cash flows at the beginning and end of the year CF_0 and CF_1, then:

$$k = \frac{CF_1 - CF_0}{CF_0}$$

e.g. $$k = \frac{1,000 - 909.09}{909.09} = .1$$

The equation only holds for a single period with cash flows at the beginning and end of the period.

What Is a Discount Rate?

Suppose we state the previous problem a little differently. You want to invest money in a bond for one year, and you want to earn a 10% rate of return on your investment. If you have $909.09 to invest today, how much do you expect to receive at the end of one year? We already know the answer will be $1,000. That is, you earn 10% on the money you invest, and you also get the amount invested back: 1.1 × $909.09 = $1,000 (after rounding).

Finally, state the previous problem this way: You have some money to invest today for one year, and interest rates for one year are 10%. How much do you have to invest if you want to have $1,000 in one year? We know that the answer is $909.09. We would get it by the same equation rearranged:

$$\$1,000 \div 1.1 = \$909.09$$

All this is very simple arithmetic, but it has several important meanings. We call the 10% interest rate the **discount rate**. The discount rate is the interest rate or rate of return that we use to equate amounts of money paid or received in different periods. We often say that the $909.09 is the value of $1,000 **discounted** at 10% for one year. The discount rate is a rate of return. The time value of money techniques are simply the arithmetic with which we convert money between periods, or calculate what rate of return is implied by a given set of cash flows. Why do we care what the value of money is in different time periods?

Opportunity Cost   What do you want to do with your money today? What would you do with it tomorrow? If you spend the $909.09 on clothes today, you have the clothes and can start wearing them now. What do you give up by spending the money now? The answer is that you give up $1,000 in one year's time. The $1,000 you give up is the **opportunity cost** of your decision. We also say that the opportunity cost of money is 10%, because that is what you can earn if you don't spend the money today. Only you can decide whether you want to spend $909.09 today or have $1,000 to spend in one year. The discount rate simply tells you in monetary value the amount that you are giving up — the opportunity foregone — in order to consume now.

Another way to look at it is to call the discount rate the rate that makes us indifferent between present and future amounts (in any pattern). That is, if we use the appropriate discount rate to calculate the present value of a future amount, we don't care whether we receive the present value now or the future value at the later date.

Who decides this discount rate? How do we know what discount rate to use?

Best Alternative Available   When we decide where to invest our money, we naturally want to get as high a return as possible. In order to compare alternative investments, we must keep everything else equal. That means that risk, income taxes and the time length of the investment must be identical. We will discuss the implications of these issues later in the chapter and in other chapters, since they are very important. For now, let us accept that we are choosing between otherwise identical investments.

Suppose we observe a bank, a trust company and a credit union, each offering us the chance to invest our money in a guaranteed investment certificate (GIC) for one year. Each one pays $1,000. To get the $1,000, we must invest $909.09 at the bank, $907 at the trust company and $905 at the credit union. We needn't think very hard to realize that the credit union is offering the best rate, since we invest the lowest amount to realize $1,000. We can convert these offers to rates of return as we did previously. The bank is offering 10%, the trust company is offering 10.25% and the credit union 10.5%. Thus, the rate of return, or discount rate, gives us a convenient way to compare the three choices, even if the amounts to invest happened to be different.

The best alternative available provides the discount rate, then. In the previous example, the discount rate is 10.5%, because that is the highest rate we can get. We would discount all other similar investment opportunities at that rate to see if they are as good.

The best rate isn't so easily determined in practice because of different risks involved in different investments. Nonetheless, we can try to use it as a benchmark. Think of the previous example again. Suppose you also owed $900 on your credit card. If you put the money into a GIC you would have to pay interest on the credit card balance at 19.56% p.a. Clearly, the discount rate for any financial decision up to $900 should be 19.56%, since you can save that amount by paying off the credit card balance, and it is higher than the interest you can earn. Once you have paid off the balance, and any other debts, then you could use the credit union's 10.5% as the best alternative rate.

Let us now turn to the mechanics of time value of money problems.

MECHANICS OF TIME VALUE

Future and Present Value — Single Period

You deposit $100 in a caisse populaire for one year at an annual rate of interest of 4%. How much money do you have at the end of the year?

You get back the $100, which is also called the **principal**, plus 4% of $100, or $4 in **interest**. Your total balance is thus $104. We call this amount the **future value** (FV) of $100 at 4% for one year.

We reverse the problem and ask how much the future value of $104 is worth today at a discount rate of 4%. We call the answer of $100 the **present value** (PV) of $104 at 4% for one year. That is, $104 ÷ 1.04 = $100.

We can express these two concepts in two equations, where k is the discount rate:

Future Value: $$FV = PV\,(1 + k)$$

Present Value: $$PV = \frac{FV}{(1 + k)}$$

e.g. $$FV = \$100\,(1 + .04) = \$104$$

$$PV = \frac{\$104}{(1 + .04)} = \$100$$

In fact, there is only one equation, rearranged for whatever we want to solve. We can also solve for the discount rate if we know the PV and the FV. Note an important mathematical fact here. Most interest rate mathematics deals with (1 + discount rate). When we invest money, the money we get back is both principal and interest. If we express discount rates as (1 + discount rate), we preserve this relationship.

Now we will look at present and future values for more than one period.

Future and Present Value — Multiperiod

Compound Interest   You deposit $100 in a bank account for five years at a rate of 5% p.a., compounded annually. What does it mean to compound? At the end of the first year you have $105 in the account. If you leave the entire amount in the account, you earn $5.25 in interest in the second year. You earn $5 on the original principal, and $0.25 on the first year's interest. Each year the interest earned increases because of interest on interest. We call this method of calculation **compound interest**.[1] Every year's ending balance is (1 + discount rate) times the previous year's balance. Thus, we can extend our previous equation to get the future value of an amount invested for any period of time we want. The actual length of the period is whatever we want it to be. Years and months are common periods in financial contracts, but any length of time could be specified as the compounding period.

---

[1] The alternative method is called simple interest. Interest is paid only on the original balance every period, with no interest paid on any interest left with the borrower. Modern financial contracts assume compound interest.

Future Value   The equation for the future value of an amount, compounded each period for t periods is:

$$FV = PV (1 + k)^t$$

Returning to the problem at the start of the section, what will the balance in the account be at the end of five years?

$$FV = \$100 \times (1.05)^5 = \underline{\$127.63}$$

Compounding means that every period, in this case every year, we multiply the principal plus interest of the previous period (i.e. the ending balance) by (1 + discount rate) to get the next ending balance. This is the same as multiplying (1 + discount rate) together five times and then multiplying by the original principal, which is what the previous equation does. We can verify the answer by doing it the long way.

FV after				
	one period	$100.00 × 1.05	=	$105.00
	two periods	105.00 × 1.05	=	110.25
	three	110.25 × 1.05	=	115.76
	four	115.76 × 1.05	=	121.55
	five	121.55 × 1.05	=	127.63

Present Value   The present value of a multiperiod stream is calculated by rearranging the equation for future value, just as we did in the single period case.

$$PV = \frac{FV}{(1 + k)^t}$$

Problem: Your great aunt Aida promises to give you $10,000 when you turn 21. You are 16 now and a five-year GIC pays 6% p.a. How much should Aida give you today to be worth as much as the future amount?

Answer: $$PV = \frac{\$10,000}{(1.06)^5} = \underline{\$7,472.58}$$

These two equations for future and present value are perfectly general and with them we can equate any pattern of cash flows in present and future time to any other. The $(1 + k)^n$ part of the future value equation is called the **future value interest factor** (FVIF). Table A2 in Appendix A shows the FVIFs for $1 for a range of interest rates and numbers of periods. The $1/(1 + k)^n$ part of the present value equation is called the **present value interest factor** (PVIF). Table A1 shows the PVIFs for $1 for a range of interest rates and numbers of periods. You can use the tables to find the PV or FV of any single amount for any interest rate and number of periods listed by multiplying the amount by the factor.

We have one shortcut method that will help us reduce the work whenever we have a series of equal payments.

Annuities

An **annuity** is any payment that is the same amount for many consecutive periods. Many pensions are paid as annuities. The rent for an apartment is an annuity until the landlord raises it. Some simple mathematical manipulation allows us to get easy formulas for annuities, instead of having to calculate a string of present or future values and add them up. We won't show the details, but in essence you add up all the FVIFs or PVIFs to get annuity factors.

One critical assumption is when the payment is made: at the beginning or the end of the period. In most finance work in North America, payments are assumed to occur at the end of the period. This is an **ordinary** or **deferred annuity**. An **annuity due** is one for which the payments are made at the beginning of the period. The formulas that follow are for deferred annuities, but the factors can be converted easily to those for annuities due simply by multiplying by $(1 + k)$. Since each payment is received one period earlier, an annuity due accumulates one more period of interest.

The **future value interest factor for an annuity** (FVIFA, also called the sum of an annuity) is:

$$FVIFA = \frac{(1+k)^n - 1}{k}$$

Problem: You send your nephew Hezekiah $100 every Christmas for 10 years. He deposits it in a bank account earning 6%. How much does he have after the 10th gift?

Answer: $FVA = \left(\frac{(1.06)^{10} - 1}{.06}\right) \times \$100 = \underline{\$1,318.08}.$

The **present value interest factor for an annuity** (PVIFA) is:

$$PVIFA = \frac{1 - \dfrac{1}{(1+k)^n}}{k}$$

Problem: Hezekiah comes to you and asks for the next five Christmas presents in advance. Leaving aside the difficulty of explaining time value to a child, how much should you give him to produce the same value as the annuity?

Answer: $PVA = \left(\dfrac{1 - \dfrac{1}{(1.06)^5}}{.06}\right) \times \$100 = \underline{\$421.24}.[2]$

Tables of present value and future value annuity factors are shown in Appendices A3 and A4.

Using a Financial Calculator

People have used the tables in Appendix A for time value calculations for many years, but the development of cheap financial calculators that do the same thing has rendered the tables obsolete. The calculators do it faster, with less chance for you to make an

---

[2] He is expecting $500. If you are a parent faced with explaining time value, you might try saying that you don't have whatever amount is demanded right now, but if you put the present value into a bank account, it will grow to the desired amount.

error. More important, calculators can handle any fractional interest rate and any fractional period, which the tables cannot do. The tables are also limited by practical space considerations and do not list every possible number of periods.

For the rest of this book we will assume that you are using a basic financial calculator. It will have buttons on it to enter the number of periods, the interest rate, the payment amount (for annuities) and the present and future values. It will have buttons that will compute annuities deferred and annuities due, whichever you need.

The best source of instruction is the manufacturer's instruction booklet. White provides excellent step-by-step guidance to financial problems on a variety of Sharp, Hewlett-Packard and Texas Instrument financial calculators.[3] We cannot replace these sources, but we will show a few solutions with the steps for a Texas Instruments Business Analyst 35 (BA-35) calculator.[4]

Details to remember:

We show the operations keys you push in **boldface**, and the numbers entered in ordinary typeface, in our examples.

1. Calculators (including the BA-35) usually treat percentages as numbers, not as fractions. .6% is .6 **%i**, NOT .006 **%i**. However, if you do something the long way, using $(1 + k)$ and the power key, y^x, then you express percentages as decimals, and .6% = .006.

2. Some calculators, not including the BA-35 model we use, require either the PV or the FV to be entered as a negative number.

Worked Examples with a BA-35 Calculator   The diskette symbol will appear in the margin beside problems you can solve using Super Rep. The appendix to Chapter 2 contains the solutions to the following three problems, done using Super Rep.

Problem: If you deposit $5,000 in an RRSP account at a guaranteed rate of 7%, how much will you have when you retire 10 years from today?

Answer: Turn on the calculator: **ON/C**
Put it into financial mode: **ON/C 2nd N**
Don't forget to clear before new calculations each time.
You have a present value, a length of time it will be invested and the interest rate. You need the future value.

5,000	**PV**	
10	**N**	
7	**%i**	
CPT	**FV**	ans. <u>9,835.7568</u>

---

[3] Mark A. White, "Financial Problem Solving with an Electronic Calculator," *Financial Practice and Education*, Fall/Winter 1991, pp. 73–88; and Mark A. White, "Financial Problem Solving with an Electronic Calculator: Texas Instruments' BA II Plus," *Financial Practice and Education*, Fall 1993, pp. 123–26. This journal grants unlimited rights to reproduce articles without asking permission, as long as the reprints are for educational purposes, are not sold, and credit is given.

[4] This choice of calculator does not imply any endorsement of the manufacturer as the preferred source.

Problem: Your fairy godmother appears at the bedside when you are born, and promises to deposit in an account paying 5% interest per annum $2,000 p.a. on each birthday from your first to 21st inclusive. What is the present value of her gift on the day you are born?

Answer: This is an annuity problem. Since it is paid at the end of each period, it is an ordinary or deferred annuity, and you will be using the **CPT** button. 1st to 21st inclusive is 21 years.

21	N	
5	%i	
2,000	PMT	*note ANN appears on display*
CPT	PV	ans. <u>25,642.305</u>

Problem: You are just dying to buy that new television set, but you have no money. The salesperson notices you reading the price tag — $779, all taxes included — with a hopeless look. She tells you she can make you a deal. If you pay just $38 down and $38 each month thereafter for a total of only 24 payments, you can walk out of the store with the set right now. Your bank will lend you money at 1% per month. If you decide to go into debt to buy the set, should you borrow from the bank or take the store's offer?

Answer: Another annuity, this time an annuity due. The calculator will handle this one in one pass, too.

779	PV	
24	N	
38	PMT	
DUE	%i	ans. <u>1.4222%</u>

You should borrow from the bank, since the interest rate implicit in the store's offer is much higher. Another way to solve this problem is to calculate the size of the payments the bank would require to repay a loan of $779 at 1% over 24 months. These payments would be at month-end, because bank loans are always deferred annuities.

24	N	
779	PV	
1	%i	
CPT	PMT	ans. <u>$36.67</u>

The payment of $36.67 is lower than the store requires, and it is deferred for one month as well.

A Note on Rounding

Electronic calculators and computers produce lots of decimal places, but the implied precision is frequently invalid. If you are planning how much you need to save for your retirement in 20 years, rounding the answers to thousands is more reasonable. Even for short-term planning we suggest that rounding to the nearest dollar is the most precise you can be. On the other hand, we would round to the nearest $0.25 when pricing bonds or shares, since that is how they are priced in the market. Mortgage rates and bond yields may need to be calculated to several decimal places, because they have considerable effect on the value of annuities that pay out over many years.

There are no precise rules. Common sense and experience will tell you how much to round or how precise you need to be in personal financial planning.

RATE OF RETURN — Multiperiod

Why Annual Rates?

When we refer to rate of return in this book, or when people refer to it in finance generally, annual rate is almost always implied. Sometimes, interest is charged or accrued for different time periods, e.g. monthly interest on a credit card debt. Since so many natural and social processes are measured at yearly intervals, finance has adopted the convention of converting discount rates/rates of return to annual rates. This conversion appears to be a simple mechanical exercise, but there are several critical issues that arise. If we are to understand the various rates quoted in the finance world, we need to look at these issues carefully.

Arithmetic and Geometric Rates of Return

Suppose we invest $100 for two years. At the end of two years, we receive $120. What rate of return did we earn?

We could start by calculating the dollar return as $20. We earned it over two years; so we divide by two to get $10 per year, which is 10% of $100.

Alternatively, we could apply the time value rules we learned in the previous section and ask: What annual discount rate compounds $100 to $120 in two years? The answer, from a calculator, is 9.5445%.

Which answer is right? This isn't an academic question, because different investment opportunities may be quoted using one or the other. Mutual funds, for example, often quote their past rates of return using the first method.

The second answer, 9.5445%, is correct, because it allows for compounding. Think of the two-year investment as two one-year investments. If the annual rate of return is 10%, then at the end of one year you have $110. After another year at 10%, you should have (110 × 1.1) or $121. Now do the same thing with the 9.5445% rate. After one year you have $109.54. After the second year you have (109.54 × 1.095445) or $120.

This difference still holds when we know the individual rate of return for each year, though it isn't so obvious. Suppose we want to know the average annual rate of return we earned over four years, with the following observed rates in each year:

Year	Return (%)
1990	17
1991	8
1992	2
1993	15

We could sum them and take the mean, which is 10.5%. This average is called the **arithmetic mean return**. In general, if k_t is the return in period t, the arithmetic mean is calculated as:

$$\text{Arithmetic mean} = \sum_{t=1}^{n} \frac{k_t}{n}$$

$$= \frac{.17 + .08 + .02 + .15}{4} = .105$$

The alternative method is to find the rate of return which would compound to the same final answer as the individual rates multiplied together. This average is called the **geometric mean return**, and it is calculated as:

$$\text{Geometric mean return} = \left[\prod_{t=1}^{n} (1 + k_t) \right]^{\frac{1}{n}} - 1$$

This equation tells us to multiply together all the factors $(1 + k_t)$ for the years and then take the nth root. For the example above, this is:

$$\sqrt[4]{(1.17 \times 1.08 \times 1.02 \times 1.15)} - 1 = 10.34\%$$

The geometric mean return is lower than or equal to the arithmetic mean return. The difference could be large. Consider a share that loses 50% of its value in one year and then doubles in the second year to return to its original price. The geometric mean return is 0, but the arithmetic mean is $(-50\% + 100\%) \div 2 = 25\%$ p.a. When the annual returns are exactly equal for every year in the sequence, the two means are equal.

We use the arithmetic mean return in analyzing investments when we want to estimate an average or expected return across different investments in the same period. For example, if we wanted to say what the average rate of return offered by bank savings deposit accounts is compared with the rate offered by trust company accounts, we would use an arithmetic mean.

Worked Example with a TI BA-35 Calculator   There are two methods to get the geometric mean. Each starts out with:

$$1.17 \times 1.08 \times 1.02 \times 1.15 = 1.4822. \text{ Then, either}$$

1.4822	y^x	.25	=	1.10338, or
1.4822	FV			
1	PV			
4	N			
CPT	%i	ans.	=	10.338

In future examples we will always use the first method with the y^x key to convert interest rates between frequencies of compounding, but both methods will always give the same answer.

COMPOUNDING MORE FREQUENTLY THAN ANNUALLY

Many loans are compounded more frequently than once a year, and this raises some interesting issues when we try to determine how to compare the discount rates. We convert the actual periodic rates to annual rates just as we do for rates over several years, and for the same reason. Virtually every form of consumer loan, including residential mortgages, is compounded more than once a year, and the loan rates that the institutions quote can be misleading if you don't know how they quote them.

Annual Percentage Rate

The **annual percentage rate (APR)** is a conventional method of quoting interest rates that ignores the compounding effect completely. The periodic rate is multiplied by the number of periods in a year. If m is the number of periods in one year and k_m is the rate of return or discount rate for one period, then:

$$APR = m \cdot k_m$$

This method is used for quoting rates for consumer loans, residential mortgages, corporate/commercial mortgages and other loans, and bond yields. Everyone is expected to understand the convention in the business world, although consumer protection legislation sometimes requires more explanation for non-business loans. Thus, the wording on a loan contract might read like this:

> The interest rate shall be 12% (twelve per cent) per annum, compounded and payable monthly...

What this wording means is that the monthly interest rate is 1%, and it is compounded every month. You are also required to make monthly payments, rather than allowing the loan balance and interest to accumulate as is usually done when a financial institution is borrowing from you.[5]

It is certainly wrong to call this interest rate 12%, since we know that the 1% interest paid at the end of the first month could have earned interest for you for another 11 months if you hadn't had to pay it to the lender. Therefore, you have a greater cost (including the opportunity cost of paying interest early) if you pay 1% per month than if you pay 12% at the end of 12 months. In the next section we introduce the effective annual rate, which is a more reasonable procedure.

Effective Annual Rate

The conventional solution is to compound the periodic rate the number of times there are periods in the year, to arrive at the **effective annual rate (EAR)**. Using the same notation as for the APR:

$$EAR = (1 + k_m)^m - 1$$

For example, an interest rate of 1% per month has an EAR of $(1.01)^{12} - 1 = .1268$ or 12.68%. In personal finance we use the EAR as a way of converting periodic rates to a common annual basis. Some types of consumer lending require disclosure of the

---

[5] That is, when you deposit money in a long-term deposit at the bank, the bank is now the borrower. Most such deposits do not pay the interest periodically, but rather compound it over the life of the certificate. When the certificate matures, the bank pays you the principal and all the interest, including compounded interest on interest, for the entire term of the loan.

EAR now, but not all of them. If you are the investor, then it is your problem to calculate rates of return. Bond yields are quoted as APRs, for example, though this fact is not evident in any table of yields. We will show examples in other applications in the chapter, but first we have some specific problems for you to solve.

Worked Examples with a TI BA-35 Calculator

Problem: You are the manager of credit card statements for the Tottery Bank Visa Card operation. Declining interest rates have led the bank to lower its monthly interest rate on unpaid balances to 1.25%. What is the APR? What is the EAR? Which rate must you disclose to cardholders?

Answer:[6]   APR: $1.25 \times 12 = \underline{15.00\%}$

EAR: $(1.0125)\ \mathbf{y}^x\ 12 = \underline{1.1608} - 1 = \underline{16.08\%}$[7]

You must disclose the EAR to cardholders.

Problem: "Yeah, 1% a day is purty high interest, sweetheart, but I guess ya gotta have that fix of Gelato Fresca Devil's Chocolate ice cream purty quick or yer gonna get the shakes — an' I don' mean McDonald's shakes, heh, heh. So let me make it real clear. I lend you four bucks, at 1% per day, and ya pay me back $4.28 in one week. Else, I start countin' the vigorish [ed. comment: vigorish is interest] on the $4.28 at the same rate, except fer I give ya a day off at Christmas, heh, heh."

Grinder McSnarl operates an unofficial financial institution out of his long black limousine. His 'chauffeur' sits in the front cleaning his teeth with a switchblade. Grinder has just explained his lending terms to nine-year old Jennie Sweettooth.

(a)   What is Grinder's compounding frequency?

(b)   What is the EAR of Grinder's loan?

(c)   If Jennie falls into his clutches and borrows $4.00 without paying it off for a whole year, how much will she then owe him?

Answer: (a)   There is a trick here. Grinder is not compounding daily, since he says she'll owe $4.28 in one week. $0.28/$4.00 is 7%, or $7 \times 1\%$; so his compounding frequency is weekly.

(b)   Since he generously charges no interest on Christmas, there are exactly 52 weeks in a standard year. Thus,
EAR $= 1.07\ \mathbf{y}^x\ 52 = \underline{33.725} - 1 = \underline{3,272.5\%}$ p.a.

---

[6] You can also do these operations on TI BA-35 using the **APR** and **EFF** keys, but we think that our method is easier, and shows more clearly the logic of the operation.

[7] Note that when you use the time value of money keys on this and most financial calculators, the answer is in % already. When you use the $\mathbf{y}^x$ key, the answer is in the form of 1 + a decimal. You must deduct 1 and move the decimal point two places to the right to convert to a %.

(c)   Either:

        4   **PV**
        52   **N**
        7   **%i**
        CPT   **FV**   ans. = $134.90

or, more simply, 4 × 33.725 = $134.90.

Reinvestment Rate Assumption   In the previous section we said that we would use the EAR to compare different rates. It, too, is just a conventionally-accepted method, and it has an assumption that is not necessarily true. The assumption concerns at what rate the periodic payments are reinvested.

The APR assumes that the periodic payments are not reinvested at all. That is, the lender hides the money under his mattress until the end of the year, then adds it up and calculates the return. Clearly, this is an unreasonable assumption. Our financial system quotes rates at the APR simply as a convention, or convenience, with the implicit understanding that the opportunity cost is something greater.

The EAR assumes that the periodic payments are reinvested at the same rate as the original loan. This assumption is more reasonable, because the lending institution will have many loans of different amounts and maturities outstanding. It will lend out the repayments as part of other loans at similar rates. However, if interest rates change, then the lender will receive a rate on the reinvested payments that differs from the rate on the original loan. Then, the EAR will give the wrong rate in economic terms, although not by much.

The same analysis holds from the borrower's viewpoint. If you could hold on to those interim payments, what would be the best alternative use of them from your point of view? If it is different from the loan rate, then the effective cost to you is different from the EAR.[8]

As a practical matter, we won't worry about this problem and will continue to use the EAR as the benchmark in this book. Interest rates do not change by large amounts nor very fast in Canada; so any imprecision is small. Furthermore, when we look at a lending or investment decision before we make it, the current interest rate is our best estimate of the average anyway. Therefore, the EAR we calculate at the start of a loan or investment is a valid measure of our best estimate of what it will cost us (or earn for us).

---

[8] The student will recognize that this is similar to the problem of using the internal rate of return (IRR) in corporate finance to make capital budgeting decisions. The IRR assumes that any interim cash flows to the investor can be reinvested at the IRR. If this IRR represents a positive net present value, that is, it is lower than the appropriate cost of capital for the company, then using IRR to make decisions assumes that there are an infinite number of such positive net present value projects available in which the company can reinvest its earnings. Such an assumption is clearly unwarranted.

Reprinted with permission — The Toronto Star Syndicate. © 1994 GREG HOWARD distributed by King Features Syndicate.

FACTORS AFFECTING DISCOUNT RATES

We observe that there are many rates of return prevailing in the market at the same time. Some of them have specific names, others are the yields on different bonds or other investments. We have already said that we obtain our discount rates by looking at the best alternative use for the money. How do we choose which of these many possible discount rates is equivalent to the best available alternative? We can collect the factors that influence these rates into four categories: pure time premium, risk, income tax and inflation.

Pure Time Premium

The **pure time premium** is the price that we demand for waiting before we consume. Since we let someone else use our money when we invest it, we need some compensation for deferring the pleasure of using it to buy something we can consume. This premium is the rate of return that would theoretically exist if there were no risk of any kind that the rate will change or not be paid, no inflation and no income taxes. Economists estimate that it is 2–4% per annum.

Risk

The many different discount rates may have different amounts of **risk**. The risk may take the form of a probability that we won't be paid a promised sum. It may be that we know an investment will produce variable returns which we can't predict in advance. An investment may pay exactly what it promised in dollar terms, but every other competing investment may do better than expected. Investors will bid more for these other investments and the market price of our investment will fall.

For example, a Canadian government bond carries very little risk of default. However, if we buy a bond paying 10% for $1,000, and all interest rates rise unexpectedly in the market the next day, the value of our bond will decline because we could have waited one day and invested at a higher rate. This **interest rate risk** is hard to avoid in debt investments at fixed rates.

We might decide to invest in the common shares of a small oil company that has very little production and reserves, but is drilling on some promising land. The common shares promise no dividends or maturity payment as bonds do. If the company finds a lot of oil, the share price will triple and we will make a lot of money. If the company finds no oil at all and runs out of money to do more drilling, our share price may drop to only pennies.

Naturally, these risks affect the discount rates we use to value the expected or possible future cash flows. We said earlier to pick the best alternative rate of return. In the case of risky investments, you would try to find the rate of return realized on other similar investments. For example, the oil company would have to offer a high rate of return (which implies a low share price), because of the high probability that you wouldn't get anything at all. Previous share prices on small oil companies would have been priced likewise to yield high returns in the event of success.

We discuss many different aspects of risk in Chapters 13–15. For now, all we wish to say is that different risk is the most important factor leading to different discount rates in the market at the same time. The other factors affect the general level of discount rates on all investments and loans.

Income Tax

We are going to state an important rule of discounting:

> *Use after-tax discount rates for after-tax cash flows. Use before-tax rates for before-tax cash flows.*

Income tax rules apply different rates to different sources of income and allow some expenses to be deducted from taxable income, but not others. The effects are often very large. We buy goods and services using after-tax dollars, but so far we have been doing time value calculations based on the before-tax rates. Insofar as market prices are concerned, this is all right — we discount the before-tax cash flows at the before-tax rates. When we make individual personal decisions, we have to consider individual tax situations. Mechanically, we must make two adjustments. We calculate the cash flows to be discounted in after-tax dollars. We discount these after-tax dollars using an after-tax discount rate. Think back to our rule that we use the best alternative rate available as the discount rate. If all we get is 60% of the dollars from an investment because of taxes, then the rate of return on the investment is only 60% of the pre-tax rate. Therefore, we use the lower after-tax discount rate when considering a choice which is expressed in after-tax dollars.

Let us consider the example of the GIC that costs $905 at the credit union and matures in one year at $1,000. We established earlier that the before-tax rate of return is 10.50%. Now suppose that a potential purchaser has a **marginal tax rate** of 40%. The marginal rate is the rate that applies to the next dollar of income. In this case we mean that the income from the GIC will be taxed at 40%. Since she only receives (100% − 40%) = 60% of the income, the after-tax rate of return *for this person only* is (.6 × 10.5%) = 6.3%.

Let us illustrate the rule by continuing the same example. The holder of the GIC collects ($1,000 − $905) = $95 in interest, but has only 60% of it, or $57 left after-tax. There is no tax on the principal amount of $905, since it is not income but a repayment of the money originally invested. The holder's total after-tax receipt is ($905 + $57) = $962. We already know that the original price is $905. If we discount $962 for one period at 6.3%, we get $904.99, which is the original price with a rounding error.

Therefore, we must use the after-tax rate to get the answer that we already know is correct.

We go into more detail on Canada's tax system and the effect it has on personal finance in Chapters 6 and 7. There we will see how different sorts of investments and other incomes are taxed, and how to evaluate decisions concerning income tax planning.

Inflation

We are going to state another important rule of discounting:

> *Use nominal discount rates for nominal cash flows and real discount rates for real cash flows.*

Let us explain what this rule means:

> Money is only a medium of exchange. We acquire money and manage it to use it to buy goods and services that we need or want.[9] **Inflation** is a general rise in the prices of all goods and services. If there is inflation present in an economy — and there has been inflation in the Canadian economy every year since 1939 — we want to measure our success in personal financial management by how much we are able to consume in physical terms, not by how many dollars we have.

For example, you want to buy a new car in three years' time. The model you like costs $15,000 today, including taxes. You don't want to borrow to buy it in three years; so you must save the entire price. You have $10,000 now, in short-term investments yielding 5% p.a. How much do you have to save each year to reach your goal of buying the car?

You might say that you would calculate how much the $10,000 will accumulate to in three years, then find the three year annuity at 5% that will make up the difference. There is a practical problem here, because the car won't cost $15,000 in three years; it will cost more if there is any inflation.

Dollars are somewhat elastic measures of value — they don't stay constant. If we want to buy something in the future, we will buy it with dollars in the future, not dollars today. We still remember when a loaf of bread cost $0.25 and a quart (not a litre!) of milk cost $0.24. Does that mean that somehow life is impossibly expensive today? Not really. When those prices prevailed, our parents' total income was well under $10,000 p.a., which would put them in poverty today in Canada. The problem is that for financial planning we have to adjust the **purchasing power** of the dollars so that we are planning for a level of consumption rather than a fixed amount of money.

There are two ways to do this. One is to inflate every dollar measure for every year of the plan by the rate of inflation expected to occur. Then, the goal is measured in **current dollars** of the future year, and all the dollar amounts in the interim are measured

---

[9] We recognize that this is a simplifying assumption. Money also fulfils symbolic functions in our society beyond the consumption it permits, and it is a key mechanism in the attainment and perpetuation of power relationships. Nonetheless, we will stick to the traditional financial interpretation in this textbook.

in the current dollars when they occur. The calculations can be very messy, although with a personal computer and a spreadsheet program they are feasible.

The alternative is to measure everything in **constant dollars**. That is, we discount all future amounts back to today's dollars (or some other fixed time point) and express all our planning as if we were doing it in today's dollars. This method generally assumes that all amounts inflate at the same rate.

The advantage of using current dollars is that we are getting the values that we expect will occur. Depending on how income taxes are levied, this may be more accurate, as long as our forecast is accurate.

The advantage of using constant dollars is that we can understand and relate to amounts expressed in today's dollars. As we update our plan in future years, we can adjust the amounts by the inflation rate so that they will then be in current dollars of each future period when we are in that period of time. Constant dollars are easier to work with, since they allow us to use annuities and we can avoid having large and messy spreadsheets.

Just as we calculated discount rates to allow for taxes, we must find the appropriate discount rates for inflated and uninflated amounts. We call the discount rate for inflated or current dollars the **nominal** rate, and the dollars that we are discounting are nominal dollars. They are expressed in the purchasing power of the period in which they occur, not any other.

We call the discount rate for uninflated or constant dollars the **real** rate, and the dollars that we are discounting **real** dollars. It may seem an odd contradiction in terminology, but real dollars don't exist. They are a fictional creation that allows us to keep money and what it buys constant. Thus, if we express a future amount in real dollars, what we are saying is that if we want to buy something in the future, it would cost us that real dollar amount if we were buying it today. If inflation is zero, then the real and nominal discount rates, and the real and nominal dollars, are equal.

There is a simple relationship between real and nominal dollars, and real and nominal discount rates. The nominal rate is simply the real rate compounded at the rate of inflation. This is exactly what inflation does to the cost of goods and services over time as well. Every year the general price level rises by the rate of inflation, and over time that rate compounds on today's prices. For example, we said that we remembered bread at $0.25. Today a comparable loaf might cost $1.59. Over a 36-year compounding horizon, that implies an inflation rate of 5.3%. If we had been planning in 1957 how we would afford to buy bread in 1993, we would have had to save enough to buy it at $0.24, compounded at a real rate, or enough to buy it at $1.59, compounded at a nominal rate. Thus, we have an inflation premium in the nominal discount rate, and it will be higher than the real rate. Letting k_{nom} be the nominal rate, k_r be the real rate, and i be the rate of inflation, the relationship can be expressed as:

$$1 + k_{nom} = (1 + k_r)(1 + i)$$

For example, suppose the inflation rate is 2% and the real rate of interest is 3%. Then

$$k_{nom} = (1 + .03)(1 + .02) - 1$$
$$= .0506 \text{ or } 5.06\%$$

This equation is called the Fisher equation, after the economist who developed it.[10] Let's return to our problem of saving to buy a car to see how all this fits together.

Let us assume that inflation is 2% p.a. In three years the car will cost $15,918 (15,000 × 1.02³). In three years the $10,000 grows to $11,576. The shortfall you must save to make up is $4,342. At 5%, the annual saving required to accumulate to this amount is $1,377. Let us analyze what we have done. We have converted the cost of the car from today's dollars into dollars of three years hence when we want to buy it. Then we compounded our current savings into the amount we would have in three years' time. Finally, we calculated the amount we would have to save annually, expressed in future dollars. If all the rates stay constant and we save exactly $1,377 per annum, we will have enough to buy the car in three years.

The one problem with the nominal approach in this example is that we expressed the savings amount in year three dollars, but we will be saving it in years one, two and three. It will be harder to save it in year one, because our income will be somewhat less in dollar terms, and relatively easier to save in year three.

If we do the same problem in real dollars, we get a different savings number, and a different interpretation. First, we need to calculate the real rate of return, given that we know the nominal rate. We rearrange the Fisher equation to get:

$$k_r = \frac{1 + k_{nom}}{1 + i} - 1$$
$$= \frac{1 + .05}{1 + .02} - 1 = .0294 \text{ or } 2.94\%$$

Now we don't have do express the cost of the car in any new dollars, because we are working in constant dollars. The present savings of $10,000 will compound at the real rate of 2.94% to yield $10,908 in constant dollars. The constant dollar amount you need to save is thus $4,092. The PV of the savings annuity, in constant dollars at 2.94%, is $1,325. If you are trying to reach the goal of buying the car, you could now ask yourself: Did I save $1,325 last year? Could I have saved that much if I wanted the car badly enough?

We don't save in real dollars, though; we save in nominal dollars each year. The solution in nominal dollars, however, is also a constant number since it is an annuity. It would work, but a more feasible plan is to save an increasing number of dollars every year to reach the final total of $4,342. We can calculate what the value in nominal dollars is each year by inflating the real dollar figure each year as we check our plan. Look at the following time line to see what will happen:

Real $				Compounds to
Save	1,325	1,325	1,325	4,092
Time 0	1	2	3	
	1,352	1,379	1,406	4,345
Nominal $				Compounds to

---

[10] This relationship assumes that we know future cash flows for certain, but it is a reasonable approximation for the level of accuracy that we can hope for in personal financial planning.

The lower half of the time line is the value of $1,325 compounded by the inflation rate of 2%. This is the amount you would have to save in each year's dollars. The first year's saving is compounded for one year because it occurs at the end of the year (using annuity deferred). If we now compound each of these savings amounts by the nominal rate of 5%, the sum is $4,345, which is the same as we got previously (with a rounding error) when we did everything in nominal terms. Thus we can see that the two approaches are equivalent.

In this simple example it wouldn't matter much which one you used, since the numbers aren't much different. If you were planning to retire in 20 years, and expected to live for many years after retirement, inflation would make a big difference. The most important lesson from this section is that you must allow for the effect of inflation. Whether you do it by keeping everything in real dollars and updating as you go, or whether you do it by creating a messy spreadsheet in nominal dollars for each of the years in the future, is not so important. We will tend to do a lot of our planning in real dollars in this book because it is easier to present that way.

SUMMARY

This chapter teaches you how to compare monetary amounts received at different times — the fundamental arithmetic of personal finance. The basic relationship between the present value (PV) and future value (FV) of cash flows received at time t in the future, at a discount rate of k, is

$$FV = PV \, (1 + k)^t$$

If we have a series of equal payments at equally-spaced intervals, we can calculate the PV and FV using annuity formulas.

A discount rate is the opportunity cost of spending your money now instead of investing it in the best available investment. You determine how much a future series of cash flows is worth to you today by discounting them at the rate that is the best alternative. Expressed differently, the discount rate is the rate of return that you expect to earn on an investment.

Comparing discount rates that are charged for different periods requires a convention. We express all discount rates as annual rates, using the effective annual rate method if the rate is applied for some period other than a year.

Discount rates are affected by the pure time premium, risk, income tax and inflation. The pure time premium is the price we demand for delaying consumption by investing money instead of spending it. Risk means the possibility of not getting what we expected. The riskier the returns on an investment, the higher the average or expected rate must be to persuade us to invest.

Income tax reduces the return that we actually receive. Furthermore, the form of the investment return — interest, dividends, capital gains, rental income — is taxed in different ways. We discount after-tax returns using discount rates adjusted for income taxes, to make them comparable with one another.

Inflation reduces the consumption value of future dollars, and therefore we use inflation-adjusted discount rates to discount inflated future dollars. We can also adjust the future dollars to be in real or constant dollars and use real discount rates.

KEY TERMINOLOGY

annuity — deferred — due — ordinary / arithmetic mean rate of return / compound interest / discount rate: — annual percentage rate (APR) — best alternative — effective annual rate (EAR) — nominal — opportunity cost — real / factors affecting discount rates — income tax — inflation — pure time premium — risk / future value / geometric mean rate of return / present value / principal / rate of return / sum of an annuity

PROBLEMS

1. You deposit $5,000 in a guaranteed investment certificate offering an escalator rate compounded annually in successive years as follows: 5%, 6%, 7%, 8%, 8%. What is the maturity value of the GIC? What annual rate of return does the GIC offer for the five-year period? Define how you calculated rate of return!

2. Great Uncle Bracegirdle deposits $1,000 p.a. in a trust fund earning 8% p.a. for you on your birthday every year up to and including your 18th birthday. How much is the trust fund worth the day after you turn 18? How much would your great uncle have had to deposit the day you were born to replace the annual deposits?

3. Bob Gibson has won the first prize in his company's annual Christmas party. The award is cash and he has three options to choose from:
   I   receive $1,000 now;
   II receive $400 at the end of each of the next three years; or,
   III receive $500 at the end of one year, $400 at the end of two years, and $300 at the end of three years.
   (a) Which of the options should he choose if the rate of interest is: (i) 6%; (ii) 10%; (iii) 12%?
   (b) If the rates of interest for one-year, two-year and three-year deposits are 6%, 6.5% and 7%, respectively, which option is the best?

4. Jill Blume inherited some money recently and is considering paying off the loan on her car with one lump-sum payment. She pays $450 per month and there are 40 payments left. The loan agreement allows her to pay off the loan at any time using a monthly discount rate of 1/12th of the prime rate, but there is an administrative fee equal to 2% of the loan outstanding. The current prime rate is 8%. Calculate the amount required to retire the loan.

5. Sheila Gilbert wants to invest $50,000 in a bank account. The following accounts are available in the local bank:

Type	Stated interest rate (% p.a.)	Frequency of compounding
1	10.00	annual
2	9.75	semi-annual
3	9.50	quarterly
4	9.25	monthly
5	9.00	weekly

   (a) Calculate the effective annual rate (EAR) for each type of account.

(b) What is the other name for the stated interest rate?

(c) Calculate the compound value of her investment at the end of one year; three years; five years.

(d) Is there any factor other than the interest rate that might enter into her decision as to which account to use?

6. David has estimated the annual rate of return for 10 years on three shares that he wants to invest in, as follows:

Year	Share 1	Share 2	Share 3
1	.10	−.02	.02
2	.15	−.04	.08
3	.02	.28	.14
4	.35	.45	.28
5	.67	.12	.25
6	−.08	.10	.27
7	.14	−.20	.11
8	.16	−.01	.15
9	.21	.00	.12
10	.05	.22	.13

Calculate the estimated arithmetic mean and the estimated geometric mean rate of return for each share.

7. An alumnus donated $40,000 to a university in 1990. The money was invested so as to provide for a $6,000 scholarship at the end of the year, forever.

(a) What rate of interest was the money earning?

(b) The interest rate changes to 10%. If the university wants to continue to award the scholarship indefinitely, what will be the amount of each scholarship?

(c) How many years can a $6,000 scholarship be awarded if the rate stays at 10%?

8. Mr. Haroun plans to make the following contributions to his Registered Retirement Savings Plan (RRSP):

Year	Amount ($)	
1	7,500	
2	9,500	
3	11,500	
4	12,500	
5	13,500	
6 and thereafter	15,500	per year

If the contributions are made at the end of each year, and the rate of interest is 12%, how much will Mr. Haroun have when he retires 30 years hence? How much would he have if he made the contributions at the start of every year (thus, the last contribution is one year before he retires)?

9. Your daughter wants to go to university. She has three years of high school left, and then she would attend university for four years. She thinks she can save $2,000 in today's dollars from her summer jobs each year, both while she is in high school, and while she is in university. Tuition fees are presently $2,500 p.a., and living costs (she will attend a university in another city) $9,000 p.a. These costs are inflating

at 5% p.a. You can earn 6% after-tax on your savings. She pays no tax and can earn 10% on her savings. How much will you have to deposit today (time 0, earning 6%) to be able to make up her shortfall in each of her four years of university? To simplify the question, assume that she receives all her earnings at the end of years one through six. She starts university at the end of year three and must pay all the fees and costs at that time; so she pays everything at the end of years three through six.

10. Lewis Broderick is the knight errant of the Puce Garter in the Court of Luxemstein. He is 60 years old, with an average life expectancy of 87, and is paid 60,000 francs p.a. King Peter wants him to resign so that a distant cousin of Peter's can have the job. Broderick refuses, since the appointment is for life. He suggests instead that he retire in five years with a pension of 50,000 p.a., with his wife (who is expected to outlive him by 20 years) getting half on his death. In addition, he wants to stay on staff for five years after his retirement as an adviser to the court on garter selection, at a stipend of 5,000 p.a. The K.E.P.G is the traditional director of Luxemstein's once a century anniversary celebrations, coming up in 10 years. He would receive an additional honorarium of 40,000 p.a. for the two years before the celebrations, and he wants to receive those payments as well. Finally, he wants to receive a lump sum payment of 100,000 at the retirement date.

King Peter makes a counteroffer: "We'll pay you an extra 130,000 p.a. for the next five years and a lump sum of 40,000 at the retirement date if you agree to retire without any further payments."

(a) All payments come at year end. The interest rate is 7%. Which alternative gives Broderick the higher present value, using expected lives?

(b) What other considerations should influence his choice?

11. Mr. Ronson, an engineer at Physicon Ltd., is planning to retire in 10 years. His current liquid savings are $525,000, and his goal is to have $1 million at retirement. He has been advised by his bank manager to put all his cash into a Guaranteed Investment Certificate (GIC) account at 6.5%, and also to contribute a small amount at the end of each year, for the next 10 years, in order to achieve his goal.

(a) If he does not make further contributions, can he reach his goal? If not, what rate of return must he earn in order to reach his goal?

(b) Calculate the annual contribution that he must make to reach his goal, given an interest rate of 6%.

(c) Answer (b), but make the contribution at the start of each year.

(d) Repeat part (b) with an interest rate of 12%.

12. Betty Au wants to invest $10,000 for a term of 30 years. How much will she have if the rate of return is (a) 4%, (b) 8%, (c) 11%, (d) 14%, (e) 18% and (f) 20%?

Suppose that in addition she will invest $2,000 per year at the beginning of each year. How much wealth will she have in 30 years? How will your answers change if the annual investments are at the end of each year?

13. Gordon Kohaku, aged 25, is planning to contribute 18% of his employment income into an investment account each year. His employment income, currently at $30,000,

is expected to increase at 5% per year, and he will increase the contribution accordingly. Assuming that he makes the contributions at the end of each year, how much will he have in 40 year's time if the rate of return is (a) 8%, (b) 10%, (c) 12%, (d) 15% and (e) 18%?

How would you answers change if the contributions are at the beginning of each year?

14. You have $9,500 which you plan to invest for a term of 5 years. The following choices are available:

(i)   You can buy a five-year GIC at the current interest rate of 10% p.a., interest payable annually.

(ii) You can buy a 5-year Miron Company bond with face value of $10,000 and it pays $375 interest semi-annually.

(iii) Your neighbour, Ronald, who owns a small manufacturing company, urges you to loan him the money. He says he will pay you an increasing stream of interest as follows:

Year 1	$ 200
Year 2	$ 400
Year 3	$ 800
Year 4	$1,600
Year 5	$2,500

At the end of the fifth year, you will get back your $9,500.

(a) Which investment will you choose?

(b) Are there any factor other than the rate of return which should affect your decision?

15. Jack and Jill Moore have just inherited a substantial amount of money and they want to put aside enough money in a special investment account earmarked for their three children's university education. Their children, David, Joe and Janet are expected to start university in 4 years, 5 years and 8 years, respectively. The Moores plan to support each child for four years of university. It is estimated that it costs currently a full-time student $12,000 per year in tuition fees, books, room and board, and other sundry expenses. Attending the local university and commuting from home will cut that to $5,000 per year. If the expected rate of return on investment is 10% and the expected rate of inflation is 3%, how much must they set aside now,

(a) if all three children go to out-of-town universities?

(b) if David goes out-of-town; and Joe and Janet attend the local university?

(c) if all three children stay home and attend the local university?

APPENDIX 2.1: SAMPLE PROBLEMS SOLVED
WITH SUPER REP

Problem: If you deposit $5,000 in an RRSP account at a guaranteed rate of 7%, how much will you have when you retire 10 years from today?

Answer: Double click on the Super Rep for Students ICON in the Window's Program Manager to launch the software.

Click any key to close the licence information window. (All future examples will assume you are in the software.)

Select Utilities, Calculators, Present & Future Values from the menu bar.

Enter a 0 for the periodic payment.

Enter 10 for the number of payments and set the frequency to annual.

Under % Interest/Yr type 7 and Enter.

Enter $5,000 as the present value, then press the $= icon beside the present value and future value to calculate the future value.

Problem: Your fairy godmother appears at the bedside when you are born, and promises to deposit in an account paying 5% interest per annum $2,000 p.a. on each birthday from your first to 21st inclusive. What is the present value of her gift on the day you were born?

Answer: Select Utilities, Calculator, Present & Future Values from the menu. The Present & Future Values calculator will open.

Type 2000 and Enter for the Periodic payment.

Type 21 and Enter for the Number of payments.

Type 5 and Enter for the % Interest/yr.

Click your mouse on the Annual radio button for Frequency.

Click your mouse on the $= Icon/button in the bottom right corner of the window across from the Present Value and Future Value fields.

The Present Value of $25,642.31 will be displayed.

Problem: You are just dying to buy that new television set, but you have no money. The salesperson notices you are reading the price tag — $779, all taxes included — with a hopeless look. She tells you she can make you a deal. If you pay just $38 down and $38 each month thereafter for a total of only 24 payments, you can walk out of the store with the set right now. Your bank will lend you the money at 1% per month. If you decide to go into debt to buy the set, should you borrow from the bank or take the store's offer?

Answer: Select Utilities, Calculators, Loan Calculations from the menu. The Loan Calculations window will open.

Leave the Description blank, then enter 779 and Enter for the Loan $ amount.

Skip the Date and type 24 in the Amort: months. You could also have typed 2 and Enter in the years field.

Type 12 and Enter in the % Interest/yr field.

As a consumer type loan, the interest is compounded monthly so the existing default is correct. Click on the $= Icon with your mouse and the payment will be calculated.

You can see that with Pay: equal to $36.67, the bank loan is the better option.

chapter **3**

Setting Goals

LEARNING OBJECTIVES

There is a lesson to be learned from the old saying: 'Knowing your destination is half the journey.' The lesson is particularly important in the area of personal finance because many people do not have a clear idea of where they want to go or what they want to achieve in their financial affairs. Some may feel that the idea of setting precise financial goals is rigid and uncreative; others may think it is easier to 'go with the flow' and assume all monetary matters will work out in the end. However, managing personal finances without well-defined goals is like driving a car without knowing where you want to go: you will never 'arrive'.

A crucial component to the success of your financial affairs is establishing well-defined goals that reflect what is important to you. Whether they realize it or not, most people have financial desires — to be rich, to be financially independent, to retire early and comfortably, to buy a better house etc. However, it is unlikely that these desires will be achieved because they are too vague and it is very difficult to formulate plans and take action to reach vague goals that are not well-defined.

Thus, we have three specific learning objectives for this chapter:

1. To distinguish between a financial desire and a financial goal;
2. To learn the process of setting goals; and,
3. To learn the process of financial planning to achieve goals.

DESIRES AND GOALS

There is some confusion about what a financial goal is and how it differs from a desire. Indeed, the key to setting financial goals successfully is to understand the difference between goals and desires. When individuals are asked to write down their financial goals, they very often come up with a list of desires. The following is just a sample:

I want:

- to be rich
- to be financially independent
- to gain financial security

Reprinted with permission — The Toronto Star Syndicate. © 1994 GREG HOWARD distributed by King Features Syndicate.

- to retire early and comfortably
- to send the children to university
- to move to a bigger and better home

None of the above items is a goal. They are all too vague and there are no deadlines for their completion. As such the likelihood of achieving them is small. A financial goal must possess two attributes: first, the goal's outcome can be measured precisely in dollars; second, there is a deadline for its completion. Thus, the statement, "I want to be rich," expresses a financial desire while the statement, "I want to have $1 million in ten years' time," expresses a clear financial goal.

The following are some examples of financial goals:

I want:

- to have $1 million in ten years' time
- to buy a house in five years' time that will cost $200,000
- to retire at the age of 55 with $700,000 cash in addition to my house, which will be totally paid off
- to send the two children, now aged nine and ten, to university, which will cost $20,000 per year
- to save ten per cent of my earnings every month and put the money in a good stock mutual fund
- to cut the family's entertainment spending by $100 per month, starting this month
- to buy a car next year that will cost $18,000

Note that each of the above items has the two attributes of a financial goal: it is expressed and measured in dollars and a completion time is set.

How to Set Financial Goals

Now that you know what a financial goal is and how it differs from a desire, how do you set it down and develop it? Is there any magic process? How many goals should you set?

The best way to start is by brain-storming. Write down all your desires and goals in your financial affairs. At this stage, don't separate the goals from the desires; just put down what you think is important. Include everything you can think of without assessing the reasonableness of it at the moment. Your goals should include both short-term ones, such as a special vacation or a new piece of furniture next year, and long-term goals, such as buying a house in five years' time. You should look at every aspect of your financial affairs and at all your desires.

Now you have a list of goals and desires. The next step is to examine each item carefully and convert every desire into a financial goal. This may be difficult for some items, such as the desire to become rich or financially independent. You have to do some deep thinking to convert that desire into a specific goal, such as having $1 million in ten years' time. At the end of this step you will end up with a list of goals only. Each goal should be expressed in dollar amounts and with a time for completion.

The Fundamental Financial Goals

Most of the financial goals that families set can be translated into the goal of achieving a specific amount of money by a certain date. For example, a goal of early retirement implies accumulation of enough savings — including pensions — to support the desired level of consumption after retirement. As we shall see in Chapter 16 (**Retirement Planning**), the goal for retirement is the present value of the desired level of consumption from the date of retirement to the expected date of death. Similarly, all expenditure goals — buying a car next year, switching to a bigger home in five years, sending the children to university etc. — can be translated into the fundamental goal of accumulating a specific amount of money by a specific date.

THE FINANCIAL PLANNING PROCESS

If goal-setting is half the journey to success in personal financial management, then the other half lies in devising a plan to achieve the goal, following through by taking action, and monitoring your progress until you reach the destination. Do you know why the majority of people never achieve their goals? First, they fail to plan. A worthwhile goal cannot be accomplished in one step. You need an action plan which takes a goal and breaks it into a series of sub-goals. By following the sub-goals, you know where you are heading day by day. Second, even if people do plan, they do not take action. The best plan in the world will not help you if you do not follow through with action. We shall now examine the important concept of the **financial planning process**.

The **financial planning process** is the system of setting goals, devising action plans and monitoring progress. It is a dynamic process that requires continuous changing and monitoring. The process has four main steps:

1. Goal Setting
2. Action Plan
3. Take Action
4. Feedback (Monitoring Progress)

The first step, **goal setting**, is essentially what we have discussed so far. We will illustrate the **financial planning process** by an example. John Ross (JR) is a 25-year-old who wants to be financially independent. He sets a goal of having $1 million by the time he reaches 40, 15 years hence. Note that this is a specific financial goal with a time for its completion. Thus, JR has completed step one in the **financial planning process**.

To reach a financial goal, an individual normally has to do two things: first, he invests the money in the right investment — one that can generate sufficient return so that the goal can be achieved. JR has $20,000 now, and he estimates that he can save $5,000 each year in the future. What must he do to achieve his financial goal? If the rate of return is too low, the goal cannot be achieved. What is the minimum rate of return on investment that must be earned to reach his goal? Let k be this minimum rate of return. If he invests the $20,000 to earn k% per year, the compound value of the investment after 15 years will be $20,000 $(1 + k)^{15}$. Also, if he invests the $5,000 that he will save every year for 15 years, the compound value of this investment — it is an annuity of $5,000 per year for 15 years — will be $5,000 $[(1 + k)^{15} - 1]/k$. Thus, the total future value of his wealth in 15 years' time is $20,000 $(1 + k)^{15}$ + $5,000 $[(1 + k)^{15} - 1]/k$. Since his goal is for this amount to be equal to $1 million, we have the following equation:

$$20,000 \, (1 + k)^{15} + 5,000 \left[\frac{(1 + k)^{15} - 1}{k} \right] = 1,000,000$$

Solving the equation by trial and error, k is equal to 23.92%, or 24% after rounding. Therefore, JR must find an investment that is expected to generate a return of 24% in order to reach his financial goal. To summarize, the first two steps of JR's **financial planning process** are as follows:

Step 1   Goal Setting:
To have $1 million after 15 years.

Step 2   Action Plan:
To invest his current wealth of $20,000, and $5,000 every year for 15 years in an investment that has an expected rate of return of 24% per annum.

The third step means JR has to take action according to the **action plan** — i.e., he must find an investment that has an expected rate of return of 24%. At this step, there are three possible cases. First, JR finds such an investment and is happy with the risk involved. In this case he simply invests his money according to the **action plan**. Second, JR cannot find an investment that can generate such a high return. The second case quite commonly occurs when a goal is set that calls for a very high rate of return. That is why the goal of making $1 million in a year from an investment of $10,000 is unrealistic: there is simply no investment vehicle in the world — except maybe the casino! — that can generate the required rate of return of 10,000%. In this case, JR must either revise his financial goal (Step 1) or revise his action plan (Step 2) or both. (More on this later.) Third, JR finds some investments that are expected to generate the required rate of return of 24%, but he finds all of them incur more risk than he likes. He is uncomfortable with the prospect of placing his money in these investments. This case is an example of how an individual's risk preference affects his financial goals and plans. Although theoretically his goal is achievable, JR's risk attitude prevents him from taking action. The third case is, therefore, similar to the second case; and JR must either revise his financial goal (Step 1) or revise his action plan (Step 2) or both.

In addition to risk preference, an individual's value standard and ethical attitude sometimes prevent her from acting according to the **action plan**. For example, some people refuse to invest in companies that are known polluters, even though the rate of return is satisfactory.

When the goals become unattainable, there are two things that you can do. First, re-examine your goal and revise it, if necessary. Second, re-examine the **action plan** to see if changes can be made so that the goal becomes achievable.

Formal Model for Analysis

We can model the financial planning process in a concise mathematical form. The mathematics should not intimidate anyone, as we use it simply to express what we have already said in words. We will use this model to show how everything in the rest of the book fits together in the process of meeting financial goals. Recall the basic equation from Chapter 1:

Financial goal (at time n)

= Existing savings + investment income for n years on existing savings

  + (Earnings − consumption each year)

  + investment income on the annual savings, n.

Let us model the plan using the following symbols to represent the elements of personal financial planning. The subscripts represent time: t is any particular future year; n is year the goal is to be met; and 0 is now, the starting point of the plan. Thus, if you plan to retire in 10 years, $n = 10$, and t runs from 1 to 10.

W_n The financial goal. This is the amount of money you are trying to accumulate for some purpose by a particular year. It might be enough savings to retire on at age 65, or perhaps the down payment on a house in five years' time.

W_0 The amount of money you have today that can be dedicated to the future goal.

k The rate of return that you earn on savings. It is expressed as $1 + k$ because you have both the original amount invested and the earnings.

E_t The money you earn in year t, other than investment income.

C_t The money you consume or spend in year t, other than that used to purchase investments.

$$W_n = W_0 (1 + k)^n + \sum_{t=1}^{n} (E_t - C_t) (1 + k)^{n-t} \qquad (1)$$

To reiterate, the left-hand side of the equation is the financial goal of the plan. The first term on the right hand side is the initial savings at the start of the plan, compounded at the rate of return, and the second term is the sum of the annual savings ($E_t - C_t$) as it is invested and compounds. Note that the compounding period for the annual savings is $n - t$, allowing for the shorter and shorter period of compounding as you approach the time of the goal. For example, if you have a 10 year horizon, the money you save in year four will earn investment income for six years (10 − 4).

Every chapter in the book relates to some part of this equation. Chapter 2, **Time Value of Money**, covers the basic arithmetic of finance that allows us to compare amounts of money received or paid at different times. This chapter, **Setting Goals**, discusses how to find a W_n that you can expect to achieve with your current and future savings. Chapter 4, **Budgeting**, shows you how to determine your present financial position (W_0) and plan for future saving ($E_t - C_t$). Chapter 5, **The Life Cycle and Financial Intermediation**, puts personal finance into the context of the family's stage in the life cycle and its relationship to financial institutions. This context determines different needs as n changes. Chapters 6 and 7, **Personal Income Tax**, and **Income Tax Planning**, provide a basic introduction to this extremely complex topic, which plays a major role in determining both k and $(E_t - C_t)$. Chapter 8, **Risk Management**, is the theoretical basis for insurance, and is thus the way you determine how certain you are that each of the specific elements of a financial plan will turn out as intended. Chapters 9 and 10, **Life, Health and Disability Insurance**, and **Property, Casualty and Liability Insurance**, are the principal means of ensuring that W_0 and E_t don't go up in smoke (sometimes, literally!). Chapter 11, **Debt and Credit Management**, deals with times in the life cycle when $(E_t - C_t)$ is negative and the family must borrow money. Chapters 12–15 deal with investing money to earn k in a wide variety of ways, including the personal residence, stocks, bonds and bank accounts.

Chapters 16 and 17 take us back to square one as we try to determine how much we need to live in retirement and how much our current savings pattern will provide. Thus, our goal of wealth available for retirement must equal the present value of all the consumption during retirement. If n is the age at retirement, d is the expected age of death and we assume that all payments or consumption expenditures occur at year-end, the previous planning equation becomes:

$$W_n = \sum_{n+1}^{d} \frac{C_t}{(1+k)^{t-n}}$$

Once we determine the desired standard of living and what it entails in wealth at retirement, we can return to the first equation and try to see if this goal is feasible. Essentially, the first steps in retirement planning are another application of the tools learned in Chapters 2–4.

We can use this financial planning model to analyze JR's options.

$W_n = 1,000,000,$

$n = 15,$

$W_0 = 20,000,$

$E_t - C_t = 5,000$; so that we have

$$1,000,000 = 20,000 \, (1+k)^{15} + 5,000 \left[\frac{(1+k)^{15} - 1}{k} \right]$$

The solution to the equation is 24%.[1]

Suppose JR has decided not to make the investment because he feels it is too risky. What can he do? He can choose any of the following actions:

1.   He can change his goal, W_n;
2.   He can change the amount of initial investment, W_0;
3.   He can change (e.g., increase) the amount of annual investment, $E_t - C_t$;

---

[1] In case you have forgotten the time value formulae, the factor $(1+k)^{15}$ is simply the future value factor, and $[(1+k)^{15} - 1]/k$ is the future value of an annuity. Not all time value calculators can solve this for k, but Super Rep or a standard spreadsheet package can.

4.   He can change the investment horizon, n;
5.   He can choose a different investment that has a different rate of return, k;
6.   Any combination of the above.

To illustrate, suppose JR changes his goal to 500,000, i.e., $W_n = 500,000$. Then, the rate of return required to achieve this goal is given by the solution of the equation:

$$500,000 = 20,000 (1 + k)^{15} + 5,000 \left[\frac{(1 + k)^{15} - 1}{k} \right]$$

The solution is $k = 17.17\%$ or 17% after rounding. An investment with an expected return of 17% is less risky than one with a return of 24%.

Goals should be reviewed periodically. If you find that the goals set in the past are no longer important to you and that there are other more important needs, you should change the goals to reflect that change. Goal setting and financial planning is a dynamic process that requires necessary changes to adjust to the ever-changing economic circumstances and to the changes in needs of the individual as he/she goes through the different stages of the life cycle.

Suppose JR does not want to change his goal (i.e., he still wants $1 million in 15 years). Suppose he cannot find any additional money to increase the initial investment (i.e., W_0 remains at $20,000), but he estimates that he can save $10,000 per year. Then equation (1) becomes:

$$1,000,000 = 20,000 (1 + k)^{15} + 10,000 \left[\frac{(1 + k)^{15} - 1}{k} \right]$$

Solving by trial and error, $k = 19.7\%$.

Priority or Ranking of Goals

You may now have a lengthy list of financial goals. Most can be combined into a few key ones, which would include two or three big savings/net worth/asset accumulation goals. There should be a good balance between short-term and long-term goals; and you have to estimate the cost of each. For a short-term goal of saving, or an asset purchase, the cost of the goal is simply the intended saving or the price of the asset. For a long-term goal, you can use the formal model of analysis and equation (1) to estimate the cost of the goal. Depending on your action plan, the cost of the goal may be one lump-sum investment right now, or a series of future investments, or a combination of the two. For example, the cost of the goal of accumulating x in ten years could be in the form of investing y now and z per year for a number of years. Every goal calls for the sacrifice of either current or future consumption, so it is unrealistic to expect yourself to be able to accept all goals. You will have to set priorities, rank all your goals, and only accept the most important ones.

SUMMARY

This chapter introduces and examines goal setting and the **financial planning process**. It is important to know the difference between desires and goals. Most goals in personal finance can be expressed in terms of the **fundamental financial goal** of achieving a specific amount on a certain date. We have examined the **financial planning process** and its four stages. Finally, we have shown how to use a simple mathematical model to analyze different aspects of goal setting and action planning.

KEY TERMINOLOGY

goal / desire / the fundamental financial goal / required rate of return on investment / risk preference / cost of goals / the **financial planning process** — goal setting — action plan — taking action — feedback, monitor progress / priority/ranking of goals / brainstorming

DISCUSSION QUESTIONS

1. Explain each of the terms under **Key Terminology**.

2. What are the two attributes of a financial goal?

3. Explain the four steps of the **financial planning process**.

4. Write down as many things as you can think of that would give you the most joy out of the financial aspects of your life. These may include wishes, desires, dreams, and goals. Separate the items into desires and goals. Change every desire into a goal. Rank your goals in the order of importance to you. Devise an action plan for each of the top three goals.

PROBLEMS

1. Woody Williams, 35, set a retirement goal of having $1,500,000 by the time he retires in 30 years. He plans to achieve this by saving $5,000 per year, which he will invest in term deposits, expected to generate an average return of 10% in the next 30 years.

    (a) Will he achieve his goal?

    (b) If not, what can he do in order to reach his goal? List all the possible alternatives of action.

    (c) For each of the alternatives that you have listed in (b), perform the appropriate mathematical analysis and present the **action plan**.

2. Mr Helliwell, a production manager at Polo Kitchens, is planning to retire in 10 years. His current liquid savings is $575,000. His goal is to have $1 million at retirement. He's been advised by his bank manager to put all his cash into a GIC that guarantees a 5% annual return, and also to contribute a small amount each year for the next 10 years, in order to achieve his goal. Calculate the fixed yearly contribution that Mr. Helliwell must make for the next 10 years.

3. After meeting with the bank manager, Mr. Helliwell decided to ask the advice of an old friend. The friend, a successful analyst at the brokerage firm owned by the bank, bombarded Mr. Helliwell with various ideas and recommendations. One of these captured Mr. Helliwell's attention: "Given the market situation, interest rates, real estate market, low mortgage rates, international mutual funds market, and etc.... I would strongly recommend to you not to lock all your money into a low interest rate. Rather, take a conservative risk and invest part of your savings in a stock

mutual fund, like Pacific Rim, which is expected to have a return of at least 16% for the next 10 years. Take advantage of low real estate prices and invest in a property that can provide you with a bit of rental income in the future, while it increases in value, even if it will produce no net cash flow for the next 10 years. Then, invest in the GIC the same annual amount you were going to anyway. You can still reach your goal of $1 million in liquid savings, plus have something extra invested in real estate."

(a) How much should Mr. Helliwell invest in the Pacific Rim mutual fund to make this plan work?

(b) Now suppose that he decides not to buy the real estate, but puts the rest of the $575,000 (that is, the part not invested in the Pacific Rim fund) into the GIC, as well as the periodic payment. How much does he expect to have in 10 years?

4. Mr. Goldman, 36, has just received an inheritance of $250,000. He wants to retire in four years' time, with $500,000. He has no other liquid assets, and cannot save anything more. Calculate the rate of return he needs in order to achieve his retirement goal.

5. Recent actuarial studies have shown that the life expectancy of a 65-year-old woman is nearly 30 years. This, combined with nervousness about the solvency of the CPP, is putting increasing pressure on individuals to save and invest for retirement. Assume you are advising a 25-year-old woman who plans to retire at age 65 and wants to provide for at least 30 years of retirement living. We shall ignore inflation in this question.

(a) If your client estimates that she will need to withdraw $40,000 annually at the beginning of each year during her retirement years, how much will she need to have in her retirement account when she retires at age 65? Her retirement account is expected to earn 8% annually.

(b) How much will she have to save annually if she invests her savings in an equity mutual fund expected to earn an average annual return of 10%? Assume she deposits her savings at the end of each year.

(c) What amount would need to be saved each year if the deposits were made at the beginning of each year?

chapter **4**

Measuring and Controlling Personal Finances

LEARNING OBJECTIVES

This chapter shows you how to do the accounting work that is essential in personal financial management. You can do very little planning unless you know the resources available, where they come from and where they are spent. Many families get into financial troubles because they do not pay attention to the basic 'housekeeping' of personal finance. Managers of financial institutions will tell you that they see this problem with their professional and small business customers all the time, even when these people earn substantial incomes and should have no difficulties in making ends meet.

You will recall that we cast the basic financial planning model in terms of your wealth today and the wealth you will accumulate in the future by saving. By the time you finish this chapter, you will know how to pull together the figures so that you have a large part of the raw material for doing personal financial management. We have four specific objectives, or tools, to master:

1. To prepare a family balance sheet that shows the resources and debts, and how much the family is worth in financial terms;
2. To prepare a family income statement that shows where the money came from and where it went during the year;
3. To prepare a budget for the next period of time that incorporates the family's objectives; and,
4. To develop control mechanisms so that the family meets its budget and continues to move towards its objectives.

ACCOUNTING AND PERSONAL FINANCE

You will notice that this chapter is very similar to financial accounting used by businesses. The similarity is deliberate. As we are using it here, planning and controlling your personal finances is nothing more than keeping track of how well you are doing, and families and businesses both need to do that. If you have previously studied accounting, you should find this chapter easy to understand, though this prior experience

47

is not necessary. Family finances are not as complicated as those of most businesses, and there are some significant differences.

First, the only reason you prepare personal financial statements is for managing the family finances. No one outside the family will use them, except to help you with your planning. Lenders will make their decisions based on some specific amounts, such as total debts and value of the house, but they won't use the entire statements. There is no such thing as generally accepted accounting principles for personal financial statements. Therefore, you prepare them in the way that works for you. We provide a detailed guide on doing them in the way that we think will be meaningful for most people, but everyone will have some differences in how they calculate, present and use their statements and budgets.

Second, the articulation that is necessary for a business balance sheet and income statement isn't critical in personal finance. **Articulation** means that the income statement items all link directly to the balance sheet, and the net worth amount (or retained earnings on a business balance sheet) is exactly the sum of all the previous incomes minus dividends paid. For example, if a business asset increases in value, then eventually the value is recorded as part of income, at which time it also increases retained earnings and the asset on the balance sheet. If your house increases in value we could record the increase on the balance sheet and in net worth without going to the trouble of recording it as income. Since you will live in the house for a long time, the value increases aren't something you can control, plan for or consume.

Third, we will tend to deal in cash rather than accrual income. For example, your investment in a university degree creates valuable human capital that increases your future earnings. A business might capitalize and amortize such an asset, but we treat it as an expense for personal planning.[1]

HOW MUCH IS THE FAMILY WORTH?

The family **balance sheet** or **statement of net worth** is a photograph of the family's financial standing at a point in time. It summarizes the major assets and liabilities, with the balancing figure being the net worth. The balance sheet is essential for two reasons.

First, it provides a **benchmark** or measure of progress in meeting the family's goals. The type of assets you have acquired relative to your goals and the net worth are the most relevant items. You may have stated one of your goals as some level of net worth at the end of the year. If you are trying to save for retirement, a comparison of this year's balance sheet with last year's will tell you how far you have progressed.

Second, the listing and valuation of assets shows what you have to manage. In particular, it will provide a listing for determining how much property insurance to carry (see Chapter 10).

The arithmetic is quite simple. The tricky questions are:

1. Who is a member of the family?
2. Which items should be included?
3. How do we value the assets and liabilities?

---

[1] Though you should see the section on human capital later in the chapter.

Defining the Family

We define a family as any group of people (including a single person) who share their wealth, revenues and expenses. By sharing we mean that they pool them, and make communal decisions about their use and management. Some members might have resources that they do not share, but the primary resources needed to live are held in common. Usually they occupy a common residence, but not always, or not at all times. This definition is broad enough to include the traditional married couple with children, same-sex couples, single parents and common-law relationships. The family can be the nuclear family or the extended family.

The problems occur when we look at the edges. A grown child who is staying at home while searching for a job is sharing finances, but not for long (the parents hope!). Dependent children in joint custody of separated parents, are part of both families, since they live in both homes and the finances are shared. Some of the planning will have to be done as if the parents were still together.

Most assets are held legally by a single individual or a couple, but for planning purposes we ignore the strict ownership, since we want to look at the joint planning decisions.

What Assets Do We Include?

The short answer is to include all assets. You must aggregate them into general categories and not try to list everything in detail. Your financial planning will not benefit from a detailed inventory of every tea towel and book you own. The most important assets are the valuable ones, and especially the ones that relate to something you can control or plan into the future.

We group assets into three categories. **Financial assets** provide income or are part of what you will consume in retirement. These are the most important for planning purposes, because they are the resources that determine progress toward financial goals. Aside from insurance and the principal residence, most of the personal financial management is directed towards these assets. **Personal use assets** are the ones you use in everyday life —the house, car, clothing etc. One of your personal goals is to have the appropriate (for your family) accumulation of personal use assets. They don't yield income, they provide consumption. **Luxury assets** are also for personal use, but they are very marginal to the family's needs. This categorization depends on what the family considers necessary. Many assets that Canadian families consider basic are luxuries for most families in less-developed countries. A major difference between luxury and personal use assets is that luxury assets are of high value if liquidated. Your kitchenware and used furniture will not bring much money, and will have to be replaced soon if you are to live any kind of comfortable existence.

Table 4.1 provides a checklist of the personal assets, but it is not meant to be exhaustive.

What Liabilities Do We Include?

You include any amount that any member of the family owes to someone outside the family. Table 4.2 contains a convenient check-list, divided into two categories.

Current liabilities are due within one month. **Long-term liabilities** are due later than one month, and often are payable monthly for many years. The current liabilities

TABLE 4.1
A Checklist of Personal Assets

Financial Assets	Personal Use Assets	Luxury Assets
Cash on hand	Principal residence	Jewellery
Deposits in financial institutions	Car(s)	Vacation property
Retirement Savings Plans	Furniture	Valuable collections
Tax refunds expected	Clothing	
Cash value of pensions	Household supplies	
Shares	Kitchenware, dishes	
Bonds	Maintenance equipment	
Mutual funds	Sporting equipment	
Options, futures, commodities	TVs, stereos, VCRs	
Precious metals, gemstones		
Real estate		
Direct business investment		

TABLE 4.2
A Checklist of Personal Liabilities

Current	Long-term
Credit card(s)	Consumer loans
Telephone	Mortgage on home
Electricity	Other mortgages
Natural gas, oil	Investment loans
Repair services	Student loans
Rent	Pledges
Property taxes, water	Amounts owed on leases
Income taxes	
Insurance premiums	
Current portion of long-term loans	

include the current month's portion of any long-term liabilities. This distinction is similar to that employed in business accounting, except that businesses treat anything due within one year as current. Most businesses operate on annual cycles. Households operate on a financial cycle determined by how often they are paid, which may be weekly, bi-weekly or monthly. While the choice of one month is arbitrary, it coincides reasonably with the cycle within which bills have to be paid, and hence is useful for decision-making. The distinction becomes most important for young families, when meeting the monthly bills is a close call. By calling debts due within one month current, we draw attention to the risk of having to liquidate investments in order to pay them if the current income is insufficient.

Valuation of Assets and Liabilities

Valuation of assets and liabilities depends on what you want the information for. This issue is highly contentious in corporate accounting, but we will try to make it fairly simple for personal finance. There are several possible valuation rules. None of them is ideal for every purpose.

Market value is what someone else would pay for the asset in a fair, arm's length, unhurried transaction. **Historic cost** is the original price. **Depreciated cost** is the historic cost minus an allowance for wear and obsolescence. Historic and depreciated cost are the principal measures used in corporate accounting. **Replacement cost** is the price to replace the asset in new condition. Replacement cost is close to market value for assets for which there is a ready market, like financial assets, homes and cars. The differences are due to depreciation, if any, and transactions costs. Personal use assets like clothing have little market value relative to their replacement cost.

Financial Assets

Value them at market, always. We hold financial assets for the purpose of their income or cash value, and thus they are a means to consumption. The historic cost is irrelevant for planning (except for calculating taxes), since what we want to know is how much we can consume by cashing them in. Transactions costs to liquidate them will range from 0.1% to 5% of the market value. It is rarely worth the trouble to estimate the transactions costs item by item; so we suggest deducting 3% if you want to be very precise, or just ignoring it, which is what we will do in our examples.

One particular aspect you can't ignore is accumulated income taxes. You will learn more about the details in Chapters 6 and 7. For now, let us say that the major tax issues for asset valuation are capital gains and sheltered retirement savings. The asset values must be recorded net of the tax payable in these cases, if the amount is material.

Personal Use Assets

The valuation rule depends upon the circumstances. The value of many personal use assets is irrelevant to financial planning, except for insurance purposes. Your future consumption depends on your future earnings from labour and investment, and not on selling the personal use assets. Therefore, if you value them at replacement cost and hence increase your net worth on the balance sheet, it is misleading. You can't consume the net worth increase, because you are already consuming it by using the personal assets. On the other hand, their ownership is an important part of your financial position. A family has to spend a lot of its early years of earnings to build up the fundamental assets like clothing, furniture, linen etc. A family near retirement has a stock of these assets, and so it is better off financially, even if it never intends to sell any of them.

Another factor is the future plans of the family, especially when approaching retirement. If the family plans to dispose of some of the personal use assets and use the money generated as part of the retirement fund, then these assets should be valued at market less cost of disposition.

We follow these general rules, though there are always exceptions:

1. Value the house and cars at market value. If you are planning to sell them and use part or all of the proceeds for something other than buying another house or car (retirement fund, purchase of a business, for example), value them at market less all costs associated with the sale.
2. Value all other personal use assets at replacement cost. Value any assets you are planning to sell and not replace, at market less all costs associated with the sale.

Don't bother with detailed valuations of every asset. Aggregate all the ordinary household assets into one estimate, with house and car(s) separated.

Luxury Assets   Value them the same as personal use assets other than the house and car. The difference between replacement cost and market is much larger for luxury assets in general.

Liabilities   Value all liabilities at the current value that you owe. This is not the same as market value, since if interest rates have changed, a loan might be worth more or less than the balance owing. For example, you would have to check the amortization schedule or calculate the balance owing on a mortgage as shown in Chapter 12, since the present value will be less than the initial loan.

A Detailed Example

You are a financial planner advising this family. You may learn more from this example if you do the suggested exercises at each step without looking at the following material.

Donalda and Harold Woodhaven ("Call us Donnie and Harry — everyone does.") have no children. They readily describe their financial position to you. Harry, 30, is a recycling supervisor in Vancouver's waste management department. Donnie, 31, is a bookkeeper for a fish processing plant. Two years ago they bought a modest house for $150,000, with a down payment of $45,000. They are very pleased that they bought when they did, since real estate prices have soared in Vancouver since then. They got a five year mortgage (25 year amortization period) at 9.25% for the balance. They have $200 in a chequing account, $500 in a savings account and $2,000 in RRSPs. Harry has some mutual fund units whose current market value is $1,500. They guess that their clothes would cost $8,000 in total to replace and that the rest of their household effects would cost $20,000 to replace. Donnie drives a 1996 model car that cost $15,000, including taxes. Harry drives a 1989 compact that is in good condition, and would sell for about $2,000.

The current month's balance owing on their credit cards is $2,500. All their utilities and property taxes are paid to date. Their joint monthly take-home pay is $3,600. Today is December 31, 1996.

Problem: Take on your role as adviser now.

Before you can answer their questions, you will need to make sense of their financial position. Start by preparing a balance sheet. Do you think there are omissions in the information they have given you? What questions would you ask? Take time now to sketch a preliminary balance sheet, and then write down your questions.

Answer: You could have asked any number of questions about missing assets and liabilities and valuation. You should have asked, at the least, if they have any luxury assets or employer pension plans, and if there is a car loan outstanding on Donnie's new car. You will want a current market value for the house, and you know how to calculate the present value of the mortgage.

Let us suppose that they have no luxury assets. They did forget about Harry's employer pension plan. The current value (total of his contributions and the employer's, plus earnings) is

$32,000. Donnie has no pension plan. They forgot the car loan, too. Donnie borrowed $12,000 on January 30, 1995, on a three-year consumer loan at 7%, payable monthly in blended payments. Given the rapid rise in Vancouver real estate prices, they guess that the house is worth $180,000 now. They could sell Donnie's car for $12,000.

Now prepare the balance sheet. Turn to page 54 for the answer.[2]

What Is Net Worth?

Can the family spend its net worth? The Woodhavens seem to be pretty well off, with a net worth of $143,269. Look again at the balance sheet. They have a total of $700 in cash, and that is what they can spend. If they sell the other assets to provide cash to spend, they lose the income, or the retirement income, or the use of the asset, whichever they sell. The house has gained $30,000 in value, but they still need a place to live. In the short-run, therefore, net worth isn't something you can spend. It is simply the excess of your assets over your debts.

In the long-run, net worth converts to cash as the family starts selling its assets. A family could sell a large house and buy a smaller one at retirement age, and sell some of the household assets. The members of the family stop contributing to pension plans and convert them into annuities to support everyday consumption.

One thing to remember is that most personal use and luxury assets depreciate over time. Maintaining and/or replacing them requires that you continue to spend part of your income. If you use all of your income for current consumption without maintaining the fundamental asset base, you will be worse off in the long-run, because you will have to replace the assets using current income. When you add inflation to the equation, you must increase your net worth in nominal dollar terms in order to maintain the same level of well-being.

Human Capital

Human capital, in financial terms, is the earning power that a person possesses. A doctor has more human capital than a carpenter, because she has spent many years to learn difficult skills that society rewards well. Even though human capital is very valuable, we don't put it on the balance sheet. Consider two people at age 18.

One becomes a carpenter, learning on the job and getting progressively higher wages. The wage level peaks in less than ten years, and after that the carpenter's income rises in real terms only by inflation or overtime work. Today, at age 35, the carpenter is earning $40,000 p.a.

The other person studies for many years, becoming a doctor. At age 28 she starts earning a reasonable income. By age 35, that income is $90,000 p.a.

At age 30, the doctor probably still has a negative net worth on the balance sheet as far as tangible assets are concerned. She has student loans and loans to set up a

---

[2] Super Rep uses a slightly different format, but the principles are the same. Super Rep shows the assets and the associated liabilities together, whereas Table 4.3 uses the more customary corporate format of assets and liabilities shown separately. The Woodhaven example is reproduced in Appendix 4.1 in the Super Rep format, which uses the term Net Worth Statement.

TABLE 4.3
The Woodhaven Family Balance Sheet, Dec. 31, 1996

Financial Assets:		Current Liabilities:	
Cash	$ 700	Credit cards	$ 2,500
Mutual funds	1,500	Car loan	371
RRSPs	2,000	Mortgage	887
Pension plan	32,000		3,758
	36,200		
Personal Use:		Long-term Liabilities:	
Clothing	8,000	Car loan	8,596
Household	20,000	Mortgage	102,577
Cars	14,000		111,173
House	180,000	Total liabilities	114,931
	222,000	Net worth (Assets – liabilities)	143,269
Total Assets	$258,200		$258,200

practice. At the same age, the carpenter has substantial net worth from 12 years of earning and saving. The carpenter's family balance sheet might look like the Woodhavens'. The balance sheets do not tell the whole story, because in the future the doctor's human capital will produce a higher income. At some point the doctor's financial net worth will exceed the carpenter's.

Why don't we correct the balance sheet by adding an estimate for human capital? The practical reason is that the estimation is very difficult and may be seriously wrong. We keep the family's human capital in mind when making decisions, though. For example, lenders extend a lot more credit to a young professional with few tangible assets than to a construction labourer with the same net worth. The difference is that the human capital provides a form of security.

There are three important personal finance decisions related to human capital. The first is the decision to acquire it. Higher material wealth is closely linked to higher levels of education. The person with grade 10 education and no other training rarely has the same material success as someone with a trade. In turn the university-educated professional enjoys even higher income, on average. In addition, higher levels of education provide non-financial satisfaction due to the achievement, status and generally more pleasant working conditions that attach to occupations requiring education.

The second decision is to protect human capital. Higher levels of human capital require more life and disability insurance, because there is more to lose.

The third decision is to maintain the human capital. Like any other asset, it depreciates over time. Perhaps there was a time in the near past when a person could acquire some trade or profession and then practise it for life without further formal study. That time has certainly passed forever. Now, you must engage in lifetime education if your skills are not to become obsolete. More people are finding that they must plan for possibly several occupations and employers during their working life.

This lifetime education, and flexibility to change work, is not necessarily formal. There are many ways to learn, including self-study, research, experimentation, formal

TABLE 4.4
Listing Assets and Documents

Houses, including vacation home

Cars: serial numbers, licence plates

Household items and personal effects

All financial institution accounts: bank, trust, credit union, broker

Insurance policies: held directly, through employer, on credit card

Investment assets held directly: real estate, securities

Safe deposit box and location of key

Last four years' income tax returns

Pension plans: employer(s'), including previous employers

Registered Retirement Savings Plans

Private business investments

Social Insurance Number, Health Card number of family members

Drivers' licences

Credit cards

Lawyer's name and address

Executor(s) name(s) and address(es)

Trustees(s) name(s) and address(es)

Insurance agent

courses and practical experience. What is critical is to realize that education in the broadest sense must continue throughout the working life, and money and effort spent on it is not a luxury, but a basic expenditure to maintain or improve the existing human capital and the income it commands.

Keeping Track of Assets

Every family needs to keep track of its assets and liabilities in another way that makes identification of them easy in the event of death or incapacity of one or more adult members. The required information includes identifying numbers, names, addresses and physical location of documents or assets. This list will also help with insurance claims.

The family should keep a copy of this list, and update it regularly. The family lawyer and the executors of the will or other family members or friends should also have copies. Thus, if anything tragic happens, at least someone will know where to find the relevant documents to handle the estate. Table 4.4 lists common items the family should record. The level of detail for household items and personal effects depends on their value and the needs of the insurance company.

THE FAMILY INCOME STATEMENT

The balance sheet shows the family's position today. The income statement shows how it got to today's position from last year's. We want an income statement so that we can see **how** we are moving towards our goals. It provides the basis for the **budget** that is the plan for next year.

We don't advise you to be too precise about the income statement. We call it income because that is the commonly-recognized term, but actually it is a **cash flow statement**, since in personal finance we don't do much accrual accounting. That is, we record income and expenditure when they are received and paid, not when they are earned. A business would capitalize a car and then depreciate its value over several years. We will record it as a cash flow in the year purchased. This makes for lumpy results, and sometimes negative cash flows, but that is appropriate. Businesses have much more flexibility to raise capital to cover the uneven cash flows. Families should recognize them directly in their planning, since they will have to either save up money in advance or reduce consumption after a major purchase.

Basic Format

We summarize the basic format in Table 4.5. Income is net of income tax and other withholdings (Canada Pension Plan, Unemployment Insurance premiums, insurance paid by the employee but administered through the payroll), including income tax paid or refunded based on the income tax return. Self-employed persons should also deduct contributions to Quebec or Canada Pension plan, since they will have to make contributions directly to cover both their personal and employer portion.[3]

Expenditures are any outlay of cash. **Expenses** are recurring expenditures made for everyday living. Defining which is which is a matter for the family. We do it because we want to control spending using a budget. **Non-discretionary expenditures** are ones over which the family has no immediate control usually repayments of debt principal. **Discretionary expenditures** are ones the family chooses, usually purchases of major assets or very large charitable donations.

The **net cash flow** that is the bottom line will add to cash reserves or be invested in income-producing instruments. It is the savings left after consumption and debt repayment.

TABLE 4.5
The Personal Income Statement

+	All sources of income, net of withholdings
–	Taxes not paid at source
+	tax refunds
=	Net revenue
–	Expenses
=	Net income
–	Non-discretionary expenditures
=	Discretionary cash flow
–	Discretionary expenditures
=	NET CASH FLOW

---

[3] We will return to the issue of non-discretionary savings later, since they do create an asset for the family.

TABLE 4.6
Family Revenues

Take-home pay from employment: Deduct everything withheld by employer — taxes, Unemployment Insurance premiums, pension contributions etc.

Self-employed net income: business, professional, commission, farming, fishing

Unemployment Insurance benefits
Welfare
Alimony and separation allowance
Child support
Old Age Security
CPP or Quebec Pension Plan
Other pensions

Investment income:
  cash dividends (actual, not grossed-up value)
  net capital gains
  rental income
  interest income
  other investment income

Deduct: Income tax payments made directly (i.e. not deducted by employer)

Add: Income tax refunds due to overpayments

Revenues

Revenue is not too hard to calculate, as you can see from Table 4.6. We do not include unrealized capital gains or windfall gains (like lotteries and inheritances) in the income statement. These do increase the value of the assets and the equity on a balance sheet, but we already said that perfect articulation of the statements is not necessary. We don't include unrealized capital gains because the income statement deals with cash flow. The chief reason to prepare an income statement is to lay the groundwork for a budget. Windfall gains are unusual and completely unpredictable; so there is no way that you can budget for them.

Expenses and Expenditures

Collecting all the expenses is quite difficult if you haven't kept detailed records. Most people don't. Table 4.7 shows a summary of the expenses a family normally incurs. If you get bank statements with all the cheques returned, and keep copies of your credit card statements, that will include a lot of the outlays. Missing will be all the cash purchases. While you can figure out how much cash you spent by going backwards — how much went into the bank accounts, and how much is there now — this doesn't help much in controlling or planning, since you need to identify what you spent the money on. You may have to guess a lot. Food, health and hygiene and entertainment are the biggest areas for cash expenditures. If you don't use credit cards, you will have even more unidentified items.

One way to collect the information is to keep very careful records for a couple of months. You can reasonably extrapolate the cash items to the full year, and use the actual amounts from the other payment records for the full year. An important consideration is

TABLE 4.7
Expenses and Expenditures

Shelter	principal residence: interest, utilities, taxes, maintenance, insurance, condominium fees; or, rent, utilities not included in rent.
Health and hygiene	personal and household cleaning materials, dry cleaning, laundry, drugs, toiletries
Alcohol and tobacco	
Food	show meals bought at work separately if material
Clothing	separately for each member of the family
Entertainment	movies, plays, cable fees, dining out, books, records, subscriptions, membership fees, sports clothing and equipment, babysitting, children's allowances, toys
Transportation	car(s): loan interest, gasoline, maintenance, licence, insurance car rentals taxis public transportation bicycle maintenance
Day care	
Insurance	not included elsewhere
Gifts and donations	
Financial and Professional	union dues, memberships, bank service charges, tuition fees
Vacations	
Vacation property	show separately from principal residence

how much use you will make of detailed expense records. If you won't change your spending habits by knowing how much you spend in particular categories, then keeping track of them is a waste of time. You do need to know how much you spend and earn in a year in order to see how much you are saving and to plot progress toward your goals, but further detail may not be useful.

Table 4.7 summarizes a categorization scheme for expenses. The family must determine its own categories.[4] Any of the items included in the main categories might be so important that it needs to be followed separately. For example, a family with four children actively engaged in a variety of competitive sports might want to records expenses for sports equipment, clothing and fees as a separate category.

As a matter of convenience, some expenses inevitably end up lumped into the wrong category. For example, some health and hygiene items are bought at the supermarket, but it is rarely worth the trouble to allocate the bills to each category, and so you include them with food.

---

[4] Personal finance software packages have a variety of categorization schemes. Appendix 4.1 shows the Super Rep version, applied to the Woodhavens.

Expenditures are a matter of definition for each family. We distinguish between **expenditures** and **expenses**, because the latter are 'used up' within the year, or at least fairly quickly. However, we call clothing and house repairs expenses, even though they do last for a long time, because they recur so regularly. A business might capitalize such expenditures and depreciate or amortize them over many years, but such a procedure is unnecessary for a family.

Two particular purchases will cause some planning problems no matter how we handle them. Most families purchase cars every few years. About half of Canadian families own their own home. Each car purchase, and the initial home purchase, will produce a very strange income statement if they are deducted as expenditures in arriving at net cash flow. The net cash flow will be a very large negative, and the money comes not out of current revenues, but from cash saved in previous years and/or money borrowed. As we have already noted, a business would capitalize such expenditures. Families are not formed to make profits; therefore, their balance sheets and income statements do not have to be linked as carefully.

Our suggestion is that a family record the purchase of cars and houses, including vacation homes, on the balance sheet, without putting them on the cash flow or income statement. Maintenance on either asset, short of full additions to a house, would be expenses. Since cars need to be replaced every few years, the wise family plans for this large expenditure, a subject we discuss further under budgeting.

Expenditures we record in two categories on the cash flow statements: discretionary and non-discretionary. The non-discretionary expenditures are primarily debt repayments. We split blended payments (which most personal debts require) into the principal and interest portions, with the interest portion as an expense and the principal repayment as an expenditure. Blended payments include interest and principal repayments in an annuity that retires a loan over a specified period (see Chapter 12).

The discretionary expenditures are items like furniture, home computers, cameras etc. The family has the greatest opportunity to change its spending habits in this category, because these expenditures are relatively large and not essential. Of course, expenses like entertainment and vacations are also discretionary, and it is the family's choice of what to call expenditures or expenses, and what is discretionary.

Detailed Example Continued

Donnie and Harry also provide some estimates of their expenses in 1996. You already know that they paid about $887 per month on the mortgage[5]. Their other shelter expenses included: taxes, $1,600; utilities, $1,800; insurance $200; and maintenance, $300. Hygiene cost $1,200; food, $4,000; clothing $3,300 for the two of them; entertainment, $4,000; gifts, $500; donations, $300; financial, $200; and a trip to the Caribbean, $2,500. They haven't saved much in the last two years, with the mortgage and car payments. Oh yes, their two cars cost $1,000 in gasoline and $600 in maintenance last year, in addition to the payments of $371 on Donnie's car. They also got tax refunds of $350. You already know their combined take home pay is $3,600 per month.

---

[5] The actual mortgage payment is $886.67. In the main text we round some of these numbers, but the calculations are done more precisely so that you can check at each stage to see that you can calculate the time values yourself. We do not need really precise personal financial statements.

Problem: Take Your Role as Advisor Again

Start to put together an income statement for them. You should find some problems, and ask them some questions. Try to see for yourself what you might ask them, before you read on to the answers.

Answer: The most important problem is that the cash flow their numbers yields is clearly wrong. They said they haven't saved much in the last two years, since they bought the house, and yet their surplus cash flow is about $8,000 on the basis of this statement.[6] Their total bank account, RRSP and mutual fund holdings are less than this amount.

This is not unusual, since most people underestimate how much money they spend. As adviser, you would ask them to consider a list of potential expenses, such as Table 4.7, and try to get the numbers closer. They could also try to get at the net cash flow by calculating how much their bank account and investments have changed since December 31st, 1995.

You should ask them about insurance on the cars, which is required by law but is not mentioned in their figures. They have indicated no asset purchases, no alcohol or tobacco, no spending on taxis and public transit. Food and health and hygiene also look a bit low, and since there are so many individual purchases made in these categories, it is easy to miss a lot.

After some more thought and checking, they added $1,600 in car insurance, another $1,500 in food, $500 in entertainment, furniture purchases of $1,500 and a compact disc player for $1,000 to the total. They don't smoke, alcohol was included in entertainment and they guess they spent about $100 on taxis and buses last year. Based on this information, you should now complete their income statement. Try it before you turn to Table 4.8 on the next page.[7]

HOW MUCH DID YOU SAVE?

Donnie and Harry seem to have saved $1,135, if their income statement is now correct. Appearances are deceiving, however, and they have saved a good deal more than that. The net cash flow is the amount of discretionary saving — the amount that they can control. However, they have been forced to save by repaying the principal on the mortgage, and by contributions to pension plans. As well, the employers have to contribute to pension plans, too. The money in the employer pension plan will be earning a return, as will any money in RRSPs and other investments. To the extent that these investment

---

[6] Try for yourself and see.

[7] The Super Rep version of this income statement appears in Appendix 4.1, where it is called the Cash Flow Statement.

TABLE 4.8
Woodhaven Family Income Statement, 1996

Take-home pay		$43,200
Tax refunds		350
Net Revenue		43,550
Expenses:		
Shelter	13,273*	
Food	5,500	
Health and hygiene	1,200	
Clothing	3,300	
Entertainment, including alcohol	4,500	
Transportation	3,972†	
Gifts	500	
Donations	300	
Financial and professional	200	
Vacations	2,500	
Total Expenses		35,245
NET INCOME		8,305
Non-discretionary Expenditures:		
Mortgage principal repayments	1,266	
Car loan repayments	3,404	4,670
DISCRETIONARY CASH FLOW		3,635
Discretionary Expenditures:		
Furniture	1,500	
Compact disc player	1,000	2,500
NET CASH FLOW		$ 1,135

---

* This amount includes 9,373 in interest, with the principal portion of 1,266 shown in Expenditures. The amortization schedule for a Canadian residential mortgage is a bit tricky. The student who doesn't know how to do it will find a detailed explanation in Chapter 12.
† The interest portion for 11 months is 672. Calculations involving consumer loans are explained in more detail in Chapter 11.

---

returns are unrealized (i.e. not included in income), they are also savings. If you estimate your total savings, as shown in Table 4.9, you may be pleasantly surprised.

You have to search for some of this information, but you can find it, or make reasonable estimates. Let us consider the Woodhavens again. Harry made the maximum contribution to CPP (no choice), as did the employer: that is, $806 for each employee and employer (5.2% to a maximum of $806). Donnie's earnings are less than the maximum pensionable earnings (MPE) and she and the employer contributed $586 each. Harry has an employer-sponsored pension. He could find out how much each contributed from his annual pension statement. Suppose he and the employer each contributed $2,000 last year, and the earnings on the accumulated value were another $2,000. They lost $400 in the mutual fund last year. The Woodhavens' savings for 1996 are shown in Table 4.10. Note that the repayment of the car loan is not counted as a saving, but the house

TABLE 4.9
How Much Did You Save?

	Canada/Quebec Pension Plan: employer and employee portions
+	Employer pension: employee's contributions + interest
+	Employer pension: employer's contributions + interest, if vested
+	Mortgage principal repayments
+	Deferred Profit Sharing Plan contributions and interest
+	Unrealized capital gains on investments
+	Net cash flow

TABLE 4.10
The Woodhavens' Savings in 1996

Canada Pension Plan	$ 2,784
Harry's pension contributions	4,000
Harry's pension plan earnings	2,000
Mutual fund loss	–400
Mortgage principal repaid	1,266
Net cash flow	1,135
	$10,785

mortgage repayment is. The car will have to be replaced within a few years, but the house, if kept in good repair, could last a lifetime. To look at it another way, if a person saves up money to buy a car and takes no loan, that person still has nothing saved once the car wears out. Therefore, borrowing to buy the car and repaying the loan does not create savings.

USING PERSONAL FINANCIAL STATEMENTS

The personal financial statements are generally useful as tools in further financial planning, rather than in their own right. For example, the income statement provides the basis for budgeting next year's spending. The balance sheet provides some information for risk management. Both statements are part of the process of setting goals. We will discuss all of these uses and others in future chapters and sections.

These financial statements do allow us to make a few statements about the Woodhavens:

1. They don't seem to have enough cash on hand for prudent management. Since their monthly take-home pay is $3,600, and they have $700 cash, they do not have enough to pay off the next month's current debts (credit cards, two loans), let alone eat. Presumably, they will pay off the minimum balance on the card, charge more, and pile up more debt.
2. When Harry's car needs replacing, they will have trouble finding the money to buy another one, and they can't cover all their debts now.
3. They will have to budget for reduced spending next year. The most likely targets appear to be entertainment and discretionary expenditures.

4. Aside from the short-term liquidity problem and the desirability of reducing spending somewhat, they seem to be in pretty good shape. They have bought a house, are paying down the mortgage, and have some other savings.

BUDGETING

The family **budget** is a projection of revenues, expenses and expenditures for a future period. It takes the same form as the income statement. The time frame may be for a week, a pay period, a month, or a year. Budgets for more than one year are not useful, except in highly summarized form, e.g. estimates of net cash flow and total savings for several years.

A family prepares a budget for several reasons: controlling spending, checking short-term liquidity and short- and long-term planning.

1. **Controlling spending**. A budget provides a benchmark against which to compare actual and planned spending. This works only if the family keeps careful track of its actual spending by category, compares it to the budget, and adjusts spending, all on a regular basis.

2. **Checking liquidity**. Liquidity relates to the ability of a family to pay its current and near-future bills without borrowing money. As we have seen, the Woodhaven family is quite illiquid, since it does not have enough money and income from the next month to pay all of the bills. When a family is illiquid, it should be preparing budgets for short periods — even weekly — in order to monitor the situation and control spending. For example, if they had seen this problem coming, they might have deferred the purchase of the compact disc player.

3. **Planning**. In the short-run, the budget focuses attention on the family's goals, since many of them relate to accumulation of money. If the family wants to take a special holiday next year, it must plan where the money will come from. In the longer-run, the net cash flow and the total savings become the planning variables for house purchases, and ultimately, for retirement. A family estimates how much it needs for long-run goals, then plans how much it must save each year to accumulate the required amount. The time value of money calculations equate the dollars over time. This long-run planning is necessarily more imperfect, since so much will change, but without it the family is unlikely to meet its goals.

The budgeting process is trial and error. The family uses its previous year's income statement (if it has one) as the starting point. The expected revenues are usually easily determined. The expenses are more difficult, and discretionary expenditures are a matter of which goals the family wants to achieve first. After the first run, the budget often fails to balance. That is, the results don't give the desired net cash flows, total savings and expenditures that are aimed to meet both the short-run and long-run goals. This process is also discussed in Chapter 3, where we show you how to set goals and monitor progress. The hard part is cutting expenses and expenditures, but it must be done. After some revisions, the budget meets the goals, or the goals must be changed to match what is feasible.

Practical Control   The textbook method to control budgets sounds easy. The family divides the annual budget into sub-periods, say monthly. Each month the results are compared with the budget. Some differences may have been unavoidable, or perhaps the family came in under the budget due to luck or good management. Maybe some expenses were deferred, but must be made in a later month. Once the differences are understood, the family decides how to change its behaviour, if necessary. Every member then implements these changes into his or her spending behaviour.

The reality is quite different. The previous paragraph refers to the way businesses control budgets.[8] A family that can follow that process and make it work probably doesn't need to put much effort into budgeting. The process of comparing actual and budgeted results is useful, but more practical controls are necessary for families who are having troubles meeting their goals.

The solution is some sort of **envelope system**. Every pay cheque is divided into the budget sections it has to cover. Once the section's money is exhausted, spending on it has to stop. The envelopes may be actual envelopes of money, or separate bank accounts. There are many variations on this system.

For example, a family might use a chequing account for deposits and regular living expenses — food, clothing etc. When every pay cheque is deposited, the budgeted amounts are left in the account. The rest is distributed into savings accounts, cash held in the home, an RRSP and a mutual fund. One account might be to save for a new car, another for major furniture purchases and home repairs. The mutual fund and the RRSP deposits are meeting the goal of saving for retirement.

Many personal financial planners recommend "pay yourself first" as a means of achieving savings goals. Set a target of how much you are going to save from each pay cheque, and then take that amount out first and deposit it outside the spending accounts. The popular advice is a target of 10% of take home pay. The difference between this and the budgeting as we have described it so far, is that saving, or net cash flow, is not allowed to become a residual, but rather is predetermined. The family is obliged to curtail its spending to balance a budget that yields the target saving.

If the family cannot control its spending without help, many employers and financial institutions have enforced savings plans. The employer deducts money from the pay cheque and puts it into Canada Savings Bonds, for example, or the institution puts part of each deposit into an RRSP automatically. In the worst case, a family can sign over

---

[8] Businesses have their own human problems with budgets, but the framework is at least honoured in theory.

its affairs to a financial counsellor who will take in all the deposits and allow the family only enough money to pay living expenses. The counsellor takes charge of paying off debts and accumulating savings. This latter alternative is both humiliating and expensive (the counsellor must be paid), but sometimes it is the only way to avoid ruin.

Credit cards are very helpful in managing personal finances, for those who can control their use. They provide a record of spending for budget purposes, and free credit for a period of time. However, the uncontrolled spender can destroy any budget created by using too much credit. One way to avoid this might be to have several cards, each with very low limits. Financial institutions may not co-operate with this plan to the extent needed to be effective. A better control is to use the credit card for only certain types of purchases. If the family is unable to control its spending on credit cards to match the budget, then it should cancel the credit cards and operate with cash and cheques only. **Debit cards**, which charge the bank account immediately, would be helpful to avoid carrying too much cash, but they are only in the early stages of introduction in Canada.

An important issue in the budgeting process is the right to privacy. We believe that every member of the family should have some amount of money, however small, that he can spend freely, without accounting for how it was spent. Children should have a small allowance to start their understanding of money, and they should be able to spend it on anything that they would ordinarily be allowed to buy. They will learn to deal with budget constraints much more effectively if they have some of their own money to spend wisely or foolishly.

Each adult should have some 'walking around' money as well. It might go on treats or a frivolous item of clothing you don't really need. What this freedom does is make the restrictions of a budget less irksome.

SUMMARY

In this chapter you have learned how to prepare three family statements: balance sheet, income statement and budget. The balance sheet shows the assets, liabilities and net worth of the family at a point in time. The income statement shows the net revenues, expenses and expenditures for the past year. The final figure is the net cash flow, which is also the family's discretionary saving for the year. As well, you learned how to calculate the family's total savings, including all the pension contributions.

The family budget projects the next period's income statement. It provides the basis for controlling spending and meeting the family's goals. Different families will use it in a variety of ways.

These statements are tools for financial planning, rather than ends in themselves. We will use them in our subsequent work in this book.

KEY TERMINOLOGY

articulation / balance sheet / budget / defining the family / discretionary expenditure / envelope system / expenditures / expenses / shuman capital / income statement / liquidity / net cash flow / net discretionary cash flow / net income / net worth / non-discretionary expenditures / personal financial statements / walking around money

DISCUSSION QUESTIONS

1. Explain the signficance of the entries under **Key Terminology**.

2. **Personal Project 1**
   Prepare a complete balance sheet for your family. Explain what valuation rules you used for each group of assets and liabilities, and why. Note any shortcuts or guesses you used to make this a manageable task, without losing too much information.

3. **Personal Project 2**
   Prepare a complete income statement for your family. Why did you choose the particular set of categories? Verify that your estimates are reasonable by comparing the net cash flow with the increase or decrease in financial assets.

4. **Personal Project 3**
   Calculate the total saving for your family for last year.

5. **Personal Project 4**
   Use the answers to the first three questions to assess whether there are any issues raised by the financial statements. Does it look as if your family is saving enough money for retirement (without getting too detailed)? Is the family sufficiently liquid?

6. **Personal Project 5**
   Prepare a budget for your family for a one-year period. Explain how you arrived at the amount in each category.

7. The savings control mechanism of "pay yourself first" means that you deduct 10% of every pay cheque (that is, 10% of pay after deductions) and put it into savings. The rest goes towards meeting all expenses and expenditures. This simple measure ignores both the family life cycle stage and the enforced savings in the routine expenses and deductions. Critically evaluate the validity of the 10% rule with respect to:
   (a) A couple with three children under 10 years old. The husband is a dock worker currently receiving unemployment compensation. The wife works as a waitress and brings home $300 per week.
   (b) A single male, aged 30, who works as a stockbroker.
   (c) A couple in their 50s, whose children have left home. He is a self-employed lawyer and she has her own consulting business. They have enjoyed a very good lifestyle for many years, including paying for all the education expenses for their children at private schools and universities.

PROBLEMS

1. It's New Year's Day, 1997, and Vincent and Anne Crago have decided to be more careful with their money. Lately, they seem to go from pay cheque to pay cheque. They want to look seriously at their financial situation and put themselves on a budget. "At the rate we're saving, we'll be 90 before we can retire!" says Anne.
   They have two children, Jenny, four years, and Ross, 18 months. They are planning to have another child in a year or so, but they would like to buy a larger home. With the way real estate prices fluctuate, they are worried that they won't be able to afford to move.

The Cragos have come to you for advice and have provided you with the following information:

(i) Vincent is a production manager in a small manufacturing firm. His salary is $54,000. His net bi-weekly pay after payroll deductions is $1371.37. Anne has a part-time job as a legal secretary and makes about $250 a week after deductions. Her gross salary is $15,700. The children stay in a home day care in the neighbourhood while Anne is working, at a cost of $65 per week.

(ii) They have a chequing account which is used to pay all their household bills and from which they draw their pocket money. The balance in the account at the end of December is $407.27. Their savings account has a balance of $4,123, and pays interest of approximately 5% p.a., on the minimum monthly balance.

(iii) Vincent always buys a Canada Savings Bond for $1,000 through his employer's payroll savings plan. When he receives the fully-paid bond in November he cashes it and the proceeds pay for all their additional expenditures during the holiday season.

(iv) Vincent gets a performance and salary review on the anniversary of his employment. He thinks he will get a 2% increase this year.

(v) Monthly mortgage payments on their $85,000 mortgage are $998.90. Monthly life insurance premiums for Vincent are $173. As of December 31, the policy had a cash surrender value of $2,133.

(vi) Monthly car loan payments are $273. License fees of $90 are due in October and March.

(vii) Anne belongs to a fitness and social club. She pays annual dues of $650 on Oct. 1. The club requires a minimum food and bar expenditure of $50 per quarter. Their payment cycle is March, June, September and December.

(viii) As one of the beneficiaries of her great-aunt's estate, Anne expects to get about $20,000 by the end of August.

(ix) Their average utility bills are:
$100 for gas, monthly
$ 80 for telephone, monthly (includes long distance)
$100 for hydro, bi-monthly (February, April, etc.)
$ 25 for water, per month, billed March, June and November
$ 25 for cable TV per month, billed quarterly (January, April, etc.)

(x) Vincent has a car valued at $13,000 with a $6,000 loan outstanding (originally taken out for a four year term). Anne's car is three years old and fully paid, with an estimated value of $10,000. Gasoline and parking costs $50 a week for both of them together, and repairs cost $1,350 last year. Vincent's car is still quite new, but Anne's is starting to show signs of age. For example, radiator problems (warranty expired) cost them an unexpected $465.

(xi) Insurance premiums are paid annually for the house and vehicles. House insurance will be $600 in May, car insurance on both cars totals $1,500 in October.

(xii) They spend about $150 per week on food, drugs and toiletries and about $10 per week on alcohol. Vincent figures he spends about $220 per month

(xiii) They have a $400 subscription for season's tickets to the symphony (paid in June). Before the concerts they treat themselves to dinner which costs about $100 for two. There are concerts in November, January, February and May. The children go a play group on Saturdays, which costs $150 every term. The term starts in September, January and May.

(xiv) Semi-annual dental check-ups for the two of them cost $100–120 in June and December.

(xv) Anne has a balance of $755 owing on her Visa card and Vincent owes $250 on his charge card. They do not always pay the full balances owing, but they try.

(xvi) There are other costs that must be covered — clothes, gifts, miscellaneous household utensils etc. Vincent says: "Thank goodness for credit cards. If there is anything left, I try to save some, but it never seems that there is anything left at the end of the month. We have tried budgets before, but it is impossible to stick to them. I guess you could say that I am a little sceptical that a budget will work for us."

(xvii) Vincent owns listed company shares worth $10,000 that paid $750 in dividends last year. He has $3,500 in Canada Savings Bonds (in addition to the payroll savings one that they just used up over Christmas), paying interest of $315 p.a., and RRSPs holding $15,000. Anne has $3,500 in her RRSPs and $5,000 in CSBs. Anne's interest income is $350 p.a.

(xviii) Household contents would cost about $40,000 to replace, according to the insurance agent. They feel that they could get about $250,000 for their house, before real estate commissions, legal fees and moving expenses. This year's property taxes will increase 2% over last year's taxes of $2,354. They are due in equal installments in February, March, April, June, July and August.

Required:

(a) Prepare a balance sheet and income statement for last year for the Cragos. Assume that they had no taxes owing or refunded.

(b) Prepare a monthly cash budget for the period of January to December, this year. State clearly any assumptions you make.

(c) Comment on the Cragos' current situation with regard to their cash budget and make recommendations on what they should do with respect to their current spending and saving habits. Discuss all issues that you feel are relevant to the Cragos' financial situation. How realistic is their desire to buy a larger house?

2. Jack and Natalie Novak, aged 32 and 30, respectively are living in a house they bought last year. They have only one child, Martin, aged 3, but they plan to have another child in two or three years. They have become a little concerned about their finances lately.

Jack is an engineer for a large auto parts manufacturer and Natalie is a legal secretary. Jack's gross salary is $65,000 per year, but after all deductions he takes home $3,700 per month. Natalie gets $31,000 per year and nets about $1,950 per month. Jack's 8 year old Volvo has been giving him lots of costly troubles in the last year, so he has asked the bank about a car-loan. Also, the Novaks are interested in getting a personal line of credit, as they sometimes experience cash-flow problems. They have been asked by the bank to supply a personal balance sheet and an income and expenditure statement. They have asked you to prepare these for them. They have provided you with a list of financial information as follows:

Cash on hand	$ 175
Bank Account Balance	950
Term Deposit	5,000
Canada Savings Bond	1,800
Home	250,000
Home Mortgage Balance	180,000
Jack's car (8 years old)	3,000
Natalie's car (1 year old)	15,000
Car-loan on Natalie's car	12,500
Monthly mortgage payment	1,292
Monthly car-loan payment	403
Bills outstanding:	
Telephone	35
Hydro	95
Visa (Minimum due $83)	2,816
Master Card (Minimum due $10)	150
Insurance (cars)	2,220
Estimated monthly expenditures:	
Groceries	800
Gas and auto expenses	180
Day-car/nursery	600
Utilities	350
Newspaper and magazines	50
Alcohol and cigarette	100
Entertainment	300
Clothes	200
Miscellaneous	200
Personal Assets	20,000
Jack's RRSP. (in term deposits)	3,000
Natalie's RRSP (in a stock mutual fund)	6,000

Jack comments further, "Before we bought the house last year we had no money problems. By the way, I have forgotten the property tax of about $1,800 and the home insurance premium of $450. Last year, I spent over $700 on landscaping. We really enjoy the home and the neighbours are nice, but it is costing us a lot more than we thought. I borrowed $25,000 from my father for the down payment. He is kind enough to charge me no interest, but I hope to pay him back as soon as possible, like several thousand dollars a year. Fortunately, I have a nice job and the benefits are good — medical and drug plan, pension plan, life and disability insurance, ... You name it, I have it! Natalie does not get any of those things, but my medical plans cover the whole family. Last year, we got tax refunds of $500 and $250, which we spent on a one-week vacation.

We usually take a vacation once a year. How much does it cost? Well, it depends on where we go...., about $2,000, I would say."

Required:

(a) Using the information provided, prepare a statement of net worth and a statement of income and expenditures for the Novaks.

(b) Based on the statements you prepared, discuss and comment on their financial situation.

(c) If their income increases by 5 percent, their total expenses by 4 percent, and their total assets (excluding personal assets and the cars) by 6 percent, what will be their net worth one year from now?

APPENDIX 4.1: FINANCIAL STATEMENTS AND BUDGETS USING SUPER REP

This appendix shows the Woodhaven examples produced using Super Rep.

NET WORTH STATEMENT FOR
Harold and Donalda Woodhaven

	Harold	Donalda	Other	Total Value	
ASSETS					
Personal Use					
Cars	2,000	12,000		14,000	
Clothing	8,000			8,000	
Household	20,000			20,000	
Residence	180,000			180,000	
Subtotal	210,000	12,000	0		222,000
Registered Investments					
Harold's Pension Plan	32,000			32,000	
RRSP's		2,000		2,000	
Subtotal	32,000	2,000	0		34,000
Non-Registered Investment					
Cash	350	350		700	
Mutual Funds	750	750		1,500	
Subtotal	1,100	1,100	0		2,200
TOTAL ASSETS	243,100	15,100	0		258,200
LIABILITIES					
Personal Use					
Credit Cards	2,500			2,500	
Car Loan		8,967		8,967	
Mortgage Loan	103,464			103,464	
Subtotal	105,964	8,967	0		114,931
TOTAL LIABILITIES	105,964	8,967	0		114,931
NET WORTH	137,136	6,133	0		143,269

PERSONAL CASHFLOW FOR 1996
Harold and Donalda Woodhaven
Prepared by Super Rep
PLANPLUS INC.

CASH INFLOW	CL.	SP.	$/MTH	$/YR	%
Investment Income					
Nontaxable income	100	0	1,800.00	21,600.00	50.00
Nontaxable income	0	100	1,800.00	21,600.00	50.00
Source Deduction					
Tax Refund	100	0	14.58	175.00	0.41
Tax Refund	0	100	14.58	175.00	0.41
NET INFLOWS			3,629.17	43,550.00	100.81

CASH INFLOW	CL.	SP.	$/MTH	$/YR	%
Family & Living					
Food & Beverage	50	50	458.33	5,500.00	12.73
Medical/Dental/Drugs	50	50	100.00	1,200.00	2.78
Transportation					
Vehicle Payment	50	50	197.67	2,372.00	5.49
Gas/Oil	50	50	83.33	1,000.00	2.31
Repairs/Maintenance	50	50	50.00	600.00	1.39
Accommodation					
Property Tax	50	50	133.33	1,600.00	3.70
Utilities	50	50	150.00	1,800.00	4.17
Misc. Housing	50	50	25.00	300.00	0.69
Property Insurance	50	50	16.67	200.00	0.46
Mortgage Principal	50	50	105.50	1,266.00	2.93
Rent/Mrtg. Intr.	50	50	781.08	9,373.00	21.70
Personal Expenditures					
Personal Debt Payments	50	50	283.67	3,404.00	7.88
Holidays/Vacations	50	50	208.33	2,500.00	5.79
Entertainment/Tobacco/Alcohol	50	50	375.00	4,500.00	10.42
Gifts	50	50	41.67	500.00	1.16
Prof. Fees	50	50	16.67	200.00	0.46
Discretionary Exp.	50	50	208.33	2,500.00	5.79
Miscellaneous Expenses					
Charitable Donations	100	0	12.50	150.00	0.35
Charitable Donations	0	100	12.50	150.00	0.35
NET OUTFLOWS			3,534.58	42,415.00	98.18

UNALLOCATED CASH FLOW			94.58	1,135.00	2.63

5

The Life Cycle and
Financial Intermediation

LEARNING OBJECTIVES

This chapter places personal finance in a theoretical context in institutions and the family life cycle. The specific objectives are:

1. To gain an understanding of the concept of the family life cycle and how it can be used to diagnose the most significant requirements of a family at different stages in the life cycle.
2. To explain the idea of financial intermediation and the role of financial institutions. Personal finance is a practical application of the concept of financial intermediation.

THE FINANCIAL LIFE CYCLE

People have a limited life expectancy, and during their lives they go through stages of differing financial position and earning power. We call the lifetime pattern of these stages the *financial life cycle*. Modigliani and Brumberg (1954) developed a formal model of it, but we will speak in more intuitive terms.

Early in your life you are totally dependent on your family for financial support, and your parents do the financial planning for the family unit that includes you. We don't consider this part of the cycle from your point of view, though we note that you are making a critical investment in your human capital during this dependent stage, and your human capital is the principal determinant of your future earnings when you are independent.

When you become independent, you have to find a way to earn enough money to at least match your consumption. Let us repeat the basic equation from Chapter 3, which provides a model of a financial goal, W_n:

$$W_n = W_o (1 + k)^n + \sum_{t=1}^{n} (E_t - C_t) (1 + k)^{n-t}$$

73

Early in the life cycle, your consumption is likely to exceed your income at least some of the time. Perhaps you are following a course of study that will raise your future earnings, even though it necessitates taking a student loan now. We consider the use of a house and other durable, long-lasting goods as consumption of their value over a period of time, rather than as consumption of the whole price in the year of purchase. You buy the durables because you want to enjoy their value over many periods, and this means you try to maximize your satisfaction over a long time frame, not for a short time only. During this early stage you are likely to have a lot of debt.

As you proceed through the life cycle, you start to earn more than you consume: $E_t - C_t > 0$. As your children grow, so likely does your earning power, until it peaks in middle age. As the children become independent and you pay your debts off, you find yourself with surplus income, or savings. The rate of savings increases every year, and of course the total balance of savings increases. Eventually, you reach retirement, and then your earning power becomes very low or zero. You start to consume the accumulated savings balance, and the savings rate is negative. If you plan perfectly, you spend your last dollar the day you die![1]

The essence of personal financial planning is arranging to meet the differences in earnings and consumption through borrowing and saving as appropriate. To some extent you plan your entire life rather than each individual step, in order to make the most of the resources you have now or may have in the future. Buying a house is a good example of the trade-offs. Most families buy their first house long before they have the money to pay for it. They borrow in the form of a mortgage, and repay the mortgage over a period of five to twenty-five years. The interest on the mortgage, plus the principal repayments, poses a heavy burden for most families, and also a significant risk if they suffer even temporary financial reverses like job loss or disability. On the other hand, as the mortgage principal declines, their earnings rise, and when it is paid off, the children (if any) will be at or close to the stage of independence. Now the family is in a good position to save for retirement, because the housing costs are quite low and will remain so, while the current saving rate is high and rising. Their pension contributions, the high savings from the time the mortgage is paid off until retirement and the house itself provide the means for a comfortable retirement.

The original idea of the financial life cycle of a person has led to many important thoughts in economics and finance. As a practical matter, we don't do our financial planning alone, however; we do it in family units. The field of marketing has developed the notion of the family life cycle, based on the pioneering work of Wells and Gubar (1966). We turn to this concept in the next section.

THE FAMILY LIFE CYCLE

Compare two individual males, each aged 35, each earning $35,000 per annum as mail carriers. The financial life cycle hypothesis would tend to treat them as identical. Now we tell you that Sam is single with no romantic attachments. Jaime is married with two children, aged 10 and seven. His wife, Sonia, is working part time as a waitress, earning $15,000 p.a. Sonia's mother also lives with them and does a lot of the child rearing.

---

[1] Assuming that you don't want to leave an estate for your children, if any.

Reprinted with permission — The Toronto Star Syndicate. © 1994 GREG HOWARD distributed by King Features Syndicate.

Even without any further information, we know that Sam and Jaime have different financial planning needs. For example, Sam and Jaime both need disability insurance, but Sam has no evident need for life insurance — he has no dependents. If he chooses to, Sam can do some discretionary saving and think about how to invest it. Jaime and his wife will be on a tight budget while the children are dependent upon them, and will have to make up their retirement savings faster when they are older.

We can group families into different categories in the family life cycle by looking at age and other factors. Marketers have found this way of identifying people is very useful for market segmentation in consumer products. Mayhew (1987) and Murphy and Rogers (1986) find that the family life cycle is more useful than age as a variable for identifying and analysing demand for consumer financial services. At the same time, the family life cycle captures the effect of the income patterns in the financial life cycle, even though they are more directly related to age.

A Modern Family Life Cycle Segmentation   We introduce the family life cycle to ease our task of diagnosing a family's personal finance requirements. The initial diagnosis based on this basic information is always subject to revision as the specific circumstances of a family become clearer, but it does help to put us on the right track.

No single scheme of family life cycle groupings is perfect, because there are always some families that don't fit into any category. Furthermore, the growing number of marriage breakdowns, changing demographics (an ageing society in North America) and reduced family sizes have altered the picture that prevailed when Wells and Gubar

---

TABLE 5.1
Family Life Cycle Categories

Category	Description
1	Younger single
2	Younger couple, no children
3	Couple, dependent children
4	Single, dependent children
5	Older couple, children independent or nearly so
6	Older single
7	Couple, retired
8	Single, retired

TABLE 5.2
Family Life Cycle and Personal Finance

Personal Finance Element	Significance of Personal Finance Issues by Stage in Life Cycle							
	1	2	3	4	5	6	7	8
Budgeting	H	H	H	H	M	L	L	L
Income Tax	L	M	M	M	H	H	M	M
Risk Management	L	M	H	H	M	L	M	L
Debt Management	M	M	H	H	M	L	L	L
Investment	L	M	L	L	H	H	M	M
Retirement Planning	L	L	L	L	M	H	H	H

Notes: L — low; M — medium; H — high. The stages correspond to those in Table 5.1.

developed their grouping pattern. Murphy and Staples (1979) propose a different segmentation that allows for single parents, for example.

Our categories, shown in Table 5.1, are a hybrid of those proposed by Wells and Gubar (1966) and Bernier and Robinson (1987).

DIAGNOSING PERSONAL FINANCE NEEDS WITH THE FAMILY LIFE CYCLE

Now we can do a rough diagnosis of the most important issues by matching the stage in the life cycle against the different elements in the book. This matching isn't perfect. The family unit may not fit in a category, or might be right on the boundary between two categories. The level of income, the expected future income and the level of liquid wealth may render a specific element more or less important than it would be for most families at a given stage in the life cycle. Nonetheless, Table 5.2 provides a good first diagnosis.

For example, consider the average single parent, life cycle stage 4. Money is tight, and so budgeting and debt management are very important. Income tax may be important if there are special considerations relating to a separation agreement, and there are the complexities of taking advantage of provisions of the income tax rules relating to child deductions. The single parent typically has little free cash for investing and can do little about retirement planning. Risk management is perhaps the most critical issue, because there may be no backup at all if the single parent becomes disabled or dies.

Let us recall where we started, with an individual or family optimizing lifetime consumption and saving. How do we accomplish this desirable situation of being able to trade off money now for money at some other time? We turn to that question in the next section.

FINANCIAL INTERMEDIATION

Financial intermediation is the process of transferring money from surplus economic units to economic units that have a productive use for the money. Intermediation takes place between sectors, and over time. Surplus units in one period may need more money for productive investments in another period. The surplus unit collects a rent on the money that economists call interest in a general sense, although it might be in another legal form, such as dividends. The financial intermediary collects a fee for effecting the transfer.

For example, you might imagine the house purchase discussed previously being intermediated this way. Jim and Tammy buy a house when they are both 25 years old. They advertise in the paper for someone to lend them the 70% of the purchase price. Ruth and Isaac are 50, and their savings are increasing at a good rate as they start planning for retirement. They lend the money to Jim and Tammy. For the next 20 years Jim and Tammy pay interest and repay the loan principal. Ruth and Isaac invest their subsequent savings into mutual funds (described in Chapter 15), retire at age 60, and finance their consumption with the mortgage payments. By the time Ruth and Isaac reach age 75, they need to start selling the mutual funds units. To whom do they sell them? Jim and Tammy, of course. They are now 50 and have savings to invest. Thus, at different stages the same family is borrower and lender.

The financial intermediation system in Canada rarely functions like the example, because we could not maintain our sophisticated economy if it did. Imagine how complicated the search for the couples to find each other would be. They would need to have the same amount in mind, and the same time frame. Ruth and Isaac would have to be able to enforce the collection of the debt if necessary, and would have to know how to write the loan contract so it would be enforceable. People would spend much more of their productive time on financial transactions, and would be able to achieve fewer objectives.

Financial institutions have emerged to act as intermediaries between all the different families and organizations that have money to invest or need money to consume. The financial institutions collect deposits or money for investment, risk pooling or transactions from all the families and organizations and repackage this money in the amounts and forms that different units need. Deficit units get money in return for paying interest that goes to the surplus units (with a cut for the intermediary). They have specialized employees to handle all the technical details. As to matching terms, a financial institution needs to make sure that the total pot of money it owes is less than the amount it holds or is owed, and that the cash flow in and out is reasonably balanced at any point in time.[2]

You can see that the financial institutions play a very valuable role in our society. Without them, our ability to save up for a rainy day would be very constrained. Money wouldn't necessarily move to the most productive uses, and thus we would all suffer from a weaker economy. A lot of the actions in your financial plans will require financial institutions for implementation.

CANADIAN FINANCIAL INSTITUTIONS

As you might imagine, the literature on this subject is enormous. We will content ourselves in this book with brief descriptions of the major kinds of institutions and the personal finance products/services they offer. A recent trend in finance is for institutions to seek the right to provide a wider range of products than previously allowed. The regulatory stance in Canada has been for specific types of products to be reserved for one group

---

[2] The details of the balancing function are too complicated to discuss in this book, not least because the amounts that will flow in or out at any time cannot be known for sure in advance.

of companies, leading to the term '**four pillars**'. The four pillars are banks, trust companies, life insurance companies and investment dealers. Separate statutes and regulatory bodies have developed for each of these groups. The reasoning is that conflict of interest and incompetent advisers are less likely that way. Canada has decided to reduce this separation a great deal, and both the Canadian and the provincial governments have been and are continuing to allow more cross-ownership and the offering of most products in most institutions. The protection for consumers is to be provided by rules governing the products and services, not just the institutions.

One response to the loosening of financial regulation in Canada and the US is the development of **financial supermarkets**. These are more or less closely-linked groups of different financial services and/or institutions in one location to serve consumers with 'one-stop financial shopping.' Since the different aspects of financial intermediation are connected, and consumers need a comprehensive financial plan, such a development seems logical. For example, you might enter a financial supermarket and go to a qualified financial planner for a diagnosis of your needs. He determines that you need more life insurance, a better deal on your home mortgage and a different house insurance package. You then go to a life insurance broker who shops the market to find the best term life insurance available for your situation, as diagnosed by the planner. The trust company that is part of the supermarket arranges for the transfer of your current mortgage when it comes up for renewal. A general insurance agent assesses your house and recommends better insurance coverage. Finally, you go to the supermarket's lawyer to have your will updated to include your newborn child. This is just one possible scenario. You can explore some of the issues by doing one of the Discussion Questions.

Chartered Banks   Everyone will be familiar with the traditional symbol of Canadian capitalism — the large national bank with branches across the country. Canada has two classes of banks: **Schedule A** and **Schedule B**. The Schedule A banks are Canadian-controlled and most of them offer a wide range of products and services to the retail customer through an extensive branch network. That range of services includes virtually any transaction service, most investment services, consumer and residential mortgage loans and a limited amount of insurance.[3] The Schedule A banks operate the payments clearing system that transfers cheques, deposits and other transactions among all the banks and other financial institutions. **The Bank of Canada**, which is controlled by the federal government, regulates the money supply, and provides temporary liquidity support to the banks. The Schedule B banks are much smaller, and much more numerous, but most of them have no retail branches at all. Their business is concentrated either in the corporate and commercial sectors, or occasionally in a particular ethnic community. A few of these banks do offer some retail services, but in general, when we refer to banks in this book, we will mean Schedule A Banks. Banks are regulated federally under The Bank Act. They must have a formal federal charter granted by Parliament.

---

[3] The insurance area is changing too quickly, and is too complicated to provide details. Until quite recently, banks could not sell insurance directly, but had found ways to offer it indirectly. For example, they offer life and disability insurance on their customers' loan balances, life and automobile insurance for rented cars through their credit cards. They are entering the retail insurance markets directly, now, but it is too early to predict how complete their coverage will be, and what it will do to competition in the market.

Trust Companies

Most trust companies are hardly distinguishable from the Schedule A banks in the services they render now. The principal difference is that they are smaller and have somewhat fewer branches, and they are often open much longer hours than banks in most communities. They do offer one other service — trust management. The trust companies manage estate and special trust funds on a fee for service basis.

There are some smaller trust companies that are located in only one city or region of the country, and they typically offer a smaller range of transactions services. Most trust companies are regulated and registered provincially, which has encouraged the smaller sizes. Some of these small trust companies specialize in financial services for the quite wealthy and they offer financial planning services as well.

Caisses Populaires and Credit Unions[4]

These are mutual associations owned by their own customers. To belong to one you buy a share or open a special account that is treated as share capital. Some or all of the interest paid on accounts will be legally a dividend. The common factor of the membership in a caisse or credit union may be the community in which it is located, the employer, the ethnic or religious group or some fraternal order. They are distinguished from other financial institutions by the collective social nature of their formation and governance. Their early success sprang from the need of people left out of the mainstream of financial power to have financial services responsive to their situation. Thus, even today there is a strong flavour of social responsibility to the community that is not present in other institutions.

The caisses and credit unions vary in size, but are generally much smaller than the trust companies and banks, and offer a more limited menu of services. The basic transactions services, term deposits, credit cards, RRSPs and consumer and mortgage loans make up most of their business. They are regulated provincially. All the credit unions in a province also belong to a co-operative 'central' that handles cheque clearing with the chartered banks and provides liquidity support in much the same way that the Bank of Canada does for the banks.

Mortgage and Loan Companies

Mortgage and loan companies, including finance companies, provide consumer and residential mortgage loans, and take deposits from the public. They do not provide any other services. Their deposits are not insured by either the Canada Deposit Insurance Corporation (CDIC) or an industry-sponsored co-operative. The retail depositor has to be wary, since they are generally quite risky, but may appear to be the same as trust companies.

Investment Dealers

Investment dealers provide primarily investment services. Their main retail service is acting as an agent to buy and sell securities — shares, bonds, and other more exotic instruments. They also provide access to other institutions' term deposits and offer self-managed RRSPs. They will manage your money and make investments using their own judgement if you wish, usually based upon some general

---

[4] They offer virtually the same menu of services in French and English regions respectively, although the origins are different. Alphonse Desjardins founded the first caisse in 1900 in Levis, Quebec. The first credit union started in 1932 in Nova Scotia, and the movement has since spread to the rest of English Canada, with its strongest representation in the West.

instructions you give them.[5] They make margin loans to their customers for security purchases. The name of the loan comes from the fact that these loans are limited to a specified percentage or margin of the value of the securities that the dealer is holding in trust for the customer. A few investment dealers offer limited cheque-writing privileges on customer accounts.

Life Insurance Companies

The principal business of life insurance companies is offering life, health and disability insurance for individuals, the subject of Chapter 9. However, the premiums paid up front accumulate very rapidly while the payouts occur later, and so life insurers have huge pools of money to invest. They invest most of their money in the corporate-commercial sector, but many companies offer residential mortgages as well. In addition, they offer a variety of RRSPs, Registered Retirement Income Funds (RRIFs) and annuities. These retirement investments are discussed more fully in Chapters 16 and 17.

General Insurance Companies

They are also called property, casualty and liability companies, describing the types of insurance they provide for individuals and companies. General insurance is the subject of Chapter 10. Like life insurers, they have a large pool of investable funds, but until recently have not been able to participate in other areas of financial services. They now have the right to offer residential mortgages, but are not yet major participants in this market.

Mutual Fund Companies

The term 'mutual fund' applies to both the company that offers it and the product itself. A mutual fund is a pool of securities held by a company. The company sells units or shares in the fund to individuals. Each unit gives the owner a proportionate share of all the securities in the fund, and is thus just another way of investing in securities. A fuller description of mutual funds can be found in Chapter 15. Many independent mutual fund companies exist to offer this service (and no other service). However, all of the previously-described institutions, except general insurers, also sell mutual fund units. Some have their own mutual funds, others act as agents to sell mutual fund units of the independent mutual fund companies, and some do both.

SUMMARY

Unlike corporations, people have limited lives, and so their patterns of financial activity follow a reasonably-predictable life cycle. Early in life, a person develops earning power, borrows money and saves little. Later in life, after he has purchased the major durable assets and paid off much of the loans, he starts to accumulate savings for retirement. Income tends to peak in middle age, usually before retirement. The retiree consumes the savings built up.

We gain further insight into the cycle when we look at family units, rather than individuals. The formation of couples and the birth of children affects the amount of saving and the sort of durable purchases. Marketing has developed the family life cycle,

---

[5] For example, a customer might specify that he wants the money invested in Canadian common shares of sound industrial companies, with the dealer to decide which shares to buy within that group.

and defined categories that are useful to predict consumption behaviour of families. We present our own set of categories, and show in Table 5.2 how personal financial needs are related to the stage of the family life cycle.

The theoretical economic relationship behind the relationship is the financial intermediation process. Early in the life cycle, families tend to consume more than they earn or can draw from savings, while later in the cycle the relationship is reversed. A complex and varied group of financial institutions exists in Canada to serve these changing intermediation needs. These institutions are specialized to some extent, but most of them are moving into different fields so that the differences between are less clear than they were even a few years ago.

KEY TERMINOLOGY

diagnosing personal finance needs / family life cycle / financial life cycle / financial institutions — bank: schedule A and B — caisse populaire — credit union — general insurance company — investment dealer — life insurance company — mortgage and loan company — mutual funds — trust companies / financial intermediation / four pillars

DISCUSSION QUESTIONS

1. Explain the significance of the entries under **Key Terminology**.

2. Which stage in the family life cycle are you in? What general categories of personal financial planning should concern you most now?

3. Discuss the appropriateness of the categorization scheme in Table 5.1. Can you think of any family situations not covered by the categories? What sort of changes would you suggest in these categories?

4. Demography is the study of the vital statistics of a population — births, deaths, age structure etc. The demographics of a given population affect the economy in critical and long-lasting ways. Once a particular trend is established in the population, it is largely irreversible. For example, the low birth-rate of the 1930s and early 1940s, plus the huge baby boom that followed that period, have created a population in Canada that has a large number of middle-aged people (the baby-boomers) who will form a large group of retired people in the next 20–40 years. At the same time, changes in health care and diet have led to much longer life expectancy for all ages. Our total population profile is thus showing rising proportions of older people in the future, with a large bulge of people aged 30–45 right now.

   (i) The above description of the demographic pattern of the Canadian population is very sketchy. Do some library research using Statistics Canada materials and anything else you can find to develop a more complete pattern. Try to include the effect of immigration and the multiethnic character of Canada's urban population in your research.

   (ii) What effect do you think the demographics of the Canadian population will have on personal financial needs?

   (iii) If you were the head of a financial institution, what long-run strategy would you consider to meet the changing demographic patterns?

5. Discuss the following statement in both practical and ethical terms:

Men make most of the significant financial decisions in Canadian households. A financial institution should develop a personal financial counselling service targeted exclusively at men in order to increase its share of the retail financial services market.

6. List the financial institutions you patronize and the services you get from each one.

7. Following up on Question 6, find a retail branch of each of: trust company, Schedule A bank, credit union or caisse populaire, large investment dealer. Obtain information about **all** of the retail services offered by each institution. Organize this information into a chart, with the columns being the four institutions and the rows, the different services. This chart will show both the extent of the overlap, and the extent of the unique services offered by different institutions. In the information you collect, try to include the fees for each service.

8. Financial supermarkets have developed to some extent in the US, though they have not been as successful as expected. The idea is well-known in Canada, but few institutions have tried it. Considering both the personal finance aspects, and the broader issues of how organizations compete:
    (i) What are the strengths and weaknesses of organizing financial services into a financial supermarket instead of independent companies and professional advisers?
    (ii) Do you have any ideas why the financial supermarket hasn't become a successful concept in Canada?
    (iii) You can organize a financial supermarket in more than one way. Suggest two different organizational structures for a financial supermarket and what advantages or disadvantages the different structures would have in competing in the retail financial services market.

REFERENCES

Bernier, Gilles, and Chris Robinson. 1987. *Personal Financial Management*, second edition, Institute of Canadian Bankers, Montreal (mimeo).

Mayhew, Barry. 1987. "Relationship banking and the life cycle concept," *Canadian Banker* May–June: 26–9.

Modigliani, Franco, and R. Brumberg. 1954. "Utility Analysis and the Consumption Function: An Interpretation of Cross-Section Data," *Post Keynesian Economics*, Rutgers University Press.

Murphy, Neil, and Ronald Rogers. 1986. "Life Cycle and the Adoption of Consumer Financial Innovation: Empirical Study of the Adoption Process," *Journal of Bank Research* Spring: 3–8.

Murphy, P.E., and W.A. Staples. 1979. "A Modernized Family Life Cycle," *Journal of Consumer Research* 6(June): 12–22.

Wells, W.D., and G. Gubar, 1966. "Life Cycle Concept in Marketing Research," *Journal of Marketing Research* 3(November): 355–63.

chapter **6**

Personal Income Tax

LEARNING OBJECTIVES

In this chapter we describe the general structure of income taxation in Canada, with some particularly important specific provisions spelled out in detail. We show you how to calculate marginal tax rates and after-tax discount rates, essential tools for financial planning.

We caution you that your understanding of income taxation will be very general indeed after you master Chapters 6 and 7. The *Income Tax Act* is a statute of Parliament, and as such you must apply it literally — by the letter of the law — including the various Regulations attached to it. Since it is a very long and complicated Act, complete mastery of it requires years of study and practice. Each province also has an income taxation statute. Except for Quebec, the provinces base their taxation on the federal rules and forms, but there are differences, and they are not consistent between provinces. Most of the topics in this book are governed by fairly basic principles of finance, and so you can understand and implement practically anything you will require after this course from a finance point of view. The specific application of the law to any given situation depends upon the facts, and you may require expert advice for any tax planning you undertake.

Furthermore, the *Income Tax Act* and Regulations change frequently, since different parts of them are affected by every federal government budget, as well as many other pieces of legislation. The Act itself is administered by Revenue Canada, which has built up a large number of procedures that are not recorded in the Act to carry out the law. Many of these procedures are documented in Interpretation Bulletins, Information Circulars and rulings on specific cases. Many years of court decisions on assessments made by Revenue Canada and disputed by companies and individual taxpayers add to the complexity, since these decisions are used as precedents in deciding future disputes. The same comments apply to the provincial statutes and revenue departments, though the complications are fewer.

We acknowledge an exhaustive review by Joanne Magee for the second edition.

We can deal with the most important considerations that will affect the majority of people in their income tax planning. We discuss the strategic aspects of planning in Chapter 7. You should view Chapter 6 as a necessary evil. It is quite technical and picky, but without it you can't understand Chapter 7, nor can you implement tax strategies. The concepts of a marginal tax rate and an after-tax discount rate, are very important in later chapters as well.

Our specific objectives are:

1. To provide you with a basic understanding of the structure of personal income taxation, including an introduction to how to fill out a personal income tax return.
2. To explain and illustrate the differences in taxation of different forms of investment income.
3. To understand and calculate marginal tax rates and after-tax discount rates.

GENERAL CONCEPTS OF INCOME TAXATION

Canadian income taxation is based on **self-assessment**. With a few exceptions, every resident — limited corporation, trust or individual — is required to complete an income tax return on **prescribed forms**. Someone else may prepare the return, but the resident is legally responsible for it. The final entry on the form shows whether the taxpayer owes money to the government or is owed money, and how much.

The fundamental rules are the same for companies and individuals, although in practice they may seem rather different, and the forms are quite different. The tax scheme is outlined in Table 6.1.

The Canadian system for individuals is **progressive**. This means that higher levels of taxable income are taxed at higher rates. The lower rate applies to all income up to a specified level, then all income above that level is taxed at the higher level. We can calculate both **marginal** and **average** tax rates. The average tax rate is simply the total tax payable divided by total income. The marginal federal rates are shown in Table 6.2.

The marginal tax rate is the rate that applies to one more dollar of income. If you are currently in the highest category or **tax bracket** and you are deciding whether to invest your money in a term deposit, the marginal after-tax rate of return you receive will be (1 − marginal tax rate) × (interest rate). Under a progressive system, the average rate will be equal to or less than the marginal rate, but only the marginal rate should enter into your decisions. If addition or subtraction of an amount of income would put you into a different tax bracket, then you have to use the two different rates pro rata on the amount of income to which each one applies. We discuss the issue of after-tax discount rates in detail in a later section.

The tax payable on taxable income in the different tax brackets is added up, and then **tax credits** are deducted. Provincial tax is calculated as a fraction of the federal tax payable after the tax credits are deducted. There may also be **surtaxes** payable. Surtaxes are taxes based on the tax, they are temporary (or so governments claim) and usually apply most heavily on upper tax brackets. Although they have a somewhat different legal form, their financial effect is identical to an increase in the basic tax rate, as far as financial decisions are concerned. Each province and the federal government have their own surtaxes.

TABLE 6.1
Basic Outline of Personal Income Taxation

1. Add all Sources of income (pg. 1 of T1)
    - Deductions (pg. 2 of T1)
    = Taxable Income (carried forward to Schedule 1)

2. Add all personal tax credits (line 335, pg. 3 of T1) = P
    Tax credit is 17%, or .17P
    Add all charitable donations = D

    Tax credit is 17% on first $200, 29% on the rest
    = .17 × MAXIMUM (D, 200) + .29 × (D − 200)

    Total non-refundable tax credits
    = .17P + .17 × MAXIMUM (D, 200) + .29 × (D − 200)

3. Federal tax calculation (Schedule 1, carried forward to pg. 4 of T1): Tax the first *x* dollars of Taxable Income at lowest rate, then the next *x* dollars at the next rate, and the remainder at the highest rate
    - non-refundable tax credits
    - dividend tax credit
    = Basic Federal Tax

    + Federal surtax (based on Basic Federal Tax)
    = Federal Tax

4. Basic Federal Tax × Provincial tax rate
    + Provincial surtax (rate and method differs by province)
    = Provincial Tax

5. Federal Tax + Provincial Tax
    - Tax withheld at source
    - Tax paid by installments
    - various other credits
    = Tax owing/Tax refundable (if negative) (pg. 4 of T1)

TABLE 6.2
1996 Rates of Federal Income Tax

Taxable income	Tax
$29,590 or less	17%
$29,591–$59,179	$5,030 plus 26% on income over $29,590
$59,180 or more	$12,724 plus 29% on income over $59,180

Finally, the taxpayer may have paid instalments or had tax withheld at source. Employers and certain institutions dealing in investments are required to withhold part of the amounts they pay out and remit them to the government on account of the taxpayer's ultimate income tax liability. These amounts are deducted from the tax payable for the year to arrive at a final balance.

Let us turn to the details of completing an income tax return to make your understanding more concrete. If you have completed your own income tax return for several years already, you will find that the next section of the chapter requires only a quick skim.

COMPLETING AN INCOME TAX RETURN

The personal Income Tax Return is the T1 GENERAL. The T1 return is slightly different for each province[1] and it changes somewhat every year. We recommend that you have on hand a copy of the most recent T1 package and read this section while following along on it. Otherwise, you are unlikely to understand much of the discussion. If you filed a T1 last year, that would be suitable. The T1 package, which includes two copies of the return and schedules and a detailed line-by-line guide to completing it, is available in post offices from about February to early May every year. During the rest of the year, you will have to obtain one from the nearest Revenue Canada office (check your phone directory).

First, some basic detail. The T1 General is four pages long[2] and all the lines that have numbers entering into the calculations are numbered. Revenue Canada employees enter each form into a computer format using these numbered lines, and the program then verifies all calculations. The line numbers are the link to the extensive Guide that accompanies the Return. For most people, all the knowledge they require to complete their returns is in the Guide. Indeed, the authors of this book rely primarily on the Guide in preparing their own returns.

On the front page the taxpayer enters some basic personal information. A taxpayer who filed the previous year will receive a T1 package in the mail in January, with two personalized labels to attach to the Return. Individuals must file their personal returns based on calendar years. For most individuals, the deadline to file the return (postmark date) is April 30 of the year following the calendar year. Taxpayers who have business income (and their spouses) get an extended deadline: Their returns are due June 15, XXXX, although they must still pay any balance owing by April 30th.

Total Income   The first section of entries accumulates all forms of income: employment, investment, business, etc. Note that several lines have both a gross and a net amount. These self-employment sources of income allow the taxpayer to deduct expenses from the gross revenue to the extent that the expenses were incurred to earn it. The unincorporated taxpayer will file an income statement and balance sheet to document this part of the return. If the taxpayer incorporated the business, then the business will have to file its own corporate income tax returns. The taxpayer-owner's income on the personal return will be salary, dividends and/or commissions paid to her by the corporation.

We will discuss the taxation of investment income: dividends (line 120); interest (l. 121); and, taxable capital gains (l. 127) in separate sections later in this chapter.

Taxable Income   The sum of the incomes is totalled and transferred to page 2. The next block of entries is various deductions from total income to arrive at taxable income. Persons can deduct from their income expenses that are incurred to earn income, although

---

[1] Quebec uses its own forms for provincial tax and we do not discuss it further in this book as the differences are beyond our scope. For the most part, the principles are the same as for other provinces, and the effects on financial decisions are the same.

[2] There is another form called the T1 Special, which is an abbreviated version designed to simplify matters for people who have no dividends, capital gains, self-employment income or other complications in their financial affairs. We will not discuss this form. The T1 Special does not involve a different set of rules at all, simply a different administrative procedure.

they are somewhat more limited in their ability to do so than are corporations. The Income Tax Act specifies particular items that are deductible, and the limits on deductibility. For example, contributions to registered pension plans (employer-sponsored plans) and Registered Retirement Savings Plans are deducted from total income, within specified limits. The contributions will be taxed later, along with accrued income, as the taxpayer receives them as part of a pension or lump sum withdrawal. The taxable income remaining after all the deductions is on line 260, and is transferred to Schedule 1. We will leave taxable income hanging in limbo for a moment while we take a look at the rest of pages two and three on the return.

Tax Credits   Page 3 contains the calculation of **non-refundable tax credits**. These tax credits are deductions from taxes otherwise payable, with a limit that tax payable cannot be reduced below zero.[3] The items include some basic deductions for the taxpayer and dependents (these deductions in effect ensure that low income taxpayers pay no tax), unemployment insurance and Canada Pension Plan[4] premiums, educational expenses, medical expenses and charitable donations. The total is multiplied by 17% (29% for charitable donations totalling in excess of $200) to get the tax credit. Now, let us turn to Schedule 1 and page 4 on the return.

Federal Tax   Schedule 1 contains the calculation of federal tax. Part 2 of the schedule is simply the calculation of tax at progressive rates. At one time there were 10 tax brackets in Canada, which led to some messy calculations and numerous tax planning opportunities. Now and for the foreseeable future[5] there will be only three brackets.

As you can see, the tax rate rises quite sharply from the first to the second bracket, but not as much from the second to the third bracket. This fact is important in tax planning, as we will discuss in Chapter 7. We expect the rates and brackets to be the same in 1997. You may wonder why everyone is complaining about high taxes, given these seemingly low rates. The answer is that we haven't dealt with surtaxes and provincial taxes. Hold on...

Continuing with the mechanics of the return, we see that (in Part 3 of Schedule 1) we deduct a variety of items from the federal income tax calculated in Part 2 of Schedule 1. The commonly-encountered ones are the non-refundable tax credits that we have already mentioned, and the dividend tax credit, whose intricacies we will discuss later in the chapter. The net of the tax payable and the tax credits is transferred back to page four of the Return (line 406). Also on Schedule 1 is the calculation of federal individual surtax. As you can see, it is a progressive marginal rate just like the ones in Table 6.2, but it is based on federal tax payable, not taxable income, and will only apply at the maximum rate to persons with quite high incomes. Now, we turn back to page four of the Return.

---

[3] At one time these items were deductions from taxable income. Credits are worth the same amount to you no matter what tax bracket you are in. Deductions are worth more to those in higher tax brackets, and the government decided, as a matter of fairness, to change to tax credits.

[4] Or, in the case of Quebec, Quebec Pension Plan premiums.

[5] Cynical observers would say that where change to tax laws is concerned, the foreseeable future is the lesser of the next election and one year!

TABLE 6.3
1997 Provincial Tax Rates

Province	Rate (%)
Alberta	45.5
British Columbia	51.0
Manitoba	52.0
New Brunswick	64.0
Newfoundland	69.0
Nova Scotia	59.5
Ontario	48.0
P.E.I.	59.5
Saskatchewan	50.0
N.W.T.	45.0
Yukon	50.0

The Federal Tax is entered from Schedule 1 and various other tax credits are now deducted, and the federal individual surtax is added to arrive at Net Federal Tax on line 420. The next two lines are important, but they have nothing to do with the *Income Tax Act*. The Income Tax Return is used as a mechanism for making certain social service collections as well. The next line is the provincial tax, and now we have to make another detour. Turn to the provincial return, T1C, that appears before the T1 and various T1 schedules.

Provincial Tax   This return will differ from province to province, and we will not discuss the differences in this book. The most important factor is the provincial rate. The provincial tax is determined by multiplying the Basic Federal Tax (from Schedule 1) by the provincial rate. Note that this is NOT the same as multiplying taxable income by the provincial rate.[6] The provincial tax as a percentage of federal tax is based on the federal tax before any surtax, but after deduction of non-refundable tax credits and the dividend tax credit. The provinces have various other provisions, including their own surtaxes in some cases. The net result is transferred to line 428 on the Return. Table 6.3 displays the current rates for provinces other than Quebec.

Quebec imposes its own direct rate of 16 to 24%, without using the federal return, and based on taxable income defined for Quebec only, which may differ from federal taxable income.

Balance Owing or Refund   In line 435 you total the Federal and Provincial taxes, plus the other social service collections, to arrive at the total payable for the year. The last block of numbers adds up the credits. The largest one for most people is the income tax already deducted at source, but there are other credits. Deduct the credits from the

---

[6] For example, the Ontario rate is 56% for 1996. If you multiplied taxable income by the federal rate (29%) and then the provincial rate, and added the two, you would have a marginal tax rate of 85% for a top tax bracket investor before considering surtaxes. Instead, you multiply the federal rate by 1 + the provincial rate. We discuss this under the heading of Combined Marginal Rates later in the chapter.

total payable for the year. If the number is positive, you owe money, and must pay by April 30th; if the number is negative you will receive a refund.

Everything Else   If you have been following along in your T1 General Return, you will have realized by now that we have only sketched in the outline. There are a host of subsidiary schedules and forms, only some of which are included with your return. For example, if you want to claim day care expenses, you will have to get form T778 plus instructions from your district office of Revenue Canada. If you want to claim moving expenses (allowable, within certain limits, if you move in order to start a new job), you need a pamphlet called *Are You Moving?* and you must complete form T1-M included in it, and so on. There can be a lot of "and so ons" in some returns, but it is beyond the scope of this book to cover them all.

What we have done is lay out the basic structure. You gain more familiarity with the details through practice — doing your own return or the problems in this chapter. For most of the important personal financial planning work, this basic structure covers the material things that will affect your decisions.

Super Rep will calculate personal income tax, though it does not print a tax return. There are many personal tax software packages that will calculate the taxes and print both the return and the schedules. We caution you that their main benefit is to avoid mistakes in the routine calculations and do them faster. If you provide the wrong data or fail to recognize specific tax planning opportunities, the software will rarely be able to do it for you.

INVESTMENT INCOME

Not all investment income is created equal in the eyes of the *Income Tax Act*. The treatment of different forms of investment income affects planning materially for most people, since you must invest your savings if you are to have enough money to retire.

Expenses incurred to earn investment income are deductible from income generally, though there are some restrictions. The most significant of these expenses are interest on investment loans and fees paid for money management by third parties.

Dividends

A limited company must pay income tax on its earnings. A dividend is a distribution to shareholders of some portion of the corporation's earnings, after it has paid tax on them.[7] The dividend on preferred shares is specified by the terms of the issue, while the dividend on common shares is at the discretion of the Board of Directors. The personal taxation situation is the same in most circumstances. When shareholders receive dividends from the company, they must pay income tax on the dividends. This is double taxation, and in order to neutralize its effect, approximately, the *Income Tax Act* includes the **dividend tax credit**. The mechanics sound deceptively simple: any dividend received from a Canadian company[8] is **grossed up** by one-quarter (that is, multiplied by 1.25) and the

---

[7] Dividends may also include a repayment of capital, but that situation is rare and we do not cover it.

[8] The dividend tax credit does not apply to dividends paid by foreign corporations to Canadian investors. These dividends are taxed at the same rate as ordinary income.

grossed-up amount, called the **taxable amount**, is included in income. The recipient deducts from federal tax payable a dividend tax credit equal to ⅔ of the gross-up. Note that this is equal to one-sixth of the actual dividend paid or .1333 of the grossed-up amount. If you receive a dividend of $100, the gross-up is $25, and the grossed-up amount that is reported on the tax return is $125. The dividend tax credit can be calculated in three identical ways:

$$\$25 \times \frac{2}{3} = \$100 \times \frac{1}{6} = \$125 \times .1333 = \underline{\$16.67}$$

The marginal tax rate is just the tax payable divided by the original cash amount of the dividend. Be careful to deduct taxes from the cash amount and not the taxable amount. The taxable amount is just a fiction used in the tax rules. See Table 6.4 for an example.

By contrast, if the dividend were taxed at the same rate as any other income in that bracket, the marginal tax rate would be (.26 × 1.69) or 43.94%. We won't show the details, but the system is set to make a small business owner indifferent between incorporating and remaining unincorporated, as far as income tax is concerned.[9]

This seemingly simple calculation leads to a great number of financial issues, because lower tax bracket investors benefit more from the dividend tax credit than do the top bracket investors. We will see more of this issue in later sections and in Chapter 7.

TABLE 6.4
Dividend Tax Credit Example

Problem:	You live in Newfoundland (which has no surtax). You receive a dividend of $100 from a Canadian company. How much income tax do you pay on it if you are in the 26% bracket, ignoring any possible federal surtax? What is the marginal tax rate you pay?		
Answer:	**Item**	**Calculation**	**Cash Flow**
	Cash received		$100.00
	Taxable amount	$125.00	
	Federal tax @ 26%	32.50	
	Dividend tax credit	<16.67>	
	Basic federal tax	15.83	
	Provincial tax @ 69%	10.92	
	Tax payable	$ 26.75	<26.75>
	After-tax receipt		$ 73.25
	Marginal tax rate		26.75%

---

[9] Active small businesses pay tax at lower rates. The dividend tax credit system leads to about the same tax on the company plus tax on dividends as the unincorporated business would pay on all the income at the owner's marginal personal rate. The dividend tax credit is too small to prevent some double taxation on shareholders in large corporations that pay tax at the full corporate rate.

Capital Gains and Losses

If you buy an asset either for the income it generates or for personal use, and subsequently sell it for more or less than you paid for it, the difference may be a **capital gain** or **capital loss**. A capital gain occurs when you sell a capital item for more than the sum of its original price and all the transaction costs of buying and selling it. A capital loss occurs when the selling price is less than the purchase and transaction costs. Capital transactions are taxed differently than income items, and so the first step is to distinguish between the two. It might sound trivial, but in fact defining what is a capital item and what is an income item raises difficult issues that lead to many disputes between Revenue Canada and taxpayers.

What Is a Capital Item?
Imagine you own a peach orchard. You sell the peaches from it every year. Your annual income from this business is the revenue minus the expenses incurred to earn it, including an allowance for depreciation. This income enters into your taxable income and is taxed in the same way as employment income.

Now you sell the peach orchard to another farmer for a price that is equal to the present value of the future net cash flows it will generate. The capital gain on the sale of the orchard is taxed differently, because the orchard is a capital item — one which involves earning capacity in its own right. The general principle that used to be invoked was that income tax applied only to periodic earnings from labour and/or capital, not to the sale of the source of the income. Therefore, capital gains used to be untaxed (at least, until 1972).

Today, most capital gains are taxed, but at a lower rate than ordinary income. Some capital gains are still tax-free. As a result, taxpayers have a strong incentive to declare any profits on investment as capital gains rather than as interest or ordinary income, and sometimes prefer to declare them as capital gains instead of dividends also.

For example, if the owner of a small company retains earnings in the company for many years, he will not pay personal tax on them, only the small business rate. If he then sells the whole company and is able to declare the profit as a capital gain, he has converted what would have been dividend income into a capital gain.[10]

Capital Gains
Capital gains, except of those that are tax free, are multiplied by 75%, and this amount is called a **taxable capital gain**. Taxable capital gains are added to income on line 127 of the T1 Return.

Tax-free Gains
The gain on the sale of a family's principal residence, including one-half hectare of land, is not taxable. If part of the residence was used to earn business or rental income, the gain may be partly taxable.

If a capital gain comes from disposition of "qualified farm property" or qualified shares of a small business corporation, a lifetime capital gains deduction of $500,000 is available for individuals. Once again, the details are quite complicated.

Capital Gains Reserves
If the proceeds from the sale of an asset are not all received within the year, the taxpayer may claim a reserve on a reasonable portion of the gain,

---

[10] This particular transaction is more complicated than we make it seem, but the principle is valid.

but it must all be included in income in equal annual amounts over the next five years, or when the rest of the proceeds are received, whichever comes first.

Capital Losses   If the sale creates a capital loss, three-quarters of it is an **allowable capital loss**. An allowable capital loss is first used to reduce taxable capital gains in the year it occurs. If there is any unused loss remaining, it may be carried back three years and carried forward forever for use in reducing taxable capital gains in other years. The effect of an amount carried back is that the taxable income and tax owing for that year would be recalculated, and a refund sent to the taxpayer in respect of the earlier year. Available allowable capital losses realized prior to 1985 may be deducted from other income to a maximum of $2,000 p.a.

Interest Income

Interest income is taxable at the same rate as all other income and interest income accrued but not yet received must be included in income. Individuals must use the "anniversary date" method to accrue income annually. For example, if you make a long-term investment on July 1, 1994 which compounds interest for five years without paying any of it to you, you will have to report the interest accrued from July 1, 1994 to June 30, 1995 in your 1995 tax return. Similarly, any interest earned from July 1, 1995 to June 30, 1996 would have to be reported in your 1996 tax return (and so on). The most common investment instrument this rule affects is compound interest Canada Savings Bonds.

CALCULATING COMBINED MARGINAL TAX RATES

The concept of 'marginal' is very important in economic theory and personal and corporate finance. Marginal revenue, or income, or expense, is the amount that is added to or subtracted from the existing cash flow because of a particular decision or event. For example, if you move $10,000 from a bank account paying 2% p.a. to a guaranteed investment certificate (GIC) paying 5% p.a., the marginal income is 3% of $10,000, or $300. The total income for one year from the GIC is $500, but only $300 of that is marginal, or *incremental* because of this decision.

The marginal tax rate is the rate that applies to the next dollar of income. It is very useful to know when you want to compare two investment opportunities that are taxed differently. The after-tax cash flow is what you receive, and so it is what you must base your decision on. The relevant marginal tax rate is the one that combines provincial and federal taxation, and allows for whatever differences apply to the particular type of income. Surtaxes have become so large that they affect the rates materially, although they are supposed to be temporary. Table 6.5 shows the current surtax rates.

The marginal rate is essential for long-term financial planning where we are trying to estimate how much a particular savings plan will accumulate, say for retirement. The savings will compound at the after-tax discount rate if they are not invested in a tax shelter. We need to know the marginal tax rate to calculate the after-tax discount rate.

The way to calculate the marginal tax rate is to model the application of the income tax rules using simple algebra. We will model them in steps so that you can see the general principles, and then can apply them to other situations. These models change as tax rules change, so that you must modify the models often. If the rates change while

TABLE 6.5
1997 Surtax Rates

Federal	3% of basic federal tax + 5% of basic federal tax over $12,500.
British Columbia	30% on B.C. tax between $5,300 and $8,745 + 54.5% on B.C. tax over $8,745.
Alberta	0.5% of taxable income + 8% of Alberta tax over $3,500.
Saskatchewan	2% of net income + 10% of basic Saskatchewan tax + 15% of Saskatchewan tax over $4,000.
Manitoba	2% of net income + 2% surtax on net income over $30,000.
Ontario	20% of Ontario tax between $4,555 and $6,180 + 46% of Ontario tax over $6,180.
Quebec	5% of Quebec tax between $5,000 and $10,000 + 10% of Quebec tax over $10,000.
New Brunswick	8% of N.B. tax over $13,500.
Nova Scotia	10% of N.S. tax over $10,000.
P.E.I.	10% of P.E.I. tax over $12,500.
Yukon	5% of Yukon tax over $6,000

the rules applying them are the same, then the models still work, but with different values for the variables.

First, we set up some notation:

t_c the combined marginal tax rate
t_f the marginal federal rate
t_p the marginal provincial rate
x the marginal $ amount of income being taxed.

We illustrate each model for an Ontario taxpayer, Mr. Dutta, with $55,000 of taxable income. Mr. Dutta is in the 26% federal bracket, and the Ontario rate is 56%.

Interest or Ordinary Income, No Surtax   The provincial rate is calculated as a percentage of the federal tax; so the combined rate will be:

$$t_c\, x = t_f\, x + t_f\, t_p\, x$$
$$= t_f\, (1 + t_p)\, x$$
$$t_c = t_f\, (1 + t_p)$$
$$= .26\, (1 + .56) = 40.56\%$$

For convenience, we drop x, the marginal amount of income, from the equations in the remainder of the chapter.

Dividends and Capital Gains, No Surtax   The grossed-up dividend, upon which the tax is calculated, is $1.25x$, the dividend tax credit is $.1667x$ and the taxable capital gain is $.75x$. For a Canadian dividend, the combined marginal rate without surtax is:

$$t_c \text{ (dividend)} = (1.25t_f - .1667)(1 + t_p)$$

Mr. Dutta's marginal rate on dividends is $t_c = [(1.25)(.26) - .1667][1.56] = 24.69\%$. For a capital gain, the combined marginal rate without surtax is:

$$t_c \text{ (gain)} = (.75t_f)(1 + t_p)$$

Mr. Dutta's marginal rate on capital gains is $t_c = (.75)(.26)(1.56) = 30.42\%$.

Interest or Ordinary Income with Surtaxes

Mr. Dutta, like most of us, pays surtaxes. The algebra gets messy, because the federal government has two rates, and the provinces all use different systems. We model the Ontario Fair Share Health Care Levy (a type of surtax) as an example, but the equations are not valid for all provinces.

The surtaxes create a new batch of tax brackets, because their break points do not coincide with the break points in the basic federal marginal tax rates. To capture them precisely, we would need an equation for each bracket, since the provincial rate is dependent upon the federal bracket. As a practical matter, the difference between the brackets is relatively small. We will illustrate in this section and the next one with Mr. Dutta's combined marginal tax rates. The basic equation is the same for each bracket in Ontario, and the other provinces that base surtaxes on provincial tax: Add the two surtaxes at the appropriate marginal rate to the combined rate without surtaxes:

t_{sf} federal surtax rate on the marginal federal tax
t_{sp} provincial surtax rate on the marginal provincial tax

$$t_c = t_f(1 + t_p) + t_{sf} t_f + t_{sp} t_f t_p$$
$$= t_f[(1 + t_{sf}) + (1 + t_{sp}) t_p]$$

To calculate t_{sf} and t_{sp}, we determine which federal and provincial surtax brackets he is in. As an illustration of how to calculate income tax payable from taxable income, we will also calculate the total tax bill for Mr. Dutta. You should follow along using Schedule 1 of the T1 General return. See Table 6.6 for a detailed example.

Dividends and Capital Gains With Surtaxes

The equations for the dividends and capital gains are changed from the equations without surtaxes in the same way. For a Canadian dividend, the combined Ontario marginal rate with surtaxes is:

$$t_c \text{ (dividend)} = (1.25t_f - .1667)[(1 + t_{sf}) + (1 + t_{sp}) t_p]$$

For a capital gain, the combined top Ontario marginal rate with surtaxes is:

$$t_c \text{ (gain)} = (.75t_f)[(1 + t_{sf}) + (1 + t_{sp}) t_p]$$

Table 6.7 gives the results of using these equations to calculate Mr. Dutta's marginal rate without and with surtaxes.

AFTER-TAX DISCOUNT RATES

Remember that we defined the discount rate for a decision as the best alternative rate available, all else equal. All else equal must include the effect of income taxes, and so we need to use after-tax discount rates, since the rates of return we receive are after-tax.

TABLE 6.6
Marginal Tax Rates Example

Problem: What is Mr. Dutta's total tax bill and his average and marginal tax rates, if he has $2,000 in non-refundable tax credits in 1996?

Answer:

	Calculations	Tax Payable
Taxable income	$55,000	
First bracket	29,590	$ 5,030.00
Tax rest at 26%	25,410	6,606.60
		11,636.60
– Tax credits		2,000.00
Basic Federal Tax		9,636.60
Ontario	.56 × 9,636.60	5,396.50
Federal surtax	.03 × 9,636.60	289.10
	(basic federal < $12,500)	
Ontario surtax	.2 × (5,396.50 – 5,310)	17.30
	(provincial tax < $7,310)	
Total tax		$15,339.50
Average tax rate	15,339.50 ÷ 55,000	27.89%
Marginal tax rate	.26 × [(1 + .03) + (1 + .2)(.56)]	44.25%

TABLE 6.7
Example of Marginal Rates with Surtaxes

Problem: What is Mr. Dutta's marginal tax rate, with and without surtaxes, for interest or ordinary income, dividends and capital gains?

Answer:

Income type	No Surtax (%)	Surtax (%)
Ordinary	40.56	44.25
Dividends	24.69	26.94
Capital Gains	30.42	33.19

To calculate the after-tax discount rate, we call k_b the before-tax rate, k_t the after-tax discount rate and t_c the combined marginal tax rate. Then,

$$k_t = k_b (1 - t_c)$$

We can demonstrate that this formula is precisely correct with a simple example. There can be only one price for a security on the market. Suppose the competitive rate for one-year Treasury Bills is 6%. Recall that a Treasury Bill is a pure discount instrument. It sells at issue at a discount priced to yield 6%, and by convention it matures at an even value. Suppose we have a $10,000 T-bill, and our marginal tax rate is 49.78%.

We know that the market is competitive; so the 6% rate is exactly the rate that makes the future payment equal to the price we pay today. What must that price be? Today's price is the $10,000 future value discounted one year at 6%, or $9,433.98.

After income tax, we won't get $10,000, because we have to pay income tax on the interest earned. The tax paid is

$$.4978 \ (10{,}000 - 9{,}433.98) = \$281.76$$

This makes the after-tax receipt $(10,000 - 281.76) = \$9,718.24$. The present value of this amount today is still $9,433.98, because that is the price on the market. If we discount $9,718.24 at 6%, we will get a much lower value. Now, discount it at the after-tax marginal rate, $(1 - .4978) \times 6\% = 3.0132\%$. The answer is $9,433.98. Conclusion: you must use after-tax discount rates to discount after-tax cash flows.

KEEPING UP TO DATE

How do you know what is happening in tax if the field changes so quickly? If your needs are very complex, or you aren't sure how complex they are, then you will have to hire professional help if you can afford it. If you can't afford it, the odds are very high that the amount at stake in your tax problems is modest.

You should be able to complete your return yourself, and do most of the tax planning. The Guide accompanying the T1 General Return is quite helpful and clearly written. There are also guides for many of the special forms required in the various circumstances. Revenue Canada also published pamphlets on some areas of income tax that many people have questions about. You can call your district office or visit it in person to get free assistance with your tax affairs. You should use this source for basic information, not for rulings on complicated situations.

If you want to learn a lot about taxation, the universities and community colleges have a variety of courses. You can get current textbooks and updates from legal publishers like Carswell and CCH. The largest public accounting firms and the provincial associations of CGAs and CAs publish fairly detailed booklets on tax planning every year. You can get these booklets free with a phone call in most cases.

SUMMARY

Rather than summarize what is already a very summarized chapter, we repeat three important lessons:

1. Income taxes affect personal financial decisions. We give you the basic outline of the effects in the chapter, and most issues you will encounter are covered.
2. Income taxation is very complicated, and we have left out a huge number of rules that will trip you up if you try to do sophisticated tax planning using only this book as a guide.
3. You must use marginal tax rates and after-tax discount rates in financial planning whenever the cash flows are affected by income taxes.

KEY TERMINOLOGY

after-tax discount rate / allowable capital loss / capital gains deduction / capital gains reserve / combined marginal tax rate / cumulative net investment loss / dividend tax credit / federal tax / grossed-up dividend / investment income / progressive / provincial tax / self-assessment / surtax / taxable capital gain / taxable dividend / taxable income / tax brackets / tax credits / tax rates — marginal and average / T1 General Income Tax Return / T1 Special Income Tax Return / total income

DISCUSSION QUESTIONS

1. Explain the significance of the entries under **Key Terminology**.

2. A popular idea among conservative tax reformers is the flat income tax. The basic notion is to remove most of the deductions and tax credits, and eliminate the progressive tax brackets. These steps would simplify the tax calculations greatly, and end many complicated income tax dodges that add nothing to real economic activity. The flat tax would be at a relatively low rate, say 20%, because of all the deductions that are removed. What do you think of this proposal?

3. The level of income for each tax bracket and some of the personal deductions and credits are partially indexed for inflation. That is, they increase each year by the inflation rate.[11]

    (a) Why is this necessary? What would happen if they weren't indexed?

    (b) At the current low levels of inflation (about 1% p.a. at the date of this book) there is no indexation. What will happen if inflation continues at 1% for the next 10 years to a pensioner with fixed taxable income of $28,000?

PROBLEMS

1. Randy Huffman has asked you to prepare his 1996 income tax return. He is president of a firm that publishes Regency romances and post-modern poetry. He has been divorced from his former wife, Sandy, for several years. His son Max (17 years old) and his daughter Min (12 years old) live with him. His household also includes his father, Mick, who is an unemployed inventor working on a new production process for sealing wax. His father's friend, Bianca, also lives with them. Max earned $3,500 in his summer job in 1996, but Randy is the only other member of the household with an income. His 1996 T4 form from the publishing firm shows the following:

Employment Income	$80,098.00
Canada Pension Plan	806.00
Unemployment Insc. Prem	1,245.24
Registered pension plan	4,000.00
Tax withheld	19,000.00

His donations receipts include:

Friends of the Earth	$300
Pollution Probe	200
York University	200
Federation of Ontario Naturalists	50
Green Party of Canada	150
	$900

---

[11] To be precise, they are indexed by any amount that the inflation rate exceeds 3% in the previous year.

His T5 slips for investment income include:

Taxable Dividends:	
Apple Computer	US$ 44.00
Bell Canada	88.46
Inco	US$ 74.00
Nova G preferred	90.00
Interest: Tottery Bank	$428.59

In December 1996 he sold 10,000 shares of Pure Gold Resources shares for $4,500, less commission of $120. He bought them in May 1996 for $2,100, including commission.

Under the terms of his original separation agreement with Sandy and the subsequent divorce, he paid her alimony of $6,000 during 1996. She got into some financial trouble when her car broke down, and he loaned her $5,000 to help her buy another one, at a zero interest rate. In December she was still having bad luck; so he forgave half the loan and she repaid only $2,500.

Randy received $400 in royalties on sales of a book of poetry he wrote. He paid $125 in annual dues to the League of Canadian Poets. He paid $25 to rent a safe deposit box at the bank.

The average exchange rate in 1996 was US$1 = CAN$1.32

Required:

Prepare his return, with schedules as needed. Assume that the necessary receipts exist. [Super Rep will calculate the tax payable, but does not print the return and schedules.]

2. Jason Barnes is the President of the Nutshell Manufacturing Company Ltd. He is a major shareholder of the company, holding 75% of the common shares. The other shareholders are his wife, Betty (20%), and his cousin (5%). Jason and Betty have three children: Jimmy (19 years old), who is a first year university student living away from home; Hanna (10 years old) and Janice (5 years old). Although Betty is a full-time homemaker, she earned $4,500 in 1996 for doing some typing and clerical work for Nutshell when the secretary went on vacation. Jimmy earned $4,100 in his summer job in 1996. The family lives in [location to be be provided by instructor].

The following information is available from Jason's 1996 T4 form from Nutshell:

Employment income	$72,000.00
Canada Pension Plan contribution	806.00
Unemployment Insurance premium	1,245.24
Income Taxes paid	18,736.00
Registered Pension Plan contribution	2,500.00

On January 3, 1997, he contributed $8,000 to an RRSP account and received a receipt for tax purposes, but he is not sure how much he can claim for 1996. His pension adjustment on his 1996 T4 was $5,250.

Jason and Betty jointly own a rental property. The relevant information for the property for 1996 is as follows:

Gross rent	$18,500.00
Mortgage interest	12,581.61
Property taxes	3,175.42
Utilities	1,578.11
Insurance Premium	1,438.92
Sundry expenses	750.13

In 1990, Jason bought $50,000 in Canadian stock mutual funds. The purchase was financed partly by a loan of $30,000 on which he pays prime plus one per cent interest. The value of the mutual funds has increased to $65,000 and the loan of $30,000 is still outstanding. The mutual funds paid dividends of $1,200 in 1996 and Jason paid $2,752 in interest on the loan. The Barnes rent a safe deposit box at an annual cost of $100. The Barnes' T5 slips for investment income include:

Dividends:

Nutshell (Jason)	$30,000.00
(Betty)	8,000.00
Canada Mutual Funds	1,200.00

Interest:

Joint bank account	361.20
Term deposit (Betty)	1,150.00

Jason donated $560 to the United Way. Betty donated $800 to their church. They sent Hanna and Janice to a day-care programme after school, at a cost of $50 per week for each child (40 weeks). Jimmy paid tuition fees of $2,500 in 1996.

Required:

(a) Prepare income tax returns for Jason and Betty, with schedules as required.

(b) [This is an advanced question, and requires you to do some research outside the textbook.] They didn't claim any capital cost allowance on their rental property. What is capital cost allowance? Why didn't they claim it?

3. Linda Resch is an investment dealer in Brockville, Ontario. She has identified two low risk investments that are appropriate for clients who want secure earnings. One is a guaranteed preferred share to be issued tomorrow by a Canadian company. The price is $25 and it pays a quarterly dividend of $0.25. It will be redeemed at par in 10 years by the company. The payment of dividends and the redemption payment are guaranteed by a large bank. The other investment is a 10-year Canada bond to be issued at par tomorrow, with a yield-to-maturity of 5.4%. It pays a semi-annual coupon. She has two customers for whom the risk level of these investments seems appropriate:

(a) Peter Poor has a marginal federal tax rate of 17% and is subject to the 3% federal surtax, but not to any provincial surtax. Which of the two securities is better for him?

(b) Wendy Wealthy has a marginal federal tax rate of 29% and pays the highest marginal federal and provincial surtaxes. Which of the two securities is better for her?

4. You are a taxpayer with a marginal tax rate of 44% (all surtaxes included) for interest income. You are considering buying a 5% bond for $950. It matures in five years and pays interest semi-annually.

    (a) What is the yield-to-maturity? What is the effective annual rate?

    (b) What is your expected after-tax EAR?

    (c) What assumption did you have to make to be able to solve this problem (No, it has nothing to do with a flat term structure)?

5.   Mary James, a self-employed interior designer in P.E.I., has earned $45,000 in consulting fees. She also received $2,000 interest income. If she has $1,800 in non-refundable tax credits, what is her total income tax bill for the year?

6.   For each part of this problem, non-refundable tax credits are $2,400.

    (a) Nick Orlando earns $70,000 p.a. at Alcan in Hamilton, Ontario. He recently received a dividend of $4,500 from Bell Canada. How much tax does he have to pay on the dividend?

    (b) How much tax does he pay on the dividend if his salary is $50,000?

    (c) How much tax does he pay on the dividend if his salary is $90,000?

7.   Syed has a federal marginal tax rate of 29% and a provincial rate of 60%, with no surtax. He is considering buying a one-year Treasury bill paying 5%. Calculate his expected after-tax rate of return.

chapter 7

Income Tax Planning

LEARNING OBJECTIVES

Now that you understand the general structure of income taxation in Canada we consider how you can legally minimize the amount of income tax you pay. The same warnings apply. The *Income Tax Act* is a complex statute of Parliament, and it changes frequently. The specific details of any situation may require more specialized knowledge than we provide in this book.

We establish the fundamental principles and provide examples of how to apply them in situations that will cover most of the tax minimization opportunities available to you. The principles hold true even when the Act changes, because they arise from three basic aspects of the nature of income taxation in Canada and most other countries:

1. The tax rates are progressive and the rate for each higher bracket applies only to the additional or marginal income.
2. Governments try to achieve several objectives at once with taxation laws: raise revenue; promote social equity; encourage/discourage certain financial actions; and manage economic trends.
3. Income tax deferred costs are less than that paid currently, because of the time value of money.

Our specific objectives are:

1. To explain the four fundamental tax minimization strategies: income deferral, income splitting, income spreading and tax shelters.
2. To illustrate these strategies with the specific techniques commonly available at the present time in Canada.

INCOME DEFERRAL

The general principle involved in **income deferral** is that if you can't use the income for consumption purposes, you shouldn't have to pay tax on it until you can use it. If

We acknowledge an exhaustive review by Joanne Magee for the second edition.

you can invest the tax-deferred income at a rate of return which is untaxed, then you get a second advantage with faster compounding.

Registered Pension Plans

A **registered pension plan (RPP)** is established by an employer to defer income payable to employees to provide retirement income for them. Such a plan may have payments made into it by either or both the employer and the employee, depending on the terms of the plan. The contributions are deposited with a plan trustee who invests them. When the employee retires, he receives a pension from the plan. We discuss pension plans in more detail in the retirement planning chapters, but the key tax aspect is that the contributions to the plan are not taxed as income in the employee's hands at the time they are put into the plan.[1] The employee pays tax on the pension as it is received. Thus, the employee's pension contributions are deductible from taxable income, and accumulate at the before-tax rate of return. The employer's contributions are not included in the employee's income until they are paid out of the plan in retirement, and these contributions also accumulate at the before-tax rate of return.

Most people will have no planning to do with respect to a registered pension plan. The contributions are fixed by the terms of employment. Occasionally, the plan may be retroactively amended to allow for higher contributions for past service, or to allow employees to join the plan who were not previously in it, and to gain credit for past service. If such an amendment allows a person to make **past service contributions**, they are almost always worth doing. In effect, you get a tax deduction for buying more pension income.

Registered Retirement Savings Plan

A Registered Retirement Savings Plan (RRSP) is a do-it-yourself pension plan. The taxpayer contributes part of her income to a trusteed fund. The contribution is deducted from income for tax purposes in the year it is paid into the fund, and income on it accumulates tax-free. When the taxpayer withdraws it for spending purposes, the entire amount, principal and accrued earnings, is taxable.[2] The amount you can contribute in a year is the lesser of 18% of your earned income in the preceding year and a specified total dollar limit,[3] plus any unused contribution allowance from previous years, starting in 1991. If you have an employer pension plan, the RRSP contribution limit is reduced according to a complex formula. We discuss RRSPs in more detail in the retirement chapters.

The RRSP is primarily for use as retirement savings, but it can be used legally to defer income tax in shorter horizons, too. If you know that you will want more cash than you will earn in some future year, you could contribute to an RRSP for the intervening years and allow the income to accumulate at the before-tax rate. You will have to pay the tax when you withdraw the money, but the increased earnings rate will leave you

---

[1] The employer can deduct the pension payments for income tax purposes as they are paid.

[2] In both RRSPs and registered pension plans, the differential treatments of capital gains and dividends paid by Canadian companies do not apply. All withdrawals are treated as ordinary income.

[3] 1996 to 2003 — $13,500; 2004 — $14,500; 2005 and thereafter — $15,500.

with more money. The one thing to be careful about is that the extra income in the later year could push you into a higher tax bracket. A taxpayer in the highest bracket needn't worry about this situation; otherwise some careful calculation is required. If tax brackets change during the intervening years, you may lose out even if you made the correct decision originally.

Example 7.1: Sarah Goldberg likes her job with the credit union, but she feels that she must finish her university degree in order to move into management. She has started the courses this year, and in three years she plans to take a year off in order to finish it, going from September of year 4 to August of year 5. Her tax bracket is 26% now, and would stay at that rate in the two years during which she is in school full time. Suppose she can save $3,000 p.a. for each of the next three years. She could do this either by depositing it into an RRSP and paying the tax in year 5; or she could invest it outside an RRSP and pay the tax each year. In the fourth year she starts school, and uses that year's savings to carry her to December. In January of the fifth year she cashes in the first three year's savings, including any accrued earnings. The time line looks like this, assuming each deposit of savings is made at year end:

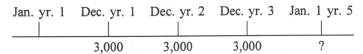

Jan. yr. 1	Dec. yr. 1	Dec. yr. 2	Dec. yr. 3	Jan. 1 yr. 5
	3,000	3,000	3,000	?

She can withdraw on Jan. 1, year 5, the accumulated value of a three year annuity of $3,000 p.a., compounded for one more year. Withdrawing the entire amount from an RRSP in year 5 wouldn't change her tax bracket. In either case, she will choose a safe credit union rate of 6% p.a. An important point that you should note concerns how you get the tax deduction for your RRSP. You can file a form with Revenue Canada declaring your RRSP contribution during the year, and get your employer to reduce the tax withheld from your regular pay by the amount attributable to the RRSP deduction. Thus, you can use your RRSP deduction to generate more cash to make another RRSP contribution. The limit of this process is (Cash saved)/(1 − tax rate). That is, if Sarah reduces her consumption by $3,000 to put into an RRSP, she can actually generate $3,000/.074 = $4,053 in tax-sheltered savings.[4] How much more will she have to spend in year 5 if she uses an RRSP?

---

[4] To implement this, she may have to take out a loan ($1,053) at the end of February and repay it when she receives the tax refund.

Answer: The RRSP is worth:

PMT	$4,053
n	3
%i	6
FV	$12,903
FV yr. 5	$12,903 × 1.06 = $13,677
After-tax	$13,677 × .74 = $10,121

The unsheltered amount is worth:

PMT	$3,000
n	3
%i	4.44
FV	$9,406
FV yr. 5	$9,406 × 1.044 = $9,819

The RRSP saving method accumulates to $320 more. The higher the tax bracket and the longer the period, the larger the value of the tax deferral.

Capital Gains Deferral

No tax is payable on capital gains until they are realized. A portfolio of shares can increase in value at the before-tax rate of return if the return consists of capital gains instead of dividends. Thus, you should invest in assets that will realize more of their rate of return from capital gains, because you can defer paying tax on the returns until you cash them in, and when you do, you will pay tax only on 75% of the gain (under the current rules).

This strategy makes two strong assumptions. First, you do not require the dividend or interest income from the portfolio for current consumption. This assumption should hold for people who are saving for future retirement.

The second assumption is that you can continue to hold the identical portfolio. In reality, you may expose yourself to a lot of risk if you do so. Some of the companies will do very well and become a larger part of the portfolio, while others will decline in value. The well-diversified portfolio you started with may not stay that way. See Chapter 13 for more on the importance of diversification.

You may also want to change your investment position because you think that the securities that have gained the most are not going to perform as well in the future. If you sell them, the capital gains will be realized. In some cases, you will have no choice about disposition — another company may take over one of yours and pay cash for the shares.

These considerations do not eliminate the deferral benefit of capital gains; they simply reduce it.

INCOME SPLITTING

If different members of the family have different marginal tax rates, it would be nice to allocate income from the higher tax brackets to the lower ones. Legal allocation of income in this fashion is called **income splitting**, and it is possible in limited circumstances.

Most of the techniques involve investment income in some way. Income splitting has become somewhat less useful in recent years because there are only three federal tax brackets, and the difference between the second and third brackets is quite small.[5]

Between Spouses

The simplest method is for the spouse with the higher income to pay all the living expenses. The lower income spouse does all the saving, and accumulates investment assets, whose income is taxed at a lower marginal rate.

Gifts between spouses are presumed to occur at their adjusted cost base. If the gift is an income-earning asset, then the income is **attributed** to the spouse who gave the gift. In other words, you can't split income simply by giving investments to the lower income spouse. The gift could be given at fair market value, with the spouse paying for it. Now, this doesn't help much, since if the spouse had the money, she could buy the asset on the open market anyway. However, the selling spouse can take payment in the form of a loan bearing interest at market rates. As long as the investment asset transferred earns more than the market interest rate (e.g. a portfolio of common shares would do so, on average), then some income is split. This is not a very efficient way to split income, however, and is quite risky. If the investment asset loses money, the income split works in reverse, because the lower income spouse will have even less income.

Income attribution does not apply to the compounding of earnings. The income earned on a gift is attributed back to the spouse who gave it every year. However, the income on that income in the second year is not attributed. Thus, a high income spouse could give a bond to the low income spouse. The low income spouse deposits each coupon amount in a separate account. The coupons will be taxed in the high income spouse's hands, but the earnings on the separate account will be taxed in the low income spouse's hands. This method requires a fairly substantial amount of assets and a lengthy time period for significant effects.

One useful device that both splits and defers income tax is the **spousal RRSP.** A taxpayer may contribute to an RRSP for his spouse, but claim the tax deduction. If the contributing spouse will be in a higher tax bracket at retirement, then the ultimate tax payable on the RRSP withdrawals will be lower. This technique is especially important in a family where one spouse has spent most or all of the potential earning years working in the household, and consequently has no pension. The limit on how much can be contributed is determined by the contributing spouse's income and RPP entitlements, just as for a regular RRSP. The total contributed to a taxpayer's own RRSP and a spousal RRSP must fall within that limit — there is no 'double deduction' by establishing a spousal RRSP. The spouse may not withdraw contributions until after two years have elapsed without triggering attribution of the income back to the contributing spouse.

An important change in 1993 is the change of definition of spouse to include common-law relationships. This new definition means that common-law relationships now encompass not only the same income splitting techniques as formal marriages, but also the same income attribution rules. A common-law spouse is eligible for the married deduction, a spousal RRSP and transfer of certain unused deductions. Complications in

---

[5] There were 10 brackets ranging from about 9% (combined) to 61% prior to 1985.

defining who is a common-law spouse will doubtless arise as we gain some experience with this situation.

Example 7.2:   Rose Vino owns and manages a winery and several vineyards. Her husband, Andres Vino, is disabled and has only a small investment income. Rose's marginal tax rate is 50%; Andres rate is 26%. Rose "lends" him a warehouse with a fixed rental income of $15,000 p.a. for 10 years. She has enough surplus income to pay the tax annually on the attributed income without receiving the $15,000. He deposits the earnings into a money market fund earning 5% p.a. At the end of 10 years he gives the vineyard back and continues to earn in his own name the interest at 5% on the accumulated money market fund. How much does he earn in the 11th year, if all payments are assumed to occur at year end?

Answer:

PMT	$15,000
n	10
%i	5% × (1 − .26) = 3.7%
FV	$177,606

Next year he earns 5% × $177,606 = <u>$8,880</u> before tax, or <u>$6,571</u> after tax. Note that Rose has paid $7,500 tax every year on the $15,000 earnings. Only the earnings on the saved earnings are taxed at Andres' lower rate.

Between Other Family Members

Income splitting between other family members is usually from parents to children, although others, such as dependent parents, may benefit from it too. There is no analog to the spousal RRSP with other persons.

The higher-income person should pay all the living expenses. This may be particularly evident when a dependent child receives inheritances or gifts from other relatives. These amounts should be invested and the parents pay expenses, as long as their marginal tax rates are higher.[6]

The income attribution rule does not apply to capital gain on a gift to a family member other than a spouse, although interest, dividends and other income are attributed. A parent can thus give a child a significant income with a gift of common shares whose future return is mostly capital gains, and pay little or no tax on attribution.

A **Registered Educational Savings Plan (RESP)** is another technique for splitting income with children and deferring some of the tax. The parent (or sometimes another relative) makes payments into a trust fund that is an RESP. The earnings compound untaxed, but there is *no* deduction from the parent's income for the principal payments. If the child then goes to a postsecondary institution, the money is used to pay tuition,

---

[6] The principle of giving children some responsibility for their affairs may well take precedence over tax minimization at some age. The parents may well decide that the child should start to pay for her own entertainment, for example. Saving taxes is not the only important issue in family life!

books and living expenses. The principal amount is not taxed, and the accumulated income is taxed in the child's hands, usually at a much lower rate than the contributing parent would have paid. In most plans, if the child does not go to a postsecondary institution, the contributor receives a refund of the principal amounts contributed, but the fund keeps the accrued income and it is part of the amount available for payment to other children who do continue their education. The exact method of arranging the payments varies between different RESPs.

Estate Freezes

This complex technique freezes the value of a property in the hands of the original owner, who places it in the estate freeze. All further appreciation in value accrues to the heir. This technique is useful for family businesses or large investment portfolios — hundreds of thousands of dollars. Depending on how it is structured, the freeze can allow the original owner to retain control of the asset during his lifetime, or receive some income from it. The control aspect is important if the asset is the family business which the original owner continues to manage. Relatively few families need estate freezes, and expert guidance is required to establish one. We discuss estate planning in a bit more detail in Chapter 17.

Single Parent Families and Marriage Breakdowns

The single parent family is becoming a common situation with the increasing rate of marriage breakdowns. The sharing of deductions and costs between two separated or divorced parents can involve significant income tax consequences, and we will cover only two here.

One simple tax-saving device is for the parent who supports the children to claim one of them as equivalent-to-married, which is explained in Schedule 6 of the General Tax Guide. Certain other dependents may also qualify for this tax credit. Since only one married or equivalent-to-married credit may be claimed in a year, you should check to see which arrangement of dependents is most beneficial.

An important planning consideration is how to structure the settlement under a separation agreement. A basic rule in the Act governs how separation payments are taxed. Such payments may be deducted by the payer and reported as income by the recipient if they meet all of these conditions:

1. When the payments were made, the spouses were living apart and continued to do so for the rest of the year;
2. The payments were made under a decree, court order, judgement or written agreement;
3. The payments were made to maintain the spouse, former spouse and/or children;
4. The payments were an allowance to be paid periodically; and,
5. The payments were made to the spouse or former spouse.

There are exceptions, but generally the rules are interpreted quite strictly. Payments not meeting these conditions are not taxable income for the recipient and are not deductible by the payer.

The separating couple can minimize income taxes by arranging that the spouse making the payments does so as an allowance if she is in the higher tax bracket, and as a lump sum payment if she is in the lower income tax bracket.[7] The correct choice reduces taxes more for the payer than it increases taxes for the recipient, and thus the two will have more after-tax income to share. The only weakness with this form of income splitting is the risk that the payer will not make all the periodic payments, and hence a lump sum is better for the recipient even if it is less tax efficient. Nonetheless, the tax benefits can be considerable.

Example 7.3: Gertrude and Claudius are separating. Claudius gets the castle, and Gertrude will also pay him some money. She offers to pay him $35,000 in a lump sum now, or to invest $50,000 in Canada Savings Bonds at 6% p.a. and pay him an annuity at the end of each of the next five years. His best alternative riskless investment is also CSBs at 6%. Her tax rate is 42% and his is 26%. They think the tax rates will stay the same for each of them for the next five years. Claudius trusts Gertrude to pay the annuity. Which way should they do it?

Answer: First, calculate the annuity payment:

PV	$50,000
%i	6
n	5
PMT	$11,870.

Next, calculate their after-tax discount rates:

Claudius: 6% (1 − .26) = 4.44%
Gertrude: 6% (1 − .42) = 3.48%.

Next, calculate their after-tax payments:

Claudius receives: $11,870 (1 − .26) = $8,784
Gertrude pays: $11,870 (1 − .42) = $6,885.

Now we can calculate what the after-tax payments are worth:

	Claudius	Gertrude
PMT	$ 8,784	$ 6,885
%i	4.44%	3.48%
n	5	5
PV	$38,626	$31,104

Thus, they should structure it in annual payments. The after-tax cost to Gertrude is less than the $35,000 lump sum, while Claudius gets more than $35,000 after-tax.

The law changes on May 1, 1997. Child support payments made pursuant to agreements or court orders made or changed on or after that date will not be deductible to the payor nor taxable to the recipients.

---

[7] Note that child support payments made or changed after May 1, 1997 will not be deductible to the payor or taxable to the recipient.

INCOME SPREADING

A taxpayer who has highly variable income may want to **spread income** over several years to reduce the marginal tax rate. This method of tax reduction does not have many applications, because the difference between the second and third brackets is now quite small, and the top bracket kicks in at a fairly modest income level. Furthermore, most people earn relatively even streams of employment income, and thus spreading income has no effect on their marginal rates.

A few people — professional athletes and entertainers, commissioned salespersons, professionals with irregular large contracts — may benefit from deferred compensation arrangements. These require carefully-structured contracts.

Anyone with substantial accrued capital gains should be careful to realize them over several years rather than all at once, to avoid a higher tax bracket. Taxpayers in this situation are most often in the top bracket anyway, and income spreading is of no value (though deferring the realization of the capital gains is still worthwhile).

One income spreading situation that many people can use occurs when a taxpayer will be earning much less income for one or two years than in the years before and after. A person might take a long maternity or paternity leave, an unpaid leave of absence, return to university or have a long period of involuntary unemployment or underemployment. In this situation, a person can withdraw part or all of the money in an RRSP for consumption and pay tax immediately, but at a lower marginal rate than the original deduction provided. This does compromise retirement savings, but it is sometimes the cheapest way of bridging a period of low income. Some people use their RRSPs deliberately for this purpose.

Example 7.4: Sarah Goldberg, from Example 7.1, now has a degree and a middle management job, but needs an MBA to move into senior management. She plans exactly the same pattern of saving and school time as in Example 7.1, but now her salary is higher. She is in the 42% tax bracket, and would drop to the 26% bracket in years 4 and 5. How much more can she save using an RRSP compared with not using it?

Answer: The annual payment, taking advantage of the tax deduction, is now

$$\frac{\$3,000}{(1 - .42)} = \$5,172$$

The RRSP is worth:

PMT	$ 5,172
n	3
%i	6
FV	$16,466
FV yr. 5	$16,466 × 1.06 = $17,454
After-tax	$17,454 × .74 = $12,916

The unsheltered amount is worth:

PMT	$3,000
n	3
%i	3.48
FV	$9,317
FV yr. 5	$9,317 × 1.044 = $9,727

The difference is now $3,189, which illustrates how much income spreading can save in the right situation.

TAX SHELTERS

In some situations a taxpayer can arrange affairs so that **tax shelters** allow a lower or zero rate of tax, without any deferral or other sacrifice required. Many shelters are transitory, because they relate to government attempts to affect the economy in some way.

Capital Gains

Capital gains have been a common shelter, with the rules varying considerably over the years. Until 1972, capital gains were tax-free.[8] The taxable portion has increased from 50% in 1972 to 75% today. During the period 1985 to February 22, 1994, an individual taxpayer could claim a lifetime exemption for a maximum of $100,000 in capital gains. A lifetime exemption for a maximum of $500,000 in capital gains on sale of a family farm or "qualifying" small business still exists (the details are too complicated for us to cover).

For most people, who don't own farms or small businesses, the untaxed 25% of a capital gain still represents a considerable potential for tax saving, and is one reason why investment in risky securities with growth potential is so popular.

The principal residence of a family is exempt from any capital gains tax (except for the portion of the gain assigned to a part of the house that has been a rental property). Given the long-run trend of property values to increase, this is a powerful incentive for a family to buy a home as early as possible and bend its savings efforts towards paying off the mortgage. Even if the capital gain doesn't materialize, the family has a place to live. Another benefit may be income splitting. If the couple sells the home at retirement and moves into a smaller home, or an apartment, the capital gain can be split between the partners to provide income for both, without income attribution.

Dividends vs. Interest Income

If you want to receive a relatively steady stream of income from investment assets, then securities paying dividends or interest are preferred. The tax treatment is different, and so the question arises as to which one you should choose, assuming risk and maturity are the same. You compare them using the after-tax cash flows (see Chapter 6). Depending on the relative pricing and your tax bracket, you may prefer either dividends or interest, and your preferences may change over time. The price you pay on the market will reflect some equilibrium average of all the market participants, but your own marginal tax may be different, and so you may be able to pay less tax by your choice of investment.

---

[8] There are transition rules that allow a taxpayer to claim part of the capital gain as tax free on assets owned prior to 1972 and sold subsequently.

Example 7.5: Dwayne Webb is in a tax bracket of 50.74% for interest income and 34.26% for dividend income. Cesa Sarmazian is in a tax bracket of 26.86% for interest income and 7.24% for dividends. Each one has $1,000 to invest, and the choice is between a bond and a preferred share of equal risk, maturing in 10 years. The bond pays interest of $100 annually; the preferred share pays a dividend of $77 annually. Which investment should each person choose?

Answer: Dwayne should choose the preferred share.

$$\text{Preferred return after-tax} = (1 - .3426) \times \$77$$
$$= \$50.26 \text{ or } \underline{5.026\%}$$

$$\text{Interest return after-tax} = (1 - .5074) \times \$100$$
$$= \$49.26 \text{ or } \underline{4.926\%}$$

Cesa should choose the bond.

$$\text{Preferred return after-tax} = (1 - .0724) \times \$77$$
$$= \$69.51 \text{ or } \underline{6.951\%}$$

$$\text{Interest return after-tax} = (1 - .2686) \times \$100$$
$$= \$73.40 \text{ or } \underline{7.340\%}$$

Specialized Tax Shelters

A specialized tax shelter is an investment that allows the investor to recover a significant portion of the initial investment very quickly through income tax reductions, regardless of the subsequent earnings on the investment. Many writers use the term tax shelter only to refer to this kind of shelter, rather than to all shelters as we have done.

These investments have five characteristics in common, regardless of their stated terms:

1. They are granted the tax shelter status because the government wants to encourage investment in that part of the economy.
2. They are exceedingly risky, which is why investment incentives are required.
3. The promoters are well aware of the advantage of the tax shelter, and price the investment to take taxes into account.
4. The tax shelters come and go as government objectives change.
5. These specialized tax shelters are very susceptible to fraud.

Our general advice is to avoid them altogether. The high risk of the investment plus the risk of fraud makes them dubious investments. A Revenue Canada registration number does not mean that Revenue Canada has approved a particular shelter. In fact, Revenue Canada tries to attack most of them after the fact. We have not met anyone who prospered from tax shelters. In some cases, the investment money never reaches the productive operation, but is wholly consumed by the organizers, the promoters, lawyers and the accountants.

If you are still determined to invest in these sort of shelters, you should only do so if you are in the top tax bracket and expect to stay there during the period when deductions are available. It is worth even more if your tax bracket will be lower when the investment starts to generate cash flow. Self-employed professionals nearing retirement fit this tax profile, if they are willing to take the risk.

Tax shelter deals usually involve either **flow-through securities** or limited partnerships. These two structures are advantageous because they allow the individual investor to claim tax shelter deductions while limiting his or her liability to the amount invested. The business giving up these deductions does so in return for capital (and because it is in an early stage of development and has no taxable income against which to apply them). The investments currently in vogue include film production, software development and mining.

Another form of tax relief for investing involves government tax credits as a proportion of the amount invested in specified sectors, usually small business. Both the provincial and federal governments have been involved in this activity at various times. Currently, Labour-sponsored Venture Capital Corporations are the popular vehicle..

SUMMARY

There are four fundamental tax minimization strategies (and sometimes combinations of them):

1. **Income deferral**, bringing income into taxable income at a future date, and so deferring the payment of income tax until later. This is beneficial because the present value of the future tax payment is less than if it were paid at once.
2. **Income splitting**, allocating income to family members with lower marginal tax rates to reduce the total family tax bill.
3. **Income spreading**, shifting income from years of higher marginal tax rates to years of lower marginal tax rates.
4. **Income sheltering**, reducing tax paid on income (usually investment income) because of some special characteristic.

The major accounting firms and associations all produce helpful tax guides that you can get at no charge. We have found these two useful and clearly-written (the 1996/97 editions should be available by the time this book is published):

Strategic Personal Tax Planning, Certified General Accountants Association of Ontario, revised annually.

Personal Tax Strategy, Price Waterhouse, revised annually.

KEY TERMINOLOGY

attribution / income deferral / income splitting / income spreading / Registered Educational Savings Plan / Registered Pension Plan / Registered Retirement Savings Plan (RRSP) / spousal RRSP / tax shelters

DISCUSSION QUESTIONS

1. Explain each of the terms under **Key Terminology**.
2. What is the dividing line between ethical and unethical behaviour in tax minimization?

PROBLEMS

1. Can you suggest an additional tax minimization strategy for Rose and Andres in Example 7.2?

2. Inmoo Kwan works as a shift supervisor in a factory for a salary of $40,000 p.a. He wants to take a one-year manufacturing technology programme that will improve his future income and job security prospects substantially. His employer has agreed to give him a one-year unpaid leave from his job, starting either immediately on January 1, or on July 1 following. From an income tax point of view, which date should he choose if:

    (a) he will finance his studies by cashing $30,000 of Canada Savings Bonds?
    (b) he will finance his studies by withdrawing money from his RRSP?

3. Refer to Problem 2 in Chapter 6. Can you provide some tax planning advice to Jason and Betty?

4. Desiree and Anita are living with their two children from their previous marriages, in a large four-bedroom apartment. Desiree (42 years old) is a lawyer, earning about $120,000 p.a. Anita (41 years old) used to be a freelance secretary and housepainter, but she has worked in the home for several years. Neither of them has a pension plan. The children are aged 13 and 10.

    On the breakdown of their marriages, each one of them negotiated lump sum settlements from their husbands in lieu of child support payments (Desiree, $60,000; Anita $150,000). Anita has used the interest income and a part of the principal to pay a reasonable share of the household expenses. The largest single expense is the apartment, at $2,000 per month. They have been quite modest in their lifestyle. As a result, Desiree has been able to save quite a bit, and she now has $140,000 in term deposits at the bank. Anita has $130,000 in certificates at a trust company. They earn about 6% on their money. They have $2,000 in a joint chequing account.

    Although they have always been careful with money, and make saving a priority, they are starting to worry about retirement and also how to help the children if they want to go to college or university. Without setting a specific dollar target, suggest how they can make the most of their savings.

5. Alas, Maggie and Pierre have separated after 10 years of marriage and three children. Maggie is a successful actress with a large income. Pierre is an unemployed former politician. He is taking custody of the children and will stay home with them for the next six years. As a fair settlement to split up their tangible assets at the date of separation, he gets the marital home. However, since he will have no income, Maggie will have to pay him an additional amount to help support him and the children until he returns to work after six years. The problem at hand is whether a lump sum or a periodic annuity is better, and how to equate the two.

    You are the adviser. You expect Maggie to have a marginal tax rate of 48% throughout the six years, and Pierre to have a marginal rate of 26%. The *Income Tax Act* makes periodic payments under a separation agreement taxable for the recipient and tax deductible for the payer.[9] Lump sum payments are not taxable for the recipient nor tax deductible for the payer. You observe that the current EAR on six-year Canada bonds is 7%. To simplify matters, assume that any lump sum is paid today, and that the first payment of any series of annual payments occurs one year from today.

(a)   What are their after-tax discount rates?

(b)   Maggie offers $65,000. What before-tax annual payment stream for six years is equivalent to the lump sum from her point of view?

(c)   Pierre asks for a lump sum of $80,000. What before-tax annual payment stream for six years is equivalent to the lump sum for him?

(d)   "You rotten free-loader," yells Maggie. "I don't have anything more than $65,000, and I don't have the house either. Why don't you go back to that Barbra Whatsername, she's got lots of money." Pierre's reply was altered in Hansard. After you cool them down, how do you advise them so that they both do better financially on this part of the separation agreement? Explain how your advice works in general for any separation.

(e)   Now, to make the problem more interesting, assume that expected inflation is 3% p.a. Pierre wants the payment indexed to the rate of inflation. That is, the payment at the end of this year will be $1.03x, the payment at the end of two years will be 1.03^2x, and so on. They agree on a payment of $21,000 in real dollars for the first year, which means the first payment at year-end will be $21,630. The marginal tax rates are unchanged. The 7% bond rate is unchanged (i.e. it is nominal). What is the expected present value of the after-tax cost to Maggie? What is the expected present value of the after-tax receipt to Pierre? You can't do this with annuities, you must do it year by year (see next part). That is, you discount the inflated (nominal dollar) amounts each year by the nominal rates.

(f)   Redo part (e) by treating the $21,000 amount as a real dollar annuity and discounting by the real after-tax discount rate.

6.   Do Example 7.3 over using the rules that will be in place after April 30, 1997?

---

[9] You will recall that this may not be the situation in the future, but assume that it will be for the purpose of doing this question.

chapter **8**

Risk Management

When families think about the financial risks they face, they turn immediately to insurance to protect themselves. In this chapter we postpone the visit to the insurance agent in order to develop a conceptual model of personal risk management. Insurance plays a critical role in the process, but it is not the only factor, nor is it the first thing you should consider.

We discuss financial risk only in this book. There are tragedies worse than losing money — who could put a price on losing an only child? — but we leave them for others more qualified to offer advice.

Our specific objectives are:

1. To develop the concept and practice of a five-stage personal risk management process: identify, evaluate, control, finance and monitor.
2. To explain the theoretical role of insurance in financing personal risks.

The risk management process we describe is equally useful in business management, which is where it developed. Although we won't discuss business risk issues much, the applications will be quite evident.

DEFINING RISK

We all have an intuitive understanding of risk — the possibility of losing something valuable. We can divide risks up into two types to understand them better.

Speculative risk involves loss and gain, but in uncertain amounts. You buy a lottery ticket, and you have a very small chance of winning a lot of money, and a big chance of losing the dollar you paid for it. You buy common shares in a company, with uncertain future dividends and capital gains prospects. You leave your secure job and start your own business. Each of these actions may make more money for you, or it may cost you money. In this formal definition, speculative does not mean gambling on something, in the way that the term is used in common language.[1] A speculative risk has a probability

---

[1] Though gambling is entirely a speculative risk, since you may win or lose.

of winning and a probability of losing. Speculative risks are generally those that you chose to accept, rather than those that you encounter simply because of your circumstances. All investments are speculative risks, for example, though some are riskier than others.

We defer consideration of speculative risk to the investments and retirement chapters. The same basic risk management principles apply, but their application is more appropriate in the context of those chapters.

Pure risk involves the possibility of loss, only. Early death, disability and theft of your car are all pure risks. Generally, pure risks are ones that happen to us without us having made a conscious choice to seek them out.

THE RISK MANAGEMENT PROCESS

Step 1: Identifying the Risks

This is perhaps the most important step, though it seems easy. Many people avoid this step because they believe: "It won't happen to me." Others fail to recognize which risks are the most serious. Regrettably, many people buy the wrong insurance, or the wrong amount, because they listen to skilled salespeople before they assess their own needs. Some of the risks are related to the life cycle stages, and must be reviewed as the family situation changes. We can group them into three general categories: personal, or life and health; property; and liability to other persons for our actions that affect them. We expand on these three categories in Table 8.1.

A table like this cannot capture all the possible risks, but it is a useful guide. The life cycle stages for health and disability risks show those risks that are most likely to be important, but others are possible. For example, a retired single could have both dependent parents and dependent children. We added a category of child to this table, because disability of a child may be a serious financial problem for the parents. The death of child is not, however, because the child is not contributing significant income to the family.

Most Canadians think the risk of liability means third party liability insurance on a car (mandatory in all Canadian jurisdictions). That is, if you cause harm to another person with your car, you may be found liable for the other person's losses. These losses might be very large, e.g. present value of lifetime earnings if you kill someone.

Other liabilities could be just as material. You are required to ensure that your property does not pose a danger to a reasonable person. If Wayne Gretzky comes to call, breaks his leg by falling over a loose step and can't play hockey again, you are in big trouble. You could be in even bigger trouble if Eric Lindros were the injured party, because he is younger and therefore has more years of future hockey earnings.

The rule governing these sort of liabilities is the common law applying to **torts** — legal wrongs or injuries one person causes another. Common law is the part of the law determined by court decisions over a long period of time, rather than by statute. The court will not find you responsible for someone else's losses, as long as you take reasonable care. For example, if a hurricane blows a healthy tree from your property onto someone's car, you wouldn't be responsible. If you knowingly left a dying and weakened tree on your property and it fell on a car in a light breeze, you probably would be found liable for the damage to the car.

TABLE 8.1
Significant Personal Risks

Life and Health

Stage in Life Cycle[1]	Risk	Possible Losses
All stages	Disability	Extra expenses, family duties
1–6	Disability	Income (limited time or permanent)
2–5	Death	Income
2–5, 7	Death	Extra expenses, family duties
Child	Disability	Extra expenses

Property

Rental residence	damage or destruction	Cost of finding other accommodation, including hotel bills
Owned residence	damage or destruction	Repair or replacement, cost of temporary accommodation
Automobile	Theft, damage destruction	Repair or replacement, cost of temporary replacement rental
Other Assets	Theft, damage destruction	Repair or replacement, additional expenses while waiting

Liability to Others

Unincorporated bus.	Liability to 2nd, 3rd party	Amount lost by other parties, legal costs
Property	Liability to 3rd party	Amount lost by third party, legal costs

[1] See Ch. 5, Table 5.1. Stages are: 1, single; 2, childless couple; 3,4, families with children; 5, older couple; 6, older single; 7, 8, couple, single retired.

Limited companies are also liable for their actions (or inaction), but the limited liability means that the investors are not responsible beyond the amount of money paid for the investment.[2] Unincorporated businesses and professionals are personally liable without limit for all losses they cause. These losses may be to their customers and creditors (second party, or contractual liability) or to a third party. This unlimited liability is the most important reason why most small businesses incorporate, since otherwise the owners put not only their direct investment at risk, but also virtually everything else they own.

Once you have identified the risks, you need to evaluate them.

Step 2: Evaluating the Risks

We did some preliminary evaluation of the risks in the previous step by listing only those that could be important. Now we evaluate them using two criteria: the size of the potential loss, and the frequency or probability of occurrence. Which risks you wish to

---

[2] Both legislatures and courts are imposing increasingly broad and significant personal liabilities on directors of companies and other organizations. This is a specialized topic beyond the scope of this book. If you are a director of any legally-constituted organization — company, charity, government agency etc., you should get expert legal advice on your responsibilities.

		Probability of Occurrence	
		High	Low
Size of Loss	Large	Insupportable	Insupportable
	Small	Supportable	Immaterial

**TABLE 8.2
Evaluation of Risks**

avoid and which you can live with is a personal decision, but Table 8.2 gives some guidance. The basic rule is that a risk is insupportable if it materially affects the family's standard of living.

The normal family cannot run the risk of very large losses, even if the probability is quite low, if it can avoid them somehow. The death of one of the parents in a family with young dependent children is such a loss. While the occurrence is not common, the lost income and family duties constitute a huge and potentially unmanageable financial loss.[3] On the other hand, small losses are not a big problem, even if relatively frequent.

We haven't defined 'large' and 'small' in terms of the size of the losses. This depends on the family's resources. Theft of a car costing $15,000 to replace is a loss some families can afford, others cannot. It is quite small compared with the potential loss if you are negligent and cause an automobile accident. Thus, if we were advising you on your car insurance policy, we would say, first take all the liability insurance you need. Then, assess how much you can afford to pay for any other problem with the car. Perhaps you have very little reserve cash and need to be insured almost totally. Perhaps you can afford to write off the car and so you take nothing but the third party liability coverage.

Probability of occurrence is not precisely defined, either. None of the events subject to risk management occur frequently — they would be part of ordinary life if they did so. Your chance of dying in an airline crash is probably even less than the proverbial one in a million. By contrast, if you drive a car 10 kilometres to work every day, you have something like a one in three chance of an accident serious enough to at least cause material property damage during your working life. Even so, a one-third probability over a 30 year period is not a high probability on a daily basis.

Once you have decided which risks are insupportable, you must consider how to control them, if possible.

Step 3: Controlling the Risks

One method is **avoidance**. For example, you can avoid the risk of injury in a dangerous sport by not engaging in it. You can avoid the risk of air crashes by taking the train. Avoidance applies to actions where we have some choice in what we do.

---

[3] This loss is quite severe even for a home-maker spouse, since the work done by him or her must be replaced. If the other spouse is to continue to be the breadwinner for the family, paid help (day care, cleaning person, occasional babysitters) is usually necessary. Even so, the surviving spouse will have a substantially greater workload to carry.

A second method for controlling some risks is **separation**. Parents who travel on different airplanes will not be killed in the same accident, leaving the children without support. Spouses who work for the same company increase the severity of the risk of job loss, since both might lose their employment at the same time. This method only applies in a few situations for families, because much of their life is spent together. It tends to be more useful for large organizations.

Prevention or **reduction of frequency** is the most widely applicable method. We reduce the risk of disability or premature death with good nutrition, regular exercise and preventive medicines. We protect property with smoke detectors, bolt locks and preventive maintenance. We reduce the likelihood of being sued for negligence by driving carefully and incorporating the family business.[4]

The size and probability of the loss will dictate the amount of time and money you will spend to control it. Another factor is the availability of a means of financing it. If there is no way to finance a risk, then you will do more to control it. If financing is readily available, then you may discard all precautions if that is the cheaper way to deal with it.

Step 4: Financing the Risks

For families, **financing** a risk means finding someone to share it with through insurance. We detour from the applications for a short explanation of the principles of insurance.

Basic Principles of Insurance   **Insurance** is based on the law of large numbers. If the occurrences of some particular event are independent of each other, then in a large population the probability of their occurring can be represented by the average observed frequency. The population can share the risk of an event involving an insupportable loss to a family by pooling its funds. Every family contributes an amount equal to the probability of the occurrence times the value of the loss. The specific families who suffer losses receive compensation from the pool and the ones who suffered no loss are poorer only by their contribution to the pool. *Ex ante* (before the fact), we don't know which families will suffer the losses. Every family finances its risk by paying the premium, which is a certain cost, but supportable.

This pooling or insurance only works under some conditions. We have already said the occurrences must be independent. If they are related in some way, then the probability is not stable, since the existence of some occurrences increases the probability of more of them. For example, private insurers do not insure against job loss, because it is not an independent occurrence. If a factory closes down in an area, other jobs are more likely to disappear too. The most dramatic example of this is the recent shut-down of much of Canada's East coast fishery. The loss of some fishing jobs signals the loss of more, since all are dependent on the same fish stocks. Then the fish-packing plants close, and then all the small retail and service businesses in the fishing communities are threatened because their customers have no work.

---

[4] The children's lemonade stand need not be incorporated, though you may wish to reduce risk by ensuring that they serve lemonade without adding anything from the liquor cabinet!

For some of these dependent conditions that are uninsurable, the government provides what it calls insurance. In the example, it is Unemployment Insurance Compensation (UIC). UIC is not insurance, because some people have virtually no chance of losing their jobs and would never choose to pay UI premiums if they had a choice. Instead, our society agrees that it has to share risk in a very general sense, and allows the government to tax and redistribute wealth through a variety of welfare mechanisms. UI premiums are a tax, and UIC is a form of welfare.

As a practical matter, the insurer must be able to establish the time, the place, the cause and the amount of the loss. In some cases less than perfect determination of some of these factors is acceptable. The time and place an illness first occurred may be uncertain. The cause of a car accident may be uncertain. The amount must be determinable, otherwise compensation is impossible.

Widespread catastrophes like war and earthquakes are not generally insurable, because no insurer is large enough to spread the risks. Risks subject to **moral hazard** are not insurable. Moral hazard occurs when the loss is due to deliberate actions or choices of the insured. For example, no one will insure you against the risk of personal bankruptcy, because such insurance would give you a terrific incentive to gamble on the lottery. If you win, you are rich; if you lose, the insurer pays off.

One myth we wish to dispel is **self-insurance**. It is not insurance at all; it is a decision not to finance a risk. If the decision is rational, then the family has judged that the loss is not great enough to materially affect its standard of living. Alternatively, a family may have money to cover only more pressing needs, and be forced to gamble on risks that it can neither afford to insure nor to incur. Once again, this is the absence of insurance, not a special kind of insurance called self-insurance.[5]

Mechanics of Insurance   In our society, insurance companies pool the risks and write contracts with many individuals and organizations. Since they have expenses in doing this work and shareholders who want profits, they charge more than the average value of the losses. They handle this intermediation of risk more efficiently than we can as individuals; so we are prepared to pay the extra cost.

An important part of their expenses lies in the determination of the premiums to be charged. Their staff use vast quantities of statistics on the occurrence of certain events in order to develop **actuarial tables** that show probabilities of occurrences for every possible combination of age, sex, occupation etc.

For example, there are **mortality tables** that show the probability that a Canadian will die within the next year, for each age up to 106 (see Appendix B). The detailed tables show the same statistic separately for men and women, smokers and non-smokers, male smokers, male non-smokers, males working in coal mines who smoke, males working in coal mines who don't smoke and so on. The life insurance company can use these tables to calculate the probability of death for an applicant during the next year.

---

[5] Some organizations are so large that they do not carry certain types of insurance, because their operations and employees are numerous enough to allow the law of large numbers to apply without pooling risks with others. For them, self-insurance is an acceptable way of avoiding paying administration costs to insurance companies.

It then adds an amount for its expenses, and offers the policy, priced at $\$x$ per $\$1,000$ of principal amount.

The insurance business has become segmented into life and health insurance, discussed in Chapter 9, and property, casualty and liability insurance, discussed in Chapter 10.

Step 5: Monitoring the Risk Profile

You don't manage your risk once and then forget about it for 20 years. The material risks will change as you move through the life cycle, both because of the risks you have, and your financial ability to support them. You needn't spend much time on revision, since all you have to do is reconsider Tables 8.1 and 8.2, with your basic work already done.

When would you be most likely to revise your estimation of your risk situation? Changes in the life cycle — marriage, birth of a child, marriage breakup, children becoming independent, retirement, death of a spouse — are the most likely triggers. When one of these occurs, you should go through the risk management process again.

Even without such obvious changes, occasional reflection is useful. Some people review their insurance coverage annually. As we have shown, risk management is more than insurance, but an annual review of both together is a good idea. Perhaps as you sit reviewing your insurance over a cigarette and your third brandy of the evening, you will remember your last medical check-up, and consider other methods of reducing your risk of heart attacks!

SUMMARY

Risk management is a life-long process that involves five steps: identification, evaluation, control, financing and monitoring. The important risks you face will change over the life cycle. You should evaluate risks based on both the possible losses and the probability of occurrence. You can manage risk with control techniques, or you can finance it using insurance. You must review your risk profile regularly, and particularly when you change stages in the life cycle.

KEY TERMINOLOGY

insurance: — actuarial tables — law of large numbers — moral hazard — self-insurance / pure risk / risk management process — identify — evaluate — control: avoidance — finance — monitor / speculative risk

DISCUSSION QUESTIONS

1. Explain the significance of the entries under **Key Terminology**.
2. Draw up a risk profile for your family, and evaluate the risks.
3. List the control measures and insurance you have for the answer to question 2. Are you satisfied with your risk management? Can you do anything about it?
4. Discuss the appropriateness of the categorization scheme in Table 8.1. Can you think of any family situations not covered by the categories? What sort of changes would you suggest in these categories?

PROBLEMS

1. Identify and evaluate the most likely material risks for these families:
    (a) Reed Chalmers is a 62-year-old professor of alchemy at York University, where he has been employed for 30 years. He will retire shortly with a comfortable pension. His wife, Florimel, is 50. She has stayed at home with the children, now independent, for almost all her adult life. She does not plan to work outside the home in the future.
    (b) Schmendrick the Magician is an itinerant performer in circuses and local fairs. His wife, Molly Grue, works the sideshows or cooks. They are both 35 years old, have no children and no assets to speak of.
    (c) Brian M. is the former prime minister of a medium-sized country. He is in his 50s, with a wife a fair bit younger and three dependent children. He has a pension that is inadequate for the family's accustomed standard of living, and no full-time job.
    (d) Salvatore Cuchimel is the former police chief of a small city in a small country where the government changes frequently. He is on a forced leave of absence at the age of 55 because of his heavy drinking and excess weight. He has no savings, a small house, and the expectation of modest pension granted by the national government's justice minister. If and when he returns to work he will receive back pay for his leave period and several years of unclaimed holidays, in addition to his generous regular salary. His wife is dead, but he has a physically-handicapped child who will be dependent on him for life.

2. Eustace Wingtip, 44 years old, is a world-famous poet, renowned for his books of Spenserian sonnets. Last year he earned $2,400. Fortunately, he is not married, has no children and is the only child of Sam and Samantha Wingtip, who made millions selling cut-rate men's shoes. His parents dote upon him, and have provided moderate income supplements for many years. They will not provide a large lump sum for him to spend. He is their sole heir (they are in their late 70s). Eustace lives with his cat, his typewriter and thousands of books in a luxurious apartment in downtown Vancouver. What are his significant risks requiring insurance? Give specific reasons for your answer.

9

Life, Health and Disability Insurance

LEARNING OBJECTIVES

Risk management is a very important component in personal financial management. Many families are exposed to risks that are insupportable. In this chapter, you will learn how to deal with two of those insupportable risks. First, you will learn how to use life insurance to finance the risk of loss of income due to premature death of a family member. Second, you will learn how to use disability insurance to finance the risk of loss of income due to the disability of a family member. The specific objectives are:

1. To evaluate who needs life insurance and who doesn't.
2. To determine the amount of life insurance coverage that a family needs by (a) the **Income Approach** and (b) the **Expense Approach**.
3. To explain the most common insurance policies sold in the market, including term life, whole life, universal life and endowment policies.
4. To describe a method that can be used to compare different life insurance policies.
5. To explain the major features of a typical disability insurance policy.

LIFE INSURANCE

Life insurance is a means of financing the risk of the premature and untimely death of a family member. Most people cannot afford the risk of very large losses which materially affect the family's standard of living. The loss of income due to the unanticipated death of a family member is an **insupportable** risk for most families. The most common way to finance such risk is, as we have discussed in Chapter 8, to find other people to share it — through insurance. A relatively small **premium** is exchanged for the insurance company's promise to pay a potentially large amount, which will ensure that income will be provided to financial dependents of the **insured** in the event that he dies. Before we proceed, we must introduce some basic terms:

Insured: the person upon whose death the death benefit (or the face value) of the insurance policy will be paid.

Beneficiary: the person(s) who receives the death benefit or face value of the policy upon the death of the insured.

Death Benefit or Face Value: the dollar amount that will be paid to the beneficiary if the insured dies.

Premium: the dollar amount that must be paid to the insurance company. The premium may be payable in one lump sum, or periodically — monthly, quarterly, semi-annually, or annually.

Owner: the person who pays the premiums. The owner can be the insured, her employer, the beneficiary or other third parties. If you buy life insurance for your son, you are the **owner** and your son is the **insured**.

Policy Term: the period during which the insurance is in force. The term can range from one year to an entire lifetime.

Rate: the cost of each unit of insurance. A rate of $2.50 per $100 unit means that the premium for $10,000 of insurance is equal to ($2.50 × 100) or $250.

Insurability: the qualification for the insured to be insurable. There are certain requirements that the insured may have to meet before an insurance policy can be bought; for example, the insured may have to pass a medical examination.

Guaranteed Insurability: this is a provision that allows the insured to buy additional life insurance at certain specified future dates without proof of insurability — e.g., without undergoing a new medical examination.

Do You Need Life Insurance?

We have already provided a framework for you to analyse and answer this question in Chapter 8. Basically, you simply evaluate the risk of your premature and untimely death and ask whether it is supportable or insupportable. The basic purpose of life insurance is to ensure that your financial dependents will be provided for financially in the event of your unanticipated death. Therefore, if you do not have financial dependents, you do not need life insurance. Still, you should not skip this chapter because it is important for you to know about life insurance for at least two reasons. First, your situation will change much sooner than you think. When you move to the next stages of the life cycle — getting married, having children and so on — you will probably need life insurance because you will then have financial dependents. Second, there are plenty of employment opportunities in the financial planning and the insurance industries, where a good knowledge of life insurance is very important.

Who needs life insurance? An individual who has financial dependents who will suffer financially (in the sense of a material fall in the standard of living) will need life insurance. Here it is important to understand the difference between "financial dependents" and "dependents". Let us take a family of four as an example. Suppose the father is the only breadwinner and the mother is a full-time home-maker. The loss of a daughter is a big emotional loss to the father, but the father does not need life insurance protection against the daughter's death because he is not financially dependent on her; however, the reverse is not true. The death of the father is not only an emotional loss to the daughter, but also a big financial loss because she relies on him financially. In this example, the father should buy insurance to protect the family in the event of his death.

Does the family need insurance on the life of the wife who is a full-time home-maker? Although she does not earn a salary in explicit monetary terms, she certainly provides valuable services that would cost money to replace. Furthermore, the odds are good that she will work outside the home later in the family life cycle when the children are able to look after themselves. Her earnings later in the life cycle will be important in building a retirement income for the couple. Therefore, it is reasonable to consider life insurance coverage based on the value of the services she performs — child care, cooking, cleaning etc. — and the possible future income.

The ultimate test of whether a family needs life insurance is whether the standard of living of the remainder of the family will fall materially in the event of the death of one family member. Does a very wealthy businessman with a full-time housewife and four young children need life insurance? The answer is no because the standard of living of the wife and the children is not expected to fall.[1] On the other hand, a childless couple, both working and each earning a good salary, may need life insurance coverage if the standard of living of the remaining spouse is expected to fall substantially.

Three Important Questions in Life Insurance

There are three important questions in life insurance that everyone should answer:

1. Do you need life insurance? Who needs life insurance?
2. How much life insurance do you need? How can people estimate the appropriate amount of insurance they should buy?
3. What kinds of life insurance are sold in the market? What kind of life insurance should you buy?

We have already analysed and answered the first question. To say it again, one needs life insurance if one has financial dependents and if the standard of living of these dependents is expected to fall as a result of one's premature and unanticipated death. We will now turn to the next two questions.

How Much Life Insurance Does a Family Need?

Many people buy too much or too little life insurance without knowing it. In fact, they do not know how to determine the right amount of life insurance. Very often, they bought their current life insurance policies as a result of chance — for example, policies are often sold to purchasers who succumb to aggressive salesmen calling at the right time and the right place. Other people may have bought their life insurance policies because they seemed to be good deals — for example, an employee says to himself, "My employer pays 70% of the premium; so how can I go wrong? Why should I buy only $30,000 just because my annual salary is only $30,000?"; or, "My employer will pay 70% of the premium on a policy amount equal to my annual salary. Anything above that, I have to pay the full premium myself. But — do I need more insurance than the equivalent of my total annual salary?"

---

[1] Many wealthy people buy a large insurance policy for the purpose of paying taxes in the event of death, but this is tax planning rather than life insurance planning.

There are many methods in the life insurance literature to calculate one's required life insurance face value. We will describe two approaches: the **Income Approach** and the **Expense Approach**. Both are very popular methods used to estimate the amount of life insurance coverage that a family needs.

The Income Approach

The **Income Approach** estimates the face value of the life insurance (i.e., the amount that the individual needs to buy) by calculating the present value of the insured's expected future income. From a conceptual viewpoint, this is, theoretically, the correct method. The present value of the insured's expected future income is conceptually the insured's **human capital**. Even though human capital cannot be traded in the market like other assets, it has a theoretical value. Life insurance can be viewed as an insurance policy that is protection against the loss of an asset, in this case, the insured's human capital. From this viewpoint, the theoretically-correct face-value amount to insure is the value of the insured's human capital, which is simply the present value of the insured's expected lifetime income.

There are three issues that must be dealt with:

1. What is the present discount rate of the insured's expected future income?
2. How do we handle inflation? The insured's income may appear to rise every year but, after accounting for inflation, there may not be any increase at all.
3. The income stream of an individual is very uncertain and hence, fraught with risk: income over one's lifetime may go up or down; indeed, it may become zero if and when the person is unemployed.

The first two issues can be easily handled by looking at real income (i.e., income after it is adjusted for inflation) and using the real rate of interest. Let us illustrate this with an example.

> **Example 9.1:** Max Brownlie, 35, is currently earning $30,000 per year. He expects his income will increase at the rate of inflation which is expected to be 5% every year. He intends to retire at the age of 65, 30 years from now. We want to use the **Income Approach** to estimate the face-value amount of the life insurance that Max should buy.

The easiest way to handle inflation is to deal with "real numbers" — real income and real interest rates. Although Max Brownlie's income increases in nominal terms, in real terms, after accounting for inflation, his income remains constant at $30,000 per year for the next 30 years. We can discount this annuity of $30,000 per year for 30 years at the real rate of interest. The **real rate of interest** is usually measured by the nominal rate of interest minus the expected rate of inflation. In Canada, the real rate of interest has been between 2% to 4% in the last four decades. Let us assume that the real rate of interest for the next 30 years to be 3%. The present value of Max's lifetime income is equal to the present value of a 30-year annuity of $30,000 per year. Using a discount rate of 3%, the present value of the annuity is equal to:

$$\$30,000 \times \left(\frac{1}{.03} - \frac{1}{.03\,(1.03)^{30}} \right) \text{ or } \$588,000 \text{ after rounding.}$$

The Basic Benchmark of the Income Approach

We will call the case in the above example the **basic benchmark**. Thus the basic benchmark is simply the present value of the insured's lifetime earnings assuming **no growth** in real earnings and using the **real rate of interest** as the discount rate. It is simple to calculate and to apply. It will take you only two minutes to calculate the basic benchmark for anybody including yourself. You simply find the present value of an annuity of your current salary. The length of the annuity will be the expected number of working years and the discount rate will be the real rate of interest, say 3%. This **basic benchmark** will be the amount of life insurance coverage that you should buy, using the **Income Approach**. In the above example, Mr. Brownlie should buy about $588,000 of coverage.

Usual Adjustments to the Basic Benchmark

The actual situation of an individual usually differs from the basic benchmark and one may want to make adjustments for those differences. The lifetime earning stream is risky and one may want to use a higher discount rate than the real rate of interest. Also, for many workers, there is usually growth in their real income streams.

The Income Tax Issue   The basic benchmark assumes that the beneficiary pays income tax on the receipts at the same rate as the insured paid on the original income. The income we used to calculate the benchmark was before-tax, and we used a before-tax discount rate. If the beneficiary now pays tax at the same rate on the amounts withdrawn from the proceeds of the policy, then doing everything before tax is correct. By replicating the lump sum amount that yields the income annuity before tax, we place the beneficiary in the same financial position after-tax as if the insured were still living.

The beneficiary will pay tax at a lower rate in most situations, however. The face amount of a life insurance policy is not taxable income for the beneficiary, because the premiums are not tax deductible.[2] The interest earned on the face amount after it is paid out is taxable like any other interest. Thus, the payments the beneficiary lives on for the years after the insured's death are partly taxable interest, and partly non-taxable return of principal (just as the blended principal and interest repayments would be for a bank or trust company). Therefore, the principal amount required to replace the insured's income is less than the amount calculated by the basic benchmark method.

We can illustrate this effect with the Max Brownlie example again. Max would have included the entire $30,000 in his calculation of taxable income. His beneficiary will not include the $588,000 lump sum in income, but will declare the interest on it each year. Suppose the beneficiary lives for 50 years more and uses the $588,000 to buy an annuity. The annual payment, in real dollars, using a 3% real rate of interest, would be $22,853. The payments the beneficiary will receive over the 50 years total 50 × $22,853 = $1,142,650. The beneficiary thus receives ($1,142,650 − $588,000) = $554,650 of taxable interest. To simplify matters, assume away the usual declining balance factor of higher interest payments in the early years. The beneficiary receives on average

---

[2] The principal exception is the company that insures a key executive and deducts the life insurance premiums for income tax purposes. The company will have to pay income tax on the policy's face value if the insured dies.

$554,650 ÷ 50 = $11,093 of income that has to be reported for tax purposes. This amount will attract a lot less tax than the $30,000 p.a. that Max was receiving. If the death benefit provides most of the beneficiary's future income, the income taxes will be very low or zero.

Rule-of-Thumb Adjustment   It is possible to account for all these factors by making the appropriate adjustments in the formula that is used to calculate the present value of the individual's lifetime earning stream; however, the insurance industry has come up with the following rule of thumb. Rather than insuring 100% replacement of the insured's income, families may want to insure only 70% to 80% of the insured's future income. Returning to our example, Max Brownlie may want to insure only 75% of his basic benchmark ($588,000), or $441,000.

The Expense Approach

The **expense approach** is another popular method to estimate the amount of life insurance coverage that a family needs. The idea of the expense approach is as follows. A life insurance face-value amount that the family needs is the amount that will provide enough funds to pay those expected expenses of the beneficiaries that are not covered by government transfer income or other income. If the insured dies, the life insurance death benefit is invested and used as the expenses occur. As we said earlier, the primary objective of life insurance should be to replace the income lost to the dependents so that they can maintain the same standard of living as before. Nevertheless, some people use insurance to provide an increased inheritance or much improved lifestyle to the beneficiaries that is in excess of their needs. This latter approach would leave the family much better off financially in the event of the insured's death. We do not think families should want this; and it would certainly make insurance companies nervous! What we will suggest then is a simple method for determining the life insurance need for the objective of expense replacement only.

The difference between the **Income Approach** and the **Expense Approach** is that the former calculates the present value of the insured's future income, while the latter calculates the present value of the beneficiaries' future expenses. The implementation of the expense approach is, therefore, very similar to that of the income approach. First, one has to estimate the beneficiaries' expected lifetime expenses. As with the **Income Approach**, one can handle inflation here by simply ignoring it. One therefore simply estimates the expected expenses in current dollars and then discounts that estimate by using the real rate of interest, say 3%.

How can one estimate the beneficiaries' expenses? Many people do not have a good idea about their current expenses: they never seem to know where the money goes. To ask these people to forecast their beneficiaries' future expenses is asking for the impossible. It is much easier for them to use the income approach because these people at least know how much they earn.

You have already learned how to prepare a statement of net worth (or balance sheet), a statement of income and expenditure, and a budget. You already have substantially more knowledge of personal finance than most people. It should therefore not be difficult for you to implement the expense approach, which is a more complete method than the income approach, for calculating the amount of life insurance that your family needs.

If you have not done so already, prepare your family's statement of net worth, its statement of income and expenditure, and its budget. To estimate your beneficiaries' future expenses in the event of your death, the best place to start is your latest statement of income and expenditure.

Examine each item on the statement of income and expenditure carefully. It may be helpful to compare each item with that of your budget. Now change each amount to the expected and desired level of expenditure assuming that you have died. Some expenses will decrease — e.g. there is one less mouth to feed; there is no need for a second car; there will be less eating out; and so on. Other expenses would increase — e.g. education and child-care expenditure will increase as the children grow older. There may be liabilities that fall due shortly after your death — e.g., mortgage on your home that is not life-insured, tax liabilities and so on. After making adjustments and changes for every item on your statement of income and expenditure, you will have a good idea of how much your beneficiaries will need in the event of your death. We shall now introduce a simple method for determining the amount of life insurance coverage that your beneficiaries need. There are six steps in our approach:

Step 1   Draw up the (projected) balance sheet of the individual at death. This must include the income taxes that will be payable with respect to the year of death. With certain exceptions, a taxpayer is deemed to dispose of all assets at death, and consequently capital gains may be realized.

Step 2   Determine the capital and the assets available that can be invested to generate an annual income for the dependents. Only the liquid and the surplus assets, at liquidation value, should be included. For example, the family home should not be included because the dependents will still be living there. Estimate the annual income that can be generated from this capital and these assets.

Step 3   Add to the above (1) all government payments, such as the survivor benefits from the Canada Pension Plan, Worker's Compensation etc. and (2) the spouse's income. Don't forget that even if the spouse is a full-time home-maker now, she can work, especially when the children grow older.

Step 4   Estimate the expenses required for the dependents to live comfortably, preferably at the standard of living currently enjoyed. This is the most important step (and we have already described how one can estimate the beneficiaries' expected expenses).

Step 5   Subtract the amount in Step 3 from that of Step 4 to get the required supplementary income. This is the amount that must be generated from the life insurance face value.

Step 6   Calculate the capital (the life insurance face value) needed to generate the supplemental income in Step 5.

Table 9.1 is a guide and a summary of this process.

Table 9.1 over-simplifies the problem in another important way. The implication is that the required expenses will continue as is until the death of the beneficiary. This is not true. The family expenses may change in the future — for example, as the children grow older, their clothing and food costs more. When the children are no longer dependent on the surviving parent, expenses decrease a lot, and they may decrease even further when the survivor retires. The largest changes will correspond to changes in the family life cycle stage.

TABLE 9.1
Calculation of the Amount of Life Insurance Needed

1. **Personal Balance Sheet (after death)**

    Assets: $ _____

        Individual life insurance   _____
        Group life insurance   _____
        CPP death benefits   _____
        Cash   _____
        Bank accounts   _____
        Cash value of pension plans   _____
        RRSPs   _____
        Investments (stocks, bonds)   _____
        Other redundant, saleable assets   _____

    TOTAL ASSETS (A) $ _____

    Liabilities:

        Funeral expenses   _____
        Immediate expenses after death   _____
        Consumer debt, income taxes   _____
        Mortgages; other non-life-insured loans   _____
        Contingency fund   _____

    TOTAL LIABILITIES (B) $ _____

2. **Available Capital (C) = (A) − (B)** $ _____

3. **Annual Revenue:**

    Income generated by capital (C) $ _____ invested at ____% yields   _____

    Plus: spouse's income   _____
           spouse's CPP pension   _____
           children's CPP pension   _____
           spouse's share of employer pension   _____
           other income   _____

    Minus: Income taxes   _____

    Total = Available Annual Income (D) $ _____

4. **Expected expenses that the dependents will incur during the period of dependence (E)**

5. **Supplementary income required (D) − (E) = (F)**

6. **An annual income of (F) _____ after taxes, at an interest rate of ____, requires a capital of (G)**

(G) is the required amount of life insurance. Leaving aside taxes, (G) is the present value of the annuity of amount (F), using the real rate of interest, say 3%, as the discount rate. As in the income method, taxes are quite tricky, since part of the payout will be tax free, part taxable. The expense method, however, underestimates the amount required, since the expenses must be paid in after-tax dollars. Hence, we must adjust the calculation of G to allow for taxes. In practice, ignoring taxes and adding 20–30% is a reasonable rule of thumb for most situations.

Table 9.1 will still give a reasonable estimate of the insurance needed using rough lifetime averages for the numbers. You can do it more accurately by re-estimating it for each different stage and then discounting the net value for each block of years. You will require a time line to keep track of all the values.

THE PRINCIPAL TYPES OF LIFE INSURANCE

There are many different kinds of life insurance that are sold in the market and new products are being developed every day. There are term life, whole life, endowment, universal life, group life, single premium, level premium, increasing premium, participating, non-participating, and decreasing term policies, to name just a few. Nevertheless, we can classify all these into two types:

1. Term life policies, which are pure life insurance policies without savings/investment features; and
2. Insurance policies that have savings/investment features. Whole life and universal life policies are examples of this second type.

Term Life Insurance

Term insurance is plain life insurance without a savings component. Term insurance pays the face value to the beneficiaries if the insured dies before the expiry date (i.e., within the term). If the insured does not die, the beneficiaries and the insured collect nothing.

There are different kinds of **term insurance** and we shall mention the most common ones. A **participating term policy** is one on which the insurance company will pay back to the insured each year an amount of money called **dividends**. A **non-participating term** policy means the policy pays no dividends back to the insured. Normally, the premium on a participating policy is higher than the premium on a non-participating policy. Dividends are derived from the investment that the insurance company makes out of the higher premiums that the **participating policy** holders pay. Dividends can be viewed as a partial return of the premium. **Net premium**, defined as the premium minus dividend, is the true annual cost of a participating policy.

If the face value of the policy stays the same throughout the term of the insurance contract, the insurance is called **level term insurance**. If the face value declines as the policy approaches expiry, the insurance is called **decreasing term** insurance. Decreasing term policies are very useful for mortgage borrowers since the principal of the mortgage declines over time.

Term insurance is pure insurance with no frills. It offers protection of the face amount of the policy and nothing more. If the insured wishes to terminate the policy, she gets nothing back from the insurance company. The word "term" in a term policy is misleading: many people think that a term policy is "not permanent" or "non-renewable". This is not true. Generally, as long as the policyholder pays premiums on time, the policy is automatically renewed each year without additional proof of **insurability** — for example, no follow-up medical examination is required.

The Pure Premium

To understand the difference between **term insurance** and insurance with an investment feature, it is important to know how insurance companies calculate premiums. If they charge premiums to the policyholders so that the present value of the revenues received by the insurance company is exactly equal to the expected present value of the benefits paid to the beneficiaries (i.e., the insurance company does not make a profit), then the premium charged is called the **pure premium**. Of course, the premium that one must pay is higher than the pure premium because the insurance companies have to pay administrative and other costs; also, they have to make a reasonable profit. In other words, the insurance premium that one pays is equal to the pure premium plus the insurance company's service costs and profit.

The **pure premium** depends on the likelihood of the insured dying during the insurance coverage period. How can one find out one's likelihood of dying? The historical death rates for many defined groups of people have been observed and reported in **mortality tables**. Mortality tables report the historical death rates of various groups of people according to specific characteristics, such as age, smoking addiction, sex, occupation and so on. Insurance companies can use these mortality tables to predict the number of deaths and the expected payout to the beneficiaries of the group of insured persons in a particular category.

Appendices B1 and B2 contain standard Canadian mortality tables for females and males, respectively. These tables follow a hypothetical group or cohort of 100,000 persons from birth to death and report the actual number of deaths each year for that year. To see how to read the table, turn to Appendix B1 and look at the first line. It says that during the first year of life, Canadian females have a .58% (or probability = .0058) of dying. The next line shows the probability of living from age one to two, given that the person has already survived to age one. The cohort at the start of the year is reduced to 99,423 (due to the 577 predicted deaths in the first year of life). The mortality during year 2 is 45 girls, or .05% of 99,423.

> **Example 9.2:** Let us illustrate how the premium of annual term insurance would be calculated. Suppose a male aged 35 wants to buy $200,000 of term insurance for a year. The mortality rate of this specific group of people — 35-year-old males — is .15% (see Appendix B2).

In that case, the life insurance company expects to pay to the beneficiaries on average an amount of:

$$\$200,000 \times .0015 = \$300$$

Thus, the insured must pay $300. This premium, paid by every other person in his category, is just enough when pooled over a large number of policies, to pay the death benefits that the insurance company expects to have to pay during the year. As we discussed in the risk management chapter, the law of large numbers implies that the actual occurrence of deaths in a large group approaches very closely to the average or expected number of deaths.

Premiums are paid at the beginning of the year, but benefits are paid throughout the year. The insurance payout must be discounted for this period. Let us assume that all benefits are paid at year end. If the appropriate discount rate is 5%, the **pure premium** that must be charged is equal to ($300 ÷ 1.05) or $285.71. Finally, service costs (including profits) will be added to the pure premium. If servicing costs are $35, then the final premium is equal to ($285.71 + $35.00) or $320.71.

From the above analysis, we see that the premium on a term insurance policy will increase with the insured's age because the probability of death increases with age. Term policies are best suited for the person who wants lower life insurance premiums in the early years of the policy in order to have more money to spend or invest. Term policies are also suitable for the person who will not need life insurance in the later years of life when the premiums become very high. For example, some people feel no need for life insurance when the children are grown up and are financially independent. In contrast, people who want very long life insurance coverage, or who want to use life insurance as a form of forced savings, will find there are other more suitable forms of insurance than term insurance.

A commonly-quoted statistic in the popular press is the "average life expectancy." Often the press actually reports the median age of death, starting from the date of birth. The median age is the age at which 50,000 of the original 100,000 cohort have died. Reading down the second column of Appendix B1, we can see that this occurs late in the 84th year for women. (The year that person is 83 years old, in common speaking, is the 84th year of life.) For males, Appendix B2, the median age of death is in the 78th year.

We rarely buy life insurance for a child at birth, however, and the more useful information is the conditional probability that a person will live to a certain age, given that he is already y years old.

Example 9.3: What is the probability of a 35-year-old woman surviving to age 65.

Answer: At age 35 there are 98,344 women surviving out of the original 100,000. At age 65 there are 88,596. The probability of survival, given that the woman has already reached 35, is: 88,596 ÷ 98,344 = 90%.

Suppose we want to apply conditional probability to an insurance premium for more than one year. How would the insurance company calculate the level pure premium for a $200,000 policy?

Each year a number of the cohort die and the insurance company pays the full face value of life insurance policies to the beneficiaries. The rest of the insured get no cash payment. The next year, only those still surviving could be eligible for a payout in the event of their death. Therefore, the probability of receiving such a payment in the second year is slightly less, because there is a possibility that you died during the previous year. Thus, we can calculate the probability of the death of an individual for each year for a specified number of future years, conditional each year on having survived to that year.

We need this probability to calculate the present value of the expected future payouts. We will not derive it formally, but using the following notation:

M	the face amount of the insurance policy
$_DP_t$	the probability of dying in year t
$_SP_t$	the probability of living to the start of year t, starting at a specified year
k	the discount rate
n	expected date of death

$$PV \text{ of Premium} = M \sum_{t=1}^{n} \frac{_DP_t \times _sP_t}{(1+k)^t}$$

The final step is to use the same interest rate and the period of support required, and convert the present value of the future payments into the equivalent annuity.

Example 9.4: A 35-year-old single mother requires a $1 million life insurance policy on herself, in favour of her son. When she reaches 40, she will no longer need it, because he will receive a trust fund. She wants to pay a level premium. The appropriate interest rate is 7%. What is the pure level premium (no costs, no saving component)?

The probability of dying from age 35 to 36 is .0007, from Appendix B2. The probability of dying from age 36 to 37 is again .0007. But the probability of the insurance company paying out is .9993 × .0007, because .0007 of the cohort are already dead. The probability of a payout from age 37 to 38 is .0008, and the conditional probability of arriving at age 37, from age 35, is .9993 × .9993 and so on. Each of these probabilities must be discounted to get a present value, and then the sum is multiplied by the $1 million face value:

$$\$1 \text{ million} \times \left[\frac{.0007}{1.07} + \frac{(.0007 \times .9993)}{1.07^2} + \frac{(.0008 \times .9993 \times .9993)}{1.07^3} \right.$$
$$+ \frac{(.0009 \times .9993 \times .9993 \times .9992)}{1.07^4}$$
$$\left. + \frac{(.0009 \times .9993 \times .9993 \times .9992 \times .9991)}{1.07^5} \right]$$

$1 million× [.00065+ .00061 + .00065 + .00069 + .00064]
= $1 million × (.00324)
= $3,240

Then to convert it to a level premium:

$$\text{PVA due} \times (7\%, 5yr) = 3,240$$
$$\text{Premium} = \$738.51$$

In the first year, the level premium is higher than the one-year pure premium. In the last year, the level premium is lower. The calculation is an annuity due, because insurance premiums are paid at the start of the period.

Term Life Insurance Premiums

Numerous factors affect the actual premium the insured pays to the insurance company:

- age
- gender
- specific health conditions

- cost of selling and administering the policy
- the ability of potential insured persons to choose policies beneficial to them.

The older the insured, the higher the probability of death. Men die earlier than women on average. Smokers die earlier, on average. These are the commonest factors that insurance companies price in their general quotations. A person who takes a medical examination that reveals some specific health risk — heart condition, diabetes, etc. — may be able to get life insurance, but the premium will be much higher.

Individual policies cost more to sell and to administer than group policies. Life insurance agents receive substantial commissions for every policy they sell, whereas large group policies are sold directly by the company for a much lower cost relative to the value of the premiums. Also, the size of the policy matters, because it takes the same time to administer a single policy, regardless of size. Therefore, all non-group term life insurance quotations apply to a policy of the specified size. The quotation always includes an implicit fixed **policy fee** and a variable premium that depends on the risk factors.

A person who takes out a policy that expires at the end of one year will get a relatively cheap premium, because the company has only one year of risk to assume. If the person wants to renew the policy, he or she must take another medical examination. A person who takes out a 10 year policy may become a serious risk after the first year, but the company cannot rescind the policy. Therefore, a 10 year policy will carry a higher annual premium than a series of one year policies for someone who is healthy at each annual renewal date, because the company cannot avoid the higher risks that some of the 10 year policyholders will pose after the initial purchase of the policy.

Group term insurance is usually renewable every year, but without further medical testing required. Group term insurance has the advantage of cheaper administrative costs, but the disadvantage of what we call **adverse selection.** Adverse selection occurs wherever something is priced to reflect an average quality. The item which is above average quality commands the same price as the item of poor quality. In this case, people who are healthy know they are healthy, but they still pay the same average life insurance premium. The ones who aren't healthy pay an average premium that is too low.

The people who are healthy can always leave the group and buy cheaper insurance as they age and the general rates rise. People in the group who are unhealthy will stay in the group and take advantage of the right to renew their insurance every year without a medical examination. As a result, as the ages rise in a group, the death rate is likely to rise faster than in the general population, since those who are least healthy have the greatest incentive to stay insured within the group. Insurance companies must price to compensate for this adverse selection.

We could say a great deal more about pricing of insurance policies, but the subject is too large for us to continue. Table 9.2 shows comparative life insurance premiums for level term insurance for 10 and 20 year terms. This type of policy is for long run coverage. The insured takes out the policy at the age shown, and pays the same premium, in nominal dollars, for the term agreed. At the end of the term, if he or she wants to renew the insurance, a new policy, a new medical examination, and a new rate schedule are all required. The particular prices shown are quotations by a variety of companies, and are the lowest available in each category at the time of writing.

TABLE 9.2
Term Life Insurance Premium Quotations
Annual Premium for $250,000 of Level Term Insurance

These premiums are for 10 and 20 year terms. The premium is the same for each year of the term, starting at the age indicated.

| | Non-smoker | | | |
| | Male | | Female | |
Age	10 Year	20 Year	10 Year	20 Year
25	$ 215.00	$ 267.50	$ 192.50	$ 250.00
30	220.00	267.50	195.00	262.50
35	222.50	297.50	197.50	267.50
40	275.00	370.00	222.50	297.50
45	390.00	555.00	275.00	370.00
50	572.50	830.00	390.00	555.00
55	825.00	1,202.50	572.50	830.00
60	1,270.00	2,032.50	825.00	1,202.50

| | Smoker | | | |
| | Male | | Female | |
Age	10 Year	20 Year	10 Year	20 Year
25	380.00	497.50	257.50	375.00
30	407.50	520.00	292.50	449.50
35	422.50	597.50	377.00	520.00
40	567.50	812.50	422.50	597.50
45	905.00	1,340.00	567.50	812.50
50	1,385.00	2,052.50	905.00	1,340.00
55	1,955.00	2,870.00	1,385.00	2,052.50
60	2,782.50	5,442.50	1,955.00	2,870.00

Source: Compulife Software Inc. The quotations are from different companies. Each quotation is the lowest available in that category at the time of writing.

Group Life insurance premiums vary greatly between groups. Such policies have annual terms, but with an option for the insured to renew each year. Each group may have a different mortality table, and there will be different features between the policies set up for the groups. The premium is usually per unit of insurance, with no difference between smaller and large policies. The premium schedule may change at the option of the insurance company at any annual renewal date. This is different from non-group term policies, other than annual ones. If the insurance is automatic for every member of the group, then there is no medical examination required. For example, many employers provide some amount of life insurance to every employee as long as he or she is employed. This insurance is usually **convertible insurance**, which means that on leaving the employer, the employee can convert the insurance to a non-group policy, provided he or she can pass a medical examination.

TABLE 9.3
Group Term Life Insurance Premium Quotations
Monthly Premium for $25,000 of Term Insurance
Institute of Chartered Accountants of Ontario

These premiums are for annual terms, but are renewable every year without further medical examinations. The premium schedule may be changed at any renewal date.

	Non-smoker		Smoker	
	Male	Female	Male	Female
Under 35	$ 1.50	$ 1.25	$ 2.00	$ 1.75
35–39	1.75	1.50	3.00	2.25
40–44	2.50	2.00	4.50	3.25
45–49	3.75	3.00	6.50	5.00
50–54	5.75	5.00	10.00	7.00
55–59	9.00	6.75	15.00	9.50
60–72	12.50	10.00	22.50	13.75

Maximum coverage is $1 million for the member and $500,000 for the spouse. There are some other special features of the policy not included in this table. The Manufacturers Life Insurance Company provides the policy.

If the members of the group have the option to take the insurance or not, then they will have to pass a medical examination when they take the insurance. Once passed, no further medical examination is necessary except for an increase in the face amount of the policy. Commonly, members of the group and their spouses are eligible to apply for coverage. Table 9.3 shows the premiums for a specific group whose members take the insurance at their option, the Institute of Chartered Accountants of Ontario.

Life Insurance with Savings/Investment Features

Are there life insurance policies whose premium does not increase with the insured's age? The answer is yes. There is a type of life insurance policy where premiums are constant, or even decreasing, each year, even though the probability of dying increases with age. Example 9.4 shows how this apparently contradictory situation can occur. The insurance company sets the premium at a level that is higher than the expected mortality costs in the early years of a policy, and lower than the expected mortality costs in the later years of the policy. In other words, the policyholder is "overpaying" in the early years and "underpaying" in the later years of the policy. The overpayment in the early years is invested and accumulated by the insurance company as a **cash surrender value** or, as it is frequently and more simply called, the **cash value**. If you cancel the policy, the cash value will be returned to you. Thus, the cash value is really your investment that is being kept by the insurance company for the purpose of keeping future premiums at the same, or at an even lower, level than they are currently. An insurance policy of this kind is actually a combination of term insurance and an investment account. There are many examples of this type of policy. We will mention the most common ones:

Whole Life Insurance This is a policy that pays the face amount to the beneficiaries when the insured dies. The face amount is paid without any restrictions because the policy remains in force for the life of the insured. The premium is constant throughout the insured's lifetime. This is called the **level premium**. When the insured cancels the policy, she gets back the **cash surrender value**, which is really the savings component of the policy.

Endowment Life Policy This is a form of insurance that will pay the face amount to the beneficiaries if the insured dies. However, unlike other insurance policies, it will also pay the face amount to the insured — the amount paid is called the endowment — if the insured lives to a certain age. How is this possible? Recall that the insurance is actually a combination of two things: a pure term insurance and a savings account. The premium of an endowment policy is set in such a way that the savings component will be invested to reach the endowment value at a specific date.

Universal Life Insurance A universal life insurance policy is a combination of a **term insurance** and a side **investment fund**. The policyholder pays a premium which the insurance company separates explicitly into an insurance component and an investment component. First, the insurance company deducts from the premium an amount for the insurance coverage plus costs plus a profit margin; the remainder becomes an investment on which the policyholder earns interest. As long as the policyholder maintains the insurance portion of the premium every year, the insurance policy is in force. The money accumulated in the investment portion of the policy can be used to pay the minimum premium required to maintain the insurance portion of the contract. This makes universal life insurance policies very flexible. After some money has been saved up in the investment fund, the policyholder can make whatever premium payment he wants — lower premium payments or even skip premium payments for a while. The insurance company prepares a report periodically which shows how much of the premium goes to pay the pure insurance premium, administrative costs, and other costs, and how much goes to the side investment fund.

Term Policy vs. Non-Term Policy

Although there are numerous different kinds of insurance policies in the market, there are only two major types. First, there are the **term policies**. These are the pure insurance policies without a savings/investment component. The premiums on such policies are based on the way **pure premiums** are calculated, as we have discussed earlier. Since the most important factor affecting the premium rate is the mortality rate of the insured, the premium rate of a term insurance policy will always increase as the insured gets older.

The second type of life insurance are the **non-term insurance** policies. These are insurance policies that have a pure insurance component and a savings/investment component. Except for the term life insurance, all the insurance products that we have described — whole life, endowment policy, universal life and so on — are insurance policies with an insurance component and a savings component. The policyholder pays a higher premium than that of a comparable term insurance in the early years of the policy because part of the premium goes into a "savings account". The money in the savings account will be used to reduce the future premiums or will be returned to the policyholder if she cancels the policy. The amount of money that the policyholder gets back when the policy is cancelled is called the **cash value** or the **cash surrender value**. Thus, the cash surrender value is actually the amount of money accumulated in the "savings account" at the point of cancellation of the policy.

Which is better: term life insurance or non-term life insurance such as whole life and universal life? Many financial experts advise that you should buy term life insurance for protection and "invest the difference" between term and whole life premiums, rather than buying whole life insurance. The argument rests on the belief that whole life (and other non-term policies) insurance is more costly, and the purpose of insurance is risk management.

Risk Management   Recall that the need for life insurance is higher during the stages of the life cycle when the family will have the greatest demands on its financial resources: dependent children, mortgage, incomes below the peak level, perhaps one spouse staying home with the children. The risk management need is to cover the loss due to the premature death of one of the parents. Most families will have only a limited amount of money that they can afford to put into life insurance. Term policies cost far less than non-term because they require only the pure premium plus costs. A family that takes on extra risk by putting its limited dollars into a non-term policy is very unwise.

On the other hand, a family may have sufficient resources that it can put some money into enforced savings at the same time as it buys life insurance. The universal policies, with their flexible savings amount, could be worthwhile. This brings us to the other considerations in the comparison.

Who Is the More Effective Investor?   First, can you invest the difference to earn a higher return than the life insurance company? Empirical studies in the past find that the rate of return on whole life is inferior to that available on comparable savings instruments. In other words, there is evidence that you would earn a higher return by putting the monetary "difference" in a chartered bank savings account than by putting it in whole life insurance. But why is that the case? We think this is due, to a large extent, to the high commission fees that insurance companies pay to agents. In general, the insurance companies pay a much higher commission fee to agents for selling whole life than they do for selling individual term life. Since the commission is a percentage on the total premium that you pay, this means that you pay a commission for saving money with an insurance company. Banks do not charge you a commission for putting your money into a savings account!

Do You Need Someone to Make You Save?   Do you have the self-discipline to invest the difference between term and whole life premiums? If you do not, many insurance agents would suggest that you may be better off buying a whole life policy that will force you to save. But automatic savings plans offered by chartered banks, trust companies and brokerage firms will do the same job. The benefits of using whole life policies as savings vehicles are not obvious.

The above discussion is just a qualitative comparison of the two types of life insurance policies: term life, which has no savings components, and non-term life, which does have such a component. The qualitative comparison does not lead to a clear conclusion of which is better. We will next describe a quantitative method to shed more light on this issue.

Buy Term and Compare the Difference

This is a quantitative method to compare term and non-term life policies. Although we will use a numerical example that compares a term policy versus a whole life policy, the method can be used to compare any two policies that provide the same death benefit. As we have seen, the question of whether term or non-term life policies are better depends on whether you would be better off buying a term policy and investing the difference of the whole life premium and the term premium. This method assumes the mortality tables do not change during the time period of the comparison.

Take a whole life policy and a term life policy both of which are similar in all respects including their face value. For each year of the policy term, write down the premium for each policy.[3] Then, calculate the difference between the whole life premium and the term life premium — this is the amount that you invest each year. Assume that you will invest this difference in premiums every year at the after-tax rate of interest, and accumulate an investment fund with these investments. Since the term policy and the whole life policy are identical in all other respects, the comparison of the two now boils down to comparing the amount accumulated in the investment fund and the **cash surrender value** or the **cash value** of the whole life policy. We will illustrate this with an example.

> **Example 9.5:**   Consider the quotes from a life insurance company for a term insurance policy and a whole life policy for a 35-year-old male who wants insurance coverage from now until the age of 54, after which he does not need the coverage because the children will be independent. The premiums for each policy are shown in Table 9.4.
>
> Let us assume that the individual can invest money to earn an after-tax interest rate of 4%. Is the term policy better or is the whole life policy better? The analysis and calculation is shown in Table 9.5.

Let us analyse the results. If the person purchases the term policy and invests the difference, he would have an investment fund of $16,097, which is already after taxes. If he buys the whole life policy, he will receive $20,200 when he cancels the policy at 54. So in our example, the whole life policy is better than the term policy. But there is one more thing to consider. Under the current tax law, the cash value is taxable. Cash value is the difference between the cash surrender value and the adjusted cost base (the premiums paid less dividends received). In our example, the adjusted cost base is the total sum of all the net premiums, i.e., column (2) in Table 9.5, and this is equal to $13,778. Thus, the amount $20,200 − $14,542 or $5,658 is taxable. Assuming the individual's tax rate at 54 is 40%, the amount of taxes paid is $2,263. So, after taxes, he ends up with $20,200 − $2,263 or $17,937. This is still better than the $16,097 in the investment fund under the "buy term and invest the difference" policy.

---

[3]   For a participating policy, you should use the net premium, i.e., subtract the expected dividends from the premium paid.

TABLE 9.4
Comparing Term and Whole Life (Face Value of $100,000)

Age	Whole Life		Term
	Net Premiums	Cash Value	Net Premiums
35	$1,316	$ 0	$163
36	1,165	0	166
37	1,127	500	169
38	1,085	1,500	176
39	1,043	2,600	185
40	994	3,740	196
41	945	4,880	214
42	896	6,020	231
43	847	7,160	249
44	798	8,300	265
45	736	9,500	288
46	672	10,700	310
47	609	11,900	336
48	546	13,100	369
49	482	14,300	406
50	407	15,480	432
51	332	16,660	461
52	257	17,840	494
53	182	19,020	535
54	103	20,200	574

TABLE 9.5
Calculating the Difference between Term and Whole Life

(1)	(2)	(3)	(4)	(5)
Age	Whole Life NP	Term Life NP	(2) − (3)	Balance in Investment Fund at A-T Rate of 4%
35	$1,316	$163	$1,153	1,153 × 1.04 = 1199
36	1,165	166	999	(999 + 1,199) × 1.04 = 2286
37	1,127	169	958	(958 + 2,286) × 1.04 = 3374
38	1,085	176	909	(909 + 3,374) × 1.04 = 4454
39	1,043	185	858	(858 + 4,454) × 1.04 = 5524
40	994	196	798	(798 + 5,524) × 1.04 = 6575
41	945	214	731	(731 + 6,575) × 1.04 = 7598
42	896	231	665	(665 + 7,598) × 1.04 = 8594
43	847	249	598	(598 + 8,594) × 1.04 = 9550
44	798	265	533	(533 + 9,560) × 1.04 = 10497
45	736	288	448	(448 + 10,497) × 1.04 = 11383
46	672	310	362	(362 + 11,383) × 1.04 = 12214
47	609	336	273	(273 + 12,214) × 1.04 = 12986
48	546	369	177	(177 + 12,986) × 1.04 = 13690
49	482	406	76	(76 + 13,690) × 1.04 = 14317
50	407	432	−25	(−25 + 14,317) × 1.04 = 14864
51	332	461	−129	(14,864 − 129) × 1.04 = 15324
52	257	495	−238	(15,324 − 238) × 1.04 = 15689
53	182	535	−353	(15,689 − 353) × 1.04 = 15949
54	103	574	−471	(15,949 − 471) × 1.04 = 16097

This is only an example to illustrate the mechanics of the "buy term and invest the difference" approach. It can be used to compare any two insurance policies.[3]

Secondary Policy Provisions

We have described the most important elements in a life insurance contract — face value or death benefit, premium, cash surrender value, term policy, whole life policy, dividends, insurability and so on. If you read a typical insurance policy, you may find a lot more terminology — usually printed in fine print, the secondary policy provisions spell out the details of the policy. We will describe briefly the more common of these clauses. Note that these are by no means standard clauses; they may be present or absent in your insurance policy.

Waiver of Premium. By this provision, premiums will not have to be paid although the policy will remain in force if the insured becomes totally disabled before a specified age, usually 65.

Guaranteed Insurability. This is a provision which allows the policyholder the right to buy additional life insurance in the future without providing evidence of insurability — e.g., without passing a medical examination.

Smoker/Non-smoker Provision. There is a recent trend in the insurance industry to reduce premiums if the insured is certified as being a non-smoker.

Reinstatement Time Limit. This is the maximum length of time before a lapsed policy can be reinstated without proof of insurability. For instance, if one becomes unemployed and cannot make premium payments, the insurance policy becomes lapsed. This provision allows for the reinstatement of the policy within time limits.

Suicide Time Limit. Believe it or not, many insurance policies pay the death benefit even when the insured commits suicide. The suicide time limit is the number of years that must pass from the date of purchase before the policy will pay death benefits in the event that the insured makes a successful attempt on his own life.

Loan Provisions. Many life policies allow the policyholder to borrow money, usually up to the cash surrender value of the policy. The loan provisions state the conditions under which the loan will be made, e.g., the interest rate charged, the amount of the loan and so on.

Settlement Options. These refer to the options available to the beneficiaries for receiving the death benefits. Two common options are to receive the benefits in one lump sum and to receive the benefits periodically, e.g., in monthly cheques, with the balance being invested in the insurance company.

Convertibility. This is a provision which allows the holder of a term policy to convert it to a whole life policy under the specified terms and time limits.

Accidental Death Benefits. This provision means that the face amount paid to the beneficiaries will be increased (usually by two or three times) to the stated amount

---

[3] This procedure is slightly biased to show the whole life policy in a favourable light. In fact, the whole life policy pays *either* the CSV or the face value, while the term policy pays the face, and the beneficiary also gets the investment account established with the net premiums saved.

if the insured dies from an accident (e.g., car accident), than if the insured dies in some other way.

Grace Period. This is the short period of time (usually 30 days) after a premium due date has been missed that the insurance policy is still in force.

HEALTH INSURANCE

This is often called medical insurance. In Canada, most basic medical procedures are provided for under the various provincial health-care plans. It is therefore not necessary for most Canadians to carry additional coverage for medical expenses; however, if you want to supplement this basic level of health care, private insurance coverage can be purchased from many insurance companies such as Blue Cross. The typical additional coverage includes semi-private or private rooms for hospital stays, prescription drugs, eyeglasses and dental care.

Health-care costs outside Canada, especially in the United States, can be very high, and may not be fully covered by provincial health-care plans. A Canadian can purchase additional protection for health-care costs incurred outside Canada from many private insurance companies at quite reasonable rates. Some credit cards provide out-of-Canada health-care coverage for limited periods of time.

DISABILITY INSURANCE

Disability Insurance protects the insured and the insured's family against the risk of serious illness or accident that would render the insured incapable, to a greater or lesser extent, of self-care or of full employment.

The risk of disability cannot be totally avoided. It depends to a large degree on one's lifestyle and one's occupation. Studies have found the probability of a significant period of disability is much higher than the probability of death at any age up to the normal age for retirement. Also, studies have found that more than half of the disabilities experienced at any age exceed one year in duration. Not many families have enough savings to support the loss of income for a full year or more. The evidence suggests that most families need disability insurance even more than they need life insurance because the cost of total disability of a breadwinner is greater to the family than death, since additional expenses may be incurred to take care of the disabled person.

In Canada, the provincial governments have established various social programmes which provide some insurance against disability — the Worker's Compensation Board is one example. The protection available varies from one province to another, and it is important for you to find out the programmes available in the province in which you reside. Also, the Canada Pension Plan (CPP) provides a disability pension, up to a maximum of $870.92 per month, to the disabled until the age of 65, at which point he or she will receive the regular CPP benefits. These government programmes, however, are totally inadequate to maintain a decent standard of living; moreover, the rules are strict and many disabilities (especially partial disabilities) do not qualify. For these reasons, the government programmes should be viewed as a supplement rather than a substitute for a disability insurance policy.

How much disability insurance coverage do you need? Theoretically, the **income approach** or the **expense approach**, both of which were described earlier, can be used.

As a practical matter, insurance companies and many financial experts recommend coverage for 60% to 80% of one's current gross income. For example, if your annual income is $40,000, you would buy a disability insurance that will pay you $24,000 to $32,000 per year in the event of disability. The amount that you receive from the insurance company is not taxable because the premium that you pay is not tax deductible. The amount you will get is therefore not too much below the amount of your current after-tax income. Of course, if the disability involves substantial additional expenses, you and your family will still be worse off.

Like any insurance policy, the terms and conditions of a disability policy are very important. The following should help you to determine whether the policy is suitable for you:

1. The definition of **Total Disability**.
   The definition is not standardized, and it varies from one insurance company to another. Ideally, it should include the loss of speech, sight, hearing, the complete loss of the use of both hands or feet, or one hand or foot. Read this very carefully in your contract.

2. The **waiting period** or **elimination period**.
   This is the period from the start of the disability to the time when the benefits begin under the policy. The shorter the waiting period, the higher the premium you pay. For that reason, if you can afford some self-insurance, you can ask for a longer waiting period.

3. The **length of the contract** or the **term**.
   It should be non-cancellable and renewable at the insured's option up to the age of 65.

4. **Period of Benefits**.
   This is the length of time over which the benefits may be payable. The longer the period, the higher the premium.

5. **Period of Deemed Total Disability**.
   This is the length of time after which the disability is deemed to have permanently prevented the insured from returning to normal work. Under this provision, a disabled person who recovers after a prolonged period is not cut off when she cannot realistically resume her previous occupation.

6. **Waiver of Premium**.
   This is a provision that allows for the cancellation of all premiums if the insured is disabled before age 65. Every disability insurance policy should contain this clause.

7. Definition of **Partial Disability**.
   This provision covers the question of whether or not you will be paid benefits if you are unable to carry on your normal occupation, but can carry on another occupation which is paid at a lower rate.

8. **Exclusions**.
   This term refers to things not covered by the policy. Usually, insurance does not cover acts of war, a state of war or a normal pregnancy. What you should be careful about is that some policies cover disability only from accidents and not

disability due to a prolonged illness. Read your policy very carefully on all the exclusions.

Many people have access to group disability insurance plans through their employers. Since the employers usually pay part or all of the premium, you should take it. Be aware, however, that the policy does not necessarily provide you with adequate coverage. Study your employer's group disability insurance contract — benefit periods, waiting periods, causes of disability, definition of disability and amount of coverage. You may have to buy additional disability insurance from an outside insurance company.

Disability Insurance Premiums

Disability insurance premiums vary widely, even for persons of the same age and gender, because of the different features a policy can have. Group disability insurance is quite a bit cheaper than an individual policy, but the provisions and premiums of group policies also vary greatly. Table 9.6 provides premiums for one group, but you should realize that this table applies only to that group with that specific set of features in the policy.

TABLE 9.6
Group Disability Insurance Premiums
Institute of Chartered Accountants of Ontario

Each unit is $100 of monthly income. Maximum coverage is lesser of (i) $8,000 per month or (ii) 50% of earned income reduced by other disability insurance other than CPP and reduced by income continued by the employer or partnership. Other key features:

- Total disability — unable to do normal duties of regular occupation
- Indexed to inflation, up to 8% p.a.
- No coverage for disabilities from self-inflicted injury, active participation in a criminal offence, insurrection or war.
- Partial payments available for partial disability.

| | Monthly Premium Per Unit | | | |
| | Waiting Period in Days | | | |
Age	30	90	180	365
Male				
Under 40	$0.85	$0.65	$0.60	$0.50
40–49	1.50	1.25	1.15	1.00
50–64	3.25	2.65	2.50	2.00
65–69	3.75	3.00	2.75	2.50
Female				
Under 40	1.00	0.85	0.75	0.65
40–49	1.65	1.40	1.25	1.10
50–64	2.90	2.35	2.25	1.75
65–69	3.25	2.60	2.50	2.25

HOW SAFE IS YOUR INSURANCE COVERAGE?

The assurance that your insurance coverage will cover you when you need it has taken on new concern with the recent insolvency of Confederation Life, one of Canada's largest life and health insurers. **The Canadian Life and Health Insurance Compensation Corporation (CompCorp)** provides partial insurance of policies of its members in the event of a company's insolvency and inability to meet its policy liabilities. Virtually all life and health insurance companies belong to CompCorp. The rules include a number of complicating features. Group insurance and joint policies can be particularly tricky. We provide only the basic outline in this book — you should contact CompCorp directly at (800) 268–8099 or, in Toronto, at (416) 777–2344.

CompCorp provides protection to policyholders of its member companies with life insurance, health insurance, disability, money accumulation or annuity policies that promise to pay either a fixed or a minimum amount of money to a person at some point in time, or on the person's death to the beneficiary. The policies are grouped into three classes with specified coverage limits. The limits apply to all policies together in each class with a single insurance company. That is, if you have three life insurance policies with a single company (Class A policies), the limit insurable is $200,000 of life insurance. If you have three insurance policies with three different companies, the limit is $200,000 for each company. If you have a class A, a class B and a class C policy with a single company, the limit is the amount for each class for each policy, taken separately.

CompCorp covers the gap between the amount paid in insolvency by an insurer, and the lesser of the CompCorp limit and the policy amount.

Class A Policies

- life insurance policies
- accumulation annuities (like bank Guaranteed Investment Certificates)
- Registered Retirement Savings Plans (RRSPs)
- Registered Retirement Income Funds (RRIFs)
- any other policies that provide life insurance or savings features.

   The limits for the class are:

1. $200,000 for life insurance;
2. $60,000 in cash withdrawal for policies registered under the *Income Tax Act*, like RRSPs, RRIFs and pension policies; and,
3. $60,000 in cash withdrawal for non-registered policies.

Class B   Life and fixed term annuities, including disability income policies, are in this class. Annuities where the annuitant can opt to take a lump sum cash payment instead of the periodic payments are included in Class A. The limit is $2,000 income per month.

Class C   Health- and dental-care benefits are included in this class, with a limit of $60,000 in total payments to each covered person, including each dependent separately.

Other Rules   The limits apply to the combined total amount payable under all policies in the same class with the same insurer covering the same *person*. What do the rules mean by "person?"

1. For Class A, insurance policy, person means the person whose life is insured. For a money accumulation policy it means the person who is owner. The beneficiary is irrelevant in determining the person covered by CompCorp. For example, one person could have policies in favour of each child in the family, but the limit would still be $200,000 for all the policies in total at a single insurer.
2. For Class B: the annuitant.
3. For Class C: the person in respect of whom the payments are made.

Only Canadian policies are covered. The policy must be in Canadian funds. The policyholder must have been a Canadian resident when the policy was issued, or now be a Canadian resident, with the policy shown on the insurer's Canadian books. The policy must not be covered by any other compensation arrangement. (There are no such other arrangements at present in Canada.)

Finally, we repeat that there are complications that can arise in various circumstances that we have not covered.

> **Example 9.6:** Colonel Mustard has a life insurance policy for $250,000 with Itsadogs Life Insurance Co. He also has a disability income policy that pays out 60% of his annual income if he becomes seriously disabled and unable to work. His wife has a life insurance policy for $100,000 with the same company. His wife also has her spousal RRSP (i.e., the Colonel made all the contributions, but she is the owner. See Chapter 16.) with Itsadogs Life, invested in a $50,000 guaranteed account of the company. Finally, they have a group health plan with Itsadogs through the Colonel's employer that covers them and their three children. The Colonel earns $60,000 p.a. If Itsadogs Life goes bankrupt tomorrow, and the trustee-in-bankruptcy pays out 50% on claims, how much are they covered for?

The Colonel is covered for $125,000 under the life policy by the trustee, and CompCorp raises that coverage to $200,000 if he dies. His disability coverage is .6 × $60,000 = $36,000 p.a., or $3,000 per month. The trustee would pay $1,500 per month, and CompCorp will raise it to $2,000 per month. His wife's insurance policy and RRSP will be covered 50% by the trustee, and 50% by CompCorp, since they are below the limits. Finally, they are covered for $60,000 in health care for each member of the family. To put the answer another way, the lost coverage is $50,000 in the Colonel's life insurance and $1,000 per month in his disability income insurance.

SUMMARY

This chapter introduces and explains two important topics in insurance: life insurance and disability insurance. Life insurance is a very useful method to protect a family from the risk of loss of income due to the premature and unanticipated death of a family member. We examine three important questions: (1) Who should buy life insurance? (2) How much life insurance coverage does a family need? (3) What type of insurance should an individual buy? Is term insurance better than whole life insurance? Several analytical tools have been introduced: the **income approach** and the **expense approach** to determine insurance needs, and the "buy term and invest the difference" approach to compare different insurance policies. Many common terminologies of the insurance industry have been described and used.

Disability insurance is the method used to protect a family from the loss of income when a breadwinner becomes disabled. Past studies have indicated that many families need disability insurance even more than they need life insurance. The important terminologies found in a typical disability contract have been introduced. After studying this chapter, the reader should have a very firm foundation of knowledge to analyse and make decisions on different life insurance and disability insurance policies.

KEY TERMINOLOGY

insured / premium / insupportable risk / beneficiary / death benefit / face value / owner / policy term / rate / insurability / guaranteed insurability / dependents / financial dependents / income approach / expense approach / real rate of interest / basic benchmark of income approach / endowment policy / single premium policy / level premium policy / increasing premium policy / pure premium / net premium / level term policy / decreasing term / mortality table / mortality rate / death rate / cash value / cash surrender value / human capital / "buy term and compare the difference" method / waiver of premium / settlement options / convertibility / no growth / term insurance / participating policy / non-participating policy / dividends of participating policy / group insurance / whole life insurance / universal life insurance / accidental death benefits / reinstatement time limit / suicide time limit / loan provisions / smoker/non-smoker provision / grace period / disability insurance / exclusions / period of benefits / period of deemed disability

DISCUSSION QUESTIONS

1. Define or describe each of the terms in the **Key Terminology** section.

For the next two projects, if you are a young student you may not have these insurance needs/policies. Use your parents or another older family member instead.

2. **Personal Project 1**
    (a) Do you need life insurance?
    (b) Using (i) the income approach and (ii) the expense approach, determine the amount of life insurance coverage that you need.

3. **Personal Project 2**
    Get a copy of the group disability insurance policy from your employer.
    (a) Go through each clause in the policy. Do you understand each one? Discuss any questions in class or with your instructor.
    (b) Do you have sufficient disability insurance coverage? If yes, why? If not, why not?

PROBLEMS

1. What is the probability of:
    (a) a 50-year-old man living to age 56?
    (b) a 30-year-old woman living to age 34?

2. Calculate the pure premium for a man buying a one-year policy at age 48, assuming payout at year end and an interest rate of 8%.

3. Calculate the pure level premium for a woman buying a policy at age 35 that will mature at age 65. The interest rate is 8%. [The calculations will be very time consuming unless you use a computer spreadsheet.]

4. Using the information and the premium quotes in Table 9.4, suppose the individual needs coverage until he is 50. Which policy is better assuming that he can invest his money at an after-tax rate of return of:
    (i)   3%;
    (ii) 6%;
    (iii) 10%?

5. Mr. Green has an annual salary of $48,000. Through his employer he has group disability insurance of 80% of his salary, with Getta Life. He also has a life insurance policy of three times his salary with Getta Life, paid by the employer. He has taken the option to add $100,000 more in life insurance with the same company. This company also insures the employer's health- and dental-care plans, with a lifetime payout limit of $80,000 per member of the insured's family. Mr. Green's wife also carries $50,000 of life insurance with Getta Life.

    Mr. Green is the beneficiary of a whole life policy issued by Getta Life on his mother for $100,000. He has placed his RRSP of $70,000 in a guaranteed account with another life insurance company. He has insured each of his children with Getta Life for $10,000.

    How secure is Mr. Green's insurance coverage?

6. Walter and Maria McKay are 30 and 29, respectively. They have children aged six and three. Walter works for the City of Regina in maintenance. He earns $31,000 p.a. and takes home $25,000. He has long-term disability insurance covering 75% of his income (and it will be tax free). He has life insurance coverage for two times his salary through an employer group plan. He has good medical coverage with the employer. They have adequate insurance on the house and car.

    Maria works part time in a local submarine shop and earns $4,000 p.a. She is paid less than the minimum wage and does not report the income for tax purposes. The employer does not claim it as an expense. She spends most of her time working in the home.

    If Walter dies, Maria and the children get Canada Pension Plan (CPP) survivor benefits, all indexed to inflation:

Lump sum to Maria	$3,000
Pension to Maria until age 65	$300/month
Pension to Maria age 65 to death	$250/month
Pension to each child to age 18	$110/month

    Maria hasn't worked legally, and so gets no CPP pension on her own account, nor would Walter get any survivor benefits. Maria would get Walter's pension value (to be rolled into an RRSP to avoid immediate taxation). Each one would get Old

Age Security (OAS) at age 65. The present rate of OAS is $4,799, and it is indexed to inflation.

They currently save only a few hundred dollars a year, what with mortgage payments, children's clothing etc. If either one dies, the family would save about $2,000 p.a. in food and other expenses, but would have extra child-care expenses for about seven years.

Maria has little education or training for work outside the home.

The mortgage on the house will be paid off in 15 years at the current interest rate of 9% p.a. Maria and Walter don't plan to finance the children's education beyond high school because they will need to save for their own retirement.

Maria and Walter McKay
Family Balance Sheet

Assets

Cash and bank accounts	$ 2,000
Walter's RRSP	3,000
Walter's pension plan	21,000
Family car (depreciated cost)	5,000
Home (market value)	80,000
Household effects (replacement cost)	15,000
Clothing	10,000
	$126,000

Liabilities and Equity

Credit cards	$ 300
Car loan	700
Mortgage on home	55,000
	56,000
Family equity	70,000
	$126,000

Required:

What do you think Walter and Maria should do about life and disability insurance? Using the premium quotation in Table 9.2, calculate the premium for the life insurance you recommend. Do you think it is feasible?

7. Your friend Laura Lobo, 32, owns $200,000 of whole life insurance at a cost of $1.70 (per thousand of coverage) per year. The policy can be cancelled and the cash surrender value is $1,500. She would like to get more coverage without increasing her premium by switching to a term insurance. Using Table 9.2, how much insurance can she buy for the same premium? What other factors should she consider before she makes the switch?

8. Mary Qi, 29, earns an annual after-tax income of $70,000 per year. If she died, her company insurance and government benefits would pay her husband and children $15,000 per year. Her husband, Tony, 31, works part-time and earns a net income of $20,000 per year. Since Tony does all the house work, if he died, the family would need an additional $12,000 a year to cover the home-making services that he currently provides for the family. The family wants to buy enough life insurance so that in the event of premature death, the remaining family members will not suffer any income loss. How much life insurance does the family need? Using the premium quotation in Table 9.2, how much does the life insurance cost?

10

Property, Home and Automobile Insurance

LEARNING OBJECTIVES

In this chapter, we describe the basic concepts, characteristics, and policy provisions of **property insurance**. In particular, we examine in depth **home insurance** and **automobile insurance** — the two major areas in which the average Canadian family is exposed to potentially large and catastrophic losses. We shall show that the concepts and theories that you learned in Chapters 8 and 9 can be applied to property, home, and automobile insurance.

Our specific objectives are:

1. To describe the basic principles and terminology in property insurance.
2. To explain the concepts and terms of home insurance. We shall pay particular attention to the characteristics and policy provisions that you will find in a typical home insurance policy.
3. To introduce and describe automobile insurance. We shall introduce and explain the terminology, the coverage available, and the provisions of an automobile insurance policy.

At the end of this chapter, you will be ready to make intelligent decisions about home insurance and automobile insurance.

PROPERTY INSURANCE

People face a vast amount of **pure risk**[1] as a result of owning or using properties — home, automobile, furniture, clothing etc. The most important risk is damage or destruction. If you own a home, it is exposed to the risks of damage by fire, lightning, explosion, windstorm, riots, vandalism etc. If you own a car, it is subject to the risk of damage

---

[1] Recall that a pure risk is one that involves the possibility of loss only.

due to theft, collision, and so on; in addition, you are exposed to the risk of body injury to yourself, your passengers and other third parties. Indeed, if you examine a typical home insurance policy or an automobile insurance policy, you will see a list of most of the risks to which you may be exposed; some of these may be familiar to you while others may not be.

Property insurance insures your physical properties — your home, clothing, furniture, appliances, jewellery and so on — against damage or destruction. For the average Canadian family, the most important property insurance is home and automobile insurance. They will be described separately in this chapter.

The theories and concepts of risk and insurance that you learned in Chapters 8 and 9 apply to property insurance. You will find a basic principle being applied over and over again in every type of insurance: One buys insurance to insure for large and catastrophic expenses but not for small ones. In other words, one transfers most of the risk to an insurance company in return for paying a premium. The required premium depends on both the statistical probability of the loss (or the expenses) and the expected amount of the loss (which may not be the same as the insured face value, since property is rarely totally destroyed).

HOME INSURANCE

Home insurance protects the family against the risk of loss, damage, or destruction of the home, its related outbuildings (e.g., a garage), its contents (e.g., clothing, furniture, appliances) and covers liability to third parties for injuries suffered on the property. There are two important questions that you must ask before buying a home insurance policy: (1) What are the risks that are covered? and (2) How much home insurance do I need?

The following is a list of typical risks that are covered by a home insurance policy. Damages or destruction due to:

- fire, lightning
- falling objects
- riots
- windstorm, hail
- explosion
- vandalism
- theft and break-in
- glass breakage, window breakage
- freezing
- water, flood
- weight of ice, snow, sleet
- collapse of building
- smoke
- aircraft or other vehicles
- faulty electrical wiring

There is no such thing as a "standard" home package; the above list is by no means complete. You should read your home insurance policy carefully to find out what is covered and what is not. Obviously, the more risks covered by the policy, the higher the premium will be.

How Much Home Insurance Do You Need?

Contents of the Home   A home insurance policy typically covers damage or destruction to the contents of your home — clothes, furniture, appliances and so on. There are two ways to estimate the amount of coverage required. One way is to estimate the value of the contents as some per cent (usually around 20%) of the value of the structure (which is the home excluding the land). For example, for a home valued at $100,000, one would buy $20,000 insurance coverage (20% of $100,000) for the contents. The second way to estimate the insurance coverage for the contents is to list and value every item. This approach is recommended by many insurance companies and agents, who have forms to help their clients to list everything. It is recommended that a copy of this list be kept in a safety deposit box or other location away from the insured property.

How Do You Value the Home Contents?   There are two forms of home insurance that you can buy: one form covers the **depreciated value** of the damaged or lost item and the second form covers **replacement value**.

The **depreciated value** of an item is the value of replacement or repair for the item to the condition it was in when lost or damaged. For example, if the lost item was a three-year-old, 28-inch colour television, the **depreciated value** is the cost of buying a three-year-old, 28-inch colour television of the same quality — and **not** the cost of a brand new television.

The standard insurance policy pays the **depreciated value**. This is usually calculated by subtracting from the price of a new item an allowance for depreciation based on the age of the item that is to be insured.

The **replacement value** of a damaged or lost item is the cost of buying a new item of the same quality. In the above example, the insured would receive the cost of a brand-new, 28-inch colour television of the same quality as the lost one.

In general, the **depreciated value** is less than the **replacement value**, so most people would probably prefer a replacement value policy. Of course, the policy for replacement value requires a higher premium.

You should be aware of how payments for damaged or lost items are made under a **replacement cost policy**. The lost or destroyed items must be replaced with new ones of comparable quality. If the insured chooses not to replace, the claim will be settled at the **depreciated value** only. In the case of damaged items, repairs must be made to return the items back to the best possible condition. Again, if one chooses not to make the repair, one will be paid the depreciated value only.

Replacement Value of a Home

The **replacement value** of a home for insurance purposes is not its current **market value**. The method to estimate the **fair market value** of a home will be described in Chapter 12, where we talk about buying one's own home. For insurance purposes, however, the fair market value of the home should not be used because it includes the value of the land and foundation. In most cases, the land and foundation of a home cannot be destroyed by typical disasters. Therefore, what you want to insure is the **replacement value** of your **home's structure**. This is what it would cost to replace the **home's structure** (defined as everything except the land and foundation) if the home were totally destroyed. In Chapter 12, we will describe a method called the **cost approach of valuation**, which is a method to determine the replacement cost of the home's structure. In general, it is quite difficult and complicated for one to estimate the replacement value of a home's structure. It is more practical to pay for an appraisal of the home, indicating to the appraiser that the appraisal is for the purpose of buying home insurance. Such an appraisal will give you a professional estimate of both the **depreciated value** and the **replacement value** of the home's structure.

Some insurance companies automatically set the amount of the home insurance equal to the amount of the mortgage on the house. Very often, the banks or the loan companies require this insurance amount to be in place before they will grant you a mortgage. While insurance set at the amount of the existing mortgage protects the lender's interest it is not intended to cover the owner's interest in the structure.

The 80% Rule

Most insurance companies will not pay the full loss on partial damage unless the insured has bought insurance to cover at least 80% of the home's replacement value. If the insured buys insurance coverage for less than that, the insurance company will only make payments proportional to the percentage of required minimum coverage taken. This practice is called the **80% Rule**; the best way to illustrate this rule is by a numerical example.

> **Example 10.1:** John and Mary Doyle own a house whose current replacement value (not including the value of the land) is $100,000. They bought a home insurance coverage equal to $70,000. Their home suffered a fire loss equal to $30,000. How much will the insurance company pay?

The Doyles have coverage for only (70,000 ÷ 100,000) or 70% of the replacement value of their home; this is below the required minimum coverage of 80%. Therefore, because the Doyles have not met the **80% Rule**, the insurance company will pay only [$30,000 × $70,000 ÷ $80,000] or, $26,250.

The next example shows that because replacement value increases over time it is advisable to check your policy periodically to ensure that you have the minimum required coverage.

> **Example 10.2:** Jonathan and Janice Carter bought a house five years ago that had a replacement value of $150,000. They bought insurance coverage for $125,000 but they have not increased the coverage since the time of the original purchase. Because of inflation and other factors, their home has a current replacement value of $180,000. Their house suffers fire damage of $10,000. How much of this $10,000 will be reimbursed by the insurance company?

The required minimum coverage is 80% of current replacement value — in this case, 80% of current replacement value is ($180,000 × .80) or $144,000. Their current insurance coverage is only $125,000, which is below the minimum required coverage. Therefore, the insurance company will only pay ($10,000 × 125,000 ÷ 144,000) or $8,681.

Note that in the example, the Carters had 83.33% coverage (125,000 ÷ 150,000) when they bought the home five years ago; at the time of purchase, then, the **80% rule** was satisfied. This example illustrates the importance of reviewing your insurance policy periodically to see if you have adequate coverage. The inflation protection that we will describe later is a very useful feature in your policy.

Finally, it is extremely important that you know exactly how **replacement value** or **replacement cost** is defined in the policy. These terms are not standardized. In some insurance policies, it refers to the structure's value without the foundation; in other policies, it refers to the structure and the foundation.

Inflation Protection Provision

Inflation and the increasing dollar value of the replacement costs of homes are very important considerations in your home insurance policy. If your policy does not take inflation into account, then the real value of your coverage will decline over time. Also, as we saw in Example 10.2, your policy may fail to meet the 80% rule in the future.

Many insurance companies offer an **inflation protection provision** that automatically increases the coverage amount each year in accordance with the increase in some inflation index such as the Consumer Price Index (CPI). Naturally, you have to pay an additional premium for this provision.

If you live in an area of the country where housing costs are expected to rise faster than the average rate of inflation (as represented by the CPI) then even the inflation protection provision may not provide adequate coverage. Most insurance companies, for additional premiums, provide additional coverage in excess of that provided by the inflation protection provision.

Deductibles

A **deductible** is the part of a claim that you must pay first before the insurance company will pay anything. For example, suppose you have a $2,000 insurable loss from your home due to theft and there is a **deductible** of $500 in your home insurance policy. In this case, you pay the first $500 on the loss and the insurance company pays the rest, or $1,500.

The higher the amount of the **deductible**, the lower the premium that you have to pay. There are three reasons why premiums will be lower if deductibles are higher. First, since you share part of the damages or loss, the insurance company does not have to pay as much on the claims. Second, the insured will try harder to avoid the damages, losses and accidents against which he is insuring valuable property if there is a significantly large deductible. Finally, there is a fixed cost of administration for settling any claim that is largely independent of the size of the claim. The insurance company would rather avoid numerous small claims, and will charge a high premium on policies with low deductibles to encourage customers to deal with their own smaller losses.

"Higher Deductible, Lower Premium" vs. "Lower Deductible, Higher Premium"

Is there any theory that will tell you the optimal amount of deductible that is the best for you? In theory, the answer is yes, but for practical purposes, the answer is no. If one knows one's utility function for money, then theoretically one can calculate the optimal amount of deductible that is the best. However, in practice, nobody knows her utility function, which means it is impossible to determine the "right" amount of deductibles.[2]

Rigorous theory aside, high deductible policies (and hence, lower premiums) make more economic sense than low deductible policies. Let us recall that the basic principle of buying insurance is to ensure against large rather than small losses. Your insurance dollars should first be spent to insure against losses that would be insupportable to you and your family. By buying a policy with a large deductible, you are spending your insurance money to cover large losses reducing the premium cost per dollar of insurance and can therefore afford a higher total coverage.

> **Example 10.3:**   Suppose Mr. Wolfgang can afford only $500 annually on home insurance. Suppose he has two choices: (1) he can buy $50,000 of coverage provided that he takes a $100 deductible; and (2) he can buy $100,000 of coverage provided that he takes a $300 deductible. Economic logic suggests that he should take the higher deductible policy of $300 because it would provide more protection against catastrophic losses.

Rule of Thumb

Although it cannot be proved rigorously, many financial experts recommend a deductible equal to 3% of your net worth. For example, if one's net worth is $50,000, one should seek an insurance policy with a deductible equal to $1,500.

The incentive aspect of a high deductible policy should be emphasized once more. If there is a high deductible, one would try much harder to avoid or reduce the risk. The home-owners will, for example, put in smoke detectors, buy more fire extinguishers, install a security system, regularly check the electrical and gas appliances for leaks and so on, to avoid or reduce the risks. They have a higher incentive to do so if there is a larger deductible in the home insurance policy.

Another incentive relates to loss of personal property away from the house, a common peril covered in home insurance policies. A home-owner with a $500 deductible will be quite careful to lock up a bicycle away from home, since he will pay most or all of the cost if it is stolen.

Third Party Liability Insurance

Apart from the home's structure and contents, a typical home policy also covers **liabilities to third parties**. This insurance coverage protects you from the liability to other people for injuries suffered on your property or by anything attached or related to your property. You are required to ensure that your property does not pose a danger to a reasonable person; however, your responsibility as a home-owner is not well defined. For example, would you be liable if someone, falling on your driveway and breaking his leg, claimed that his accident was caused by your fault in not clearing the driveway sufficiently of snow accumulated during the previous week's heavy snowstorm (even though you had used the snowblower to clean it twice)?

---

[2] A utility function is a mathematical representation of the risk-return preferences of an individual. In the case of an insurance deductible it would indicate for every combination of deductible (or potential loss) and premium, how much each are is valued by that person.

There are many "grey" areas in **third party liability** that make it almost impossible to determine how much **liability insurance** one should buy, especially in view of the changing court decisions in recent years. Some factors that you should consider are: the nature of any non-household activities carried out in your home; whether or not there are any domestic servants; whether or not there is a swimming pool; whether or not there are any dogs or other pets; and anything else that you can think of which might increase your risk exposure to third party liability.

Once again, the basic principle that one should insure for potentially catastrophic losses applies here. Home-owner's liability insurance is still fairly cheap because claims against home-owner policies are quite infrequent. Many insurance agents advise the average family to carry $1,000,000, which does not cost a lot more than $500,000 in coverage.

Types of Home Insurance

The home insurance market has developed to the extent that it can provide a policy tailored to almost any need. Clauses and provisions with the appropriate premiums can be added or deleted from a policy to suit a family's particular need. Nevertheless, we can classify all home insurance policies into three types: (1) **comprehensive home insurance**; (2) **fire insurance**; and (3) **tenant's insurance** (also called the renter's insurance).

The most common type is the **comprehensive** home policy which covers the three major sources of risk: the home structure, its contents, and third party liability. It covers all the risks listed earlier. Other provisions are usually added to suit the insured's specific needs. The following is a list of additional provisions that can be added to a comprehensive policy at the insured's option:

- damaged property removal
- removal of debris
- trees, shrubs and plants — usually covered up to a certain maximum, e.g., a maximum of $200 per tree, or a maximum aggregate value of 5% of the home insurance
- fire department surcharges — up to a specified maximum amount
- expensive jewellery, furs and other valuable personal properties
- earthquake
- temporary repairs to prevent further damage to the property

Fire Insurance

This is a no-frills insurance policy that provides the most basic protection: mainly fire, lightning, smoke damage as well as other specifically listed perils. It usually excludes the risks of theft, window breakage, goods in transit and third party liability. This policy is only advisable for families who have separate liability coverage and little risk of theft.

Tenant's Insurance or Renter's Insurance

Tenant's or **renter's insurance** covers the contents in the home, excluding the home structure. If you rent an apartment or a house and it burns down, the landlord loses the apartment or the house but you lose your possessions. The landlord is not liable to reimburse you for the loss of your possessions; you therefore need a **tenant's insurance** package. Your tenant's insurance policy should include **third party liability** coverage.

If someone is hurt in your apartment and has sustained significant injury, you may be liable for substantial expenses; you therefore need a liability protection provision in your policy.

AUTOMOBILE INSURANCE

Automobile insurance covers a number of risks, the damages from which are potentially very large. First, there is the risk of injury or death of the owner and his or her passengers. Second, there is the risk of damage, destruction or theft of the car. Third, and most important, there is the potential liability to others (third parties) for injury, death, or damage to their cars or property. This third party liability — injury to others caused by you and your car — is the largest potential claim on you. **Liability insurance** is the means to finance this potentially devastating risk. Furthermore, the probability of a car accident in which significant losses are incurred is much higher than the probability of major damage to your home.

Most provinces require that the registered car owners carry liability insurance and a few additional coverages; however, the minimum amount of insurance required by the provincial legislatures is usually not the optimum amount of insurance. The concepts and theories that you have learned should be used to assess the amount of auto insurance that you need. Again, the basic principle is: insure large losses and pay for small expenses yourself.

Types of Automobile Insurance

Liability Insurance (Auto)   **Liability insurance** covers the injury, death, and damage to the property of other persons (third party). There are two components to this coverage: bodily injury coverage and property damage coverage.

Bodily Injury Coverage covers the injury or death of other people (e.g., people in your car, people in other cars, pedestrians) resulting from the accident that you caused. The car owner's policy covers the car owner and persons using the car with the car owner's permission. If you drive someone's car with permission and have an accident in which you caused bodily injury to other people, the liability claim will be settled under the **bodily injury coverage** of the owner's auto policy. If the car owner is uninsured, then your own policy will cover you.

Property Damage Coverage covers the damage your car causes to someone else's property in the event you were the cause of the accident. For example, if you ran the red light and hit another car, you were clearly at fault (that is to say, you were the cause of the accident). If $5,000 of damage resulted from the accident, the bill less the **deductible** will be paid by the **property damage coverage** of your auto insurance policy.

How Much Liability Insurance Do You Need?   Liability to others is an insupportable risk to most people. It could instantly wipe out your wealth and your future if you were the cause of a severe injury or death to another person in an accident. Admittedly, the probability of such a serious injury happening is very small, especially if you are a careful driver; nevertheless, because this is a potentially catastrophic loss, you should buy enough **liability insurance**.

But how much is enough? First, the minimum coverage for bodily injury liability required by each province (except Quebec) is $200,000. If your net worth is small (and you have to determine what is small), there is no financial need for you to buy more coverage than this minimum amount required by the law. Ethically, you might prefer to carry more insurance. If you do cause serious harm or death through careless driving, you might be found liable for a very large amount — even a sum equal to the expected lifetime earnings of the person injured. If your net worth is large enough that you don't want to lose it, it is advisable to purchase a lot more than the minimum liability insurance (which includes bodily injury liability). The common amount for prudent car owners in Canada is now $1 million. It is conceivable that you could be found liable for a greater amount, but such cases are quite rare. Since major losses are infrequent, insurance companies do not charge a lot for the higher liability coverage.[3]

Other Auto Insurance Coverages

Collision Coverage   This coverage pays for damage to your car from an accident in which you are at fault. (Recall that if the other driver is at fault, the damage will be paid by his insurance policy under the **property damage coverage** already described.)

The **collision coverage** normally pays only the **depreciated value** of the car. For example, your 15-year-old car, worth $200; is damaged in an accident in which you are at fault. If it would cost $3,000 to repair the car, the insurance company will only pay you $200 minus deductible. Therefore, you should periodically reduce your **collision coverage** to reflect the car's current value. Considering the purpose of risk management is to eliminate or finance insupportable risks, you should probably drop collision coverage altogether on older cars. Collision coverage is quite expensive, because of the large number of relatively small claims that insurance companies have to settle.

Comprehensive Coverage   The **comprehensive coverage** pays for the damage to your car resulting from "non-accidents" — theft, vandalism, fire etc. This coverage pays only the **depreciated** value of the car; for this reason, you should periodically reduce this coverage to reflect the decrease in the value of the car.

Medical Payment Coverage or Medical Insurance (Auto)   This coverage pays for the medical costs for you and your passengers as a result of an accident in which you are at fault.

Uninsured Motorists Coverage   This provision covers you and your family for bodily injury caused by another driver who is either uninsured or does not have enough insurance. **Uninsured motorists coverage** also covers you and your family members in the case of injuries caused by a hit-and-run driver. Usually only bodily injury is covered and not the damage to the car.

No-fault Insurance   No-fault insurance allows you to collect insurance payments from your own insurance company even if the accident is someone else's fault. Some provinces (e.g., Ontario) have imposed laws that require insurers to offer **no-fault insurance**. The idea is that if fault did not have to be proved in accidents, legal costs would be saved and car insurance premiums would be lowered. As a result of recent

---

[3] Car accidents are common, but serious personal injury or death, coupled with demonstrable negligence by the other driver, are infrequent. Hence, the losses spread over a large population are quite small.

legislation, some provinces even require the insured to give up her right to sue, thereby reducing legal fees even more and lowering premiums further. Nevertheless, there are counter-arguments insisting that **no-fault insurance** will not lower premiums: first, no-fault insurance gives many drivers less incentive to be careful; second, insurance companies have less incentive to penalize drivers who have frequent accidents because they will not always pay for the accidents caused by the persons they insure. Whether **no-fault insurance** will lower insurance premiums or not is an empirical question that requires further study.

Deductibles in Car Insurance

As in home insurance, taking a bigger **deductible** will lower your premiums. **Deductibles** are available with the **collision coverage** and the **comprehensive coverage** parts of your car insurance policy. If you follow the basic principle of buying insurance only, then you should increase the amount of **deductible** and use the savings in premiums to buy more coverage for the potentially big losses; for example, you should use the savings to buy more coverage for bodily injury and uninsured-motorists insurance.

Rental Car Insurance

If you rent a car, you should be aware of the insurance coverage, since you face the same risks as if you owned the car. In Canada, and most other jurisdictions, the rental fee will automatically include liability insurance. You should make sure of this, however, and find out the amount covered. In our experience in Canada, it is usually $1 million.

All other perils are at your risk, unless you specifically request coverage, have coverage through your insurance policy on your own car,[4] or have coverage on a premium credit card. You can opt to pay an extra fee for extra insurance, and also for some life insurance. This extra insurance is quite expensive. Since you should have planned your life insurance coverage according to the principles in Chapter 9, you should not need the life insurance offered by the car rental agency (and it, too, is quite expensive).

SUMMARY

In this chapter we examine **property insurance**, which protects your properties such as clothing, furniture, car and home against the risk of damage or destruction. In particular, we introduce and discuss two important property insurances: **home insurance** and **automobile insurance**. Most of the concepts and theories that we have discussed in Chapter 8 and Chapter 9 can be applied to property insurance as well. For example, the basic principle that you buy insurance for large and catastrophic losses only, has been applied to both home insurance and automobile insurance.

Home insurance protects your home and its contents against the risk of damage and destruction, and protects you against third party liability. A home and its contents can be covered either by a **depreciated value** policy or a **replacement value** policy. Some important characteristics of home insurance — **deductibles**, **inflation protection provision** and so on have been introduced and described. If you rent an apartment or a house, you should buy a **renter's insurance** policy to protect your possessions.

---

[4] Many automobile insurance policies now contain a special rider that extends collision and theft coverage to cars rented by the family that buys the policy.

Automobile insurance provides the protection in three major areas: (1) liabilities to third parties; (2) the injury or death of the owner and the passengers; and (3) the damage, destruction or theft of the automobile. A typical auto insurance policy has the following coverages: **bodily injury coverage**, **property damage coverage**, **collision**, **comprehensive**, **medical payments coverage**, and **uninsured motorists coverage**. The concept of a **no-fault insurance** policy has also been discussed.

KEY TERMINOLOGY

property insurance / home insurance / automobile insurance / pure risk / damages to property / home's structure / home's contents / depreciated value / replacement value or cost / depreciated value policy / replacement value policy / 80% rule / required minimum coverage / inflation protection provision / deductible / third party liability / liability insurance (home) / comprehensive home policy / fire insurance policy / tenant's insurance / renter's insurance / liability insurance (auto) / bodily injury coverage / bodily injury liability insurance / property damage coverage / property damage liability insurance / collision coverage / comprehensive coverage / medical payment coverage / medical insurance (auto) / uninsured-motorist coverage / no-fault insurance

DISCUSSION QUESTIONS

1. Explain or describe all the key words and terms under **Key Terminology**.

2. If you have a limited budget for property insurance, which would you prefer: a "higher deductible and lower premium" policy or a "lower deductible and higher premium" policy? Why?

3. What are the three basic components of a comprehensive home policy?

4. "No-fault insurance was introduced in Ontario because it was expected that premiums would drop very significantly."
   (a) What are the reasons to expect a drop in the premium?
   (b) Are there any reasons to believe that premiums may increase rather than decrease?

5. What is the basic principle in insurance that has been applied many times in this chapter?

6. What are the major components of a car insurance policy?

PROBLEMS

1. **Personal Project 1**
   Get a copy of an actual home insurance policy — yours, your parents' or a friend's. Read the policy from the beginning to the end.
   (a) Describe the coverages of the policy in terms of the home, its contents, and liability insurance. Be as specific as possible; for example, does "home structure" include the foundation?
   (b) Jot down all the new terms that were not discussed in this chapter. Find the definitions of these terms in the insurance policy.
   (c) If this is your home policy, assess whether it has the right coverage for you.

2. **Personal Project 2**

    Get a copy of an actual automobile insurance policy. Read the policy carefully from the beginning to the end.

    (a) What are the coverage limits and the deductibles (if any) for each major coverage component — bodily injury coverage, property damage coverage, collision etc.

    (b) Find out the premium for each of the items in (a).

    (c) If this is your car insurance, assess whether it has the right coverage for you.

    (d) How do you know whether the insurer is charging you too much?

3. What is the 80% rule? Mr. J.J. Thompson owns a home with a current replacement cost of $210,000. He has insurance coverage for a replacement value of $100,000. If he suffered fire damage of $10,000, and if the deductible is $500, how much of the loss will the insurer pay?

4. Mr. and Mrs. Copperfield bought a house for $95,000 ten years ago; they then bought a home insurance policy to provide coverage for $80,000 replacement value. There is an inflation protection provision in the policy so that the amount of insurance automatically increases every year at the rate of inflation. The current replacement cost of the house is $180,000. The average annual rate of inflation in the last ten years has been 5%. Recently, their home suffered fire damage which resulted in a loss of $80,000. How much of the loss will the insurance company pay?

11

Credit and Debt Management

LEARNING OBJECTIVES

Most problems in a family's financial affairs arise from the improper use of credit and debt. In order to manage your personal finances successfully and to achieve your financial goals, you must be able to manage debt effectively. We hope that this chapter will make you a better borrower. More specifically, our objectives are:

1. To discuss ways of assessing your debt capacity.
2. To suggest ways of efficient credit management.
3. To discuss the common forms of consumer financing, especially the use of credit cards.
4. To explain the difference between consumer credit and investment loans.

In general, the most important debt commitment that one makes during one's life is the mortgage that is used to buy a home. This is a very important topic but we feel it is more natural to postpone it until Chapter 12 when we talk about investing in a home. Right now, it suffices to say that most of the concepts discussed in this chapter apply to a home mortgage.

DEBT CAPACITY

Why Use Credit?

You may have heard of stories about families ruining their lives by living beyond their means on credit. In fact, many books on personal finance recommend to those people who have overextended themselves in debt, to first of all destroy all their credit cards. In the nineties, the word **debt** is perhaps the ugliest four-letter word in finance. Why in the world then would anyone use consumer credit? Isn't credit the reason for most financial problems? For many people, the question is easily answered. There is no cash available, so credit must be used if the product is to be purchased. When you borrow,

Reprinted with permission — The Toronto Star Syndicate. © 1994 GREG HOWARD distributed by King Features Syndicate.

the lender is giving you a credit, or trust, against your future earnings. You get to use the credit to buy something now. Without credit, you have to wait until you have saved enough money to pay cash, and you must postpone the use and enjoyment of the product. In the early stages of your life cycle, income is typically below consumption needs, whereas in later years, it normally rises above those needs. Borrowing allows the income stream to match the desired consumption stream. By using credit prudently and creatively, you can acquire assets sooner and in larger amounts then you otherwise might. Therefore, if credit is properly used, it can serve a very valuable function.

Many people, however, overuse their credit. The problem of overindebtedness or borrowing too much initially starts out harmlessly when people borrow an amount that they can handle easily. Then they begin to borrow more and more until they become overindebted and, as a consequence, fall into despair and crisis. We are less concerned about people who become overindebted through circumstances beyond their control, such as unanticipated loss of employment or reduction of income. We are more concerned about people who become overindebted through careless and impulsive use of credit. To ensure that you don't fall into this trap, it is important for you to gain the proper knowledge of debt management. There is a right way and a wrong way to use consumer credits, such as a credit card. The right way is to take full advantage of the many attractive features that the credit card provides — such as the free-loan grace period, detailed record keeping, no need to carry quantities of cash etc. The wrong way is to build up a large debt balance and pay over 18 per cent non-tax-deductible interest.

Debt Capacity

If overindebtedness is the biggest potential problem in the use of debt, then the natural questions to ask would be:

- How much debt can one take?
- Is there an optimal level of debt that one can take?
- What are the factors that affect this optimal level of debt?
- How can one manage one's credit and debt effectively?

These are interrelated questions. Before we can answer any of these questions, we must first introduce the important concept of **debt capacity**. A borrower's debt capacity is defined as the amount of debt that he can reasonably expect to be able to repay under the terms of the loan agreements, given his current and expected future financial situations

— assets, liabilities, cash-flows, income, expenditures etc. Normally, the borrower's obligation is to make future payments (interest and principal) to the lender, so debt capacity does not look only at what the borrower has today but also at what she will have in the future. The most important determinant of one's debt capacity is therefore one's expected future net cash flow, or more specifically, one's ability to generate sufficient cash flow after living expenses and required capital outlays, to pay the interest and principal of all loans to maturity. The lender is interested in both the borrower's short-run and long-run ability to pay interest and principal.

Liquidity and Solvency

Liquidity is the ability of a family to meet its debt service payments in the short run. **Solvency** is the long-run ability of the family to pay its debts. A young dentist who has just started a new practice may have good long-run expectations but may not be able to meet next month's interest payment — that is, she may have liquidity problems. On the other hand, a factory worker who will be retiring next year may have no problem in meeting month-to-month interest payments but may have some difficulty in paying off the loan when it comes due.

Assets vs. Cash Flow

The lender is concerned about both the liquidity and solvency of the borrower. The borrower has two sources of cash to pay off the loan: net cash flow and asset sales. For example, you can pay off your loan from your employment income or out of the proceeds of the sale of the antique furniture which you inherited recently. Thus, the most important factors that affect your debt capacity are: first, your expected net assets or net worth; and second, your expected net cash flow each year. Other things being equal, the higher the expected net assets and net cash flow, the higher the debt capacity.

Risk

If the future is known with certainty, determining liquidity, solvency, future cash flows and future asset values would be trivial. Since the future is uncertain, we have to assess how risky the future cash flows and future asset values are. We will discuss risk in a theoretical context later in the chapters on investment. For now, we will think of risk as how likely the cash flow is to fail to provide for all **debt service charges**. In this sense, risk comes from the variability of cash flow from one period to another, and it is during the time when cash flow is low that the individual would have problems meeting his debt obligations.

The variability of the cash flow (the risk) can come from many sources. The biggest variation comes from the changes in earning streams. The following are some causes that can affect changes in earnings:

- loss of employment
- pay cut
- death of a breadwinner
- disability or poor health
- failure of a small business
- withdrawal from work for pregnancy

Asset values can and usually do change over time. Depreciable assets like furniture, cars and household appliances normally decrease in value over time. Investment assets like houses, stocks, bonds and mutual funds generally appreciate in value in the long run, but in the short run, they can go up or down. As before, this variation in asset values causes the risk to your ability to service debt obligations. The following are some examples that can cause the decrease in asset values:

- depreciation due to wear and tear
- negative changes in the economy
- increases in interest rates
- disasters such as fire, burglary or termite infestation
- closing of a major factory in a small town
- obsolescence of one's professional skills (this leads to a decrease in the value of one's human capital)

Finally, we will point out that a lot of the variability in cash flows and asset valuation can be reduced to manageable levels with appropriate insurance. For example, you can buy insurance to cover the risks due to death or disability and the risk of loss to property value due to fire. The risk of job loss may be partially covered by Unemployment Insurance Compensation, if you are an employee.

How Much Debt Can You Afford?

We have seen that there are three characteristics of a family's assets and cash flow — liquidity, solvency and risk — that affect the borrower's debt capacity. In practice, however, since these characteristics are difficult to assess and measure precisely, there is no rigorous theory that determines a precise value of debt capacity, nor is there any method to determine a family's "optimal" level of consumer debt. To a large extent, the amount of debt that a family can assume depends on the spending objective and the risk tolerance of the family. It is conceivable that a family with gross earnings of $50,000 would assume a larger amount of debt than a family with twice that amount of gross income ($100,000) because they have different spending habits and risk preferences (i.e., comfort zones of debt levels). If a family assesses its financial situation according to the three characteristics — liquidity, solvency and risk — it should be able to come up with a comfort zone of debt for the family.

The most useful tool for assessing debt capacity is a budget of income and expenditure. The technique of preparing a family budget has been discussed in Chapter 4. When you do a budget for the entire period of the loan, the budgeting process will cover both the liquidity and the solvency aspects of your debt. You simply add the proposed debt payments to the expenses in the budget and see if it still balances. Don't forget to include all the additional expenses or revenues caused by whatever the borrowed money is spent on. For example, if the borrowed money is spent on buying a new car, you must include in your budget the additional expenses of running the car. If your budget shows surpluses in every month of the entire loan period, you can afford the loan.

Debt Service Ratios

Most people obtain their consumer credit and debt from the conventional sources — banks, credit cards, department store charge cards, finance companies etc. It is important to know how these institutions make decisions in their consumer lending practices. A commonly used quick-scoring method for loan applications is the debt-service ratio. The two popular debt service ratios are: the **Gross** Debt Service ratio (GDS ratio) and the **Total Debt Service ratio** (TDS ratio). They are defined as follows:

$$GDS = \frac{\text{annual mortgage payments} + \text{property taxes}}{\text{gross family income}}$$

$$TDS = \frac{\text{mortgage payments} + \text{property taxes} + \text{other debt payments}}{\text{gross family income}}$$

See Example 11.1 for an illustration.

Example 11.1: Mr. and Mrs. Smith have an annual gross income of $80,000. There is a first mortgage on their house and the monthly mortgage payment is $1,800. Last year they paid $2,400 in property taxes. Their other debt obligations include a car loan (monthly payment is $210) and a credit card balance (monthly payment is about $150). They have no other debt outstanding.

$$GDS \text{ ratio} = \frac{(1,800 \times 12) + 2,400}{80,000} = 30\%$$

$$TDS \text{ ratio} = \frac{(1,800 \times 12) + 2,400 + (210 \times 12) + (150 \times 12)}{80,000} = 35.4\%$$

The two benchmarks most often cited are: Gross Debt Service (GDS) ratio of not over 30% and Total Debt Service (TDS) ratio of not over 40%. The GDS and TDS ratios of the Smith family in the example are within those limits.

These ratios and benchmarks are developed by statistically analysing a large number of previous credit files for which the payment histories are known. They may be useful for financial institutions that require a quick-scoring method to process a large number of loan applications. They make a good rule of thumb for families in the average income brackets, say $40,000 to $60,000. However, for the purpose of assessing your debt capacity, the budgeting process is still superior to these ratios for the following reasons. First, ratios do not allow for risk. A physician and a salesman may have the same expected gross income but the doctor's income is probably much more stable and can therefore support a higher level of debt. Second, these ratios are based on gross income and therefore do not allow for the effect of taxes. After-tax income will be significantly higher with two workers each earning $20,000 than with one earning $40,000. Third, these benchmarks are normally applicable for average incomes only. At the low end, a family of four with an income of $15,000 cannot possibly afford to pay 40% of the family income in debt servicing. At the high end, a four-member family with a $200,000 gross income can afford to spend more than 40% of the family income on debt servicing because most living costs do not rise proportionately with income. Finally, ratios do not give information about the short-run liquidity and long-run solvency that a budget would give.

In spite of these disadvantages, debt service ratios are easy to calculate and financial institutions use them. Therefore, if you want to assess your debt capacity, it is advisable to prepare a budget for the entire loan period and, in addition to that, to calculate these ratios to see if they are within the current benchmarks. At least they would give you an indication of how much you can borrow from a conventional financial institution.

Matching Assets and Debts

There is a rule of thumb in corporation finance that can be applied easily to personal finance. This rule, sometimes called the Matching Principle in Finance, suggests that one should match the expected economic life of an asset to the term of maturity of the financing. Assets with long expected economic lives (e.g., real estate) should be financed by long-term debt. For example, if the expected economic life of an asset is 20 years, it should be financed by a loan that matures in 20 years. This is what the banks do with people's term deposits; when banks lend money, they match the term of the loan with the expected economic life of the asset. For groceries and perishables that are consumed right away (i.e., their economic life is close to zero), you should pay cash. It does not make sense to use credit card loans to buy groceries or other perishables. Of course, if you always pay off the credit card balance in full, you are using the credit card for convenience and that is a different matter. If you must borrow to buy a car, the term of the loan ideally should be four to six years, which is the average economic life of a car. How about your home? The expected economic life of a home is 25 years or much longer. Therefore, it makes sense to pay off the loan in 25 years — technically, this is called amortizing the loan in 25 years.

CONSUMER CREDIT

When people borrow money to purchase consumer goods or services, they are making use of consumer credit financing of one form or another. Examples of consumer credit financing are personal loans, auto loans, credit cards, and home equity loans. Borrowing money to invest, a topic which we will discuss later, does not fall under consumer credit. We restrict the meaning of consumer credit finance to the case where an individual borrows money to purchase consumer assets or services. Thus, borrowing money to acquire a washing machine, furniture or to take a vacation in Europe, is consumer credit, while borrowing money to invest in a stock mutual fund is an investment loan. The differences between a consumer loan and an investment loan are substantial, so we will discuss the two topics separately in this chapter.

Consumer Loans and Time Value

In order to budget for them, we need to know how to handle the time value calculations. A consumer loan is almost invariably repayable in equal monthly instalments of blended principal and interest. Thus, it is compounded and payable monthly. The loan rate may be quoted as an APR or as an EAR, depending on the applicable legislation, but increasingly the EAR is the norm.[1] Example 11.2 illustrates the application of the time value mechanics to a consumer loan.

---

[1] The APR (annual percentage rate) does not allow for the monthly compounding, while the EAR (effective annual rate) does. See Chapter 2 if you need to review time value of money.

Example 11.2: Mwangi Ndegwa offers the best price in town on used cars. Even better, you can pay in 36 easy, low, low, monthly instalments, at an effective annual interest rate of only 11.22%.

(a) What is the monthly rate Mwangi charges?

(b) If you buy a used Bentley for $70,000 and finance the whole purchase price, what is your monthly payment?

(c) How much do you still owe after 24 months of payments?

(d) Suppose you could deduct the interest expense on the first year as an expense on your tax return because you were using the car for business travel exclusively. How much interest expense would you report?

Answer:

(a) You reverse the compounding process to find the 12th root of 1.1122. $(1.1122)^{1/12} - 1 = .89\%$.

(b) PV = 70,000. i = .89%. n = 36. Payment = $2,281.12

(c) You now owe 12 months of payments of $2,281.12, at .89%. The PV of this loan = $25,853.52.

(d) The quickest way to find the interest for a specific time period during a loan is to calculate the amount of principal owing on the loan at the start and end of that period. The difference is the amount of principal repaid. Now add up the total payments during that period. Subtract the principal from the total payments and you get the interest you paid.

PV of loan with 24 months to go = $49,099.20. Total payments 12 × $2,281.12 = $27,373.44. Amount of principal repaid $70,000 − $49,099.20 = $20,900.80. Amount of interest paid $27,373.44 − $20,900.80 = $6,472.64.

Personal Credit Management

Personal debt plays an important role in your personal financial affairs. It is important that you learn some crucial techniques in personal credit management and start to build positive credit habits as soon as possible. The following are the critical areas in which you have to gain knowledge in order to be successful in managing your debt and credit:

1. How do you get credit?
2. How do you build up and maintain positive credit habits?
3. How do you maintain a good credit record?
4. How do you spend the money that you have to borrow?

How Do You Get Credit?

There are many sources of consumer credit. You can get credit from banks, trust companies, credit unions, finance companies, department stores, oil and gas companies, to name a few. Usually the lenders target their loans towards specific risk classes of borrowers. Banks, trust companies and credit unions normally specialize in lower risk loans. Finance companies and loan companies that are tied to specific sellers (such as department stores like the Bay or Eaton's, or automobile manufacturers like General Motors and Ford) normally specialize in slightly higher credit risk loans. On the other end of the scale you would find small finance companies, pawnshops or even loan sharks who specialize in very high credit risk and, hence, high-interest-rate loans.

As a borrower you want to pay as low an interest rate as possible on a loan. Whether you will be successful in getting the best deal depends on how you present yourself to the lender. The lender generally requires you to fill out an application form for credit or for a loan; and she assesses you on the basis of the information given on that form as well as on the basis of your credit history.

Credit Scoring

Lenders use a pre-determined scoring system to make credit decisions. Points are added or deducted for various characteristics elicited by the application form. The typical questions that are asked cover your age, marital status, annual income, number of years in your current job, whether you rent or own your home, age of your cars, your bank accounts, amount of existing debt, type and amount of investment you own, whether you have declared bankruptcy before, and general credit references. Each characteristic will be given a score based on some credit standard. If you score high enough, you will get the credit or the loan.

Lenders view an individual's character as a key factor in deciding whether to grant the loan. Therefore, it is important that you tell the truth. Deceit is not only costly in the short term (you do not get the credit) but in the long term as well (future chances of getting credit are jeopardized). Evidence of deception will remain in your file and become part of your credit history for a long, long time.

Your Credit File

Whether they know it or not, most consumers have credit files in the local credit bureau, which is a credit reporting agency. If you have applied for or used any form of credit before, you can be sure that there is a credit file on you. Do you have a phone? If you do, we are almost certain that there is a credit file on you.

Lenders routinely make a credit check on anyone who applies for a credit card, a loan, a mortgage, or any form of financing; and the local credit bureau is the first place the lender will check. There are many credit reporting agencies; they provide different kinds of credit information to members for a fee. It is easy to find out all the local credit reporting agencies in your city. Simply look under the credit reporting agencies section in the Yellow Pages of your local telephone directory: every major city in Canada has a credit bureau.

Credit reporting agencies do not evaluate your credit file. Their job is to record all relevant information in your file and make the information available to credit bureau members — a group which includes banks, mortgage companies, trust companies, insurance companies and other lenders and issuers of credit.

If there is one single factor which affects your future borrowing, it is your credit report. An unfavourable credit report will almost certainly jeopardize your future credit and loan applications. Therefore, if you suspect, for whatever reason, that there is incorrect or negative information in your credit file, you owe it to yourself to correct the mistake as soon as possible. By law, you can request any credit bureau to give you a complete, accurate copy of your file. You can request reverification by the credit bureau if information is incorrect and you have the right to ask that missing data be added to your file. You also have the right to know exactly why you were refused credit. These are just a few examples of the rights that you have with respect to your credit file. Indeed, all provinces, except Alberta and New Brunswick, have legislation to protect your right to know what is in your credit file and which lenders have requested information about your credit-worthiness.

COMMON TYPES OF CREDIT AND LOANS

Open Account Credit and Credit Cards

The most common type of credit is the open account credit. It is a form of credit extended to the consumer in advance of any transactions. Typically, a bank, a lender, a retail outlet, or a utility company agrees to let the consumer buy up to a specified amount on open account. The consumer's obligation is to make payments in accordance with the specified terms. Many people often maintain a variety of open accounts. For example, nearly everybody uses one-month charge accounts to pay their phone bills, utility bills, retail purchases etc. In addition, many people have one or more bank credit cards, such as MasterCard or Visa. In general, using open account credit is a good idea if you pay the full amount of the account balance before the due date. You do not have to pay any interest charges. In essence, you are getting a free loan from the bank or the issuer. However, open account credit cards generally charge a very high rate of interest on balances that are not paid in full on the due date. In fact, you will find that they are the most expensive kind of debt. You should avoid using credit card financing as much as possible.

What Kinds of Credit Cards Are Best?

There are hundreds of credit cards on the market and new ones are introduced almost daily. Very often the same bank or institution offers several types of credit cards. How do you decide which card is the best for you?

The features of a credit card can be divided into four major categories:

1. the annual fee;
2. the grace period or the free loan period;
3. the interest rate charged on the unpaid balance and how it is calculated; and,
4. the additional features, such as free life insurance, air mileage entitlement, cash machine linkage, amount of credit available and so on.

How important each of these factors is to you depends on how you use the credit card.

The annual fee is simply a fixed flat fee paid each year.[2] Other things being the same, you would choose the card that charges the lowest annual fee. However, other

---

[2] Some cards offer a second card, usually for a spouse, without an additional fee; others charge a supplementary fee.

things are seldom the same: the cards that charge higher annual fees usually provide you with more and better features such as a higher credit limit (e.g., in the case of gold cards), longer grace periods and so on. Your choice then depends on whether you can take advantage of these additional features.

If you use credit cards for convenience only — that is, you always take advantage of grace periods and always pay off the previous balance by the due date — you will prefer a card with a low fee, a high interest rate, and a long grace period. You would not mind the high interest rate because interest charges are never incurred. In contrast, if you always carry a loan balance and seldom pay the previous month's balance in full, you would prefer a card with a high annual fee and a low interest rate — of course, the trade-off depends on your average outstanding balance.

Cost and Benefit Analysis

You can use the old common-sense cost and benefit analysis to choose the best credit card for yourself. Go through the list of features that the credit card provides. Delete all the features that are irrelevant to you. For example, if you are always able to pay the balance in full by the due date, the interest charges would be irrelevant. If you do not drive, a car collision waiver insurance on rental cars would be irrelevant. On the other hand, the annual fee affects you because every user must pay the fee.

Now, you are left with a list of features that are relevant to you. The next step is to price each item according to your expected usage. For example, suppose you expect an average balance of $2,000 every month. That is, every month you spend $2,000 on the card, and pay it off at the end of the grace period. If the opportunity cost of your money is 10% per annum and the grace period is one month, you can price this benefit at $2,000 × 10% or $200 per year. As another example, suppose the credit card provides you with free car collision insurance on rental cars. Each year you expect to rent a car for two weeks on average and the car collision insurance premium that the car rental company will charge is $12 per day: then, the benefit of having free car collision insurance from your credit card can be priced at $12 × 14 or $168. Thus, every relevant feature of the credit card that affects you could be priced according to your expected usage. The net benefit is then equal to the total of all the benefits less the total of all costs. Similarly, you can perform the same cost and benefit analysis on each and every credit card in which you are interested. The best card for you is the one that gives you the maximum net benefit. See Problem 4 at the end of the Chapter.

Other Kinds of Credit or Consumer Loans

Interest charges on credit card balances are very high, making them a very expensive form of financing. There are other forms of personal credit available. These are often a much better deal because they offer a higher credit limit and at a lower interest rate.

Unsecured Personal Credit Line   You can apply for a personal line of credit at your bank. A line of credit is the maximum amount that you can owe at any point in time. Interest will be charged only on the amount that you have actually borrowed. Normally, these credit lines are set up so that interest charged on the amount borrowed is a function of the prime rate, such as the prime rate plus 3%. Repayment is set up on a monthly instalment basis, and the loan is normally repaid in two to five years. The

advantage of a personal credit line is that it provides a higher credit limit at a lower rate of interest than credit card financing. Thus, if you have a credit card balance that you cannot pay off in one or two months' time, it is usually cheaper for you to arrange a personal credit line to pay off the credit card balance.

Home Equity Credit Line

If you own a home, the equity on your home can be used as collateral to secure a line of credit. This is called a home equity credit line. There are two major advantages of using a home equity line of credit. First, the lender will charge a much lower rate of interest than that charged on other personal loans. If you own your home free and clear of debt and mortgages, you can get a home equity line of credit at a rate of interest that is very close to the current rate of interest on first mortgages. Second, you can borrow a lot more by taking out a home equity credit line than you can draw on from an unsecured credit line. In general, the amount you can borrow is a fraction (which could go as high as 90%) of your equity in your home.

The majority of banks and financial institutions set their maximum credit lines at 75% of the market value of the home. Example 11.3 illustrates the typical situation.

Example 11.3: A couple bought a home for $100,000 15 years ago. The home is now worth $200,000. They still have not paid off the mortgage on the house. Let us say the amount of the mortgage still outstanding is $50,000. This means that the couple has built up $200,000 − $50,000 = $150,000 of equity in their home. Suppose now they want to use the home equity as collateral to secure a home equity line of credit. What is the maximum amount of home equity loan that they can get from a bank?

Assuming that the bank will lend up to 75% of the market value of the home, they can expect to borrow (75% × $200,000) less the $50,000 of the first mortgage, or a maximum of $100,000. This does not mean that they can automatically borrow up to this maximum amount. The bank will assess them on their ability to service the debt, using the debt-service ratios or the scoring systems that we have discussed before.

Overdraft Protection

An overdraft protection is a kind of unsecured line of credit. Normally you apply for overdraft protection on your chequing account. You fill out an application form, which will be evaluated by the bank according to some credit scoring system. If your application is approved, you can overdraw your chequing account up to a pre-determined point. Funds advanced from an overdraft protection line carry a very high rate of interest, usually not much lower than that of a credit card advance. Therefore, an overdraft should be used only as an emergency source of funds. Any funds advanced should be repaid as quickly as possible. Some people use it for the convenience of not having to monitor the chequing account balance every time they write a cheque.

Secured Personal Line of Credit

Credit card loans, overdraft protection advances and credit lines are expensive sources of consumer credit. This is so because these loans are risky from the lenders' viewpoint; and the lenders charge a relatively high rate of interest to compensate for the risk they are taking. If the borrower owns assets and is willing to use them to secure the loan, this will reduce the lender's risk and the lender will charge a lower rate of interest on the loan. This is the concept of a secured loan or a collateral loan. The asset used to secure the loan is called collateral. In the event of the borrower defaulting, the lender has the right to sell the collateral to get back her money.

Not every personal asset is suitable for collateral. Lenders want reasonably high-valued assets that they can seize and sell easily. They are not interested in your personal belongings (clothing, kitchen utensils etc.), your stamp collection or your bicycle. They want security against cars and investment assets (shares, bonds) if they can get it. A company selling furniture is relatively comfortable lending you the money to buy it, since it can resell the furniture if it has to repossess it. Banks will lend you money to buy furniture only if they think the probability of default is very low, since for them seizing the furniture is often more trouble than it is worth.

INVESTMENT LOANS — BORROWING MONEY TO INVEST

There are two kinds of assets that we can buy with borrowed money: assets for consumption purposes and assets for investment purposes. Up to this point, we have been talking about consumer credit financing, which refers to borrowing money to acquire assets for consumption purposes. In general, consumption assets depreciate in value over time.

You can also borrow money to acquire investment assets. These are assets that in general increase in value over time, and they usually generate cash flow in the future. Examples of investment assets are stocks, bonds, term deposits, mutual funds, real estate, options and futures. There are significant differences between consumer debt and investment debt. You must understand the distinction between them before you can manage your personal debt successfully.

First, the use of consumer loans will normally decrease your net worth over time, whereas the use of investment debt will normally increase your net worth. Consumer goods — cars, appliances, groceries, clothes, furniture — depreciate in value over time while the debt obligation remains unchanged. Since net worth is the difference between assets and liabilities it is obvious that the use of consumer loans to acquire consumption goods will decrease your net worth. In contrast, investments — stocks, real estate, mutual funds — generally appreciate in value over time, while the face value of the debt obligation remains constant; therefore, you can expect your net worth to increase over time. Of course, financial leverage — that is to say, using borrowed money to acquire investments — is risky. We will discuss the risk of financial leverage when we talk about investments. But, to draw conclusions from the above brief analysis, it is clear that you should pay cash for consumption and use debt to acquire investments, if you are going to borrow at all.

There is a second reason for doing this. If you borrow money to invest, the interest expense is tax deductible — you will pay less income tax, whereas if you borrow money to consume (or purchase consumer goods), the interest expenses are not tax deductible. Suppose you can borrow at a 10% rate of interest and your marginal tax bracket is 50%. If you use the borrowed money to buy consumer goods, the interest expense is not tax deductible and the cost of borrowing is 10%. If you use the borrowed money to acquire investments such as stocks or mutual funds, the interest expense is tax deductible and the cost of borrowing is 5%. In addition, lenders usually charge a higher interest rate on consumer loans than on investment loans.[3]

It is advisable for you to adopt the following good habits of debt management:

1.   As far as possible, pay cash for consumption and borrow money for investments.
2.   If you have investment assets and consumer debt, convert the consumer debt into investment debt. (For example, you can sell your investment, pay off the consumer debt, then borrow again to acquire the investment).

Why Borrow Money to Invest?   There are three main reasons for people to borrow money to invest:

1.   Although there is financial risk involved, if it is done prudently and properly, borrowing money to invest in good investments will result in the growth of the family's net worth.
2.   Borrowing is a way to magnify the after-tax investment return in order to reach specific financial goals.
3.   If it is done correctly, borrowing is a good way for high-income earners to create their own tax shelters, thereby reducing or deferring taxes.

We have already discussed the first reason for borrowing money to invest. To reiterate the main point, if the investment increases in value faster than the debt obligation, the family's net worth will increase in the long run. For example, if you borrow money at a 10% interest rate and the money is invested to earn an expected rate of return of 15%, your net worth will increase over time. Of course, there is financial risk involved because the rate of return is uncertain. Although over the long term, you expect to earn 15% on your investment, the rate of return in some years will be low. If the rate of return is lower than the rate of interest of 10%, there is insufficient cash from the investment for you to pay the interest. Therefore, you may need other sources of income to make interest payments during the lean years when return on your investment is low.

Borrowing to Reach Specific Financial Goals   Borrowing could be a powerful way to magnify the rate of return on investment so that you can reach specific financial goals. In Chapter 3, on goal setting, we saw that to reach certain specific financial goals may require the individual to earn a very high rate of return. For example, if your goal is to have $1 million in twenty years' time and you want to achieve this goal by investing your initial wealth of $10,000, then you must earn a rate of return of 25.89%. (By now, you should be able to calculate this. If you can't, you should review Chapter 2). Suppose you cannot find any investment that has such a high rate of return and the closest investment you can find is a mutual fund that has a very good track record but the expected rate of return is only 20%. However, this is not good enough because you need a return of 26% to reach your financial goal.

If you are willing to take more risk, there is a way for you to reach your goal and that is by borrowing money. Suppose you can borrow money from a bank at the rate of interest of 10%. (Usually, it is quite easy to arrange such a line of credit if the mutual

---

[3] The risk they take is quite low, and since the investment asset is supposed to generate income, the loan is self-liquidating — it produces the cash flow to pay the lender.

funds acquired are used as collateral to secure the credit.) You borrow just enough money to reach your required rate of return, 26%. How much do you have to borrow?

Suppose for each dollar of your own money (your equity) you will borrow $x from the bank at 10% interest. The ratio $x/$1 or x is called the debt-to-equity ratio. That is, if you borrow $0.40 for every $1 you have already, your debt-to-equity ratio is .4, or 40%. This is exactly the same concept as a debt-to-equity ratio in corporate finance. There is a debt-to-equity ratio at which you can reach your financial goal, which requires you to earn 26%. How do you calculate this debt-to-equity ratio, x?

For each dollar of your money, you borrow x dollars and you invest the $(1 + x)$ dollars into the mutual fund, which is expected to earn a 20% return. At the end of the year, the expected value of your investment is $\$(1 + x)(.20)$, from which you must pay interest equal to $\$(x)(.10)$. Your rate of return on equity is therefore $[(1 + x)(.20) - x(.10)] \div 1$ and you want this return to be 26%. Therefore you can set up the equation:

$$\left[\frac{(1+x)(.20) - x(.10)}{1} \right] = .26$$

Solving the equation, $x = .6$. This means that at the debt-to-equity ratio of .6 — borrow 60 cents for each dollar of your equity — the expected rate of return on your investment is 26% and you can reach your financial goal.

We can generalize the above analysis.

Let r = the required rate of return in order to reach the individual's financial goal;
k = the expected rate of return on the investment opportunity, e.g., mutual fund;
i = the rate of interest charged on borrowed funds;
x = the debt-to-equity ratio required to magnify the rate of return on investment to reach the required rate of return, r.

Generalizing our analysis, we have the equation:

$$(1 + x)\,k - xi = r \tag{1}$$

$$(1 + x)(.20) - x(.10) = .26$$

$$x = .6$$

To get a feel of how borrowing can magnify a given rate of return on investment to any high required rate of return, you can put some reasonable numbers into equation (1) and examine the results. We want to emphasize that financial risk increases with the amount of borrowing (see Chapter 15). Indeed, many personal and corporate bankruptcies are the direct result of overindebtedness. Nevertheless, it should be clear that borrowing is a powerful tool to help people to reach certain specific financial goals. See Example 11.4 for an illustration.

Borrowing Money to Create Tax Shelters

Borrowing money to invest can be a very useful strategy for some people, especially high-income earners, in setting up their own tax shelters. Recall that a good tax shelter must first of all be a good investment. Regardless of how much tax you can save or defer, if the money is invested in bad investments, you will end up losing money. Many people make the mistake of looking only at the tax aspect of tax shelters — how much money that would otherwise be taxed away can be saved or deferred — and they forget about the investment aspects of tax shelters. Tax considerations aside, there remains the question of whether or not a particular tax shelter is a good investment, whether or not it is too risky.[4]

The idea of using borrowed money to create your own tax shelter is actually very simple. It is based on two facts:

1. Interest expense on money borrowed for investment purposes is tax deductible: you can deduct the interest against your other sources of income and so save taxes; and,

2. capital gains from investments are taxed at a lower rate than other income; and, more important, capital gains are not taxed until you sell the investment so that taxes can be deferred by holding on to the investment.

If you borrow money and put it into investments that have a good potential of growth, you save current taxes because the interest expense is tax deductible, and the capital gains on the investments are not taxed until you sell. Ideally, you will be in a lower tax bracket when you sell the investment.

We show how to borrow to reach a financial goal with an example.

Example 11.4: Dr. Anderson is a surgeon who has a well-established practice in downtown Toronto. Mrs. Anderson is a full-time home-maker and they have a six-year-old child, Janet. They have just paid off the mortgage on their house and are debt-free. Here is a summary of the Anderson's financial situation from the most recent information that they provide:

Net professional income	$250,000
Taxes paid last year	100,000
Consumption	90,000
Savings (including RRSP contribution)	60,000

Dr. Anderson wants to invest his money to achieve two objectives: long-term growth of net worth and tax savings. Currently, he puts his savings in several growth mutual funds. The funds pay very little in the way of dividends, but over the long term they are expected to generate an average rate of return of 16% in the form of capital gains.

Let us analyze Dr. Anderson's current investment programme. To make things simple, assume that he will save and invest $40,000 per year into a basket of several mutual funds. The mutual funds do not pay dividends but their expected rate of growth is 16%. The value of his portfolio in ten years' time is equal to $40,000 $\times$ [$(1.16^{10} - 1) \div .16$] = $852,859.

The values of his portfolio in 15, 20, and 25 years are $2.06 million, $4.62 million, and $9.97 million, respectively. As long as he does not sell the investments, there are no taxes payable. Although the above values seem attractive or even enviable for many

---

[4] Revenue Canada challenges some complicated tax shelters, adding to their risk. Even if you successfully defend your position, the cost in legal fees and your time may exceed the tax savings.

people, Dr. Anderson is not happy with the amount of taxes that he pays every year; and he wonders if he can do better. "It would be nice if I can cut taxes by 40%, or $40,000," he complains. Let us assume that his goal is to cut taxes by $40,000. If he can create an investment loss of $80,000 by borrowing money, then at his marginal tax rate of 50%, the loss would save him $40,000 of taxes. How can he create an investment loss of $80,000? We will give you two minutes to suggest an answer.

Yes, your answer is right! Dr. Anderson should go to the bank and get an investment loan. Using the mutual funds that he will be buying as collateral, and with the healthy cash flow from his professional practice, it would not be difficult for him to get an investment loan to buy the mutual funds. Some banks are more conservative and may require Dr. Anderson to provide additional collateral, such as his home.

Suppose that he can get an investment loan at the rate of interest of 10%. If his goal is to generate an investment loss of $80,000, he must borrow $80,000 ÷ .10 or $800,000, so that the interest expense is $80,000 and since the mutual funds do not pay dividends, that will give him a loss of $80,000, as follows:

Investment Income	$ 0
Interest Expense ($800,000 × .10)	80,000
Investment Loss	($80,000)

If he borrows $800,000 now and invests the money in the basket of mutual funds that is expected to generate a 16% return, the value of his portfolio in 10 years will be:

$$[(\$800,000 \times 1.16^{10}) - 800,000] \text{ or } \$2.73 \text{ million}$$

This is substantially higher than the value of his portfolio if he does not borrow ($852,859). Of course, when he sells the investment he has to pay capital gains taxes. Still, the difference is significant. Here is a summary of the values of his portfolio:

Programme I: save and invest $40,000 per year in mutual funds with expected return of 16%

Programme II: pay $80,000 interest per year to service the investment loan, with a net after-tax expense of $40,000 per year. The investment loan of $800,000 is invested in the same mutual funds.

Value of Portfolio

Number of Years After	Programme I (millions)	Programme II (tax shelter) (millions)
10	$ 0.853	$ 2.73
15	2.060	6.61
20	4.620	14.77
25	9.970	31.90
30	21.210	67.88

Caution!   Borrowing money to invest is risky and is not for everyone. We used the above example only for the purpose of describing the use of financial leverage to create a tax shelter. Its suitability depends on each family's financial situation (e.g. cash flow, net worth) and risk preference. Indeed, in the example, we cannot say Programme II (the tax shelter) is better than Programme I. Certainly, the expected portfolio values under Programme II are much higher than those under Programme I but the risk is also higher. The return on the mutual fund is not certain and interest rates may increase in the future (which makes servicing the debt more difficult). If you are considering the use of borrowed money to invest, we advise you to check your cash-flow situation before and after the borrowing. To illustrate, let us look at Dr. Anderson again. The family's cash flow before and after setting up the tax shelter is as follows:

	Before	**After**
	(Setting up Tax Shelter)	
Net Professional Income	$250,000	$250,000
Taxes	100,000	60,000
Consumption	90,000	90,000
Ann. contribution to mutual funds	40,000	0
Interest expense	0	80,000
Other savings (RRSP etc.)	20,000	20,000

As you can see, the Andersons do not have to sacrifice any consumption to support the tax shelter investment. They are simply channelling tax savings to support an investment programme that will increase their net worth faster.

SUMMARY

In this chapter we have discussed personal debt management. There are two kinds of personal debt: consumer debt or credit, and investment debt. They are different concepts and call for different methods of management. Normally, you are advised to use cash to buy consumption goods and to borrow money to invest, if you borrow at all. There are three main reasons for this: first, interest charges on consumer loans are much higher than those on investment loans; second, interest expenses on consumer loans are not tax deductible whereas interest expenses on investment loans are tax deductible; third, borrowing money to acquire consumption goods will normally decrease net worth while borrowing money to invest will normally increase net worth.

It is important that one does not overextend oneself. We recommend that you evaluate your debt capacity, liquidity and solvency in order to arrive at a comfort zone of debt. How much you should borrow to a large extent depends on how much the banks and other financial institutions will lend to you. Understanding the scoring systems and the debt service ratios that the lenders use is therefore very helpful.

There are many sources and types of consumer loans and credit, including credit card loans, unsecured personal credit line, overdraft protection, secured personal credit line, and home equity credit line. In order for you to get a loan easily, it is important that you maintain a good credit history. We recommend a cost and benefit analysis if you want to evaluate the numerous credit cards that are available.

There are three main reasons why people want to borrow money to invest: (1) borrowing to invest normally leads to an increase in net worth; (2) borrowing to invest is a powerful tool for people to use in reaching certain specific goals; and (3) borrowing to invest is a useful method for creating tax shelters for some people.

KEY TERMINOLOGY

consumer credit and debt / debt capacity / solvency / liquidity / debt service ratios / gross debt service ratio / unpaid balance / free loan period / grace period / line of credit / collateral / secured credit line / unsecured credit line / home equity credit line / cost and benefit analysis — total debt service ratio — credit scoring system — credit file — credit bureau — overindebtedness — credit card / investment loan / financial risk / rate of return required to reach a financial goal / debt-to-equity ratio / magnifying a rate of return / financial leverage / tax shelter through financial leverage / matching assets and debts / matching principle in finance

DISCUSSION QUESTIONS

1. Explain all the key words and terms under **Key Terminology**.

2. **Personal Project 1**
    Go to several banks or financial institutions and get information about the credit cards that they offer. Take any two credit cards you like, e.g., Visa and MasterCard, or Visa and Visa Gold.
    (a) Put down all the features that each card offers, including grace period, interest rate etc.
    (b) Based on your expected usage, delete all the features that are irrelevant.
    (c) Price all the remaining items that are relevant to you.
    (d) Use the cost and benefit analysis to examine which card is better for you.

3. **Personal Project 2**
    Find the addresses and phone numbers of all the local credit bureaus in your city. (The Yellow Pages in the phone book is a good place to start). Request a copy of your own credit file. Record what you had to go through (e.g. what forms have you filled out?) before the credit bureau gives you a copy of your credit file. Examine your credit file. Are there any missing data or incorrect pieces of information? What is your right, as provided by the provincial legislations, if there are incorrect or missing data in your file?

PROBLEMS

1. Refer to Dr. Anderson and his family in Example 11.4 in the chapter.
    (a) Using the usual benchmark for GDS ratio and TDS ratio, what is the maximum amount of cash flow that the Andersons can apply to service debt?
    (b) If the rate of interest is (i) 8%; (ii) 10%; (iii) 12%, and if he can get a loan that requires him to pay interest only, what is the maximum amount of the loan that he can get?
    (c) How would your answer to (b) change if the bank requires him to amortize the loan in 10 years?

2. (a) Goal Setting
        Mr. Johnston wants to have $1 million when he retires in 25 years. He plans to achieve this goal by saving and investing $3,000 per year at the end of each

and every year for 25 years. What is the required rate of return that he must earn in order to reach his goal?

(b) Investment Loan

He wants to invest his annual savings of $3,000 in a mutual fund. The expected rate of return on the fund is 14%. He can borrow from the bank at an interest rate of 8%, provided that he uses the mutual fund as collateral. What is the debt-to-equity ratio that Mr. Johnston must maintain in order to reach his goal in (a)?

3. Friendly Freddie always has his customers' best interests at heart. They want to know exactly what they have to pay without any tricky financial calculations. Friendly Freddie charges 24% p.a. on consumer loans. To make it easy for his customers, he divides the interest and principal into 12 equal monthly amounts. Thus, on a $1000 loan you pay $103.33 monthly [(.24 ÷ 12) × 1000)] + (1000 ÷ 12)] and just as easy as anything you've paid off the whole loan.

(a) What would your loan payment be if it were calculated in the usual way for consumer loans at 24%, compounded monthly?

(b) What is the effective annual rate of Freddie's loan?

4. Kurt Mountain and his wife, Larissa Valley, are thinking of switching from their Bank of New Brunswick basic Visa credit card to a CIBC gold card. Their average month-end balance on the credit card is $2,000, which they pay off on the last day of the grace period. Each of them owns a car. They work very hard at their jobs, and spend most of their holidays doing repairs to their house. Every winter they fly to Florida, rent a car, and spend a week sightseeing. They keep their extra cash reserves in a broker's account yielding 5% p.a. Here are the relevant features of the two cards:

	CIBC Gold	BNB Basic
Grace period	17 days	25 days
Rebate on every purchase[1]	.5%	no
Card fee at start of year	$175	$12
Monthly interest rate on overdue balance	2%	1.5%
Collision damage waiver on rental cars[2]	yes	no

Notes: In reality there are other differences between basic and premium cards. Consider only the ones listed for this question.
[1] Paid at year-end.;
[2] The car rental agencies usually charge $12 per day to insure you against collision.

Which credit card is better for them?

5. The due date for the balance of $2000 on your credit card is tomorrow and you have only enough money to survive the next six months without paying this debt. In six months you will have enough money to pay off the debt. The credit card company charges 18% p.a., compounded monthly. Kneecap Finance offers a better rate, 16%, compounded weekly (assumes 52 weeks in a year).

(a) Should you borrow $2000 from Kneecap to pay the credit card bill? Assume there are 26 weeks in six months.

(b) Suppose you were earning enough money each week during the next six months that you could repay a loan in the usual form of blended payments (principal and interest). How much would you pay each week if you borrowed $2000 for six months from Kneecap?

(c) In reality, there is a bit of a problem comparing the two alternatives by assuming there are 26 weeks in six months. You can do it mechanically, but do credit card companies all charge interest on part months?

6.   Marge Ciccone has applied to you, the assistant manager at her trust company, for a three year loan to buy a car. She wants $7,000 at the current rate of 1% per month. She and her husband Lou have four children, aged 6–13, with the youngest about to start Grade one in a few days. Lou earns $32,000 a year as an accountant for a factory. He is in the fourth year of the certified management accountants' (CMA) programme, and expects to finish in less than two years.

Marge wants the car so that she can start working outside the home again, after being out of the labour force for almost 10 years. She can work as a commission salesperson for a small food processing company that is just starting to expand its lines. Up to now, it had concentrated on restaurants and caterers; now it wants to sell to small speciality food retailers in the Montreal area. Marge has worked in the food business as both a food store clerk and a sausage stuffer, and she feels she understands the business well enough to sell successfully. She speaks French, Italian and English fluently.

She talked to the two salesmen who currently handle the restaurant clientele, and discovered they make "about $35–40,000" before automobile expenses, which they must pay themselves. She would sell to the proposed new target market; so she wouldn't be in competition with them. They warned her that it would take at least a few months to make any reasonable level of sales, and several years to build up a good clientele with repeat business. She cannot work a full day for at least two or three years, because she still wants to be home when the children aren't in school. She figures that gives her about five hours on the road, compared with their eight hours, but she can do some of the paperwork and telephoning from home.

Marge and Lou own their own house in a pleasant suburb of Montreal. The mortgage payments of $748 per month run for four years to renewal, and the mortgage has 10 years after that. They pay property tax of about $1200 p.a. and $180 per month on another car loan that has two years to run. Lou's take-home pay is $25,000. They put $1000 into an RRSP for Lou in 1994 (in several installments), the first such deposit they have made. They keep $1,000 in a savings account for contingencies, and they have saved up another $3,500, which Marge plans to use for the rest of the $10,500 purchase price of the car.

(a) What advice would you give her?

(b) Will you grant the loan?

7.   Annette earns a gross income of $45,000 p.a. She owns a condominium in North Vancouver, valued at $218,000. She still has a mortgage on it, with 11 years of monthly payments of $650. The annual property taxes are $3,000 and the condominium fee is $250 per month. She has no other debts, and $10,000 invested in a

mutual fund. Recently, she has been longing to buy a car that costs $28,000. The current interest rate is 8.5% for a four year term.

(a) If she has to meet the standard bank lending tests, can she finance the entire purchase price of the car?

(b) How much is the minimum down payment she should make?

8. Tom Radcliffe has $20,000 to invest and can save $5,000 at the end of each year. He will invest it all in a stock mutual fund that is expected to return 13% p.a.

(a) Calculate the value of his total investment after 10 years. After 20 years.

(b) Suppose Tom's goal is to have $1 million in 20 years. You should see from part (a) that this goal is infeasible. What can he do to reach the goal?

(c) If he doesn't change the goal, how long does he take to reach $1 million, rounded to the nearest year?

(d) If he changes his goal to having $1.5 million in 22 years, with the same starting point and savings, what is the required rate of return that he must earn? (Hint: the answer is between 15% and 20%).

(e) If he can borrow from the bank at 8% p.a., what is the leverage ratio necessary to reach his goal in (d)?

(f) How much is his goal in (d) worth in current dollars, assuming an inflation rate of 3%?

chapter 12

Buying a Home and Mortgage Financing

LEARNING OBJECTIVES

For most people, expenditures on housing — whether as a home owner or as a tenant — take the largest bite of the family's monthly income. Decisions concerning housing represent some of the biggest financial decisions that people have to make in their financial affairs. For example, the family must decide whether to own or to rent, where to live, the size and the type of the dwelling to choose, how to finance a home purchase and so on. Many people also want to know whether buying a house is a good investment.

Since very few people are fortunate enough to be able to come up with one lump-sum of cash to buy a home, most people must deal with a mortgage. Financing a home and mortgages have become a complex and confusing task for many people since so many types of financing and mortgages have been developed in recent years. It is important for a home-owner or potential home buyer to have the basic knowledge of how a standard mortgage works.

The specific learning objectives of this chapter are as follows:

1. To introduce the most common form of mortgage financing and go through the calculation of the major costs.
2. To discuss how large a house a person can afford.
3. To evaluate home ownership as an investment.
4. To introduce methods for valuing a house.
5. To introduce a framework for making the rent versus buy decision.

MORTGAGE FINANCING

For most people, buying a home is such a big financial commitment that they must borrow money to finance the purchase. **Mortgage financing** is the traditional way of borrowing money to purchase a home; however, many people do not understand the basic terminology of a mortgage contract. Most do not know how the monthly mortgage payments are calculated and simply assume the numbers given by the lenders as correct.

Although most lenders — the banks, trust companies, insurance companies, credit unions, and most private lenders — are trustworthy and will not cheat the borrowers on the mortgage payments, the individual is still better off and can make much better decisions if he or she has more knowledge about **mortgage financing** and the calculation of the monthly mortgage payments. This is especially true because there are so many different types of mortgages to choose from.

In this section, we will first introduce some basic concepts and terminology. The mathematics of mortgages will be described so that at the end of this section you will have enough knowledge to make the right decision about **mortgage financing**. You will know the relationship between the key variables: the monthly payment, the rate of interest, the term, the amortization period, and so on.

Home Mortgages

To many people, a **home mortgage** is a real estate loan with equal monthly payments. They know that the monthly payments may increase or decrease according to changes in interest rates but they do not know precisely how the monthly payments are calculated. Most people also know that they must keep paying the lender each month for twenty or twenty-five years, after which, they will own the house "free and clear." In the interim, if they do not keep up with the monthly payments, they may lose their homes. The above description is essentially correct by and large but that is not what a **mortgage** actually is. We will now describe more precisely how a mortgage works.

Mortgage   A **mortgage** is defined as the transfer of an interest in property to a creditor as security for payment of a debt with a **right of redemption** by the borrower upon repayment of the debt. In other words, if you get a mortgage from a bank to purchase a home, the title of ownership of the home is actually conveyed to the bank and what you have is a right to reclaim clear title to the home upon full repayment of the debt. This right to reclaim title from the lender is called the **equity of redemption**. Thus, a **mortgage** is not in fact a loan **per se** but rather, it is the security for a loan (see Example 12.1).

> **Example 12.1:**   John and Janet Coulson have bought a house from Paul Evans for $200,000. The Coulsons paid Mr. Evans $80,000 cash and assumed his first mortgage of $120,000. The mortgagee, the Bank of Nova Scotia, had approved the latter transaction — that is to say, the Bank had allowed the Coulsons to assume the mortgage.
>
> Mr. and Mrs. Coulson, like many home buyers, believed that they had acquired a new home, including the title to the home. In fact, however, the Bank has title and what had transferred between the Coulsons and Mr. Evans was the possession and use of the home and the equity of redemption.

The two parties to a **mortgage** transaction are called the **mortgager** and the **mortgagee**. The **mortgager** is the person who gives the security to obtain the loan — in other words, the mortgager is the home owner. The mortgager receives funds and maintains possession (but not the legal title) of the property. The **mortgagee** is the lender who receives the title to the property until the debt is fully repaid.

There can be only one legal mortgage with respect to any particular piece of property because title can be conveyed only once. The mortgage where the conveyance of title is involved is commonly called the **first mortgage**.

Second Mortgage

If there can be only one legal mortgage for a particular property (since title of a property can be conveyed only once), then what security do second and third mortgages have? From the foregoing discussion it should be clear that when one mortgages one's home a right known as the **equity of redemption** — the right to reclaim the title to the home upon full repayment of the loan — is retained by the mortgager. Clearly then, this right is an asset that has value of itself and it too can be used as security for another loan. Therefore, the act of making a **second mortgage** consists of using the **equity of redemption** as security or collateral for a loan. In fact, the **second mortgage** conveys the right to a further equity of redemption which can again be mortgaged — and if this further equity of redemption is mortgaged, the resulting mortgage is called a **third mortgage**. There can be successive mortgages of equities of redemption following the first mortgage and the borrower retains at all times an equity of redemption in the **last** mortgage given. In a red-hot real estate boom, it is not uncommon to hear of borrowers with fourth and fifth mortgages on their properties!

Some Basic Concepts and Terminology

Principal   This is the amount of money that is being borrowed.

Interest   Interest is the price paid by the borrower to the lender for the use of the lender's money.

Amortization   This is the gradual retirement of a debt by means of partial payments of the principal at regular intervals.

Amortization Period   This is the time period required to retire completely a debt through scheduled repayments of principal.

Blended Payments   This is the method of repayment of a debt where the periodic repayments are constant and each payment includes interest and repayment of part of the principal.

Term   This is the actual length of time for which the money is loaned at a particular rate of interest. The most common terms for home mortgages are 6 months, 1 year, 2 years, 3 years, 4 years and 5 years.

Maturity Date   The final date in the **term** of the mortgage is called the maturity date.

Conventional Mortgage   This term is used to describe a first mortgage granted by an institutional lender such as a bank, mortgage, loan, or trust company where the amount of the loan does not exceed 75% of the appraised lending value of the property.

High Ratio Mortgage   A mortgage that exceeds 75% of lending value and must be insured, via a National Housing Act loan or a private insurer. The insurance is paid by the borrower in favour of the lender to protect the lender against default.

Default   This is failure to meet the obligations imposed by the debt (an example is failure on the part of the mortgager to make monthly payments)

Foreclosure   Remedial court action taken by a mortgagee, when default occurs on a mortgage, to cause forfeiture of the equity of redemption of the mortgager.

Power of Sale   The right of a mortgagee such as a bank to force a sale of the property should default occur is called a **power of sale**.

Mortgage Financing Mathematics

Mortgage financing is another application of time value calculations. If you mastered Chapter 2, then this section should be easy for you. There are five important **elements** in a mortgage. They are stated in the mortgage contract between the **mortgager** and the **mortgagee**. Once they are known, you can carry out the following calculations to make the right decisions about mortgage financing. These five elements are:

1.   The **Principal**.
2.   The **Term**.
3.   The **Rate of Interest** and the compounding frequency.
4.   The **Period** of payment, usually a month.
5.   The **Amortization period**.

Example 12.2:   Mr. Wong has just bought a house. He obtained a three-year first mortgage of $100,000 from the Bank of Montreal at an interest rate of 7% p.a., compounded semi-annually. The loan is to be amortized over 25 years by blended monthly payments. What is the amount of each monthly payment?

The five **elements** in this mortgage are:

1.   The **Principal** = $100,000.
2.   The **Term** = 3 years.
3.   The **Rate of Interest** = 7% p.a., semi-annual compounding. This is equivalent to a monthly compounding rate of 0.575%. We explain why in the next section.
4.   The **Period** of Repayment = a month.
5.   The **Amortization Period** = 25 years or 300 months.

Answer: The monthly payment is $700.41.

Here is how you get the answer from your calculator:

100,000	**PV**
300	**N**
.575	**%i**
CPT PMT	answer = <u>700.41</u>

We will now go through the mathematics and the theory that provide the above calculation.

Canadian Home Mortgage Rates

In Canada, mortgage rates are stated as an annual rate with semi-annual compounding but the loan is normally repaid by monthly payments.[1] Thus, the **compounding period** (6 months) is different from the **repayment**

---

[1] By law, residential mortgages may not be compounded more frequently than semi-annually.

period (1 month). How can we translate the stated rate — such as 7% p.a., semi-annual compounding — to an effective monthly rate with monthly compounding?

■   The Stated Rate and the Equivalent Monthly Compounding Rate

Let k =   the stated annual rate, with semi-annual compounding
       m =   the equivalent monthly compounding rate

Because of the semi-annual compounding, the effective annual rate of interest is equivalent to:

$$\left[1 + \frac{k}{2}\right]^2$$

Since we want the equivalent monthly rate to compound to this effective annual rate, we can set up the following equation:

$$(1 + m)^{12} = \left[1 + \frac{k}{2}\right]^2 \tag{1}$$

In Example 12.2, $k = 7\%$, so from equation (1),

$$(1 + m)^{12} = \left[1 + \frac{0.07}{2}\right]^2$$

$$m = .00575 \text{ or } .575\%$$

How to Calculate the Monthly Mortgage Payment   If you recall the basic concepts in Chapter 2, the answer is based on the simple logic: "The mortgage payments should be such that the present value of the stream of mortgage payments, when discounted by the appropriate interest rate, equals the amount of the loan (i.e., the principal)." Now go back to Example 12.2 again, the **principal** = $100,000, the **equivalent monthly compounding rate** = .00575, the number of months = 25 × 12 or 300 months. Let $x = the monthly mortgage payment. The present value of an annuity of $x for 300 months at the discount rate of .00575 is equal to:

$$(x)\left[\frac{1}{.00575} - \frac{1}{.00575 \times 1.00575^{300}}\right]$$

Since this is equal to the amount of the loan of $100,000, we can set up the equation:

$$(x)\left[\frac{1}{.00575} - \frac{1}{.00575 \times 1.00575^{300}}\right] = 100,000$$

$$x = 700.41$$

This is the theory behind the programs in your calculator and in Super Rep; it is important that you understand the theory before you use them.

How to Calculate the Outstanding Principal at Any Future Point In Time   The **outstanding principal**, or the **outstanding balance** of the loan, is equal to the present value of the remaining stream of mortgage payments, discounted at the

equivalent monthly compounding rate. Let us continue with the above example. What is the **outstanding balance** of the loan after two years?

After two years, Mr. Wong would have paid 24 monthly payments so that there will be (300 − 24) or 276 monthly payments remaining. The outstanding balance is the present value of an annuity of 276 monthly payments of $700.41 each. Using the equivalent monthly compounding rate of .00575 as the discount rate, this is equal to

$$\$700.41 \times \left[\frac{1}{.00575} - \frac{1}{.00575 \times 1.00575^{276}} \right]$$

$$= \$96,782 \quad \text{after rounding.}$$

Only if you understand the theory, are you entitled to use your calculator. The procedure is:

276	**N**
700.41	**PMT**
.575	**%i**
CPT PV	answer = $96,782

Change in Mortgage Rate   The rate of interest is guaranteed and fixed only for the **term** of the mortgage. Thus, the rate of 7% p.a. in Example 12.2 is fixed for three years only. At the end of the three-year term, the mortgage has to be renewed or refinanced at the rate of interest that applies at that time. Since the future rate may rise or fall, the future mortgage payment may rise or fall accordingly. How do you calculate the new monthly payment? The procedure is illustrated in Example 12.3.

> **Example 12.3:** To continue with Example 12.2, suppose at the end of three years the rate of interest for a three-year term has increased to 9% p.a., semi-annual compounding. What is the new mortgage payment?

After three years, the remaining number of monthly payments is equal to (300 − 36) or 264 months. The outstanding balance of the loan is equal to:[2]

$$\$700.41 \times \left[\frac{1}{.00575} - \frac{1}{.00575 \times 1.00575^{264}} \right]$$

$$= \$94,999$$

Next, we have to calculate the new equivalent monthly rate, by using equation (1), that is,

$$(1 + m)^{12} = \left[1 + \frac{.09}{2} \right]^2$$

$$m = .00736.$$

---

[2] The outstanding balance is equal to the present value of an annuity of 264 monthly payments of $700.41 each, at the discount rate of .00575.

Finally, let y be equal to the new monthly payment. The present value of an annuity of 264 months of $\$y$ is equal to:

$$y \times \left[\frac{1}{.00736} - \frac{1}{.00736 \times 1.00736^{264}} \right]$$

and we want this to equal $94,999. We therefore have:

$$y \times \left[\frac{1}{.00736} - \frac{1}{.00736 \times 1.00736^{264}} \right] = 94,999$$

$$y = 817.09$$

Make sure that you understand the theory before you use the calculator to find the answer, which is as follows:

264	N
.736	%i
94,999	PV
CPT PMT	answer = $817.09

Therefore, as a result of the increase in the interest rate from 7% to 9%, the monthly mortgage payment would increase from $700.41 to $817.09.

Problem: In Example 12.2, if the three-year mortgage rate falls to 5% after three years, what is the new monthly mortgage payment?

Answer: $591.26.

Summary of Mortgage Financing Mathematics

There are **five elements** in a mortgage: the **Principal**, the **Interest**, the **Term**, the **Period** of payment (a month, a week and so on), and the **Amortization Period**. All these can be easily found out from the mortgage contract.

Based on these five elements, we can calculate

1.   the equivalent monthly compounding rate;
2.   the periodic mortgage payment;
3.   the outstanding balance of the principal at any point in time; and
4.   the new mortgage payment when there is a change in the rate of interest or in the amortization period. Such changes usually occur at the end of the term of the mortgage.

HOW MUCH HOME CAN YOU AFFORD?

Since very few people can afford to pay cash for a home, how much home one can afford depends on how much mortgage financing one can obtain. The traditional sources of mortgage financing are provided by the financial institutions such as the banks and trust companies. In the course of the discussion in Chapter 11, we noted these institutions use certain criteria to qualify potential borrowers. One of the more popular criteria is the **gross debt service (GDS) ratio**. You may recall this rule says that your monthly mortgage payment plus property taxes must be less than a certain percentage (usually 30%) of your monthly gross income. Based on this, the lender will calculate the maximum amount that you can borrow, subject to other criteria if applicable. Example 12.4 illustrates the calculations.

Example 12.4:   Brenda and Bobby Black both work for the federal government. Their jobs are stable and last year they earned a combined household gross income of $75,000. They are very careful with their personal finances and have no debt. They want to buy a house and wonder how much they can borrow based on their income. They have saved $80,000 which they are willing to use as a down payment. The current home mortgage rate for a three-year term mortgage is 8% p.a. The houses that they have been looking at require about $3,000 in annual property taxes.

Based on a **GDS ratio** of 30%, the amount of **principal, interest**, and **property tax** payment that the Blacks can afford is equal to (30% × $75,000) = $22,500/year or $1,875/month. Since property taxes amount to $3,000/year or $250/month, the maximum amount of **principal** and **interest** that lenders would allow is equal to ($1,875 − 250) or $1,625/month.

The **equivalent monthly compounding rate**, m, is calculated from equation (1), as follows:

$$(1 + m)^{12} = \left[1 + \frac{.08}{2}\right]^2$$

$$m = .00656 \text{ or } .656\%$$

Assuming a 25-year amortization period, the maximum amount of mortgage that the Blacks can get is equal to the present value of an annuity of 300 months of $1,625 each, using .656% as the discount rate. This is equal to:

$$\$1,625 \times \left[\frac{1}{.00656} - \frac{1}{.00656 \times 1.00656^{300}}\right]$$

$$= \$213,000 \quad \text{rounded to the nearest thousand.}$$

If you want to use your calculator, the sequence is:

300	**N**
.656	**%i**
1625	**PMT**
CPT PV	answer = $213,000 (rounded to the nearest thousand)

The amount of housing that they can afford = $80,000 + $213,000 = $293,000, or about $300,000.

Minimum Down Payment

The financial institutions in Canada normally will not lend more than 75% of the appraised value of the house. This means that to buy a house, one normally needs a **minimum down payment** equal to 25% of the value of the house. Suppose the Blacks in Example 12.4 do not have any savings — in other words, they have no down payment. In that case, even though their income qualifies them to borrow $213,000, in practice, they will not get any mortgage from the banks or other conventional sources.

Saving Up for a Down Payment

For young families in the early stages of their life cycle, it is unlikely that they have enough money for the minimum down payment. If they want to buy a home in the future, their short-term financial goal should be to save up money for the down payment of the house. The above analysis should give you some idea of how to set this financial goal. To summarize, this is what you have to do:

1.   estimate the amount of mortgage that you can get, based on your expected gross income, the current GDS ratio (say 30%) or TDS ratio (say 40%), and the current mortgage rate.[3]
2.   this amount of mortgage is approximately equal to 75% of the value of the house; for this reason, you can find the amount of housing you can theoretically afford.
3.   the minimum down payment is equal to 25% of the value of the house obtained above.
4.   you set up a deadline for acquiring this minimum down payment.

See Example 12.5 for an illustration.

Example 12.5:   Suppose the Blacks in Example 12.4 have no down payment. They want to save up enough money for the minimum down payment in five years' time. Based on their current income and the current mortgage rate, what is the amount that they must have for the minimum down payment in five years time?

First, as shown in Example 12.4, they can borrow about $213,000 from the bank. Second, as this is about 75% of the value of the house, the theoretical home value that the Blacks can afford is equal to ($213,000 ÷ .75) or $284,000. Third, the minimum down payment is equal to 25% of $284,000, which is $71,000. Finally, their financial goal would be to have $71,000 in five years' time. You may recall from Chapter 4 that this is a financial goal because the amount is precise ($71,000) and there is a deadline (five years for its completion).[4]

Balancing the Budget

The rules we have presented on how much mortgage you can afford have been constraints imposed by outside lenders. These are rough approximations of the true limit, which is how much money you can afford in your budget. For most families, these rules are a

---

[3] If you can forecast the future mortgage rate, that is what you should use. Empirical studies have, however, found that forecasting future interest rates is very difficult. Many economists think the current rate is the best estimate for the future rate.

[4] The next thing the Blacks should do is to set up an action plan, take action and so on to reach their goal. In other words, they should follow the Personal Financial Process described in Chapter 3 in order to reach their goal.

reasonable guideline. However, suppose a family enjoys being able to travel to Europe every summer and ski at Whistler every winter. The members eat at the best restaurants and stay in four-star hotels. Their budget may not support even 30% GDS. Conversely, we know many families that carry 50% GDS and manage to pay off the home by being very thrifty.

What it comes down to is a choice of goals. If owning your own home is the first priority, then you may have to give up some other goals, at least temporarily. Bankers tell us that they are more likely to find well-off families getting into debt troubles because they couldn't cut their luxury spending, than they are to find modest income families who took on too much.

The mechanical solution to this problem is in Chapter 4. In addition to the tests presented in this chapter, the prospective home buyer needs to balance the budget. All the costs of home ownership — mortgage, utilities, taxes, repairs and maintenance, and insurance — must be factored in. The cost of renting (including utilities, if they are separate from rent) are deducted. One issue to watch out for is inflation. On average, the cost of renting rises over time. The mortgage amount is fixed, and hence it is in nominal dollars already. Thus, the budgeting exercise, if done in nominal dollars, will include the inflation hedge of buying over renting.

Other Sources of Financing and Mortgages

So far we have described the conventional mortgages which are the major sources of first mortgages provided by banks and other financial institutions.

If one wants to borrow more than what is allowed by the constraints of the GDS ratio or the 75% value criterion, one has to look for other sources of financing. These are usually provided by private lenders who do not use the stringent criteria of the banks. In return for the higher risk, these lenders normally require a higher rate of interest. The more common sources of financing are higher mortgages — second mortgage, third mortgage and so on. Another very popular source is a vender-take-back (VTB) mortgage.

A **vendor-take-back (VTB) mortgage** is a mortgage which the seller of a home has taken from the purchaser as part payment of the purchase price for that property. This is sometimes called **seller financing**, since in essence the seller acts as the lender to the buyer. The seller offers a mortgage (or a loan) to the buyer, usually a short-term loan, at a below-market interest rate. Thus, instead of receiving in a lump-sum the sales price of the home, the seller receives monthly mortgage payments from the buyer over a specified period of time. A high-ratio first mortgage can be covered with mortgage insurance, providing yet another alternative for those who cannot raise a 25% downpayment.

> **Example 12.6:** Lynn Buyer wants to buy a home from Jill Vendor for the price of $80,000. Since Lynn Buyer has $10,000 for a down payment, she cannot get a first mortgage of $70,000 from any financial institution. (Why?)

Since Jill Vendor really wants to sell her house, she accepts a **VTB mortgage** of $70,000 for a three-year **term** and 7% **interest** and **amortization period** of 25 years. The monthly payment is $490.29 (you should check this!) and since this is within Lynn Buyer's budget, the transaction is closed.

As this example shows, using non-conventional sources of financing allows a buyer to acquire a more expensive home than that which a conventional lender would normally allow.

Summary: How Much Home Can You Afford?

How much home one can afford depends to a large extent on how much mortgage money one can get from the banks or loan or trust companies. This in turn depends on the usual qualifying rules — GDS, TDS, etc. — that these institutions have used. The major factors affecting the lender's decision are the family's income, the value of the home, the current mortgage rate and the institution's credit criteria (such as the GDS ratio of 30%). Also, it depends on how much money the buyer has for the down payment. We have gone through the basic analysis of how to estimate the value of the home that you can afford. The estimate is nothing more than a **benchmark**. You can buy a more expensive home than the benchmark by using non-conventional sources of financing — but this is usually more risky. On the other hand, you are free to buy a smaller home than the benchmark. In fact, you can even choose not to buy a home. We shall discuss the rent versus buy decision later in this chapter.

VALUATION OF A HOME

For most people, buying a home is the biggest investment in their lives. Until recently, most people believed that houses are the best investments one can buy; indeed, real estate was a good investment during the boom of the 1970s and the early part of the 1980s when house prices skyrocketed in many parts of Canada, especially in large cities like Toronto and Vancouver. In the "go-go" years of the real estate market, some went so far as to think that a person was financially ignorant not to own a home. Many so-called financial experts advised people to buy the biggest possible home that they could afford — which meant borrowing up to a family's debt capacity. Realtors would say that the best time to buy a house was always "NOW": prices of houses would keep on climbing.

The collapse of the real estate market in the late 1980s and the early 1990s in most of Canada[5] reminds us of something that the shrewd investors have always known — that investing in a home, just like investing in any other type of investment, is a **risky** business. There is always a possibility of losing money. The value of a house, like almost any investment, can rise, fall or remain constant over time.

The House as an Investment

There are two important characteristics of any investment: (1) the **return on investment** and (2) the **risk**. Investing in one's home certainly has these characteristics, too.

There are two sources of return from a home. First, there is the potential capital gain. If you buy a home today for $100,000 and sell it in five years for $150,000, then you will have earned a capital gain of $50,000. Under current Canadian tax law, the capital gain on your home — formally, it is called your **principal residence** — is tax exempt. Second, if you invest in a home, you save on the rental expenses you would otherwise have to pay. This is called the **imputed rental income** of your home. Under

---

[5] In the same period, the real estate market suffered major setbacks in the U.S.A. and Japan as well.

the current tax law, the imputed rental income is also tax exempt; therefore, by investing in a home, you expect to earn an after-tax rate of return on your investment which is composed of the total **imputed rental income** plus the total expected **capital gain**.

Example 12.7: Ronald and Catherine Allan are the proud owners of their three-bedroom detached house which they bought recently for $200,000. To rent a similar house in the same neighbourhood would cost about $1,500 per month, exclusive of utilities. On the other hand, if the Allans were renting such a home, they would not have to pay the property taxes and maintenance of $2400 per annum ($200 a month). Furthermore, historical data show that the prices of homes in that neighbourhood have been increasing at about 3% per year. What is the expected rate of return on the Allans's investment?

The expected rate of return

= the return from the imputed rental income

  + the expected capital gain

$$= \left[\frac{(\$1,500 - 200) \times 12}{200,000} \right] + 3\%$$

$$= 7.8\% + 3\%$$

$$= 10.8\%$$

Since the imputed rental income and the capital gain income are both tax exempt, the 10.8% is the after-tax rate of return on investment.

Is this a good investment for the Allans? The answer depends on two things: (1) How risky is the home? What is the historical price variation of home prices in that neighbourhood? (We will discuss the nature of risk in greater depth in the next chapter.); and (2) Can the Allans earn an after-tax rate of return of 10.8% on investments of similar risk as their home? If they cannot, then the home is a good investment.

Although the return from a home investment is tax-exempt, the expenses are not tax-deductible. The usual expenses associated with home ownership are: interest on mortgages, insurance, property taxes, utilities and maintenance. A landlord renting the property to you can deduct these expenses, however. Part of this tax shield is reflected in the level of rents; so there are also implicit tax advantages to renting.

Non-financial Aspect of Home Ownership

A home is not just an investment. It is one of the few investments that has both utilitarian and enjoyment value: in short, it is a place to live that provides its owner with a very real and personal pride of ownership. And even though a similar home in the same neighbourhood can conceivably be rented more cheaply, renting a property does not give a person the same unquantifiable pride of ownership as does owning a home. Consequently, it may very well be the case that it is partly for this reason that studies have found that most people prefer home ownership to renting shelter; it may very well be that the superior performance of real estate over other investments in the 1970s and the first half of the 1980s does not constitute the entire reason for this finding. Home ownership also offers security of tenure, and the right to decorate as you please. These subjective values may not have measurable market values by themselves, but they do affect house prices.

HOW DO YOU VALUE A HOUSE?

The market value of most investments such as stocks and bonds are readily observable. You can find out the latest price of a stock by calling a stockbroker. In contrast to that, the price of a home is not observable. The market value of a home must be estimated and the process of estimating a home's value is called **appraisal**. If the market value of a home is not observable, what do people mean when they use the term **market value**?

Market Value

The **market value** of a home is defined as the highest price that a willing buyer will pay if the house is exposed for sale in the open market allowing a reasonable time to find a willing buyer with neither the buyer nor the seller acting under necessity, compulsion or any peculiar circumstances.

The above definition suggests that one can find good deals (or undervalued properties) if the seller is under financial pressure or distress. For example, one may find good buys if there is a power of sale, loss of employment, or a marriage break-up.

Valuation Approaches

There are two common methods for valuing a home: the **Direct Market Comparison Approach** and the **Cost Approach**. We will describe each method and use a numerical example to illustrate how each method works.

The **Direct Market Comparison (DMC) Approach** is a method of valuing properties by comparing the prices at which similar properties have been sold. Because no two homes are exactly the same, one must make adjustments to the various differences that exist among the properties.

Major Factors that Affect House Value

You have probably heard about the three major factors that affect home value: location, location, location. Clearly, when you buy a house, you are also "buying" the surrounding neighbourhood: the quality of the schools, the crime rate, the neatness of adjacent yards, the quality of the air and so on.

The following is a list of other factors that affect house values:

- lot size
- building size
- number of rooms
- number of baths
- type of construction (e.g., all brick, brick veneer, aluminum siding etc.)
- number of garages
- number of fireplaces
- family or recreation room
- deck
- recent sale prices of homes in the area
- other factors

To apply the **direct market comparison approach** to value a home, you must first locate a number of properties that are as similar as possible to the **subject property** (i.e., the home that is to be appraised) and have recently been sold in the local market. Detailed information for each sale can be acquired from the city, county, township, registry or land title offices, and the local real estate board. The best way to illustrate the **direct market comparison approach** is by an example.

The following information has been gathered by David Hudson who wants to appraise a house that he intends to buy (the subject property). He has also collected information on four comparable homes that have been sold in the last year.

The subject property is a three-year-old, all-brick home located on a 45' × 110' lot in a good residential subdivision. The house size is 2240 square feet; it has a finished recreation room, one four-piece bathroom and no garage. There is a fireplace in the living room which is estimated to add $3,000 to the value of the house. The information about the four comparable sales is summarized as follows:

Sale 1:   sold six months ago for $167,400. All features are similar to the subject property except the following: house size = 2120 s.f.; lot size = 40' × 100'; it has one four-piece bathroom and one two-piece bathroom, and a single-car, attached garage which is expected to add $3,000 to the sale price.

Sale 2:   sold recently for $189,000; it has no fireplace or recreation room; lot size = 50' × 110'; house size = 2340 s.f.; the property has a heat pump which is expected to add $2,000 more to the house's value; other things are similar to subject property.

Sale 3:   sold 12 months ago for $165,000; lot size = 55' × 105'; it has a recreation room but no fireplace; it has a single garage; it is on a corner lot and corner lot properties sell for about $3,000 less than similar houses; other features are similar to subject property.

Sale 4:   sold last week for $192,000; it is on a ravine lot which is quantifiably superior to the subject property by about $4,000; lot size = 45' by 110'; it has one four-piece and one two-piece washroom; there is no recreation room or garage but there is a walkout basement which is expected to add $2,000 to value; other features are similar to the subject property.

An analysis of the real estate market indicates that a two-piece washroom adds $1,500 to value, recreation rooms, $2,000, and sales prices have risen gradually and evenly by 10% over the last year. Lots in the area sell for $500/front foot and the depth of the lot does not add much value. The present construction cost for this type of dwelling is $40/s.f.

Summary of Data

It is useful to summarize the relevant information in a table, such as Table 12.1. The table is very useful because it shows clearly how each comparable sale differs from the subject property. We have to make an adjustment for every difference.

The Adjustment Process

Adjustments are made for each of the differences between the comparable sale and the subject property. The idea is to adjust the comparable properties so that they become as similar as possible to the subject property. Let us illustrate this by comparing the subject

	Subject Property	Sale 1	Sale 2	Sale 3	Sale 4
	TABLE 12.1				
	Summary of Relevant Information				
Sale Price	N/A	167.4M	189.0M	165.M	192.0M
Sale Time	now	6 mon.	recent	1 yr.	recent
Location	address	similar	similar	corner	ravine
Lot size	45 × 110	40 × 100	50 × 110	55 × 105	45 × 110
House size	2240sf	2120sf	2340sf	same	same
Washrooms	1	1 1/2	1	1	1 1/2
Garage	0	1	1	1	0
Fireplace	1	1	0	0	1
Rec. room	1	1	0	1	0
Extras	—	—	Heat Pump	—	Walk-out bsmt.

property to Sale 1. First, Sale 1 was sold six months ago, at a time when there was an increase of 5% in selling prices; therefore, we have to add a time adjustment to its sale price. The time adjustment is equal to ($167,400 × .05) or $8,370. This is an "add" adjustment because if the house were to be sold today it would be sold for a 5% higher price. Second, the Sale 1 property has a smaller lot size (40' × 100') than that of the subject property (45' × 100'). We have to "add" a lot size adjustment to Sale 1 to bring it to the same as the subject property. Since lots sell for $500/front foot, we "add" ($500 × 5) or $2,500 to Sale 1. The third difference is in the home size — the subject property has 2240 s.f. versus Sale 1's house size of 2120 s.f. Since construction cost is $40/s.f., the home size adjustment is [(2240 − 2120) × $40] or $4,800. We have to add this to Sale 1 to bring it to the same home size as the subject property. The fourth difference is in the number of washrooms — subject property (one four-piece) versus Sale 1 (one four-piece and one two-piece). We have to "subtract" a two-piece washroom from Sale 1, or $1,500, to make it similar to the subject property. The result of all the adjustments as shown in Table 12.2.

> **Exercise:** Make the necessary adjustments to each of the comparable properties — Sale 2, Sale 3 and Sale 4 — and check your answer in Table 12.2.

Reconciliation — the Final Step

If you look at the bottom line of Table 12.2, you will see four different adjusted sale prices: each one is an indicated value of the **market value** of the subject property. The process of reducing this series of value indications to a final estimate of value is called **reconciliation**.

In order to reconcile the adjusted sale prices, you should:

- check all calculations
- discard sales that require extreme adjustments
- choose the sales with the highest degree of comparability with the subject property
- make the final value estimate

TABLE 12.2
Adjustments for Direct Market Comparison

	Sale 1	Sale 2	Sale 3	Sale 4
Sale Price	167,400	189,000	165,000	192,000
Time	+ 8,370		+ 16,500	
Location			+ 3,000	− 4,000
Lot Size	+ 2,500	− 2,500	− 5,000	
Home Size	+ 4,800	− 4,000		
Washrooms	− 1,500			− 1,500
Garage	− 3,000	− 3,000	− 3,000	
Fireplace		+ 3,000	+ 3,000	
Rec. Room		+ 2,000		+ 2,000
Extras		− 2,000		− 2,000
Total adjustments	+ 11,170	− 6,500	+ 14,500	− 5,500
Adjusted Sale Price	178,570	182,500	179,500	186,500

In our example, Sale 1 and Sale 3 are not recent sales and therefore cannot be considered as ideal comparables. Of the remaining two, Sale 4 requires the least number of adjustments. Thus, the indicated value of the subject property is $187,000 (to the nearest thousand). The direct market comparison approach can be used only if there are sales of comparable homes in the recent past and the data about those sales are available. Sometimes there are homes that are quite unique in their features — e.g., a newly-build "monster" home with unique structures — for which there are few, if any, comparable sales available. In this case, the **cost approach** can be used to value the home.

The idea behind the **cost approach** is that at any point in time, home values cannot rise above their **reproduction cost**. The cost approach involves four basic steps:

1. Estimate the value of the land.
2. Estimate the cost of reproducing the existing home as though it were new.
3. Estimate the accrued depreciation suffered by the home from all causes — such as wear and tear, obsolescence, and so on.
4. Add the value of the land (Step 1) and the value of the reproduction cost (Step 2), then subtract all accrued depreciation (Step 3) to arrive at an estimate of the **market value** of the home.

Before we proceed, it is important to distinguish between **reproduction cost** and **replacement cost**.

Reproduction Cost — This is the cost of exactly reproducing the subject property using identical or highly similar materials at current costs.

Replacement Cost — This is the cost of replacing the subject property with a new structure of the same size and utility using current technology, materials and equipment instead of trying to reproduce it detail by detail. In the **cost approach**, it is the **reproduction cost** that we are using in Step 2. We will now use an example to illustrate the cost approach.

Example 12.8: You are asked to estimate the market value of a bungalow (using the cost approach). You find that the present construction cost per square foot (s.f.) for this type and quality of structure[6] is $54.94. After measuring the bungalow very carefully, you estimate that its area is approximately 1250 s.f. The lot size is 55′ × 105′ and lots in the area sell for $350/front foot. Your personal inspection of the house reveals the need for interior and exterior painting which will cost $1,450 and $1,960, respectively. A window is damaged and the estimated replacement cost is $420. The flooring is broadloom and you notice that about 700 s.f. is worn out. The cost of replacing it with similar quality broadloom is $2.50/s.f. There are no other indications of depreciation that you can find.

Since there have been no transactions — buying or selling of similar types of homes — in the last two years, you cannot use the direct market comparison approach to estimate the home's value; consequently, you have decided to use the cost approach.

Step 1   Estimation of land value
= $350 × 55 = $19,250

Step 2   Estimation of reproduction cost
= ($54.94 × 1,250) = $68,675

Step 3   Estimation of all accrued depreciation:

Interior painting	$1,450
Exterior painting	1,960
Replacing window	420
New broadloom ($2.5 × 700)	1,750
Total accrued depreciation	$5,580

Step 4   Market value by the cost approach
= land value + reproduction cost − accrued depreciation
= $19,250 + $68,675 − $5,580
= $82,345

SHOULD YOU BUY OR RENT?

You can either rent or buy a home. Is there a theoretical framework whereby one can analyze this buy versus rent decision? The answer is yes. It turns out to be a very simple cash-flow analysis of the two alternatives. You list all the cash flows required under home ownership and also all the cash-flows required under renting and compare the two. We shall illustrate by an example.

Example 12.9: Jack and Jill are considering buying a $150,000 two-bedroom condominium and living in it for three years. They have saved up $48,000 to be used for a down payment and for covering

[6] There are many sources of information about the construction cost of various types of homes and buildings (for example, the Schedule of Unit Costs 1993 published by the Toronto Real Estate Board).

closing costs (estimated to be about $3,000). They will take out a first mortgage at an interest rate of 8% p.a., to be amortized over 25 years. Apart from the monthly mortgage payments, there are other home ownership costs which are estimated as follows:

Property taxes	$2,400/year
Insurance Premium	360/year
Condominium Maintenance Fee	3,600/year

Alternatively, they can rent the condominium at $1,200/month. If they rent, they do not have to pay property taxes, insurance, and condominium fees — the landlord will pay. They can invest money to earn an after-tax rate of return of 5%. They expect that rent will increase at a rate of 4% per year; likewise, the same rate of increase is expected for property taxes, insurance premiums and condominium maintenance fees. Should they buy or rent?

Assume that the value of the condominium will appreciate at 4% per annum. There is also an initial one-time cost of home ownership: the down payment of $45,000 plus the closing cost of $3,000 = $48,000.

If they choose to rent and not buy, they can invest the $48,000 to earn 5% after-tax return. After three years, the compound value of the $48,000 will be ($48,000 × 1.05^3) = $55,566.

Their annual home ownership costs are summarized in Table 12.3.

The last row in Table 12.3 represents the money available for investment every year if they choose to rent instead of buy. At an after-tax rate of return of 5%, this stream of investment will become:

$$\$1,576.49 \times 1.05^2 + (1,254.89 \times 1.05) + \$920.43$$

$$= \$3,976.14.$$

TABLE 12.3
Jack and Jill
Annual Home Ownership Cost

Annual Cost	Year 1	Year 2	Year 3
Mtg. Payment*	$ 9,616.49	$ 9,616.49	$ 9,616.49
Property taxes	2,400.00	2,496.00	2,595.84
Insurance	360.00	374.40	389.38
Condo Fees	3,600.00	3,744.00	3,893.76
Gross Home-ownership Costs	$15,976.49	$16,230.89	$16,495.47
Rent	(14,400.00)	(14,976.00)	(15,575.04)
Net Home-ownership Costs	$ 1,576.49	$ 1,254.89	920.43

* Principal = $105,000; interest = 8%; amortization = 25 years.

The total amount of money that they will have at the end of three years if they choose to rent instead of buy = \$55,566 + \$3,976.14 = \$59,542.

If they buy the condo unit, the value of the condo after three years = (\$150,000 × 1.04^3) = \$168,730.

The amount of the mortgage outstanding after 3 years = \$100,438 (You should be able to check this by now!)

The amount of home equity that they will have = \$168,730 − \$100,438 = \$68,292.

Their equity under the "buy" is therefore greater than their equity under "rent" (\$68,292 versus \$59,542). Thus, in this example, Jack and Jill are better off buying than renting.

The above example is used to explain the framework to analyse buy versus rent. Clearly, it is not always true that buy is better than rent. Indeed, we want you to show in the following exercise that renting is better than buying.

Exercise: Assuming all the information of Example 12.9 holds except that the value of the condominium increases at the rate of 2% per year, and that Jack and Jill can rent the condominium unit for \$1,000/month. Should they rent or buy?

Answer: They should rent.

OTHER ISSUES IN BUYING A HOME

How Do I Know It Isn't a Lemon?   You don't. You have to do your homework, but there are no guarantees. Questions such as the suitability of the location, the number and type of rooms etc., are personal matters that you should judge for your own family interests.

What you may not be capable of judging is more technical matters, like the soundness of construction. Perhaps you have a good friend or relative who is knowledgeable and will look over a prospective house with you. If you have found a house that suits all your other needs and all you are worried about is if it really is what it appears, most urban areas have firms of consulting engineers or home-assessment experts. The sorts of things these assessors do is look for signs of structural damage or flaws, e.g. termites, concealed fire damage, crumbling foundations, leaks, rotted beams. One of them will examine the house in some detail and write a report on good or bad items, for a fee of \$200–\$500. If you are concerned about someone else buying the house while you wait for the report, you can make an offer conditional on an acceptable assessment.

Another way to protect against specific problems is to include a **warranty** in the offer to purchase the home. The warranty says that the purchase is conditional on certain conditions being met. For example, the seller might warrant the house against containing any asbestos insulation (which is very messy to check for, and both expensive and hazardous to remove). If it subsequently proves to have asbestos, the buyer has legal recourse against the seller for the cost to remove it and any other expenses. Sellers are rarely willing to accept many warranties, however.

If you can't afford the cost of an assessor and have no relatives or friends who can help, you may wish to learn more about how to assess a house. There are books written on the subject, but we will confine our discussion to personal finance, and leave you to pursue this at your local library.

Lawyers and More Lawyers   You don't need a lawyer to handle the purchase or sale of a house, but we would advise that you hire one. Real estate transactions are bread and butter for most lawyers, and they know all the pitfalls. The most important job they perform is the **title search**. They check the land records to ensure that the seller owns the property and that there are no undisclosed debts or restrictions on it. In most cases they guarantee the validity of the transfer of the property, so that if you later discover some further debts or liens, or a defect in the title, and you lose money, they will reimburse you.

In addition, lawyers will help you file the various legal documents required, and will advise you on things like land-transfer taxes or other taxes exacted by the provincial government.

As there is quite a bit of competition for legal business these days, you should shop around a bit to get a reasonable fee. Some lawyers will quote fixed fees for standard real estate transactions. The fee will still be several hundred dollars.

If you are determined to do the legal work yourself, be prepared to spend some time reading, and then some time going to various offices. Any business bookstore carries one or more books that contain detailed instructions and appropriate forms to enable you to do the legal work yourself. Personally, we prefer to hire lawyers.

SUMMARY

This chapter covers one of the biggest commitments in many people's financial affairs — buying a home and taking out a mortgage. The most common type of mortgage is the **conventional mortgage** loaned by the banks, loan and trust companies. These institutions use credit standards such as **GDS** or **TDS** ratios to qualify potential borrowers. The usual rule of thumb is that they will lend up to 75% of the home's value and up to 30% of the borrower's GDS ratio. There are five important **elements** in a mortgage: the **Principal, Interest, Term, Payment Period,** and **Amortization Period.** These elements can be found easily from the mortgage contract. Based on these five elements, we can carry out all the mathematics on **mortgage financing**. We can calculate the **equivalent monthly compounding rate**, the **monthly mortgage payments**, the **out-standing principal** and so on. We can also examine the effect of changes in the interest rate and the amortization period on the monthly payments.

How much home you can afford depends upon (1) how much money you have that can be used as **down payment** and (2) how much you can borrow. If you do not have enough down payment, you should set that as one of your financial goals. You are free to buy a smaller home than you can afford. You can even choose to rent instead of buying. A framework to analyse the rent versus the buy decision has been discussed.

The **market value** of a home is not observable. The process of estimating the market value of a home is called **appraisal**. Two methods of valuing a home have been described — the **direct market comparison approach** and the **cost approach**.

Finally, a home is not just an investment. It is also an asset that you can enjoy. It provides the pride of ownership and other utilities. A home generates a rate of return on investment in two ways: there is the **imputed rental income** and the potential **capital gain**. Both are tax-exempt income. On the other hand, interest expenses on the home mortgages are not tax deductible. Investing in a home, just like any other investment, is a **risky** business. There is no guarantee of a positive return on investment.

KEY TERMINOLOGY

mortgage financing / home mortgage / mortgage / right of redemption / equity of redemption / mortgager / mortgagee / first mortgage / second mortgage / third mortgage / principal / interest / amortization / amortization period / blended payments / term / maturity date / conventional mortgage / default / power of sale / five elements of a mortgage / compounding period / repayment period / stated rate of interest / equivalent monthly compounding rate / outstanding principal / outstanding balance / GDS ratio / TDS ratio / down payment / minimum down payment / vendor-take-back (VTB) mortgage / seller financing / return on investment / principal residence / imputed rental income / capital gain / appraisal / market value of a home / direct market comparison approach / subject property / the adjustment process / reconciliation / comparable sales / the cost approach / replacement cost / reproduction cost / buy versus rent decision / gross home ownership costs / net home ownership costs

DISCUSSION QUESTIONS

1. Define or explain each of the terms under **Key Terminology**.
2. What is used as security in (i) a first mortgage (ii) a second mortgage and (iii) a third mortgage?
3. Describe how each of the following would affect one's blended monthly mortgage payments:
    (i) an increase in the mortgage rate of interest;
    (ii) a decrease in the amortization period;
    (iii) an increase in the length of the term without a change in interest rates.

PROBLEMS

1. The current mortgage rates on three-year and five-year mortgages are 8% and 8.5% respectively. Both rates are semi-annual compounding rates.
    (a) Calculate the equivalent monthly compounding rates.
    (b) If you borrow $150,000, what is the monthly payment under each alternative?
    (c) What will be the outstanding balance of the mortgage at the maturity date if you:
        (i) borrow the three-year term?
        (ii) borrow the five-year term?
    (d) What are the advantages and disadvantages of a three-year term (at a lower rate) versus a five-year term (at a higher rate)?

2. A bank quotes a rate of 7.75% for a three-year residential mortgage of $100,000, with a 25-year amortization period.
    (a) What is the effective annual rate?
    (b) How much are the monthly payments?
    (c) How much will you owe at the end of one year? At the end of three years?
    (d) How much interest will you pay during the second year of the mortgage?

3. Joe and Maria Vincente recently bought their dream home. They financed it with a two-year mortgage loan from the Royal Bank of Newfoundland for $170,000. The

nominal rate of interest on the loan is 8.75%., compounded semi-annually. They chose a 25-year amortization period.

(a) Calculate the monthly blended payment.

(b) Calculate the balance of the loan outstanding at the end of two years.

(c) If they renew the mortgage at the end of two years at a new rate of interest of 11% p.a., what will be the new monthly payment, given an amortization period of 23 years?

4. You have a five-year mortgage on your house with two years remaining on it with the Tottery Dominion Bank (TD). The quoted interest rate is 11.25%, the principal amount when you took out the mortgage was $90,000 and the amortization period was 25 years.

(a) How much are your monthly payments?

(b) How much principal do you owe now?

(c) Collapsible Trustco (CT) offers to pay you $300 to switch your mortgage to it. You would get a five-year mortgage with a 22-year amortization at 8.25%. TD would charge you a three-month interest penalty (i.e. the next three months of interest you would have paid on its mortgage) and $100 in legal fees to cancel its mortgage. Should you make the switch?

(d) In case you didn't notice it, you had to make a critical assumption to answer part (c). What was it? [**Hint**: Think about why we specified CT's mortgage to have a 22-year amortization instead of the more usual 25 years. It was one step in making the question easier.]

5. The Canadian Imperialist Bank of Capitalism (CIBC) offers Muhammad Datoo a rate of 8.5% on a $100,000 mortgage on his home. The term is five years; the amortization period is 25 years. Mortgage broker 'Honest' Hovig Moushian finds him an otherwise identical private mortgage at 8.375%, but he will charge Muhammad a $400 finder's fee.

(a) Which mortgage should Muhammad take?

(b) What assumption did you make to be able to solve part (a)?

(c) How much would Muhammad owe at the end of five years if he took the CIBC mortgage?

6. Jonathan and Janice Bromstein have just bought a $200,000 house. They paid $70,000 cash for a down payment and took out a first mortgage for the remainder of the price. It is a five-year term mortgage with an interest rate of 9% p.a. semi-annual compounding, to be amortized over 25 years. The Bromsteins expect their house will appreciate in value at 5% per year.

Required:

(a) What is the monthly mortgage payment?

(b) What is the outstanding principal at the end of the term?

(c) What is the Bromsteins's equity in their home at that time?

(d) Is this house a good investment for the Bromsteins? If your answer is "it depends," what does it depend on?

7. Robert and June Campbell have a combined income of $80,000. They always wanted to own their home some day and have saved up $50,000. The property tax of the

kind of homes they are interested in is about $3,000/year. The recent mortgage rates for different terms are quoted by the Royal Bank

Term	Rate % (Semi-annual compounding)
1 year	7.00
2 years	7.50
3 years	8.00
4 years	8.25
5 years	8.50

(a) Using a GDS ratio of 30%, calculate the amount of first mortgage they can get under each term (5 answers).

(b) Now impose the 75%-appraised value rule. Can they get the loan in (a)?

8. Mr. Brian Turner has recently inherited $200,000. Since he does not own a home, he is contemplating buying one in the $200,000 price range. The property tax on the house is about $2,400/year. To rent a house of the same quality in the same neighbourhood costs $1,300/month plus utilities. If he does not buy a house, he plans to invest the money in a term deposit yielding about 5% p.a. His marginal tax rate is 40%. Do you think a home is a good investment for Mr. Turner? Why?

9. Noemi graduated last year from York University with an MBA and is currently working for an environmental consulting firm. Her salary is $44,000, she has savings of $16,000 and no debts. She wants to buy a condominium in downtown Toronto, but the cheapest she can find is $120,000 with property taxes of $2,200 p.a. and condominium fees of $200 per month. The banks rejected her application for a first mortgage, and so she has decided to save her money and buy a similar condominium in three years time. She estimates the rate of inflation of real estate prices will be 3% p.a., and she can earn 6% by investing her savings in Treasury bills. She will also have to pay about $3,000 in legal and moving costs in three years time when she buys the condo.

(a) Why did the banks reject her mortgage application?

(b) How much does she need to save each year to qualify for the first mortgage in three years?

10. Gilles and Lisette are planning to buy a new house in Outremont. They have seen their dream house, which is offered at $300,000. Taxes are currently $3,000 p.a. on this house. Their current home on the south shore is fully paid, and they have received an offer to purchase for $120,000, which leaves $110,000 after paying the realtor and legal fees. They are planning to use this for the down payment, and they will cover other costs from their savings. The residential mortgage rate for a five year term is 7.9%. Their combined gross income is $65,000 p.a. and they will be paying off a student loan for the next six years, at a rate of $229 per month.

(a) How much will their monthly mortgage payment be if they take a five-year term, amortized over 25 years?

(b) Will they qualify for a first mortgage of $190,000 under normal bank lending practices?

(c) If they do get a mortgage, what will be the outstanding balance after four years?

(d) At the end of five years, they can change the terms of the mortgage. Suppose that the interest rate is 7% in five years, and they change to bi-weekly payments of $700. How long would it take them to retire the mortgage?

(e) Suppose that at the end of three years after the initial mortgage, interest rates are 6.5% for a two-year mortgage. For a penalty payment equal to the next month's interest added to the principal, Gilles and Lisette can switch to this rate for the two years remaining in the term of the mortgage, while continuing to make the same monthly payment. Thus, they would pay off the principal faster for two years, until the renewal date. At that time, the terms would again be open, and the bank would adjust the interest rate to the market rate. Should they make the switch?

11. Lillian Thong and Garsen Yap have been married for several years, and have good jobs with a joint income of over $85,000 p.a. They are each 28 years old, and wish to buy a house in Toronto by the time they are 30. The house they want would cost about $250,000 in current dollars, plus $5,000 for moving and legal expenses. Taxes and utilities would cost $3,000 p.a. They live now in a two-bedroom apartment renting at $900/month, heat, light, water and taxes included. They are presently saving about $6000 p.a. They have no children, but plan to have children in their early thirties. Their balance sheet follows:

Lillian Thong and Garsen Yap
Family Balance Sheet

Cash and bank accounts	$ 500
Portfolio of shares and options	85,000
RRSPs	0
Company Pension Plans:	
Lillian	18,000
Garsen	15,000
Two cars (replacement cost)	30,000
Personal stuff	20,000
Liabilities	
Credit cards	3,000
Car loans	8,000

Assume that inflation is expected to be 2% p.a. for the next five years. The investment portfolio is shown at market.

Required:

What advice would you give them about planning for their house purchase? You are responsible for estimating their tax bracket. Five year mortgage rates are currently 8.25%. See also Problem 5 in Chapter 13.

12. John and Lara are considering buying a house, now that their combined gross income is $72,000. They have no debts and no savings to use for a downpayment. Their goal is to buy a house in five years, financed with a first mortgage and no second mortgage. Currently, taxes are $300 per month on houses in the neighbourhood and price range they want. The legal fees, moving costs and other costs are $4,000 in today's dollars. The inflation rate is 4% p.a., and they expect their salaries to rise

by 5% p.a. This question could be done in either real or nominal dollars — explain which you are using and how to interpret the required savings figure in part (b).

(a)   What is the maximum they can afford to pay for a house and still qualify for the first mortgage, assuming they have saved a 25% downpayment?

(b)   How much do they have to save each year to make the downpayment?

13. When Sally and Harry started looking for a house a few months back, they were looking to spend a maximum of $220,000, based on having a $70,000 down payment and being able to afford a $150,000, 8.5% mortgage, amortized over 25 years. With recent reductions in mortgage rates, to 7.4%, they know they can afford a larger, more expensive house; they just don't know how much they can spend.

(a)   What are the monthly payments on an 8.5% mortgage, amortized over 25 years?

(b)   How much mortgage can Sally and Harry afford now that rates have fallen to 7.4%?

(c)   Assume they would have a 5-year renewal term, for each mortgage
   (i)   how much principal would they be owing at renewal?
   (ii)   how much interest would have been paid over the first five years?

14. You are asked to appraise a 15-year-old two-storey house with a double garage on a 35-feet frontage lot. It has two 4-piece and one 2-piece bathrooms. It has a finished recreation room which adds $10,000 to its value. It does not have central airconditioning, and also it does not have a walkout basement. It has a fireplace, and the kitchen has recently been modernized at a cost of $5,000.

In analysing the M.L.S. statistics for this area you found the following average house prices:

1 month ago	$237,500
2 months ago	$236,300
3 months ago	$235,100
6 months ago	$231,700

Using the following comparable sales, determine the market value of the subject property.

Sale #1   Sold 3 months ago for $222,0000. Its age, condition, design, location, number of bathrooms are similar to the subject property. It had a frontage of 32'. In this area each front foot cost $1,000. It had a single garage, a walkout basement, and central airconditioning. Central airconditioning adds $2,000 to the value of the house. Its kitchen had not been upgraded, and the recreation room was unfinished. It also didn't have a fireplace. It had a walkout basement which adds $7,000 to the value.

Sale #2   Sold 1 month ago for $231,000. It had 35' frontage. Its location and design were similar to the subject property. Its condition was inferior to the subject property, requiring an adjustment of $6,000. It didn't have a fireplace or a walkout basement. It had two 4-piece bathrooms and two 2-piece bathrooms. It had a double garage, a finished recreation room and central airconditioning. Double garage requires an adjustment of $3,000 and an additional 2-piece bathroom adds $1,000 to the value. It had original kitchen.

Sale #3   On a 35' frontage lot sold 2 days ago for $239,000. It had a better location, requiring an adjustment of $5,000. Its condition and design were the same as the subject property. It had a double garage and two 4-piece and two 2-piece bathrooms. It had a fireplace which added $2,000 to the value. It also had a finished recreation room and a modern kitchen. It didn't have central airconditioning or a walkout basement.

Sale #4   This house on a 30' frontage lot, with a double garage, central airconditioning, walkout basement, and a finished recreation room sold 6 months ago for $227,000. Its kitchen was never upgraded and it had no fireplace. Its location, design, condition, and number of bathrooms were similar to the subject property.

Summary of Relevant Information

	Subject Property	Sale #1	Sale #2	Sale #3	Sale #4
Sale Price	N/A	$222,000	$231,000	$245,000	$227,000
Sale Time	Now	3 months ago	1 month ago	2 days ago	6 months ago
Location	Address	Similar	Similar	Better	Similar
Lot Size	35'	32'	35'	35'	30'
Physical		Similar	Inferior	Similar	Similar
Washrooms	2-4 & 1-2	2-4 & 1-2	2-4 & 2-2	2-4 & 2-2	2-4 & 1-2
Garage	Double	Single	Double	Double	Double
Fireplace	Yes	No	No	Yes	No
Finished Recr. Rm.	Yes	No	Yes	Yes	Yes
Modern Kitchen	Yes	No	No	Yes	No
Airconditioning	No	Yes	Yes	No	Yes
Walkout Basement	No	Yes	No	No	Yes

15. You are asked to estimate the market value of a 2800 square feet 2-storey house. You find that present construction cost per square foot for this type and quality of structure is $78. The lot size is 46' × 110', and the lots in the area sell for $870 per front foot.

   The personal inspection of the property reveals that a storm door is damaged beyond repair and estimated replacement cost is $350 installed. A window in the living room is damaged and it will cost $900 to replace it.

   House also needs exterior and interior painting which will cost about $4,600. About 200 square metres of broadloom is worn to the point of requiring immediate replacement. The cost to replace it with similar quality broadloom is $39/square metre. No other depreciation is evident.

chapter 13

Principles of Investment

LEARNING OBJECTIVES

Investing is a very important part of personal finance. When people think of personal finance, they immediately think of investing. Of course, you now know that investing — although it is very important — is, nevertheless, just one of the components of personal finance. Most of us have some kind of investments at any point in time. If you have some money in a savings account, you have an investment.

There have been two major developments in the investment world in the last three decades. First, there has been an enormous expansion in scholarly knowledge about investments. Hundreds of research studies about investing have been done both in the business and academic world. As a result, we can fairly say we now know a great deal more about investment than we did 30 years ago. The second development is the enormous explosion of investment products available, even for the small investor. As a result, even the experts find it difficult to keep up with all of the new investments that come to the market every day.

This is the first of three chapters about investing. This chapter describes the fundamentals of investing and discusses the three most important concepts and findings of over 30 years of research. We will call these the **three basic principles of investment**. These principles and the concepts therein are the basic knowledge that you should have before you venture out into the investment world. The next chapter, Chapter 14, introduces and describes the different types of investments available in the Canadian market. Finally, in Chapter 15 we introduce and discuss mutual funds, which provide the most efficient means for small investors to implement their investment programmes.

The specific objectives of this chapter are:

1. To discuss the first basic principle in investment: the **risk-return trade-off**. The basic concepts of **return**, **risk**, **risk premium**, and **risk aversion** will be described.
2. To discuss the second basic principle in investment: "one should diversify." The various aspects of diversification — **diversification over time**, **portfolio diversification**, **international diversification**, and **asset allocation diversification** will be discussed.

211

3.   To discuss the third basic principle in investment: the **efficient market hypothesis**. We shall answer some frequently asked questions such as:
   • Is it possible to make a killing in the stock market by picking the right stocks?
   • Is it possible to time the market (i.e., buy at the bottom and sell at the top)?
   • Can one benefit from looking at charts?
   • Is there any way to "beat" the market?
   • Is it possible for one to get rich from the stock market?

At the end of this chapter, you will have a firm foundation of knowledge about investment. This knowledge is a summary of a substantial part of over 30 years' research in investments. You will then be ready to go to Chapter 14 to examine the different types of investments available in Canada.

Investing and Saving

First, **investing** and **saving** are two different concepts. **Saving** is simply the money that you did not spend; it is money left over after your consumption. Thus, the money that you take from under a pillow and put into a safe or safe-deposit box is **savings**.

What is **investing** then? Investing means using the **savings** that you have and "making it work" — putting it in investments to earn a rate of return. Normally saving money by itself will not be enough to achieve your financial goals. As we have seen in Chapter 3, in goal setting, in order to reach your financial goal, normally you have to earn a minimum rate of return. The only way to earn the required rate of return is by putting money into the right investment that is expected to generate the required rate of return. Thus, you invest because you want to reach your financial goals.

BASIC CHARACTERISTICS OF AN INVESTMENT

All investment — stocks, bonds, real estate, term deposits, gold and so on — have some basic characteristics which affect your investment decisions. The following are the more important characteristics:

1.   Return
2.   Risk
3.   Liquidity
4.   Marketability
5.   Term (short term, long term)
6.   Management
7.   Tax Considerations
8.   Divisibility

While all these characteristics affect an investor's investment decision, the first two — **return** and **risk** — are the most important.

Return on Investment

There are two ways that an investment can earn a return for you: an **income return** and a **capital gain return**. The **income return** is the periodic cash flow that the investor receives. For example, if you have a rental apartment, the periodic rental income (net of all expenses) is the income return. If you own a bond, the interest income that you receive is the income return. In the case of a stock, the dividend income is the income return. A **capital gain return** of an investment is generated when you sell it for a price higher than what you paid for it. For example, if you sell a stock for $20 and you bought it for $15, the **capital gain return** is ($20 − $15) or $5. The **total return** is defined as the **income return** plus the **capital gain return**.

Rate of Return

In order to compare returns of different investments, it is more useful to define **return** in terms of a rate, as follows. The **rate of return** (r) or holding period return (*HPR*) is defined as:

$$r \ (or \ \text{HPR}) = \frac{P_1 - P_0 + D}{P_0} \qquad (1)$$

where P_0 = the price at the beginning of the holding period;
       P_1 = the price at the end of the holding period;
       D = the income return (interest or dividend) during the holding period.

> **Example 13.1** John bought a stock at the beginning of the year for $20. At the end of the year he sold it for $25. During the year he received total dividend income of $1. The rate of return (r) or the holding period return (*HPR*) is equal to [($25 − $20 + $1) ÷ $20] or 30%.

Note that for a bank account or a Canada Savings Bond (because there is no capital gain) the rate of return is simply the rate of interest.

Expected Return *E(r)* vs. Realized Return   The **realized rate of return** is the rate of return that has actually occurred in a past period. If we look at any historical period — such as the year January 1, 1991 to December 31, 1991, or the period from February 15, 1990 to March 31, 1990 — all the prices and the income are known with certainty, so we simply calculate the rate of return actually earned during that period, using equation (1). The **realized rate of return** can be positive, zero, or negative.

The **expected rate of return** is the return that is expected to happen in the future. It is what we are expecting to earn for buying and holding the investment. More precisely, the expected rate of return, *E(r)* is defined by:

$$E(r) = \frac{E(P_1) - P_0 + E(D)}{P_0} \qquad (2)$$

where P_0 = the price today, or the beginning of the period;
       $E(D)$ = the expected income during the period.

> **Example 13.2:** Tony received a call today from his stockbroker who recommended a stock currently selling for $10. The stockbroker said his company's research department had just published a very favourable forecast on the stock. According to the report the stock price is expected to rise to $20 after one year. Last year the stock paid a dividend of $1. It is not expected that the

company will increase its dividend in the near future. Based on the stockbroker's information, what is the expected rate of return?

Assuming Tony forms his expectation according to the broker's research report, then he would expect the stock price, $E(P_1)$, to be $20; and he would expect to receive dividends, $E(D)$, of $1. Hence, the expected rate of return is

$$E(r) = \frac{E(P_1) - P_0 + E(D_1)}{P_0}$$

$$= \frac{(20 - 10 + 1)}{10} = 110\%$$

Note that in the above example, the rate of return is not guaranteed because the future price and dividends are uncertain. The actual rate of return may turn out to be higher or lower than 110% — this is what risk is about.

INVESTMENT RISKS

What do people mean when they say an investment is **risky**? To some people, this simply means the probability of losing their invested money. In other words, risk means the probability of a negative rate of return on investment: the higher the probability of a negative rate of return, the higher the risk of the investment. This, however, is only one type of risk.

Suppose the rate of return on a stock was 6% during a period when the rate of return on a term deposit was 8%. Even though the rate of return on the stock was not negative, it was still a "loss" because you could have earned a higher return of 8% in a term deposit. You would not have put your money in the stock if you had known for sure that the return would be 6%. This suggests a more precise definition and measure of risk.

Risk is the uncertainty about the rate of return that you will earn from an investment. One way to measure risk is the **variability** in an investment's rate of return. Investments with more variability in their rate of return are riskier than investments with less variability, because the larger the variability, the higher the probability of getting a rate of return lower than the expected rate of return.

A more formal treatment is to look at the rate of return, r, defined in equation (1), as a random variable. At the time you make the investment, only P_0 is known; P_1 and D are future values and, as such, are uncertain. Because P_1 and D are random variables r is also a random variable. The expected value of the random variable r is the expected rate of return, $E(r)$. The most commonly-used measure of the variability (or the spread) of a random variable is the *standard deviation*.[1] In the investment literature, one of the popular measures of risk is the standard deviation of the rate of return.

---

[1] We assume that the reader knows the basic statistical concepts of expected value (or mean) and standard deviation. See next section for formulas.

TABLE 13.1
Annual Return Series 1950–1995

Investment	Arithmetic Mean (%)	Standard Deviation (%)
Treasury Bills	6.41	3.89
Long Cda Bonds	7.40	10.65
Common Stocks	11.99	17.10
U.S. Stocks	13.58	17.25
International Stocks*	16.71	14.33
Inflation	4.36	3.52

* Morgan & Stanley World Index 1971–1995.
Source: PlanPlus Inc.

TABLE 13.2
Range in which 68% of the Investment Returns Would Fall

Investments	Range
Treasury-Bills*	6.41% ± 3.89% = 2.52% to 10.30%
Long Cda Bonds	7.40% ± 10.65% = –3.25% to 18.05%
Common Stocks	11.99% ± 17.10% = –5.11% to 29.09%
U.S. Stocks	13.58% ± 17.25% = –3.67% to 30.83%
International Stccks	16.71% ± 14.33% = 2.38% to 31.04%

* least risky

Table 13.1 shows the historical average rate of return and standard deviation of some major Canadian investments.

The last column is the **standard deviation**, based on historical data from 1950 to 1995, of the different investments. Using the standard deviation as a measure of risk, we see that stocks are the riskiest, long-term bonds are less risky and, as expected, government Treasury bills are the least risky.

To further elaborate on why the standard deviation is a measure of risk, let us assume that the rates of return are normally distributed for all four investments: Treasury bills, long-term bonds, common stocks and small company stocks. From basic statistics, 68% of the investment's returns over the period will fall between the mean minus the standard deviation and the mean plus the standard deviation. Table 13.2 shows the ranges for the four investments. Note that the bigger the standard deviation, the bigger the range (or spread) and the bigger the **variability** in the investment's rate of return. In other words, the bigger the standard deviation, the greater the risk of the investment.

Another Measure of Risk: Beta

In the academic investment literature, there is another measure of risk of an investment. This measure of risk is called **beta**. It measures the co-movement of the stock's return with the stock market's return. Beta measures the risk of the investment relative to the risk of the market. The higher the value of beta, the more sensitive the stock is to moves in the market. Beta is defined in such a way that the stock market has a beta of 1. Here, the stock market is usually represented by a market index; the TSE 300 is an example. If a stock has a beta of .5, this means its risk is only half that of the TSE 300. If the stock has a beta of 2, this means its risk is two times that of the TSE 300.

Total Risk

The idea of using the **standard deviation**[2] of an investment's **rate of return** is a fundamental concept in academic investment literature. The **total risk** of an investment is defined as the **standard deviation** of its rate of return. Thus, the total risk measures the total variability or volatility of an investment. Since investment decisions are based on future returns, much care must go into estimating the expected returns and the expected risk statistics (i.e., standard deviation, or beta) for all the investments under consideration. This is the security analyst's job. There are books that describe explicitly the techniques and the procedures that security analysts use to estimate risk and return statistics;[3] it is beyond the scope of this book to go into these estimation techniques in depth.

For most investments, there are two ways to formulate a probability distribution (including the expected value and the standard deviation) of the possible rates of return. First, an **objective probability distribution** is formed by measuring objective historical data. For example, one can estimate the mean and the standard deviation of the rate of return on a stock (for example, the common stock of the Bank of Montreal) by using five years of monthly data. In other words, one calculates the actual rate of return for each month of an historical five-year period and then uses basic statistical formulae to calculate the mean and the standard deviation. One then uses this historical probability distribution as an approximation for the future probability distribution. This approach is useful only if the investment's rate of return probability distribution is stationary — in other words, if it does not change — over time. Fortunately, empirical studies have found that most firms' probability distributions of rates of return and the statistics describing them (e.g., the mean and the standard deviation), do not seem to change very much over time. Thus, using **objective probability distribution** is very popular, at least as a first approximation.

The second method for estimating an investment's probability distribution is to forecast the future in some way. A **subjective probability distribution** is formed by writing down one's perception of all the possible rates of return of the investment and then assigning probabilities to them. Table 13.3 is an example of a subjective probability distribution of the rate of return on an investment.

Recall from basic statistics that the expected rate of return, *E(r)* (i.e., the expected value) and the standard deviation (*S.D.*) are given by (1) and (2):

$$E(r) = \sum_i P_i r_i \qquad (1)$$

---

[2] Some people use the variance, which is simply the square of the standard deviation.
[3] For example, J.C. Francis and E. Kirzner, *Investments Analysis and Management*, First Canadian Edition, McGraw Hill Ryerson 1988.

TABLE 13.3
Example of a Subjective Probability Distribution

Outcome (possible rate of return), r_i	Subjective probability of the outcome, p_i
.35	.10
.25	.15
.15	.20
.10	.30
−.05	.15
−.20	.10
	1.00

$$S.D. = \left[\sum_i P_i[r_i - E(r)]^2 \right]^{1/2}$$

(2)

The expected rate of return of the investment in Table 13.3 is:

$= (.35 \times .10) + (.25 \times .15) + (.15 \times .20) + (.10 \times .30)$
$- (.05 \times .15) - (.20 \times .10)$
$= .105$ or 10.5%

The standard deviation (*S.D.*) on the rate of return, using equation (2), is:

$= \{[.10 \times (.35 - .105)^2] + [.15 \times (.25 - .105)^2]$
$+ [.20 \times (.15 - .105)^2] + [.30 \times (.10 - .105)^2]$
$+ [.15 \times (-.05 - .105)^2] + [.1 \times (-.20 - .105)^2]\}^{1/2}$
$= (.0225)^{1/2}$
$= .150$ or 15%

Most financial and scientific calculators have functions that will calculate mean and standard deviation for you. To get them to calculate expected values using probabilities, you may need to trick the calculator by multiplying the probabilities by 100 and calling them frequencies. The mean and standard deviation of a distribution of 10 outcomes at 35%, 15 outcomes at 25% etc., are the same as for a distribution of 10% chance of 35% return, 15% chance of 25% return etc. The exact keys and steps vary by calculator.

The Risk-free Asset

There are investments whose rates of return are guaranteed. In other words, the rate of return is equal to a certain guaranteed rate of return with a probability of one. For this type of investment, there is no variability in the rate and the standard deviation is zero. Such an investment is called a **risk-free asset**. The best example of a risk-free asset is a short-term government **Treasury-bill** or **T-bill**. This is a short-term note issued by the government. T-bills are sold in the money market and are priced in such a way that if you hold them until maturity, the rate of return is guaranteed.

If you invest your money in T-bills, the so-called **risk-free asset**, is your investment really risk-free? The answer is no. First, it depends on inflation. Although T-bills guarantee a nominal rate of return on your investment, it does not guarantee the purchasing power of your money — that would depend on the rate of inflation during the holding period. This is called **inflation risk**. Second, if your investment horizon is longer than the maturity period of the T-bill, which usually has short maturities of 60 days, 90 days, 120 days, and so on up to one year, then you have to reinvest your money into another T-bill when the first one matures. The rate of return on the future T-bill is uncertain. It could be higher or lower than the current rate. This is called **interest rate risk**.

Other Risk Factors

This section introduces some other investment risk factors. The variability of an investment's rate of return is not the only source of risk, even though it is a very important one. As we have discussed, even putting money in the **risk-free asset** is not necessarily risk-free!

Default Risk   **Default risk** is the risk of losing part or all of the future cash flow that the investor expects to get when making the investment initially. For example, when one buys a corporate bond, one expects to receive the promised interest income periodically and the principal when the bond matures. The company may become bankrupt, or run into financial difficulty and therefore be unable to make payments. In this latter case, we say the company has defaulted on its obligation. Other default risks are systematically related to the economy, which affect almost all companies. Some default risks are caused by factors that are unique to the afflicted company, such as losing a lawsuit.

Interest Rate Risk   This is the risk that is caused by the changes in the level of market interest rates, which affect the values of all assets. In general, asset values will rise when interest rates fall and they will fall when interest rates rise.

Liquidity Risk   This is the risk of not being able to cash in your investment in time of need. For example, it may take a long time to sell investments like real estate.

Reinvestment Risk   This is the risk associated with the uncertainty of not knowing at what rates of return your money can be reinvested in the future. Suppose you have a term deposit that will mature next month. Since you do not need the money, you plan to reinvest it then but you do not know the rate of return on your reinvestment.

Inflation Risk   This is the risk that the return on your investment will not keep up with inflation. Investments that are expected to keep pace with inflation are called **inflation hedges**. Normally, short-term financial investments like short-term T-bills or money market funds have little **inflation risk** because their rates will change fast enough to reflect the changing inflation rates.

Risk and Return Trade-off

Risk Aversion   People do not like risk. Given two investments that are identical in every respect except for risk, people will choose the investment with the lower risk. This behaviour is called **risk aversion**.[4] This does not mean that people will not take risk. **Risk aversion** implies only that people require higher returns for taking greater risks.

Return: An Increasing Function of Risk

Assuming that all investors are risk-averse, investments will be priced in the marketplace to reflect this behaviour. In order to induce investors to take risk, some incentive will be given in the form of a higher return. Given two investments, one riskier than the other, they will be priced in the marketplace so that the rate of return on the riskier investment will be higher than that of the less risky one. Over 30 years of research effort has been devoted to establishing this fact rigorously. We will call this the **first fundamental principle in investment**: the expected rate of return on an investment is an increasing function of its risk. The higher the risk of an investment, the higher the expected rate of return. Thus, risk and rate of return go hand in hand. If you want a higher rate of return on your investment, you will have to accept a greater exposure to risk.

Dominance

Given two investments, A and B, if A is always preferred to B for all investors, then we say A **dominates** B. We will provide two examples. First, suppose A and B have the same expected rate of return but B is riskier than A. Then A is always preferred to B by all investors. As a second example, suppose A and B have the same level of risk but A has a higher expected return than B. Then A is always preferred to B by all investors.

We cannot, however, rank all investments by the **dominance** concept. Suppose there are two investments, C and D, and that C is riskier than D but C has a higher expected return. In this case, we cannot make any statement about which dominates which. In the last 30 years, much research effort has been devoted to comparing investments with different risks and returns, and we have now some well-known theories and economic models which measure the **risk-return trade-off**.[5] These theories are quite popular in the academic world and some professional investment managers use them. However, using these theories requires a great deal of data, time and effort: unless you have a huge multi-million-dollar investment portfolio to manage, these theories will not be very useful to you.

As a practical matter, it is more important for you to remember that there are two important attributes of any investment — **risk** and **return** — and they go hand in hand. High returns are generally associated with high risks; this being the case, remember the next time you get a cold call from a stockbroker who recommends a stock that he says will double in a week, the word **risk** should immediately come to your mind. One of the biggest mistakes you can make in the world of investment is to fall for stockbrokers' phone pitches: it is this mistake that causes the investor to end up with a substantial portion of his or her net worth invested in a very risky proposition. We summarize the

---

[4] People who choose the riskier of the two investments are said to be risk-loving. People who are indifferent between the safer investment and the riskier one are said to be risk-neutral. From casual observation, very few people are risk-loving or risk-neutral.

[5] The Capital Asset Pricing Model (CAPM) and the Arbitrage Pricing Theory (APT) are two well-known examples. While they can be used to price any investment, empirical studies found that they are more accurate when used to compare portfolios.

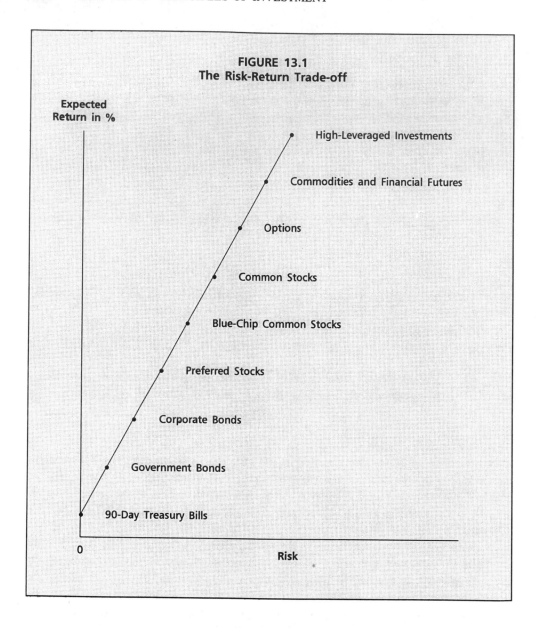

FIGURE 13.1
The Risk-Return Trade-off

Expected
Return in %

High-Leveraged Investments

Commodities and Financial Futures

Options

Common Stocks

Blue-Chip Common Stocks

Preferred Stocks

Corporate Bonds

Government Bonds

90-Day Treasury Bills

0

Risk

risk-return trade-off in Figure 13.1. To reiterate, in the field of investments, there is a positive relationship between **risk** and **return**. The more risk you take, the higher the return that you should expect to get from the investment.

DIVERSIFICATION

Is it possible for one to lower one's investment risk exposure without sacrificing one's expected return on investment? The answer is yes; this is done by the strategy of diversification. **Diversification** means putting one's money into a broad basket of different investments. As we will explain later, for diversification to work, the investments chosen must not be perfectly correlated: this means that the stock prices of the investments chosen do not always move in the same direction (up or down) at the same time.

Diversification is such an important concept in investment that we will call it the **second basic principle of investment**. This principle simply says that you should avoid putting all of your investment eggs in one basket — i.e., you should avoid putting all of your money into a single stock or a single bond issue. By spreading your investment funds among several different issues, you are proving the wisdom of the old saying, "Do not put all your eggs in one basket." Diversification is the risk-averse approach to investing because it involves reducing your risk exposure without necessarily sacrificing expected return on investment.

How Does Diversification Work? An Example

Suppose there are two investments, X and Y. Suppose your expectation of their rates of return are as follows: For half of all the future years, X will give an annual rate of return of 20% and half of the years it will give an annual rate of return of –5%. Y is expected to produce the same pattern: half of the future years it yields 20% and half of the future years it yields –5%. Suppose further that when the rate of return on X is 20%, the rate of return on Y is –5% and when the rate of return on X is –5%, the rate of return on Y is 20%. In other words, we suppose that X and Y are **perfectly negatively correlated** — i.e., they move in exactly opposite directions. When X is at its best, Y is at its worst and vice versa. The expected rates of return on X and Y are, using equation (1), respectively:

$$E(r) \text{ of } X = (.05 \times .20) + (.05 \times -.05) = .075$$

$$E(r) \text{ of } Y = (.05 \times -.05) + (.05 \times .20) = .075$$

The standard deviations of the rates of return of X and Y are, respectively, and using equation (2):

$$\text{S.D. of } X = \{[.05 \times (.20 - .075)^2] + [.5 \times (-.05 - .075)^2]\}^{1/2} = .125$$

$$\text{S.D. of } Y = \{[.05 \times (-.05 - .075)^2] + [.05 \times (.20 - .075)^2]\}^{1/2} = .125$$

Thus, X and Y have the same expected rates of return of 7.5% and the same standard deviations (risk) of 12.5%.

Suppose you have $1,000. If you put all the $1,000 in either X or Y, you will expect to earn 7.5% and your risk exposure will be 12.5%. Now, suppose that you diversify, and allocate your $1,000 equally between X and Y — i.e., suppose that you invest $500 in X and $500 in Y. There are two possible outcomes on your investment. First, the rate of return on X is 20% and the rate of return on Y is –5%, then the rate of return on your investment is equal to:

$$\left[\frac{(\$500 \times .20) + (\$500 \times -.05)}{\$1000} \right] = .075$$

Second, the rate of return on X is –5% and that on Y is 20%, then the rate of return on your investment is equal to:

$$\left[\frac{(\$500 \times -.05) + (\$500 \times .20)}{\$1000}\right] = .075$$

Therefore, you will earn .075 or 7.5% with certainty.[6] This example shows that you can reduce risk — from 12.5% to zero — without sacrificing return, which stays at 7.5%. This is the benefit of diversification. In fact, you can often increase return and reduce risk.

Portfolio Theory

A **portfolio** is a collection of securities, so it is diversified in more than one asset. For example, you can have a stock portfolio which contains 10 stocks, or you can have a bond portfolio which contains five bonds. In the last four decades, economists have built rigorous **portfolio theories** which examine various ways of investing and diversifying efficiently. Such theories can be found in any standard textbook about investment.[7]

The idea behind diversification and portfolio theory, however, is actually very simple. You choose investments that are not highly correlated with each other — that is to say, they do not move at the same time with the same magnitude. When one of the investments in the portfolio experiences a bad year, hopefully there are other investments in the portfolio that are having good years.

From basic statistics, the relationship between the returns on any two investments is expressed by the **correlation coefficient**, which measures the extent to which two sequences of numbers (in this case, the rates of return of two investments) move together. The correlation coefficient can range from −1 to +1. It is usually greater than zero for returns on investments, because most investments are affected in the same way by the same economic factors such as interest rates and the rate of inflation. A correlation coefficient of zero means that the two investments are **uncorrelated**. For **diversification** to work effectively, ideally you should choose investments that are uncorrelated, or better still, **negatively correlated** with each other. Indeed, in our example, the investments X and Y are perfectly negatively correlated and for that reason we are able to derive the maximum reduction in risk — we ended up with a risk-free portfolio whose standard deviation is zero! In practice, however, returns on assets are almost always positively correlated because to some extent they depend on the same economy. Still, for diversification purposes, you should select assets that have low correlation coefficients with each other.

Figure 13.2 shows the reduction in **portfolio risk** (measured by the standard deviation of the rate of return of the portfolio) as assets are added to the portfolio. Empirical studies have found that the bulk of the benefit from diversification is achieved by investing in 15 to 20 stocks. In other words, the major reduction in risk (or standard deviation) is achieved by including about 20 stocks in your portfolio. Further addition of investments in the portfolio will still reduce portfolio risk, but at a much slower pace.

Notice in Figure 13.2 that the risk of the portfolio does not become zero, regardless of how many assets or stocks are added to the portfolio. This means that there is a certain amount of risk which cannot be reduced, no matter what kind of assets, and how many, are added. Thus, even if you hold every asset and every stock in the market, your

---

[6] The standard deviation on the rate of return is zero. Why?

[7] For example, J.C. Francis and E. Kirzner, *Investments Analysis and Management*, First Canadian Edition, McGraw-Hill Ryerson, 1988.

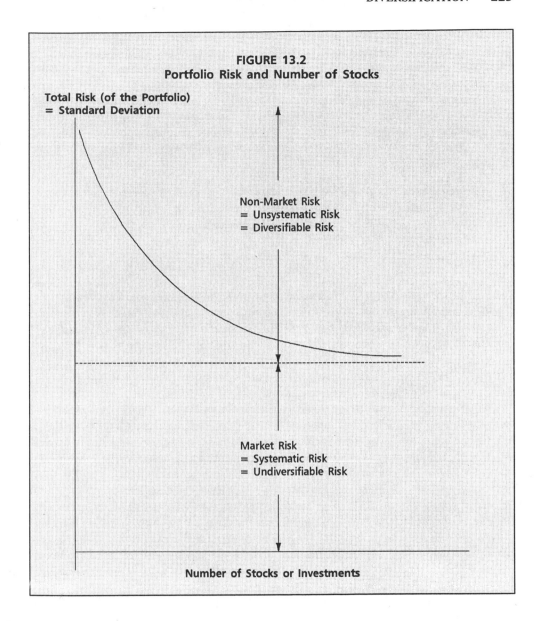

FIGURE 13.2
Portfolio Risk and Number of Stocks

Total Risk (of the Portfolio)
= Standard Deviation

Non-Market Risk
= Unsystematic Risk
= Diversifiable Risk

Market Risk
= Systematic Risk
= Undiversifiable Risk

Number of Stocks or Investments

portfolio is still risky because the entire market and the entire economy are risky. The risk that cannot be diversified away is called the **market risk**, **systematic risk** or **undiversifiable risk**.

Three Dimensions of Diversification

There are three important reasons why you want to diversify your investments. First, you diversify to avoid having your money all tied up in one or a few investments that might do very poorly and wipe out your entire wealth.

Second, you diversify because you cannot perfectly predict the "hot" and the "cold" years of each investment category. In this case, the benefit of diversifying over time is that you avoid doing all the transactions in years with big losses so that you do not lose much on the average annual rate of return over a long time period. Third, you diversify globally to reduce the market risk (or systematic risk or undiversifiable risk or country risk) of the portfolio. As noted earlier, general economic conditions affect most investments within a single country, like Canada. Diversifying across Canadian-based investments will not eliminate or reduce those general market factors — that is why the risk is called **undiversifiable risk** — but investing on an international scale will help. We will call these three reasons and the strategies for dealing with them, the **three dimensions of diversification**:

1. Diversification within each type of investment; e.g., diversification between stocks.
2. Diversification between types of investments. This is sometimes called **asset allocation**; e.g., diversification in bonds, stocks and real estate.
3. Diversification across different countries. This is sometimes called **global diversification** or **international diversification**.

Diversification in Stocks

If you want to invest in the stock market, you should allocate your money among a portfolio of stocks. Two questions must be answered: (1) How many stocks should be bought? (2) How should one choose those stocks?

Recall from earlier discussion (also see Figure 13.2 again) that the major reduction in portfolio risk comes from the first 20 stocks that you include in your portfolio. Thus, you should buy at least 20 different issues. Further addition of stocks to the portfolio will reduce the portfolio's risk but at a slower rate.

Most portfolio managers recommend at least 30 stocks in a portfolio so that the portfolio can be well-diversified, meaning that the **diversifiable risk** (or **unsystematic risk** or **non-market risk**) is almost totally diversified away; however, buying 30 stocks (or even 20) requires a substantial amount of investment capital that is beyond the means of most people. There is another effective way of achieving diversification and that is by purchasing **mutual funds**, a topic which we will leave for Chapter 15.

How should the set of 20 to 30 stocks be picked? As we shall see later, when we introduce the **efficient market hypothesis**, the answer is surprisingly simple. One way to select a well-diversified portfolio is to randomly select the stocks. Although empirical studies have found that this random selection method works very well, most people think that it is counterintuitive. Another way of choosing the stocks is the "armchair" way: let professional experts choose them for you. Once again, this may involve buying one or more **mutual funds**. The matter of selecting mutual funds for investment is a very important topic which we will cover in Chapter 15.

Finally, if you really want to choose the stocks yourself, you may want first to divide the stocks into business or industrial groups (e.g., banks, utilities, consumer products, oil and gas, transportation, gold etc.) and then randomly select two or three stocks within each group. Again, let us emphasize that empirical studies have found that there is little additional benefit from doing this.

Diversification between Types of Investment

Investments are classified into different types. The most common types of investments are cash (short-term safe investments like Treasury bills), bonds and stocks. One can add more to the above list — such as real estate, one's own home, foreign stocks, options, futures, collectibles and so on — but traditionally the above three represent the most common way of classifying investments. In the long term, the rates of return on stocks are higher than those on bonds which in turn are higher than Treasury bill rates. (Of course, the riskiness of these assets is correspondingly correlated.) However, over any short period in time, the rates of return may not follow the above order; indeed, there have been many periods in the past where bonds realized a higher return than stocks. If one could predict perfectly what investment type would do best at any point in time, one would invest all one's money in that type of investment and then move money from one investment type to another to maximize return. This is called **market timing**. This investment concept means that the investor moves his money into the investment type when the value is low, sells when it reaches its highest point, moves the proceeds of the sale into another investment type whose value is low, and so on and so forth. It is important to remember, however, that this ideal strategy requires perfect prediction of what will do best in any given point in time. Studies have found that such perfect timing is almost impossible.

If one cannot predict what investment type will perform the best at any point in time, a natural approach will be to diversify across asset types — that is, have some of one's money invested in each major investment type at all times. Diversification between different types of investments is called **asset allocation**. **Asset allocation** works because the major asset types — stocks, bonds and cash — are not perfectly positively correlated. In fact, returns on cash (Treasury bills) are very often negatively correlated with stocks and bonds; therefore, the concept of portfolio diversification can be applied. You create a portfolio of cash, bonds and stocks to achieve the desired "risk-return mix." In other words, you choose a portfolio that is expected to generate the rate of return that you want and the risk that is within your comfort zone.[8]

Diversification across Different Countries

As discussed earlier, even if you hold every stock in the Canadian stock market, there is still the **market risk (systematic risk)** that will remain. This is the risk of all the economic conditions within Canada that affect all investments. Broadening your horizons by investing in the investments of other countries will help because their economic conditions are not perfectly correlated with those of Canada. By combining investments of different countries whose patterns of return are different, an international portfolio achieves a less volatile rate of return and hence reduces your risk exposure. This is called **international diversification** or **global diversification**.

Can the Average Person Do It?

The **second fundamental principle** of **investment — diversification —** has many implications as to what you should do with your money. First, you should put some money into each of the major types of investments — cash, bonds, stocks, foreign stocks etc. Second, within each type of investment, you should diversify; for example, where feasible, you should hold about 20 to 30 stocks in the stock portfolio.

---

[8] Computer software, such as Super Rep, will compute the allocation among cash, stocks and bonds. You may add other investment types such as foreign stocks. The program requires historical data or information about asset returns, and your acceptable level of risk (or your required rate of return).

Can an individual who is thinking of saving at most a few hundred dollars a month benefit from these recommendations? How can she afford to buy so many stocks? The answer may lie in **mutual funds**. Mutual funds allow a person with modest savings to benefit from all the knowledge and most of the investment products developed in recent years. Indeed, with the proper knowledge of how to use mutual funds, an average person (in terms of wealth) is no more disadvantaged than a very wealthy person.

THE EFFICIENT MARKET

The stock market is said to be an **efficient market** if current stock prices always reflect all information (past, current and future) about the company, the industry and the general economy. If there is good news or bad news that affects a stock, this information will be immediately incorporated into the stock price. The implication is that for a small investor, there are no bargains available.

Is the market efficient? This is the question that hundreds of research studies have tried to answer in the last 20 or 30 years. Their findings are so important that we will call this the **third fundamental principle of investing**. The efficient market hypothesis says that the financial markets (which include the stock market, the bond market, the option market and the futures market) are efficient: stock prices reflect all the relevant information at any point in time.

There are several implications for the investor:

1. Stocks are fairly valued at any point in time. The bad news about this is that there are no undervalued stocks but the good news is that there are no overvalued stocks either. This means that you will never have to second-guess the fair value of a stock.
2. There is no need for you to spend time on drawing charts, analysing stocks, learning fancy techniques for picking stocks, or forecasting the turning points of the market because none of these will help you to gain any superior performance on your investment.
3. The best investment strategy is a **buy and hold strategy**. You simply buy a stock that fits your desired risk-return mix and hold that stock until the end of your investment horizon. More important, you should not trade actively, because trading will not improve your investment performance. Rather, trading will incur heavy commissions or transaction costs.
4. Do not buy stocks because of news or "hot tips." By the time you know the information everybody in the market also already knows it.

What Should an Investor Do in an Efficient Market?
The **efficient market** implications do not negate what we have discussed so far. In other words, you should still concentrate on doing the right things:

1. Based on your financial goal and your risk preference, determine your desired risk-return mix. For example, do you prefer a portfolio with $E(r) = .15$ and $S.D. = .20$ or a portfolio with $E(r) = .10$ and $S.D. = .15$?
2. Buy a diversified portfolio of investments to achieve your desired risk-return mix.
3. Diversify along the three dimensions of diversifications — within the type of investment, across different types of investment, and diversify internationally.

4. Reduce the costs of buying and selling investments — for example, by trading less, using a discount broker, adopting a buy-and-hold strategy etc.

5. Reduce taxes on investment returns — for example, by comparing the after-tax return from different sources of income — interest, dividends, capital gains.

6. Learn how to choose the proper **mutual funds**, which will be covered in Chapter 15.

Market Inefficiencies   The stock market is not perfectly efficient. A few techniques have been found to select stocks that give above-average returns on investments, even after adjusting for risk. However, these **market inefficiencies** are relatively small and, unless you have a large portfolio, it is quite uneconomical for a small investor to exploit any of them. The potential benefits are normally not enough to justify the time and effort that must be spent to exploit these market inefficiencies.

The best-known ones are the **small firm effect** and the **January effect**. Researchers have discovered that smaller companies listed on stock exchanges tend to have higher than average returns, even after adjusting for their risk. The evidence isn't perfect, however, because the methods of adjusting for risk and the statistical techniques are contentious. Many mutual funds have developed small cap funds. Nonetheless, the average excess returns are not enormously greater and the risk seems to be higher as well.

Researchers have also found that share prices tend to be lower in December and then rise in January. The effect is not large, but the small retail investor who can afford to time purchases might try to do them in late December. The often-cited reason for this is people selling losing holdings at year-end to establish capital losses to set against capital gains. More careful research does not support this as the only cause; so we still don't know why we see this pattern.

THE LONG vs. THE SHORT RUN

One thing we haven't discussed is your time horizon. We all have a limited life span, and so we have finite horizons. A company, or a mutual fund with an ever-renewing supply of investors, has infinite horizons, and should always look to the long run. The average life span of a North American male is over 70 years and a female can expect to live to her late 70s. If you are now 50 years old, you can expect to live to an even greater age, on average, since you have successfully escaped such common killers as childhood diseases, childbearing and military service in a war. Therefore, you should look to the long run in your investment decisions now.

In the long run, we have an effect that some authors call **time diversification**. If you hold riskier assets over a long time period, they will almost certainly return more than a less risky portfolio. We are not suggesting an undiversified portfolio within an asset class, but rather a diversified portfolio concentrated on the riskier classes, like real estate and equity. The effect is that over time, the losses from the bad years are more than overcome by the good years, and you should get the higher mean return shown in Table 13.1. A portfolio of bonds cannot offer very high returns over 30 years, but a portfolio of common shares likely will. As long as your holding period is expected to exceed 10 years, the portfolio of risky assets will almost certainly yield you more money at the end than a portfolio of safe assets.

For most people in the early and middle stages of the life cycle, therefore, investment in equities is preferred. If you will have an early need for money you might wish to stick to a low risk, liquid portfolio, but such a situation is not common. We think that a planned purchase of a house or other major asset is the most likely exception. We will deal with the question of time diversification in more detail when we talk about retirement planning.

SUMMARY

In this chapter, we introduce and describe many basic concepts in investment. We summarize the most important findings of over 30 years of research in three **fundamental principles of investment**:

1. The most important attributes of any investment are its expected return and risk. Return and risk go hand and hand. If you want to earn a higher return you must take more risk.

2. An investor should diversify according to the three dimensions of diversification:
    (a) Diversify across assets within the same investment type;
    (b) Diversify across different types of investments;
    (c) Diversify internationally.

3. The financial markets, and especially the stock markets, are fairly efficient.

We explain the importance of these three **basic investment principles** and how they would affect your investment programme. We provide a list of basic instructions on how to invest in an efficient market. Finally, we point out that if you have a long investment horizon (over 10 years), you should concentrate your investments in the riskier asset classes, since they will give you a higher return almost always, as long as you hold them for a long time period.

KEY TERMINOLOGY

return / rate of return / income return / capital gain return / holding period return / investing / saving / characteristics of an investment / liquidity / marketability / term / management effort / tax consideration / divisibility / standard deviation / beta / risk aversion / risk-return trade-off / risk-free asset / total risk / objective probability distribution / subjective probability distribution / Treasury-bill or T-bill / inflation risk / inflation hedges / default risk / interest rate risk / reinvestment risk / liquidity risk / risk neutral / risk loving / risk premium / dominance / diversification / portfolio / portfolio theory / correlation coefficient / uncorrelated / perfectly negatively correlated / portfolio risk / market (non-market) risk / systematic (unsystematic) risk / diversifiable (undiversifiable) risk / diversification between types of assets / asset allocation / mutual fund / global diversification / international diversification / efficient market / market inefficiency / buy-and-hold strategy / time diversification

DISCUSSION QUESTIONS

1. Define or explain each of the terms under **Key Terminology**.
2. How do we measure the risk and the return of an investment?

3. Why are investments issued by the government default risk-free?
4. What is the advantage of investing in stocks as compared to investing in bonds?
5. Is investing in a government Treasury-bill risk-free? Discuss.
6. Your stockbroker called you with a "hot tip" and he said the stock would double in one month. How are you going to respond?
7. "The efficient market implies that you can never get rich by playing the stock market." Comment and discuss.
8. Discuss the concept of dominance of one stock over another.
9. How does diversification help investors?
10. How can investors diversify?

PROBLEMS

1. Calculate the expected rate of return and standard deviation of the following stock:

rate of return	probability
−.015	.08
−.010	.12
0	.25
.12	.20
.17	.20
.20	.15

2. Calculate the expected rates of return and the risk of the following investments:

Investment A		Investment B	
rate of return	probability	rate of return	probability
−.10	.05	−.20	.05
−.05	.10	−.10	.10
0	.15	−.05	.10
.08	.30	0	.15
.14	.25	.10	.20
.20	.10	.20	.25
.25	.05	.30	.10
		.40	.05

Can you say anything about dominance?

3. **Personal Project 1**
   Assessing your risk-return preference.

   (a) Choose one of your financial goals. If you do not have one yet, go back to Chapter 3, follow the suggestions there and set a financial goal.
   (b) Based on your current wealth and expected future savings, what is the required rate of return to achieve this goal?
   (c) Find out from the newspaper at least three mutual funds that historically have generated your required rate of return in (b). Find out their historical standard deviations.
   (d) Assuming that all the returns on the mutual funds are normally distributed, find the probability that you will lose money if you invest in each of the funds.

(e) For each of the three mutual funds, what is the probability that you will earn less than (i) 3%, (ii) 6%, (iii) 10%?

(f) Are the mutual funds' return-risk characteristics within your comfort zone?

4. Nathan, 33, recently won a lottery prize of $26,000. His goal is to retire at age 65, with $3 million in addition to his pensions (the contributions for his pension plans are automatically deducted from his pay cheques). He is considering whether to invest his winnings in bonds or stocks.

(a) What rate of return must he earn in order to reach his goal?

(b) How would you advise him to invest the $26,000?

5. In Problem 10 in Chapter 12, you advised Lillian Thong and Garsen Yap on planning for a house purchase. Their balance sheet included a portfolio of securities at market value, but with no details. Now suppose that the portfolio is as follows:

Lillian Thong and Garsen Yap
Schedule of Investments

Common Shares
100	Barrick Gold
2,000	Royal Oak
2,000	Pure Gold Resources
2,000	Morrison Petroleum

Call Options
20 contracts	Placer Dome, January 1998, $35
10 contracts	Barrick Gold, January 1998, $35

Find the current prices for these securities. All of the companies are listed on the Toronto Stock Exchange. Your instructor will provide replacements for any that are missing for any reason. Advise Lillian and Garsen on the suitability of their portfolio, given their goal of buying a home in two years.

14

Types of Investments

LEARNING OBJECTIVES

In the last chapter, we introduced and discussed some fundamental concepts and theories in investment. We emphasized three particular topics that are very important in the investment literature. These three topics are summarized in terms of three fundamental principles in investment:

1. **Risk-return trade-off**
    Every investment has two important characteristics — **return** and **risk**. This principle says that return is a positive function of risk; the higher the risk of the investment, the higher the expected return.

2. **Diversification**
    This principle states that (i) one should allocate one's money among the major types of investments — cash, bonds, and stocks; (ii) one should also diversify within each type of investment (for example, one is well-advised to invest in a portfolio of common stocks rather than to hold one stock only); and (iii) one can benefit from global diversification.

3. **Efficient markets**
    This principle states that financial markets are efficient, by and large. Stocks and bonds are fairly valued at any point in time. One cannot outperform or "beat" the market by picking stocks, by timing the market or by switching one's investments from one to another. Although some market inefficiencies have been detected, it is very difficult for a small investor to exploit these inefficiencies because he does not have the time or the financial resources.

In this chapter, we will apply these investment principles to evaluate different kinds of investments. There is no such thing as a perfect investment. Each one has its own characteristics in terms of risk, return, liquidity, maturity and so on. The investor must choose the investments that fit her economic circumstances (such as wealth, income, age and stage in the life cycle) and her risk preference.

This chapter is **not** about picking the right stock or about choosing the right time to switch one's investment from one category to another. By virtue of the principle of efficient markets, we have emphasized that a small investor cannot expect to benefit much from such activities. On the other hand, we believe that one should have a good understanding of the characteristics of each type of investment — stocks, bonds, mutual funds and so on, so that one can make the right choice of investment that will achieve one's financial goals. The specific objectives of this chapter are:

1. To describe the major investments such as Treasury bills, Canada Savings Bonds, government and corporate bonds, preferred shares, common shares, mutual funds, and so on.
2. To describe the characteristics of each investment — risk, return, liquidity, maturity, etc.
3. To introduce very briefly other investments like options.

You have already learned that there are many kinds of risk and that technically speaking there is no such thing as a risk-free investment.[1] The major kind of risk that worries most people is **default risk** — the risk of losing part or all of one's investment due to the inability of the issuer to honour the obligations of the security. We shall introduce various types of investments in order of their default risk; in other words, we will first go through investments with little or no default risk and continue by describing investment with increasingly higher default risk. In this chapter, we will describe the three major categories of investments: cash and cash equivalents, bonds and stocks, with a brief reference to options, futures and commodities. We will leave mutual funds to Chapter 15.

CASH AND CASH EQUIVALENCES

Federal Government of Canada Securities

The federal government borrows money by selling securities. It borrows money when current revenue from taxes is not sufficient to meet all expenditures. When the government runs a deficit, it funds the deficit by borrowing money through the issuance of government securities. These government securities are considered to have virtually no default risk because the federal government can always get money to pay its debt — by virtue of its legal right to levy taxes on its citizens and resident corporations as well as its ability to create money.

There are three major types of securities sold by the federal government: **Treasury bills**, **Canada Savings Bonds**, and **Government of Canada Bonds**. Each has its own investment characteristics — return, risk, liquidity, maturity and so on. The first two are cash equivalents.

Treasury Bills (T-Bills)
Treasury bills are short-term debt obligations issued normally in denominations ranging from $1,000 to $1 million, and with 91-day, 182-day, and occasionally, one-year terms. They are issued by auction once every week. In the past, T-bills were mainly of interest to large institutional investors such as banks, loan and trust companies but recently, they have become accessible to small investors since

---

[1] Government securities are default risk-free; however, one is still exposed to inflation risk in government securities.

many investment dealers have begun offering them in small packages. These dealers buy T-bills in large quantities and then sell them in small packages to individual investors, making a small profit by paying a slightly lower interest rate than they receive from the government.

T-bills have no **default risk**; however, if you want to cash them before the maturity date, you may suffer a capital loss or enjoy a capital gain. They are very liquid; you can therefore normally sell them through the same investment dealer from which you bought them.

T-bills do not pay interest; instead, they are bought at a **discount** from their **face value**. The face value is the amount that the federal government will pay on the maturity date, and is in denominations ranging from $1,000 to $1 million. Buying at a discount means that you pay a lower price than the face value. This makes the calculation of the rate of return on a T-bill a little complicated.

Example 14.1: The current market price of a $10,000 Treasury bill is $9,500. The bill matures in 181 days. What is the effective annual rate of return?

The holding period is 181 days, and the holding period return (HPR) is equal to:

$$[(\$10,000 - \$9,500) \div 9,500] = 5.26\%$$

This is the rate of return for a holding period of 181 days. The effective annual rate of return is therefore equal to:

$$[(1.0526)^{(365/181)} - 1] = [(1.0526)^{2.0166} - 1] = 10.89\%$$

Even though T-bills do not pay interest, the difference between the face value and the initial price paid, is considered as interest income for tax purposes. Thus, in Example 14.1, the $500 (which is the difference between the face value of $10,000 and the initial price of $9,500) would be considered as interest income for the investor and would be taxed at the investor's marginal tax rate.

The rate of return on T-bills is usually higher than the rate of inflation. For individuals who pay little or no taxes, or non-profit organizations, T-bills are good hedges against the risk of inflation. For people in higher tax brackets, however, T-bills may not be good inflation hedges, as the following example will show.

Example 14.2: Mr. Wong, a relatively well-off retired man, is very worried about the erosion of his wealth by inflation. The expected rate of inflation is 8% for the coming year and Mr. Wong is contemplating buying the T-bill in Example 14.1. If Mr. Wong's marginal tax rate is 53%, is the T-bill a good hedge against inflation?

The before-tax rate of return is 10.89%, which is higher than the expected rate of inflation of 8%. Thus, for people or organizations that pay little or no taxes, the T-bill would be a good inflation hedge; however, that is not the case for Mr. Wong. After paying taxes on interest income at the rate of 53%, the after-tax rate of return on the T-bill is equal to:

$$[10.89\% \times (1 - .53)] = 5.12\%$$

This is lower than the expected rate of inflation of 8%. Mr. Wong would lose 2.88% in terms of the purchasing power of money. This example illustrates that even though T-bills are considered as the "risk-free" investment in the investment literature, T-bills are actually free of default risk only.

Canada Savings Bonds (CSBs)

Canada Savings Bonds (CSBs) are sold once a year with the actual issue date and the maturity date falling on November 1. For example, Series 42 was sold on November 1, 1987 and will mature on November 1, 1997. CSBs offer a fixed rate of interest compounded annually and the interest rates are normally adjusted for later years.

There are two types of CSBs: the **regular interest bond** and the **compound interest bond**. The **regular interest bond** pays annual interest either by cheque or by direct deposit into the investor's bank account on November 1 each year. This type is available in denominations of $300, $500, $1,000, $5,000 and $10,000; you must pay cash to purchase them. The **compound interest bond** does not pay annual interest but reinvests the interest payable automatically until maturity or redemption. This type is available in denominations of $100, $300, $500, $1,000, $5,000 and $10,000 and can be purchased by cash, by a monthly installment plan through banks and other financial institutions or through payroll savings plans offered by many companies in Canada.

CSBs are sold to Canadian residents and registered in the names of individuals.[2] There is a maximum limit of any one series that an individual is allowed to hold. Ownership of a CSB cannot be transferred or assigned; therefore, they are not traded in the market like other bonds. The only seller is the government and the only legal buyer of bonds already issued is the government.

If the holder of a new CSB issue cashes the bond within a few months — usually the first three months — from the issue date, he normally receives the face value without the payment of interest. After this initial "waiting period," CSBs can be redeemed at any time for the face value plus accrued interest. You can cash the bonds at any bank in Canada on any business day.[3]

A CSB is a very unusual investment. It is free of default risk. It is perfectly liquid and the value of the bond is always equal to the face value. There is no down-side risk because when the market interest rate rises, the CSBs are still worth their face value. The prices of all other bonds rise when interest rates fall and vice versa. See next section on Bonds. In fact, the government usually adjusts the interest rate on the CSBs upward to prevent high redemptions of the bonds. On the other hand, when the market interest rate falls, the rate on the CSBs remains unchanged until the next November. In addition, the government pays all the commissions for the buying and the selling of the CSBs through financial institutions; for this reason, the individual investor does not have to incur any commission expense. The yields of CSBs are usually slightly lower than that of Treasury bills and other government bonds; nevertheless, investors should realize that

---

[2] CSBs can also be held by the estate of a deceased person or a trust for an individual.

[3] Redemption of CSBs should be done on the first business day of a month for maximum interest advantages because the government pays accrued interest as of this date.

they hold a valuable option — namely, investors can force the government to redeem the bond at face value at any time they want. The redeemability of CSBs therefore justifies their lower return. Overall, the conservative investor who wants perfect liquidity and zero default risk should find CSBs to be suitable investments. Many financial experts advise a family to set aside an emergency fund equal to three to six months' take-home pay. This emergency fund should be put in a low-risk and liquid investment. CSBs are excellent investments for this particular purpose.

Deposits with Financial Institutions

Deposits with banks and other financial institutions are one of the most popular investments for Canadians. They are easy to understand and, in terms of investment characteristics, they are **safe** (very low risk), **liquid**, and **convenient**, but the **rate of return** is low. The most common types of deposits are: interest-bearing savings and chequing accounts, term deposits, and guaranteed investment certificates.

Bank Accounts   Three basic types of accounts are available at banks, loan and trust companies, and credit unions. They are chequing, chequing-savings and savings accounts. **Chequing accounts** usually do not pay interest. You are allowed to write cheques on the account and the cheques can be returned to you with a monthly statement. There is a service charge which is usually a function of how many cheques you write and the amount of money you have in the account. **Savings accounts** do not allow chequing but pay interest to the account holders. The **chequing-savings account** has the attributes of the other two; it allows chequing but pays a lower interest rate than savings accounts. These three accounts are the basic types although financial institutions offer many varieties of accounts, each with slightly different features and charges.

Bank accounts are safe and almost default-risk-free — in terms of relative default risk, they are next in line after Treasury bills and CSBs. They are also perfectly liquid. Banks and financial institutions have always honoured investors' withdrawals even though legally they can ask you to wait several days on withdrawals from savings accounts. Bank accounts are also very convenient with the numerous branches that banks have all over the country. In addition, the introduction of **automated teller machines**,[4] which offer 24-hour service, has made banking more and more convenient. Indeed, it is expected that in the near future one can take care of all one's banking needs without ever leaving home. A limited range of such services is already available with some financial institutions.

In return for the safety, liquidity and convenience for the consumer, bank accounts offer a low rate of interest — lower than CSBs and T-bills, for example. In some ways, the consumer is paying for the convenience and other services by accepting a lower rate of return. Many institutions calculate the interest on savings accounts on the minimum monthly balance and compound it semi-annually. For example, if you have $10,000 in a savings account from the beginning of the month until the 30th day when you must withdraw $9,999 because of an emergency, the interest for the month will be based on the minimum balance of the month which is the $1 on the last day of the month. What this means in effect is that you lose interest for the entire month! It is therefore important

---

[4] An automated teller machine is a terminal that allows you to get cash, make deposits, pay bills, and transfer funds between accounts.

for you to find out how interest is calculated for each type of account. The retail banking industry has become more competitive and most financial institutions now offer **daily interest accounts** where interest is calculated daily and compounded semi-annually. If you expect many fluctuations in your savings account balance, these accounts may be more suitable for you.

Term Deposits   In contrast to savings accounts, which have no guaranteed interest rate and no set term, you can deposit your money in **term deposits** which guarantee a rate of interest for a specified **term**. You give up some liquidity[5] in return for a higher rate of interest. The typical terms range from 30 to 364 days and, usually the longer the term, the higher the rate of interest. Interest is normally paid semi-annually or annually. In some cases, there may be a minimum deposit required and the amount of the deposit usually affects the rate of interest. In terms of investment characteristics, **term deposits** are as safe as savings accounts, less liquid than savings accounts and capable of earning a higher rate of return than savings accounts.

Guaranteed Investment Certificates (GICs)   GICs are really long-term term deposits. These certificates have terms ranging from one to five years. During the term, the interest rate is guaranteed. In most cases, a minimum deposit will be required. Interest is usually paid semi-annually or annually and some GICs have automatic compounding of interest. GICs are as safe as savings accounts and term deposits. They are less liquid because they have longer terms but you can normally expect a higher interest rate on GICs.

Deposit Insurance   How safe are savings accounts, term deposits and GICs? Is their default risk equal to zero, just like T-bills and CSBs? What happens to a depositor's money when a trust company goes bankrupt? These questions bring us to the deposit insurance that the federal government provides to most financial institution depositors.

The federal government in 1967 established a Crown Corporation, the **Canada Deposit Insurance Corporation (CDIC)**, to provide the investor with insurance against any loss on his deposits should a member institution become insolvent or bankrupt. Who are the members of CDIC? Membership in the CDIC is restricted to banks, trust companies and mortgage loan companies.[6] Thus, not all financial institutions are members of the CDIC. To check the status of an institution in this respect, you should ask a senior officer at the institution, or call the CDIC directly at 800–267–1999. The CDIC publishes a list of its members which is available upon request.

The CDIC insures savings and chequing accounts, term deposits, guaranteed investment certificates, debentures and other obligations issued by member institutions. The maximum coverage is $60,000 for each person in each member institution; this amount applies to the combined total of principal and interest. The deposit insurance does not cover investments in stocks, bonds, mortgages or mutual funds. Joint accounts and joint deposits are separately insured from the individual's accounts. For example, if you have

---

[5] Money is put in for a specified term. If you withdraw before the term, there is usually a penalty.

[6] CompCorp provides investors with insurance against any loss on deposits, RRSPs and RRIFs of life and health insurance companies. See Chapter 9.

a term deposit under your own name and a joint savings account with your spouse and another joint account with your sister, the term deposit will be covered up to $60,000 and each joint account will also be covered up to $60,000. If you have more than $60,000 to deposit, you should spread it around so that no more than $60,000 is deposited with any one CDIC-member institution. Are deposits to Registered Retirement Savings Plans (RRSPs) or to Registered Retirement Income Funds (RRIFs) insured? If the monies are invested in a type of deposit that qualifies for deposit insurance, they are insured to the $60,000 maximum. In addition, the deposits are separately insured from any regular deposits or other types of registered plan deposits the person may have in the same member institution.

Example 14.3:   Edward Booth has a term deposit in his name for $50,000, a joint savings account with his wife for $25,000, another joint savings account with his son for $10,000, an RRSP account for $45,000 invested in stock mutual funds and an RRIF account for $20,000 invested in a mortgage mutual fund. All the accounts are with a bank which is a CDIC member. Are Edward's accounts fully covered by CDIC insurance?

Edward's term deposit is covered up to $60,000. Each of the joint accounts are also fully covered, up to $60,000 for each account. The RRSP account is not covered because the money is invested in "unqualified" investments.[7] For the same reason, the RRIF account is not covered. If the monies in the RRSP and the RRIF accounts had been invested in qualified investments — term deposits, GICs etc. — both accounts would be covered up to $60,000 for each account.

Example 14.4:   Leslie Carter is a loyal customer of a local trust company. In addition to a savings account with a $35,000 balance, she has three term deposits of $10,000 each. She also holds a two-year GIC of $20,000. Are Leslie's investments fully covered?

First, she should check to see if the trust company is a CDIC member. Assuming that it is, the insurance coverage is $60,000 for each person in each member institution. Her total investments amount to [$35,000 + (3 × $10,000) + $20,000] or $85,000, which exceeds the $60,000 limit. Thus, her investments are not fully covered. She is well-advised to put at least $25,000 in another CDIC-member institution.

BONDS

Bonds are fixed income securities issued by various levels of governments — federal, provincial and municipal — and corporations. When corporations and governments need long-term financing, they borrow money by selling bonds. When you buy their bonds, you become their creditor and you receive a bond certificate by which the issuer promises that the principal (or face value or par value) will be repaid on the maturity date and that interest will be paid on stated dates. The following important items of information are stated on the bond certificate:

---

[7] The CDIC does not cover investments in stocks, bonds, mortgages or mutual funds.

Face Value — This is also called the **principal**, the **par value**, or the **maturity value**. It is the amount that the issuer has promised to pay on the **maturity date**. It is usually in denominations of $500, $1,000, $10,000 or more.

Maturity Date — This is the date on which the **face value** will be paid.

Coupon Rate — This is the rate which forms the basis for calculating interest. The annual interest payable is the coupon rate times the face value. For example, if the face value of a bond is $10,000 and its coupon rate is 8% p.a., the annual interest payable is ($10,000 $\times$ .08) = $800.00. Interest is normally paid semi-annually on the stated dates. In many bonds, there are **interest coupons** attached to the bond certificate; they can be clipped and cashed on the stated dates.

Coupon Bonds — These are bonds with a series of interest coupons attached to the bond certificate itself. On the coupon is printed the value of the interest in dollars, the date when the coupon can be cashed and the financial institution at which the coupons can be cashed.

Investing in Bonds

Bonds are bought and sold in the **bond market** through bond brokers. The **bond market** is not a physical place where brokers meet; it is rather a communication system where brokers put orders to buy and orders to sell together.

There are some major security firms that act as **investment dealers** (or **bond dealers**) in the bond market. These **dealers** hold hundreds of millions of dollars of bonds in inventory and they buy or sell bonds on their own account. On any trading day, the investment dealers will set a price list for the bonds. This price list is called **bond quotations**. There are two prices for any given bond. The **bid price** for a bond is what the dealer will pay to buy the bond; the **ask price** is the price at which the dealer will sell the bond. Table 14.1 shows typical bond quotations that you can find in the business section of many daily newspapers.

Let us look at the first row in Table 14.1. This is the quotation of a Canada Government Bond with coupon rate of 9.50% which matures on October 1, 2001. The bond could be sold for $116.35 per $100 of face value or bought for $116.75 per $100 of face value. The **spread**, which is the difference between the **ask price** and the **bid price**, represents the dealer's gross profit margin. Higher spreads are quoted on bonds which are traded infrequently and hence are of poor liquidity. The bond quotations that you find in newspapers normally apply to large lots which may be as high as $250,000; additional spreads or commission may be charged on smaller trades.

TABLE 14.1
Example of Bond Quotations

Issue	Coupon	Maturity	Bid Price	Ask Price	Bid Yield	Ask Yield
CDA	9.50	01Oct01	116.350	116.750	6.80	6.74
CDA	12.00	01Mar05	137.350	137.600	7.14	7.11
ALTA	7.75	05May03	103.750	104.000	7.20	7.16
B.C.	10.15	29Aug01	117.800	118.100	7.14	7.10
T-D BANK	13.15	15Sep03	119.026	120.026	10.06	9.92

Basic Bond Pricing Mathematics and Yields

Accrued Interest   The prices quoted for bonds are all calculated as of the previous interest date for convenience's sake. When you buy a bond, you have to pay the ask price plus all interest accrued from the previous interest date to the closing date of the transaction. The following example will illustrate this point.

> **Example 14.5:** Anthony Schilling bought the following Canada Government
> Bond to settle on June 15:
> Face Value of the Bond: $10,000
> Coupon Rate: 10%
> Interest payable on Mar. 15 and Sept. 15
>   How much accrued interest must Mr. Schilling pay to
> the seller?

When Sept. 15 next arrives, Mr. Schilling can clip the interest-coupon and get six months' interest, which is equal to $500. But he will have held the bond for only three months and, therefore, he should not receive six months' interest. Mr. Schilling is obligated to pay to the seller of the bond $250, or three months' interest, in addition to the value as if the bond were priced at March 15 (the previous interest date).

Yield to Maturity   The **yield to maturity** is the average rate of return that will be earned on a bond if it is bought now and held until maturity. It is also called the **return to maturity** or the **internal rate of return**. You pay the current price to buy a bond and if you hold it until maturity, you will receive (1) an annuity of interest income and (2) the face value at maturity. In theory, the current bond price is equal to the present value of the interest-annuity plus the present value of the face value of the bond. This is called the **bond price equation**.

■ Bond Price Equation
First, we define the following symbols:

P = the current price of the bond
C = the coupon rate, expressed in % p.a.
M = the par value or face value of the bond
n = the number of years to maturity
k = the discount rate

One pays P dollars to buy the bond. If one holds the bond until maturity, one will receive an annuity of interest income of $c(M)$ dollars for n years, plus the face value, M, on the maturity date. The present value of the annuity of interest is equal to $cM(PVIFA)$. The present value of the face value is equal to $M(PVIF)$. Recall that in Chapter 2, *PVIFA* is defined as the present value interest factor for an annuity, and PVIF is the present value interest factor. In other words:

$$PVIF = \frac{1}{(1 + k)^n}$$

$$PVIFA = \frac{1}{k} - \frac{1}{k(1 + k)^n}$$

The bond price equation equates the current bond price to the present value of the annuity of interest and the present value of the face value. It can be written as equation (1) or equation (2).

$$P = CM\,(PVIFA) + M\,(PVIF) \tag{1}$$

$$P = CM\left[\frac{1}{k} - \frac{1}{k(1+k)^n}\right] + M\left[\frac{1}{(1+k)^n}\right] \tag{2}$$

We can calculate the **yield to maturity** by solving the **bond price equation** for the discount rate k, given the bond's price P.

Example 14.6:   What is the yield to maturity of the following Canada Government Bond?
Face value = $1,000
Coupon rate = 9.5%, payable semi-annually
Current price = $1,030
Maturity = 20 years

First, note that the bond pays $47.50 in interest every six months for 40 periods. The bond price equation is:

$$1,030 = 47.5\left[\frac{1}{k} - \frac{1}{k(1+k)^{40}}\right] + 1000\left[\frac{1}{(1+k)^{40}}\right]$$

We can solve for k by trial and error, or we can use the calculator, as follows:

1,030	**PV**
40	**n**
47.50	**PMT**
1,000	**FV**
% i	Answer = 4.58%

Note that the 4.58% is the rate for the half-year period. The bond's **yield to maturity** will be quoted in the financial press at an **annual percentage rate (APR)** of $(0.458 \times 2) = 9.16\%$, despite the fact that its effect annual rate is actually $(1.0458)^2 - 1 = 9.37\%$. The latter is the correct annual yield to maturity even though it is not reported in the newspaper.

Current Yield vs. Yield to Maturity   Some financial press reports another yield called the **current yield**. It is the bond's annual coupon payment divided by the bond price. For example, the current yield of the bond in Example 14.6 is equal to $(95 \div 1,030)$ or 9.22%. Clearly, the **yield to maturity** is not the same as the **current yield**. The **yield to maturity** is widely accepted as the measure for the average return on investment if the bond is held to maturity. It can be interpreted as the compound rate of return of one's investment over the life of the bond, under the assumption that all interest coupons can be reinvested at an interest rate equal to the bond's yield to maturity. If this assumption does not hold, the yield to maturity will not be the same as the return over the bond's life.

Investment Risk of Bonds

There are risks associated with investing in bonds. Unlike term deposits or guaranteed investment certificates, the market value of bonds can fluctuate. Even if the bond is issued by the federal government and is therefore free of default risk, the bond's price is guaranteed only at maturity. Before then, the bond's price can go up or down. We will discuss four important risks of bonds: **default risk**, **interest rate risk**, **reinvestment risk**, and **option features** (such as callable, retractable, extendible features which may make the bond more or less risky to the investor).

1. Default Risk

Default risk refers to the risk that the issuer may not be able to pay part or all of the interest and face value. In the case of bonds issued by the federal government, the default risk is zero. Bonds issued by the provincial and municipal governments are not free of default risk although they are usually considered to be less risky than corporate bonds. The **default risk** of bonds depends largely on the quality of the assets and cash flows of the issuer. As long as the issuer (company or government) is not in financial difficulty, the bondholders will get their interest and principal as promised.

Assessing the **default risk** of different bonds is a very complicated matter; therefore, there are **bond rating agencies** who specialize in rating the credit risk of different issuers. In Canada, the largest bond rating agencies are Canada Bond Rating Service and Dominion Bond Rating Service. Studies have shown that bond ratings are very reliable and many investors use them as measures of the default risks of bonds. In other words, the **bond ratings** can be used as indicators of the probability of uninterrupted payment of interest and principal repayment. Ratings classify bonds from investment grade to speculative grade and relate one company's ability to meet its debt obligations to those of other companies.

■ Dominion Bond Rating Service — Ratings

The following are the bond ratings[8] assigned by the Dominion Bond Rating Service:

AAA — Highest quality: The protection of principal and interest is of the highest order.

AA — Superior quality: The protection of principal and interest is high.

A — Higher medium-grade securities: The protection of principal and interest is substantial but less than AA.

BBB — Medium-grade securities: The protection of principal and interest is adequate but some areas of potential weakness exist.

BB — Lower medium-grade securities: These are mildly speculative securities; the protection afforded interest and principal is uncertain.

B — Medium speculative-grade securities: The ability of the company to meet interest and principal obligations on a continuing basis is uncertain.

CCC — Highly speculative securities: These are securities in danger of default of interest or principal.

CC — Securities in default: This rating is assigned to securities in default of either interest or principal or with other serious problems.

---

[8] Canada Bond Rating Service uses different symbols but the basic idea is the same.

C   — Securities in serious default: These securities are similar to CC securities but they have different liquidation values.

■ High or Low

The above rating may also be modified by "high" or "low" to indicate the relative standing within a classification and an improving or declining trend within that classification.

2. Interest Rate Risk

Interest rate risk refers to the volatility or fluctuation of the bond's price due to the fluctuation in interest rates. The coupon interest is fixed for most bonds but the market interest rate can and does change. If, in the course of time, interest rates available on bonds rise, the price of the bond held in your portfolio will fall since the coupon interest it bears is not as attractive as those on other bonds. On the other hand, if interest rates fall, the same bond's price will rise.

If you intend to hold the bond until maturity, then the interest rate risk is irrelevant to you: what matters is the price at maturity which is known to be par value. Most people, however, may want to sell the bond before maturity and for that reason they face an uncertainty about the bond's price because of possible interest rate changes. Even with zero default risk — as in the case of Canada Government Bonds — bonds could therefore be risky investments. Moreover, the longer the **term to maturity** of the bond, the greater the **interest rate risk** for the obvious reason that the bondholder is locked into a fixed rate for a longer period of time. Because most investors are risk-averse, they will pay a little less for "longer" bonds. The relationship between a bond's price and the rate of interest can be analysed by the **bond price equation**, as the following example will illustrate.

Example 14.7: Mr. Lopez has invested in the Canada Government Bond in Example 14.6 — face value = $1,000, coupon rate = 9.5%, maturity = 20 years, market price = $1,030, yield to maturity = 9.16%. He has held the bond for one year, during which time the rate of interest in the market has increased substantially. As a result, the required yield to maturity of the bond has increased to 10.04%. Required:
(a) What is the bond's price at the end of the year?
(b) If Mr. Lopez sold the bond, what would be his holding period return (HPR)?

Answers: (a) After one year, there are 19 years remaining to maturity. The bond's price is equal to the present value of an annuity of 38 interest payments (each = $47.50) plus the present value of the face value of $1,000. The discount rate is equal to (10.04% ÷ 2) = 5.02%. Using a calculator, we get:

47.5	PMT
1000	FV
38	n
5.02	%i
PV	Answer = $954.58

The price of the bond has fallen from $1,030 to $954.58 in one year's time.

(b) Mr. Lopez's holding period return (HPR)
= (95 + 954.58 − 1,030) ÷ (1,030)
= 1.9%

Note that Mr. Lopez has a capital loss of $75.42. Investment in Government of Canada Bonds is not risk-free! We have observed from historical data that there were periods of time when long-term government bonds were more volatile (and hence, more risky) than stocks.

3. Reinvestment Risk

As mentioned before, coupon interest is paid semi-annually or annually to the bondholders and not reinvested in the bond. This means that the bondholder must find somewhere else to invest the interest. Of course, the rate of return on future reinvestments of the coupon interest is uncertain; it could be higher or lower than the current yield on the bond. **Reinvestment risk** refers to the risk of not knowing the interest rate that will be earned on future interest earnings. Other things being the same, the higher the **coupon rate** of the bond, the higher the **reinvestment risk**. Thus, a bond that does not pay interest year to year has no reinvestment risk.

■ Zero-Coupon Bond

A **zero-coupon bond** is a bond that pays no interest — in other words, the coupon rate is zero: it has no **reinvestment risk**. It is the only long-term investment where the **yield to maturity** is guaranteed. A **zero-coupon bond** thus has the advantage of producing a specified amount of money at a specified future date and is therefore a very useful investment vehicle for the goal setting and personal financial planning process that we discussed in Chapter 3. Zero-coupon bonds, nevertheless, do have their disadvantages: the major one is that their market price is very sensitive to interest rates — in other words, they have high **interest-rate risk**.

■ Strip Bonds

The Canadian government issues very few zero-coupon bonds; instead, it allows investment dealers to "re-package" regular government bonds and sell them in the form of zero-coupon bonds. For example, a 20-year Government of Canada Bond has 40 semi-annual coupons plus one principal payment; each of these 41 cash flows can be re-packaged and sold as 41 different zero-coupon bonds, with maturities ranging from six months to 20 years. Such a re-packaged zero-coupon bond is called a **strip bond**.

You may want to invest in a **zero-coupon bond** or a **strip bond** if (1) you want no reinvestment risk, (2) you want a guaranteed yield to maturity or (3) you want a specific amount of money at a specified future date and you want to achieve this goal without uncertainty.

4. Option Features of Bonds

Many bonds today have certain features in addition to the basic variety that we have described so far. Some of the features are beneficial to the issuer; others are beneficial to the bondholders. Usually, if the issuer has the option to exercise the feature, the feature is beneficial to the issuer; on the other hand, if the bondholder has the option to exercise the feature, then it is beneficial to the bondholders. What follows here is a list of some of the more common option features.

■ Call Provision and Callable Bonds

A **call provision** allows the issuer the option of buying back the bonds at a specified price before maturity. A bond with a call provision is called a **callable bond**.

■ Retractability Provision and Retractable Bonds

A **retractability provision** provides the bondholder with an option to sell the bond back to the company for a specified price before maturity. A bond with a retractability provision is called a **retractable bond**.

■ Extendibility Provision and Extendible Bonds

An **extendibility provision** allows the bondholder the option of extending the maturity of the bond for another fixed period of time at a specified interest rate (often the same rate as before). Such a bond is called an **extendible bond**.

■ Conversion Provision and Convertible Bonds

A **conversion provision** gives the bondholder the option of exchanging the bond for a fixed quantity of stocks of the company. Such a bond is called a **convertible bond**.

STOCKS

Stocks are probably the premier kind of investment: when people think of investments, they usually think of stocks and the stock market. Technically, the common stockholders as a group are the owners of the firm; they have a claim on the net earnings of the company after the claims of the creditors and other claimants have been satisfied. Common stocks are the riskiest of all the investments that a company issues — promissory notes, short-term and long-term debt, bonds, preferred stocks and common stocks — but their expected returns are also the highest. The common stockholders are protected by the **limited liability** provision of the stocks; they are not personally liable for the financial obligations of the company. The most that a stockholder can therefore lose is 100% of what she has invested in the stock.

Stock Markets

Shares in public companies are traded on what we call **stock markets**. When a company issues new common or preferred shares, it normally does not sell directly to the public; rather, it sells the shares to investment dealers. This is called the **primary market**, where new issues are brought to the market for the first time through investment dealers. After buying the new securities, the investment dealers then sell them to the public through their network of stockbrokers. This process of buying new issues from the company and then selling them to the public is called **underwriting**.

A private company's shares are held by only a few people — usually the executives and/or members of a founding family. The shares are not traded on a stock exchange and are thus very illiquid.

Most of the publicity about the stock markets concerns the **secondary market** where previously issued stocks are traded. The secondary market includes the **stock exchanges** and the **over-the-counter (OTC) market**.

Stock Exchange   A **stock exchange** is a place where members of the exchange buy and sell stocks. A limited number of memberships are available in a stock exchange and these memberships are called **seats**.

Over-the-counter (OTC) market   The **OTC market** is not a physical place where people trade stocks; rather, it is an informal network among the security firms which allows trading in securities that are not formally listed on a stock exchange. This market operates very much like a bond market.

Stock Quotations

Stock quotations are reported in the financial press every day. The following is a typical quotation which you can find in the business section of most newspapers. We look at the Canadian Imperial Bank of Commerce (CIBC) as it was shown in a newspaper's weekly report of stocks.

Weekly Trading Report

52-Wk High	52-Wk Low	Company	High	Low	Close	Sales 000's	Chg	Ind. Div.	Yield	Share Profit	P/E
33	22	CIBC	30 ¾	30	30 ½	884	+ ¼	1.32	4.3	3.84	7.9

Let us explain the information from the stock quotation. The first two numbers are the highest and lowest prices at which the stock has traded in the last 52 weeks; for the CIBC, they are $33 and $22, respectively. The next four numbers provide information on the trading in the week just ended: the highest price and lowest price per share at which the stock traded in that week were $30 ¾ and $30, respectively. The last trade was at a price (the closing price) of $30 ½ which was up ¼ of a dollar from the closing price of the previous week. The **sales volume** is reported in thousands of shares and there were 884,000 shares traded during the week. The 1.32 figure that follows the sales volume is the indicated dividend which means that the dividend payout to the shareholders over the last quarter was $1.32 per share on an annual basis. CIBC, which was last sold for $30 ½, has a **dividend yield** of (1.32 ÷ 30.5) = .043 or 4.3%. The **share profit** is the **earnings per share** which is calculated as the company's net income for the last four quarters divided by the number of shares outstanding. The share profit of the CIBC was $3.84. The last number is the **P/E ratio**, or **price-earnings ratio** which is defined as the closing price divided by last year's earnings per share. For CIBC, the P/E ratio is equal to (30.5 ÷ 3.84) or 7.94. The P/E ratio tells you how much you must pay per dollar of earnings that the firm generates for each share. If the dividend yield or the P/E ratio is not reported in the stock quotation, then that means the firm has zero dividends, or zero or negative earnings.

Stockbrokers

You will need a stockbroker to assist you to buy or sell stocks. There are two kinds of brokers: **full-service brokers** and **discount brokers**. A **full-service broker** will execute your buy and sell orders and will also provide you with advice or guidance about what to buy and what to sell and when. A **discount broker** will only execute your buy and sell orders: he will not give investment advice. Obviously then, you will pay a higher commission for the full-service broker because part of the commission fee goes to pay for the investment advice that you get from your agent. If you are a knowledgeable investor and know what to buy and sell, you do not need any investment advice. Therefore, you should find a discount broker, particularly as their commission can be 70% lower than that of full-service brokers.

Commissions are now negotiable in Canada but that does not mean that they are inexpensive: in fact, the small investor has very little bargaining power and her commissions have gone up since the advent of negotiated commission rates. Typically, **commissions** have two components — a fixed minimum commission per trade and a variable component based on the value of the trade. The average total commission ranges from 1% to 3% of the value of the trade, buy or sell.

Stock Market Indices

How do you keep track of what the entire stock market is doing? How do you measure the historical performance of the stock market? The answer lies in the use of **stock market indices**.

TSE 300 Composite Index

The TSE 300 Composite Index is Canada's best-known stock market indicator.[9] It contains the 300 largest securities, in terms of market value, traded on the Toronto Stock Exchange. It is computed by calculating the total market value of the 300 stocks in the index every day. The percentage increase (or decrease) in the total market value from one day to the next represents the increase (or decrease) in the index. The rate of return of the index is the rate of return that would be earned by an investor who holds a portfolio of all 300 stocks in the index in proportion to their market value — except that the index does not reflect cash dividends paid out by those stocks. In other words, the TSE 300 index tracks the capital gains of the TSE 300 stocks.

TSE 35 Index

This is a 35-stock index composed of 35 of the largest Canadian companies drawn from a variety of industrial groups.

Other Stock Indices

The TSE also calculates about fifteen stock indices based on narrow industry groupings such as the Oil and Gas Index, the Gold and Silver Index, the Merchandising Index and the High Technology Index.

The Montreal Stock Exchange computes the 25-stock Canadian Market Portfolio Index which is sometimes called the MSE Index. The MSE also computes several industrial indices. The Vancouver Stock Exchange calculates its own VSE Index which is based mainly on low-capitalization stocks (i.e., small companies) that are traded there.

Investing in Stocks

Are stocks good investments? How do stocks compare with other investments, like bonds, with respect to their return-risk characteristics? Should one include stocks in one's investment portfolio?

Historical Performance of Stocks

Over long periods of time, stocks have consistently paid returns higher than that of bonds. For example, over the period 1954 to 1980, the return on stocks was 10.02% and that for long-term corporate bonds was

---

[9] TSE stands for Toronto Stock Exchange.

only 3.93%. This finding confirms the first basic principle in investment that the higher the risk the higher the return that one can expect to earn. In other words, although stocks are riskier than bonds, there is a higher reward for investing in stocks. A very important feature of stocks is that the longer the holding period, the less fluctuation there is in the rate of return. Researchers have found that the spread between highest and lowest returns shrinks dramatically with longer holding periods. This means that the risk of investing in the stock market decreases as the holding period increases. If you are investing for long-term purposes (such as saving for a comfortable retirement) then you have a long holding period and the stock market can be a rewarding place to be, in spite of its short-term volatility.

There is one more important finding: researchers have found that over long periods of time, stocks have consistently generated returns much higher than inflation. For example, the real rate of return (after inflation) of the TSE 300 stocks was 3.07% per year during the 20-year period from December 1961 to December 1981 and it was 2.92% for the 10-year period from December 1971 to December 1981. Thus, over the long term, stocks have proved to be good inflation hedges.

Although history may not repeat itself, there are three lesson that we have learned from past performances:

1.   Stocks outperformed the other two major categories of investments — cash equivalents and bonds. Nevertheless, stocks are also more risky in the short term.
2.   The risk of investing in stocks is substantially reduced if one has long holding periods. In fact, the risk is a decreasing function as the holding period increases. The implication is that long-term investors should include stocks in their portfolios.
3.   Over long periods of time, stocks are good hedges against inflation risk.[10]

Investment Risks of Stocks

There are a number of risks involved with stock market investing. The three most important risks associated with "playing the market" are:

Price Volatility Risk   This is similar to the default risk of bonds. It is the risk of losing part or all of one's initial investment. As discussed in Chapter 13, there are two measures of this risk — the **standard deviation** of the rate of return and **beta**. The former measures the total risk of the stock whereas the latter measures its systematic risk (or market risk).

One way to reduce the price volatility risk is to diversify. It takes about 15 to 20 stocks to achieve the full benefit of diversification. Another way to reduce this risk is by buying mutual funds, which we will discuss in Chapter 15.

---

[10] We hasten to add that this is not the case in the short term. In fact, researchers have found that there is a short-term negative relationship between stocks and inflation. The reason for this is that interest rates increase as inflation increases; consequently, stock prices tend to fall when interest rates increase. This means that, in the short run, stocks may not be good inflation hedges.

Inflation Risk   This is the risk that the return on investment cannot keep up with the rate of inflation. In the long run, stocks are good hedges against inflation risk but in the short term, there is substantial inflation risk in stock investments.

Liquidity Risk   This is the risk of not being able to liquidate or cash in one's investment within a short length of time and at a reasonable price. Most stocks are very liquid, for example, you can sell a large amount of a blue-chip stock within a matter of minutes. On the other hand, there are stocks (usually of smaller companies) that are thinly traded in the market. These stocks will have some liquidation risk.

Selecting Stocks

There are two primary reasons motivating people to spend time and effort in selecting stocks. First, many people believe that there are ways to discover undervalued stocks that would give them an above average return. Second, one has to choose the stock that has the right "risk-return mix." This means choosing the stock which is compatible with one's financial circumstances and risk preferences.

As for the first motivation, by virtue of the third investment principle of **efficient markets**, finding undervalued securities is very difficult. Although the market is not perfectly efficient, it is very difficult for a small investor to exploit these market inefficiencies. The individual would likely be disappointed if her objective is to find undervalued stocks. We believe that, by and large, stocks are fairly valued.

Nevertheless, even if every stock is fairly valued in the market, that does not mean that every stock is suitable for any one individual investor. Each stock has its own characteristics in terms of return, risk, liquidity and so on. It is up to the investor to choose stocks which are compatible with his risk preferences and financial circumstances. Go back to Chapter 13 and review how one estimates the **expected rate of return** and the **risk** (either the **standard deviation** or **beta**) of a stock. Using historical data to estimate an objective probability distribution for the rate of return is usually a good starting point. Full-service brokers normally have all kinds of research reports or forecasts that help individual investors to assess the risk and return of a company. There are also investment newsletters and advisory services which forecast the future returns (and risks) of stocks. You can also learn security analysis techniques for the purpose of making your own analyses. Regardless of the method you use, the basic idea is to come up with a reliable measure of a stock's **risk** and **return** so that you can choose stocks that fit your risk-return preference. We will go through this in more detail in Chapter 15 when we discuss choosing a mutual fund.

OTHER INVESTMENTS

Up to this point, you have learned a lot about the traditional types of investments — short-term near-cash investments, bonds, stocks, real estate, international securities, mutual funds etc. These are the basic investments which should form all or at least a major part of your investment portfolio. There are, however, many other more complicated investment vehicles such as **options** and **futures** that have gained substantial popularity in recent years. We shall describe the major ones in the remainder of this chapter, but before doing so, let us make an important comment. Most of these investments are very sophisticated and carry high risks. You should commit at most a small portion of your portfolio to them and then only if you have learned more about them and can afford to lose everything invested.[11] Do not touch these investments just because of the recommendation of a broker or a so-called financial expert.

Options

An **option** is the right to purchase or sell an asset at a stated price for a specified period of time. A **call option** is the right to buy the asset and a **put option** is the right to sell the asset. Every option is written on an asset which is called the **underlying asset**. An option is always a contract between two parties.

Theoretically, the **underlying asset** can be anything that the two parties of the contract have agreed upon. The most common underlying assets are stocks and, in this case, the option is called a **stock option**. **Index options** are based on a well-established stock market index such as the TSE 300 or the Dow Jones Industrial Average. **Currency options** and **commodity options** are options based on currencies and commodities, respectively.

Exchange-traded Options

Exchange-traded options are options that are traded on an exchange. The best-known ones are **stock options** which are traded on the Toronto Stock Exchange (TSE), the Montreal Stock Exchange (MSE) and the Vancouver Stock Exchange (VSE). Only firms that meet certain quality standards can have their options listed.

For **stock options**, an option contract generally covers 100 shares of a stock at a fixed price per share — this is called the **exercise price** — within a certain period of time. Stock option prices are quoted in the financial press.

> **Example 14.8:** Mr. Carl Copeland bought a call option of the LMN Co. Ltd. three months ago. He paid a **premium** (which is just another name for the option price) of $2 per option, or $200 for the full contract ($2 × 100 shares). The exercise price of the option is $15 per share. The stock price of the LMN Co. Ltd. has increased from $14 to $21 since the time he bought the option. If he exercises the option now, how much money would he make? What is the rate of return on the investment? Ignore broker's commission.

He would make ($21 − $15) = $6 per share, minus $2 per share for the cost of the option. This is equal to $4 per share for a total profit of 100 × $4 = $400. The rate of return on investment = $400 ÷ $200 = 200% in three months, which translates into a rate of return of 800% per annum.

Let us warn you once more that options could be very risky. In Example 14.8, suppose the stock price of the LMN Co. Ltd. never increased above the exercise price of $15; then, in nine months' time, Mr. Copeland would have lost $200, or 100% of his investment.

---

[11] Options and futures can be used for the purpose of hedging. If used as such, they may play an important function in one's investment plan. Again, the first basic principle in investment applies: what is the risk-return trade-off? Are you comfortable with the risk?

Futures Markets

A **future** is a standardized contract to buy or sell a specific quantity of a commodity on a specified future date at a price agreed upon today. The word, "commodity," includes agricultural products (e.g., wheat, corn, coffee, pork bellies etc.), metals (e.g., gold, copper, silver, nickel etc.), other natural resources (e.g., lumber, oil, gas etc.), foreign currencies (e.g., Japanese Yen, Deutsch Mark, British Pound etc.) some financial instruments (e.g., government bonds, Treasury bills), and financial futures (e.g., interest rate futures, stock index futures). You can buy and sell commodities in a futures market whether or not you own the particular commodity. In fact, physical deliveries of the commodity are rare because most futures-contract buyers and sellers close out their contracts before the delivery date.

The individual investor is normally a speculator in the commodity market because he tends to put down a small margin to buy or sell a large amount of commodities. In other words, one's investment position is always highly leveraged. As a result, even a small price fluctuation can wipe out the investor's entire investment principal. Sometimes one cannot limit one's losses: unlike the option markets where one can lose at the most 100% of one's principal, in the commodity markets one can lose more than 100% of one's initial principal.[12] The commodity markets are very volatile for the most part and they are dominated by professional traders who have a lot of knowledge and experience. They make their living in trading and have better information sources than the average investor. Past studies of the performance of the average investor have shown that the odds against the individual are overwhelming. You should not put more than a small portion of your portfolio in the commodity markets.

SUMMARY

In this chapter, you have learned the three fundamental types of investments — **cash equivalent investments**, (such as T-bills and term deposits), **bonds** and **stocks**. Each has been described in terms of their investment characteristics — risk, return, liquidity and so on.

Treasury bills and Canada Savings Bonds are investments with zero default risk. They are both very liquid, however, the return is usually quite low. They are good places to park a family's emergency funds. Next in line in terms of default risk are savings and chequing accounts, term deposits and guaranteed investment certificates. All are very liquid and the default risk is close to zero. Longer-term GICs usually offer a higher interest rate than T-bills and CSBs. All these investments are generally called cash-equivalent investments. Every family have should some money invested in cash-equivalent investments — at least three to six months' take-home pay as an emergency fund.

The next investment category is bonds. Bonds are issued by the three levels of government as well as by corporations. There are various measures of rate of return — the holding period return (HPR), the yield to maturity and the current yield. Bonds are risky investments. Even Government of Canada Bonds are not risk-free investments; they

---

[12] If you do not understand this last sentence, you should take it as proof positive that you are not knowledgeable enough to touch the commodity markets. Do not put any money in the commodity markets until you acquire more knowledge about the risk involved.

are only free of default risk. The major risks associated with bond investments are default risk, interest rate risk, reinvestment risks and option features (such as call provisions) which make the bonds more or less risky to the bondholders.

The third category of investments is stocks. The stock market performance can be measured by stock market indices such as the TSE 300 Composite Index. Stocks are riskier investments than bonds and their risk can be measured by the standard deviation of the rate of return or by their betas. The major reasons for investing in stocks are:

1. Over long periods of time, stocks provide higher returns than cash-equivalent investments and bonds;
2. The risk of investing in stocks is substantially reduced for long holding periods; and
3. Over long periods of time, stocks have generated returns that are substantially higher than inflation.

Finally, some complex investments have been described. We introduced the **options markets** and the **futures markets**. These are normally very risky investments and the markets are dominated by professional traders. You should allocate at the most only a small fraction of your portfolio to these risky investments but only after you learn more about them.

KEY TERMINOLOGY

principle of risk-return trade-off / principle of diversification / principle of efficient markets / market inefficiencies / default risk / Treasury bills (T-bills) / face value / buy at a discount / inflation hedge / Canada Savings Bond (CSB) / regular interest bond / compound interest bond / savings account / chequing account / chequing-savings account / automated teller machines / term deposit / daily interest account / term / guaranteed investment certificate (GIC) / deposit insurance / Canada Deposit Insurance Corporation (CDIC) / face value (par value or principal) of bonds / coupon rate / maturity date / coupon bonds / bond quotation / investment dealer, bond dealer / ask price / bid price / bond market / spread (of bid and ask) / accrued interest / yield to maturity / return to maturity / internal rate of return / bond price equation / default risk / interest rate risk / option features / bond ratings / bond rating agency / reinvestment risk / zero-coupon bonds / strip bonds / callable bonds / extendible bonds / retractable bonds / convertible bonds / common stocks / limited liability / primary market / secondary market / underwriting / stock exchange / over-the-counter (OTC) market / seats in a stock exchange / stock quotations / closing price / sales volume / indicated dividends / dividend yield / share profit / earnings per share / price-earnings ratio (P/E) / full-service broker / discount broker / commission (for stock trading) / TSE 300 Composite Index / TSE 35 index / price volatility risk / beta / inflation risk / option / stock option / call option / put option / underlying asset / index option / currency option / commodity option / exchange-traded option / exercise price / futures market / future / commodity future

DISCUSSION QUESTIONS

1. Define or describe all the terms under **Key Terminology**.

2. **Personal Project 1**
   Get a copy of the business section of today's newspaper. Examine (i) the bond quotations and (ii) the stock quotations. Go through each column heading and

explain in your own words what each term means. Now pick randomly ten bonds from the bond quotation and ten stocks from the stock quotation list. Go through the numbers for each bond and each stock. Describe in your own words what information has been conveyed by the market quotations. Verify some of the numbers if possible — e.g., P/E ratio, bond yield etc.

3. T-bills have zero default risk and savings accounts are a little more risky. The interest rate of T-bills is often higher than that of savings accounts. Is this inconsistent with the basic principle of risk-return tradeoff?

4. Are securities sold by the federal government always default-risk free?

5. Are Treasury bills good inflation hedges? How does income tax affect your answer?

6. How safe is one's money in a bank? Describe how the CDIC works. What is the maximum insurance coverage available to an individual depositor?

PROBLEMS

1. The current price of a 91-day T-bill is $9,750. Its face value is $10,000. What is the effective annual rate of return?

2. (a) Find the yield to maturity of the following bonds:
   (i) Price = $9,500, coupon = 9.5%, maturity = 20 years, face value = $10,000.
   (ii) Price = $10,500, coupon = 10.25%, maturity = 30 years, face value = $10,000.
   (iii) Price = $10,000, coupon = 10%, maturity = 10 years, face value = $10,000.

   (b) Are these yields to maturity guaranteed? Explain.

3. For each of the bonds in Question 2, if the yield to maturity changes to 11% after one year, calculate (i) the new bond price and (ii) the holding period return during this year.

4. Joe and Mary Whitehall have the following accounts/investments at a trust company which is a CDIC member.

In Joe's name:	
Savings Account	$40,000
Chequing Account	$ 5,000
Term Deposit	$15,000
RRSP (in GICs)	$35,000
In Mary's name:	
Savings Account	$ 5,000
Chequing Account	$ 1,000
GICs	$67,000
RRSP (in mutual funds)	$90,000
Joint names:	
Savings Account	$10,000
Term Deposit	$30,000

Discuss the CDIC insurance coverage for the Whitehalls.

5. Mr. Wolfe's stockbroker recently sent him a research report on a stock that is currently selling for $25. According to the report, the stock will pay $2 per share of dividends next year and the target stock price after one year is $30. The commission for trading stocks is 1.5% of the stock price, for either buy or sell.

   (a) Calculate the expected rate of return, after all commissions, if Mr. Wolfe buys and holds the stock for one year.
   (b) What is Mr. Wolfe's expected after-tax rate of return if he lives in Ontario and is in the 26% federal tax bracket?

6. An 8% Canadian Pacific Railway bond with a quarterly coupon costs $1,172.50 and matures in nine years. What is the yield to maturity? What is the effective annual rate of return (EAR)?

7. Currently the 11% semi-annual bonds of Smith and Daughters have eight years to maturity and are selling at 85.83 ($858.30 per $1,000 of face value).

   (a) Calculate the yield to maturity on the bonds.
   (b) If interest rates do not change, at what price will the bonds sell two years from today?
   (c) Suppose interest rates do change over the next two years. At the end of two years, the bond is priced to yield 12%. What will be the bond's price on that day?
   (d) Given the information in (c), what is the expected before-tax rate of return if the bond is bought today and sold two years from today? State clearly your reinvestment assumptions.
   (e) If your marginal tax rate is 40%, what is the expected after-tax rate of return corresponding to part (d)?

8. (a) A Government of Canada Bond (called a Canada for short) with one year to maturity pays a semi-annual coupon of $65. The current price of the bond is $1,064.56. What is the yield to maturity (YTM)? What is the effective annual rate (EAR)?
   (b) A Canada with 10 years to maturity has a YTM of 7.26% and a semi-annual coupon of $40. What is the current price?
   (c) Interest rates rise in such a way that the required yield (that is, the best alternative rate for this risk and maturity) rises by 1% for all bonds (this is also called a parallel yield shift). What is each bond worth now? Explain the difference in the price changes.

9. Ives and Staicu Ltd. has an outstanding 10% bond issue trading at $1,092.50. It pays interest semi-annually and has seven years to maturity.

   (a) What is the yield to maturity?
   (b) What is the effective annual rate of return?

10. Laura Parker buys for $952.38 a Treasury bill that matures in one year at $1,000. She lives in Ontario. She is in the 26% federal income tax bracket, the 3% federal surtax bracket and the 20% Ontario surtax bracket. What is her after-tax rate of return on the Treasury bill?

11. You are a Prince Edward Island investor in the top tax bracket trying to decide between two investments of equal risk. One is a five-year bond, trading at par, with an 8% coupon, paid semi-annually. The other is a preferred share that will be redeemed at $25 in five years. It pays a dividend of $0.35 every quarter, and is trading at $25. Ignore transactions costs and surtaxes.

    (a) In which security should you invest your money?
    (b) The calculated returns would be different if you included surtaxes, but the decision in part (a) would be the same. Why?
    (c) If the securities were not trading at par, the calculations would be much more complicated. Explain briefly how you would do the calculations for part (a).

chapter 15
Mutual Funds

In Chapter 13 we described the basic concepts in investments. We summarized the major developments in the investment literature in terms of three **basic principles in investment**. In Chapter 14 we described the three most important types of investments: **near-cash investments**, **bonds** and **stocks**. In this chapter, we will put everything together and develop an investment strategy that is suitable for most people, especially the average Canadian investor. The investment strategy is built on a firm theoretical foundation; more specifically, it is built on the three fundamental principles of investment. This investment strategy will allow you to allocate your investment money among three basic types of investments — cash, bonds and stock. If you like, you can easily add other types of investments, such as real estate, your own home, options, foreign stocks and so on. There is plenty of flexibility in the investment strategy to allow you to choose the proper risk and return mix — at the level you are comfortable with — to reach your financial goals. The things that make our investment strategy possible are **mutual funds**. We will argue that **mutual funds** are the best investment choice for most Canadians. Mutual funds provide an opportunity for even a small investor with limited financial resources to build an investment plan that satisfies the three fundamental investment principles and, at the same time, allows the person to reach his financial goals.

The specific learning objectives are:

1. To describe the major types of mutual funds;
2. To discuss the advantages and the disadvantages of investing in mutual funds;
3. To explain how you can compare the fees of different mutual funds;
4. To explain how you can read the daily, weekly and monthly mutual fund reports;
5. To assess the total risk exposure of a portfolio of several mutual funds;
6. To describe how you should go about buying a mutual fund.

TYPES OF MUTUAL FUNDS

A **mutual fund** is a financial organization that accepts funds from hundreds and thousands of investors, pools these funds and invests them in bonds, stocks, real estate, precious metals or other investments. It issues shares or units to investors in proportion to the funds each investor contributes. Each of the investors owns a fraction of all the investments in the mutual fund.

Conceptually, a mutual fund is not like a stock or a bond; rather, it is a way of investing. Investing in mutual funds provides small investors with an opportunity to hold many different securities, thereby achieving a much higher degree of diversification than they could achieve by investing on their own. While a mutual fund offers investors other benefits which we will discuss later, we want to stress here that the main contribution of mutual funds is that they provide investors with ready-made diversification at a low cost.

There are many types of mutual funds. They are classified by the way they are organized; for example, **closed-end funds** and **open-end funds**. They can also be classified by what they invest in. There are mutual funds that invest in stocks, bonds, gold, real estate, Treasury bills and so on. With stock mutual funds, there are those that invest primarily in conservative stocks and funds that specialize in risky stocks. In fact, there is probably a mutual fund for just about every type of investment. The following is a list of the more common mutual funds:

Open-end Fund
This is a mutual fund that continuously sells its own shares or units to the public. Its investors or shareholders have a continuing right to sell their shares back to the fund itself. This right is called the **right of redemption**. The number of shares or units of the fund changes continuously as shares are being sold and redeemed. Examples: any of the funds in Table 15.1.

Closed-end Fund
This is a mutual fund that offers its shares or units to investors at the time the fund is set up; after that, the fund normally will not sell or buy back its shares or units. Proceeds from the initial sale of shares are then invested in a diversified portfolio of investments consistent with the fund's objective. Thus, a closed-end fund's equity base is relatively fixed and seldom change materially. The shares can be traded among investors in an "after-market"; in fact, the shares or units of most of Canada's closed-end funds trade on the stock exchanges or the over-the-counter market. Example: Canadian World Fund, traded on the TSE.

RRSP Eligible Funds
Because of the foreign investment restriction for RRSPs and RRIFs, not all investments are eligible. An RSP-eligible fund is one that has enough Canadian investments in the fund to avoid contravening the RRSP and RRIF foreign investment restriction. Examples: all the funds marked RSP-eligible in Table 15.1.

Treasury Bill Fund
This is a mutual fund that invests exclusively in Treasury bills issued by the government of Canada. Example: Green Line Canadian T-Bill Fund.

Money Market Fund
This is a mutual fund that invests in safe, short-term, liquid investments such as Treasury bills, term deposits, commercial paper (short-term corporate debt), and short-term bonds. The fund generates a floating rate of return which rises or falls with the rate of inflation. Money market funds (as well as Treasury bill funds) are normally good investments when the rate of inflation is rising. Example: AGF Money Market Fund.

Mortgage Funds
This is a mutual fund that invests primarily in high-quality conventional mortgages (i.e., first mortgages). It may also invest in short-term bonds. It

generates a higher rate of return than Treasury bill funds and money market funds do, albeit at a slightly higher risk. Example: Green Line Mortgage Fund.

Income Fund or Bond Fund

This is a mutual fund that invests primarily in government bonds, high-quality, high-yielding corporate bonds, some high-yield preferred and common stocks and mortgages. The objective of the fund is to maintain the safety of principal and high income. Example: CIBC Canadian Bond Fund, Dynamic Income Fund.

Dividend Fund

This is a mutual fund that invests primarily in Canadian preferred and common stocks with high dividend yields. The preferential tax treatment of dividends over interest-bearing investments makes this type of fund highly attractive to some investors. Example: Prudential Dividend Fund, Royfund Dividend Fund.

Balanced Fund

This is a mutual fund that allocates its money among the three basic types of investments — cash equivalent investments, bonds and common stocks. In some balanced funds, the portfolio mix remains fairly stable from one period to another and the fund's manager adopts a more or less "buy-and-hold" investment strategy. In other balanced funds, the manager changes the portfolio mix continuously, putting more weight on the investment type that is expected to outperform the other two for the coming period. This strategy of changing the portfolio mix continuously to increase the return on investment is called the **asset allocation** strategy; it is a kind of market-timing strategy. Example: MacKenzie Industrial Balanced Fund, CIBC Balanced Fund.

Equity Fund or Stock Fund

An equity fund invests primarily in common stocks, although short-term notes and other fixed income securities may be held to maintain liquidity. Because common stock prices are more volatile than those of other fixed income securities, equity funds tend to be more risky than income or balanced funds.

Equity funds have a great range in the degrees of their risk and growth potentials. Some are heavily invested in blue-chip, income-producing common stocks and are quite conservative. Example: Royfund Equity Fund, Green Line Blue Chip Equity Fund.

Other equity funds take a more aggressive investment stance. They invest in companies with higher risk but greater growth potential. These funds are often called **growth funds** and their objective is to achieve above-average growth of capital. Example: Royfund Canadian Growth Fund, Cambridge Growth Fund, Dynamic Canadian Growth Fund.

Index Fund

This is a stock index mutual fund that holds a representative sample of the entire stock market. The objective of the fund is to give the investor the average return yielded by the stock market, no more and no less. Example: Green Line Canadian Index Fund.

Real Estate Fund

This is a mutual fund that invests primarily in income-producing real estate (such as rental apartment buildings, office buildings, shopping malls, industrial buildings) in order to achieve long-term growth through capital appreciation and reinvestment of income. Example: Investors Real Property Fund, MD Realty Fund.

Specialty Funds

These are mutual funds that concentrate on shares of a group of companies in one industry (e.g., Oil and Gas), in one geographic location (e.g., Japan), or in one segment of the capital market (e.g., Natural Resources). Although there is diversification in their portfolios, these funds tend to be more risky and speculative than most types of common share funds. Examples: AGF Canadian Resources, Saxon Group Small Capitalization Fund, Scotia Bank Precious Metal Fund.

Ethical Mutual Funds

These are funds whose investment decisions are guided by some moral criteria which may vary from fund to fund. One ethical fund may avoid investing in companies that profit from tobacco or armaments, whereas another fund may avoid companies that pollute the environment. Example: Dynamics Green Fund.

International Funds

These are mutual funds that primarily invest in securities of countries other than Canada. Some international funds focus on one single country. In Canada, the most popular single-country funds are the **US Funds** which invest in US securities. Both US bond funds and US equity funds are offered by many mutual fund companies. Examples of other single-country international funds include Investors Group's Japan Growth Fund and Fidelity Investments' Japanese Growth Fund.

Some international mutual funds focus on a certain region of the world, such as Europe, Asia or South America. Examples: Altamira European Equity Fund, Dynamic Europe Fund, Fidelity Investments' Far East Fund and Royal Trust Asian Growth Fund.

Some international mutual funds invest in a well-diversified world portfolio. They invest in every major economic region of the world, including North America, Europe and Asia. They are often called **Global Funds**. Example: Templeton Growth Fund, MD Growth Fund, AGF Global Fund, Royfund International Equity Fund and CIBC Global Fund.

Finally, there are the international specialty funds which concentrate on a certain narrow sector or on a certain theme. For example, the **emerging market funds** invest primarily in small countries that are expected to grow very fast — e.g., Templeton Emerging Market Fund.

MUTUAL FUND COSTS

Buying mutual funds entails a variety of fees or costs. These fees can be classified into three groups: (1) fees charged when one buys mutual fund shares — these are called the **front-end load** or **front-end fees**, (2) fees charged when one sells the mutual fund shares — these are called the **back-end fees**, **rear-end fees** or **redemption fees**, and (3) management fees charged each year — these are called **annual fees**.

No-load Funds

No-load funds are mutual funds that do not charge a front-end fee; however, they can still charge back-end and annual fees.

Are No-load Funds Cheaper Than Front-load Funds?

In the past, **front-load mutual funds** charged a very high front-end fee. Sometimes the fee could be as high as 9% of the purchase price. For example, if you purchase $1,000 of a front-end fund which charges a 9% front-end fee, then (9% × $1,000) or $90 would be deducted up front, leaving you with a net investment of only $910.00. Because of this, front-load funds give most people the impression that they are more expensive than no-load funds.

Nevertheless, if a no-load fund charges a higher annual fee or back-end fee than a front-load fund of similar quality, then it is not clear which fund is the cheaper. You should look at the entire fee structure — front-end fees, annual fees, rear-end fees — of each mutual fund, and you should use the analysis employed in Example 15.1 to decide which fund has the lowest set of fees. You may be surprised to find that some so-called no-load funds are actually more expensive than some front-load funds.

Back-end Fees

Many mutual funds charge back-end or redemption fees according to a sliding scale: the longer you hold the fund, the less will be charged. Because its purpose is to encourage long-term holding, the back-end fee normally is waived after one has held shares in the fund for longer than a specified number of years (usually five). The following is a typical back-end fee structure:

if it is sold in the first year:	5% (of selling price)
if it is sold in the second year:	4%
if it is sold in the third year:	3%
if it is sold in the fourth year:	2%
if it is sold in the fifth year:	1%
if it is sold after the fifth year:	0%

Thus, whether you have to pay a rear-end fee and how much depends on your holding period. Long-term investors normally do not have to pay the rear-end fee.

Example 15.1: ABC Fund and XYZ Fund are two Canadian equity funds of
(comparing   similar quality and past performance. Suppose the ABC Fund
mutual fund   has a front-end fee of 8%, an annual fee of 1.25% and no
fees)   rear-end fee, whereas the XYZ Fund has no front-end fee but
                    it does have a rear-end fee of 5% and an annual fee of 2%.
                    If Mr. Stargill's holding period is 10 years, which fund has
                    a lower fee structure?

Suppose the discount rate that Mr. Stargill uses is 10%. We will convert all fees into annual fees and then compare them for the two funds. In other words, we will convert the front-end and the rear-end fee, which are both one-time fees, into annual fees.

Let us first consider the ABC Fund. The 8% front-end fee should be spread out (or, more precisely, amortized) over the 10-year holding period in order to obtain an annual cost. If x% is the annual "amortized" cost of the front-end fee, we have the following equation:

$$x \times \text{PVIFA} = 8\%$$

$$x \times \left[\frac{1}{.10} - \frac{1}{.10 \times 1.10^{10}} \right] = 8\%$$

$$x = 1.3\%$$

The annual cost of the ABC Fund equals the annual front-end cost plus annual fees plus the annual back-end fee cost which equals:

$$1.3\% + 1.25\% + 0\%$$
$$= 2.55\%.$$

Let us now consider the XYZ Fund. The rear-end fee is a one-time fee and we will spread it over 10 years. If we let y equal the annual cost of the back-end fee, we have the following equation:

$$y \times \text{FVIFA} = 5\%$$
$$y \times \left[\frac{1.10^{10} - 1}{.10}\right] = 5\%$$
$$y = .31\%$$

The annual cost of the XYZ Fund equals the annual front-end cost plus annual fees plus the annual rear-end fee cost which equals:

$$0\% + 2\% + .31\%$$
$$= 2.31\%.$$

Thus, XYZ Fund has a cheaper set of fees than does ABC Fund.

MUTUAL FUND TAXATION

The investment income rules from Chapter 6 apply to the income you earn in a mutual fund. The mutual fund administrator records your share of the interest, Canadian dividends, foreign dividends, net realized capital gains and losses and net unrealized capital gains and losses. In February you receive T5 information slips reporting your interest, dividends and realized capital gains for the previous year. You report the income exactly as you would if you had received the amounts directly, and pay tax on them. The mutual fund's management fees are tax deductible.

When you sell the mutual fund units, your share of the unrealized capital gains and losses is realized. The front-end and the back-end load fee reduce the capital gain (or increase the capital loss). Technically speaking, the front-end fee is added to the adjusted cost base, and the back-end fee is deducted from the proceeds on disposition of the mutual fund units.

Thus, all of the tax strategies apply to mutual funds in the same manner as direct investments. For example, if you are saving for retirement a long time in the future and do not need income from the investments now, a growth mutual fund with low dividends is more tax efficient. Most of the return is capital gains, and to the extent that they remain unrealized, the income tax is deferred.

WHY INVEST IN MUTUAL FUNDS?

It has been noted previously that mutual funds are not, conceptually speaking, types of investments like stocks or bonds; rather, they are a way of investing. We shall go on to argue that for the average investor, especially small investors with limited resources, mutual funds are the best way to invest one's money to achieve one's objectives.

Let us examine what a typical investor should do in view of what we have learned so far. First, one should set financial goals and have action plans to reach those goals (see Chapter 3). Second, one should find an investment approach with which one is comfortable and to which one can commit oneself with follow-up action. The investment approach should be based on firm investment principles — the three fundamental principles described in Chapter 13. Finally, one should choose the types of investments which give the desired risk-return mix. The three basic types of investments have been covered in Chapter 14 — cash equivalent investments, bonds and stocks. Some people may (and usually do) include other investments in addition to the three basic types — for example, one's own home, real estate, precious metals, futures, options and so on.[1]

The three fundamental principles in investment speak very strongly for the use of mutual funds in one's investment plan. First, one needs reasonably reliable estimates of the risks and the expected returns of investments before one can make decisions. The historical data of a mutual fund give reliable and objective estimates of the fund's risk and return. Since a mutual fund is normally a diversified portfolio, the risk and return do not shift over time as erratically as that of a single share. In other words, not only is it easier to estimate the risk of a mutual fund than it is to estimate a stock's risk, the estimate made on a mutual fund's risk and return is much more reliable.

Second, the principle of diversification dictates that one should diversify across major investment types (i.e., cash, bonds and stocks); that one should diversify within each investment types (i.e., hold a stock portfolio instead of just one stock); and that one should diversify across different economies (i.e., hold a global portfolio rather than a portfolio of a single country's issues). Although the benefits to be derived from following the principle of diversification in one's investment decision making are substantial, because the required degree of diversification requires a substantial capital outlay, these benefits are unavailable to a small investor: for example, even one who saves and invests several hundred dollars a month cannot achieve all the objectives of diversification. The average small investor's monthly savings are not enough to buy even a single bond! To make matters worse, the average small investor has little time to manage her investments; moreover, a non-professional investor's knowledge about investment is too limited to make good investment decisions. **Mutual funds** provide the solution to the problem of how to achieve well-selected and well-managed diversification with limited funds, time and knowledge. The minimum investment required for most mutual funds is quite small: it can go as low as $50. Thus, with several hundred dollars, one can easily buy five or six mutual funds — say, a money market fund, a bond fund, one or two equity funds, a global fund and a specialty fund — and achieve all the benefits of diversification available. You need not worry about time and knowledge because the mutual fund managers will do all the investing for you.

It is almost impossible for a small investor to achieve better stock selection than a mutual fund manager; it is highly unlikely that a small investor will outperform a professional fund manager even over the short term. The principle of efficient markets supports both of these assertions. Furthermore, even if there are market inefficiencies (empirical studies have detected some), professional fund managers are in a better position

---

[1] Every person's investment portfolio also includes human capital — the value of education, occupational training and experience.

than are small investors to exploit these market inefficiencies in order to produce better returns. Professional investors are more knowledgeable than small investors and they have more resources (i.e., time, money and information) than do small investors.

Advantages of Mutual Fund Investment

To summarize, the following are the chief advantages:

1. Professional Management
Mutual funds are run and managed by professional managers who make all the day-to-day decisions about buying and selling. If you believe that the markets are inefficient and that it is possible to outperform the market (either by timing, picking stocks or some other technique), the professional manager should stand a much better chance of doing the job well. Even if you believe the market is efficient and that professional managers cannot outperform the average investor, you still benefit from professional management because hired professionals reduce the amount of time and effort that you must devote to investing your money.

2. Broad Diversification
The mutual fund has more dollars with which to purchase a wider range of investments than any one investor can independently provide. A typical fund has a portfolio of over 50 stocks in 15 to 20 industries. By purchasing several mutual funds, a small investor can achieve all the objectives of diversification — to diversify among the major investment types; to diversify within each investment type; and to diversify across different countries.

3. More Reliable Estimates of Risk and Return
Studies have shown that risk measures — whether using standard deviation or beta — are more stable and hence, more reliable in the case of portfolios than individual stocks. You can use a fund's historical data to come up with objective and reasonably reliable estimates for the fund's return and risk. In contrast, it is much more difficult to assess the risk of your total investment position when you buy your own stocks and investments.

4. Past Performance Record
You can check a fund's past performance record relative to the market or relative to other mutual funds of similar quality and with similar investment objectives. Many newspapers keep track of the performance of mutual funds. These records are reported regularly and are easily available.

5. Record Keeping and Safekeeping
The mutual fund manager keeps the records of all buying and selling of securities and other relevant transactions. You do not have to worry about cashing interest coupons or dividend cheques. You do not have to bother about keeping stock and bond certificates safe. A summary record will be mailed to you before the deadline for filing your tax return.

6. Flexibility of Purchase and Sale
A variety of purchase plans are available, ranging from one-time, lump-sum purchases to regular purchases in small amounts under **automatic contribution plans**.[2] Similarly, various withdrawal plans are available,

---

[2] You can preauthorize a specific amount to be deducted from your bank account for the purchasing of a mutual fund.

which are very convenient to retirees who want to cash in a fixed amount every month for consumption.

7. Automatic Reinvestment Plan   You can automatically reinvest your dividends and capital gains. This is a very useful feature because continuous reinvestment and compounding is the key to success in investment.

Disadvantages of Mutual Fund Investment

1. High Cost for Short-term Investment   Many mutual funds charge a front-end fee or a rear-end fee or both. The fees could be very high for short-term holding periods. For example, how can one justify paying a 9% front-end fee for holding a mutual fund for six months? Mutual funds are therefore more suitable for investors who adopt a long-term, buy-and-hold strategy. Mutual funds are not suitable for investors who have short-term holding periods or who trade frequently. The exceptions are T-bill and money market funds, which are cash equivalents and do not charge as high fees.

2. Vulnerable to Massive Redemption   Financial markets are very sensitive to mass psychology of the market's investors. Investors notoriously move as a crowd and this phenomenon may result in a massive request for redemption. This would force the fund manager to sell stocks and investments at the wrong time in order to meet redemption requests. Thus, your investment could be very vulnerable to the mass psychology of the marketplace.[3]

3. Professional Management Is Not Infallible   Although we believe professional management is by and large an advantage for mutual fund investment, there is a counterargument that says there are certain small investors who may have an advantage over large mutual funds. It has been argued that fund managers are subject to tremendous peer pressure because they are constantly being compared to each other. As a result, some tend to emphasize short-term performance rather than long-term results. Also, most mutual funds are very large and they must buy and sell in large quantities so that any significant shift in portfolio holdings necessarily influences market prices; therefore, managers may not always be able to buy at the lowest price or sell at the highest price.

The Average Investor's Responsibility

The advantages of mutual funds outweigh the disadvantages and we think mutual funds are the best way for the average investor to invest his money. The investor nevertheless must choose the right mutual funds from the hundreds that are available. How do you choose the right mutual funds? There are several things that you must do and know. First, you must gather information which means that you must know how to read the daily/weekly market quotations as well as the prospectus of any mutual fund you contemplate purchasing. Second, you must know how to evaluate the risk and the return of each fund that you are considering. Third, you must know how to calculate and

---

[3] In the early 1990s, due to the decline of the Canadian real-estate market, many real-estate mutual funds experienced massive redemption requests from shareholders who wanted to reduce their exposure to the real-estate market. Some funds were temporarily forced to stop redeeming shares because they ran out of cash and could not sell their illiquid real-estate assets quickly enough to meet the demand for redemption.

evaluate the risk and return of your portfolio which may be comprised of several mutual funds and other investments. This is important because you have to choose the "risk-return mix" that is consistent with your financial goal and your risk preference. Fourth, you must monitor your investment results periodically and make adjustments if necessary. These topics will be discussed in the remainder of the chapter.

READING DAILY/WEEKLY MARKET QUOTATIONS

Daily Quotation

Table 15.1 is the typical information given by the daily financial press; obviously, there may be slight variations among different newspapers. The mutual funds are grouped under the fund management companies. In Table 15.1, the management companies are AGF Group, Canadian International, CIBC Funds and Hyperion Funds, etc. The **daily quotation** reports the following information:

1. Name of the fund — usually the name gives some indication of the type of investment in which the fund specializes (e.g., stocks, bonds).
2. Load — whether the fund charges a front-end or a redemption fee.
3. RSP eligibility — whether or not the fund is eligible for RRSP contribution.
4. Distributor — whether the fund is sold by the fund sponsor or by independent brokers/dealers.
5. Value — the value is the **net asset value per share** or unit last calculated. The net asset value per share is defined as total assets minus current liabilities divided by the number of shares outstanding. Investors buy at this value plus the sales charge, if any, and sell at this value minus redemption fees, if any. The **net asset value per share (NAVPS)** is calculated daily for most funds and weekly for some.
6. Change — the last column usually gives the change in value since the last calculation.

> **Example 15.2:**   Let us examine the first fund under the AGF Group in Table 15.1. The name of the fund is the American Growth Fund; it is quoted in Canadian dollars. The fund has an optional front-end or a redemption fee — you have to call the company, the AGF Group, to find out further details. It is not RRSP-eligible, because it exceeds the foreign content rule. It can be bought through independent brokers/dealers. Its last net asset value per share was $10.12 which represents an increase of $0.06 from the previous report.

Weekly/Monthly Performance Report

A more detailed **performance report** is published weekly or monthly by some financial papers such as *The Globe and Mail* or *The Financial Post*.[4] Table 15.2 is part of the monthly performance survey published by *The Financial Post*. We will go through the

---

[4] *The Globe and Mail* publishes the Report on Mutual Funds on the Thursday of the third week of every month. *The Financial Post* publishes the Mutual Funds Performance Survey once a month.

TABLE 15.1
Daily Mutual Fund Quotations*
Canadian Mutual Funds

Recent prices of investment funds supplied by Fundata Canada Inc. at 5:30 p.m. Oct. 28. Prices reported by funds are the net asset value per share of unit last calcualted and are for information purposes only. Confirmation of price should be obtained from the fund. Chg —penny change from last valuation; D —distributed by fund sponsor; G —redemption charge; I —distributed by Independent dealers; L —sales charge; N —no sales charge; O —optional front — end or redemption charge; R —eligible for RRSPs; Z —not available for sale; m —minimum purchase of $150,000; u—U.S. currency; x —ex —dividend; (n) —not a member of IFIC; (Date following fund denotes last valuation).

Fund	Load	RSP	Dist	Val	Ch
A.P.P.Q.(n)					
Equilibre (21/Oct)	N	R		12.40	—
ABC FUNDS					
mFully-Mgd (30/Sep)	N	R	D	7.96	+.05
mFund-Value (30/Sep)	N	R	D	9.72	+.02
ADMAX REGENT GROUP					
A.AmerPerf C$	O			5.08	+.05
uA.AmerPerf US	O			3.84	+.02
A.Asset All (27/Oct)	O	R		11.99	+.01
A.Cdn Income (22/Oct)	O	R		5.23	—
A.Cdn Perf	O	R		6.08	+.05
A.Glot 11th C$				5.54	+.00
uA Glot 11th US	O	R		4.19	-.01
A.Poly perf	O	R		5.19	+.02
A.US Poly C$				5.42	+.3
uA.US Poly US	O			4.10	+.01
R.Europa (27/Oct)	O			9.79	+.03
R.Intt (27/Oct)	O			6.21	-.01
R.Korea (27/Oct)	O			11.13	-.00
R.Nippon (27/Oct)	O	R		11.71	-.06
R.Tiger (27/Oct)	O	R		12.88	+.06
R.World Inc (27/Oct)	O	R		12.33	-.02
AGF GROUP					
Amer Gth C$	O			10.12	+.06
uAmer Gth US	O			7.65	—
Asian Gth C$	O			9.21	—
Cdn Equ	O	R		5.52	unch
Cdn Gth	O	R		7.01	+.09
Cdn Res	O	R		16.03	+.08

Fund	Load	RSP	Dist	Val	Ch
Ev US Equity	D			14.73	+.11
CANADIAN INTERNATIONAL					
Cdn Balanced	O	R		6.45	+.05
Cdn Bond	O	R		5.31	-.01
Cdn Growth	O	R		6.53	+.07
Enterprise				10.34	+.09
Emrg Asian				7.94	+.07
Emrg Mkt				5.62	+.01
European	L	R		5.01	+.01
Glob Bd RSP				5.04	+.01
Glob Eq RSP		R		9.10	+.02
Global	G			10.01	unch
Latin American				7.61	+.06
North Amer				15.98	+.17
Pacific				5.51	unch
World Bond				8.93	+.08
sect Amer				4.97	+.03
sect Cdn				6.71	+.01
sect Em Mkts				5.77	+.01
sect European				9.33	+.02
sect Global				6.69	+.05
sect Nth Amer				10.97	+.11
sect Pacific				8.66	+.02
sect Resource				6.65	unch
sect Sht-Term					
CDN NATURAL RESOURCES(n)					
Can Nat Res (27/Oct)	L	R		6.12	+.01
CAPSTONE GROUP(n)					
Internat'l	N			7.93	+.11
Investment	N			7.32	+.05
CENTURY					
DJ	L			10.65	+.01
CHOU ASSOC MGT					
Associates (22/Oct)	L	R		20.70	—
RRSP (22/Oct)	L	R		11.27	—
CHURCH STREET					
Balanced	N			12.54	unch
Equity	N			12.28	unch
Income	N			10.93	unch
CIBC FUNDS					
Balanced	N	R		12.63	+.03
Cap App	N	R		17.54	+.14
Cdn Bond	N	R		12.02	-.03
Cdn Equity	N	R		11.81	+.01
Cdn Income	N	R		10.10	-.01
Equity Inc.	N	R		11.91	+.10
Far East	N	R		9.40	+.09
Global	N	R		14.43	-.02
Mortgage	N	R		12.06	+.00
US Equity	N	R		12.28	+.08
CLEAN ENVIRONMENT					
Balanced	O	R		7.01	+.03
Equity	O	R			+.06

Fund	Load	RSP	Dist	Val	Ch
Amer Equity	O	R		10.69	+.04
Balanced	O	R		17.67	+.06
Canada Bond	O	R		10.32	+.01
Cdn Equity	O	R		5.94	+.05
Enterprise	O			12.45	+.13
Glo Equity EAFE	O			5.00	+.02
Gth Equity	L	R		8.33	+.05
Intl Bal	L	R		5.96	-.01
Intl Income	N			10.29	-.01
North Amer	N	Z		8.52	+.03
Pld Div	G			20.31	+.13
Vantage US	G	Z		9.27	+.01
				5.45	+.02
GUARDIAN TIMING SERVICES(n)					
mCdn Protect (30/Sep)	G	D		13.04	—
First Amer (30/Sep)	G	R		12.21	—
mProtect Amer (30/Sep)	L	R		12.73	—
HODGSON ROBERTON LAING					
HRL Balanced	N			11.18	+.08
xHRL Bond	N			10.02	-.11
HRL Canadian	N	R		9.88	+.12
HRL Overseas	N	R		13.59	-.07
HONGKONG BANK CAN.					
Balanced (27/Oct)	N	R		13.08	+.04
Equity (27/Oct)	N	R		15.05	+.06
Mortgage (27/Oct)	N	R		10.27	-.03
HYPERION FUNDS					
Hyp Asian	O			19.14	+.36
Hyp Euro	L			12.02	+.01
Hyp Fixed	L	R		12.02	-.03
Hyp Mogd	L	R		12.58	+.08
Hyp Vall Inc				15.80	—
INVESNAT BANQUE NATIONALE					
Act Equ Cdn	N	R		6.56	unch
Act Equ Eur	N	R		10.69	unch
uAct Equ US	N	R		10.96	unch
Equ Bal	N			5.89	+.03
Hypo Mort	N			10.50	+.14
Oblig gouv	N			5.57	-.03
INVESTORS GROUP					
Bond	G	R		4.90	-.00
Cdn Liquity	G			8.82	+.07
Dividend	G			11.06	+.10
European	N			6.29	-.02
Global	N			5.39	-.04
Global Bond	L			7.54	+.00
Growth	G			6.56	+.01
Growth Plus	L	R		5.58	+.00
Income	G	R			

Fund	Load	RSP	Dist	Val	Ch
MAWER INVESTMENT FUNDS(n)					
xBond (22/Oct)	N		D	11.39	+.01
xCdn Bal RSP (22/Oct)	N		D	11.42	-.05
xCdn Divers (22/Oct)	N		D	11.65	-.05
xCdn Equity (22/Oct)	N	R	D	10.99	-.05
xCdn Income (22/Oct)	N		D	10.61	+.02
xNorth Amer (22/Oct)	N		D	16.73	+.31
xUS Equity (22/Oct)	N		D	10.06	-.28
xWorld (22/Oct)	N		D	12.60	-.20
NATCAN BANQUE NATINALE					
Act-Equ CDN	N	R	D	11.63	+.06
uAc-Equ US	N	R	D	10.99	+.07
Dividendes	N	R	D	10.64	+.03
Oblig-Bond	N	R	D	10.22	unch
NATIONAL TRUST					
American Eq (27/Oct)	N	R	D	11.96	+.06
Balanced (27/Oct)	N	R	D	12.73	+.03
Dividend (27/Oct)	N	R	D	11.12	+.04
Equity (27/Oct)	N	R	D	12.21	+.04
Income (27/Oct)	N	R	D	12.08	+.01
Mortgage (27/Oct)	N	R	D	10.26	+.00
Special Eq (27/Oct)	N	R	D	14.37	+.16
NORAM(n)					
Canadian (14/Oct)	L	—		7.99	—
Internat'l (14/Oct)	L	—		11.39	—
N. AMER TRUST/CORNERSTONE					
Balanced	N	R		5.97	+.03
Bond	N	R		5.68	+.00
Cdn Growth (27/Oct)	N	R		6.06	—
Global	O	R		10.25	+.03
US Bond				19.12	+.11
O.I.Q. FERIQUE(n)					
Actions (22/Oct)	N			33.76	—
Equilibre (22/Oct)	N			39.12	—
MM (22/Oct)	N			37.88	—
OHA GROUP					
Balanced (21/Oct)	N	R	D	11.18	+.04
Bond (21/Oct)	N	R	D	11.35	+.01
Cdn Equity (21/Oct)	N	R	D	14.16	+.05
Foreign Equ (21/Oct)	N	R	D	11.26	+.01
ONTARIO TEACHERS GROUP					
Balanced (22/Oct)	N	R		13.10	unch
Diversified (22/Oct)	N	R		11.65	+.03
Global Value (22/Oct)	N	R		12.52	+.07
Growth (22/Oct)	N	R		12.68	+.04
	N	R		11.69	+.02
OPTIMA STRATEGY(n)					
Equity	O			6.46	+.01
Income	O	R		5.19	-.00
ShTerm	O			5.17	+.00
ORBIT GROUP (n)					

TABLE 15.2
Mutual Fund Performance Survey*

CANADIAN EQUITY FUNDS 30 April, 1993

Fund name	Notes	Fund sponsor	RRSP/ RRIF	% for.	Total net assets $mil.	NAV per share $	Simple rate of return 1 mo.	6 mo.	1 yr.	Avg. annual compound return 3 yr.	5 yr.	10 yr.	Std. var. 3 yr.	Expense rate %	Load F	Load B
Average					112.3		+4.6	+20.0	+22.6	+9.7	+6.8	+8.4	38.1	2.00		
ABC Fundamental-Value	b	I.A. Michael Inv. Couns	R	2	3.5	6.69	+11.9	+37.7	+35.1	+22.0	n.a.	n.a.	51.2	2.00	N	N
AGF Canadian Equity		AGF Mft. Ltd.	R	9	638.0	9.80	+3.3	+12.3	+14.1	+6.0	+2.6	+8.1	35.5	2.61	O	O
AGF Canadian Resources	f	AGF Mgt. Ltd.	R	3	86.9	13.47	+9.3	+55.8	+93.3	+17.7	+10.1	+7.0	60.1	3.22	O	O
AGF Growth Equity		AGF Mgt. Ltd.	R	4	203.9	15.90	+5.1	+40.0	+40.1	+20.1	+10.4	+10.4	43.2	2.50	O	O
AIC Advantage		AIC Ltd.	R	11	40.4	16.31	+1.4	+19.9	+16.6	+19.2	+11.0	n.a.	55.8	2.92	O	O
Admax Canadian Performance		Admax Regent Int'l Mgt.	R	7	7.8	5.49	+3.8	+12.3	+14.2	+6.3	n.a.	n.a.	29.5	2.40	O	O
All-Cdn. CapitalFund		All-Cdn. Mgt.	R		13.8	10.59	+5.1	+13.9	+16.2	+6.4	+5.8	+7.3	27.0	2.00	Y	N
All-Cdn. Compound	n	All-Cdn. Mgt.	R		13.8	14.56	+5.0	+13.9	+16.2	+6.4	+5.8	+7.3	26.8	2.00	N	N
All-Cdn. ConsumerFund		All-Cdn. Mgt.	R		1.1	3.41	-0.9	n.a.	+16.1	+6.4	+5.8	+7.3	n.a.		Y	N
All-Cdn. Resources Corp.	f	All-Cdn. Mgt.	R	11	4.1	3.06	+18.6	+23.9	+31.0	+1.0	-3.0	+0.1	71.7	1.98	Y	N
Altafund Investment Corp		Altamira Inv. Svcs.	R		104.5	14.86	+4.6	+29.4	+40.3	n.a.	n.a.	+9.3	n.a.	1.88	N	Y
Altamira Capital Growth		Altamira Inv. Svcs.	R	2	30.5	11.48	+5.9	+15.1	+16.3	+13.9	+11.6	n.a.	33.3	2.25	N	N
Altamira Equity		Altamira Inv. Svcs.	R		1141.0	29.40	+5.8	+28.4	+37.5	+31.3	+29.1	n.a.	43.9	2.09	N	N
Altamira Resource		Altamira Inv. Svcs.	R		749.9	13.94	+8.1	+53.8	+86.8	+42.7	+19.7	n.a.	59.1	2.50	N	N
Altamira Special Growth		Altamira Inv. Svcs.	R	1	268.1	15.38	+4.0	+35.4	+42.7	+30.0	+5.9	+8.1	46.1	2.50	N	N
Associate Investors		L. Frazer & Assoc.	R		7.9	7.10	+3.8	+7.2	+8.4	+6.8	+5.9	+8.1	27.7	1.83	N	N
BNP (Canadian) Equity		Corporate Inv. Assoc.	R	15	6.2	28.33	+4.1	+13.4	+16.2	n.a.	n.a.	n.a.	27.7	2.06	N	Y
BPI Canadian Equity		BPI Capital Mgt.	R	14	2.8	10.75	+4.2	+19.6	+17.1	+5.1	n.a.	n.a.	38.4	2.45	O	N
Batirente Section Actions		Corp. fin. St-Laurent	R	12	7.8	12.94	+3.9	+8.6	+7.7	+2.1	n.a.	n.a.	29.6	2.90	N	O
Beutel Goodman Cdn. Equity		Beutel Goodman	R		12.3	10.34	+5.7	+10.3	+8.8	n.a.	n.a.	n.a.	n.a.	1.50	N	N
Bissett Canadian Equity		Bissett & Assoc.	R	13	4.4	19.19	+4.1	+18.2	+21.7	+13.3	+9.6	+11.1	32.3	1.36	N	N
Bissett Small Cap	b	Bissett & Assoc.	R		0.7	16.31	+12.4	+67.5	+71.1	n.a.	n.a.	n.a.	n.a.	1.47	N	N
BT Canada Cumulative		Bolton Tremblay Fds.	R	14	48.7	16.99	+3.0	+19.2	+20.1	+7.8	+6.4	+6.4	31.9	0.50	N	N
BT LDMK Canadian		Bolton Tremblay Fds.	R	12	134.8	6.56	+2.7	+20.8	+24.2	+13.0	n.a.	n.a.	27.9	2.66	Y	N
BT LDMK Small Cap		Bolton Tremblay Fds.	R	1	43.8	7.01	+3.4	+33.0	+37.2	+18.4	+8.8	n.a.	40.0	2.62	O	Y
BT Planned Resources	f	Bolton Tremblay Fds.	R		37.7	21.04	+10.6	+45.3	+80.9	+27.6	+16.5	+9.9	51.1	2.95	O	N
Bullock Growth		Spectrum Mutual Fds.	R	10	47.2	3.06	+3.0	+25.9	+7.5	+13.4	+5.3	+5.6	36.6	2.00	Y	O
CCPE Growth Fund "R"	am	Nth. American Life	R	12	29.5	65.23	+3.6	+8.7	+18.4	+5.5	+7.4	n.a.	30.0	2.25	O	N
CDA Common Stock	am	CDA	R	12	43.9	20.52	+4.1	+15.8	+14.0	+10.3	+8.5	+11.3	28.6	0.27	N	Y
CDA		CDA	R		151.1	10.87	+4.0	+15.0	+14.0	+4.3	n.a.	n.a.	32.3	0.95	N	N
CIBC Canadian Equity		CIBC Sec's. Inc.	R		210.8	15.63	+1.9	+11.3	+13.2	n.a.	n.a.	n.a.	n.a.	2.25	N	N
CIBC Capital Appreciation		CIBC Sec's. Inc.	R		26.0	10.68	+3.4	+28.5	+38.4	n.a.	n.a.	n.a.	n.a.	1.50	N	N
CIBC Equity Income		CIBC Sec's. Inc.	R		9.7	5.11	+5.9	+10.6	+6.4	n.a.	n.a.	n.a.	n.a.	2.00	N	N
Caldwell Securities Associate		Caldwell Secs.	R	18	43.3	8.87	+8.8	+22.6	+20.7	+13.6	+11.2	+15.9	26.5	2.34	N	N
Cambridge Growth		Sagit Inv. Mgt.	R	1	25.9	3.94	+15.5	+134.	+122.	+22.8	+10.1	+11.0	91.4	2.87	Y	Y
Cambridge Resource		Sagit Inv. Mgt.	R		10.1	8.57	+10.6	+80.3	+28.3	-1.3	+1.9	+10.3	106.5	2.87	Y	Y
Cambridge Special Equity		Sagit Inv. Mgt.	R		44.7	8.57	+3.4	+12.1	+14.5	+9.6	+7.2	n.a.	35.3	2.87	Y	Y
Canada Life E-2	im	Canada Life Inv. Mgt.	R	15	267.8	219.74	+3.1	+11.6	+12.2	+9.6	+7.2	+10.3	35.3	1.00	N	D
Canada Life S-9	im	Canada Life Inv. Mgt.	R	15	267.8	97.36	+3.1	+11.6	+12.2	+8.0	+6.4	+9.4	36.3	2.00	N	D
Canada Trust Equity		CT Fund Svcs. Inc.	R	10	26.6	66.30	+4.5	+17.7	+21.2	+9.3	+7.1	+7.7	29.7	2.23	N	N

* Published monthly by *The Financial Post*. Excerpt reprinted with permission.

key terms contained in the report and later discuss how to use the information to help you with your investment decision.

The **Mutual Funds Performance Survey**, which is published monthly by *The Financial Post*, classifies mutual funds by the following categories: Canadian Equity Funds, US Equity Funds, Balanced Funds, International Equity Funds, Dividend Funds, Bond & Mortgage Funds, Real Estate Funds, Money Market Funds and Specialty Funds. Each category of funds is reported in a separate table, such as Table 15.2, which is a report on Canadian Equity Funds.

The following data are reported for each fund:

1. Fund Name — listed in alphabetical order.
2. RRSP and RRIF Eligibility — An 'R' indicates that the fund is both RRSP- and RRIF-eligible.
3. Fund Sponsor — the name of the group that sponsors and manages the fund.
4. Percentage of Foreign Securities — the percentage of foreign content in the mutual fund.
5. Total Net Assets — the total assets minus the current liabilities; indicates the size of the fund as of the date of the survey.
6. Net Asset Value Per Share (NAVPS) — total net assets (see immediately above) divided by the number of shares outstanding.
7. Simple Rates of Return for one month, six months and one year — the holding period returns for one month, six months and one year; the figures represent changes in asset value, including reinvestment of dividends and capital gains and excluding sales or redemption charges during the holding periods, and they are not to be confused with annual rates of return.
8. Annual Average Compound Rates of Return for three, five and 10 years — each of these figures measures the average annual change in net asset value per share, assuming all dividends and realized capital gains are reinvested on the date of distribution or realization, respectively; no sales or redemption charges are figured into these calculations.
9. Standard Deviation — the annual variability of the return; this figure provides a measure of volatility and hence, risk.
10. Expense Ratio — the total operating costs (including annual management fee but excluding front-end and rear-end fees) as a percentage of assets; for example, if the annual operating cost of the fund is $1,500,000 and the total assets of the fund are $100,000,000, then the expense ratio is equal to (1,500,000 ÷ 100,000,000) = 1.5%.
11. Front-end and Rear-end Fees — indicates whether or not the investor pays up front for the privilege of investing in the fund or pays when he cashes out.

> **Example 15.3:** Let us examine the fifth row in Table 15.2. The fund's name is AGF Growth Equity. We know that it is a Canadian equity fund because it is reported under the Canadian Equity Fund Table. The fund's sponsor is AGF Management Limited. It is RRSP- and RRIF-eligible; its foreign content is 4% of the fund which is within the 20% limit prescribed by law for foreign investments. The total net asset value of the fund is

$203.9 million. The net asset value per share is $15.90. The simple rates of return (i.e., the holding period return) are 5.1%, 40% and 40.1% for holding periods of one month, six months and one year, respectively. The average annual compound rates of return are 20.1%, 10.4% and 10.4% measured over periods of three, five and 10 years, respectively. The standard deviation on the rate of return, measured over the last three years, is 43.2%. It has an expense ratio of 2.5%. The fund has an optional front-end and rear-end fee.

ASSESSING THE RISK AND RETURN OF A MUTUAL FUND

As mentioned before, the most important characteristics of any investment are its risk and expected return. The monthly **mutual fund performance survey** (Table 15.2) provides historical, and hence objective, estimates of these two characteristics. As a general rule of thumb, many financial experts recommend that one should use historical data of at least 10 years to estimate risk and return because a longer time period provides more reliable estimates of these two characteristics.

If you look down the column of "average annual compound rate of return for 10 years" in Table 15.2, you will notice that a lot of numbers are missing — "n.a." in the table means "not available". The reason that these numbers are not available is that the funds to which the numbers would apply are relatively new funds and they do not have a 10-year history. If you look down the "3 year" and "5 year" columns (for average annual compound rate), you will find still a substantial number of missing values (or n.a.). In general, the shorter the history of the fund, the poorer the quality and reliability of the estimates for the rate of return and standard deviation. You should bear this in mind when you use the information from the monthly mutual fund performance survey.

The risk of the mutual fund is measured by the standard deviation of the rate of return. *The Financial Post* (see Table 15.2 again) uses a three-year time period to estimate the standard deviations. Once again, this falls short of the recommended 10-year period by a large margin; therefore, the three-year standard deviation should be viewed as a very crude measure of the mutual fund's risk.[5] We will continue to use the data from Table 15.2 for the purpose of illustration only; we are not endorsing the accuracy or reliability of the numbers.

Let us use the AGF Growth Equity again — the fifth row in Table 15.2. The average annual compound rate of return and the standard deviation are 20.1% and 43.2%, respectively, both estimated from three-year data. How do we interpret these numbers?

Empirical studies have found that the rate of return on a well-diversified portfolio is normally distributed; therefore, we can assume that the rate of return on the AGF Growth Equity Fund is normally distributed, with an expected rate of return of 20.1% and a standard deviation of 43.2%. We can use the statistical properties of the normal

---

[5] You are advised to focus on funds with longer histories. You can calculate the standard deviation yourself by using at least 10 years of data. You can calculate the standard deviation easily from most business calculators. You can also use the Super Rep software.

distribution to assess the risk of the mutual fund. For example, we can find the probability of losing money: it is equal to the probability of getting a rate of return less than zero. The point, zero, lies at (20.1% ÷ 43.2%) or .47 standard deviation on the left-hand side of the expected value (20.1%), and from a normal distribution table such as Appendix C, the probability of getting a value less than .47 standard deviation from the expected value is equal to .3192.[6] In other words, there is a 32% chance that you will earn a negative rate of return (i.e., lose money) in the AGF Growth Equity Fund in the coming year. Similarly, given any target rate of return (e.g., this could be the minimum rate of return that you require), you can calculate the probability of earning less than that target rate of return. By doing this kind of analysis, you can assess the riskiness of each mutual fund that you are considering.

A simpler, albeit less accurate, way to assess the risk of a mutual fund is as follows. The probability of the rate of return falling within one standard deviation below or above the expected value is equal to 68%, or roughly two out of three times. In other words, in two years out of three, the rate of return on the AGF Growth Equity will fall between (20.1% − 43.2%) = −23.1% and (20.1% + 43.2%) = 63.3%.

Example 15.4: Using the three-year average annual compound rate of return and standard deviation from Table 15.2, the rates of return for the following mutual funds will fall within the indicated lower bounds and upper bounds for two years out of three (i.e., with a probability of 68%).

Name of Fund	Lower Bound	Upper Bound
Altamira Capital Growth	13.9% − 33.3% = −19.4%	13.9% + 33.3% = 47.2%
Altamira Equity	31.3% − 43.9% = −12.6%	31.3% + 43.9% = 75.2%
BPI Canadian Equity	5.1% − 38.4% = −33.3%	5.1% + 38.4% = 43.5%
Bissett Canadian Equity	13.3% − 32.3% = −19.0%	13.3% + 32.3% = 45.6%
CDA Common Stock	10.3% − 28.6% = −18.3%	10.3% + 28.6% = 38.9%
Cambridge Growth	13.6% − 26.5% = −12.9%	13.6% + 26.5% = 40.1%

Further Risk Reduction

Even though each mutual fund in Example 15.4 is a well-diversified portfolio and hence, substantially less risky than a single stock, investing in any one of them still seems to be quite risky; the range for the rate of return is quite large in all cases; and to make things even worse, in one year out of three, the rate of return is expected to fall outside the range which is already quite wide. Fortunately, there are two more ways to reduce risk substantially: (1) hold the mutual fund for the long term rather than the short term and (2) hold a basket of mutual funds that are not highly correlated (i.e., low correlation can be had by diversifying the specialization of one's mutual fund holdings across the three main asset types of cash, bonds and stocks). Let us elaborate on these two topics.

---

[6] This assumes you have some knowledge about basic statistics and the properties of a normal distribution.

Reducing Risk by Investing for the Long Term

Holding a mutual fund for 10 years is substantially less risky than holding it for one year. The reason for this is that there will be some good years and some bad years and the good years tend to cancel the bad years out so that over the 10-year period, the rate of return grows at the expected rate with less variability. In fact, the longer the investment horizon, the less risky the mutual fund will become.

Suppose the mutual fund's rate of return is normally distributed with expected value $E(r)$ and standard deviation s. It has been proved that if the mutual fund is held for n years, the annual standard deviation will be reduced to s divided by the square root of n.

Example 15.5: What is the standard deviation of the rate of return of the AGF Growth Equity Fund in Example 15.3 if the holding period is (a) one year, (b) two years, (c) five years, (d) 10 years and (e) 20 years?

Answer: The answers are:
(a) 43.2%
(b) 43.2% ÷ $\sqrt{2}$ = 30.55%
(c) 43.2% ÷ $\sqrt{5}$ = 19.32%
(d) 43.2% ÷ $\sqrt{10}$ = 13.66%
(e) 43.2% ÷ $\sqrt{20}$ = 9.66%

Thus, longer investing periods make riskier investments more attractive. The Super Rep software can display this graphically.

Reducing Risk by Asset Allocation

Asset Allocation   **Asset allocation** can be defined as the allocation of one's invest-ment money among the major asset types — non-cash investments, bonds and stocks. Since these three investment types are not highly correlated, a substantial reduction in risk can be achieved by asset allocation.

Even with a modest amount of investment money, **asset allocation** can easily be done by buying a money market fund, a bond fund and a stock fund. Many people include other investment types such as real estate, US stocks and bonds, international stocks and so on. All these can be included by selecting the appropriate mutual funds.

Formal Analysis of Risk Reduction

Two-asset Portfolio   Suppose you have $10,000 and you want to invest part of it (say, 30%) in a T-bill mutual fund and the rest (say, 70%) in a Canadian stock index fund. What is the expected rate of return on your portfolio? What is the risk (the standard deviation of rate of return) of your portfolio?

To answer these questions, we have to introduce some results from the portfolio-investment literature. Suppose there are two mutual funds with expected rates of return $E(r_1)$ and $E(r_2)$, and the standard deviations of their rates of return are s_1 and s_2. Suppose further that the correlation coefficient between the two rates of return is r_{12}. Let x_1 be the fraction of investment money to be invested in the first mutual fund and x_2 be the fraction of investment money to be invested in the second mutual fund. Let $E(r_p)$ be the expected rate of return of the portfolio, and s_p be the standard deviation of the rate of the portfolio's return. The following equations will give the expected rate of return $E(r_p)$ and the risk s_p of the portfolio:

$$E(r_p) = x_1E(r_1) + x_2E(r_2) \tag{1}$$

$$s_p^2 = x_1^2s_1^2 + x_2^2s_2^2 + 2x_1x_2r_{12}s_1s_2 \tag{2}$$

Example 15.6: Suppose you want to invest 30% of your investment money in a T-bill mutual fund and the rest (i.e., 70%) in a Canadian Stock Index Fund. The following information is given:

Expected rate of return on the T-bill Fund, $E(r_1)$ = 6%
Expected rate of return on the Stock Index Fund, $E(r_2)$ = 12%
Standard deviation of $r_1 = s_1$ = 2%
Standard deviation of $r_2 = s_2$ = 16%

Correlation coefficient between r_1 and $r_2 = r_{12}$ = .10

What is the expected rate of return on your portfolio, $E(r_p)$? What is the risk (the standard deviation) of your portfolio?

From equation (1), the expected rate of return on the portfolio is equal to:

$$E(r_p) = (.30 \times .06) + (.70 \times .12) = 10.2\%$$

From equation (2), the standard deviation of the return on the portfolio:

$$s_p = [(.30^2 \times .02^2) + (.70^2 \times .16^2) + (2 \times .3 \times .7 \times .1 \times .02 \times .16)]^{\frac{1}{2}}$$

$$= .1128 \text{ or } 11.28\%$$

Three-asset Portfolio   Suppose you want to invest in three mutual funds; as in the previous case, suppose you will invest a fraction x_1, x_2, and x_3 of your investment money in the first, second and third fund, respectively. The expected rate of return of your portfolio, $E(r_p)$, and the risk (standard deviation) of your portfolio are given by the equations (3) and (4), respectively:

$$E(r_p) = x_1E(r_1) + x_2E(r_2) + x_3E(r_3) \tag{3}$$

$$s_p^2 = x_1^2s_1^2 + x_2^2s_2^2 + x_3^2s_3^2$$
$$+ 2x_1x_2r_{12}s_1s_2 + 2x_1x_3r_{13}s_1s_3 + 2x_2x_3r_{23}s_2s_3 \tag{4}$$

where r_i =   expected rate of return of the ith fund, i = 1,2,3.
s_i =   the standard deviation of the rate of return of the ith fund
r_{ij} =   the correlation coefficient between the ith fund and jth fund.

Example 15.7: Winnie Dagmer wants to diversify her investment across the traditional three types of investments — cash-equivalent, bonds and stocks. She has decided to put 20%, 30% and 50% of her investment money into a money market fund (r_1), a

Canadian bond fund (r_2) and a Canadian stock index fund (r_3), respectively. The following information is given:

$E(r_1) = 7\%$ $s_1 = 2\%$
$E(r_2) = 9\%$ $s_2 = 11\%$
$E(r_3) = 12\%$ $s_3 = 16\%$

r_{12} = correlation coefficient between r_1 and r_2 = .2
r_{13} = correlation coefficient between r_1 and r_3 = −.1
r_{23} = correlation coefficient between r_2 and r_3 = .06

What is the expected rate of return on her portfolio, $E(r_p)$?
What is the risk (standard deviation) of her portfolio, s_p?

From equation (3), the expected rate of return on her portfolio:

$$E(r_p) = (.2 \times .07) + (.3 \times .09) + (.5 \times .12)$$

$$= .101 \text{ or } 10.1\%$$

From equation (4), the standard deviation on the rate of return of her portfolio:

$$s_p = [(.2^2 \times .02^2) + (.3^2 \times .11^2) + (.5^2 \times .16^2)$$

$$+ (2 \times .2 \times .3 \times .2 \times .02 \times .11) + (2 \times .2 \times .5 \times -.1 \times .02 \times .16)$$

$$+ (2 \times .3 \times .5 \times .06 \times .11 \times .16)]^{\frac{1}{2}}$$

$$= .007811^{\frac{1}{2}}$$

$$= .088 \text{ or } 8.8\%$$

N-asset Portfolio

The above analysis can be extended to a portfolio of more than three assets (say, N assets). For example, if you invest in six mutual funds, then you hold a six-asset portfolio ($N = 6$). The expected rate of return $E(r_p)$ and the risk s_p of an N-asset portfolio are given by equations (5) and (6), respectively:

$$E(r_p) = x_1 E(r_1) + x_2 E(r_2) + \ldots + X_N E(r_n) \tag{5}$$

$$s_p^2 = \sum_{i=1}^{N} x_i^2 s_i^2 + \sum_{i \neq j}^{N} 2x_i \, x_j \, r_{ij} \, s_i \, s_j \tag{6}$$

where x_i =   fraction of investment invested in the ith asset
        $E(r_i)$ =   expected rate of return of the ith asset
        s_i =   standard deviation of the rate of return r_i
        r_{ij} =   correlation coefficient between r_i and r_j
        N =   the number of assets or mutual funds in the portfolio

There are many computer software packages[7] at reasonable prices which will help you with the calculation of equations (5) and (6).

---

[7] For example, the Super Rep software.

Where to Get Information

The application of the equations (1) to (6) requires some necessary information: the rate of return and the standard deviation of each underlying mutual fund and the correlation coefficients between them. In Examples 15.6 and 15.7 we assumed that these statistics are given. In practice, you have to find these numbers or you must estimate them yourself.

The financial press, such as the monthly **Mutual Fund Performance Survey** (see Table 15.2), publish the historical rates of return and the standard deviations of the rates of return of most mutual funds; however, as we have noted before, the quality and the reliability of the numbers are questionable because they are calculated from three-year data which is insufficient to give reliable estimates. Another problem is that the correlation coefficients between each pair of funds are not reported. Thus, even if the rates of return and the standard deviations are reliable, you still do not have enough information to use equations (1) to (6) in your analysis.

Fortunately, it is not difficult to estimate these numbers from historical data. Financial experts advise investors to invest in funds with a long track record and usually that means 10 or more years. You are well advised to select your investment from mutual funds that have existed for at least 10 years. For each of the mutual funds that you are considering, obtain or calculate the annual or monthly rate of return for at least the last 10 years.[8] You can then use any of the many computer software packages or financial calculators on the market to generate the average rates of return, the standard deviations and the correlation coefficients from the historical data.[9]

Risk of a Leveraged Portfolio

When you borrow money to invest, your portfolio is called a **leveraged portfolio**. In Chapter 11, we discussed the motivation for people to borrow money to invest. Examples of **leveraged portfolios** include buying stocks on margin, purchasing your home with a first mortgage and borrowing money to create a tax shelter. If you borrowed money to invest in mutual funds, your investment would also be a leveraged portfolio.

Leveraging, or borrowing money for investment purposes, is a double-edged sword. On the one hand, it magnifies the expected rate of return on your portfolio; on the other hand, it also magnifies the risk (or the standard deviation of the rate of return) of the portfolio.

Suppose you have W dollars to invest and you borrow B dollars more, agreeing to pay the lender the rate of interest = i% p.a. You may recall that the ratio $x = B \div W$ is called the **debt-to-equity ratio**. Suppose you invest the $(B + W)$ dollars in an investment, say, a mutual fund, that has an expected rate of return, $E(r)$ and standard deviation, s_r. Now you have a **leveraged portfolio**. It can be shown that the expected rate of return $E(r_p)$ and the standard deviation s_p of the leveraged portfolio are given by the equations (7) and (8):

$$E(r_p) = E(r) + x[E(r) - i] \tag{7}$$

---

[8] If you personally call the mutual fund companies, they will usually mail you the historical record of the fund, including NAVPS (net asset value per share), dividend payments, and even the monthly rate of return.
[9] For example, the Super Rep software will calculate these statistics from the data you provide.

$$s_p = (1 + x)s_r \tag{8}$$

Clearly, both the risk s_p and the return $E(r_p)$ are increasing functions of the debt-to-equity ratio x.

Example 15.8: Mr. Bartel has $20,000 to invest. He has an account with a full-service broker who allows him to buy stocks or mutual funds with a 50% margin. This means that he can borrow up to a maximum of $20,000 from the broker and buy a maximum amount of $40,000 worth of stocks or invest $40,0000 in a mutual fund. Of course, he is free to borrow less. The broker will charge 10% on any amount borrowed. Mr. Bartel is interested in a mutual fund that has an expected rate of return of 16% and a standard deviation of 25%.

What are the expected rate of return and the standard deviation of the **leveraged portfolio** if he borrows (i) $5,000; (ii) $10,000; (iii) $15,000 and (iv) $20,000?

Answer: (i)   If he borrows $5,000, the debt-to-equity ratio is
$x = 5,000 \div 20,000 = .25$.

From equation (7),
$E(r_p) = .16 + [.25 \times (.16 - .10)] = 17.5\%$.

From equation (8),
$s_p = [(1 + .25) \times .25] = 31.25\%$.

(ii) $x = (10,000 \div 20,000) = .5$
$E(r_p) = .16 + [.5 \times (.16 - .10)] = 19\%$
$s_p = (1 + .5) \times .25 = 37.5\%$

(iii) $x = (15,000 \div 20,000) = .75$
$E(r_p) = .16 + [.75 \times (.16 - .10)] = 20.5\%$
$s_p = [(1 + .75) \times .25] = 43.75\%$

(iv) $x = (20,000 \div 20,000) = 1$
$E(r_p) = .16 + [1 \times (.16 - .10)] = 22\%$
$s_p = [(1 + 1) \times .25] = 50\%$

Note that both the expected returns and the risks increase with borrowing.

HOW DO YOU SELECT MUTUAL FUNDS?

In spite of the tremendous progress made in knowledge about investments, investing is still an inexact science. There is no foolproof way to select the best mutual funds. Numerous methods to measure the performance of mutual funds have been suggested in investment literature but academics are still not very satisfied with the existing methods and theories.[10] Although there is no sure-fire method   in selecting mutual funds, it is

---

[10] For example, even the Capital Asset Pricing Model (CAPM), on which many mutual fund performance measures are based, has become suspect in the minds of many people.

quite easy to be "approximately right". For example, if you are young and saving up for your retirement, you will be "approximately right" regardless of which equity growth fund you happen to choose; by the same token, you will be "approximately wrong" if you put your money in a savings account earning 2% interest. If, however, you are saving to buy a car next year, putting money in that savings account makes more sense than putting your savings in an aggressive equity growth fund. Even better would be a Treasury-bill maturity at the time you want to buy the car. We shall now describe some guidelines about how to select "approximately right" mutual funds.

1. Diversify across the major asset types: money market, bonds, stocks. You can add real estate, international stocks and bonds, one or two specialty funds such as growth funds, natural resource funds, small company funds and so on.

2. Decide how to allocate your investment money among the asset types — in other words, decide how much to put in money market funds, bond funds, equity funds and so on. Your allocation depends on several things. First, it depends on your goals. For example, if one of your goals is to buy some furniture in six months' time, then the money set aside for this purpose should be put in money market funds. As explained in Chapter 3, your goals dictate the rate of return that you must earn. Second, your investment allocation depends on your risk preference. You have to find your own "comfort zone". With the assistance of computer software packages, it should be easy to perform the risk and return analysis — equations (1) to (8) — explained in this chapter. Try different allocations, create different portfolios and perform the risk and return analysis.[11] Use the normal distribution table to find out the probability of losing money for each portfolio mix. Can you tolerate the loss? Do you think the expected rate of return can justify the risk that you will take? Only you can determine where your "comfort zone" of risk lies.

3. Make a short list of the mutual funds that are potential candidates for your investment. First, examine the long-term and short-term performances of all the funds on the mutual fund reports, such as Table 15.2. A fund with a solid 10-year record should be the first thing to look for. Ideally, this should come together with a good short-term record. Second, look at the risk (standard deviation) and compare it with those of the other funds on the same table. Clearly, a fund with an above-average long-term rate of return (at least 10 years) and a relatively low standard deviation would be a prime candidate for your short list. To illustrate, let us look at Table 15.2. Look down the column which is headed "average annual compound rate of return, 10 years": the largest number is 15.9%, the rate of return for the Cambridge Growth Fund. Now, look down the column headed "standard deviation, three years": the lowest number is 26.5% which also belongs to the Cambridge Growth Fund. Clearly, this fund should go into your short list. But are there areas of concern about the Cambridge Growth Fund? We discover that the answer is yes: the fund seems to be costly as its expense ratio of 2.87%

---

[11] At this initial stage, you can use the numbers in Table 15.4 as the estimates for the rates of return, standard deviations and correlation coefficients for the major asset types. Later on when you have selected all the mutual funds and decided on the allocation of investment money among the funds, you can do the calculations again.

is quite high and, moreover, there is a front- or rear-end loading. Nevertheless, the apparently high fee structure should not prevent you from including it in your short list. At this stage, you are looking for potential candidates and not a firm commitment.

4. Go for funds without front- or rear-end loads. Although sometimes it is worthwhile to pay a low front-end load for truly exceptional performance, normally you will do better with no-load funds. To be avoided as well are funds with high expense ratios: only a truly superlative past performance can outweigh the disadvantage of a high expense ratio.

5. For the funds in your short list, call or write to the funds to get the sales literature and the **prospectus**[12] and read them. Always ask for a record of the annual rates of return for as long a time period as possible — the time period examined should be a minimum of 10 years in length. Without these numbers it is impossible to do the kind of quantitative analysis described in this chapter.

6. After obtaining the prospectus and the information about the past record from each fund, read the prospectus carefully and do a quantitative analysis such as the risk and return analysis described in this chapter. The objective here is to cut down the short list of the mutual funds that you will buy.

7. When you read the prospectus there are a few things to bear in mind. First, read the **fund's stated objectives** and see if they fit your personal needs: is the fund's attitude toward the relative importance of income, safety, capital gains and growth similar to your own attitude towards the relative importance of these investment variables? Second, carefully examine what any given fund invests in: what will it buy and what will it not buy? Have its past purchases been consistent with its stated policy? Third, find out all the charges and fees such as front-end load, annual fees, rear-end fees, deferred sales charges, commission on reinvested income and other charges: are you happy with the fee structure? How does it compare with the fee structure of other funds of the same type that are in your short list? Finally, read and analyse each fund's financial results. Normally, the prospectus does not provide you with the recommended 10-year historical record. You may have to make an additional request that this information be sent to you.

8. Buy the funds you like the best. Start a **record-keeping system**. For each fund, put down how much money you invested, the number of shares you bought and the price at which you purchased them. Arrange to have all the future income and dividends reinvested automatically unless you need this income to live on. In the future, when you receive reports periodically, update your records according to the information contained in these reports.

9. Sit back and relax: remember that, except for short-term money market funds, investing in mutual funds is a long-term proposition. In other words, do not sell out just because the market falls. Needless to say, however, a caution against premature selling does not mean that you should stick with a loser forever: if,

---

[12] The prospectus is a legal document which describes the securities or mutual funds to be offered for sale to the public.

over the course of two or three years, you find your fund's performance is substantially worse than that of other funds of the same type, start searching for another fund to replace it.

10.   How safe is your money in the hands of fund management companies? Can fund managers or other people loot the fund? For practical purposes, you need not worry about this because the law requires that all securities are held by a third party custodian, usually a trust company: even if the mutual fund **management company** goes bankrupt, your investments should be safe because they are segregated from the assets of the **management company** itself.

SUMMARY

In this chapter we put the basic theories learned in Chapter 13 and the major types of investments described in Chapter 14 together. We developed an investment strategy whereby even a small investor can make investments in all the major investment categories, choose her desired risk-return mix and reach her financial goals. The investment strategy is to invest through **mutual funds**. We believe that mutual funds are the best investment choice for most Canadian investors.

A **mutual fund** accepts funds from hundreds or thousands of investors and uses the funds to make investments. There are many different types of mutual funds. They can be classified by the kinds of investments they make; the major types are Treasury-bill funds, money market funds, mortgage funds, income or bond funds, dividend funds, balanced funds, equity or stock funds, index funds, real estate funds, international funds and other specialty funds.

The advantages and disadvantages of investing in mutual funds have been discussed. The most important benefits that mutual funds offer are professional management and broad diversification that an individual investor cannot otherwise obtain by himself. The major disadvantage is that there are fees. We described a framework for you to analyse and compare the fee structures of different mutual funds.

Mutual fund quotations are reported daily in newspapers. More detailed reports are published weekly or monthly. We have described the key terms that appear in these reports and you should be able to read them without difficulty.

Investing in one mutual fund is still rather risky. Further risk reduction can be achieved by (1) increasing your investment horizon or holding period and (2) investing in a basket of mutual funds that are not highly correlated with each other. The expected rates of return and the risks of different portfolios can be calculated by the equations (1) to (8) described in this chapter. Using these numbers and the normal distribution table, you can assess the risk level of various portfolios and discover your own risk preference (in terms of a risk 'comfort zone').

An investor's responsibility is to allocate her investment money among the major asset types — near-cash, bonds, stocks, real estate, international securities and so on. The allocation depends on one's financial goals, risk preference and economic circumstances. There is no foolproof method to determine the 'exactly right' allocation and to choose the 'exactly right' mutual funds; however, if you follow our guidelines, it is not difficult to be 'approximately right' in your investment decisions.

KEY TERMINOLOGY

mutual fund / open-end fund / closed-end fund / right of redemption / money market funds / income fund or bond fund / balanced fund / equity fund or stock fund / growth fund / index fund / real estate fund / specialty fund / ethical fund / international fund / emerging market fund / front-end load or fees / back-end or rear-end fees / redemption fees / annual fees / no-load fund / front-load fund / professional management / broad diversification / automatic contribution plan / automatic reinvestment plan / daily quotation of mutual funds / weekly report of mutual funds / RRSP-eligible fund / net asset value per share (NAVPS) / weekly/monthly performance report / fund sponsor / simple rate of return (for one year) / average annual compound rate of return / standard deviation / expense ratio / mutual fund performance survey / asset allocation / risk reduction (by long-term holding) / risk reduction (by asset allocation) / n-asset portfolio / leveraged portfolio / debt-to-equity ratio / prospectus / mutual fund's stated objectives / your record-keeping system

DISCUSSION QUESTIONS

1. Define or explain each term under **Key Terminology**.

2. For each of the following statements, say whether you think it is true, false or uncertain, and explain why. Marks will be given mainly for your explanation.
    (a) There is no risk-free investment in this world.
    (b) Since no-load funds are cheaper than loaded funds, you should never choose a fund with front-end or rear-end loads.
    (c) Since mutual fund managers are full-time professionals with lots of knowledge and experience, they can outperform the small investor nine out of 10 times.
    (d) The best investment strategy is to buy an index fund.
    (e) How you allocate your investment money among the different asset classes depends on your financial goals.
    (f) Mutual funds are for long-term investors only. You should not touch mutual funds if your financial goal is short term.
    (g) Buying a bond fund is always less risky than buying a bond.

3. "According to the principle of efficient markets, one mutual fund cannot consistently outperform another one. Therefore, the time and effort spent in selecting mutual funds is wasted." Comment and discuss.

4. Refer to Example 15.1. Why aren't the front-end and back-end loads amortized on a straight-line basis, by dividing by the number of years? The front-end load would be 8% ÷ 10 = .8% p.a. and the back-end load 5% ÷ 10 = .5% p.a.

5. **Personal Project 1**
    Get a copy of the latest Mutual Fund Performance Survey from the library. For each of the fund categories — Canadian Equity Funds, Balanced Funds, International Equity ... and so on, prepare a short list of three mutual funds. Find out the address and telephone number of each fund's sponsor. Write or call for a prospectus and the historical rates of return since the fund's inception. Did you have any difficulty in getting the information? Report to the class or your instructor your experience

in getting the required information. Explain how and why you have chosen the funds in your short list.

6. **Personal Project 2**
    State all your financial goals on a piece of paper. What are your action plans to achieve these goals? Write them down as well. Using the numbers in Appendix D as the estimates for the expected rates of return, the standard deviations and the correlation coefficients of the major asset categories, describe how you would allocate your investment money and your future savings among the major asset categories to achieve your goals. Your answer should include an analysis of your risk preference: e.g., how do you assess your own risk 'comfort zone'?

7. **Personal Project 3**
    Choose arbitrarily one bond fund, one Canadian equity fund and one international fund (if you have done Question 4, you can choose these from your short list) that have at least 10 years of data. Obtain the data necessary to calculate the monthly rates of return for the last 10 years. Use a computer software package (e.g., the Super Rep program) to generate the average rates of return, the standard deviations and the correlation coefficients between the three funds. Construct three portfolios from these mutual funds. For each portfolio, calculate the expected rate of return and the standard deviation using equations (3) and (4), respectively.

PROBLEMS

1. Compare the fee structure of the following mutual funds, A and B, which are very similar in terms of quality and past performance.

	Fund A	Fund B
front-load	5%	0%
annual fee	1%	1.5%
rear-load	0%	2.0%

    (a) Mr. Fong's holding period is 10 years and his discount rate is 10%. Which fund has the cheaper fee structure?
    (b) Mr. Goldberg's holding period is three years and he uses a discount rate of 8%. Which fund has the cheaper fee structure?
    (c) In general, are no-load funds always cheaper than front-load funds?

2. The GLE Mutual Fund has a front-end fee of 2%, a rear-end fee of 5% and an annual fee of 1.75%. Convert this fee structure to a single annual fee using an 8% discount rate and a three-year holding period.

3. The following information about the expected rate of return $E(r_i)$, the standard deviations s_i, and the correlation coefficients r_{ij} of three mutual funds (r_1, r_2 and r_3) are given:

$E(r_1) = 10\%$	$s_1 = 12\%$	$r_{12} = .5$
$E(r_2) = 13\%$	$s_2 = 15\%$	$r_{23} = .7$
$E(r_3) = 18\%$	$s_3 = 20\%$	$r_{13} = -.1$

If x_i = the fraction of initial wealth allocated to the mutual fund r_i, calculate the expected rate of return and the standard deviation of the following portfolios:

(a) $x_1 = .5$ $x_2 = .3$ $x_3 = .2$
(b) $x_1 = .2$ $x_2 = .5$ $x_3 = .3$
(c) $x_1 = .1$ $x_2 = .2$ $x_3 = .7$
(d) $x_1 = .25$ $x_2 = .25$ $x_3 = .5$
(e) $x_1 = .40$ $x_2 = .15$ $x_3 = .45$

4. (a) Assuming that all the portfolios in Question 3 are normally distributed and using the normal distribution table in Appendix C, calculate the probability of earning a negative rate of return for each of the five portfolios.

    (b) If you buy any of the five portfolios on a 50% margin, calculate the standard deviation of each leveraged portfolio.

5. Go to Appendix D. Using the data from years 1973 to 1995 (i.e., 23 years),

    (a) Calculate the average rate of return and the standard deviation for each asset class.

    (b) Calculate all the correlation coefficients. You may use a computer software package or a sophisticated calculator to do this question.

6. You wish some international diversification in your portfolio and you have narrowed your selection to three funds with similar risk and return histories. Your discount rate for fund costs is 8%. The funds have the following fee schedules:

Fund	Front-load (%)	Back-load	Management Fee (%)
Dune	7	0	2.3
Middle Earth	0	0	4.0
Narnia	0	9	3.3

Which fund would be the best for investment horizons of three, six and 10 years?

7. Mr. Wedgebarry has $50,000 to invest. He picks a portfolio of three mutual funds with different return patterns, and allocates his $50,000 as follows:

Fund	Return (%)	Standard Dev. (%)	Allocation (%)	Correlations
Angmar	7.9	3.6	20	$r_{12} = -0.1$
Gondor	11.9	16.7	45	$r_{13} = -0.2$
Mordor	17.0	29.0	35	$r_{23} = +0.3$

(a) What is the expected rate of return and standard deviation of return of his portfolio?

(b) The statistics he has are based on three year compound rates of return. Assume that the portfolio returns are normally distributed. What is the probability that he will lose money on his investment during the next year?

<u>chapter</u> # 16

Retirement Planning

LEARNING OBJECTIVES

Retirement planning isn't a separate topic; it is a combination of all the topics we have discussed in the previous chapters. To plan for retirement, you need goals and budgets. You must manage tax, risk and investment problems, and sometimes even debt. The retirement plan applies everything we have studied so far. The particularly critical aspect of it is that when the day of retirement dawns, you don't have any chance to correct mistakes. Your earned income has ended, and you must rely upon the assets you have built up during your working life.

We consider retirement planning in two steps. This chapter takes you through your working life to the time when you retire. Chapter 17 deals with managing financial affairs at the time of retirement and through the retirement years, and also discusses estate planning briefly.

We can summarize retirement planning in three phrases:

- How much have you got now?
- How much will you need at retirement?
- How do you get from here to there?

Our specific learning objectives for this chapter are:

1. To determine the financial resources a family has now that can be used for retirement;
2. To set goals for retirement and translate those goals into the financial requirements at retirement date;
3. To estimate how much the family must save to meet the retirement goals;
4. To explain how to save and invest to provide the estimated financial requirements; and,
5. To explain the nature of government and employer pension plans.

THE RETIREMENT PLANNING MODEL

Let us model the basic retirement plan as we did earlier in the book, using the following symbols to represent the elements of personal financial planning. The subscripts represent time: t is any particular future year; n is year of planned retirement; d is the number of years from date of retirement to date of death; and, 0 is now, the starting point of the plan. Thus, if you plan to retire in 10 years and expect to die 20 years after that, $n = 10$, $d = 20$, and t runs from one to 10.

W_n The amount of money you are trying to accumulate to provide for retirement.

W_0 The amount of money you have today that can be retained and used to provide retirement consumption. For example, an RRSP is part of W_0, but a savings account that will be used to put a child through university is not.

k The discount rate. It may be different for different periods or different parts of the equation.

E_t The money you earn in year t, other than investment income.

C_t The money you consume or spend in year t, other than that used to purchase investments that will eventually contribute to savings in retirement.

The following equation summarizes the retirement planning problem. The left-hand side is your current savings and expected future savings each year (earnings less consumption) compounding at the rate of return. The middle term is the amount of wealth required at retirement. The right-hand side is the consumption during retirement that you have to fund in order to live at the standard of living you specify:

$$W_0(1 + k)^n + \sum_{t=1}^{n} (E_t - C_t)(1 + k)^{n-t} = W_n = \sum_{t=n+1}^{d} \frac{C_t}{(1 + k)^{t-n}} \qquad (1)$$

Essentially, the first steps in retirement planning are another application of the tools learned in Chapters 2–4. Once we determine the desired standard of living and what it entails in wealth at retirement, we juggle saving and consumption in the time left from now until retirement to see how much we must save and whether the goal is feasible. There are no easy ways to make the equation balance. A family can consume less now in order to save more for retirement, or can decide to consume less in retirement. Investing to reach a higher rate of return will involve more risk. In principle, the adult members could try to increase their earnings, but this option isn't entirely within their control by the time they are making serious plans for retirement. Earlier choices in education and occupation determine most of the earning potential. A home-maker spouse could enter the work force, but that will entail extra costs, especially if there are children in the family.

Retirement planning involves very long time periods, and hence is very uncertain. We use specific numbers and equations in this chapter, but you must understand that the answers are only rough estimates. A person at age 35 should at least think about provision for retirement, but that implies planning for a period of 50 years or more. Many of the assumptions of any financial plan will change. We should not be misled by the apparent precision of the answers that time value calculators and computers can produce.

We need to travel down some side roads for a while before we can use the model, because we need to understand very clearly the principles involved in finding the inputs. Three problem areas stand out: discount rates, life expectancy and pension plans. We discuss each in turn.

INFLATION, TAXES AND DISCOUNT RATES

As we have already seen in Chapter 2, taxes and inflation affect discount rates. We explain the complications, then provide some reasonable principles to follow, since we need approximate rather than precise solutions. We use the following additional notation:

k_{nom}	nominal discount rate before tax
k_{real}	real discount rate before tax
$k_{nom,AT}$	nominal discount rate after tax
$k_{real,AT}$	real discount rate after tax
T	tax rate
i	inflation rate

Inflation

Inflation prevents us from comparing amounts in future years with current amounts, because what they will purchase has changed, and consumption is what we value, not the actual dollars. We usually think in terms of our cost of living today. We can express everything in today's dollars (constant or real dollars) by discounting the future nominal amounts by the inflation rate. This brings up a crucial rule of discounting:

Discount real dollars using a real discount rate, and discount nominal dollars using a nominal discount rate.

Recall from Chapter 2 that you convert between real and nominal discount rates, using the Fisher relationship, as follows:

$$\frac{1 + k_{nom}}{1 + i} = 1 + k_{real}$$

A common serious mistake in financial planning is the use of nominal discount rates for real cash flows, or real discount rates for nominal cash flows. For example, if you buy a life annuity that pays a fixed amount of $1,000 per month, that is a nominal cash flow, and to value it you would discount the payments at a nominal rate.[1] The Old Age Security (OAS) pension is indexed for inflation. That means that every period (quarterly for OAS) the amount paid is multiplied by (1 + inflation rate). Therefore, the specific amount paid at any one time is in real dollars, because it will increase in nominal dollars to match inflation. To value this pension, you would discount an annuity of the present amount by the real discount rate.[2]

---

[1] Remember, nominal rates are the rates that we actually observe in the marketplace. Therefore, the rate to discount this annuity would be somewhere around a government bond rate.

[2] Alternatively, you could inflate every year's payment and discount at the nominal rate, but it would be more time-consuming to do so.

Since retirement planning covers such long time periods, we should use long-run average inflation rates. At the time of writing this book, the inflation rate in Canada was around 1%, which is the lowest rate in many years. On the other hand, in the 1970s and early 1980s it exceeded 10% in some years. What rate should you use in a retirement plan that could stretch for 50 years? The average inflation rate for 1950–95 was 4.3% (see Appendix D).

Even in real dollars, there is still a positive interest rate, since we have to be compensated for deferring consumption. Estimates of the real risk-free interest rate range from 2–4%. The risky real rate depends upon how much risk you assume. Corporate bonds would start at 4%, and rise as the creditworthiness of the company declines. A well-diversified Canadian common equity portfolio provided a real return of 6.1% in the period 1950–95 (see Appendix E).

Income Tax

Discount after-tax dollars using an after-tax discount rate, and discount before-tax dollars using a before-tax discount rate.

Recall from Chapter 6 that the after-tax discount rate is:

$$k_{nom,AT} = k_{nom} (1 - T)$$

where T is the tax rate. Applying these discount rates to retirement planning is complicated, and we will have to be satisfied with a rough approximation. The tax rate applied to the savings portion of equation (1) (the left-hand side) is the **marginal** rate, because the earnings on the savings are on top of the regular earnings of the family. This marginal rate is not easy to calculate, however, because it depends on whether the saving is invested in a tax-sheltered or unsheltered form. Contributions to pension plans and RRSPs are deducted from taxable income and income inside them accumulates tax free until withdrawn; so the marginal tax rate is zero. Investment earnings on savings outside the sheltered plans are taxable, but at different rates for dividends, capital gains and interest. Thus, the marginal tax rate will be some average of the rates on each part of the savings. Furthermore, the tax rate for the first term on the left side, the wealth already accumulated, will probably differ from the tax rate for the future accumulations.

The tax rate applied to the consumption portion of equation (1) (the right-hand side) is the **average** rate, because in retirement, the investment income (including pensions) is the entire income of the family. We cannot calculate the average rate using the formulae in Chapter 6 — the average rate is the total tax divided by the total income. Once again, the source of the income affects the rate, because the payments from pensions and RRSPs are fully taxable (since the contributions were tax deductible). The gain on sale of the family home is not taxable. Income from investments outside pension plans and RRSPs is taxable, but the principal amounts are already after-tax, and are not taxed when the retiree cashes in the investment for consumption purposes. The tax credits (personal, old age, pension etc.) further complicate the calculation of the average tax rate. Fortunately, the after-tax average rate is calculated the same way as the after-tax marginal rate.

To get the theoretically-correct tax rate you prepare a mock tax return for the proposed future situations, and calculate the marginal and average rates that arise. This procedure can be quite time-consuming. A reasonable estimate of the average rate is

TABLE 16.1
Average Tax Rates for Retirees

Family Income	Single %	Couple %
$ 10,000	0	0
15,000	9	0
18,000	12	2
20,000	14	5
25,000	16	10
30,000	19	13
35,000	23	15
40,000	26	19
45,000	28	22
50,000	30	24
55,000	31	26
60,000	33	28
65,000	35	30
70,000	37	32
75,000	38	33
80,000	39	35
90,000	41	37
100,000	42	39
120,000	44	41
150,000	46	44
200,000	48	46
300,000	49	48

Assumptions

This table estimates average tax rates for retired couples and singles aged 65 and over, using 1995 Ontario tax rates. The income is pension and interest income (no dividends or capital gains). For the couple column, the lower income earner of the two receives $6,000 of income, which means the higher earner has no tax credits for the lower earner and no transfer of deductions, and the lower earner pays no tax. To get the average rate for a couple, each member receiving more than $6,000 in annual retirement income, take the weighted average of the values from the Single column. For example, if they receive $30,000 and $40,000, respectively, the average rate for the family is [(30,000 × .19) + (40,000 × .26] ÷ 70,000 = 23%.

This table was compiled using Hometax[TM] *provided by Softkey Software Products Inc.*

usually all that you need, given the imprecision of such long-range planning, and Table 16.1 gives the average, based on 1995 Ontario tax rates, for a number of income levels. You can use interpolation to arrive at the approximate tax rate for other situations. Tax rates change over time, but using the current rates is the best we can do.

Income tax is calculated on nominal earnings, not real earnings. This means that you pay tax on the inflation component of your savings, even though you aren't actually any better off. As long as we keep all the values in after-tax nominal dollars, we can use $k_{nom,AT}$ for all cash flows. Sometimes, we can do calculations more easily in real dollars to use the convenience of annuities.

To reflect the taxation of inflation correctly in a real rate, we have to convert a before-tax nominal rate of return into an after-tax real rate by applying the tax factor first, then converting it to real terms:

$$k_{real,AT} = \frac{1 + k_{nom}\,(1-T)}{1+i} - 1$$

For example, suppose you expect to invest in a diversified portfolio of common equity. The long-run average rate of return could be 12%. The long-run average inflation you expect is 4%, and you will be in a 40% marginal tax bracket. The after-tax marginal rate of return is then:

$$\frac{1 + .12\,(1-.4)}{1.04} - 1 = 3.1\%$$

The same calculation applies to both the average and the marginal tax rates.

A PRACTICAL APPROACH TO DISCOUNTING RETIREMENT CASH FLOWS

In theory, we could discount post-retirement cash flows before or after-tax, and in real or nominal dollars. In practice, we standardize on one method of discounting to avoid confusion. We are going to convert all our calculations to before-tax dollars, and to real dollars whenever possible. This approach has some advantages and disadvantages:

1.   We can relate to real dollars in the context of costs today more easily.
2.   We can use annuities instead of a spreadsheet with different nominal figures for every year.
3.   There is no such thing as a truly after-tax annuity. Any lump sum, even if all the tax has been paid up to the date of retirement, will still attract tax on the income earned on it as it is drawn down in retirement. Notionally, we are making the lump sum equal to an annuity in retirement, but the payments are blended principal (tax-free) and interest (taxable). Calculating a blended tax rate is beyond the scope of this book.[3]
4.   The disadvantages all relate to income tax. Taxes are levied on nominal income, and if the brackets are not perfectly indexed, then the effective tax rate is understated. Canadian tax brackets, tax credits and deductions are indexed, but not perfectly. However, capital markets evaluate investments in after-tax dollars, and if the tax system starts to weigh more heavily on nominal income because of inflation, the rates of return before-tax will rise. While we will use real dollars, in practice more precise results may be obtained by using nominal dollars.

Our practical approach works like this. There are four components to value in a retirement plan.

Consumption Needs in Retirement

We could estimate them in before-tax dollars, or after-tax dollars. To convert after-tax dollars to before-tax, use the formula:

---

[3] Revenue Canada provides prescribed annuities that level out the taxes over the life of the annuity, but we cannot use those calculations when we are notionally annuitizing a mutual fund portfolio.

$$\text{Before–tax income} = \frac{\text{After–tax income}}{1 - \text{Tax rate}}$$

and Table 16.1. This process requires trial and error. For example, suppose a single person wants \$30,000 p.a. after-tax income. The tax rate from Table 16.1 is 19%, and \$30,000 ÷ (1 − .19) = \$37,037. This level of income attracts a higher tax rate, however; so we need a somewhat higher income. We try \$40,000 × (1 − .26) = \$29,600, which is close enough. Therefore, the single person requires \$40,000 in before-tax income to generate \$30,000 after-tax.

Pension Plans

Indexed pension plans are already in before-tax real dollars. We subtract them from the required before-tax income. Indexed pensions include CPP, OAS, the future Seniors' Benefit and some employer pensions. In practice, some plans are fairly well indexed, and most have some degree of indexation. For example, some employer plans have excess interest provisions. At retirement, the retiree receives an annuity calculated at, say, 6% rate of return. If the plan's earnings exceed 6% for a number of years, then the pension is increased slightly. Since a pension fund with a mix of equity and bonds should earn more than 6% nominal in the long run, the pension should keep increasing. Moreover, it will increase more in the long-run if inflation is higher, because financial markets will adjust to provide higher long-run nominal returns.

Unindexed pensions are in before-tax nominal dollars. Pensions are relatively safe, since they are guaranteed by the annuity issuer or the employer, and there are investment portfolios backing the claim. We calculate the present value of the unindexed pension using the long-term Canada bond rate. The long Canada rate is a nominal rate with little default risk, but it is long term and hence carries interest rate risk, thus matching the long time period of a pension. We use d, the number of years planned for in retirement, as the number of years to value the pension. If the spouse receives a survivor's pension, we take the expected present value of that too. We add the present value of these unindexed pensions to W_n.

Unsheltered Savings

Savings outside pensions, RRSPs, RRIFS and DPSPs are mostly after-tax. Prior to retirement, they compound at the after-tax marginal rate. After the tax is paid on any capital gains, the net amount is in after-tax dollars; hence it will generate more after-tax consumption dollars than the same amount of sheltered savings. It will attract some tax on the income amount. The conversion of the lump sum value at retirement date to before-tax dollars uses the same formula as we used for after-tax income, but the tax rate will be much lower to reflect the fact that only the income on the principal is taxed. This future value, grossed-up to be in before-tax dollars, is then added to W_n.

Sheltered Savings

These amounts are all before-tax. They accumulate at the before-tax rate prior to retirement, and are then added to W_n.

We will illustrate all these points with numerical examples, but first we must discuss how we determine d, the number of years to discount the cash flows.

LIFE EXPECTANCY

In the model, we assume a known value of *d*, but the date of death is uncertain, or probabilistic. Therefore, we have to make some estimate or approximation, and this estimate creates additional risk. Suppose you outlive the estimated death date and run out of money? Alternatively, suppose you try to provide for a very long life, and have to practically starve yourself and work until age 75, when you really didn't need to? We can't eliminate those risks, but we do have to pick a number in order to plan at all. Let us see what we can learn from the statistical likelihood of death at any age in Canada.

In Chapter 9, you learned how to use the standard mortality tables to calculate the probability of a Canadian male or female dying at a given age, from any starting age.[4] Appendix B of the book contains the two standard life tables, one each for females and males. If you look at the probabilities of death you see that the likelihood of dying in any given year is very small until quite late ages. For example, a woman who turns 70 has a 1.67% chance of dying within the year. A male who turns 70 has a 3.20% chance of dying within the year.

However, what interests us in this chapter is the cumulative likelihood of surviving to any given age, since that is what we have to plan for in retirement. The cumulative probability combines what happens every year until some specified date. This probability is also conditional on the age that is the starting point. If we start considering the future today, then the probability of surviving for 10 years relates to what happens in each of those 10 years. For every year the horizon extends, the probability of dying at or before that horizon increases. The date at the starting point also affects the probability, but in a non-linear fashion. The probability of dying in any one year declines for the first eight years of life, then increases every year thereafter. The life tables stop at 106, because the percentage of Canadians who live beyond 106 is insignificant.

For retirement planning, we want to know how many years of retirement we have to provide income for, the *d* in equation (1). We can't give a certain answer, because the date of death is uncertain, but we can show the probability distribution. Consider a 65-year-old female. If she wants to be virtually certain of having enough retirement income, she must provide for 41 years.[5] She might reasonably say that the chances of living past 100 are negligible, but that still leaves 35 years. What age does she have an 80% chance of reaching? a 70% chance? We can calculate the deciles quite easily, and that is one way to present the risks of outliving your money.

More formally, we want to answer the question, by what age is a woman 50% likely to die, given that she has already reached the age of 65. This is a conditional probability calculation. We note that at age 65, there are 88,596 women remaining of the original 100,000. The 50% percentile is reached when only half that number alive at 65 are still living, or 44,298. Repeating the same calculation for different percentiles yields Table 16.2.

---

[4] If you have forgotten how to do this, review the section of Chapter 9 on calculating the pure premium of a life insurance policy.

[5] Absolute certainty presumably requires provision for about 55 years, since we understand that the limit of the human body is about 115–120 years, even with modern medicine.

TABLE 16.2
Probability of a Person Aged 65 Living to a Given Age

Probability (%)	Ages	
	Female	Male
50	85	80
40	88	83
30	90	85
20	92	88
10	96	91

How much risk you want to take of running out of money in retirement is a personal decision. You can guarantee some level of lifetime consumption with a life annuity, a topic we discuss in Chapter 17. All Canadians have some minimum level of income guaranteed in retirement by the government, and most have additional pensions. For any amount of retirement income required in excess of pensions, regardless of whether you finance it with an annuity or with self-managed investments, you will have to provide for quite a few years. We would suggest that a woman would have to have provided for at least 25 years, and a man for at least 20, to retire at age 65. Even at these values of *d*, there is still a 30% chance of running out of money, if they spend at exactly the planned rate.

We now return to the main road, where we apply the results of our analysis of discount rates, inflation and life expectancy.

HOW MUCH WILL YOU NEED?

Mechanical Calculations

Now we put these different pieces into numerical examples to show how they work.

> **Example 16.1:** Rose and Samwise want to retire when they reach 65 (they are the same age). They want an after-tax income of $30,000, in today's dollars. The income will be split equally for income taxes. Assume they will have no pensions. They will invest half in GICs and half in equity for an expected before-tax real rate of return of 4% p.a. How much will they need to have saved when they retire? They are very unwilling to risk running out of retirement income.

We need to calculate three things (the discount rate is given):

- The length of time to discount the cash flows
- Their average tax rate in retirement, and hence the before-tax cash flow
- The PV of the annuity of required cash flow.

Rose has a 10% chance of living 31 years, and Samwise a 10% chance of living 26 years. We will calculate PVs for 25 and 30 years.

Returning to Table 16.1 and iterating, we find that if they each receive $16,500 and pay an average tax of 10%, they will have an after-tax income of $29,700. The tax rate on $15,000 each is 9%; on $18,000 it is 12%. Since part of their earnings are from equity, and Table 16.1 assumes no equity earnings (which entails a lower tax rate), this is a conservative estimate of the tax rate. We assume, therefore, that they need $33,000 (or $16,500 each) before-tax income.

Taking the PV of the annuities of $16,500 at 4%, we find that to provide for 30 years (25 years) they would have to have accumulated $570,637 ($515,529) in real dollars, by the time they retire.[6]

> **Example 16.2:**   Now suppose that Rose and Samwise expect they will receive $22,000 in indexed pensions at retirement. How much will they need to have saved when they retire to generate an after-tax income of $30,000 in real dollars?

We can deduct the pensions from the expected consumption in real before-tax dollars, because the pensions are indexed to inflation. They need to save enough to provide $33,000 − $22,000 = $11,000 in before-tax income. The PV of $11,000 at 4% for 30 years (25 years) is $190,212 ($171,843), which gives the range of saving required by retirement, expressed in today's dollars.

> **Example 16.3:**   Now suppose that Rose and Samwise also will receive $8,000 in unindexed pensions (expressed in today's dollars) when they retire. How much will they need to have saved when they retire to generate an after-tax income of $30,000 in today's dollars?

The long-term average nominal bond return in Canada was 6.91% from 1950–95 (See Appendix D). Using that as the discount rate we find a PV of the unindexed pension[7] for 30 years (25 years) of $100,176 ($93,898). Deducting these values from the values calculated in Example 16.2, we find the required savings of $190,212 − $100,176 = $90,036 for 30 years and $171,843 − $93,898 = $77,945 for 25 years.

How Much Is Enough?

Do you want to travel around the world and stay in the best hotels when you retire? Keep a big house in the city and a cottage at the lake, and two cars? Or do you want a small house with a large garden that provides most of your food? Personal goals determine how much you have to save for retirement. Careful financial planning transforms personal goals into financial goals and shows what you must do to reach them.

How do we know what we need in retirement income? We could use some rules of thumb, such as taking 70% of our current income. The Canadian Life and Health Insurance Association suggests that high-income families could use a lower level of 50%,

---

[6] We are discounting the before-tax real cash flows ($16,500/year) by the before-tax real rate (4%).

[7] We are discounting nominal dollars (i.e., unindexed pension) by a nominal rate (i.e. the nominal bond yield).

TABLE 16.3
Changes in Expenses After Retirement

Reductions:

car expenses — don't drive to work, sell second car
food — the older you get, the less you eat
meals away from home — no work-day lunches
clothing and dry-cleaning — no business suits and dresses
house cleaning (maybe!)
shelter — move to smaller house or apartment
mortgage payments — mortgage is fully repaid
recreation — sports

Increases:

health care (although worst costs are covered by provincial plans)
employer-paid benefits — drug plans, dental plans, company car, etc.
home maintenance — as you age, you can do less of it yourself
recreation — travel, entertainment (more time to enjoy them)

while lower-income families (below $50,000) should aim for as high as 85%. Such rules do not allow for individual situations. Earlier in the life cycle, all the income might be going towards paying off a mortgage, and only 50% would be necessary once the house is paid. On the other hand, a family with no house will need to save a higher percentage of its income because it won't have the inflation protection of a house. The more accurate approach is to determine your goals in retirement, and then price the desired consumption necessary to achieve those goals. This is not an easy process for most people, especially if retirement is many years away. How do you know what you will want?

The best starting point is current expenditures, because they are the best clue to your preferences. Realistically, you can't expect to live better in retirement than before, but you can expect that your expenses will have changed in some or all of the ways outlined in Table 16.3. Of course, not everyone will change in these ways. If your goals include living in the same house, then those expenses won't decline. If you have always taken a home-made lunch to work, then food costs won't decrease as much.

The stage in the life cycle at which you are doing the planning will affect the numbers. For example, a family with young children and a large mortgage will have much higher expenses than it should expect in retirement. A couple nearing retirement, with the mortgage paid and the children gone, will have expenses that are much closer to what should be expected in retirement.

Financial needs are not the only retirement needs that require planning. Retirement involves a significant change in your pattern of life. Most of us will have been working for many years and the behaviour involved is ingrained. Suddenly, no one is telling us to be at work for a large part of our time, and we no longer can define ourselves by our occupation. For some people, retirement is a wrenching blow to their self-image, and they are unable to enjoy it. We do not discuss how to deal with the psychic needs of retirement in this book, but we remind you that they are just as important as financial needs. You should plan what you will do in retirement just as you plan how much money you will need.

Reprinted with permission — The Toronto Star Syndicate. © 1994 GREG HOWARD distributed by King Features Syndicate.

Before we deal with the other side of the coin — how much have you got? — we must take another detour to learn about pension plans and RRSPs in more detail.

PENSION PLANS

There are different ways to characterize pension plans. In the next section we explain characteristics that can apply to both government and employer-sponsored plans. In the subsequent sections, we discuss government and employer plans.

Types of Pension Plans

Defined Benefit and Defined Contribution   A defined benefit plan specifies the pension the employee receives upon retirement. There are two common methods:

1. The benefit is a specified number of dollars (per annum, per month, per week) times the number of years of service, to a specified maximum number of years or maximum dollar amount. This type of plan is often part of a labour contract, and the dollar amount is amended every time a new contract is negotiated or is subject to an agreed formula for change (normally, with respect to inflation).

2. The benefit is a specified percentage of the employee's earnings times the number of years of service, to a specified maximum number of years. The 'earnings' portion of the calculation may be defined in various ways, but the commonest way is as the average of the best five years earnings.

Defined benefit plans are less risky to employees and more risky to employers, since the latter bear the investment risk of the funds invested in the plan. On the other hand, risk has a price, as you learned in Chapters 13–15, and an employer will presumably pay less in other forms of compensation if it provides a defined benefit plan.

A defined contribution or money purchase plan specifies a per cent of earnings which both the employer and employee contribute to a fund. When an employee retires, he gets whatever pension (annuity) the accumulated contributions and earnings will buy. A defined contribution plan leaves the investment risk with the employees.

Indexation   A defined benefit plan may be indexed to inflation, usually as measured by the Consumer Price Index. Indexation refers to what happens to the payments to the employee after retirement. An indexed plan will increase these payments for inflation every year. An unindexed plan leaves the payment determined at retirement constant.[8] An indexed plan is more desirable from the employee's point of view, but it is very expensive and risky for the employer.

In practice, a plan which is not indexed formally may well keep pace with inflation. Defined contribution plans assume an interest rate below their usual experience when they set the pension amount. Many of them have excess interest provisions that increase the pension payments over time as the pension fund receives returns greater than the discount rate originally assumed in setting the pension amount. In other cases, the company may provide a guaranteed defined benefit that is also less than amount that the pension is likely to be able to provide. If the returns experienced are larger than needed for the payout level, the company may raise the payouts voluntarily.

Vesting and Portability   The employer's contributions to a plan do not belong to the employee until they are "vested." The vesting period is specified by the plan, and in the past could have been as long as 10 years. Any employee who leaves the employer, voluntarily or involuntarily, prior to vesting, gets no pension. The vesting period has become much shorter in recent years, usually only a year, due partly to provincial legislation.

Even when the employer's contributions are vested, the employee cannot simply withdraw them at will. Ordinarily, pension plan money is locked in until retirement, or can be transferred only to another locked-in fund.

A problem arises when employees with vested pension credits change employers. If the pension is defined contribution, this presents only a minor inconvenience. The employee can leave the money where it is to accumulate, and use it as part of retirement income later. Alternatively, it may be transferred to a locked-in RRSP from which a retirement income can be derived.

The problem of portability is much more serious when the employee leaves a defined benefit plan. The defined benefit will not be indexed for an employee who leaves, and if the employee is relatively early in her career, the earnings on which the benefit is based will be lower in both real and nominal dollars. Let us illustrate with an example:

> **Example 16.4:**   Miklos Georgas worked for 15 years for Skull and Crossbones Chemical in Quebec. It has a defined benefit pension paying 2% of best five year average earnings times years of service, up to a maximum of 70%. In 1968 he left SCC to join a consulting firm, with no pension plan. In 1972 he joined the Ontario government, and retired after another 15 years. The Ontario government pension plan is identical to the SCC plan.

His best five years earnings in 1968 averaged $1,000 per month. His best five years earnings at the government averaged $5,000 per month. Thus, his monthly employer pensions are:

---

[8] As previously stated, plans may be amended every year for determining the value of benefits prior to retirement, but this is not the same thing as indexing them for what happens after retirement.

SCC:	$1,000 \times .02 \times 15$	=	\$ 300
Ontario:	$5,000 \times .02 \times 15$	=	1,500
Total:			\$1,800

Suppose he had stayed at SCC for 30 years and retired at the same $5,000 average earnings? His total pension would be $5,000 \times .02 \times 30 = $3,000 per month.

Governments and private-sector employers are working on this problem of lack of portability of pensions, because it is in everyone's interest to have worker mobility. There are no easy solutions, and every worker who is depending on employer plans for part of his retirement income must be aware of this problem when considering changing jobs. In fact, since losing your job would have the same effect, you need to consider that risk with respect to your pension plan when you choose your occupation and employers all through your work life.

Non-contributory Plans
A few employers have pension plans to which employees make no contributions. If the employer really contributes enough to make up for the employee's contributions, then presumably take-home pay is lower than it would be otherwise.

Government Pension Plans

In this section we discuss the universal government plans, not those plans offered by governments to their employees. To determine the exact numbers applying in any situation, a person must consult Human Resources Development Canada, which has toll-free telephone lines and offices across Canada (listed in the Blue Pages of the telephone directory). We have summarized the maximum amounts available from the different government plans in Table 16.4. These numbers are all indexed for the previous period's changes in inflation (subject to some limitations), and hence are subject to changes, in addition to any legislative changes. The pensioner, or a representative in case of incapacity, must apply for each of these pensions — they are not automatic.

Canada Pension Plan
In 1966 the federal government started a mandatory contributory defined benefit indexed pension plan for all Canadians. Employees and employers make equal contributions. Self-employed persons must make contributions equal to the sum of the employee and employer contributions. The Canada Pension Plan (CPP) has been very successful for a large sector of the population that previously had insufficient retirement income because of a lack of employer plans. However, more recently, the contribution rate has been raised substantially, it will have to be raised even more, and the plan is still under-funded due to insufficient contributions in earlier years.

The 1996 deduction rate was 2.8% × (earnings − $3,500), up to the limit of Maximum Pensionable Earnings, which was $35,400. Thus, employee and employer each contributed up to $893.20 p.a. There are also death benefits payable to the spouse and dependent children. The details on how to qualify, and how much pension you receive, are quite involved. CPP is an important part of the retirement income package, and we will assume reasonable numbers in our examples in the textbook. CPP indexation is adjusted annually in January. The deduction rates are 2.93% for 1997, 3.05% for 1998 and 3.18% for 1999.

Old Age Security
The **Old Age Security (OAS)** pension is available to Canadian citizens and legal residents of Canada aged 65 or over, who have lived in Canada for

TABLE 16.4
Maximum Government Pensions

Maximum monthly	Details
Canada Pension Plan	
$727.08	For a person retiring at age 65 who contributed at the maximum rate on the MPE for the majority of his career. Actual amount varies according to lifetime profile of contributions, and age of retirement. Reduced/increased by 0.5% for each month retired before/after month of 65th birthday.
$3,540 (lump)	Lump sum death benefit to spouse or estate.
$164.17	Survivor benefits to dependent children, to age 18, or to age 25 while full time in school.
Old Age Security	
$399.91	Every Canadian at age 65, provided they have lived in Canada for a sufficient number of years.
Guaranteed Income Supplement	
$469.13	Available on a reducing scale to those who need it. For example, the cut-off for a single person is $11,016 in income the previous year exclusive of OAS.
OAS + GIS Minimum Income Floor	
$875.16	OAS + GIS for a single person with no other income. A retired Canadian aged 65 or over is entitled to this minimum level of income, with some qualifications.

at least 10 years since turning 18. Those who met those qualifications at the time they left Canada, but no longer reside here, must have resided for at least 20 years after turning 18. Residence in countries with which Canada has a social security pension agreement may also count towards the 20-year qualifying period. OAS is not dependent upon previous employment. OAS indexation is adjusted quarterly. OAS is included in taxable income.

The **spouse's allowance** is an income-tested monthly benefit payable to a 60–64 year old spouse of an OAS pensioner who is also entitled to a GIS. The **widowed spouse's allowance** is an income-tested monthly benefit payable to a 60–64 year old widowed spouse of a person who was eligible for OAS, or would have been had he survived to age 65. Ten years of residence in Canada after age 18 are usually required. A spouse is a legal or common-law spouse.

Guaranteed Income Supplement

The **Guaranteed Income Supplement (GIS)** is an income-tested monthly pension supplement for OAS pensioners who have little other income. The actual amount received is adjusted every year for changes in the pensioner's financial circumstances and marital status, and the pensioner must reapply every year. Only OAS recipients who are resident in Canada are eligible, which distinguishes it from OAS, which can be paid to non-residents. GIS is **not** included in taxable income. GIS indexation is adjusted quarterly.

TABLE 16.5
Proposed Seniors Benefit

These are the benefit levels that are projected to occur in 2001, but they are not certain. Inflation and future government policies may change them, or change the rules governing them.

Income	Tax-free Seniors Benefit	
	Single	Couple
$ 0	$11,420	$18,440
10,000	6,420	13,440
20,000	5,160	10,320
30,000	4,350	9,510
40,000	2,350	7,510
51,721	0	4,710
60,000	0	3,510
70,000	0	1,510
77,521	0	0

Seniors Benefit

The 1996 federal budget proposed to replace OAS and GIS with a new plan called Seniors Benefit. This benefit would be tax-free, but paid on a reducing scale related to family income of the previous year. As a transitional measure, OAS would remain available to anyone who was aged 60 or over at the end of 1995. Table 16.5 shows the projected benefit level for different levels of income. Since this programme is still in the development stage, the final form and level of benefits may differ quite a bit. In particular, we note that financial advisors have already commented on a tax problem with it. Because of the loss of benefits tied to income, those seniors who have some ability to time their income can reduce taxable income in some years and thus receive more Seniors Benefit than would be possible with their income spread evenly. Some experts advise those near to retirement to stop contributing to RRSPs, since additional taxable retirement income will reduce the available Seniors Benefit.

Registered Pension Plans

A **registered pension plan (RPP)** or **employer pension plan** is established by an employer to defer income payable to employees to provide retirement income for them. Such a plan may have payments made into it by either or both the employer and the employee, depending on the terms of the plan. The contributions are deposited with a plan trustee who invests them. When the employee retires, she receives a pension from the plan. The employee pays tax on the pension as it is received. Thus, the pension contributions provide a deduction from taxable income, and also accumulate at the before-tax rate of return.

Most people will have no planning to do with respect to a registered pension plan. The contributions are fixed by the terms of employment. Occasionally, the plan may be retroactively amended to allow for higher contributions for past service, or to allow employees to join the plan who were not previously in it, and to gain credit for past service. If such an amendment allows a person to make **past service contributions**, they are almost always worth doing. In effect, you get a tax deduction for buying more pension income.

Employer plans may be indexed or unindexed, and defined contribution or defined benefit. The specific terms of the plan and the eventual benefits the retiree will receive are entirely a matter of contract, either between the employee and the employer directly, or between a union and the employer. There are laws that require the employer to fund a defined benefit plan to meet the expected future liabilities, as determined by actuarial consultants. However, if circumstances change, the fund may have **unfunded liabilities**, and the employer will have some time to make up the difference. Employers must also be reasonably current in making their contributions to a defined contribution pension plan. The employee contributions go directly into the fund. In all cases, the money in the pension fund is under the care of an independent trustee. The trustee will retain actuaries to estimate the liabilities, and in the process they will determine the estimated future pension payable to each employee. The employer provides this information to the employees annually, and this amount of expected pension is an important input into retirement planning.

REGISTERED RETIREMENT SAVINGS PLAN (RRSP)

A **Registered Retirement Savings Plan (RRSP)** is a do-it-yourself pension plan. The taxpayer contributes part of his income to a trusteed fund. The contribution is deducted from income for tax purposes in the year it is paid into the fund, and income on it accumulates tax free. When the taxpayer withdraws it for spending purposes, the entire amount, principal and accrued earnings, is taxable.[9] An RRSP is distinguishable from a defined contribution RPP because the person retains control of how the assets are invested, and can withdraw assets before retirement. In the terminology of Chapter 7, an RRSP is an income deferral strategy.

Legally, an RRSP is a trust, an arrangement in which certain property is given by a **settlor** to a **trustee**, an independent third party, who holds the property on behalf of the **beneficiary** (or beneficiaries) who will receive income and/or capital from the trust. In an RRSP, the settlor is the person who makes the tax-deductible contributions, and we will use the common term — contributor — instead of settlor. The beneficiary is most often the contributor, but may also be the spouse, if it is designated as a **spousal RRSP**.

RRSPs constitute an important part of Canadians' retirement savings, and there are many important complications and opportunities. We will provide the major features in the following sections.[10]

Contribution Limits   The limit that you can contribute to an RRSP and deduct from taxable income is 18% of **earned income**, minus the **pension adjustment (PA)**

---

[9] Note that in both RRSPs and registered pension plans, the capital gains exemption, the 3/4 of capital gains rule and the dividend tax credit do not apply. Capital gains, dividends and interest income are treated identically upon withdrawal.

[10] For complicated problems, you may want to consult an expert financial adviser, or perhaps read more about it in a book dedicated to RRSPs.

and contributions to a **Deferred Profit Sharing Plan (DPSP)**, up to a legislated maximum amount, plus any **unused contribution room** carried forward from previous years.[11] Earned income and the adjustments refer to the previous year's figures; e.g. the limits for 1997 will be based on 1996 income and pension contributions. This allows contributors to make the full contribution early in the year if they can, to gain the maximum benefit of compounding income in a tax shelter. In mathematical form, the contribution limit is:

Max [ceiling, .18(earned income)] – PA – DPSP deposits + unused contribution room

Let us consider the terms one at a time.

The contribution ceiling has been $11,500 in 1991, $12,500 in 1992, $13,500 in 1993–94 and $14,500 in 1995. From 1996–2003, it will be $13,500. In 2004, it will be $14,500 and in 2005, it will be $15,500. Thereafter, it will be indexed to inflation.[12]

Earned income is:

- employment income (including taxable benefits)
- supplementary unemployment benefits
- alimony and maintenance payments received
- royalties
- research grants
- business and net rental income
- taxable disability benefits

minus:

- union and professional dues
- alimony and maintenance payments made.

Earned income excludes retirement income sources, investment income, child tax credits, unemployment insurance, adult training allowances, bursaries, scholarships and payments from a Registered Educational Savings Plan.

Pension adjustments are calculated by the employer and reported on the next year's T4 slip. They limit the employee in an RPP to about the same amount of tax-deferred saving as someone who has no RPP can achieve at the same income level by using exclusively RRSPs. For contributions to a DPSP or a defined contribution RPP, the limit is simply the amount contributed by both parties in the previous year. For a defined benefit plan, the calculation is more complex.[13]

---

[11] A person may contribute up to $2,000 over the limit during his lifetime without penalty, but overcontributions are not tax deductible, and are taxed upon withdrawal. The overcontribution accumulates at the before-tax rate, however, and if left in the plan for long enough, will overcome the disadvantage of non-deductibility. It is not an important issue, especially since most Canadians have trouble finding enough money to contribute to the limit. Overcontributions greater than $2,000 are penalized.

[12] Every year or two the federal government promises a specific schedule of future RRSP ceilings, only to change them a year or two later.

[13] Determine **benefit entitlement**, which is earned income from the previous year times the **benefit accrual rate** (provided by the employer, based on the plan rules). The benefit accrual rate is a fraction of your previous year's earned income that cannot exceed .02. Multiply the benefit entitlement by 9 and subtract $1,000. This value is the limit of the RRSP contribution for this year.

A Deferred Profit Sharing Plan (DPSP) is a form of retirement saving set up for contributions from the employer only, based on the company's net income according to an agreed-upon formula. It enters the calculations for limiting RRSP contribution room because payments into are tax deductible for the employer and are only taxed in the employee's hands when withdrawn, just as in an RPP.

Example 16.5: Johanna Vision earned $32,000 in wages and $1,000 in overtime in 1996. She earned $125 in interest on her Canada Savings Bonds and received $1,500 in UIC while briefly unemployed. She also got a $500 training allowance during this period. She paid union dues of $400. On her tax return, she also reported lottery winnings of $100, under Other Income. On her 1996 T4 slip, the employer reported her pension adjustment (PA) of $3,300. She contributed the maximum amount to her RRSP every year since she left school. How much can she contribute to an RRSP for the 1997 year?

Answer: Earned income = $32,000 + $1,000 − $400 = <u>$32,600</u>.
.18 × $32,600 = <u>$5,868</u>.

Since this is less than $13,500:
Maximum contribution = $5,868 − $3,300 = <u>$2,568</u>.

A person may carry forward unused contribution room for seven years. That is, if you don't have enough money to contribute to the limit in one year, you may make up the lost contribution during the next seven years, by contributing more than the limit in those years, up to the amount of the unused contribution. This carryforward is available only from 1991 and future years. Large carryforwards are not very valuable for three reasons. First, they may reduce the tax bracket if all taken in one year, and thus make the tax saving on the deduction less valuable. Second, too large a deduction in one year may trigger **alternative minimum tax**, a complex issue we have not discussed in this book. Third, the point of an RRSP is to get the money into it as quickly as possible in order to receive the maximum benefit of tax-free earnings accumulation. Nonetheless, families will have periods when they don't have the cash to make all their RRSP contributions.

Example 16.6: Lally Lolly started work as a retail representative for an investment dealer in 1994. She earned $15,000 in commissions. In 1995 she earned $62,000 in commissions, $4,000 in capital gains and $500 in dividends. She joined a professional association with annual dues of $800. In 1996 she earned $117,000 in commissions, lost $6,000 in capital gains, earned $1,000 in dividends and paid dues of $900. The investment dealer contributed $4,000 to a DPSP on her account. The investment dealer does not offer a pension plan, and Lally made no RRSP contributions in 1994–96, because it was her first job and she was paying off student debts, buying furniture etc. How much can she contribute to an RRSP in 1997? Should she contribute the maximum?

Earned income (1994) = $15,000
Unused contribution (1994) = .18 × $15,000 = $2,700
Earned income (1995) = $62,000 − $800 = $61,200
Unused contribution (1995) = .18 × $61,200 = $11,016
Earned income (1996) = $117,000 − 900 = $116,100.
Unused contribution (1996) = .18 × $116,100 = $20,898

Since the 1996 amount exceeds the limit, the limit is $13,500, and the unused contribution = $13,500 − $4,000 = $9,500

The maximum contribution possible is $2,700 + $11,016 + $9,500 = $23,216. Assuming we have all the information necessary, this would give her a taxable income after RRSP deductions (ignoring CPP and UI premiums) of:

Commissions		$117,000
Taxable Dividends		1,250
− dues	−	900
− RRSP contribution	−	23,216
Taxable income		$ 94,134

This income is in the top tax bracket, and so long as there is no problem with alternative minimum tax, she should contribute the maximum.

Spousal Plans

A contributor may make part or all of the annual RRSP contribution to an RRSP specifically designated for his spouse. In the terminology of Chapter 7, this is both an income deferral and an income splitting technique. It is especially useful if one spouse will have little or no retirement income other than OAS. Then, splitting the income into two streams may lower the marginal tax rate on the family income, and also allows both spouses to claim a deduction for pension income when the RRSP is turned into an annuity or a Registered Retirement Income Fund (RRIF). Common-law spouses qualify for spousal RRSPs.

The contribution limit applies to the contributor's income, not the recipient's. However, a person's contribution limit to RRSPs applies to the combined amount contributed to her own RRSP and a spousal RRSP. You cannot 'double up' your contributions by putting money into both.

An obvious tax loophole beckons — contribute to a spousal RRSP for a spouse with no income, who then withdraws it immediately at a lower marginal tax rate. This loophole is illusory. If a taxpayer makes a contribution to a spousal RRSP in the two taxation years prior to any withdrawal, or in the year of the withdrawal, the lesser of the amount withdrawn and the amount contributed by the taxpayer is taxed in the contributor's hands.

Investment Restrictions

We discuss investment and saving principles in retirement more generally in a subsequent section. However, the law restricts RRSPs to **eligible investments**. The details are complicated, but in general, eligible investments are:

- savings accounts, term deposits and GICs
- shares of Canadian companies listed on Canadian exchanges
- some shares of foreign companies listed on Canadian exchanges, some unlisted and foreign shares
- federal and provincial bonds, some Canadian corporate bonds, stripped bonds

- certain types of mortgages, including your own
- mutual funds investing in eligible investments
- specified foreign investments, to a maximum of 20% of the RRSP
- covered call options, warrants and rights issued by Canadian companies listed on a stock exchange.

Note that you need not contribute cash to an RRSP. A contribution could be any of the above eligible investments, and the contribution will be valued at market price. A taxpayer who transfers an asset into an RRSP at a market price higher than the original cost will have to declare capital gains.

What Happens in Death, Dissolution or Maturity?

An RRSP must be wound-up by December 31st of the year in which the beneficiary turns 69. The beneficiary may terminate it earlier, and it will be terminated involuntarily when the beneficiary dies. There are three ways to terminate an RRSP voluntarily:

1. Buy an annuity, either life or term certain, using all the money in the RRSP. The annuity payments are taxed when received.
2. Withdraw the funds and pay tax immediately.
3. Transfer the money to a Registered Retirement Income Fund (RRIF) from which taxable payments will be received until the beneficiary dies or the money runs out.

Option 2 is rarely a good idea, since it raises the marginal tax rate for the beneficiary. Options 1 and 3 are different ways of providing a steady retirement income, which is the government's purpose in creating RRSPs. We discuss them in more detail in Chapter 17.

If the beneficiary dies, the RRSP is considered to be terminated in the year of death and is included in income, except under these circumstances:

1. The spouse of the beneficiary is named as the beneficiary in the event of death. A spouse may elect a tax-free roll-over of the RRSP into his own RRSP. This is a tax deferral strategy. If the spouse is over age 69, the roll-over would be to an RRIF.
2. The deceased beneficiary had no spouse at the time, and a dependent child or grandchild was named as the beneficiary in the event of death. The child will pay tax, but may elect to buy an annuity whose term is no longer than 18 years minus the child's age. This is an income spreading technique, and is only useful if the RRSP is large enough to put the child into a high tax bracket if it is received all in one year. An important consideration is the possible loss of provincial family benefits if the child's income becomes too high.

RRSPs are part of the family property, and if spouses end their marriage, a court may order the transfer of assets from an RRSP in one spouse's name to the other spouse's RRSP. Such a transfer occurs tax free.

Withdrawals from a fund other than the tax-free roll-overs or conversion to an annuity are taxable, and are subject to a **withholding tax.** A withholding tax is one which is deducted by a financial institution from some amount it is paying to a person or company, and which is then submitted directly to the taxing authority. The withholding

TABLE 16.6
Withholding Taxes on RRSP Withdrawals

	Withholding Tax (%)	
Amount Withdrawn	Quebec residents	Others
up to $5,000	21	10
$5,001–$15,000	30	20
over $15,000	35	30

tax is credited to the account of the person who received the balance of the payment. When that person files a tax return for the year in which the withholding occurred, the amount withheld is treated as an installment payment; so the taxpayer is not penalized. Table 16.6 shows the present withholding tax rates.

Self-Administered RRSPs   The beneficiary may allow the trustee to make the detailed investment decisions, or may make them herself. Financial institutions offer plans that invest in pooled portfolios of bonds, shares and/or Treasury bills, according to your preferred allocation. The specific selection of the securities is left to the institution. Alternatively, the beneficiary can have a **self-administered plan**, and choose which securities to buy and sell inside the plan, just like a regular account with an investment dealer. The trustee will require an annual fee in addition to transactions costs and investment management fees. This trustee fee is not tax deductible, although it used to be.

HOW MUCH HAVE YOU GOT?

We discuss how to prepare and use a family balance sheet in Chapter 4, and it provides the basis for this aspect of retirement planning. The net liquid assets that can be maintained and invested as part of the eventual retirement income are the W_0 of the planning equation. Net worth is an essential figure to balance the balance sheet, but it is not the same as W_0, except by coincidence. Net worth relates to all the assets, not just to those that will provide retirement income.

Table 16.7 lists the sources of retirement income. Technically, the current pension fund balances are part of current wealth — that is, they are part of "How much have you got?" We incorporated them into the plan in a convenient way by:

- deducting indexed pensions from the required annual consumption in real dollars.
- adding the present value of unindexed pensions to W_N.

The items on the right-hand side of Table 16.7 are left to be valued today. These amounts and savings from future earnings, together with compounded income on them, are what the family will have available to cover any shortfall from required income minus pensions.

Example 16.7:   Let us return to Rose and Samwise, from Example 16.3. They are 55 years old. In addition to the pensions noted earlier, they have $10,000 in an RRSP invested in Government of

TABLE 16.7
Sources of Retirement Income

Pensions	Non-Pension Savings
Old Age Security (OAS)	Registered Retirement Savings Plan (RRSP)
Guaranteed Income Supplement (GIS)	Deferred Profit Sharing Plan (DPSP)
Canada Pension Plan (CPP)	House (if you trade down)
Employer's Registered Pension Plan (RPP)	Vacation property (if you will sell)
Seniors Benefit	Tax shelters
	Reverse mortgage
	Unsheltered savings
	Locked-in funds

Canada bonds and $10,000 outside their RRSP, in a Canadian equity mutual fund. They own a modest home worth $110,000 in Saint John, New Brunswick. There is a mortgage of $25,000 outstanding on the home that they expect to have paid off before they retire. They also have $15,000 in a separate bank account to help their youngest son pay for university. How much do they have now for retirement, in addition to their pensions?

They need to live somewhere and the house is modest; so it will not provide an extra income stream for retirement. The mortgage is to be paid from saved income prior to retirement; so it is not deducted. The money for the youngest son is already committed. While a balance sheet would show a net worth of $120,000, for retirement income calculations they have $10,000 in before-tax dollars and $10,000 in after-tax dollars.

HOW TO GET FROM HERE TO THERE

In this section we complete the time value mechanics of calculating W_n and discuss the tax and investment aspects of saving for retirement.

Today, the family has W_0 and it expects to receive various pensions in retirement. Will W_0 compound to a large enough amount to cover any shortfall in consumption provided by the pensions? If not, how much more must the family save? Once again, we illustrate the method with an example:

Example 16.8: Rose and Samwise have a shortfall of about $90,000 from pensions alone (See Example 16.3). Will their current savings (See Example 16.7) be enough to cover it if they retire in 10 years? If not, how much will they have to save each year for the next 10 years, in real dollars? Assume their marginal tax rate now is 20% on equity earnings and 30% on other earnings.

We calculate the FV of their current retirement savings, in real before-tax dollars, assuming that they maintain the same investment policies.

1. $10,000 in an RRSP. It compounds before-tax at the real long bond
    rate of 2.5% (see Appendix E), for 10 years, to yield $12,801
2. $10,000 in an equity mutual fund. It compounds after-tax at the
    real after-tax equity rate of .061 × (1 − .20) = 4.9%, for a value
    of $16,134. To be consistent with the rest of our calculations we
    need this amount in before-tax dollars. Since the tax is already
    partly paid and their tax rate in retirement is quite low, the difference
    is not great. Their average tax rate in retirement is about 10%; so
    let us guess at a 5% gross-up. Then: $16,134 ÷ (1 − .05) =   16,983
    Total value of current savings compounded to retirement date $29,784

Therefore, they are $90,000 − $27,984 = $60,216 short.

If they save and invest in equity in an RRSP at the before-tax real rate of 6.1%, they need to save $4,547 more p.a. in real dollars. Since deposits in an RRSP reduce taxes, they reduce consumption by a lesser amount. Specifically, the tax reduction is (T × contribution); so the net amount they must save to make the RRSP contribution is $4,547 × (1 − .3) = $3,183 p.a.

If they invest the initial savings in the RRSP into equity as well, they can reduce even further the amount they should expect to have to contribute. If the initial $10,000 is invested in equity, it compounds at 6.1% over 10 years to $18,078. Following the same steps as above, we find the net amount they must save to make the RRSP contribution reduces to $2,904.

Income Tax Implications

Chapter 7 pointed out four main tax strategies: deferral, spreading, splitting and shelters. All four apply with respect to retirement saving. The basic principle is to save using up all tax assistance opportunities first. Once you have exhausted all the tax strategies, save in unsheltered form. The three main savings vehicles are employer pension plans, RRSPs and the family home.

An employer pension plan defers income tax until it is paid out in retirement. The employee makes few decisions.[14] One important one is the purchase of past service credits. When a company that has not had a plan institutes one, or a company amends an existing plan, there may be an opportunity for the employee to "buy more pension." By paying some money into the plan now, some past years of service that were not credited are added into the calculation of the final pension. The employer usually contributes as well for these past service periods, and so the employee should almost always take advantage of it, even ahead of RRSP contributions.

RRSPs allow both deferral and splitting (through a spousal RRSP) of income. To a small degree, they may allow some income spreading, for a self-employed person with irregular income. The new carryforward rules are helpful in this regard. You should use

---

[14] The critical decision may have been the original choice of employer. Few people think about the value of their pension plan when they start working, yet it is a significant portion of the compensation package, or a significant lack, if there isn't a pension plan.

up all RRSP contribution room for retirement saving before any unsheltered savings are accumulated.

The family home provides a tax shelter. Neither the implicit income nor the capital gain on a home are taxable. By contrast, a renter must pay tax on investment income (the alternative place for the funds that could have been used to buy a home), then pay rent from after-tax income.

The family home also provides a tax-splitting mechanism. If a couple buys a home, with both contributing to the down payment, and one has significantly lower retirement income than the other, the ultimate capital gain on disposal can be split equally to provide retirement income. This is a bit of a grey area, since technically they should contribute equally to all payments. However, the interest portion is a debt that the higher income spouse can pay, with the lower income spouse paying only principal. In practice, it seems that even a home-maker spouse can share equally in the capital gain, since the family home is joint property.

Once you have exhausted the basic retirement tax shelters, you put additional savings into unsheltered investments. Shares are preferable, at least from a tax point of view. First, capital gains are taxed at 75% of the rate that interest is taxed. Second, capital gains accumulate untaxed until they are realized. Preferred shares and bonds are priced in the market so that the after-tax yield on dividends and interest are approximately equal for someone in the top tax bracket. If you are in a lower tax bracket, the dividend tax bracket will provide a slightly higher after-tax return than debt instruments of equal risk.

Rental properties are a retirement investment for a significant number of Canadians. Real estate can provide very high rates of return, and it has two significant tax advantages, related to deferral and spreading. First, the capital gain accumulates untaxed until the property is sold, just as with securities.

Second, rental properties often operate at low income for income tax purposes, or even a loss during the early years of ownership. Thus, a taxpayer aged 55, at the peak of the earnings curve, could invest in a rental property and pay no tax on the income, or even have a loss to deduct from other income. Then, in retirement, when the taxpayers income and tax bracket are lower, the taxable income from the rental property is higher. This levels the income over time, and defers tax as well.

Two tax aspects create this situation. A taxpayer may claim **capital cost allowance (CCA)** on the building, and deduct it from the rental income along with other expenses. We will not describe the capital cost allowance system in detail in this book, but the reference sources mentioned in Chapters 6 and 7 provide more information. The fundamental tax-spreading aspect is that CCA charges depreciation at higher rates in the earlier years, because it is a declining balance system. You can claim up to the maximum rate every year, but need not claim any more than enough to create zero rental income. In the later years, when you are retired, you have less income from other sources, but now the CCA on the rental property is lower and the taxable income is higher. There is one limit to the use of CCA on a rental property. A taxpayer may deduct losses due to cash expenses on a rental property, but may not deduct a loss caused by a CCA claim. Thus, if interest and other expenses are quite high in the earlier years of ownership, the CCA deduction will not be claimed.

A single rental property will usually absorb part or all of a family's savings, and usually requires a mortgage loan at first. The interest on a loan used to buy an income property is also deductible from the rental income. As the loan is paid down, the interest portion of the blended principal and interest payments declines, and the taxable income from the property rises. Once again, this pattern offsets the decline in other sources of income in retirement, and spreads and defers the tax burden.

Investment Principles

Chapters 13–15 provide both practical application and the three basic principles:

1.   Risk-return trade-off;
2.   Diversification; and,
3.   Efficient markets hypothesis.

The risk-return trade-off when saving for retirement extends over a very long period of time. The k required to meet your goals must be related to the trade-off. For example, if you need to earn a 13% nominal rate of return in order to have a comfortable retirement income, you won't find it by investing in Treasury bills.

There are essentially two risks in the long run that you must steer a course between: the risk of not earning a high enough rate of return to accumulate the needed retirement fund, versus the risk of losing part of your capital because of investing in high risk, high return investments. Researchers in capital markets have found that the risk of investing in equity for the long-term is not as high as the simple measures of risk suggest. Over a long period of time, the higher average return more than compensates for the bad years, and the compounded return is almost certain to outperform the lower, steadier returns in government bonds and bills. This effect is called **time diversification.**

Any portfolio attempting to take advantage of time diversification must be diversified across securities in the class. If it is a portfolio of equities, then numerous different companies must be included. The total value of most RRSPs is too small to allow effective diversification except through a mutual fund. An index fund or an equities fund would be appropriate. The foreign content is restricted to 20%.

Investment in rental property almost always violates the diversification principle for a single family. A large part of the family's net worth is in a single asset, or perhaps two or three at most. Even if there is more than one property, they are usually in the same area or city. The family probably also has a family home. Thus, the retirement income outside of pensions is dependent on a single volatile market, and this is quite risky.

Rental property also carries another disadvantage. The owner must manage it actively, and this takes time and some skill. For those who have the skill and enjoy the work associated with a rental property, this is not a disadvantage, but others should beware. Investment in a portfolio of securities, or a mutual fund, requires much less management.

SUMMARY

Retirement planning answers three questions:

1.   How much do you need? Price the level of consumption you want in retirement, estimate the number of years you will need it for, and calculate the amount needed to finance it at retirement age.
2.   How much have you got? Identify and value the present and expected future sources of retirement income. These include government pensions, employer

pensions and family savings in the form of RRSPs, the family home and unsheltered savings. The pensions may be indexed or unindexed, and defined benefit or defined contribution.

3.   How do you get from here to there? Using time value calculations, find how much the family needs to save from now until retirement to meet its retirement income goal. The savings should be first in the tax-assisted vehicles — employer pension, RRSP, family home. Then, use the tax advantages of investing in shares or rental property. Be careful to be diversified in securities holdings.

KEY TERMINOLOGY

retirement planning model / inflation / real discount rate / nominal discount rate / before-tax discount rate / after-tax discount rate / life expectancy / financial goals / pension plans — defined benefit — defined contribution — indexation — vesting — portability — Registered Pension Plan (RPP) / Canada Pension Plan (CPP) / Old Age Security (OAS) — spouse's allowance — widowed spouse's allowance / Guaranteed Income Supplement (GIS) / Registered Retirement Savings Plan (RRSP) — contribution limits — spousal plan — eligible investments — death, dissolution and maturity — withholding tax — self-administered / Registered Retirement Income Fund (RRIF) / income tax implications / time diversification

DISCUSSION QUESTIONS AND RESEARCH PROJECTS

1.   Explain each of the terms under **Key Terminology**.

The primary information source for the next three projects is the nearest office of Health and Welfare Canada. You can write, telephone or visit in person.

2.   Prepare a two-page summary of the Old Age Security benefits. Your summary should include eligibility conditions, the most recent amount per month, the indexation rules, the rules on claw-back (the government recovers part of OAS from higher income recipients) and any other features you think are important.

3.   Prepare a two-page summary of the Guaranteed Income Supplement benefits. Your summary should include eligibility conditions, the most recent amount per month, the indexation rules and any other features you think are important.

4.   Prepare a summary of not more than four pages of the most important features of the Canada Pension Plan at retirement age. Your report should include the rules under which the pension is calculated, eligibility, portability, taxation treatment, survivor benefits, indexation rules and the current maximum pension receivable. Choose the important features for financial planning relevant to most people to stay within the page limit.

5.   Both the Canadian government and various private actuaries and pension experts have noted for some time that the Canada Pension Plan is under-funded relative to expected future payouts. Government deficits compound this problem. The government may decide to restrict the amounts it pays out under OAS, GIS and CPP in the future.

Investigate this topic. Write a report that should consider the issues, and at least these three questions:

(a) How serious is the under-funding of our retirement system?

(b) What methods do you think the government will use to reduce its payments to seniors?

(c) How would your answer to (b) affect your financial planning advice for people at preretirement ages planning for their retirement?

PROBLEMS

Note: You can use Super Rep to assist in solving many of these problems, but the student version is not designed to provide complete solutions.

1. Construct a table like Table 16.2, for males and females who retire at age 60, for probabilities of 50%, 40%, 30%, 20% and 10%. What are the implications of the results for personal finance?

2. Louise Hammer is a taxpayer who will be in the 40% marginal tax bracket for the next 40 years. She looks at her budget and sees that she will have $2,400 left from her take-home pay, after expenses. She will save everything of this by putting it in an RRSP. The money in the RRSP will be invested in a diversified portfolio of shares. The long-run return on these shares is expected to be 12% p.a. capital gains and 3% p.a. dividends, for a total before-tax return of 15%. At the end of 40 years she will withdraw all the money in a lump sum, and pay tax on it at a rate of 50%.

    Ed Anvil is a taxpayer who has the identical tax situation and budget expectations as Louise. He has decided to invest his savings outside an RRSP to take advantage of the capital gains' lower rate and dividend tax credit. He plans to do this for 18 years, using the same diversified portfolio as Louise. The after-tax dividend yield is 2%. The after-tax capital gains yield is 8%. From year 19 to year 40, he does exactly the same as Louise with his savings. At the end of 40 years he collapses his investments and pays tax as applicable, at the rate of 40%. His rate is lower than Louise's because she has put herself into a higher tax bracket by not paying taxes earlier.

    Neither Ed nor Louise has an employer pension plan.

    (a) What does Louise have left in 40 years, after paying taxes?

    (b) What does Ed have left in 40 years, after paying taxes?
         Be very careful! The tax rules have an immediate effect on their savings.

    (c) What is the present value of the taxes Louise will pay in 40 years?

    (d) Ed recognizes he can do better than in part (b). He earns $50,000 every year; so his contribution limit is $9,000 p.a., or $63,000 for the seven years he is allowed to backdate. He decides he will contribute $21,000 to his RRSP in each of years 19, 20 and 21 and get the tax deductions at 40%. He will use part of the accumulated investment pool to provide the cash flow. The rest of the pool will continue to accumulate at 10%. He will contribute the $4,000 based on current income as in part (b), from years 19 to 40. How much will he have after paying taxes at the end of year 40?

(e) When is a capital gain taxed? This question is not related to instalments. When does the 8% after-tax rate of return quoted above assume the capital gain is taxed? How does this affect your answer to part (b)?

3. Elizabeth Maynes wants to plan how much she and her husband Bruce should save for retirement. They have no pension plans because she is an independent consulting economist and he owns his own computer company. Both have contributed the maximum to the Canada Pension Plan so far, and they expect to earn enough to continue to do so. Both are Canadians who plan to continue to live in Canada. They are now 35 years old, and they think they would like to retire at age 60. They would like an after-tax income of $40,000 p.a., in today's dollars. They have almost finished paying for their house. Elizabeth has $5,000 in an RRSP, invested in a GIC. Bruce has $10,000 in Far East mutual funds.

(a) Estimate their required savings p.a. in today's dollars to retire at age 60. At age 65. Explain your assumptions.

(b) Do you have any advice on how they should save?

4. Joan wants to retire in 22 years. She expects to receive a combined government and employer indexed pension of $25,000 p.a. Her son, who is articling with a professional accounting firm, has estimated that she would need an after-tax pension income of $30,000 in today's dollars to maintain her current lifestyle at retirement. She expects to live for 30 years after retirement. Assume a marginal tax rate of 40% for the next 22 years, and current savings of $20,000. How much does she have to save each year, at a nominal rate of return of 10% p.a., to meet her objective?

5. Mark and Ann are planning to retire in 25 years. Mark makes $65,000 p.a. before taxes and Ann is a housewife with no income of her own. Mark's marginal tax rates are currently at the 38% level, and he anticipates no future increases until his retirement. Mark has no employer pension, but contributes the maximum allowable every year to an RRSP, and uses the tax savings for recreation and entertainment. They figure that they would need an after-tax income of $35,000 in today's dollars at retirement, to live comfortably for 25 years. Their current RRSP has accumulated to $100,000, invested in balanced mutual fund with an average rate of return of 9% p.a. What do you advise?

6. Jim Scott is 26 years old and has been working for the Ace Manufacturing Company for five years. His gross income in 1995 and 1996 was $23,000 and $26,000, respectively. He is a member of the company's registered pension plan and has contributed $1,100 and $1,200 to it in 1995 and 1996, respectively. The (PA) pension adjustment on his T4 slips showed $2,400 and $2,500 for those two years. The company had no pension plan before 1995. He earned $18,000 in 1992, $20,000 in 1993 and $21,000 in 1994. Jim does not have any RRSP because he never seemed to be able to save any money. In January, 1997, he inherited $40,000 from a distant relative. He wants to contribute the maximum amount possible to an RRSP.

(a) What is the maximum amount that he should contribute before March 1, 1997?

(b) What advice would you give him about RRSP contributions in the future?

7. Alan is 50, Joanne is 51. They have a large house worth $800,000 in Toronto and a cottage worth $200,000 in Muskoka. Mortgage payments on these properties are $42,000 p.a. and they will be paid off in 10 years. They have no other debts, although they just finished paying off a car loan. They each own a recent model car, and they replace their cars every three or four years because they do not want to be seen driving older models. Alan's net income or take home income was $100,000 last year, after taxes, CPP, UI premiums, medical insurance, etc. Joanne takes home $40,000 p.a. after the same set of deductions and contributions to her employer pension plan. They have two children whom they are currently helping through school, at a cost of $25,000 p.a. This cost will continue for another five years, after which the children are on their own. They are both carrying substantial life insurance and disability insurance, all of the cost of which is deducted from their gross pay in arriving at the net income reported above.

   They have $10,000 in a chequing account and a substantial line of credit at the bank if they need it. Alan has $30,000 in an oil and gas mutual fund. He has no pension plan. Joanne has $20,000 invested in GICs in an RRSP. She expects an indexed pension plan of $25,000 (in today's dollars) if she retires at age 61. They would each qualify for only 80% of maximum Canada Pension, and that would be further reduced if they start receiving it before age 65.

   Alan has been earning gross income over $100,000 p.a. for five years, and he expects the $100,000 net income of last year to be sustainable until he retires. He started saving money only in the last two years. Last year he deposited $15,000 in the mutual fund (this amount is included in the $30,000 balance). Joanne has been contributing $1000–$2,000 p.a. to her RRSP for 10 years.

   They would like to retire in 10 years. Advise them in their retirement planning.

8. Etaoin Shrdlu and his wife Qwerty wave goodbye to their daughter Spellcheck as she leaves for the residence at York and her fourth year in the BBA programme. After a long shopping trip to replace their depleted stock of linen, soap, liquor and food, and a trip to the post office to send off a package of pens, pencils, calculator, textbooks and other trivia she forgot, they get the locks changed on the doors and settle down to plan their retirement. At last, peace and quiet after raising three children!

   Etaoin is 54 years old and they want to retire when he is 62. Qwerty is 50. They expect to need 60% of their current income before tax when they retire, and to maintain that amount even for a single survivor. Here is their financial situation:

	Etaoin	Qwerty
RRSP balance	$25,000	$ 25,000
Company pension balance	nil	100,000
Pay into pension p.a.:		
company gives		3,000
deducted from her pay		3,000
RRSP deposit	5,000	1,000
Net income	40,000	50,000
Canada Pension Plan pension	6,000	5,000

The Canada Pension Plan (CPP) amount shown is the annual pension each would get in today's dollars if starting at age 62 for him, 60 for her. This projection assumes that each continues to contribute the maximum amount each year. Qwerty's pension plan is defined contribution, invested half in bonds, half in equity. When she retires she will transfer the accumulated amount to a locked-in RRSP. Their RRSPs are invested in money market funds, GICs and bonds, with an average real return of 2.25% p.a.

They have a house in Thunder Bay and a cottage in Nipigon, both mortgage free. The house is worth $100,000 and the cottage $25,000. They plan to travel a lot during the winter after they retire. Their initial plan is to continue saving at the rate they have been doing.

(a)   By how much will they fall short of their goal of retiring at his age 62 if they continue their current savings plan?
(b)   Outline three courses of action that could make the goal achievable.
(c)   Do the calculations for the choices suggested in (b).

REFERENCES

Pape, Gordon. 1991. *Retiring Wealthy*. Prentice-Hall Canada.

Income Security Programs, Human Resources Development Canada provides pamphlets and telephone consultations regarding CPP, OAS and GIS. Check the Blue Pages of your telephone directory for the office nearest to you. Rates change often, and sometimes rules and forms for application change.

chapter 17

Maturation of the Retirement Plan

LEARNING OBJECTIVES

Financial planning changes once the family retires. Risk management issues are fewer, though still important. There are fewer taxation problems to consider, and debt management should be at an end. Budgeting is less important, because the family is no longer saving for a distant retirement objective. In some ways, the planning is simpler, but also more important, because in retirement, the family has no chance to make up for mistakes by earning more in the future.

Our specific learning objectives are:

1.   To describe the maturity choices available for different forms of savings at retirement and explain how to match them to a retirement situation.
2.   To show how basic principles of taxation, investment and risk management apply to decisions in retirement.
3.   To provide a basic guide to estate planning.

Shortly before the retirement date of each member of the family, key decisions have to be made, and some of them are irreversible. There are different ways to receive payouts from the retirement income sources like pension plans and RRSPs, and these maturity options can affect the family considerably, although they may appear relatively unimportant at first. In this chapter we first provide a description of some specific instruments that we haven't explained in earlier chapters. Then, we examine the different sources of retirement income and the choices available for payment during retirement. We return to some basic principles of goal setting, risk management, tax minimization and investment to determine how to choose among the different payment forms.

The last part of the chapter discusses estate planning in fairly general terms. Wills, taxation of estates, trusts, the role of an executor and probate fees are the chief topics. Estate planning becomes a complex matter, beyond the scope of this book in certain situations, primarily when there is a lot of money involved. We give you the outline so that you know what sort of questions to ask the experts.

SPECIAL RETIREMENT INSTRUMENTS

Annuities

Annuities are cash flows with periodic payments. In Chapter 2 we defined them as having equal periodic payments, which allows simple formulas for time value. Annuities may have differing payments per period, however. In this section, we are discussing annuities which are defined by whatever law or contract applies, and so they may have equal or differing payments. The person who receives the payments from an annuity is called the **annuitant**. He pays a principal amount to an insurance company or other insurer and gets regular annuity payments in return. The government pension plans and defined benefit employer plans are annuities.

A common class of annuities are **life annuities**, which pay the agreed amount to the **annuitant** until her death. A life annuity is a kind of life insurance policy, in reverse. The risk that the annuitant insures against, is outliving his money. The insurance company pools a large number of such people's money together. The financial losers are those who die earlier than expected. Their losses provide the extra money to pay the winners, who live longer than expected. Insurance companies have always had to cope with the odd complaint from an heir that the insurance policy "cheated" the annuitant and her heirs, when the annuitant dies very soon after buying a life annuity. We can understand that the losers and winners must balance out, after allowing for the insurer's costs and required rate of profit.

To meet the demand for different patterns of retirement income and risk management, the financial markets have developed the following types of annuities. Generally, they are available with monthly, quarterly, semi-annual and annual payment arrangement.

Straight life. The annuitant receives the agreed level payment until death, with nothing to the estate. This pays the highest rate of all annuities, per $ of principal.

Life with guaranteed term. The annuitant receives the agreed level payment until death. If the annuitant dies before the end of the guaranteed term, the beneficiary gets the balance. If the spouse is the stated beneficiary, the arrangement may allow the spouse to receive the rest of the payments as scheduled, or to receive the **commuted value** at once. The commuted value is the present value of the future payments, at the interest rate set in the policy. The guaranteed period is set by agreement, and is usually five or 10 years. The guaranteed period cannot extend beyond the later of age 90 of the annuitant or the annuitant's spouse. Payments are lower than a straight life policy, and decline as the guaranteed term increases.

Joint life and last survivor. This annuity names an annuitant and a second person, usually the annuitant's spouse. If the annuitant predeceases the second person, that person continues to receive payments for life. The annuitant can specify equal payments throughout, or reduced payments after his death. A guaranteed term is also possible. Payments from this annuity are lower than straight life on either party.

Substandard health. A person who can demonstrate a sufficiently-serious health problem that lowers life expectancy significantly, may be able to qualify for an annuity with a higher payment than straight life.

Term certain. This annuity pays a level amount to a specified date. This is not a life annuity and has no insurance aspect to it.

Indexed. An indexed annuity increases the payment each year by an agreed value, up to 4%. The word "indexed" may be misleading, because the annuity is not indexed to any inflation measure, it simply increases every year by a fixed percentage. The earlier payments are lower than a straight life annuity and the later payments (if the annuitant lives long enough) are higher. It does provide a reasonable inflation hedge, because inflation has been positive for a long time. It helps with taxes, since the higher tax on the higher nominal amount is deferred, relative to taxes on the straight life annuity.

Registered. If an annuity is purchased with money upon which tax has already been paid, then only the interest portion of the payments is taxable in the future. You will recall from Chapter 2 that the interest portion of any blended payment is higher in the early years. A registered annuity is arranged so that the interest portion is level each year, to avoid high tax burdens in the early years. If the annuitant is close to the threshold for one of the tax brackets, a registered annuity may help keep her in the lower bracket.

Three factors determine annuity payment amounts. The expected length of time it will be paid is calculated from the mortality tables.[1] The initial amount contributed depends on the annuitant's own savings. The interest rate is set by the marketplace, and since it fluctuates considerably over time, the annuity payments set by contract vary likewise. As a result, a given life expectancy and initial contribution will yield very different amounts depending on when the annuity was purchased. Interest rates in Canada reached very high levels in 1981–82, and people who retired then (or locked their retirement savings into annuities in anticipation of later retirement) received very good incomes. People who retired during the low interest rate period of the 1990s received much lower incomes, in nominal terms.

This difference may be an illusion, since what matters is future inflation. If the future inflation continues at the level built into the interest rates, then an annuitant is indifferent. However, if you think that inflation rates (and hence interest rates) are relatively high as you approach retirement, then annuities are the best choice. If you think that rates are very low, relative to what they will be in the future, then you should try to delay or avoid annuities.

As a practical matter, retirees who are buying annuities should check with a number of different companies or use an annuity broker to do it for them.

Registered Retirement Income Fund (RRIF)

All RRSPs must be wound up by December 31st of the year in which the beneficiary turns 69. A **Registered Retirement Income Fund (RRIF**, pronounced "riff") is the continuation of an RRSP and its mirror image. The RRSP funds can be partly or wholly transferred to a RRIF. The funds accumulated are withdrawn in future years to provide retirement income. Income on the balance in the RRIF accumulates tax-free, but all payouts are fully taxable. A trustee holds the RRIF, and the person whose RRSP created it can either manage the money in a **self-administered RRIF** or use a guaranteed rate

---

[1] The calculations can be quite complex for anything other than a straight life annuity, and we do not deal with them in this book.

TABLE 17.1
Minimum RRIF Withdrawal As a % of RRIF Assets

Age	Minimum Annual Withdrawal
65	4.00
66	4.17
67	4.35
68	4.55
69	4.76
70	5.00
71	7.38
72	7.48
73	7.59
74	7.71
75	7.85
76	7.99
77	8.15
78	8.33
79	8.53
80	8.75
81	8.99
82	9.27
83	9.58
84	9.93
85	10.33
86	10.79
87	11.33
88	11.96
89	12.71
90	13.62
91	14.73
92	16.12
93	17.92
94+	20.00

RRIF provided by the trustee. The **investment restrictions** on the RRIF are essentially the same as those on an RRSP.

The beneficiary may withdraw as much from a RRIF as desired, but there is a minimum withdrawal required, shown in Table 17.1. The minimum is based on the market value of the assets in the plan at the start of the year.

A person may have more than one RRIF. The income from a RRIF is pension income. The funds in a RRIF in excess of the minimum withdrawal for the year can be used to buy a life annuity. However, such an annuity cannot have a guaranteed term extending beyond age 90 of the annuitant or spouse.

Locked-in Pension Funds

In Chapter 16 we mentioned the problem of pension portability for those who change employers. One way of making a pension transferable is for the employer to deposit the value of the accumulated contributions[2] of both employer and the employees into a **locked-in RRSP** or a **Locked-in Retirement Account (LIRA)**. A person may use

---

[2] For a defined contribution plan, the calculation is easy. For a defined benefit plan, there can be complications, which we do not explore.

these vehicles only to buy a life annuity because this is essentially what the pension fund would have done. No cash withdrawals are permitted. The locked-in fund need not be transferred at once to an annuity and would ordinarily be held until retirement, during which time it accumulates income tax-free.

Recent changes in provincial pension legislation have created new types of funds for conversion of locked-in pensions. These funds are essentially types of RRIFs. A **Life Income Fund (LIF)** operates like a RRIF from inception. The minimum and maximum payments are set by the pension legislation of each province. The funds left in the LIF at the end of the year in which the purchaser turns 80, must be used to purchase an immediate life annuity. Pension legislation in all provinces except Newfoundland and P.E.I., permits LIFs.

Alberta and Saskatchewan have created the **Life Retirement Income Fund (LRIF)** which does not require annuitization at age 80. The minimum withdrawal is the same as in a RRIF. The maximum is the greatest of the accumulated income, the preceding year's income, and, in the first two years of the plan, 6% of the plan value. If the minimum exceeds the maximum, the withdrawal is the minimum.

Reverse Mortgage

A **reverse mortgage** is a mechanism for a family to realize part of the equity on its fully-paid principal residence while continuing to live in it during retirement. There are two kinds of reverse mortgages:

1.   A **term** or **straight** reverse mortgage provides a lump sum of cash to the owner. At the end of the term, the principal and the interest that has accrued on it are due. The family can pay off the mortgage, or sell the house and pay the mortgager from the proceeds. If the mortgage is greater than the value of the house, the lender is limited to receiving the value of the house.

2.   A **reverse annuity mortgage (RAM)** provides a life annuity to the owner. At death, or when the house is sold, the mortgage must be settled. The estate or the retiree (if the RAM is settled before death) receives the difference between the value of the house and the mortgage. The lender (mortgagee) cannot recover more than the value of the house.

Only a few small institutions, including some credit unions, offer reverse mortgages. There is a serious public relations problem, similar to that with life annuities. In a term reverse mortgage, the amount owing seems to grow quite quickly, because it is accumulating without any repayments. In a RAM, if the annuitant (mortgager) dies early, the heirs often feel cheated, since the annuity provides no value to the estate and the value of the house is much less after retiring the mortgage. Neither of these problems seems too serious when real estate prices are rising, but if they fall, the effect is severe.

Reverse mortgages are very complex. They are mortgages, because the security is the equity of redemption. However, their value is not fixed as it is in a conventional mortgage; it is contingent on the value of the house and, in the case of a RAM, on the life of the annuitant. Conceptually, the mortgager has a put option to make the issuer of the reverse mortgage take either the house or the value of the mortgage, whichever is less. The value of the put option rises with the length of time to expiry. In a RAM, that time is uncertain. A retiree at 65 has a long life expectancy, and hence the pot option is expensive. Reverse mortgage issuers will not offer very large mortgages or favourable terms until the retiree is much older, because of the significant risk that the mortgage will exceed the house value when the retiree dies.

The way to think of a reverse mortgage is to consider the alternative way of extracting equity from a home, which is to sell it and live in rented quarters. The proceeds from the sale provide cash income to pay the rent, and other expenses. The inflation protection that owning a home brings is gone but so are the operating costs.

With the reverse mortgage, the retiree continues to live in the home, which may have important psychological benefits. At the same time, the risk of value changes is partly shared with the mortgager, since the repayment is limited to the value of the home. The retiree will not face inflationary increases in rent, although some expenses will rise with inflation.

Reverse mortgages are so complicated that we cannot offer clear advice on them in this book. Furthermore, the terms are specific to the contract and vary with different companies offering them. A term reverse mortgage doesn't seem to offer the pattern of retirement income that is useful, except for someone who is very unlikely to want to occupy the house after the term expires. The RAM seems a perfectly reasonable way to spend the equity, although the home-owner must realize that this is what is happening. We don't have a good way to compare the cost of a RAM with an outright sale and rental. We think that the psychological need of the retiree to stay in the same home for as long as possible, or the absence of such a need, should be the determining factor.

SOURCES OF RETIREMENT INCOME

With the description of the special retirement options complete, we can turn now to the sources of retirement income and how they are paid out during the period of retirement. Table 17.2 summarizes this information. We have discussed most of the sources already with respect to how they are accumulated.

Government Pensions   There are no maturity choices for OAS, GIS and the future Seniors Benefit. They start at age 65 and you qualify or not according to the rules. CPP requires two choices. The pensioner can choose to split the CPP with the spouse while both are alive. The survivor benefit is specified as 60% of the pension. There is also a choice of when to start receiving CPP between the ages of 60 and 71. The current maximum pension of $727.08 assumes that the pensioner starts receiving payments at age 65. An earlier start lowers the pension by .5% for each month prior to age 65; a later start increases it by the same factor.

One specific aspect of the government pensions that many people overlook is the requirement for an application. They are not automatic, and it can take up to six months for them to start. Income Security Programs of Human Resources Development Canada provides extensive information by mail or phone (check the Blue Pages of the telephone directory for the nearest office).

Employer Pension (RPP)   Some employer plans promise a set percentage of the pension as a survivor pension to a spouse. Other plans allow the employee to choose from several percentages, the most common being 50%–75%. If there is an option, the employee must choose before the pension starts, and the election, or any subsequent change, may require the spouse's signature.

TABLE 17.2
Retirement Income Sources and Maturity Options

Source	What it Provides	Maturity Options
CPP	• indexed life annuity	• split with spouse • date to start receipt
OAS	• indexed life annuity	• no choices
GIS	• indexed supplement • non-taxable • annual means test	• no choices
Seniors Benefit	• replaces OAS and GIS in 2001 • reducing amount based on previous year's family income • Indexed	• no choices
RPP	• life annuity • taxable	• % to spouse on death of annuitant
locked-in RRSP, LIRA	• lump sum • taxable	• LIF or LRIF • life annuity(ies).
RRSP	• lump sum • taxable	• withdraw as needed • annuity(ies) • transfer to RRIF
Home equity	• lump sum • non-taxable	• trade down or sell • reverse mortgage
Endowment Life Insurance	• lump sum • non-taxable	• annuity
Tax shelters	• various	• spend as received • annuity(ies)
Regular savings	• lump sum • capital gains taxable	• spend as needed • annuity(ies)

Locked-in RRSP, LIRA   The beneficiary may choose between a LIF or LRIF, in the provinces where they exist, and one of the life annuities. The election must be made before December 31st of the year the beneficiary turns 69.

RRSP   The beneficiary has three choices: withdraw and pay tax, roll over into a RRIF by age 69 or buy one or more annuities. All the annuity choices listed earlier are allowed, or a combination of all three is possible. For example, a couple might withdraw a substantial part of an RRSP the year after retirement to finance a world tour. When they return, they could convert half of the remainder into an annuity that would pay a fixed sum and the other half into a RRIF.

Home Equity   The choices are threefold: sell and move into an apartment; sell and buy a cheaper house; reverse mortgage. The advantages and disadvantages seem to relate more to personal goals than to financial values. The sell and rent option appeals to those who want to avoid shovelling snow and cutting grass or who want to travel without worrying about a house. However, those who are attached to a home could well find themselves very unhappy after a move.[3]

The sell and trade-down options do raise more money, and do save money on operations, to some extent. If the trade down involves a condominium, the fees will eat up a lot of the savings. The value of this option is probably overestimated by most people, because they forget all the costs involved. These include real estate agent's commission, legal fees, land transfer tax (or its equivalent in some provinces) and moving costs. A large piece of the expected differential on a trade to a cheaper home may disappear, although there is no tax on the gain. If the move is to an apartment, the automatic indexation of home ownership also disappears, although rent control may help.

With these considerations, a reverse mortgage may be a good compromise, bearing in mind the complexity we have discussed already.

Endowment Life Insurance
Endowment life insurance matures at a set date, usually age 65, providing a lump sum which can be annuitized. The usual annuity options are possible. Since the insurance premiums were not tax deductible, the proceeds at maturity are not taxable.

Tax Shelters
These are so specific to the particular loony piece of legislation that created them, that we cannot offer general comments. They do not have a maturity that is connected to retirement date necessarily, though they may coincide. There are no special maturity options. The general option of cashing them in for either spending or annuitization always exists, providing they are liquid enough to permit realization.

Regular Savings
There is no required maturity date for unsheltered savings either. In fact, they are the most flexible part of the retirement funds, which makes up for at least part of the tax disadvantage. Since they are in lump sum form, they can be annuitized or spent at any time. Registered annuities might be preferable, since only the interest is taxable.

CHOOSING THE RIGHT MATURITY OPTIONS

We have outlined a large array of situations and maturity options. How does a retiree pick a path through this maze? We return to the basic principles of earlier chapters. They provide guidance, but also sometimes conflict, and differing interpretations are possible.

Goals in Retirement
There are three financial goals in retirement. For most families, we think they are, arranged in descending order of priority:

1. Minimize the risk of outliving your money. That is, minimize the risk that either spouse, a permanent dependent or the family unit will have inadequate income at any time during retirement;

---

[3] We understand that moving seniors out of a home that they have occupied for many years also shortens their life expectancy.

2.   Maximize the income available to a single survivor and to the family unit; and

3.   Maximize the bequest to the heirs.

The definition of a family unit is spouses and children who are permanently dependent by reason of handicap. The spouses could be same-sex, which means that certain legal aspects are different, but the principle is the same. If the family unit is a single person, then the first goal is to minimize risk of inadequate income for that person.

The importance of a bequest varies greatly among families. We think that it should be of lesser importance in retirement planning except for those families for whom the first two goals are easily met. Since "inadequate income" depends partly on your definition of an acceptable standard of living, we think that most families need to consider the first two goals as the critical ones.

Goal one, minimizing the risk of shortfall, is not the same as maximizing retirement income, since there is variation in investment returns. A family might sacrifice the chance of a very high standard of living in order to ensure that the future is at least comfortable. Furthermore, decisions that maximize income for a two-person family may not lead to adequate income for the survivor if one dies prematurely.

> **Example 17.1:** Georgina retired after a long and successful career as a restaurant owner. She assured her husband Nial that her retirement income would be more than enough for both of them. Nial's career as an abstract painter had provided no retirement income other than OAS. For two years, there was plenty of money and they travelled and partied happily. Then Georgina died, and Nial discovered she had provided the large income by putting everything she had saved into straight life annuities in her name. Even the money from the house they had sold went into a registered life annuity, with no guaranteed term. Now he had to live on OAS plus the survivor benefit from her CPP. Even after the addition of some GIS, he still faced a meagre existence, compared with what he had expected.

Clearly, this family made serious errors. Most important, the maturity option for at least some of the savings should have been joint and last survivor annuities, or a RRIF, where the remaining principal would provide for the survivor. Long before retirement, Georgina should have set up a spousal RRSP for Nial to create retirement income for him. This would have reduced their overall tax costs even in retirement. The proceeds of the house sale should have been shared between them, to allow Nial to create more income. The CPP should have been split. They should have planned together, so that Nial would know what to expect.

Risk Management

Three financial risks face the family in its retirement:

1.   The family unit as a whole has insufficient income;

2.   A survivor spouse or dependent will have insufficient income after the death of the person and loss of pension benefits; and,

3.   The annuities may not be secure.

Insufficient income for the whole family unit is largely the result of earnings and savings prior to retirement, and maturity choices cannot help that. However, there are two actions that may matter. First, inflation will affect consumption available by a large amount over the long time period of most retirements. If the family receives a material part of its income in unindexed pensions, or is relying on fixed income instruments, the planning for future consumption must take account of it. The family cannot consume all of its current nominal income, but must save some even in retirement in order to provide for inflation. Conversion of unsheltered savings or RRSPs into indexed annuities can provide the enforced saving discipline, if necessary, as well as deferring income tax. A RRIF with minimum withdrawals in the early years will achieve the same result.

Second, if income in later years may prove to be a problem, the family should place its non-pension savings in life annuities or RRIFs to guarantee long-run income. There should be no guaranteed period in the annuities, because that would reduce the periodic payments. The same principle applies to a retired single. In other words, the goal of income security dominates the goal of providing a bequest to the next generation.

Even if a couple has enough income, the death of one may reduce pensions to an unacceptable level. Furthermore, the loss of the individual tax credit, old age credit and pension income credit of the deceased spouse may increase the average tax rate for the survivor. This occurrence matters most at the very low income levels, as Table 16.1 shows.

The maturity choices do matter in this sort of situation, and it is common where only one spouse has earned income outside the home and a pension. The couple must estimate the income available to them jointly, and to either as a survivor, for each future year. If there is enough income for the couple, but not enough for one or both as survivor, the maturity options should be changed to minimize this risk. For example, the election for survivor benefits on an employer pension could be increased (must be done prior to retirement). This will reduce the family's income while both are alive, but will increase the survivor's income later.

Example 17.2: Wolfi M. is retiring from his occupation as a lounge pianist next month when he turns 65. He will have an indexed RPP of $10,000 if there is no pension allocated to a surviving spouse, and he will get full CPP. If he elects to have a surviving spouse receive 75% of his annual pension after his death, he will receive only $8,000 instead of $10,000. His wife Stanzi has a spousal RRSP with $25,000 in it. He has $20,000 in Canada Savings Bonds in his own name. Stanzi is 60 years old, and if Wolfi dies before she turns 65, she is eligible for a Widowed Spouse's Allowance equal to OAS until she turns 65 and can receive OAS on her own account. They estimate that they need $22,000 after-tax to live comfortably as a couple and $18,000 after-tax for a single survivor. (This example uses 1995 CPP and OAS rates.)

First, we must see what these retirement amounts would be. Everything is indexed; so we work in real dollars without any conversions. Stanzi will get OAS in five years, and Wolfie should elect to split his CPP with her now. If he dies after she reaches 65, she gets a survivor pension of 60% of his CPP. If he dies before she reaches 65, the pension is reduced by a factor related to her age. Since she is already 60, the reduction will be fairly small. She would also receive a lump sum death benefit of six times his monthly Canada pension.

Most of the income will still be in Wolfi's hands until Stanzi reaches 65 and starts receiving OAS. Some of their income will come from her RRSP, at her lower tax rate, and from his CSBs, which will attract tax only on the interest. A tax rate of 12% is reasonable. The pre-tax income required is [$22,000 ÷ (1 − .12) = $25,000]. For either one as a single, the tax rate on $18,000 would be lower, say about 10%. This yields a required pre-tax income of [$18,000 ÷ (1 − .1) = $20,000]. The following table shows what their family and her single income would be, using 1995 pension amounts.

Election of Pension to Surviving Spouse

	none		75%	
his age	65	70	65	70
If Wolfi lives:				
OAS	$ 4,653	$ 9,306	$ 4,653	$ 9,306
CPP	8,328	8,328	8,328	8,328
Pension	10,000	10,000	8,000	8,000
	22,981	27,634	20,981	25,634
If Wolfi dies:				
OAS		4,653		4,653
Widowed Allow	4,653		4,653	
CPP	4,997	4,997	4,997	4,997
Pension			7,500	7,500
	9,650	9,650	17,150	17,150

Wolfi's income as a sole survivor is not shown in the table, since it is clearly sufficient. He would get at least $8,000 in pension and full CPP and OAS. While they are both alive, the income from his age 65 to 70 is below their required minimum if he elects that she can receive a survivor's pension, but their $45,000 in other savings is clearly enough to bridge that temporary gap. If he elects for a 75% survivor pension for her, she will be below the required $20,000 by somewhat more. Savings of $45,000, turned into an annuity at 5% for 20 years, yields $3,611 p.a., which is enough to bridge that gap. However, if he elects no survivor pension for her, her income falls far below the level they have specified (and, indeed, below the poverty line). She would receive some GIS probably, but she would still not be very well off. The future Seniors Benefit may change this result, but it is risky to rely on a social programme whose implementation is several years in the future.

The maturity choice, then, is quite clear. Wolfi must choose the 75% surviving spousal pension option. They will have enough income while he lives and if he dies before Stanzi (which occurrence is likely), she will have enough, too.

Taxation

Three of the tax planning principles from Chapter 7 apply: spreading, deferral and splitting.

Spreading is not often important, except perhaps in the year of retirement. Pre-retirement income is usually higher than retirement income, and occasionally the retiree can avoid moving up a tax bracket by deferring receipt of income until the next tax year. The retiree shouldn't cash in RRSPs or RRIFs all at once, either. The withholding taxes constitute an immediate cost for an RRSP withdrawal, and a large withdrawal of RRSP or RRIF funds may raise the tax bracket.

Deferral of taxes is possible in retirement, often related to the order in which savings vehicles are liquidated to provide income. The general rule is to use up the funds on which no tax will be payable first. The retiree has no choice with pensions, but discretionary savings can be deferred even further if there is no immediate need for the cash.

The first thing to cash is unsheltered savings instruments that have no capital gains or accrued interest. The second thing to cash is unsheltered savings with accrued capital gains or interest. Since capital losses can be offset against capital gains, but not against other income, the two should be matched to use up the losses. The third thing to cash, if it doesn't interfere with other goals, is the family home.

Leaving RRSP and RRIF funds to accumulate at the before-tax rate for as long as possible maximizes the after-tax retirement income. The investments outside the RRSP and RRIF were purchased out of after-tax income, and therefore only the gains are taxable. However, the entire withdrawal from an RRSP or RRIF is taxable. The longer that tax is delayed, the less it costs. Another deferral tactic is to delay moving funds from an RRSP into a RRIF or annuity for as long as possible. Once again, as soon as payouts start, taxes start, too.

The most important tax-splitting mechanisms are pre-retirement, or at least need to be set up then. If both spouses are in the same tax bracket, tax splitting is irrelevant. The common situation of one spouse who stayed in the home and one who earned a cash income leads to several opportunities. The basic one for all families is sharing Canada Pension. This involves an election in which all CPP payments for both spouses are shared. The percentage shared is equal to the fraction of the years the spouses have been together divided by the number of years they have been contributors.

> **Example 17.3:**   Leon and Alana were married for 10 years before they retired. They had contributed to CPP for 28 years. Leon has a CPP of $8,000, and Alana has $5,000. If they elect to share their CPP, how much does each one receive?
>
> Leon gets 18/28 of his CPP plus 10/28 of hers, or [(18/28) × $8,000 + (10/28) × $5,000] = $6,929. Alana gets 18/28 of her CPP plus 10/28 of his, or [(18/28) × 5,000 + (10/28) × $8,000] = $6,071.

A major source of income splitting is the sale of the family home and reinvestment of the proceeds in income assets, divided between the spouses. Both spouses must have contributed to the purchase and maintenance of the home, but the contributions need not be financially equal.

In general, you should maintain the investments of the lower income spouse for as long as possible, allowing him longer time to accumulate principal. That is, the higher income spouse should cash investments first to pay for living expenses. This is simply a way of equalizing future income.

Death of one spouse does create a particularly bothersome tax problem for people with very modest retirement income. The tax credits and deductions for persons over 65, persons receiving pension income and persons with disabilities, disappear on the death of the spouse. In Table 16.1 we showed the different tax rates for families with a given income all in one spouse's hands or split between the two spouses. At quite low income levels, the death of a spouse doesn't reduce living expenses much, but the lost credits can cost over $1,000, which is a lot for someone already in a low tax bracket.

Example 17.4:   Next month Peer will retire at age 60 years, four months, from his job as a tour guide, because the work has become too strenuous for him. He will be eligible to receive CPP of $500/month if he starts now, $694 if he starts at age 65, and $903 if he defers starting until age 70. He has no employer pension. He has $30,000 in an RRSP (all invested in equities) and $40,000 in stock mutual funds. His wife Anitra is 58 and has no CPP or employer pension plan entitlement. She has $30,000 in a spousal RRSP. They are each eligible for OAS of $4,653 at age 65. They need $18,000 p.a. in before-tax income, and a sole survivor would need $15,000 p.a. In any case, they will pay little or no tax at these income levels, with part of the income coming from equity. The real equity discount rate is 6%.

Peer could work at less demanding jobs for the touring company, on a part-time basis, for a net pay of $20,000 p.a. after deductions, except for tax. He would deposit $3,000 in an RRSP each year, and make up the shortfall in consumption from his other sources (he can't receive CPP until he stops working). These other jobs would last till he turns 65.

(a)   Can the family manage if Peer retires early, or should he take the part-time work?

(b)   Describe all the actions they should take to optimize their retirement position under either answer to part (a).

Answers: (a)   To find out if they can afford to retire early, we need to calculate their income at various ages.

1. *Assuming they both survive to age 90*

His age	60–65	65–67	67–90
CPP	$ 6,000	$ 6,000	$ 6,000
OAS	0	4,653	9,306
Total	6,000	10,653	15,306
Need	18,000	18,000	18,000
Shortfall	12,000	7,347	2,694

PV of shortfall today @ 6%:	
12,000 for 5 years	$50,548
7,347 for 2 years, discount 5 years	10,066
2,694 for 23 years, discount 7 years	22,044
Total PV (total savings required)	$82,658

2. *Assuming he dies just after early retirement.*

Her age	58–63	63–65	65–88
CPP	$ 3,600	$ 3,600	$ 3,600
OAS			4,653
Widow allowance	0	4,653	
Total	3,600	8,253	8,253
Need	15,000	15,000	15,000
Shortfall	11,400	6,747	6,747

PV today of annuities @ 6%:

11,400 for 5 years	$ 48,021
6,747 for 25 years, discount 5 years	66,664
Total PV (total savings required)	$114,625

They have $100,000 in savings outside the pension, compared with the savings required in the two parts of the table. If they both survive, they seem to have some room for error. If he dies soon, the non-pension savings are not enough. We don't show the case if he is the sole survivor, but since he would lose only her OAS, he would clearly also have enough alone. The decision on whether to retire early will depend on their tolerance for risk, but it seems he should work part-time for at least one or two years.

(b) Whenever they choose to retire, there are both risk-minimization and tax minimization issues.

1. Split CPP.
2. Liquidate the mutual funds before the RRSP, to allow the income to accumulate untaxed as long as possible.
3. Convert all unused RRSP funds into a RRIF at age 71 to continue tax-free compounding.
4. Liquidate his RRSP or RRIF before hers, to allow her to accumulate capital as long as possible.
5. If Peer continues to work, he should contribute the maximum to a spousal RRSP, even if it means liquidating other investments. This continued income splitting, and creation of a tax deferral shelter, will reduce income tax. He should use any carry forwards from 1991 to contribute more to a spousal RRSP. He should cash some of the mutual funds to do this, and then reinvest the tax refunds.
6. When he reaches age 71 and must terminate his RRSP, he should choose either a joint life annuity or a RRIF, so that Anitra has sufficient income in the event of his death. The calculations in the table assumed he did so.

Investment Principles

How should the retired family invest the funds that now provide the income? Some of the investment decision rests with pension trustees, and the family has no say in the matter. The family's own savings are in its control, however, and the same general principles apply as in Chapters 13–15. We identify three specific problems that apply to retirement investment: risk management, liquidity and financial institution failure.

Risk Management

We can restate the risk-return trade-off question in a way somewhat unique to retirement planning. Which risk is more serious: outliving your money invested in low risk, low return assets, or losing your money because it is invested in high return, high risk assets? Ho et al. (1994a) and Milevsky et al. (1996) provide an answer to this question that contradicts the accepted wisdom of other personal finance books.[4]

They find that for most levels of liquid wealth and consumption, retirees well into their 70s should invest primarily in high risk, high return securities. As Table 16.2 shows, there is a substantial probability of living for a long time after normal retirement age. The low risk, low return assets are less likely to accumulate enough income to last people through the long years of retirement than is the risky stock market. This effect is especially pronounced for women, because they live longer. Table 17.3 provides a rough guide for the allocation between riskless Treasury bills and a diversified Canadian stock portfolio. This table should be taken as an approximation, since there are a variety of other combinations that are possible. What it shows, though, is that significant allocations to equity are preferable until quite late in life for most people.

Read Table 17.3 like this. Across the top are the age and gender categories. These are the two factors that principally affect how many years you can expect to need income. Down the side of the table are the wealth to consumption (W/C) ratios, in real dollars. For example, if you have $400,000 in retirement savings (W_n in equation (1) in Chapter 16), and your goal is to be able to consume $40,000 p.a. in real terms, then $W/C = 10$. This means constant real consumption of $40,000, not constant consumption of 10% of your wealth. As you consume the income plus some of the principal, your W/C ratio will rise each year, unless you consume less than the income. Suppose you are a male retiring at age 70 in this situation. Table 17.3 advises that your portfolio should be 90–100% equity to minimize the probability of not reaching your goal. Even so, you will have a 34% chance of not being able to consume $40,000 p.a. in real terms.

Part of the required consumption will be provided by pension plans in the form of annuities. The present value of these annuities is part of wealth, but it is easier to incorporate them by deducting the periodic payment from the required consumption, C. If the pension is indexed (CPP, OAS, GIS, some employer plans), then the initial value is in real dollars, and can be deducted from C directly.

Unindexed pension plans are in nominal dollars. The conversion to real dollars can be only an approximation, because the annuity is for life, but the life span of the retiree is unknown at the start of the plan. We approximate it by using the median life span, which you already know how to calculate. Then, take the PV of the annuity, discounted at a nominal rate. Convert this PV into a real dollar annuity using the same median life span and the real discount rate. Deduct this estimated real dollar annuity value from the real dollar required consumption.

---

[4] A professional summary of these academic papers appears in Ho et al. (1994b).

TABLE 17.3
Optimal Asset Allocation for Retirees

W/C is the wealth-consumption ratio in constant $. The first (top) number in each cell is the optimal percentage (or range of percentages) of equity. The second (bottom) number is the probability of shortfall if this optimal percentage is chosen. For example (in boldface), a male aged 70 with a wealth-consumption ratio of 12 should invest 80–85% of his liquid wealth in equity, to have a 20% chance of shortfall in his desired consumption over his remaining life if he does so. Equity investments outside that range increase the probability of shortfall. The historic real rates of return for the TSE 300 and Canadian 91-day T-bills for 1950–95, and the 1990–92 Canadian Life tables were used to construct this table.

| | Age and Gender | | | | | | | |
| | 60 | | 65 | | 70 | | 75 | |
W/C	M	F	M	F	M	F	M	F
10					90–100 .34	100 .47	80–100 .23	90–100 .34
12			100 .30	100 .42	**80–85 .20**	95–100 .32	65–90 .12	80–100 .21
14	95 .29	100 .41	90–100 .20	90–100 .31	70–80 .13	85 .21	55–60 .06	70–90 .12
16	80–95 .20	95–100 .28	55–100 .14	70–85 .21	60–75 .07	70–80 .13	35–60 .03	55–75 .07
18	50–90 .14	90–95 .19	55–60 .07	65–80 .14	45–55 .03	55 .07	20–55 .01	30–55 .03
20	45–75 .08	65–70 .13	35–60 .04	45–75 .08	40–50 .01	25–60 .04	0–95 .01	20–50 .01
22	30–45 .04	55–70 .08	20–60 .02	30–50 .04	10–70 .01	25–40 .01		
24	20–45 .02	30–60 .05	10–55 .01	20–50 .02				
26	15–55 .01	30–50 .02						

Once the pension plan payments are deducted from C, the adjusted C is the consumption that must be funded from the non-pension savings — RRSPs, RRIFs, cashing in the house, unsheltered savings. This table then provides guidance on how to make these discretionary investment decisions. It must be remembered that it is only an approximation. It does not consider the effect of couples, each person with different mortality tables. However, it does show the importance of equity in the investment portfolio until quite late in life.

A second, and equally important, risk management technique is diversification. As discussed in Chapter 13, risk reduction by holding a well-diversified portfolio is essential. The equity returns used in constructing Table 17.3 come from the return on the TSE 300, which is a well-diversified portfolio that includes most of the value of the companies listed on the TSE.

Liquidity   In retirement, the family has less flexibility in financial terms. There is no more earned income, just income from various investments. If the family needs a short-term increase in income, say for a trip, or a large lump sum, it can be difficult to manage if the investments are not liquid. You cannot draw on future pensions, and banks won't lend on them as security, because they can't seize them. Therefore, some of the unsheltered investments must be in a form that can be liquidated readily. As well, some of the investments must be ready for sale each year in a RRIF, in order to be able to make the minimum withdrawal.

Most shares listed on major stock exchanges in Canada or other developed countries, bonds of governments and large companies, Treasury bills and bank and trust company deposit accounts and instruments, are highly liquid. The principal investments that are illiquid, or at least require more than a few days to realize, are securities of private companies, direct interests in unincorporated businesses, real estate and collections (stamps, coins, art etc.). A retiree with most of her assets in these illiquid categories may never have a problem, but if a sudden need for a substantial sum of cash arises, it may be very difficult to meet. These illiquid assets are frequently in large units so that division of them to provide only partial realization is impossible. Listed securities can be divided easily into 100 share, or even single share, lots, by contrast.

Modern financial intermediation is providing some relief from liquidity problems for persons, just as they have for many years for corporations. People with identifiable valuable assets (including the value of future income implicit in valuable human capital) can get a personal line of credit, credit cards and loans based on home equity. All of these allow the family to spend money it doesn't have in the short-term, but money which it expects to receive in the long-term.

Failure of Financial Institutions

Recent events in the insurance industry have caused a wider recognition of the risk of failure of the financial institutions that are holding retirement funds for individuals. In 1993 Confederation Life failed, and it was Canada's fourth largest life insurance company at the time. In the 1980s Canadian Commercial Bank and Northlands Bank failed. Since the 1970s several trust companies have failed, too, including Financial Trust and Standard Trust.

The accounts of persons dealing with banks and trust companies are protected by the Canada Deposit Insurance Company, to a limit of $60,000 per account, per person, per institution. There are some ways of arranging affairs with joint accounts to increase the effective limit, but the coverage is limited. The limit is also $60,000 on each RRSP or RRIF account.

The Canadian Life and Health Insurance Compensation Corporation (CompCorp) insures the policies and deposits with almost all life and health insurance companies in Canada. The limits on the accounts are $60,000, just as with banks and trust companies. The insurance limits are $200,000 per person, per institution. That is, any aggregate of policies up to $200,000 is covered. The limit for fixed and life annuities is $2,000 per month.

The implications for retirement planning are quite clear, and they are most serious as retirement approaches. Large lump sums held in any institution do face some risk. Particularly risky is taking an annuity with a life insurance company for more than $2,000. If you have a deposit in a bank, you can always move it to another institution if you think your present bank is becoming a risky place to leave money. You will have great difficulty moving an annuity in the same way, and annuities may be committed for life.

ESTATE PLANNING

This entire section is a slightly-edited version of "Estate Planning, Wills and Executors," an information guide produced by Royal Trust, Toronto, 1994. Royal Trust provides estate planning, executor and trustee services, investment management services and retirement planning, in addition to many other financial intermediation services. The authors are grateful to Royal Trust for permission to use this copyright material.

Estate planning and wills are not subjects most people like to talk about. They are easy to ignore or put off to another day. Unfortunately, that is exactly what half of all Canadians are doing. Even among those individuals who have made wills, a significant portion have not had them professionally reviewed in the past three years. Dying without a will (or with one that is out of date) risks needless taxation, legal challenges, delays, and family strife while the estate is being settled and perhaps beyond. There is also a common misconception amongst some Canadians that estate planning is only needed by the wealthy. But even individuals with a modest or straightforward estate can benefit from up-front planning, thus ensuring nothing unexpected will happen to their plans. The only way to ensure that your wishes will be followed, and that your assets will be passed on in a timely, tax-effective manner, is to have a valid, up-to-date will with proper consideration given to your choice of executor. For individuals with no will at all, this means having an estate plan developed and a will prepared. Those who have an outdated will must get it professionally reviewed and updated.

In this book we provide you with an overview of will and estate planning and the duties of an executor. It is important to stress that this is not a complete guide. As the laws pertaining to estate planning and administration are complex, substantial professional training is required before you can prepare and execute estate plans. Furthermore, many gray areas in which professional judgement is required make it impossible to set out precise rules. However, this overview introduces the important issues and the various techniques for resolving them.

What Is Estate Planning?

Estate planning is a process which ensures your assets are distributed in accordance with your wishes for the maximum benefit of your heirs. A well-planned estate will ensure your assets are transferred to the individuals you wish to provide for in a timely, orderly and tax-efficient manner. On a more practical level, estate planning is often viewed as ensuring funds are available to provide your spouse or other family members with sufficient income to meet their needs should you happen to die.

In this book we deal primarily with the issues related to assets that pass through an estate under the terms of a will. This is the most common way Canadians choose to pass on a property to a surviving spouse or other family member. It should, however, be mentioned that there are five different ways property can be transferred to your beneficiaries:

> **TABLE 17.4**
> **Estate Planning Considerations**
>
> Record of personal affairs
> Pre-planned funeral arrangements
> Gifts to family members
> Planned giving to charity
> Joint property
> Living trusts
> Life insurance
> Preparation of a valid will
> Letter of wishes
> Taxes
> Incapacity — power of attorney and living wills

1. Gifts during your lifetime;
2. Living (*inter vivos*) trusts;
3. Non-probatable assets (that is, not through the will);
4. Directly through a bequest in a will; and,
5. Indirectly through a testamentary trust created in a will.

Each method of passing on assets has advantages and disadvantages. Gifting property during your lifetime may have some tax benefits, but it means relinquishing control over the asset (e.g. family cottage or business). Establishing a living or *inter vivos* trust, a trust which is established during your lifetime, may enable you to retain some control over the asset, but it could have some unfavourable tax implications unless properly structured by a trust professional. Registering assets as joint tenants with another individual so that upon your death ownership passes directly to the other individual without forming part of your estate (i.e. a non-probatable asset) may save executor and probate fees, but it could create unintended income tax problems. It also limits your control of the asset.

All five methods of passing on assets should be considered part of any estate plan. However, most individuals wish to retain control and direct ownership over their property for as long as possible and very often want to keep their intentions regarding the disposition of their property confidential until their death. The only way to ensure this happens is to have a will prepared.

Estate Planning Considerations

Many Canadians mistakenly believe that as long as they have a will they have a complete estate plan in place. While an up-to-date will is probably the most important aspect of an estate plan, it is by no means the only thing. Table 17.4 lists some of the areas that should be considered when developing your total estate plan. It should be emphasized that proper estate planning requires careful consideration of many factors given the wide range of objectives you may wish to achieve. Often, in an effort to minimize taxes or avoid probate fees, another objective is thwarted. It is therefore important to weigh and balance the costs and benefits of different courses of action.

Record of Personal Affairs

Anyone who has ever acted as the executor of someone else's estate knows how time-consuming it can be to locate important documents, certificates, lists of advisers and other items. It is in the best interests of your family that your executor be able to act quickly to protect your assets. To assist your executor with this task, a complete estate plan should include a complete listing of your financial affairs. This record will include information on the following:

- location of original will (not a copy)
- location of trust documents
- list of advisers
- names of guardians for children (if not set out in your will)
- information on pre-planned funeral arrangements
- birth and marriage certificates
- bank accounts/GICs/safety deposit boxes
- insurance policies
- pension plans
- real estate titles
- investment portfolio records
- stock certificates
- mortgages/loans
- credit cards
- club memberships

By having this information readily available, your executor will be better able to fulfill his or her duties and manage your affairs.

Pre-Planned Funeral Arrangements

When funeral arrangements are pre-planned there is considerably less potential for stress, confusion and mistakes. Anyone who has ever had to put together arrangements for a loved one in a rush knows the pain and added costs that last minute arrangements can cause. For this reason more and more Canadians are considering pre-planned funeral arrangements as part of their estate plan. It allows for family input, minimizes the chances of additional costs, ensures your wishes are followed and relieves family members from having to make decisions at a difficult time.

Gifts to Family Members

The most straightforward method of accomplishing a number of estate planning goals is to gift assets to your potential heirs during your lifetime. Gifting property can be done without incurring executor or probate fees. However, you will give up ownership and control and in some situations where the recipient is either your spouse or is under age 18, any income from the property could be attributed back to you and taxed in your hands. If you gift an asset to any person, except your spouse, you are deemed to have received proceeds of disposition equal to the fair market value of the asset and you must report any resulting capital gain or loss. In other words you might be taxed as though you sold the asset at fair market value even though it was a gift!

Gifts of sentimental property such as jewelry, art or furniture can also lead to conflict between beneficiaries if gifted property is also listed in the will. Disputes can occur between beneficiaries over whether the deceased really intended to gift the property during her lifetime.

Planned Giving to Charity

Planned giving is when a charitable gift is made in such a way that you maximize the tax and estate planning benefits. Planned gifts can be a "present gift" the charity can use now or a "deferred gift" available in the future, usually from your estate. Planned giving is an important consideration to charitably minded individuals who are revising their estate. For more information see the Royal Trust booklet, "Planned Giving — Helping others while saving taxes."

Joint Property

There are two ways of registering legal ownership of property. One is as "joint tenants"; the other is as "tenants-in-common." There is a distinction between the two at death. In the case of joint tenants, the deceased's ownership automatically goes to the survivor without forming part of their estate. In the case of tenants-in-common, the deceased's interest in the property forms part of their estate and is passed on to his beneficiaries. The above applies not only to real estate but also to bank accounts, GICs, investment portfolios etc.

Registering property as "joint tenants" is a useful way of avoiding the estate process as the property automatically goes to the survivor. This helps reduce probate fees and estate administration costs but can lead to other problems. This is discussed in more detail in a later section.

Living Trusts

A trust is created when a "settlor" transfers property to a "trustee" who holds property for the benefit of a "beneficiary." In its simplest form, a trust merely involves the holding of property by one person for the benefit of another person. A trust may be either "testamentary" (i.e. arising upon your death), or "*inter vivos*" or "living" (i.e. established during your lifetime). In this section of the book we will focus on living trusts. Testamentary trusts are discussed in a later section.

A living trust can be a very flexible financial tool that allows you to transfer beneficial ownership of the asset to an intended heir while you maintain control over the asset. For example, you can provide a beneficial interest in the income of a trust to your spouse while retaining control via the express terms of the trust as to who will ultimately receive the capital. There are a number of reasons for considering a trust during your lifetime. Some of these reasons are for estate planning purposes only while others also provide a benefit from a tax planning perspective. Typical uses include:

- to provide long-term income and protection for minor children or dependents who are not able to look after themselves or handle financial matters
- to provide protection of family assets for professionals (e.g. doctors) who may be exposed to lawsuits in excess of insurance limits
- to create a trust for charitable purposes
- to avoid probate and provide secrecy on death
- as part of an estate freeze structure where your asset value is "frozen" and future asset growth is transferred to the next generation
- to achieve income splitting with adult family members with lower marginal tax rates to the extent that attribution rules allow

For more information on trusts see the Royal Trust booklet entitled "Understanding Trusts and Their Uses." A trust is a sophisticated planning instrument and you will need a lawyer's assistance to establish one.

Life Insurance   Life insurance can:

- provide liquidity in an estate to pay off liabilities such as tax or mortgages. This will ensure non-liquid assets like a cottage or business do not have to be sold, but can be left to an heir
- establish a fund to provide income for an individual you wish to support (e.g. spouse, children or grandchildren)

Premiums for life insurance are generally not tax deductible. The benefits paid from life insurance are generally not subject to tax whether they are left to the estate or to a named beneficiary. However, if the benefits of an insurance policy are left to the estate they will be subject to provincial probate fees and executor fees. Despite this, there are some solid reasons for considering life insurance as part of your estate plan. An insurance professional can explain the cost/benefit for your personal situation and advise you as to which kind of policy will not give rise to a tax liability on your death.

Preparation of a Valid Will   The most important element of any estate plan is the preparation of a valid will. Wills are discussed in more detail in a later section.

Letter of Wishes   A letter of wishes can be a valuable part of your estate plan. A letter of wishes is normally written by you, sometimes with the assistance of your lawyer. It can provide assistance to your executor and heirs in explaining your wishes and desires, provide comfort to the family, and assist your executor in finding assets. A letter of wishes is not legally binding and cannot override your will, which is the official document that is probated by the court. Contents of the letter can include your wishes regarding funeral services, reasons why certain assets were given to a particular individual or how you would like to see a cherished family asset such as the cottage, farm or business handled in the future.

Taxes   A key estate planning objective is to reduce or defer the tax that would otherwise be payable at death. Currently, the federal and provincial governments do not impose estate taxes or succession duties. However, provisions within the Income Tax Act can create a tax liability which will significantly reduce the proceeds of your estate which are to be passed on to your beneficiaries. In the year of death, your taxation year would run from January 1 to the date of death. A final or "terminal" return would have to be filed by your executor. All income earned to the date of death must be reported. This includes interest, rents, annuities, employment income and other amounts due but not paid. Also included are taxable capital gains or losses realized prior to death and not included in income in a previous year.

In addition, the deceased is deemed to have disposed of all capital property immediately before death. Any net gains (gains less losses) are to be included as capital gains in the individual's final tax return. In other words, even though there had not been an actual sale of property, your estate will be taxed as though your property had been sold just prior to death. For individuals with assets that have accrued capital gains (e.g. cottage, business, stock portfolio) the potential tax liability can significantly affect their plans. Fortunately there are some planning techniques which can help reduce these taxes. Since tax law is very complex, it is strongly recommended you seek professional advice when considering these tax saving strategies.

1. *Spousal rollover of property.* The Income Tax Act allows a tax deferral when property is transferred from the deceased to their spouse. Essentially this means the surviving spouse will take ownership of the property at the deceased's cost base and will not have to pay capital gains tax until the property is disposed of or until the surviving spouse dies.

2. *Spousal rollover of RRSP/RRIFs.* The Income Tax Act also allows RRSPs and RRIFs to be rolled over to the surviving spouse's RRSP, RRIF or annuity without triggering any tax liability. Careful consideration should be given to the named beneficiary on your RRSPs and RRIFs. If the named beneficiary is not a spouse your estate may be responsible for the tax liability upon deregistration of the entire fund.

3. *Spousal Trust.* A trust can be established that would provide your spouse with income for life but leave the capital for other beneficiaries (e.g. children or grandchildren). The Income Tax Act allows the transfer of property from the deceased to a spousal trust on a tax-deferred basis. This would be an option to consider if you did not want to distribute outright to your spouse.

4. The filing of a deceased taxpayer's income tax returns can be a complicated matter. There are special rules relating to prior years returns, the "Terminal Return," and up to three separate "optional returns" depending upon your assets and circumstances. Knowledge of these rules and the various elections available can result in considerable tax savings to your estate.

Planning for Incapacity

■ Enduring Power of Attorney

When developing your estate plan you should also give consideration to how your affairs would be handled in the event you were mentally incapacitated. The best way to address this concern is to have your lawyer draft an enduring power of attorney.

A power of attorney is a legal document that gives one or more people the power to manage your financial affairs (not necessarily your lawyer). A power of attorney can be "general" (covering all aspects of your financial affairs) or "limited" in the scope of the powers given to the attorney(s). Normally it will only be valid while you are mentally competent. However if you have an "enduring" power of attorney prepared, it will continue to be valid in the event you become incapacitated. It is important to note that all powers of attorney terminate if a court-ordered committee or guardian is appointed, or the person you appoint as attorney dies or upon your death. You can revoke a power of attorney at any time if you are mentally competent.

It is important to seek legal advice before preparing a power of attorney. The attorney has broad powers and a person should understand the nature of the document. Limitations can be included to prevent many problems from occurring.

■ Living Wills

If you want to leave instructions regarding heroic medical care, you may wish to have a living will prepared. Living wills express a person's wishes on what kind of medical treatment they wish or do not wish to receive when they are not able to speak for themselves. Living wills are not binding at the present time but should be discussed with your doctor and family so they are aware of your wishes. A lawyer can assist you with the preparation of a living will and advise you of the limitations that may apply in your province.

How to Establish Your Estate Plan

There are three basic steps to establishing your estate plan:

1.   Prepare an inventory of your assets and liabilities.
2.   Identify your estate planning objectives.
3.   Prepare your will.

Step 1: Prepare an Inventory of Your Assets and Liabilities   Your assets will include such things as:

*   RRSPs, RRIFs or pensions
*   personal property such as cars, furniture, jewelry and fine art
*   real estate such as your home and other properties (e.g. cottages, chalets and investment properties)
*   investments such as stocks, bonds, GICs, mutual funds and any interests you have in partnerships

It is also important to list how various assets are registered (e.g. joint tenants or tenants-in-common) and to list the beneficiaries of life insurance policies and retirement plans etc. Your liabilities will include such things as the mortgage on your home, investment-related debts and other personal obligations. For a sample worksheet detailing how your inventory can be organized, see Table 17.5.[5] You should find this straightforward, now that you have mastered Chapter 4.

Step 2: Identify Your Estate Planning Objectives   Your objectives will depend on a number of factors, including:

*   your age
*   the ages of your family members and other beneficiaries
*   the needs of your beneficiaries
*   the current value of your estate
*   your beneficiaries' ability to handle their own financial affairs
*   your tax situation

Every situation is unique. A young couple with children will have different concerns from a wealthy widow or widower without children. Most people have estate planning objectives which can be broken down into things they want to "achieve" and things they want to "avoid". Some common estate planning objectives are listed below.

Things people want to achieve:

*   maximize estate proceeds for heirs
*   distribution of assets in accordance with wishes

---

[5] You could use the balance sheet in Super Rep as well.

TABLE 17.5
Estate Planning Asset/Liability Worksheet

	in your name	in spouse's name	joint names
ASSETS			
Your home (current market value)	$	$	$
Other real estate	$	$	$
Bank accounts (chequing and saving)	$	$	$
Other cash accounts (brokerage accounts, savings bonds, money market funds)	$	$	$
Stocks, bonds and mutual funds	$	$	$
Term deposits	$	$	$
Life Insurance (face value)	$	$	$
Business partnership interests	$	$	$
Retirement plan accounts:			
RRSP	$	$	$
RRIF	$	$	$
Company Pension Plan	$	$	$
Other	$	$	$
Personal property (jewelry, autos, household furnishings, etc.)	$	$	$
Annuities or other assets	$	$	$
Collectibles (market value of fine art, precious metals, etc.)	$	$	$
TOTAL ASSETS	$	$	$
LIABILITIES			
Mortgages	$	$	$
Other loans or debts	$	$	$
Contingent loans (loan guarantees)	$	$	$
TOTAL LIABILITIES	$	$	$
NET ESTATE (assets less liabilities)	$	$	$

- provide for loved ones in the event of death
- ensure adequate liquidity in estate to pay taxes and any liabilities
- ensure guardian for minor children

Things people want to avoid:

- needless taxation
- family strife
- delays in settling the estate
- costly legal challenges
- probate fees charged by provincial courts
- loss of control of family asset such as cottage property, farm or family business

You should list and prioritize your objectives before meeting with your professional adviser. This will help ensure your estate plan and will reflect your objectives and wishes.

Step 3: Prepare Your Will   After reviewing your assets and liabilities, and tax and insurance situation, your most important step is to have a will prepared, taking into consideration your wishes and objectives. Wills are discussed in detail in the next section of this book. If you already have a will, you should have it professionally reviewed to ensure changes in government legislation or your personal situation have not adversely affected your plans. An important signal of when to review your will is a change in the family life cycle stage (see Chapter 5).

Wills

A **will** is a legal document, signed in accordance with specific rules, that is essential to ensuring your wishes are carried out with minimum expense and delay. Your will won't become effective or public until your death. Until then, you can change the terms or revoke it, as long as you are mentally competent. Your will should be reviewed at least every three years to ensure it has not been impacted by changes in government legislation or your family situation. In some situations a badly out-of-date will can be worse than no will at all.

Why Is a Will Important?

- It is the only way of ensuring your property will be distributed according to your wishes. If you die without a will your assets will be distributed according to a government formula (See Table 17.6).
- It names your executor, the individual or institution who will act on your behalf and carry out your wishes. Without a will the courts will appoint someone as an administrator of your estate who may not be the exact individual you would have chosen.
- Your choice of guardian for minor children will be clearly stated and considered by the provincial courts, who make the ultimate decision.
- It helps ensure that sufficient income is provided for your spouse and children.
- It helps ensure tax saving strategies are considered and can be implemented by your executor.

  Table 17.7 summarizes the contents of a basic will.

Types of Wills   A **holographic** will is a will written entirely in your own handwriting and signed by you. No witness is necessary. This type of will is not recommended as it may leave your family with a legal minefield as the legal interpretation of how you expressed your wishes may well differ from what you had in mind. In fact, some provinces do not even recognize a will of this kind.

A **formal** will is typed and you sign it in the presence of at least two witnesses. Neither witness can be one of your beneficiaries or their spouse. Most formal wills are drafted by lawyers because they are trained to ensure the legal drafting of your will meets your needs.

Testamentary Trusts in Your Will   As mentioned earlier there are two kinds of trusts. Living (or *inter vivos*) trusts are established while you are alive, while testamentary

TABLE 17.6
This Is What Happens If You Die Without a Will

Province	Spouse Only	Spouse, Relative(s) But No Children	Child or Children Only	Remaining Family		No Spouse or Children
				Spouse and One Child	Spouse and Children	
Newfoundland	All to spouse	All to spouse	All to children[1]	Split equally[1]	1/3 to spouse; 2/3 to children[1]	All to closest next of kin, usually in this order: parents; if neither survives, brothers/sisters[8]; if none survive, nephews/nieces; if none survive, next of kin. If there is no traceable next of kin, it all goes to the government.
Nova Scotia	All to spouse	All to spouse	All to children[1]	1st $50,000 to spouse[2]; rest split equally[1]	1st $50,000 to spouse[2]; 1/3 rest to spouse; 2/3 to children[1]	
Prince Edward Island	All to spouse	All to spouse	All to children[1]	Split equally[1]	1/3 to spouse; 2/3 to children[1]	
New Brunswick	All to spouse	All to spouse	All to children[1]	Marital property to spouse; rest split equally[1]	Marital property to spouse; 1/3 rest to spouse; 2/3 to children[1]	
Quebec	All to spouse	2/3 to spouse; 1/3 to parents or brothers and sisters[9]	All to children[1]	1/3 to spouse[7]; 2/3 to child[1]	1/3 to spouse[7]; 2/3 to children[1]	
Ontario	All to spouse	All to spouse	All to children[1]	1st $200,000 to spouse; rest split equally[1,4]	1st $200,000 to spouse; 1/3 rest to spouse; 2/3 to children[1,4]	
Manitoba	All to spouse	All to spouse	All to children[1]	Either all to spouse[5], or greater of $50,000 or half of estate to spouse[10], 1/2 rest to spouse;	Either all to spouse[5], or greater of $50,000 or half of estate to spouse; 1/2 rest to children[6]	
Saskatchewan	All to spouse	All to spouse	All to children[1]	1st $100,000 to spouse; rest split equally[1]	1st $100,000 to spouse; 1/3 rest to spouse; 2/3 to children[1]	
Alberta	All to spouse	All to spouse	All to children[1]	1st $40,000 to spouse; rest split equally[1]	1st $40,000 to spouse; 1/3 rest to spouse; 2/3 to children[1]	
British Columbia	All to spouse	All to spouse	All to children[1]	1st $65,000 to spouse[3]; rest split equally[1]	1st $65,000 to spouse[3]; 2/3 rest to children[1]	

Notes: (a) In some cases provincial Family Law Acts can override these distribution formulas.

(b) The formulas on the chart are based on Provincial laws in effect at time of printing.

[1] Issue of a deceased child (grandchildren, great grandchildren) take that child's share.
[2] Spouse may elect to receive house and contents in lieu of $50,000.
[3] Plus household furniture and life interest in family home.
[4] Subject to possible equalization claim under Family Law Act.
[5] If all the children are also children of surviving spouse.
[6] If any of the children are not also children of surviving spouse. Children of deceased child (grandchildren) share in the estate.
[7] Subject to provisions of Bill 146 [Economic Equality between spouses].
[8] Children of deceased brothers and sisters share their parent's share.
[9] Depends on who the other survivors are.
[10] Life interest in the home plus a possible equalization payment under the Marital Property Act.

TABLE 17.7
What's in a Will?

A will requires careful planning to ensure all aspects are covered. The chart below outlining the contents of a basic will clearly demonstrates this point.

Common Clause	Purpose of the Clause
Identification and Revocation Clause	Identifies you and your residence. Declares that this is your last will which revokes all prior wills.
Appointment of Executor(s)	Designates the individual or institution you appoint as your executor. May also designate alternate and successor executors if your original executor cannot act. The clause may provide for the payment of compensation to the executor for the their services.
Payment of Debts	Directs your executor to pay all debts such as mortgages, loans, and funeral and estate administration expenses.
Payment of Taxes and Fees	Authorizes your executor to pay income tax or probate fees that may be due.
Specific Bequests	Outlines the distribution of specific personal property such as furniture, jewellery, cars. May also refer to your RRSPs, RRIFs and pensions.
Legacies	Directs specific cash amounts to be paid.
Residual Estates	Outlines the distribution of your remaining property after all the specific bequests have been made.
Trusts	Sets out the terms of any trust created by your will.
Power Clauses	Enables your executor to exercise various powers in the management of your estate without the approval of the court.
Life Interest Clause	Used when you want to leave someone the income or the enjoyment of the asset, rather than the asset itself. Upon the life tenant's death, the asset would pass on to another beneficiary.
Encroachment Clause	Used in a trust when you want the trustee to be able to give the life tenant or a capital beneficiary additional funds for special circumstances or needs.
Common Disaster Clause	Outlines the distribution of your assets if an intended beneficiary dies at the same time as you.
Survival Clause	States that a beneficiary must survive you for a set period of time (often 30 days) before he or she can benefit from your estate.
Guardian Appointment	Names the individual(s) who would be appointed guardian of your minor children.
Testimonium and Attestation Clauses	These clauses are found at the end of your will. They ensure the legal requirements for a validly executed will are met.

trusts take effect upon your death. The legal clauses for the establishment of a testamentary trust are included in your will. These clauses will indicate what assets are to go into trust, who the trustee(s) will be, and who the beneficiaries will be. In addition, special provision can be given to the trustee for the management and distribution of the trust assets.

A testamentary trust enables you to earmark assets for specific family members, and place restrictions on how the money is to be used. It also ensures that the money will be managed professionally by a competent trustee — an individual or trust company of your choice.

Many people set up a trust to ensure that the money being left to a spouse is properly managed, and that adequate income is provided in later years. Then on her death the remaining capital passes outright to children or grandchildren. If you have minor children to whom you want to leave money, a trust is required to hold and manage their inheritance, at least until they reach the age of majority. But many people leave assets in trust for older children as well. Trusts can provide for a child's education, assist in purchasing a first home, or any other valid purpose.

Some people want to accustom their children to handling money, but are reluctant to leave them a large amount of cash. So they set up a trust that turns over part of the inheritance when the child reaches certain ages. For example, a child could receive a third of the inheritance at age of majority, another third at 25 and the balance at 30. Provincial laws are structured such that you can keep assets in your family for an extended period. However, for trusts that last longer than a beneficiary's lifetime, it's best to consult an estate and trust professional to ensure tax implications are considered.

All this is accomplished through your will: You state what type of trusts you wish to create, specify any conditions, and indicate how much money is to be allocated to each trust.

How to Get Your Will Prepared
Will planning is important, even for individuals who will have a fairly straightforward or modest estate. Will planning is done before the actual legal document is drafted by a lawyer, usually as part of the estate planning process. Pre-planning ensures all your assets and liabilities are properly identified, tax saving strategies are considered, and your wishes and objectives clearly identified. Up-front planning can assist your lawyer in the preparation of your will, saving him time and you legal fees. It also helps ensure you end up with a will that accurately reflects your needs.

Will planning is done by trust companies, financial planners, and lawyers who specialize in wills and estates. Trust companies such as Royal Trust provide up-front will and estate planning free of charge to clients who appoint them to act as their executor or co-executor. Trust companies cannot draft your will, but they will work closely with your lawyer in the legal preparation and any subsequent revisions.

If your estate is fairly straightforward and you are planning on appointing a family member as your executor, you are probably best to go directly to a lawyer who specializes in wills and estates. Ideally, you should get a personal referral from someone you know, as the lawyer who handled your home sale may not specialize in the estate area. The legal fees for drawing up a will can range from a couple of hundred dollars, to seven or eight hundred dollars for a husband and wife with a moderately complex estate. Legal fees will vary depending on the complexity of the will and the legal fees in your area. Although the cost of having a will prepared is not cheap, it is small when compared to

TABLE 17.8
Is Your Will Up-to-Date?

	Yes	No	Don't know
1. Is it current for:			
(a) executor suitability? (see Table 17.11)	☐	☐	☐
(b) guardian suitability?	☐	☐	☐
(c) changes in tax laws?	☐	☐	☐
(d) changes in provincial laws?	☐	☐	☐
(e) changes in marital status?	☐	☐	☐
(f) birth/death of an heir?	☐	☐	☐
(g) province of residence?	☐	☐	☐
2. Does the will have an alternate or contingent executor in the event your original executor cannot act. (example: both spouses die in a common disaster)?	☐	☐	☐
3. Can your executor act impartially towards all your beneficiaries?	☐	☐	☐
4. Have specific powers been granted to the executor to deal with special assets such as a private business, real estate, investments?	☐	☐	☐
5. Does the will provide direction on how assets are to be distributed in the event one of your beneficiaries dies before you?	☐	☐	☐

If you scored predominantly "No" or "Don't Know" responses, your will may be in need of a professional review.

the value of the assets being passed on and the fact that your will may be the most important document you ever sign in your life. Like many other things in life, you get what you pay for.

Is Your Will Up-To-Date?   Estate planning and preparation of a will is not something done once and then forgotten. Changes in government legislation or your family situation can impact your will, making it out-of-date. In some situations a badly out-of-date will can be worse than no will at all. If you have a will that has not been reviewed in the past three years, complete the chart in Table 17.8 to determine if it is still up-to-date.

TABLE 17.9
Provincial Probate Fees*

Province	Probate Fee
Newfoundland	$50 for first $1,000. $4 per $1,000 thereafter. No maximum fee.
Nova Scotia	$800 for first $200,000, and $5 per $1,000 thereafter. No maximum fee.
Prince Edward Island	Progressive rates starting at $50 for the first $10,000, increasing to $400 for estates of $100,000, and $4 per $1,000 thereafter. No maximum fee.
New Brunswick	$5 per $1,000. No maximum fee.
Quebec	No probate fees.
Ontario	$5 per $1,000 for first $50,000; $15 per $1,000 thereafter. No maximum fee.
Manitoba	$25 for first $5,000; $6 per $1,000 thereafter. No maximum fee.
Saskatchewan	$7 per $1,000. No maximum fee.
Alberta	Progressive rates start at $25 for first $10,000, increasing to a maximum of $6,000 for estates in excess of $1,000,000.
British Columbia	$200 for estates of $10,000–25,000. $6 per $1,000 thereafter. No maximum fee.

* Based on information available at time of printing. Probate fees are subject to change.

Probating a Will   **Probate** is a legal process that confirms a will. Normally your executor, in conjunction with a lawyer, will file for probate with your provincial court. When your will has been probated, the court will issue a Grant of Probate, which essentially confirms that your will is valid. Often financial institutions will not release assets of an estate to an executor unless they receive a Grant of Probate; so it is likely your executor will have to go through the probate process. Provincial probate fees at the date of writing are shown in Table 17.9. Probate fees are payable to the court, not your executor, and are paid out of the proceeds of your estate.

Reducing Probate Costs   In recent years several provincial governments significantly increased their probate fees. These higher costs have prompted many people to seek ways to reduce the amount of their assets that fall into their estate, where they would be subject to probate fees. The lower the total value of the assets that become part of the estate, the lower the probate costs are likely to be. Reducing the size of an estate also cuts executor fees, which are normally 3% to 5% of the estate's value, depending on the province of residence. If you're interested in reducing these costs, here are some strategies to consider:

• Make your spouse your RRSP/RRIF beneficiary. This measure should make it possible for the funds in your retirement plan to pass directly to your spouse without tax, and without becoming part of your estate and incurring probate costs. Note, however, that some provinces do not have clear-cut rules on this point.

- Name an adult person, not your estate, as beneficiary of life insurance policies and annuity contracts. The proceeds will then pass directly to the beneficiary without probate fees. If the estate is named as beneficiary, the funds will be included in the probate process. Make sure the insurance proceeds are not "earmarked" for specific purposes, e.g. meeting a tax liability or funding a specific gift. If they are, then they should be left to the estate.

- Hold real estate as joint tenants. This allows your home, cottage or other property to pass directly to your surviving joint tenant on your death.

- Have bank accounts and other investments under joint tenancy agreements, with a right of survivorship. Here again, the assets will automatically pass to the surviving owner if one dies, without falling into your estate. Danger: joint ownership means joint control; make sure you and your spouse (or any other joint owner) share the same financial objectives.

- Set up a living trust. Assets held in a trust do not fall into your estate after death. A trust is an effective estate-planning device that can be tailored to your needs. For example, the trust could allow you access to its capital or income during your lifetime. On your death, assets pass to your intended beneficiaries as per the terms of the trust document — not your will. However, you should investigate the tax implications before you act.

Beware   Transferring assets into joint names and other techniques may have other implications that should be fully explored with an estate planner or legal adviser. Some factors to examine are:

Estate taxes and liabilities. There will probably be some taxes to be paid upon death, no matter how well you structure your affairs. Make sure the estate will have adequate funds to cover these taxes; otherwise Revenue Canada will go after the beneficiaries for the money. Remember, too, that taxes on assets passing outside the estate will be borne by the estate's beneficiaries — reducing the net proceeds. This factor must be considered in estate planning.

Consider family law. Provincial family laws can also upset your estate planning when you try to reduce probate costs. For example, suppose you and your spouse jointly own a cottage. If you die, the cottage passes directly to your spouse without probate. If your spouse then remarries, the new husband or wife may have a claim on the value of the cottage and it will bypass your children. Consider the impact of family law before you decide.

Tax consequences. Transferring property into joint ownership with someone other than a spouse may trigger tax consequences if the property has appreciated in value. Also, income attribution may apply if property is held jointly with a spouse or minor child.

Executors

An executor (executrix, if female) is the individual or institution you name in your will who is responsible for administering your estate. It is possible to name more than one executor. They will act on your behalf to carry out your wishes as stated in your will.

Co-executors are often appointed when an individual wants to combine professional estate administration expertise (e.g. trust company) with someone who is knowledgeable about their personal and family situation (e.g. spouse or child). Before choosing executors it is important to understand their duties and responsibilities, as this will assist you in determining if they have the necessary time and skills to look after your affairs.

Duties of an Executor   Table 17.10 lists some of the more common duties executors must perform. These duties will vary depending on the complexity of your estate. However, even the simplest of estates require great care and skill from your executor for a wide range of duties.

Executor Duties — Tax Returns   When an individual dies, three different "taxpayers" may have to file a return and pay taxes. They are:

1. the deceased
2. the estate of the individual between the date of the death and the date when assets were distributed
3. any trusts set up under the terms of the will

It is the responsibility of the deceased's executor and trustee, if there is a trust, to file tax returns within the time parameters set out under the Income Tax Act. Unfortunately many non-professional executors, administering an estate for the first time, can be overwhelmed with the number and complexity of these tax returns.

Tax Returns for the Year of Death. A final tax return must be filed for the period beginning January 1 to the date of death. Special rules apply upon death relating to:

- deemed disposition of capital property
- spousal rollover of property
- collapsing of RRSPs/RRIFs or transferring to a spouse
- income accrued to the date of death
- medical and charitable deductions

Tax Return for Year Prior to Death. If an individual dies before April 30th and has not filed a return for the preceding year, the executor of the estate will have to file one on his or her behalf in addition to the terminal return mentioned above.

Tax Return for "Rights or Things." Executors may also choose to file a separate return for amounts owed to the deceased at the time of death but not received. Such "rights or things" include income such as matured but uncashed bond coupons and declared but unpaid dividends. By filing a separate return for these rights or things it may entitle the deceased taxpayer to additional tax credits for the year of death and attract a lower marginal tax rate.

Tax Return for Business Income. If the deceased taxpayer had an interest in a proprietorship or partnership it may be possible to file a separate return to report business income earned to the date of death.

Tax Return for Trust Income. If the deceased was a beneficiary of a testamentary trust with a non-calendar year end, it may be possible to file a separate return to report the trust income to the date of death.

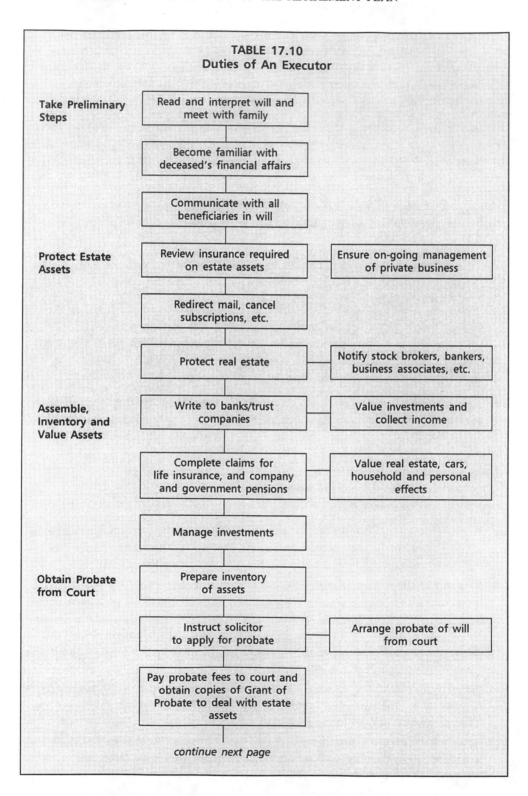

TABLE 17.10
Duties of An Executor

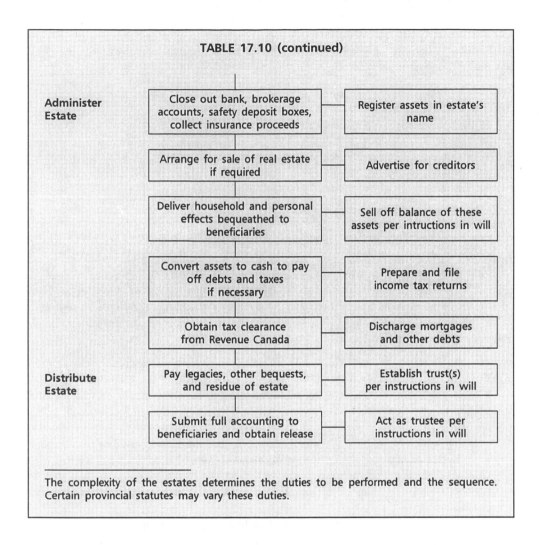

TABLE 17.10 (continued)

Administer Estate	Close out bank, brokerage accounts, safety deposit boxes, collect insurance proceeds	Register assets in estate's name
	Arrange for sale of real estate if required	Advertise for creditors
	Deliver household and personal effects bequeathed to beneficiaries	Sell off balance of these assets per intructions in will
	Convert assets to cash to pay off debts and taxes if necessary	Prepare and file income tax returns
	Obtain tax clearance from Revenue Canada	Discharge mortgages and other debts
Distribute Estate	Pay legacies, other bequests, and residue of estate	Establish trust(s) per instructions in will
	Submit full accounting to beneficiaries and obtain release	Act as trustee per instructions in will

The complexity of the estates determines the duties to be performed and the sequence. Certain provincial statutes may vary these duties.

Tax Return for the Estate. Not only do the executors of an estate have to file a tax return for the deceased individual up to the date of death, they will also have to file a separate return for the estate itself for the period from the date of death until the date all assets are distributed to the beneficiaries. Estates are taxed like individuals with progressive marginal rates of taxation but cannot claim personal tax credits. Special tax rules apply to estates which may enable taxes to be reduced. Such rules are complex and not widely known by inexperienced executors. For this reason professional advice is a must for estates with potentially significant tax liabilities.

Tax Return for the Trust. If under the terms of the will a trust is established, it will be the responsibility of the trustee to file annual tax returns for the trust. Like estates, special tax rules apply to trusts and elections are available to reduce taxes in many situations.

Choosing the Right Executor   A crucial estate planning decision is your choice of executor. Even the best laid plans will fail if the individual you select is not up to the job. An executor should be:

- trustworthy
- willing, and have the time to act
- impartial toward all beneficiaries
- able to make decisions in a timely fashion
- proficient in business, investment and administrative matters at a level sufficient to handle your estate
- understanding of estate and trust law and administration

Who Can You Choose as Executor?   There are two types of executors: professionals, such as trust companies or lawyers, and individuals, such as family members or close friends.

■   Individual Executors

It may seem that naming a family friend or relative as your executor is like bestowing an honour on them. In reality it is a heavy imposition. They will be required to devote substantial time and effort to the task. In addition they can encounter many potential problems such as:

- personal liability for mistakes made while administering the estate (For example, this can happen if they distribute proceeds of the estate and then find out a creditor has a legal claim. Or they can be liable for taxes if they distribute the estate before obtaining tax clearance from Revenue Canada and then find out additional taxes are due.)
- personal criticism from family members and friends who disapprove of how things have been handled, no matter how well intended the executor's actions were
- challenges from family members excluded under the will
- conflict of interest from being appointed executor and also being a beneficiary or business partner
- difficulty in administering the estate due to location, lack of time or ability
- difficulty handling financial matters at such an emotional time

Appointing your spouse or children as executor is appropriate if you are convinced that they are capable of handling the duties and can act in an unbiased manner to all beneficiaries and can be available. If your estate is fairly straightforward, it is likely they can attend to most matters by themselves or can seek out professional legal and accounting advice at a reasonable cost. It is important to remember that all executors, even family members, are entitled to be paid for their work.

■   Professional Executors

Given the complexities and responsibilities of executorship, many individuals appoint a lawyer or trust company to act as their executor. Some of the more common reasons why you might want to choose a professional executor include:

- you do not wish to burden family members or friends
- you do not have immediate family members living close by or do not wish to have them involved

- the family members you would consider do not have the time or expertise to administer your estate
- the individual you are considering would likely pre-decease you
- you are concerned family members appointed as co-executors would not get along and have difficulty making decisions
- you are in a second marriage and you want an impartial executor who will balance the needs of your second spouse and the children from your first marriage
- your will provides for the establishment of a trust which requires professional management by a permanent trustee.

In some situations it may be appropriate to appoint a lawyer or trust company as co-executor along with a family member. This would combine the expertise of the professional executor along with the knowledge of your family situation by one of its members.

The fees charged by a professional executor are the same as can be charged by an individual (set by provincial legislation). Executor fees are paid out the proceeds of your estate on the basis of time and effort required to settle your estate. Often, these fees can be more than offset by savings in income tax and legal fees which may be incurred by less experienced individuals. Non-professional executors, who have never administered an estate before, sometimes have to hire outside professionals or miss tax saving opportunities which can result in higher costs to the estate. In many cases, where a professional executor is involved, and where provincial legislation permits, the fees can be set out in an agreement which is signed by you. In this way you will know in advance what the cost to your estate will be.

Glossary of Terms for Estate Planning
prepared by Royal Trust

Administrator: The person appointed by the court to administer the estate when there is no will, the will did not name an Executor or the named Executor has died or is unwilling to act. Also referred to as a "personal representative".

Agent for Executor: Where a trust company like Royal Trust is hired by the named executor for a fee to provide advice and administration services.

Alternate Appointment: An alternate Executor appointed if the first named Executor cannot or will not act.

Attribution Rules: The attribution rules, under the Income Tax Act, provide that where property is transferred, directly or through a trust, for the benefit of a spouse or certain minor children, the income (and in some cases, capital gains) on that property may be deemed to be income or gains of the transferor and not of the person holding the property.

Beneficiary: A person who receives a benefit or gift under a will, or a person for whose benefit a trust is created.

Codicil: An amendment to a will which makes changes or additions. It's executed with the same formalities as a will.

Estate: The right, title or interest which a person has in any property.

Glossary of Terms for Estate Planning (continued)

Executor: The person or trust company named in a will responsible for the management of the deceased's assets and the ultimate transfer of the property; also commonly referred to as a "personal representative."

Fiduciary: An individual or institution under a lawful duty to act for the benefit of another party.

Grant of Probate: A certificate confirming the authority set out in a will to administer a particular estate; issued to an Executor by the court. Also called Grant of Letters Probate and Letters Probate.

Guardian: The person named to be legally responsible for the minor children should both parents die.

***Inter vivos* Trust:** Also known as a living trust, *inter vivos* trusts come into effect during the lifetime of the settlor.

Intestate: A person who dies without a will. A partial intestacy is where a valid will does not dispose of the whole of the estate.

Irrevocable Trust: A trust which cannot be revoked (cancelled) by the person who created the trust (settlor).

Issue: All persons who have descended from a common ancestor. It is a broader term than children which is limited to one generation.

Joint Tenants: A form of joint ownership in which the death of one joint owner results in the immediate transfer of ownership to the surviving joint owner or owners.

Probate of Will: Formal proof before the proper officer or court that the will offered is the last will of the testator and confirming the Executor(s) named. (See also: Letters Probate)

Revocable Trust: A trust that gives the settlor the power to revoke the trust.

Settlor: The individual who establishes a trust.

Tenants-In-Common: A form of joint ownership in which two or more persons own the same property in equal or differing proportions. At the death of a tenant-in-common, ownership of the deceased's share transfers to that person's estate, not to the other joint owner.

Testamentary Trust: A trust set up in a will that only takes effect after death.

Testate: A person who dies having left a valid will.

Testator/Testatrix: The individual who makes a will.

Trust: A legal arrangement in which one person (the settlor) transfers legal title to a trustee (a fiduciary) to manage the property for the benefit of a person or institution (the beneficiaries).

Trustee: The person or trust company that manages property according to the instructions in the trust agreement and the laws governing trustees.

Will: A legal document, prepared by a person in compliance with formal requirements, which takes effect on his/her death and which states what he/she wants to happen to his/her property on death.

How Suitable Is Your Executor?   To assist you in evaluating your choice of executor, complete the chart in Table 17.11. Ultimately your decision will be a personal one based upon the complexity of your estate, the abilities of your potential executor,

---

TABLE 17.11
How Suitable Are Your Executors?

	Yes	No
1. Are they knowledgeable about:		
(a) estate & trust laws?	☐	☐
(b) taxation of estates and trusts?	☐	☐
(c) asset valuation?	☐	☐
(d) insurance?	☐	☐
(e) real estate?	☐	☐
(f) investments?	☐	☐
(g) accounting?	☐	☐
2. Will they:		
(a) be available when the time comes to act?	☐	☐
(b) live in the same province as you?	☐	☐
(c) likely out-live you?	☐	☐
(d) be able to take time off work to settle your estate?	☐	☐
3. Will they be able to act impartially towards all beneficiaries?	☐	☐
4. Will they be able to work together with other co-executors you may appoint?	☐	☐
5. Are they aware they could be held personally liable for any mistakes they made in settling your estate?	☐	☐
6. Have you advised them of the location and contents of your will and have they agreed to act?	☐	☐

If the executors you have chosen score predominantly "no" to these questions they may not be able to do the job as you would want — especially if your estate is not a straight-forward one.

their willingness to act and your family situation. To help you make your decision, ask a friend or family member who has been involved in a complex estate whether or not they would do it again.

SUMMARY

The family has three goals when it comes time to use its retirement savings to provide retirement income. In order of priority, they are:

1.   Minimize risk of inadequate income for the family at any time, including after the death of a member;
2.   Maximize income; and,
3.   Maximize the bequest to the heirs who are not dependent members of the family.

The family has a variety of sources of retirement income — government pensions, employer pensions, home equity and its own savings in tax shelters and unsheltered investments. The family must choose among the various maturity options to optimize its chance of meetings the three goals. It must consider risk management, investment, taxes and liquidity in the management of its retirement income.

Estate planning requires attention to a lot of detail. The most important aspect is the preparation and maintenance of an up-to-date will that arranges for each adult family member to distribute his assets according to his goals. Issues around the will and estate planning include taxes, selection of an executor, incapacity of one of the adults and probate fees.

KEY TERMINOLOGY

annuities — life — commuted value — guaranteed term — indexed — joint and last survivor — registered — straight life — substandard health — term certain / investment principles — risk management — liquidity — CompCorp / Locked-in Pension Funds — Life Income Fund (LIF) — Life Retirement Income Fund (LRIF) — locked-in RRSP — Locked-in Retirement Account (LIRA) / maturity options / Registered Retirement Income Fund (RRIF) — self-administered / Reverse mortgage — equity of redemption — reverse annuity mortgage (RAM) — straight or term / risk management / taxation — deferral — splitting — spreading / see also Glossary of Terms for Estate Planning

DISCUSSION QUESTIONS

1.   Explain each of the terms under **Key Terminology**.
2.   A debate has arisen over the reasonableness of the OAS being paid to taxpayers with substantial income from other sources. The same question is being raised with respect to the future Seniors Benefit. Do some research and discuss this issue. You should find out the current level of "claw-back" of OAS, and consider both the ethical and practical issues in the context of increasing government deficits.
3.   How would you protect your family at retirement from the risk of failure of financial institutions?
4.   What are the two situations in which the deceased's assets go directly to a beneficiary independent of her will?

5. What would happen to your estate if you were to die intestate?

6. How did you choose your executor/executrix? Do you think this person is the best choice, in light of what you have read in Chapter 17? If you do not have a will, explain how you would choose an executor/executrix. If you don't have enough assets for a will to be necessary, then answer this question from the point of view of one of your parents, or some other person for whom a will is relevant.

PROBLEMS

1. Claudette and Onesime are planning to retire soon. Claudette will be 59, and Onesime, 64 when they retire. Both have lived in Canada all their lives. Neither one has an employer pension. Claudette has an RRSP of $50,000, and has a full CPP entitlement. She will defer taking her CPP until she reaches age 65. Onesime has $100,000 in his RRSP, and full CPP entitlement. Assume that both RRSPs will continue to earn a 6% real rate of return. At age 69, they convert their RRSPs into RRIFs, and start withdrawing the minimum amount.

    (a) Estimate their pre-tax retirement income for the following years: first year of retirement, Onesime's age 65, Claudette's age 65, Onesime's age 69, Claudette's age 69.

    (b) Estimate their after-tax retirement income at each point in time.

2. Janet retires next month at age 63. She has been divorced for many years, and receives no support payments from her ex-husband. Her severely-handicapped son, Joseph, lives with her. She will receive an employer pension of $50,000 p.a., unindexed. There is no way to provide for a survivor pension for Joseph. She is entitled to full CPP and OAS. She has a house in a nice Vancouver neighbourhood worth about $250,000. It has been specially adapted so that Joseph can live in it comfortably. She has an RRSP with $40,000 in it, and mutual funds worth $10,000. Joseph has a trust fund of $200,000, all invested in GICs of the trustee, a local trust company.

    Joseph's handicaps are physical, and he will never be able to earn a living. He has completed high school, and is fully competent to make decisions. However, he will have to have constant physical care for as long as he lives. The medical advice is that he can expect to live to his 50s. However, a few people with his disabilities have lived into their 70s. He is 30 years old.

    Janet estimates that she needs $25,000 p.a. after-tax, in today's dollars (i.e. real dollars) for her own needs in retirement, as long as they live in the house. Although she can now provide care for Joseph to a greater extent in retirement than she did when working, she is also growing older and will not be able to do so forever. Furthermore, she needs quite a bit of time away, because of the draining nature of the care required. Accordingly, she estimates that she will need another $25,000 p.a. after-tax to care for him. In the event of her death, she would like him to be able to receive care in a good institution, at a cost in today's dollars of $40,000 p.a.

    Provide advice to Janet and Joseph on all aspects of the maturation of her retirement plan, including his trust fund.

3. Running Bear has $200,000 in savings bonds, a house worth $80,000 and three dependent children. Running Bear has an insurance policy of $100,000 payable to his estate. His wife, Judy Ermineskin, has a spousal RRSP of $10,000, with one of the children named as the beneficiary. The house is listed in his name only. They live in Yorkton, Saskatchewan.

    (a) If Running Bear dies intestate, how will the estate be divided?
    (b) If Running Bear and Judy made wills and took other actions, what would be the minimum probate fees they could arrange to pay on the death of either of them?
    (c) Answer parts (a) and (b) as if they lived in Fernie, British Columbia.

4. Kenneth Wallingford died without a will in Prince Edward Island, at the age of 60. He is survived by his wife Jill and three adult children: John, Janet and Bill. He left behind the family home, which he bought 40 years ago and which is now worth $200,000. The house is registered in Kenneth and Jill's names as joint tenants. He also left behind a portfolio of shares with a current market value of $400,00 and an adjusted cost base of $150,000. He was entitled to full CPP at age 65, and would have been entitled to OAS. Jill is also 60 years old.

    (a) How much will Jill and each of the children inherit, after probate fees and income taxes? Assume the estate pays executor and legal fees of $5,000.
    (b) Answer part (a) as if they lived in Corner Brook, Newfoundland.

5. Mike and Betty Gordon are both 66 years old. Mike will retire Jan. 1, 1997 from his position as a professor of radical social thought. He will be eligible for a pension of $50,000 p.a., indexed to the Consumer Price Index. He will receive maximum CPP, and is already receiving full OAS. He has $200,000 invested in ethical mutual funds (adjusted cost base $150,000). Assume Mike will receive about $5,000 in dividends from the mutual fund in 1997 and $2,000 in realized capital gains. Betty has no pension, but is receiving full OAS. Betty has $100,000 in a spousal RRSP, invested in Canada Trust GICs. They jointly own a condominium in Toronto worth $250,000 (no mortgage). Their planned donations for 1997 include $2,000 to registered charities, and $200 to a registered federal political party. They have two children. One of them is married, with three children of his own.

    (a) How should they structure their retirement planning both now, and for the rest of their retirement? There are some decisions they must make now, and others that will have to be made within the next six years.
    (b) What will be their marginal and average income tax rates for 1997? Assume that they take no payments from the RRSPs into income in 1997 and do not sell any mutual fund units. Other than that assumption, assume that you have done the best job of planning in (a). To do this question, you must calculate taxable income for each one of them.

6. Theodore Horstmann is 65 years old and will retire in six months' time. He and his wife Astrid (60 years old) currently live in a three-bedroom house in Calgary that is worth $450,000. The house has been totally paid off. Theodore has in his name a bank account of $5,000, RRSPs of $75,000, GICs of $75,000, stock mutual funds of $20,000 and a solarium containing $10,000 in orchids. Astrid has a spousal

RRSP worth $50,000. Astrid's RRSP is invested in an index mutual fund at the Toronto Dominion Bank. All the other financial assets are at a local trust company. Their two children, David and Mary, are working in Montreal and are financially secure and independent. The Horstmanns currently spend about $27,000 a year, categorized as follows in monthly amounts:

Property taxes	$ 250
Insurance	30
Utilities (water, gas, hydro)	200
Cable	30
Phone	50
Food and grocery	600
Clothes	200
Transportation (5 year old Ford)	200
Gifts	100
Entertainment	200
Medicine and health care	100
Books, subscriptions	50
Miscellaneous	200
TOTAL	$2,210

Theodore will not have a company pension, but he will be eligible for maximum CPP and OAS. Astrid has no pension credits. They wish to travel during their retirement, and estimate that trips would cost $10,000 annually. You may assume that expected inflation is 4%, GICs earn 5.5% and stock mutual funds are expected to return 11% after management fees. The Horstmanns don't wish to plan for living beyond age 90 of each of them.

Analyze the Horstmann's financial situation in retirement and make recommendations. Be thorough. State any further assumptions you make.

7. Archie Goodwin is 68 years old and retired. He has indexed pensions of $15,000 p.a. and $300,000 in GICs inside RRSPs at a bank and a trust company. He owns a two-bedroom condominium that he lives in, and another unit in the same building that he rents out for $1,000 per month, net of all expenses. He bought the condominiums two years ago for $150,000 each, and he could sell them for that now, after legal and real estate fees. He is currently living on an income of $50,000 p.a.: $15,000 pensions, $12,000 net rent, and $23,000 withdrawal from the RRSP. Next year he will move the RRSP into a RRIF. He has no dependents and no wish to leave a bequest to anyone. Advise him how he should invest his retirement wealth.

REFERENCES

Ho, Kwok, Moshe Arye Milevsky and Chris Robinson. 1994a. "Asset Allocation, Life Expectancy and Shortfall," *Financial Services Review* 3(2): 109–26.

———. 1994b. "How to Avoid Outliving Your Money," *Canadian Investment Review* Fall: 35–38.

Income Security Programs, Human Resources Development Canada, provides pamphlets and telephone consultations regarding CPP, OAS and GIS. Check the Blue Pages of your telephone directory for the office nearest to you. Rates change often, and sometimes rules and forms for applications change.

Milevsky, Moshe Arye, Kwok Ho and Chris Robinson. 1996. "Asset Allocation via the First Exit Time *or* How to Avoid Outliving Your Money," working paper, Schulich School of Business, York University, forthcoming in *Review of Quantitative Finance and Accounting*.

Pape, Gordon. 1991. *Retiring Wealthy,* Prentice-Hall Canada.

Royal Trust. 1994. "Estate Planning, Wills and Executors."

———. 1994. "Planned Giving — Helping others while saving taxes."

———. 1996. "Understanding Trusts and their Uses."

chapter 18
Comprehensive Planning

LEARNING OBJECTIVES

Now that you have learned all the elements of personal financial planning, the final challenge is to integrate them into a comprehensive plan. Retirement planning involves all the elements at once and covers long time periods; so chapters 16 and 17 will have forced you to take a more comprehensive view. In this chapter we focus on the process of comprehensive planning, using the case study as the teaching method.

Our specific objectives are:

1. To outline a process of comprehensive financial planning.
2. To illustrate the comprehensive planning process by application to a practical case study.
3. To provide a model for reporting to a client.

COMPREHENSIVE PLANNING PROCESS

Different planners use different versions of this process, but the consistent link among them is that they organize the analysis of the client's affairs to conclude with a set of feasible recommendations for the client to follow in reaching family goals. Furthermore, you must realize that the steps are not completed sequentially in neat order. For example, a planner may collect what appears to be all the relevant information, only to discover something vital is missing at a later stage of the analysis. Then, a phone call to the client reveals not only the missing information, but also implies that the family goals are different than originally thought. The entire process has to be revisited to incorporate a change in both goals and the family situation. When we do a case study in a learning setting, like this textbook, some of this uncertainty and constant flux is removed, but in real life it will always occur.

Here, then, is a process to follow in financial planning for a family, in the order in which the steps should occur:

1. Determine the family's goals. Remember that goals require both a monetary value and a time.

2.   Collect information: assets, liabilities, insurance coverage, spending plans, occupations, education, ages of family members, etc.

3.   Diagnose the family's current situation. What are their indicated major areas of need? Prepare a balance sheet and last year's cash flow statement.

4.   Prepare a detailed analysis of their future financial position based on their current situation and projected cash flows. What is the shortfall, or does a policy of continuing as they have been reach their goals? This step involves the greatest part of the analysis. You create a pro forma spreadsheet of cash flows for a number of years in the future. The starting point is today, and the various goals will appear at the indicated future times. Common ending dates of a plan are the purchase of a house, retirement and death of surviving spouse.

     Implementation of recommendations can complicate this step. Some of the obvious recommendations to the family should be included in the analysis as if they have been done, unless the planner thinks the family will refuse to accept them. For example, if the family has been saving money outside RRSPs without using the tax deferral allowed by them, they should change that. The planner should accumulate future savings at the before-tax rate to reflect that in the plan. There is a fine line to tread here, since the client should also see what effect different recommendations will have on the future position of the family.

5.   List the feasible alternatives that allow the family to overcome the shortfall indicated by step 4, or to secure the plan in step 4 if it shows no shortfall. These alternatives are ones that could all be reasonable, and the plan must test them to find the best one. This contrasts with the obvious recommendations we mentioned in the previous step, where the advised action is the only reasonable one to take. A family could project a higher rate of savings, a different investment mix or a later date of retirement, for example. This step might involve more spreadsheets, identical in form to those in step 4, but with different values entered.

6.   Make recommendations for action. Which of the feasible alternatives in step 5 does the planner recommend? Why? Some of these recommendations will be specifically aimed at overcoming a shortfall, and some will be general advice that applies to the family regardless of the detailed plan chosen. For example, a specific action might be to buy a smaller house than planned, in order to avoid a potential shortfall when one spouse stays home for five years with dependent children. A more general piece of advice would be to make sure that both spouses have disability insurance covering at least 70% of income. This latter counsel applies whether or not they buy a house, and regardless of the size and cost of the house.

7.   Monitor the progress of the plan. How will you know if the plan is working as time goes by? Some monitoring mechanism and interim goals may be needed. For example, a family wants to retire in 10 years with 70% of its current pre-tax income. A plan covering 10 years needs regular evaluation to see if the situation still allows it to be achieved. After a few years, the family may find that circumstances — reduced saving, unexpected expenses, job loss — prevent it from achieving the goal of retirement in 10 years. Either a new plan that does reach the goal must be designed, or the family will have to delay retirement.

8.   Write an action plan or report to the client. We will discuss this point in a later section.

COMPREHENSIVE CASE ANALYSIS

The ideal educational experience at this stage in your learning would be a live subject family. You would interview them, collect the information, prepare a preliminary analysis, visit them again for more information and to review the analysis and then develop a complete plan. We can't do that in a textbook; so we simulate the process with case studies. Since a case study must contain all the information that interviews would provide, the first step in doing a case study is to read it thoroughly, and the second step is to determine the family's goals. After that, the steps proceed in the same way as already listed.

We use the following case study to illustrate the process. Read it carefully, and then continue with the step-by-step solution.

Before you go further, make sure that you have read the case thoroughly. If you can discipline yourself to attempt a complete solution before you read our solution, you will benefit even more from the rest of the chapter.

The Case of the Ottawa Doctor

Dr. Ricardo Maple is a specialist in Ottawa who treats federal politicians for unusual ailments common in that occupation (foot-in-mouth disease, digestive problems from eating their words, *etc.*).[1] He is 49 years old, and has a stable practice with gross billings of $200,000 last year. That provided a net income (*i.e.* after paying all office expenses, but before personal income tax and CPP) of $100,000 last year. He paid $1,612 in CPP premiums and $38,000 in income tax.

His wife, Yumei Willow, is 47 years old and is a nurse. She is not working outside the home, but she did work for her husband for a number of years part-time, and accumulated CPP credits worth about $1,000 in real dollars of annual pension when she reaches age 65. Her income during recent years has been negligible.

Their son, Oakley, is 23 years old and working as an actor in Vancouver. Acting is a risky occupation. So far, Yumei and Ricardo have had to help him with living expenses.

Their 16-year old daughter Sugar attends a local high school. She is a shy, good-natured girl of very limited intelligence. The teachers do not think she has the capability to complete high school, nor has she shown any aptitude for any non-academic activity or work. Her parents expect that she will continue to live with them as an adult and depend on them for support.

Ricardo owns their home in Ottawa outright, with no mortgage. The estimated market value is $350,000. Yumei owns a family cottage in the Gatineau Hills outside Ottawa. The estimated market value is $150,000, and it has a mortgage on it with monthly payments of $753.39 at 9%. The mortgage has 15 years left in the amortization, and they will renew it in a week's time for five years at 9%.

Ricardo owns a 10% interest in a commercial building occupied entirely by medical offices (including his own) and a pharmacy. The tenants are the co-owners. The partners pay rent to the partnership at market rates for the space they occupy. The revenue last year was $240,000, the operating expenses $140,000 and the capital cost allowance

---

[1] Ottawa physicians always do well because of the weak Constitution.

$40,000. The interest expense was $100,000 on a $1 million loan. In one year, when Ricardo is 50, the partnership must repay half the loan, or $50,000 each. Ten years later the remainder is due. The original cost of the building was $2,000,000, allocated $1,200,000 to land and $800,000 to building. The CCA rate is an average of 5%, straight-line. The market value is presently estimated at $1.8 million. Should he wish to borrow against his equity in the building for investment purposes, his bank would lend up to 50% of his share of the equity, at a rate of 10%. Partners are free to sell their share in the partnership, without giving up their tenancy rights. Finding a buyer would take anywhere from one to six months.

Ricardo has contributed $7,000 to his RRSP each year for a while now. The RRSP has accumulated to $90,000, all invested in GICs at Canada Trust. They have a joint chequing account at Canada Trust that has an average balance of $2,000. They owe $20,000 on their credit card (in addition to a small current balance) and the interest rate is 2% per month.

Ricardo inherited $40,000 from his maiden aunt Dora some years ago. He invested it in the following portfolio (current market value is $62,250, dividends last year were $1,300):

5000	units Trimark Indo-Pacific Canadian $ fund
1000	common shares Total Pet(roleum) NV
1000	common shares TransCanada Pipeline (TCPL)
1000	common shares Ulster Pet(roleum)

Ricardo and Yumei would like to retire at his age 60, maintaining the same standard of living. That is, they would continue to spend the same money on living expenses, but the financing charges and principal repayments would be finished for the commercial building and they would retire the mortgage on the cottage. Other than the contributions to the RRSP, everything goes to consumption: operating the house and cottage, food, clothing, health and hygiene, transportation (they have two cars), gifts, vacations and entertainment. Their expenses wouldn't drop in retirement as most people's would. Sugar will continue to live with them, and they want to do more travelling and take up some new activities.

Ricardo can sell his practice when he retires. The usual price is one year's billings. He would sell equipment, furnishings, etc., but the value is not enough to be worth including in the analysis. They have no wills. Ricardo says: "Why bother? I have all the money and it will go automatically to Yumei if I die first."

They have full replacement cost insurance and $1 million liability insurance on the house, the cottage and the cars. Ricardo carries substantial malpractice insurance. They have no life or disability insurance. All the members of the family are in good health and are non-smokers.

Required: Advise them on all aspects of their financial planning as appropriate.

A Suggested Solution

Step 1: Determine the Family's Goals

1. Provide reasonable and secure retirement income to maintain the same standard of living as at present, with retirement at Ricardo's age 60.

2. Provide for Sugar while her parents are alive and after their death. Actual amount that is "reasonable" to be defined.
3. Help Oakley? Inheritance for Oakley? We would make it a very low priority at best, or eliminate it altogether. Perhaps a residual after other goals are met.

Step 2: Collect Information

In the context of a case study, read the case. We organize the information in subsequent sections.

Step 3: Diagnose the Family's Current Situation

We will do this in several discrete steps. First, we identify the stage in the life cycle and which personal finance issues are likely to be most important for a family at that stage.

It isn't clear what stage they are in, because Sugar will be dependent for life. The stage is a combination of parents with dependent children, and parents without a dependent child heading towards retirement. They need to consider:

* risk management
* investment
* taxation
* retirement planning, including estate planning
* debt management, though it is not a big issue

To get more specific, we must organize and analyze the data in the case. The first step is a family balance sheet, in Table 18.1.

At this point we can see they should sell the shares and mutual fund units, netting $53,000, to pay off the credit card and part of the mortgage. This action follows the general rule of repaying debt that is not tax-deductible. We assume that they follow this advice and incorporate it into the plan at once. Assume the mortgage becomes $45,000, with the $3,000 surplus cash kept as emergency fund. They lose $1,300 p.a. in dividends but gain $4,800 in after-tax interest no longer paid and reduce income tax by about $300. Assume the cottage mortgage amortization is set for 10 years now (to get it paid off by

---

TABLE 18.1
Balance Sheet

ASSETS		DEBTS AND EQUITY	
Cash	$ 2,000	Debts:	
Shares, mutual fund[1]	53,000	Credit card	$ 20,000
RRSP	90,000	Cottage mortgage[2]	75,000
House	350,000	Med Bldg mortgage	100,000
Cottage	150,000	TOTAL DEBTS	195,000
Share of Bldg	180,000		
Equity in practice	200,000	EQUITY	830,000
TOTAL	$1,025,000	TOTAL	$1,025,000

[1] Market value is $62,250. Adjusted cost base is $40,000. Capital Gain $22,250. Taxable gain (.75 × $22,250) = $15,500. Tax at about 50% would be $7,750. Allow $1,500 disposition, rounding, for net of $53,000.

[2] PMT $753.39; N = 15 × 12 = 180. %i = $(1.045)^{1/6} - 1 = .73631$; PV = $75,000.

TABLE 18.2 Cash Flows and Forecast		
	Last Year	Next Year
Net income from practice	$100,000	$100,000
Dividends	1,300	0
Income tax	38,000	37,700
CPP	1,612	1,612
Take home income	$ 61,688	$ 60,688
Expenditures and Saving:		
Medical bldg	0	0
Cottage mortgage	9,041	6,793
RRSP	7,000	7,000
Credit card interest	4,800	0
Consumption	40,847	40,847
Added saving	0	6,048
Total	$ 61,688	$ 60,688

the desired retirement date). Thus, n = 120 and the new payment amount is $566.05. This action reduces annual spending by ($753.39 – $566.05) × 12 = $2,248.

Table 18.2 formats the cash flow information in the case. The consumption of $40,847 is calculated as the residual, since all the other expenditures are given. For the one year forecast shown in Table 18.2, we have assumed no inflation, since the effect of normal Canadian inflation rates would be negligible. The forecast of next year's income and spending assumes they sell the portfolio of shares, pay off the credit card debt and pay off part of the mortgage.

Note that with a small additional reduction in consumption, the family can reach $13,500 saving p.a., which is the RRSP limit. The additional $6,500 generates a tax refund of about $3,300, which can be saved each year at an after-tax rate of return. Of course, the build-up of a VISA loan suggests that they consumed more than $40,847 last year (or in some previous year).

Now we can make a more thorough diagnosis, before proceeding to a detailed plan:

1. Retirement and Investments: The family has a lot of property, but little other savings to provide retirement income. Another way to say this is that the family is illiquid and poorly-diversified.
2. Risk management: They have no life or disability insurance.
3. Taxation: The spouses have a great difference in marginal tax rates between them, both now and in retirement. Ricardo has a higher tax rate now than he will have in retirement. Income splitting and deferral strategies are indicated.
4. Estate Planning: How will they provide for Sugar? She will probably outlive them by a long period. Both pre-retirement planning for the amount needed and estate planning for how to transfer it to her hands are needed.
5. Debt management isn't a major issue. We assumed repayment of a lot of it as a first step in the diagnosis.

Step 4. Prepare a Detailed Analysis of Their Future Financial Position, Based on Their Current Situation, Projected Cash Flows and Goals   Recall our planning equation (1) in Chapter 16. We have to determine the value of k. We already have a first estimate of the value of W_0 (from the balance sheet), annual savings and the time to retirement. Our plan may change any or all of these parameters in order to meet their goals, or perhaps to show that the goal of early retirement on the desired income is unlikely to be met.

At this point the analysis becomes complicated. The student might be tempted to develop a spreadsheet that simply projects the adjusted savings rate of $13,048 (i.e. $7,000 + $6,048), plus the current RRSP balance. However, to draw any conclusions from such a spreadsheet, you must have the discount rate, k, to compare future savings with desired consumption in retirement. Determination of a discount rate requires analysis of marginal and average tax rates, and the family's investment policy. Since we have already said that the investment policy is wrong, our recommendations will change the discount rate. Accordingly, we analyze the various issues that affect the spreadsheet first.

■ Investments
The family has violated every rule of sound investment:

- undiversified: $680,000 of $1,025,000 total assets is in real estate. The equity portfolio is concentrated in only a few holdings in oil and gas and a Far East mutual fund.
- illiquid: real estate plus the practice is $880,000 of the total of $1,025,000.
- invested in non-tax-sheltered investments while also paying non-tax-deductible interest on consumer debt.
- invested in low return GICs instead of equity, even though they have a very long time horizon (the estate must provide for Sugar to the end of her life).
- exceeded the $60,000 CDIC insurance limit on the GICs at Canada Trust.

We have already resolved the undiversified equity portfolio by selling it to repay consumer debt. In addition, we recommend that the doctor sell the medical building and invest the net proceeds (after his share of the loan) in a diversified equity portfolio. He wouldn't be able to do this fast enough to repay the rest of the cottage mortgage with the proceeds at this renewal date; so we leave the mortgage to be paid off over 10 years as a simplification of the spreadsheet analysis. However, the family should take only a one or two year mortgage (or an open mortgage) and repay the rest of it as soon as possible, since the interest is not tax-deductible.

For the formal analysis, we assume he nets $60,000 after selling costs and repaying the debt. We ignore the tax effects, which would be small and very complex.[2] Selling the building is both better financial management, because of the lack of diversification, and simpler from a planning point of view. Real estate is a high return, high risk

---

[2] For those who know more tax than this textbook covers, the issues to be resolved include original cost, the split between land and building, capital gain/loss on the land portion and capital gain or terminal loss on the building portion. It seems he would have some loss to claim against other income, but the amount is not large enough to affect the planning materially.

investment, just like equity, but the concentration in one property makes it much riskier without either liquidity or the opportunity to diversify. Even after selling the building, the family will have half its assets in real estate.

The lack of liquidity is not important now. The sale of the building improves liquidity, and in any case a retirement plan is for the long run, during which time they can arrange to sell property in an orderly manner.

We have already dealt with the issue of holding taxable assets and non-tax-deductible debt at the same time.

The RRSP should be invested in equity at least partly, and probably completely. If the family refuses to change its investment policy, it must at least move $30,000 from Canada Trust GICs into something else, since it is over the CDIC limit.

We will have more to say about investments and taxes in a minute, but this discussion leads to using an equity discount rate during the savings accumulation period. A reasonable sensitivity analysis would use a GIC rate as an alternative. If this rate were good enough to reach their goals, then they could take this lower risk alternative.

■ Income Tax

Dr. Maple is in the top tax bracket now, and doesn't need all the income. He must contribute the maximum to an RRSP, which he isn't currently doing, and pay off all consumer debt. Another basic deferral mechanism is to invest in equity and hold it, deferring capital gains tax.

Yumei has no taxable income and expects only $1,000 p.a. in retirement. Unfortunately, Ricardo has not contributed to a spousal RRSP so far. All future contributions must be to a spousal RRSP, which would reduce the joint tax burden in retirement. In addition, he should use up his carryforwards (he has contributed only $7,000 p.a., while the limit is now $13,500). The limits in previous years have been less; so let us assume that he can contribute a total of $25,000 to a spousal account for Yumei. The remaining $35,000 from the sale of the building goes into an unsheltered equity mutual fund in Ricardo's name.

The effect of all this on the tax rates we use in the plan is as follows. His tax rate pre-retirement is the top one — use 50% for simplicity. Most of his saving will be pre-tax in the RRSP, but some will be after-tax. Yumei's rate pre-retirement is irrelevant, since she has no unsheltered savings.

In retirement they want an income of about $40,847 in real, after-tax dollars. A steady diet of contributions to a spousal RRSP plus splitting CPP in retirement allows them to reduce their tax rate somewhat, though we cannot be precise. If they take our advice and contribute as much as possible to Yumei's spousal RRSP, she accumulates about $225,000 (see Table 18.6). If we spread this as an annuity over 35 years, the annual real amount before tax is $15,519. In addition, by splitting CPP with Ricardo, she gets over $4,000 more. If Yumei receives $20,000 income, she pays tax of 14%, for an after-tax income of $17,200. If Ricardo receives $30,000 income, he pays an average tax rate of 19%, for a net of $24,300. This yields a family income of $41,500 in real before-tax dollars. Leaving a bit of room for error, we can plan for $50,000 p.a. required before-tax income.

The effect of the income-splitting is very evident in this case. If they continue to accumulate all the savings in Ricardo's name, they will pay tax on most of the income in his name. On Table 16.1, they would then be in the right-hand column. We can see that after-tax income from $55,000 × (1 − .26) = $40,700. Therefore, without splitting their income, they need about $5,000 more per year in retirement income to have the same standard of living.

■ Discount Rates

We will do the analysis for two different investment assumptions: all in equity, or all in T-bills. Rounding off the mean rates of return from Appendix E, we see a Canadian equity fund might provide 6% p.a. and T-bills 2% (very similar rate to GICs) in real terms. Ricardo's marginal tax rate is about 50% now and their joint average tax rate will be 27% in retirement. Yumei's rate is irrelevant, since she has no taxable income. The pre-tax discount rates apply to the savings inside the RRSPs. We will estimate the pre-tax income required to fund the desired consumption level in retirement, and then discount that income at the pre-tax rate. The after-tax rate will apply to the compounding of the amount in the unsheltered mutual fund. The value of the medical practice is after-tax, but constant in real $.

If Ricardo invests the unsheltered portion in an equity mutual fund, the effective tax rate will be lower than 50%, because of the dividend tax credit, the capital gains rate and the deferral of capital gains tax until the gains are realized. Combining this all with considerable changes in taxation of dividends every few years, it is very hard to predict a rate. The upper bound is 36%, which is roughly the 1996 rate for Ricardo's tax bracket for dividends. If we used this rate, we would be assuming that all the income is received as dividends. We use 1/3 as a slightly lower rate, allowing for some capital gains and deferral, but it is still quite conservative. This yields an after-tax discount rate of 4%. The tax rate on interest income is 50%; so the after-tax T-bill discount rate is 1%.

■ Risk Management

Neither Yumei nor Ricardo carries any life or disability insurance. All the property and liability risks are covered. Their principal risk is loss of Ricardo's income due to illness or disability. A lower-cost risk is the risk of the loss of the household services Yumei provides, due to death or disability. There is no insurable risk related to Sugar, since she has no income and they are planning to provide for her for her lifetime anyway.

For the purposes of this case, we use a rough approximation of the required insurance. Ricardo's death would reduce expenses, and would also generate survivor benefits from CPP. He brings home $62,000 after tax, and we assume his death would leave Sugar and Yumei with a shortfall of $52,000 in after-tax income for 10 years. From that, they would save for retirement, just as they would if he were alive and earning. For disability, we will allow for 60% or $60,000 of income, which would be after-tax.

For Yumei, life insurance is very much a matter of family preference. If she dies, Sugar might do some of what her mother now does in the household. On the other hand, perhaps they will wish to hire a housekeeper. We assume that they decide to provide for the equivalent of $20,000 p.a. for 10 years, while recognizing that there is no established method to calculate this figure. Yumei cannot get disability insurance, because she has no income.

The planner must also consider the cost of the insurance, which must be added to the budget. Insurance rates vary for individuals, but the best rates are usually group term insurance, if the person qualifies. Most professions, including medicine and nursing, have group plans for all their registered members and their spouses. When the planner asked

TABLE 18.3
Insurance Needs

Insurance	Annual Amount	Present Value at 2%, 10 yrs.	Rounded Value	Cost
Life, Ricardo	$52,000	$467,000	$450,000	$1,350
Life, Yumei	20,000	180,000	175,000	294
Disability, Ricardo	60,000			1,740
Total Cost				$3,384

TABLE 18.4
Revised Balance Sheet

ASSETS		DEBTS AND EQUITY	
Cash	$ 5,000	Debts:	
Mutual fund, Ricardo	35,000		
RRSP: Ricardo	90,000	Cottage mortgage	$ 45,000
RRSP: Yumei	25,000		
House	350,000		
Cottage	150,000		
Equity in practice	200,000	Equity	810,000
TOTAL	$855,000	TOTAL	$855,000

Ricardo about this, he provided a schedule of insurance rates from the Ontario Medical Association that both he and his wife can obtain. One year renewable term insurance for him is now $75 per unit of $25,000, and $42 for her. Disability insurance is on a reducing scale depending on the exclusion period: 30 days, 3.5% of the insured income; 90 days, 2.9%; 180 days, 2.75%. Given their strong financial position after they pay off the credit card debt, the planner recommends that a 90 day exclusion period is reasonable.

Since these are after-tax amounts, we need an after-tax discount rate, and it is in real dollars, because we will use today's net income without inflation adjustment. Table 18.3 summarizes the calculation: $450,000 life insurance for Ricardo; $175,000 life insurance for Yumei; $60,000 disability for Ricardo. The premiums total $3,384 for the first year. Premiums will increase in real dollars as they age, but the face value required can be reduced, because the needs will decrease.

■ Retirement Planning: How Much Have They Got?

Now we can put the pieces together. First, we present a revised balance sheet in Table 18.4 that incorporates the initial recommendations, including sale of the medical building.

In addition, they will earn income on the current investments, save more in the future, and receive Seniors Benefit in retirement. We assume that the value of the practice remains constant in real dollars. There should be no tax implications on its sale, because it is eligible for the capital gains exemption on a small business.

TABLE 18.5
Revised Budget

	Last Year	Budget
Net income from practice	$100,000	$100,000
Dividends	1,300	0
Income tax	38,000	34,450
CPP	1,612	1,612
Take home income	$ 61,688	$ 63,938
Expenditures and Saving:		
Insurance		3,384
Cottage mortgage	9,041	6,793
RRSP	7,000	13,500
Credit card interest	4,800	0
Consumption	40,847	40,847
Total Expenditures	$ 61,688	$ 64,524

We will prepare a revised budget for next year that incorporates the changes already made by paying off debt, includes an additional tax reduction from increased RRSP contributions and additional expenses for the recommended life and disability insurance (see Table 18.5). The increase in RRSP contributions by $6,500 provides a tax reduction of $3,250 at the assumed marginal tax rate of 50%. We are making a strong assumption about future RRSP contribution limits here. The 1996 budget reduced the limit, with eventual future increases. We cannot predict what the actual deduction limits will be for the next 10 years because the rules are changed almost every year, but the current limit of $13,500 seems a reasonable minimum expectation. The budget is out of balance by $586 which is too small an error to matter, given the inevitable imprecision of forecasting a whole year's cash flows.

Table 18.6 shows the details of the savings accumulation. The money in the RRSPs accumulates before-tax, and the two columns show the values at retirement in real dollars, for 2% (invested in T-bills) and 6% (invested in equities). The value of the practice stays the same in real after-tax dollars, and the mutual fund accumulates at 2% after-tax (equity investment). All the amounts on the balance sheet have 11 years to compound. The added saving of $13,500 p.a. lasts only 10 years, since this year's contribution is included in the balance sheet (or, to look at it another way, we follow the usual convention of assuming all payments occur at year-end).

Since some values are before-tax and others are after-tax, they cannot be added. The consumption required in retirement will be calculated in before-tax dollars; so we convert all the after-tax amounts into before-tax dollars, to make the two comparable. The withdrawals from the RRSPs will be fully taxable; so those funds are already in before-tax dollars. The medical practice amount will not be taxed and hence it is already in after-tax dollars. The amounts originally placed in the unsheltered mutual fund were saved after-tax, and the income was taxed. Therefore, it is in after-tax dollars. As these after-tax amounts are liquidated to provide income in retirement, however, the payments

TABLE 18.6
Savings Accumulation at Date of Retirement in Real Dollars

	Value Now	Years	Discount Rate	
			Equity	T-bill
Before-tax amounts:			6%	2%
RRSP: Ricardo	$ 90,000	11	$170,847	$111,904
RRSP: Yumei	25,000	11	47,457	31,084
RRSP: annual contributions	13,500	10	177,941	147,821
A. Total before-tax			397,245	290,809
After-tax amounts:			2%	1%
Mutual fund: Ricardo	35,000	11	43,518	39,048
Medical practice	200,000	11	200,000	200,000
Total after-tax			243,518	239,048
B. Gross-up after-tax @ 20% average rate (i.e. (after-tax amount)/(1 − .2))			304,398	298,810
Total before-tax = A + B			$701,643	$589,619

will be partly the after-tax principal, and partly the subsequent taxable income on them. Calculating the correct tax rate on this blended stream of tax-free principal and taxed earnings is too complex for the level of accuracy required, and we assume that a tax rate of 20%, which is lower than the average rate they will pay in retirement, is reasonable. Thus, we finally arrive at before-tax savings accumulations in real dollars of $701,643 (invested in equities) or $589,619 (invested in T-bills or GICs). We must remember that there is a somewhat higher variability around the equity value than around the T-bill value.

Now we turn to calculating how much they need to fund their retirement.

■ Retirement Planning: How Much Will They Need?

Return to the cash flow statement, where the right-hand column shows a forecast after paying off some of the debts. The usual rule of thumb is that retirement income needs to be 70% of pre-retirement income. We have drawn up a detailed cash flow that shows they are now consuming about $40,847 p.a. The gross is much larger because of savings and mortgage payments. They will not be able to go below $40,847, because Sugar will continue to live with them, and the other expenses that will disappear in retirement are already accounted for. We have already calculated that $40,847 after-tax is about $50,000 before-tax. When one parent dies expenses will reduce. When both parents are gone, Sugar should need less. On the other hand, with one parent or both parents gone, the average tax rate will rise somewhat (fewer tax credits, perhaps less effective income-split). Sugar should be able to sell the family home and live in a smaller home, if there isn't enough money left. As a reasonable approximation, assume Yumei and Sugar would require $45,000 before-tax, and Sugar $40,000.

How long will they need these amounts? From his age 60, Ricardo would have a 10% chance of living to 91. Yumei would be 58 at retirement, and she would have a

10% chance of living to 95. Sugar would be 27 when her parents retire. She would have a 10% chance of living to 95. We plan for both Sugar and Yumei to live to 96.

What government pensions will they get?

- Full CPP for Ricardo. $8,725. We assume he starts receiving it at 65 and uses other assets for income until that age. Since they have tax-paid investments, this is the most tax-efficient way to structure the retirement.
- CPP of $1,000 for Yumei at age 65.
- They split the CPP equally. For Ricardo's ages 65 and 66, they each receive $4,363. When Yumei turns 65, they each receive $4,863. When Ricardo dies, Yumei receives a 60% survivor's pension plus her own, for a total of $7,781.
- The 1996 federal budget provided for the OAS and GIS to be replaced by the Seniors' Benefit. This system will apply to all those who retire after 2001, but it is rather hard to be precise in planning for it, since there is neither experience nor legislation. Under the proposed rules, we make the following rough estimates. When Ricardo reaches 65, he is eligible for $2,350. Estimating what Sugar will qualify for is a shot in the dark! For the plan, we assume they and Sugar qualify for $4,000 p.a. for every year after Yumei turns 65 until Sugar dies.

The details of how much they need in retirement are summarized in Table 18.7.

■ Retirement Planning: How Much Is the Shortfall?

We can see from the totals on Tables 18.6 and 18.7 that if the family invests wholly in low-risk interest-bearing investments, the shortfall is so large as to be unmanageable — over $800,000. We assume, therefore, that they will invest primarily in equities. In that case the plan projects a surplus of $701,643 − $651,949 = $49,694. We must recognize that this number is much more imprecise than it appears. Even a 1% difference in the rate of return realized on their investments over the time frame of the plan would change it by more than $100,000. Nonetheless, the family has to plan under uncertainty, and in Step 5 we turn to the possible actions they could take to ensure this plan succeeds.

Step 5 List the Feasible Alternatives   This step could also be entitled: How do they get from here to there? In this case, we are trying to ensure that if they don't make a 6% real rate of return, they will nonetheless enjoy a comfortable retirement.

1. Save more during the next ten years. This saving will have to take place outside the RRSP, and hence will accumulate at only 2%, the after-tax rate. For example, annual saving of $4,700 accumulates to $51,460. This is certainly feasible, taken from consumption of $41,000 p.a. with no mortgage included in that amount, and it doubles the projected surplus.
2. Reduce planned spending in retirement. This requires no action now. Reducing spending in retirement is a flexible choice, but it presupposes there is room to reduce spending. If the other factors changed against them, they might not have enough slack.
3. Retire later. This increases the saving and reduces the present value of retirement costs that must be funded. This is a very flexible option, because as long as Ricardo is able to continue working, it can be used or not, depending on the

TABLE 18.7
How Much Will They Need in Real Before-tax Dollars?

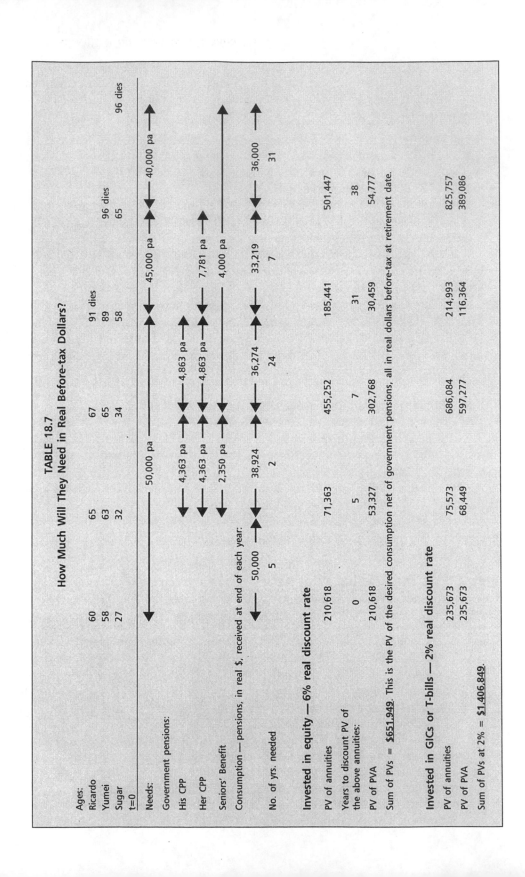

	t=0			(Ricardo 91 dies)	(Yumei 96 dies)	(Sugar 96 dies)
Ages:						
Ricardo	60	65	67	91 dies		
Yumei	58	63	65	89	96 dies	
Sugar	27	32	34	58	65	96 dies

Needs:	50,000 pa →			45,000 pa	40,000 pa	
Government pensions:						
His CPP			4,363 pa	4,863 pa		
Her CPP			4,363 pa	4,863 pa	7,781 pa	
Seniors' Benefit			2,350 pa		4,000 pa	
Consumption — pensions, in real $, received at end of each year:	50,000	38,924	36,274	33,219	36,000	
No. of yrs. needed	5	2	24	7	31	

Invested in equity — 6% real discount rate

PV of annuities	210,618	71,363	455,252	185,441	501,447
Years to discount PV of the above annuities:	0	5	7	31	38
PV of PVA	210,618	53,327	302,768	30,459	54,777

Sum of PVs = <u>$651,949</u>. This is the PV of the desired consumption net of government pensions, all in real dollars before-tax at retirement date.

Invested in GICs or T-bills — 2% real discount rate

PV of annuities	235,673	75,573	686,084	214,993	825,757
PV of PVA	235,673	68,449	597,277	116,364	389,086

Sum of PVs at 2% = <u>$1,406,849.</u>

situation as he gets close to 60. For a quick way to check feasibility, adjust only the savings components. Assume he works to age 62, with the same values otherwise. The savings accumulate to $779,625, which provides a substantial margin for errors, given that this must provide for fewer years of retirement as well.[3]

4.   Sell one property when necessary. This provides cash and reduces expenses considerably. If the cottage is suitable for year-round living and they are comfortable with that option, the sale of the house provides a very large contribution. This and the next option involve costs in selling, land transfer tax, etc., but the proceeds are not taxable. Sale of the cottage also puts the money into Yumei's hands, and she will pay tax at a lower rate on the investment income.

5.   Sell the house and move into a cheaper one, or a condominium. This action also provides cash, and will probably reduce expenses somewhat. A good house is available in Ottawa for much less than $350,000.

6.   Yumei could return to work. This action would generate income at a low tax rate, increase the cash available for saving and also increase her CPP in retirement. Sugar is now old enough for her mother to do this. However, this option does involve a significant change in their lifestyle. Yumei may not wish to do so, or she may be unable to find work or unqualified, since she has been out of the work force for a long time.

Step 6. Make Recommendations for Action   If the family remains invested in equities, then it has the luxury of being able to choose among several feasible plans to secure its retirement. The safest plan is to increase saving during the next 10 years, because that allows them more slack if something else goes wrong. We do not recommend that Yumei return to work unless she wishes to, since there are good alternatives available to fund the retirement plan. Therefore, our principal recommendations are:

- Put the maximum amount allowable into a spousal RRSP for Yumei every year, and make the deposit as early in the year as possible. The RRSP should be invested fully in equity.
- Save an additional amount every year and deposit it into equity mutual funds. The goal should be $4,700 for next year, and increasing by inflation every year thereafter.
- Invest in equities generally, because lower rates of return will make any retirement plan infeasible.

The family may choose to rely on retiring later, spending less in retirement or selling the house or cottage to help finance retirement. These actions will only be sufficient if there is saving currently, but they can replace part of our main recommendations. However, regardless of which option or combination of options they choose, they should adopt the following recommendations.

---

[3] We leave it to the student to verify that adding two more years of savings accumulation to Table 18.6 gives this result.

1. Pay off non-tax-deductible debt. Pay the credit card first, because it has the highest interest rate. Next, reduce the mortgage on the cottage at the renewal date. Sell the securities outside the RRSP to provide the cash.

2. Take an open mortgage on the cottage at the next renewal to allow faster repayment as savings continue to accumulate. Make the RRSP deposits first, but use all saving above the RRSP limit to pay off the mortgage first.

3. Write wills for both parents. Ricardo's money will not all go to Yumei under Ontario law.

4. Estate planning generally. This is very important because Yumei has almost no income of her own, and they need to provide for Sugar, who is apparently going to be dependent on them throughout her lifetime. Their wills should contain the following provisions:

    *   Testamentary trust for Yumei — life income on property with right to encroach on the capital. The balance then goes into trust for Sugar after both parents are dead. The will should name trustees for Sugar.
    *   The trust for Sugar ends on her death, with the balance passing to Oakley if he is still alive.
    *   The residual left after Ricardo and Yumei die should go to Oakley if Sugar predeceases him.

    In addition, they should take the following estate planning actions:

    *   Put all assets possible into joint ownership to reduce probate fees. This also makes it easier for the surviving spouse to make decisions and access cash before the estate is wound up. At the very least, the house and cottage should be jointly-owned.
    *   Name the other parent as beneficiary on insurance policies and RRSPs. When one dies, change beneficiary designation to Sugar. These steps reduce probate fees.
    *   A complex planning technique would be a trust now for Sugar, or shortly before they retire. The parents would be the trustees. It should be possible to structure it to split income with her, thus reducing taxes. This will be most useful after one parent dies, since if the survivor inherits all the income-producing assets, his or her tax rate will rise. An alternative would be to leave part of their estate to her on the death of either one, rather than when both are deceased. The details of how to accomplish this estate planning action are beyond the scope of this book.
    *   The student might be tempted to put the cottage in Sugar's name to reduce capital gains taxes on its subsequent disposition. If she is not mentally competent to manage the estate, then this step creates other problems, and we do not recommend it.

5. Investments:
    *   Invest the RRSPs in equity. We assumed they do so in the numerical analysis. If they insist on leaving it in GICs, they need more than one institution to stay within CDIC coverage limits.
    *   If they ignore Recommendation #1 and keep the securities, at least they should diversify. Perhaps a well-diversified mutual fund.

- Sell the medical building interest. The family's investments are too concentrated in real estate, which is undiversified and too risky. Use the proceeds first to pay off the rest of the cottage mortgage, then to deposit to Yumei's spousal RRSP using Ricardo's unused contribution room carried forward. Make the RRSP deposits over more than one year to avoid alternative minimum tax, if necessary. The sale of the building interest, with its capital loss, will offset the capital gains on the sale of securities (this detail is not explicitly incorporated in the numerical analysis).

6. Risk management:
   - $450,000 term life insurance for Ricardo with the Ontario Medical Association plan. Cost in first year: $1,350.
   - $175,000 term life insurance for Yumei with the Ontario Medical Association plan. Cost in first year: $294.
   - $60,000 annual disability insurance for Ricardo with the Ontario Medical Association plan. Cost in first year: $1,740. Insurance should have a 90 day exclusion period and provide full coverage if he is unable to work as a physician.

7. Taxes:
   - All savings should go into RRSPs, up to the $13,500 limit. Use a spousal RRSP, to put income into Yumei's hands.
   - If they don't accept the recommendation to sell the medical building, borrow more on the equity in medical building and use the proceeds to pay off the mortgage on the cottage. This transaction will require careful structuring to make sure the interest is tax-deductible.
   - When they do retire, split the CPP between them to increase income in Yumei's hands.

Step 7. Monitoring the Plan

Ricardo and Yumei are in a much better situation than most people, and monitoring need not be a frequent activity. Nonetheless, the planner should try to get them to agree to return in six months to a year, in order to confirm that they have taken the following actions:

- No overdue credit card balance or other consumer debt, other than the cottage mortgage.
- Cottage on an open mortgage, and the balance substantially reduced.
- Sold the medical building.
- Started a spousal RRSP for Yumei, with all of Ricardo's contributions going into it.
- All investments in well-diversified equity mutual funds.
- Life insurance for Ricardo and Yumei, and disability insurance for Ricardo
- Wills for both of them.

Once these steps are completed, it is simply a matter of seeing how the savings accumulate. Every year or two, the planner needs updated balance sheets and cash flows to see if the initial plan is still valid. As they approach their desired retirement date, the uncertainty will lessen and they can make more precise decisions then.

This concludes the comprehensive case analysis. However, you would not report to the client in quite the same format, and we turn briefly to that topic now.

WRITING A REPORT

Our discussion of the case study included various asides as part of the learning process, and these would not be included in the report. The field of financial planning is still developing, and there is no standardized format for how to report to a client. Various organizations and professional bodies use their own formats for this important part of the process. We do not presume to have a better format, nor do we wish to recommend any one format. A good report will always follow one key rule of writing:

■ Place the Most Important Things First

This rule implies many things. A summary of the problem and the recommended solution must appear first, and it should be brief. In business reports, this is usually called the executive summary. The client must know what you are advising him or her to do. We suggest that the following ordering of the different elements we have already written is suitable.

- Summary of the client's goals and the planner's major recommendations to meet those goals.
- Alternative actions the planner analyzed.
- Detailed recommendations for action by the client. This section will include the recommendations in #1, plus more detail and other recommendations that the client should follow, regardless which alternative is chosen to try to meet the goals.
- Statement of the basic information, restatement of the client's goals and the planner's diagnosis of the situation.
- Analysis of the current situation and how to move towards the goals. This section involves most of the detailed numerical work.
- Monitoring the plan. Times and benchmarks to be achieved. This may be fairly general, as in our plan, or quite specific.

Note that the conclusion is essentially the first item in the report. Reports should not be murder mysteries — the reader should know the answer from the start. While every report should be designed to meet the needs of the particular situation, this principle of putting the answer first must never be forgotten. Of course, the planner writes it last, after all the other work is done.

As a final step, we provide a short summary as the first item in the report to Ricardo Maple and Yumei Willow (see Figure 18.1). This is the part that they read first, and it sets the tone for the rest of the report.

SUMMARY

Comprehensive planning involves eight steps:

- Determine the family's goals.
- Collect all the relevant information.
- Diagnose the current situation.
- Prepare a detailed analysis of how they can move from the current situation to meet their goals.
- Determine feasible alternatives to realize the plan prepared in step 4. If there is a shortfall, what means are available to overcome it? If there appears to be no shortfall,

---

FIGURE 18.1
Financial Plan for Ricardo Maple and Yumei Willow
Executive Summary

You wish to retire when Ricardo reaches age 60 and enjoy the same level of spending as at present. You also wish to provide for your dependent daughter Sugar for the rest of her life. You have assets worth just over $1 million, exclusive of personal and household items and cars. Ricardo's net income is presently $100,000 p.a. from his medical practice.

Your goals are quite feasible, and several different options are available to meet them. My principal recommendations are:

- Put the maximum amount allowable into a spousal RRSP for Yumei every year, and make the deposit as early in the year as possible. The RRSP should be invested fully in equity.
- Save an additional amount every year and deposit it into equity mutual funds. The goal should be $4,700 for next year, and increasing by inflation every year thereafter.
- Invest in equities generally, because the lower rates of return on GICs or similar instruments will make any retirement plan infeasible.

Alternative plans could include selling one of your residential properties, retiring two years later, planning to spend less in retirement or part or full-time work outside the home for Yumei. In addition, I have a number of other important recommendations for actions with respect to your investments, insurance coverage, income taxes, debt management and estate planning. The details of all these, and the analysis underlying them, are in the remainder of this report.

---

how can they be sure it will work? Sometimes, there may be only one feasible alternative. If so, the analysis should show that only one meets the goals.

- Provide detailed action recommendations. There are two types. One is the overall plan or major alternative chosen. The second type of recommendation is an action that the family should take no matter which alternative it chooses.
- Provide a monitoring schedule to make sure the plan unfolds properly.
- Write the results of your work in a report to the client.

In this chapter, we illustrated this process by going through a comprehensive case study in detail. While the exact method may vary with the situation, the principles remain the same.

CASE STUDIES

1. **MAKING ENDS MEET IN SMALL TOWN ONTARIO**

Abzal and Carmina are planning for a big change in their financial situation as their two young children race around the backyard pelting each other with snowballs in January 1997. Loris is 7, in grade two, and Rosa is 5, in kindergarten. In September Rosa will be in school all day, and she and her brother will be in the school daycare. Abzal and Carmina do not plan to have any more children. They are both 30 years old.

This change will allow Carmina to work more than the part-time hours she has done for the last year, although daycare fees for before and after school, and lunch, are $300/month, per child. She thinks she can earn about $22,000 p.a., taking the summer off to be with the children. She will have to pay UI premiums of 3%, and CPP, and her taxes will increase, although $4,000 of the daycare fees is deductible from her income. Aside from that deduction from taxable income, she will have a tax credit of about $1,200.

They live in a rented house in Hanover, a town several hours northwest of Toronto. Abzal is foreman of a maintenance crew for the county government, and Carmina has been working part-time in a grocery store. Their T4 income summaries for 1996 are shown in Table 1. Now they want to plan to buy a house of their own. They want a three bedroom, detached house with a modest lot and a dry basement. They are both good at repairs, carpentry, etc., and they would take a house that requires lots of work. They have seen houses that fit their needs selling for about $85,000.

Summary of 1996 Income from T4 Slips

	Abzal	Carmina
Gross income	$36,000	$12,000
Deductions:		
Unemployment insurance premium	1,080	
Canada Pension Plan	893	238
Long-term disability insurance	200	
Extended health care and drugs, dental care	700	
Income tax	8,500	1,400

The big question on their minds is whether they can afford to buy a house. They pay $700/month rent now for a smaller house, but that includes taxes and maintenance. If they own a house, their utilities would increase from $200 to $300 per month, and they would have to pay taxes of $1,200 p.a. Even with their skills, maintenance would cost another $1,000 p.a., and there is always the risk of something serious happening that isn't covered by insurance. A reasonable insurance package on the house costs another $800 p.a. In addition, the legal and moving costs will add up to about $1,500. House prices do not change quickly in their area, and they expect they would continue to rise at about the current rate of inflation, or 2%, for some years.

"We can't forget about retirement, either," says Carmina firmly. "Nobody is going to look after us if we don't look after ourselves first. You have about $5,000 in your RRSP, but you wouldn't have even that if I didn't keep nagging you to put some away. At least it is safe in bank term deposits. And I have that $10,000 that Aunt Annie left to me invested in five year GICs at Victoria and Grey Trust."

They also have $15,000 in a joint savings account that is their house savings account. They have $500 in a chequing account, and no debts. They do not use credit cards. They have a 10 year old station wagon that is getting close to the end of its useful life. They have their eye on a used car dealer who occasionally has minivans for about $12,000, including taxes. Last year they deposited $800 in Abzal's RRSP and $2,000 in the house account.

"We need a family vacation, too," insists Abzal. "We haven't had much holiday since the kids were born. You know you need to see some place more exciting than

Hanover's main street, Carmina. We should plan a trip to the west coast of Vancouver Island, to Clayquot Sound, to see the rain forest before the loggers strip it all. I know it would cost about $5,000 for three weeks, but it would be worth it."

"How soon do you want to buy a house?" asks the financial planner.

"Within five years," says Carmina, and Abzal adds, "Sooner, if we can."

"Where does all the money go?" wonders Carmina. "I do the food shopping; so I know that we spend about $260 week on food and some of the other supplies, like soap and food for Fuzzball (the family cat)."

"The car cost a little over $4,500 last year, with that big bill for the transmission included," says Abzal. "But there are clothes, and toys and games for the kids, and the cable TV bill, and the telephone and it just seems to go on and on."

Required:
You are the expert financial planner at the kitchen table with them. Develop a plan to meet their goals, or advise them what is beyond their reach. You may rest assured that they have estimated and reported numbers fairly accurately, though of course they didn't provide details of all their expenses. If you think anything important is missing, that means it doesn't exist. For example, they didn't mention inheritance possibilities, because they aren't likely to receive any material bequests. They have no tax refunds coming.

2. **THE SOBERING STORY OF THE SEVERED CIVIL SERVANT**
Rommie Bhutani is a 48 year old civil engineer who has been working for the Ministry of Government Services in Ontario as a project manager for 15 years. Mike d'Knife has cut his position, and he will shortly have to leave. We take up our story at the start of 1997, as Rommie and his wife Rachel Benlolo, age 47, are assessing their financial situation.

"At least I get some money to help adjust," says Rommie. He receives a severance package of $80,000 in 1997, which is taxable. He can roll $2,000 times years of service into an RRSP in addition to the usual limit. Other than tax, nothing is deducted from the severance payment. He has pension credits for his 15 years of service. The pension is a defined benefit plan, and leaving the money in it would be unwise, since the pension will be determined on best five years income while with the Ministry, and inflation will erode that value considerably before he retires. He can place the commuted value of the pension, $120,000, in a locked-in RRSP.

Rachel started working as a teacher only four years ago, one of the few hired that year by her Board. She hasn't received a layoff notice, but her job is definitely at risk, and she would receive no severance, just 16 weeks notice. The commuted value of her pension is currently $23,000, which could also be transferred to a locked-in RRSP. If she were able to maintain a job as a teacher anywhere in Ontario, her pension would amount to about $18,000 p.a. in today's dollars, after 22 years of service.

Their T4 income summaries are shown in Table 1. They contributed $1,600 to Rachel's RRSP and $3,000 to Rommie's RRSP for 1996. They have about $20,000 of unused contribution room from past years relating to Rommie's income. Rommie has a $50,000 term life insurance policy through the engineer's association, costing $150 p.a. He put $10,000 into the mutual fund last year.

Summary of 1996 Income from T4 Slips

	Rachel	Rommie
Gross income	$36,000	$80,000
Deductions:		
Unemployment insurance premium	1,080	1,271
Canada Pension Plan	893	893
Long-term disability insurance	200	500
Income tax	7,300	26,000
Registered pension plan	2,675	4,100
Union dues	350	0

"I don't know what is going to happen with my career, now," sighs Rommie. "There aren't many jobs in Canada for project managers, and I don't want to travel like a gypsy doing one or two year contracts all over the world. I know I can get about $20,000 a year in business doing contract work for my various client Ministries. They are laying off a lot of engineers, but they still need jobs supervised. No benefits, though. I could look for business elsewhere too, because I have a wide variety of experience. I know a fellow who is making $70,000 a year now doing that, after expenses. There are lots of unemployed engineers out there, though, and the competition is getting tougher. I always figured we would retire early, but now 65 looks more realistic."

If he did work for himself, he would have to pay Canada Pension contributions for 1997, but there would be no other deductions.

Rachel says, "We do have other assets. Our house is worth about $450,000, and it is a big, new, four-bedroom executive house with a lovely family room and a study. Rommie still has a defined contribution pension plan at the company where he worked before the government, and it is now worth $80,000. I have $8,000 in my RRSP and he has $42,000 in his, all invested in GICs at Royal Trust. Rommie also has $100,000 in a Far East mutual fund that has done very well for us in the last few years. Rommie's BMW is only three years old, and my Audi is new last fall. We pay off our credit card balance every month — it is $4,000 this month. We do have a three year car loan of about $10,000 on the Audi. I don't know how much the mortgage on the house is, but the payment is $1,500 per month at a rate of 8-3/4%, and it has eight more years on the amortization schedule."

They have two children. Their daughter, Nadia, is in an MBA programme and they aren't providing significant support once she graduates in the spring. Their son, Christopher, is only 15 and lives at home. They would like to help him with a first university degree, since he wants to become an engineer like his father and his grandmother.

"We have to provide for our retirement, because no one else is going to do it," says Rachel. "Look what the government is doing to our jobs. We've been living very well, and I guess that will have to change some, but we aren't sure how much. I think we could live in retirement on half the amount that we have been spending."

Rommie isn't so sure that much change is needed. He is still optimistic that they can buy a cottage in a few years. They want just a cheap one that needs lots of work, which they are good at doing. "Perhaps $80,000, not in the most popular areas. That would give us a place to enjoy with the grandchildren you're going to have," he says, only half-jokingly, as he looks to Christopher, who has just dropped in on the conversation at the kitchen table.

Required:

You are the expert financial planner at the kitchen table with them. Develop a complete plan.

3. Laura Ng, 35 years old, is a lawyer in the office of the Attorney General of Alberta. Her husband, Stephen Ng, 32 years old, is a car salesperson. They adopted twins, Faith and Gaia, at age one, three years ago. They do not plan to have more children.

Laura earns $65,000 p.a. with $38,000 of that being take-home pay. Her deductions provide full family health coverage (medical, drugs, dentist, optical) with $100 deductible per family member each year. She has disability insurance for 70% of her salary and three times her salary in life insurance. Her marginal tax rate is 48%. She has a reasonably secure job, but she does not expect any raises, even for inflation, for at least a while. During 1995–96, civil service salaries were cut or frozen in Alberta. She does not expect any promotions, either. She is good at her job, and well regarded by her superiors. She already works some long hours, staying late some nights and taking work home on weekends. To move up in the organization, she would have to work even more hours, and she refuses to sacrifice her family.

Stephen's commission income is quite variable, ranging from $25,000 to $60,000 in recent years. In 1996 he grossed $50,000, with a take-home pay of $36,000. He has no benefits. Unlike many commission salespersons, he has no significant expenses not covered by the dealership. He expects he will make $45,000 to $50,000 next year. His job is fairly secure as long as the dealership doesn't fail. The owners of the dealership are fairly conservative, and he thinks they are in good financial shape, even with the recession. Stephen usually works one day on the weekends, and one or two evenings a week, but also takes one weekday off. His marginal tax rate varies, but was 42% in 1996.

Laura and Stephen Ng
Balance Sheet December 31, 1996

Assets:		Liabilities:	
Chequing account	$ 500	Current credit card balance	$ 3,000
Car savings account	6,000	Credit card debt at 21%	6,000
Securities	5,000	Car loan	12,000
Two cars, original cost	50,000	Mortgage on house	140,000
House, current market	220,000		161,000
	$281,500	Equity	120,500
			$281,500

They have a housekeeper who does the cleaning, a bit of shopping and cooking, and looks after the children. Gaia and Faith will start half-day kindergarten next year. The housekeeper lives in a self-contained apartment with a separate entrance at the side of the house. Her salary and benefits cost $17,000 p.a. On the housekeeper's tax form (T1) they report a taxable benefit of $350 per month for the apartment she occupies. They expect to retain a housekeeper until the children are 12, and then switch to a cleaning service for $100/week. They can't do without her now, because of their inflexible working hours.

They have a lot of trouble saving money. They bought the securities before the twins arrived. Their credit card debt has increased in each of the last three years. They don't keep detailed account of their expenses, but they have sorted them out a bit by using different credit cards and the chequing account for different things.

The car loan has two years left, at .75% per month. The balance shown is the current amount owing. They spent about $6,000 last year on gasoline, maintenance, insurance and licenses for the cars, all charged on one credit card. Laura has a two-year-old van that will last for perhaps five more years. Stephen drives a relatively old Cadillac loaded with all the extras. He got it for only $27,000 originally because he works for a GM dealer. He expects to replace it with another one within two years. Their insurance covers $1 million in liability and has a $50 deductible for collision.

The house is in good repair, and is located in a nice neighbourhood in Edmonton, two kilometres from the government building where Laura works and four kilometres from Stephen's job. They just renewed the mortgage for five years at 8.25%, with a 20-year amortization. They spent $3,000 on taxes and utilities last year, and $1,000 on maintenance and insurance.

Other than the items already noted, they used cheques, and cash withdrawals from the chequing account to pay another $10,000 last year. Food was the biggest item, but they aren't sure what else was included.

They used several other credit cards for a total of $19,000 last year. This included clothing, household purchases, furniture, entertainment, life insurance and vacations. They take two or three holidays per year. Last year they spent one week in Hawaii (without the children), one week at Whistler ski resort, and a week camping.

Stephen has a $100,000 term life insurance policy. The securities are a portfolio of oil exploration companies (listed on the Alberta Stock Exchange). They pay no dividends, but they increased in value by 20% in 1996.

They want to retire around the time they turn 60. If Laura stays with the government, she will have a pension in today's dollars of $40,000 before-tax, including both her employer and Canada Pension Plan. Stephen will qualify for the maximum Canada Pension Plan.

They would like to maintain a similar lifestyle in retirement. They are concerned about the possibility that their pension plans will be reduced by government cut-backs or tax claw-backs. They have read that there is some risk that the government won't be able to pay full Canada Pension Plan in the future, because it hasn't been sufficiently funded, and the population of retirees is growing rapidly.

They also want to buy a vacation property in a few years, when their current debts are more manageable. They are thinking of something in the foothills, in the $100,000 range. They might retire to it and sell the house in Edmonton, but it's too far in the future to be more than an idea.

Required:

Act as an adviser to Laura and Stephen. Help them to meet their goals. They don't have a precise plan, nor do they (or you) have every number you might need. You will have to work within those limitations. Cover any aspect of personal financial planning you think is relevant to them.

chapter 19

Probabilistic Financial Planning

LEARNING OBJECTIVES

1. To understand the difference between deterministic and probabilistic planning.
2. To understand and apply the probabilistic planning models to practical situations.

This chapter is more theoretically advanced than the rest of the book. The material in it reflects the most recent academic research in the field of personal financial planning. These concepts are not yet generally incorporated into the practice of financial planning.

DETERMINISTIC vs. PROBABILISTIC PLANNING

Let us return to some of the ideas in Chapter 3. First, we will look again at the simple problem of John Ross, with one change. In Chapter 3, he was 25 years old, saving towards a goal at age 40. In this chapter, John Ross will be 50 and saving towards retirement at 65, but otherwise the problem is unchanged.

Example 19.1: John Ross (JR) is a 50-year-old who wants to retire comfortably. He sets a goal of having $400,000 by the time he reaches 65, 15 years hence. JR has $20,000 now, and he estimates that he can save $5,000 each year in the future. What must he do to achieve his financial goal? If the rate of return is too low, the goal cannot be achieved. What is the minimum rate of return on investment that must be earned to reach his goal? Let k be this minimum rate of return:

PV	$ 20,000
PMT	5,000
n	15
FV	−400,000
k	**14.98%**

This chapter is co-authored with Moshe Arye Milevsky, Schulich School of Business, York University.

In round numbers, we see that JR must find an investment that is expected to generate a return of 15% in order to reach his financial goal. Such a high rate of return is very unlikely.[1] Can he modify his plan to make it feasible? Let us assume that he can earn 10% p.a. with a reasonable level of risk. He has three choices:

- Reduce the goal to a feasible level. If he saves as planned, and earns 10%, he will have $242,407.
- If this reduced goal provides too little for his retirement, he could choose to retire later. If he can work until 70, he will accumulate $420,925. Since he is retiring later, he should require less than the original goal, and this solution is feasible.
- If he doesn't want to retire later, or he can't work longer, then he can try to save more during his working years. To accumulate $400,000 by age 65, he needs to save $9,960 p.a.

We turn back to Chapter 3 and model the plan using symbols to represent the elements of personal financial planning. The subscripts represent time: t is any particular future year; n is the year the goal is to be met; and, 0 is now, the starting point of the plan. Thus, if you plan to retire in 10 years, $n = 10$, and t runs from 1 to 10.

W_n The financial goal.
W_0 The amount of money you have today to invest.
k The rate of return that you earn on savings, assumed to be constant.
S_t The money you save in year t, other than investment income. That is, earnings from your occupation minus all consumption. We assume it is all received at year end.
C_t The money you consume or spend in year t, other than that used to purchase investments. We assume it is all spent at year end.

$$W_n = W_0 (1 + k)^n + \sum_{t=1}^{n} S_t (1 + k)^{n-t}$$

The left hand side is the goal. The first term on the right hand side is the initial savings at the start of the plan, compounded at the rate of return, and the second term is the sum of the annual savings as it is invested and compounds. The compounding period for the annual savings is $n - t$, allowing for the shorter and shorter period of compounding as you approach the time of the goal.

W_n, *the goal of wealth available for retirement, must equal the present value of all the consumption during retirement. If n is the age at retirement, d is the age of death* and we assume that all payments or expenditures occur at year-end, then:

---

[1] Note that this is all in nominal dollars. We leave the problem of inflation aside for the moment and accept that his goal is in nominal terms.

$$W_n = \sum_{n+1}^{d} \frac{C_t}{(1+k)^{t-n}}$$

This is what we call **deterministic planning**. We assume a given rate of return will be achieved with certainty, and then assess various plans. If we decide to invest in a different asset mix, the discount rate changes, but it is still assumed to be earned with certainty. This assumption violates everything that we learned in the investments chapters, but until now it has been part of all personal financial planning. Variations in results due to different discount rates can be viewed as different scenarios, but no-one knows how likely any given scenario is.

Every single variable in the model is uncertain, or risky, except for initial wealth. Ideally, we would like to know for any given plan how probable success or failure is. In practice, we cannot possibly know the distribution of some of the variables. The amount saved each year depends on the willpower of the family and its ability to maintain its projected earnings. While the family can insure against disability and premature death, it cannot insure against job loss or salary reductions. Consumption in retirement is a matter of family lifestyle choices to some extent, though some minimum level is necessary for survival. The date of retirement is partly a matter of choice, at least in some occupations. Solid information on the probability of such occurrences doesn't exist. Furthermore, these are the variables that the family can manipulate in trying to meet its goals; so any generalized probability distribution is ineffective in capturing the actual probability that a particular family will or won't meet its goals.

We do have reasonable probability information for two of the uncertain factors, however: rate of return on investments, and date of death.[2] The family's choice of investments affects the expected return, and you would like to know how that affects the likelihood of success with any given financial plan. The life span of the members of the family also affects how much you need to save, but you don't know that in advance.

In this chapter we use the distribution of rates of return and the mortality tables, instead of deterministic numbers. One model allows individuals to estimate the probability of maintaining a desired level of consumption in retirement with different investment decisions. The second model allows a family to estimate the probability of reaching a specified goal with different combinations of the date of the goal, annual amount saved, initial wealth and investment allocations. Used together, the two models allow development of **probabilistic financial planning.**

Implicit in this probabilistic financial planning is the concept of **shortfall probability.**[3] The family sets a goal, and tries to minimize the probability that it won't make that goal. Therefore, in probabilistic financial planning, every plan, action or choice has associated with it a probability of reaching or not reaching the goal. If the family doesn't

---

[2] Appendix B contains Canadian mortality tables, while Appendices D and E contain nominal and real rates of return from 1950–95.

[3] Shortfall probability is one possible measure of risk relative to a goal. Other measures are possible. Utility maximization is another approach that finance research has also explored. We use shortfall because we think it is closest to the way most people think in setting personal financial goals.

like the probability of shortfall associated with a specific plan, it must change the variables it can control to reduce the shortfall risk to an acceptable level.

This field is a new area of research, and consequently not all problems have been solved. We make simplifying assumptions and you should interpret the results as estimates, even though they have the appearance of mathematical precision.

In the rest of the chapter, we describe the two models and show how they are used to resolve practical personal finance problems. We start at the end of the life cycle with planning in retirement, because ultimately all financial plans must provide for retirement. Once we solve the asset allocation and consumption decisions for a retiree, we can then step back and use that information to quantify an appropriate retirement goal. Then, the next model takes the retirement goal as one input for determining if a family's plan is suitable for reaching that goal.

Think of your financial planning towards retirement goals in this way. If you don't survive to retirement, then you don't care if you saved enough.[4] However, if you do survive to retirement, then you want to have saved enough to live comfortably through retirement, given that you have reached that age. Once you reach retirement, it is too late to amend a pre-retirement plan!

Before we tackle the retirement problem, we take a brief excursion into the question of inflation.

Adjusting for Inflation

JR's goal was apparently set in nominal dollars. We have learned how to deal with inflation in other chapters, and we recognize that this means the $400,000 in the future will buy a lot less than it would now. We also know that it is easier to plan in real dollars, because we can relate the amounts to today more easily in our minds. Real dollars buy the same goods and services at any date, and hence we can estimate the income needed in retirement using our present consumption as a starting point. Furthermore, we can reasonably assume that consumption stays fixed in real dollars during retirement, and this simplifies the calculations.

Accordingly, we use real dollars and real rates of return for the rest of the chapter. In practice, we would expect that a family could save an increasing amount of real dollars as it approaches retirement, but we will show how to adjust for that problem when we present the model for pre-retirement planning.

ASSET ALLOCATION AND CONSUMPTION IN RETIREMENT

Once a family reaches retirement, a lot of the variability in financial planning disappears. In its simplest form, the problem is to maintain a desired level of consumption from a known initial wealth, until death. We will cast this problem in its most basic form to develop a model.

Think of a single person who has just retired, with an amount W_0 that must provide all consumption through retirement. That is, we assume there are no pensions. We explain how to incorporate pensions into the model in a later section. The person has a goal of

---

[4] Of course, the financial dependents should have been taken care of, via insurance or other means.

being able to receive C in real dollars every year until death. The receipts are paid from both principal and income. All of W is invested in an RRSP, and after age 69, in a RRIF. Therefore, the form of the income is irrelevant for income tax purposes, because all withdrawals are taxed as ordinary income. Thus, we would interpret C as a before-tax income amount.

In mathematical terms, we say that the person wants to minimize the probability of falling short of C of income in any year prior to his or her death.[5] There are two probabilistic (also called stochastic) variables in this problem: the rate of return and the date of death. The retiree can affect this probability by the choice of investments, and that is the financial planning problem we want to solve — how to invest retirement wealth to minimize shortfall.[6]

We will not discuss the mathematics of the solution here.[7] You can think of it in terms of a present value calculation. If we know the number of years that we want to consume C and the rate of return we will earn on the remaining invested wealth each year, then we can calculate the PV of the annuity. If this PV is greater than W_0, we know that we will suffer a shortfall.

However, we know neither the exact date of death nor the rate of return that will be earned. If we know the distribution of the rates of return, and the distribution of the date of death, then we can calculate the statistical distribution of the present values. Any specific realization of this distribution of present values is a possible value of W_n. We can calculate from the distribution of the present values the probability that the present value of all the future consumption will be greater than the amount saved at retirement to provide for it. This is the shortfall probability. The rates of return can be of any combination of assets, but to simplify the presentation, we show them for different allocations between T-bills and Canadian equity. We use the mortality tables for men and women from Appendix B, and the returns distributions in Appendix E.[8]

Table 19.1 shows the shortfall probabilities for different percentages of assets allocated to equity for a male and a female aged 65 with W/C ratios of 14 and 20. Because we are doing all the calculations in real dollars with a constant level of consumption, we get the identical result for all persons with the same ratio of W to C. We use a simulation of the solution to obtain actual numbers, and hence the optimum may not appear to be unique. This table shows several characteristics that apply to the results generally for a wide range of wealth and ages.

- Women must invest more in equity, all else equal, because they live longer.
- The largest reduction in shortfall probability occurs in moving from a 100% investment in T-bills into an allocation with at least some equity.

---

[5] We discuss the goal to leave a bequest to the heirs in a later section.

[6] The retiree can also affect shortfall probability by lifestyle decisions that change the mortality table applying to him or her. A retiree who smokes, drinks alcohol heavily and takes no exercise has a lower shortfall probability than one who lives a very healthy lifestyle, given the same initial wealth. We do not incorporate different mortality schedules, but it could be done easily.

[7] See the references at the end of the chapter.

[8] To be precise, we use the continuously compounded rates of return for 91 day Canadian T-bills and the TSE 300. We use the entire period 1950–95 for our estimate of the distribution.

TABLE 19.1
Probability of Shortfall with Different Asset Allocations

W/C is the wealth-consumption ratio in real $. This table shows the probability of shortfall for different allocations to equity, with the remainder in T-bills, for two situations of persons aged 65. Thus, an allocation of 0 is 100 T-bills, an allocation of 40% is 40% equity, 60% T-bills. For example, A male with W/C = 14 has a 30% chance of being unable to consume the desired amount throughout retirement if he invests 40% of wealth in equity. Another way to say this is that he has a 30% chance that the present value of his consumption will be greater than his initial wealth. The historic rates of real returns on the TSE 300 and 91 day Canadian T-bills for 1950–95 were used to construct this table. Note that because it report simulation results (3000 trials per entry), the values do not plot smoothly. The theoretical curve we are simulating is smooth.

% in Equity	W/C = 14		W/C = 20	
	Male	Female	Male	Female
0	48%	68	15	29
5	46	65	11	26
10	44	62	9	22
15	42	61	8	18
20	40	58	6	14
25	35	54	5	11
30	31	54	5	9
35	33	48	4	9
40	30	47	4	9
45	28	45	4	8
50	26	43	5	9
55	26	38	4	9
60	24	37	4	9
65	22	37	5	9
70	21	36	5	9
75	23	32	5	8
80	22	34	5	10
85	22	32	6	10
90	20	30	5	11
95	23	32	5	11
100	19	31	6	10

- For situations with relatively higher *W/C* ratios, that is, relatively wealthy persons, the shortfall curve is almost flat for a range around the optimum, and it increases only slightly for higher equity allocations. The same is true, although you cannot see it in Table 19.1, for older retirees with even moderate values of *W/C*.

Table 19.2 (which is the same as Table 17.3) shows the optimal allocation of investment assets to Canadian equity, with the remainder in T-bills, for a whole range of *W/C* ratios, and ages of retirement at five year interval from 60 to 75, for males and females. The shortfall probability is shown below each optimal asset allocation. The optimal allocation to equity is shown as a range, because around the optimum there is usually a difference in shortfall probability of less than one percentage point for several allocations. You can see this in Table 19.1 also.

TABLE 19.2
Optimal Asset Allocation for Retirees

W/C is the wealth-consumption ratio in constant $. The first (top) number in each cell is the optimal percentage (or range of percentages) of equity. The second (bottom) number is the probability of shortfall if this optimal percentage is chosen. For example (in boldface), a male aged 70 with a wealth-consumption ratio of 12 should invest 80–85% of his liquid wealth in equity, to have a 20% chance of shortfall in his desired consumption over his remaining life if he does so. Equity investments outside that range increase the probability of shortfall. The historic real rates of return for the TSE 300 and Canadian 91-day T-bills for 1950–95, and the 1990–92 Canadian Life tables were used to cosntruct this table.

| | Age and Gender | | | | | | | |
| | 60 | | 65 | | 70 | | 75 | |
W/C	M	F	M	F	M	F	M	F
10					90–100 .34	100 .47	80–100 .23	90–100 .34
12			100 .30	100 .42	**80–85 .20**	95–100 .32	65–90 .12	80–100 .21
14	95 .29	100 .41	90–100 .20	90–100 .31	70–80 .13	85 .21	55–60 .06	70–90 .12
16	80–95 .20	95–100 .28	55–100 .14	70–85 .21	60–75 .07	70–80 .13	35–60 .03	55–75 .07
18	50–90 .14	90–95 .19	55–60 .07	65–80 .14	45–55 .03	55 .07	20–55 .01	30–55 .03
20	45–75 .08	65–70 .13	35–60 .04	45–75 .08	40–50 .01	25–60 .04	0–95 .01	20–50 .01
22	30–45 .04	55–70 .08	20–60 .02	30–50 .04	10–70 .01	25–40 .01		
24	20–45 .02	30–60 .05	10–55 .01	20–50 .02				
26	15–55 .01	30–50 .02						

The general message of Table 19.2 is quite clear, and it contradicts a lot of 'folk' wisdom in financial planning:

- Most retirees should have substantial amounts of their retirement assets invested in equity, up to quite late ages, in order to minimize the probability that they will run out of money.
- Retirees with lower *W/C* ratios and early retirees need quite large allocations to equity, sometimes 100%.

Perhaps the best known folk wisdom is that your percentage allocation to equity should be equal to 100 minus your age. This rule of thumb fails to consider gender, wealth and desired level of consumption. As Table 19.2 shows, this rule significantly underestimates the amount of equity required for most retirees. Very wealthy retirees may fit it closer, but their likelihood of shortfall is so low that the investment decision isn't very important.

We emphasize that Table 19.2 shows estimates of shortfall probabilities and optimal allocations. We don't know the true distribution of future returns, especially since we are talking about very long time periods. Mortality tables change as actuaries gather more recent information, and the average life expectancy of Canadians has been rising steadily.[9] Furthermore, we are using mortality tables for the general population, with the only distinction being between men and women. However, there are mortality tables available for all kinds of subdivisions of the population. Perhaps the best known distinction is between smokers and non-smokers. For example, a non-smoking, well-educated female in a professional or managerial job, would have a significantly longer life expectancy than the average shown in Appendix B. Therefore, she would have to save even more and/or invest even a higher proportion of her retirement assets in equity, than is shown in Table 19.2.

Although we do not present the results in the textbook, the research indicates that using bonds instead of T-bills changes the equity allocation very little. Including international equity in the equity portfolio would reduce the shortfall probabilities somewhat, because international portfolios, and US portfolios, give somewhat higher returns. The biggest question mark in all this research is how much we can rely upon historic rates of return to provide the distribution of future or expected rates of return. While we cannot answer that question, we can say that the information contained in Table 19.2 allows better planning under uncertainty than a model that assumes the date of death and rate of return are known for certain.

Bequests

Many people wish to leave a bequest to their heirs or to specific charities. The model underlying Table 19.2 assumes that the goal is to minimize the probability of running out of money during the person's lifetime, with no value attached to the bequest. We can calculate the distribution of the bequest function, too, since it is what (if any) is left over at each possible date of death, under each possible return.

We do not present tables of results, but the general message is quite simple. The median[10] and the first and third quartiles of the bequest are higher with higher allocations to equity, regardless of age, *W/C*, and gender. This should be intuitively obvious, since equity has a higher expected return.

For the family planning to minimize shortfall and leave a bequest, there may be a trade-off. If the family's optimal asset allocation to minimize shortfall is at or close to 100% equity, then there is no tradeoff. The family whose shortfall-minimizing allocation is well below 100% equity can choose to increase the shortfall probability and the expected bequest by increasing the equity allocation. Since the shortfall curve is quite flat around the shortfall-minimizing optimal allocation, and does not rise sharply for higher allocations to equity, this trade-off involves little increase in risk.

---

[9] The articles in the references and the first edition of this book showed tables different from Table 19.2, partly because they used the 1985–87 mortality tables. In this edition Table 19.2 is based on 1990–92 mortality tables, the most recent available.

[10] The mean is not a useful statistic, because the very small possibility of very high returns makes it an enormous number if there is any significant amount of equity. For such a skewed distribution the median and the quartiles better describe a measure of central tendency.

As a practical matter, if a family has enough money in retirement that trying to maximize the bequest is a sensible goal, it probably also owns a house and other valuable personal assets. These other assets are not included in the retirement plan, since the retirees normally plan to use them in retirement. These assets, principally the family residence and any vacation property, form the bulk of the bequest, as long as the retirees do not run out of pension money and investment assets during their lifetime.

Applying the Model

The model exists in a somewhat unrealistic world, and to apply it in practice we have to fiddle with it a bit:

1. Consumption is expressed in real dollars.
2. The consumption in real dollars is assumed to remain constant. This implies a constant standard of living. In reality, consumption does vary from year to year, but it is reasonable to plan for an average level.
3. Table 19.2 applies to single men and women, not to couples. A joint mortality table for a couple would be somewhat different. We estimate this be taking a position somewhere between the allocations for the two members of a couple. While this is not perfect, it is a reasonable compromise.
4. All the returns are before-tax, and so C must be the before-tax income required to fund the desired lifestyle. Some of the wealth may be in after-tax dollars (e.g. unsheltered investments, proceeds from selling the family home). We gross it up the same way as we did in Chapter 16, to turn it into a before-tax amount.
5. Almost all families have some pension income — OAS, CPP, employer. Table 19.2 assumes all wealth is captured in W_0. Pensions are life annuities, and hence taking the PV of them introduces another element of uncertainty. Some pensions are indexed to inflation, which means they are in real $. Almost all employer pensions now feature some indexation. We assume that all pensions are indexed for the application of this model. We can deduct the pensions from C, to get an adjusted C. This adjusted value is the part of our retirement income that the assets under our control must support.

   Sometimes the pension plan allows the pensioner to receive the present value of the pension — called the commuted value[11] — and deposit it in a locked-in RRSP. In this case, we can add the commuted value to W_0, because the wealth is under the pensioner's control for investment decisions.
6. Differential taxation of dividends and capital gains means the percentage of equity in the portfolio changes the before-tax amount required to fund a given after-tax consumption level. We deal with this problem in two ways:
   • Pensions and RRSP/DPSP/RRIF withdrawals are taxed the same regardless of the form of the investment income; so we have no problem with them. The bulk of most people's retirement income comes from these sources.

---

[11] This value is calculated as the sum of the expected values paid each year, discounted at the risk-free long-run rate, usually from Canada bonds. The expected cash flow each year is the probability of survival to that year (from the mortality tables) times the promised pension payment for that year.

- The income on unsheltered investments is taxed at the differential rates, which relates also to point 4. In grossing up the after-tax amounts that are part of the wealth at retirement, a tax factor that reflects the type of investment must be used. This will necessarily be a crude approximation.

Let us turn to a concrete example.

Example 19.2: Jim and Donna are each 65 years old, and have just retired. They have $25,000 p.a. in indexed pensions (CPP, OAS and employer). Jim has a $10,000 unindexed employer pension that pays 50% to Donna if he predeceases her. They have $220,000 in RRSPs, all invested in GICs and $200,000 in a T-bill fund outside the RRSPs. They wish to receive $50,000 in annual income, in real dollars. The income will be approximately equally split between them. Assume their effective tax rate on withdrawals from the equity fund is 10%, allowing for the effect of the dividend tax credit, capital gains and the untaxed principal amount. Advise them on how to invest their assets to minimize the probability of running out of money in retirement, assuming they consume at the desired level every year. Estimate the probability of shortfall.

Answer:

1. Estimate the average tax rate in retirement and total income required before-tax. They want to receive $50,000 after-tax, and the income is approximately evenly split. By trial and error from Table 16.1, we see that the tax rate would be 19% on $30,000 (each). This yields $60,000 × (1 − .19) = $48,600, which is a bit low. At $63,000, the tax rate would be about 20% (interpolating between $30,000 and $35,000 on Table 16.1), which yields $50,400. We use a 20% tax rate, and required income = $63,000.

2. Adjust the required income for the indexed pensions, to yield $C = $63,000 − $31,000 = $32,000.

3. Calculate W_0 in before-tax dollars:

   (i) RRSP $220,000
   (ii) Gross-up after-tax savings as done
        in Chapter 16: $200,000 ÷ .9 =   222,222
                                                                     $442,222

4. Calculate W_0/C and find the entry in Table 19.2. W_0/C = 13.8. For a value of 14, a woman of 65 has an optimal allocation of 90–100% in equity, with a shortfall probability of 31%. A man of 65 has an optimal allocation of 90–100% in equity, with a shortfall probability of 20%. The advice to them, very clearly, is to invest in a portfolio of Canadian equities. Even so, they have a significant shortfall probability, and should consider limiting their consumption somewhat.

Setting Goals under Uncertainty

We can use Table 19.2 in a slightly different way to set retirement goals. Most people have in mind a standard of living in retirement, rather than a lump sum savings amount at the start of retirement. If you are planning during the years of saving up to retirement, you could set the goal as a constant real consumption amount in retirement, and specify the age at which you want to retire. Then, you consider your risk tolerance and decide what probability of not reaching that goal is acceptable to you. If you plan this way, you can then calculate a lump sum goal using Table 19.2. We suggest that a 5% shortfall probability is a reasonable target. For example, in testing hypotheses in statistics, we usually define 5% as an acceptable probability of error.

Example 19.3:	Suppose John Ross, whom we met earlier, decides that his goal is $45,000 p.a., before-tax, throughout retirement. This amount is in real dollars. He expect to have $25,000 in indexed pensions. What is the amount he must save by age 65 if he wants to have no more than a 5% chance of falling short of this goal?
Answer:	He needs to save an amount that will yield $45,000 − $25,000 = $20,000 p.a. From Table 19.2, we see that a *W/C* ratio of 20 for a male aged 65 gives a shortfall probability of 4%. Therefore, we would estimate that he should set as his goal a total of $20,000 × 20 = $400,000 in real dollars by age 65. We assume that he invests it optimally in retirement, in 35–60% equity.

Now we turn to a probabilistic planning model of the decisions on saving and investment during the working part of the life cycle, when you are aiming for retirement savings or other goals.

PLANNING FOR SPECIFIED GOALS

When we plan for a specific goal, it must have both an amount and a date or time to achieve it. The rate of return on savings is uncertain, and so we have a probabilistic model. Because we model only one stochastic factor, we get a relatively simple closed form solution, which we present shortly. In the previous section, the solution to the asset allocation problem in retirement had to be determined by simulation, which is why we provided a table of results.[12] Here, you can use the pre-retirement planning equation with a calculator and a normal distribution table, or with a good spreadsheet programme.

This model allows us to vary the key elements in our financial plan: the annual savings, the date of the goal, the amount of the goal, the initial wealth and the investment allocation of the savings. In this model, we set the objective as maximizing the probability of reaching the goal, which is identical to one minus the shortfall probability. We can determine the best investment allocation between a risk-free asset and a risky asset, the probability of reaching our goal and the expected amount we will have at the goal date.

---

[12] The authors are working on a closed form solution, but it is currently an open problem.

Alternatively, we can fix the asset allocation and determine the probability of success and the expected wealth, allowing the user to see if a strategy that doesn't maximize the chance of reaching the goal nonetheless gives enough higher expected wealth to be worth taking the extra risk.

In what follows, we use more sophisticated mathematical notation than has appeared so far in the textbook. The only skill you will need to use the model is the ability to recognize what the symbols mean and how to substitute appropriate numerical values for them.

We define the following variables and terms:

T number of years to the goal

G the goal in real \$

W_T stochastic wealth at time T in real \$.

W_0 initial wealth

k_t stochastic rate of return in period t, and $k_{T+1} = 0$.

S_t amount saved from earned income each year, in real \$.

μ expected real rate of return on the risky asset, continuously compounded

σ standard deviation of the real return on the risky asset

r real risk-free rate of return

α fraction of the portfolio invested in the risky asset, $0 \leq \alpha \leq 1$.

ln the natural logarithm (function on all financial calculators)

$N(\bullet)$ the normal distribution evaluated at $\bullet$.

e the exponential function (function on all financial calculators).

G is identical to the W_n that we used in our earlier deterministic model. We use a different notation now because we want to keep the different W variables distinct. W_0 is the initial liquid wealth — RRSPs, etc. — that accumulates toward the goal, in addition to the annual saving, S_t. W_T is a random variable, which means we don't know what value it will take. It is the unknown wealth that a family will actually have when the date of the goal is reached. Our problem is to maximize the probability that W_T is equal to or greater than G. W_T is random because the rate of return is a random variable.

We go about this problem in somewhat the same way as before. If we take the present value of all the future savings plus the amount already saved, and compare it with the present value of the goal, we know if we can be certain of reaching the goal. To do this, we use the real risk-free rate as the discount rate. If investing 100% at the real risk-free rate would provide at least enough to reach the goal, then clearly we are certain to reach the goal.[13] However, if we can't get to our goal with a risk-free asset, then at least some part of our money must be invested in a risky asset with a higher return, and a standard deviation of return.

---

[13] Of course, the assumption that a real risk-free asset exists is a strong one, but no solution is possible otherwise. In fact, complete certainty is never possible, but it is a reasonable approximation. The real T-bill rate has a much lower standard deviation than any other available investment, and we use it to proxy for the risk-free rate.

We convert the problem into a continuous time framework, with the details of the mathematical derivation provided in Milevsky et al. (1996). Assuming that the annual savings is $\$S$ per year, we define another variable:

$$\widetilde{W}_0 = W_0 + \int_0^T S e^{-rt}\, dt = W_0 + \frac{S}{r}[1 - e^{-rT}]$$

This is just the expression for the present value of the current and future savings, as we already explained in words. If accumulation at the risk-free rate will reach the goal, then the allocation to equity is 0; otherwise, at least some of the investment will be in equity. The solution is an optimal:

$$\hat{\alpha} = \min\left(1, \sqrt{\frac{2 \ln [G/\widetilde{W}_0] - 2Tr}{\sigma^2 T}}\right)$$

and the probability of reaching a specified goal with any given α is:

$$P[\widetilde{W}_T \geq G] = 1 - N\left(\frac{\ln\left[\dfrac{G}{\widetilde{W}_0}\right] - \left[\alpha\mu + (1-\alpha)r - \dfrac{1}{2}\alpha^2\sigma^2\right]T}{\alpha\sigma\sqrt{T}}\right)$$

Given any alpha, we can also calculate the expected wealth at the date of the goal. This amount is not what *will* occur, but rather the expected value. Even when the expected value is well above the goal, there will be a probability of shortfall if any of the investment is in equity. Since we are working in continuous time, we use continuously compounded rates of return, but otherwise the result is similar to taking the future value as we did in Chapter 2. First, we need to calculate the weighted mean return:

$$k = \alpha\mu + (1 - \alpha)r$$

Then,

$$E[W_T] = \widetilde{W}_0\, (e^{kT})$$

Two aspects of this solution require comment. First, μ does not appear in the expression for the optimal allocation, which seems totally counter-intuitive. The reason for this is that once the risk-free rate is insufficient to allow the investor to reach G with certainty, then some amount of equity is required. The standard deviation of the equity is what matters in the allocation, since that is what allows the equity to reach G at least some of the time. Therefore, a greater σ is better for avoiding shortfall risk.

The second aspect of this seemingly counter-intuitive result is that the higher the σ, the smaller the allocation to equity. The higher swings allow the investor the best probability of reaching the goal with a smaller amount invested in equity. This is much like an option pricing argument. If you need to reach a goal and cannot do it with the return from a risk-free asset, then the more variance you introduce on the risky asset, the better the chance that at least some of the time you get enough on the positive side to reach the goal. The equity return is important in the probability of reaching the goal, however. An increase in μ, all else held constant, increases the probability of reaching G.

Let us see how this works with a detailed example. We will solve it by calculator, but you can do it more easily, and then try variations, if you program it into a spreadsheet.

Applying the Model

Refer back to the case of John Ross in the previous section. In Example 19.3, we found that a goal of $400,000 in real dollars would give him a low enough shortfall probability. Now we can substitute the values into the equations:

W_0	$ 20,000
S	5,000
G	400,000
T	15 years
r	.0193
μ	.0594
σ	.1601

First, we calculate the present value of all the savings, discounted at the risk-free rate:

$$\tilde{W}_0 = 20,000 + \frac{5,000}{.0193} (1 - e^{-(.0193)(15)})$$

$$= 20,000 + 259,067 (1 - e^{-.2895})$$

$$= 85,120$$

Next, we find the optimal allocation to equity that minimizes shortfall:

$$\alpha = \min\left(1, \frac{\sqrt{2 \ln\left[\frac{400,000}{85,120}\right] - 2(15)(.0193)}}{(.0256)(15)}\right)$$

$$= \min\left(1, \frac{\sqrt{219.72 - .58}}{.384}\right)$$

$$= \min (1, 23.89)$$

$$= 1$$

He should invest wholly in equity. His probability of shortfall comes from the following:

$$1 - N\left(\frac{\ln (4.70) - \left[.0594 - \frac{1}{2}(.0256)\right] 15}{.1601 \sqrt{15}}\right)$$

$$= 1 - N\left(\frac{1.55 - .70}{.62}\right)$$

$$= 1 - N (1.37)$$

As it happens, Appendix C is set up to give the value of $1 - N(x)$. Turn to Appendix C, look for the value of 1.3 down the left-hand side, and read across to the .07 column. The value of .0853 is the probability of success. Therefore, even with 100% of his investments in equity, John Ross has only an 8.53% chance of reaching his retirement goal with his current plan.

Finally, we can calculate expected wealth under this plan.

$$E[W_T] = \$85,120 \ (e^{(.0594)(15)})$$
$$= \$207,693.$$

What should John Ross do about this dismal situation. Let us suppose that he reconsiders his goals in life. He still wants to retire at 65, but he needs to somehow save more. He looks at his various assets and decides that his big luxury will have to go. He owns a vacation condominium at Whistler ski resort, but he doesn't go there that often. If he sells it, he can realize $150,000 after all costs and taxes. In addition, he will save money on the condominium fees, and on the travel. However, he will now have to vacation somewhere else and pay for hotels. After he figures out the details, he estimates that he can save another $3,000 p.a., including the tax refund on extra RRSP contributions.

We leave it as an exercise for the student to recalculate his position. You should find that the optimal allocation is now 92% equity, with a 65% probability of meeting his goal of $400,000. The expected wealth is $592,000. The upside of this changed plan is that if things go reasonably well, he may still be able to buy back the condominium, or enjoy some different form of consumption in retirement, above what he has planned.

As a final word on the practical application, we note that the assumption of a constant savings rate is not necessary. Most families will in fact save more in both nominal and real terms as they get closer to retirement, because debts are paid down and children cease to be dependent. We did it as an annuity, but the value of W_0 can be calculated year by year from different values, just as we have been doing throughout the textbook when determining the value of future savings.

Now that you have seen a detailed example, we present some general results.

Generalizing the Results

We illustrate them with Table 19.3, which shows a range of values for savings, goals and time to the goals, with the initial wealth assumed to be 0 and the rates of return being the 1950–95 average. Remember that you must use the continuously compounded rate of return and the standard deviation of the continuously compounded rate of return in these formulas. In Appendix E we show the geometric mean, not the continuously compounded rate. We use a continuously compounded rate of return of 1.93% for T-bills and 5.94% for equity, in Table 19.3. The standard deviation of the continuously compounded mean return of equity is 16.01%.[14]

With the initial wealth held to 0, we can collapse G and S into a single ratio, with the results identical for any savings and goals in the same proportion. This is the situation facing a family that is just starting to save for retirement. Table 19.3 shows the optimal allocation to equity (α), the probability of reaching or exceeding the goal ($\Pr[W_T \geq G]$) **and the expected wealth at time T**, $E[W_T]$, for retirement date horizons from 15 to 35

---

[14] You can calculate the continuously compounded real rate of return from Appendix E by calculating $(1 + ln(\text{real rate}))$. The arithmetic mean of this sequence is the expected continuously compounded rate.

TABLE 19.3
Asset Allocation to Maximize Probability of Reaching a Goal with No Initial Wealth

G/S		Years to Retirement				
		15	20	25	30	35
80	α	1.0	1.0	1.0	1.0	1.0
	$Pr(W_T>G)$	0.04	0.19	0.39	0.56	0.70
	$E[W_T]$	32	54	88	135	203
60	α	1.0	1.0	1.0	1.0	0.64
	$Pr(W_T>G)$	0.09	0.31	0.53	0.69	0.81
	$E[W_T]$	32	54	88	135	122
50	α	1.0	1.0	1.0	0.73	0
	$Pr(W_T>G)$	0.15	0.41	0.62	0.77	1.0
	$E[W_T]$	32	54	88	98	50
45	α	1.0	1.0	1.0	0.52	0
	$Pr(W_T>G)$	0.19	0.46	0.67	0.82	1.0
	$E[W_T]$	32	54	88	76	50
40	α	1.0	1.0	0.83	0	0
	$Pr(W_T>G)$	0.25	0.53	0.72	1.0	1.0
	$E[W_T]$	32	54	74	41	50
35	α	1.0	1.0	0.52	0	0
	$Pr(W_T>G)$	0.32	0.60	0.80	1.0	1.0
	$E[W_T]$	32	54	54	41	50
30	α	1.0	0.90	0	0	0
	$Pr(W_T>G)$	0.41	0.68	1.0	1.0	1.0
	$E[W_T]$	32	50	32	41	50
25	α	1.0	0.31	0	0	0
	$Pr(W_T>G)$	0.53	0.82	1.0	1.0	1.0
	$E[W_T]$	32	31	32	41	50
20	α	0.85	0	0	0	0
	$Pr(W_T>G)$	0.67	1.0	1.0	1.0	1.0
	$E[W_T]$	29	24	32	41	50
18	α	0.42	0	0	0	0
	$Pr(W_T>G)$	1.76	1.0	1.0	1.0	1.0
	$E[W_T]$	22	24	32	41	50
17	α	0	0	0	0	0
	$Pr(W_T>G)$	1.0	1.0	1.0	1.0	1.0
	$E[W_T]$	17	24	32	41	50

G/S is the desired future goal divided by annual savings. α is the percentage invested in equity that maximizes the chance of reaching G, with the probability shown in the line below. $E[W_T]$ is the expected wealth at time T, in the same magnitude as G and S. The assumed return distribution, using continuously compounded real rates for Canadian T-bills and equity, is $r = 0.0193$, $\mu = .0594$, $\sigma = .1601$.

years. The assumed return distribution is that of Canadian T-bills and the return on the Toronto Stock Exchange 300 from 1950–95, both deflated by the Consumer Price Index to approximate real returns.

To see how to use Table 19.3, consider a family that has decided it needs $350,000, in real dollars, in addition to government pensions and the family home. The parents are 40 and want to retire at age 65. They have almost finished paying off the mortgage and expect to start saving $10,000 p.a. $G/S = 35$, and $T = 25$. According to Table 19.3, they should invest 52% of their current and future savings in equity. If they do so, they have an 80% chance of at least reaching their goal. Their expected wealth at retirement, $E[W_T]$, is $540,000. $E[W_T]$ as shown on the table is of the same order of magnitude as the goal and the annual savings amount.

Many of the solutions shown in Table 19.3 are either all equity or all T-bills. As we vary the goal, the annual savings and the time to retirement within reasonable bounds, there is a smaller range inside the bounds of the table, where the asset allocation includes both a risky and a risk-free asset. If $G/S > 80$, the risk of not reaching the goal is always significant, and 100% equity is required. Likewise, only those with a very high savings function can reach reasonable retirement goals if they start saving with 15 years or less remaining to the retirement date.

There may seem to be a conundrum in this table. As the horizon to retirement increases, the allocation to equity declines. The time diversification argument seems to fail. This failure is an illusion, because we aren't holding the cash flow constant. As the horizon increases, the family saves more, and hence the goal becomes easier to reach without the high returns from equity. In the standard time diversification literature, there is no constant goal, but simply a comparison of identical cash flows (whether from a single amount invested at $t = 0$, or any other pattern) invested in different kinds of assets.

A family that wishes to increase the likelihood of reaching its goal can change its plan in any or all of three ways:

1. Reduce G, planning to consume less in retirement;
2. Increase S, either by consuming less now, or working harder; or,
3. Increase T, by postponing the retirement date.

On Table 19.3, reductions in G/S to increase the probability of reaching a goal move the family down the chart, while increases in T move the family to the right. Consider the family with $G/S = 35$ and $T = 25$. The probability of success is 80%. If the family wants a better shot at reaching the goal, it can postpone retirement to age 70 of the parents and be certain of reaching the goal with a policy of investing solely in T-bills. Alternatively, the family can reduce the G/S ratio to 30 through any combination of increased saving and reduced retirement consumption, and also be certain of reaching its (possibly changed) goal with a 100% allocation to T-bills.

Once again, this result may seem anomalous to some readers. If the family has a difficult goal to meet, the recommended allocation is usually 100% equity, as we can see by looking at the upper left part of Table 19.3. At the same time, as they get to a position in which the goal is easier to attain, Table 19.3 says the optimal allocation is little or no equity. The reason is the assumption of a totally riskless real asset, that is, no variance at all. As a practical matter, there is always some variance, and certainty is not possible, although the probability of reaching the goal would be very high. Note also that the expected wealth at the retirement date is much lower for the 100% T-bill allocations, even though the probability of success is high. For the family in the example, postponement of retirement to age 70, with 100% invested in T-bills, reduces the expected wealth at retirement to $410,000 from $540,000, even though there is a longer savings period. The investment of 100% in T-bills while keeping the age of retirement at 65 reduces the expected wealth further, to $320,000.

This brings up the question of the tradeoff between the higher expected wealth from equity and the higher probability of attaining at least the desired minimum. The family has to decide this question based on its risk preferences. A family that is very risk intolerant would decide on some combination of lower goals, higher saving and later retirement in order to stay in T-bills and get the almost certain success in reaching the goal. A family with higher tolerance for risk would choose a higher equity allocation and shoot for the higher goal. For most families earlier in the life cycle there won't be a lot of choice. Most families do not have enough wealth and cannot save enough for what they would regard as reasonable retirement income to be able to put all of their savings into low risk, low return assets. Typically, most families should be completely invested in high risk, high return assets, just to get reasonable probabilities of meeting their goals.

For short-run goals, this procedure is not really necessary. If a family cannot save enough to meet a goal in three years using a low-risk, low return asset, investing in equity will increase the chance of achieving the goal. The short time frame means that the time diversification effect is relatively weak, however, and no investment combination will produce a very high probability of success unless the family would fall only a very small amount short using low risk investments. Thus, you needn't use this table for short-run problems. If discounting at the risk-free rates reveals a significant shortfall, then the family has to lower the goal or increase its savings rate.

STRENGTHS AND WEAKNESSES OF THE PROBABILISTIC PLANNING MODELS

The strengths of these models are quite evident. They provide a suitable measure of the risk implicit in any plan, as well as the best investment allocations to minimize the shortfall risk. Instead of calculating different scenarios, without knowing how likely they are, a family can estimate how different planning choices will affect the likelihood of their success in meeting their goals.

The weaknesses may not be so evident.

- The models use shortfall minimization as the criterion, but they do not distinguish between different degrees of shortfall. Missing by $1 is the same as $1 million. As a practical matter, if the probability of success is high, then the most of the outcomes that fall short do so by only a small amount.
- These are mathematical models that assume constant consumption and well-behaved statistical distributions of asset returns. The mathematics gives the impression of great precision, but they are only estimates.
- The return distributions we have used are the historic rates of return in Canada. If the future distribution is significantly different, then of course the outcomes will not conform to our probability estimates. You can insert your own estimates for ours,

but any conclusions are always partly dependent on the distribution of returns that you assume. We do note that in tests of the sensitivity of the models, we found much the same results for a significant shrinkage in the risk premium of equity over T-Bills.

SUMMARY

Deterministic planning assumes that the rate of return and date of death of the family members is known. The risk of the plan can be assessed only by calculating different scenarios, but the probabilities of these scenarios are unknown. Probabilistic planning assumes that the rate of return is uncertain or stochastic, but that the distribution of returns is known. Probabilistic planning assumes that the date of death is also uncertain, but the distribution is as in some known mortality table.

To make it operational, we seek to minimize the probability of falling short of the family goals.

Probabilistic planning then allows the family or the planner to formulate plans with probabilities attached. A retired person can estimate the best allocation of investments between equity and T-bills. Alternatively, a retired person could decide that the risk of a given level of consumption is too high, and choose a less costly life style. Finally, the retirement model can be used to determine what is a reasonable lump sum goal necessary to finance the standard of living desired in retirement.

Pre-retirement, the family can change the variables under its control — savings (earnings – consumption), time to retirement, initial investment and desired retirement standard of living. It can find the best investment allocation, and it can see the probability of success under any given plan. If the chance of success is deemed to be too low, it can seek ways to vary the plan until it is satisfactory.

KEY TERMINOLOGY

asset allocation / probabilistic financial planning / deterministic financial planning / shortfall / shortfall probability

DISCUSSION QUESTION

1. Explain each of the terms under Key Terminology.

PROBLEMS

1. Woody Williams, 35, sets a retirement goal of having $1,500,000 by the time he retires 30 years hence. He plans to achieve this by saving $5,000 per year. (This question was set as a deterministic one in Chapter 3).
    (a) What is his chance of reaching his goal if he invests entirely in T-bills, using 1.93% as the continuously compounded rate of return?
    (b) What is his chance of reaching his goal with the optimal allocation to equity? Use a continuously compounded rate of return of 5.94% and standard deviation of 16.01%. What is his expected wealth at retirement?
    (c) Suggest an action plan that will give him a higher probability of reaching his goal and calculate the probability of success and the optimal allocation.

2.   Iris and Stanley Yuen immigrated to Canada in July 1994. Stanley is 63, Iris is 56. They have three children aged 34, 32 and 24, all working. They sold their business in Hong Kong before they left, they are now fully-retired and do not wish to work again. Both are in good health.

- Stanley's investments — CDN$500,000 mainly in T-bills, CSBs and money market funds
- Stanley owns the house, worth $380,000, no mortgage
- No other dependents
- No insurance policy
- No pension income. Ineligible for OAS.
- No other investments or debts
- Monthly expenses $2,500

Stanley is considering changing the mix of his investment portfolio in order to minimize taxes paid each year, but he is not willing to take too risky investments. What would be the best strategy for him to diversify his investments, to earn a higher return and to minimize taxes?

He is considering buying a $150,000 apartment and renting it out to earn a stable income each month. Would you recommend this strategy?

This problem involves more than just a mechanical application of Chapter 19. There are investment, retirement planning and taxation issues that you will have to resolve before you can apply the model.

3.   Provide a probabilistic solution to the Case of the Ottawa Doctor that formed the bulk of Chapter 18. You may use all the calculations from that Chapter where they are helpful. You will need to make some approximations and further assumptions. State them clearly.

REFERENCES

Ho, Kwok, Moshe Arye Milevsky and Chris Robinson. 1994a. "Asset Allocation, Life Expectancy and Shortfall, *Financial Services Review* 3(2): 109–26.

———. 1994b. "How to Avoid Outliving Your Money," *Canadian Investment Review* Fall: 35–38.

———. 1996a. "Risk-adjusted Retirement," *Canadian Investment Review* Spring: 19–27.

———. 1996b. "Targeting Retirement," York University Schulich School of Business working paper #17-95, revised.

Milevsky, Moshe Arye, Kwok Ho and Chris Robinson. 1996c. "Asset Allocation via the Conditional First Exit Time, *or* How to Avoid Outliving Your Money," York University Schulich School of Business working paper #24-94, revised, forthcoming in *Review of Quantitative Finance and Accounting*.

Appendices

APPENDIX A1

Present Value of $1 Received n Periods in the Future

$$PVIF = \frac{1}{(1+k)^n}$$

Period	1%	2%	3%	4%	5%	6%	7%	8%	9%	10%	11%	12%	14%	16%	18%	20%	25%
1	0.9901	0.9804	0.9709	0.9615	0.9524	0.9434	0.9346	0.9259	0.9174	0.9091	0.9009	0.8929	0.8772	0.8621	0.8475	0.8333	0.8000
2	0.9803	0.9612	0.9426	0.9246	0.9070	0.8900	0.8734	0.8573	0.8417	0.8264	0.8116	0.7972	0.7695	0.7432	0.7182	0.6944	0.6400
3	0.9706	0.9423	0.9151	0.8890	0.8638	0.8396	0.8163	0.7938	0.7722	0.7513	0.7312	0.7118	0.6750	0.6407	0.6086	0.5787	0.5120
4	0.9610	0.9238	0.8885	0.8548	0.8227	0.7921	0.7629	0.7350	0.7084	0.6830	0.6587	0.6355	0.5921	0.5523	0.5158	0.4823	0.4096
5	0.9515	0.9057	0.8626	0.8219	0.7835	0.7473	0.7130	0.6806	0.6499	0.6209	0.5935	0.5674	0.5194	0.4761	0.4371	0.4019	0.3277
6	0.9420	0.8880	0.8375	0.7903	0.7462	0.7050	0.6663	0.6302	0.5963	0.5645	0.5346	0.5066	0.4556	0.4104	0.3704	0.3349	0.2621
7	0.9327	0.8706	0.8131	0.7599	0.7107	0.6651	0.6227	0.5835	0.5470	0.5132	0.4817	0.4523	0.3996	0.3538	0.3139	0.2791	0.2097
8	0.9235	0.8535	0.7894	0.7307	0.6768	0.6274	0.5820	0.5403	0.5019	0.4665	0.4339	0.4039	0.3506	0.3050	0.2660	0.2326	0.1678
9	0.9143	0.8368	0.7664	0.7026	0.6446	0.5919	0.5439	0.5002	0.4604	0.4241	0.3909	0.3606	0.3075	0.2630	0.2255	0.1938	0.1342
10	0.9053	0.8203	0.7441	0.6756	0.6139	0.5584	0.5083	0.4632	0.4224	0.3855	0.3522	0.3220	0.2697	0.2267	0.1911	0.1615	0.1074
11	0.8963	0.8043	0.7224	0.6496	0.5847	0.5268	0.4751	0.4289	0.3875	0.3505	0.3173	0.2875	0.2366	0.1954	0.1619	0.1346	0.0859
12	0.8874	0.7885	0.7014	0.6246	0.5568	0.4970	0.4440	0.3971	0.3555	0.3186	0.2858	0.2567	0.2076	0.1685	0.1372	0.1122	0.0687
13	0.8787	0.7730	0.6810	0.6006	0.5303	0.4688	0.4150	0.3677	0.3262	0.2897	0.2575	0.2292	0.1821	0.1452	0.1163	0.0935	0.0550
14	0.8700	0.7579	0.6611	0.5775	0.5051	0.4423	0.3878	0.3405	0.2992	0.2633	0.2320	0.2046	0.1597	0.1252	0.0985	0.0779	0.0440
15	0.8613	0.7430	0.6419	0.5553	0.4810	0.4173	0.3624	0.3152	0.2745	0.2394	0.2090	0.1827	0.1401	0.1079	0.0835	0.0649	0.0352
16	0.8528	0.7284	0.6232	0.5339	0.4581	0.3936	0.3387	0.2919	0.2519	0.2176	0.1883	0.1631	0.1229	0.0930	0.0708	0.0541	0.0281
17	0.8444	0.7142	0.6050	0.5134	0.4363	0.3714	0.3166	0.2703	0.2311	0.1978	0.1696	0.1456	0.1078	0.0802	0.0600	0.0451	0.0225
18	0.8360	0.7002	0.5874	0.4936	0.4155	0.3503	0.2959	0.2502	0.2120	0.1799	0.1528	0.1300	0.0946	0.0691	0.0508	0.0376	0.0180
19	0.8277	0.6864	0.5703	0.4746	0.3957	0.3305	0.2765	0.2317	0.1945	0.1635	0.1377	0.1161	0.0829	0.0596	0.0431	0.0313	0.0144
20	0.8195	0.6730	0.5537	0.4564	0.3769	0.3118	0.2584	0.2145	0.1784	0.1486	0.1240	0.1037	0.0728	0.0514	0.0365	0.0261	0.0115
25	0.7798	0.6095	0.4776	0.3751	0.2953	0.2330	0.1842	0.1460	0.1160	0.0923	0.0736	0.0588	0.0378	0.0245	0.0160	0.0105	0.0038
30	0.7419	0.5521	0.4120	0.3083	0.2314	0.1741	0.1314	0.0994	0.0754	0.0573	0.0437	0.0334	0.0196	0.0116	0.0070	0.0042	0.0012
35	0.7059	0.5000	0.3554	0.2534	0.1813	0.1301	0.0937	0.0676	0.0490	0.0356	0.0259	0.0189	0.0102	0.0055	0.0030	0.0017	0.0004
40	0.6717	0.4529	0.3066	0.2083	0.1420	0.0972	0.0668	0.0460	0.0318	0.0221	0.0154	0.0107	0.0053	0.0026	0.0013	0.0007	0.0001
45	0.6391	0.4102	0.2644	0.1712	0.1113	0.0727	0.0476	0.0313	0.0207	0.0137	0.0091	0.0061	0.0027	0.0013	0.0006	0.0003	*
50	0.6080	0.3715	0.2281	0.1407	0.0872	0.0543	0.0339	0.0213	0.0134	0.0085	0.0054	0.0035	0.0014	0.0006	0.0003	0.0001	*
60	0.5504	0.3048	0.1697	0.0951	0.0535	0.0303	0.0173	0.0099	0.0057	0.0033	0.0019	0.0011	0.0004	0.0001	*	*	*

* less than .0001

APPENDIX A2
Future Value of $1 Compounded for *n* Periods

$$FVIF = (1 + k)^n$$

Period	1%	2%	3%	4%	5%	6%	7%	8%	9%	10%	11%	12%	14%	16%	18%	20%	25%
1	1.0100	1.0200	1.0300	1.0400	1.0500	1.0600	1.0700	1.0800	1.0900	1.1000	1.1100	1.1200	1.1400	1.1600	1.1800	1.2000	1.2500
2	1.0201	1.0404	1.0609	1.0816	1.1025	1.1236	1.1449	1.1664	1.1881	1.2100	1.2321	1.2544	1.2996	1.3456	1.3924	1.4400	1.5625
3	1.0303	1.0612	1.0927	1.1249	1.1576	1.1910	1.2250	1.2597	1.2950	1.3310	1.3676	1.4049	1.4815	1.5609	1.6430	1.7280	1.9531
4	1.0406	1.0824	1.1255	1.1699	1.2155	1.2625	1.3108	1.3605	1.4116	1.4641	1.5181	1.5735	1.6890	1.8106	1.9388	2.0736	2.4414
5	1.0510	1.1041	1.1593	1.2167	1.2763	1.3382	1.4026	1.4693	1.5386	1.6105	1.6851	1.7623	1.9254	2.1003	2.2878	2.4883	3.0518
6	1.0615	1.1262	1.1941	1.2653	1.3401	1.4185	1.5007	1.5869	1.6771	1.7716	1.8704	1.9738	2.1950	2.4364	2.6996	2.9860	3.8147
7	1.0721	1.1487	1.2299	1.3159	1.4071	1.5036	1.6058	1.7138	1.8280	1.9487	2.0762	2.2107	2.5023	2.8262	3.1855	3.5832	4.7684
8	1.0829	1.1717	1.2668	1.3686	1.4775	1.5938	1.7182	1.8509	1.9926	2.1436	2.3045	2.4760	2.8526	3.2784	3.7589	4.2998	5.9605
9	1.0937	1.1951	1.3048	1.4233	1.5513	1.6895	1.8385	1.9990	2.1719	2.3579	2.5580	2.7731	3.2519	3.8030	4.4355	5.1598	7.4506
10	1.1046	1.2190	1.3439	1.4802	1.6289	1.7908	1.9672	2.1589	2.3674	2.5937	2.8394	3.1058	3.7072	4.4114	5.2338	6.1917	9.3132
11	1.1157	1.2434	1.3842	1.5395	1.7103	1.8983	2.1049	2.3316	2.5804	2.8531	3.1518	3.4785	4.2262	5.1173	6.1759	7.4301	11.6415
12	1.1268	1.2682	1.4258	1.6010	1.7959	2.0122	2.2522	2.5182	2.8127	3.1384	3.4985	3.8960	4.8179	5.9360	7.2876	8.9161	14.5519
13	1.1381	1.2936	1.4685	1.6651	1.8856	2.1329	2.4098	2.7196	3.0658	3.4523	3.8833	4.3635	5.4924	6.8858	8.5994	10.6993	18.1899
14	1.1495	1.3195	1.5126	1.7317	1.9799	2.2609	2.5785	2.9372	3.3417	3.7975	4.3104	4.8871	6.2613	7.9875	10.1472	12.8392	22.7374
15	1.1610	1.3459	1.5580	1.8009	2.0789	2.3966	2.7590	3.1722	3.6425	4.1772	4.7846	5.4736	7.1379	9.2655	11.9737	15.4070	28.4217
16	1.1726	1.3728	1.6047	1.8730	2.1829	2.5404	2.9522	3.4259	3.9703	4.5950	5.3109	6.1304	8.1372	10.7480	14.1290	18.4884	35.5271
17	1.1843	1.4002	1.6528	1.9479	2.2920	2.6928	3.1588	3.7000	4.3276	5.0545	5.8951	6.8660	9.2765	12.4677	16.6722	22.1861	44.4089
18	1.1961	1.4282	1.7024	2.0258	2.4066	2.8543	3.3799	3.9960	4.7171	5.5599	6.5436	7.6900	10.5752	14.4625	19.6733	26.6233	55.5112
19	1.2081	1.4568	1.7535	2.1068	2.5270	3.0256	3.6165	4.3157	5.1417	6.1159	7.2633	8.6128	12.0557	16.7765	23.2144	31.9480	69.3889
20	1.2202	1.4859	1.8061	2.1911	2.6533	3.2071	3.8697	4.6610	5.6044	6.7275	8.0623	9.6463	13.7435	19.4608	27.3930	38.3376	86.7362
25	1.2824	1.6406	2.0938	2.6658	3.3864	4.2919	5.4274	6.8485	8.6231	10.8347	13.5855	17.0001	26.4619	40.8742	62.6686	95.3962	264.6978
30	1.3478	1.8114	2.4273	3.2434	4.3219	5.7435	7.6123	10.0627	13.2677	17.4494	22.8923	29.9599	50.9502	85.8499	143.3706	237.3763	807.7936
35	1.4166	1.9999	2.8139	3.9461	5.5160	7.6861	10.6766	14.7853	20.4140	28.1024	38.5749	52.7996	98.1002	180.3141	327.9973	590.6682	2465.2
40	1.4889	2.2080	3.2620	4.8010	7.0400	10.2857	14.9745	21.7245	31.4094	45.2593	65.0009	93.0510	188.8835	378.7212	750.3783	1469.8	7523.2
45	1.5648	2.4379	3.7816	5.8412	8.9850	13.7646	21.0025	31.9204	48.3273	72.8905	109.5302	163.9876	363.6791	795.4438	1716.7	3657.3	22958.9
50	1.6446	2.6916	4.3839	7.1067	11.4674	18.4202	29.4570	46.9016	74.3575	117.3909	184.5648	289.0022	700.2330	1670.7	3927.4	9100.4	70064.9
60	1.8167	3.2810	5.8916	10.5196	18.6792	32.9877	57.9464	101.2571	176.0313	304.4816	524.0572	897.5969	2595.9	7370.2	20555.1	56347.5	652530.4

Present Value of an Annuity of $1 Per Period for n Periods

$$PVIFA = \frac{1 - \left[\dfrac{1}{(1+k)^n}\right]}{k}$$

Period	1%	2%	3%	4%	5%	6%	7%	8%	9%	10%	11%	12%	14%	16%	18%	20%	25%
1	0.990	0.980	0.971	0.962	0.952	0.943	0.935	0.926	0.917	0.909	0.901	0.893	0.877	0.862	0.847	0.833	0.800
2	1.970	1.942	1.913	1.886	1.859	1.833	1.808	1.783	1.759	1.736	1.713	1.690	1.647	1.605	1.566	1.528	1.440
3	2.941	2.884	2.829	2.775	2.723	2.673	2.624	2.577	2.531	2.487	2.444	2.402	2.322	2.246	2.174	2.106	1.952
4	3.902	3.808	3.717	3.630	3.546	3.465	3.387	3.312	3.240	3.170	3.102	3.037	2.914	2.798	2.690	2.589	2.362
5	4.853	4.713	4.580	4.452	4.329	4.212	4.100	3.993	3.890	3.791	3.696	3.605	3.433	3.274	3.127	2.991	2.689
6	5.795	5.601	5.417	5.242	5.076	4.917	4.767	4.623	4.486	4.355	4.231	4.111	3.889	3.685	3.498	3.326	2.951
7	6.728	6.472	6.230	6.002	5.786	5.582	5.389	5.206	5.033	4.868	4.712	4.564	4.288	4.039	3.812	3.605	3.161
8	7.652	7.325	7.020	6.733	6.463	6.210	5.971	5.747	5.535	5.335	5.146	4.968	4.639	4.344	4.078	3.837	3.329
9	8.566	8.162	7.786	7.435	7.108	6.802	6.515	6.247	5.995	5.759	5.537	5.328	4.946	4.607	4.303	4.031	3.463
10	9.471	8.983	8.530	8.111	7.722	7.360	7.024	6.710	6.418	6.145	5.889	5.650	5.216	4.833	4.494	4.192	3.571
11	10.368	9.787	9.253	8.760	8.306	7.887	7.499	7.139	6.805	6.495	6.207	5.938	5.453	5.029	4.656	4.327	3.656
12	11.255	10.575	9.954	9.385	8.863	8.384	7.943	7.536	7.161	6.814	6.492	6.194	5.660	5.197	4.793	4.439	3.725
13	12.134	11.348	10.635	9.986	9.394	8.853	8.358	7.904	7.487	7.103	6.750	6.424	5.842	5.342	4.910	4.533	3.780
14	13.004	12.106	11.296	10.563	9.899	9.295	8.745	8.244	7.786	7.367	6.982	6.628	6.002	5.468	5.008	4.611	3.824
15	13.865	12.849	11.938	11.118	10.380	9.712	9.108	8.559	8.061	7.606	7.191	6.811	6.142	5.575	5.092	4.675	3.859
16	14.718	13.578	12.561	11.652	10.838	10.106	9.447	8.851	8.313	7.824	7.379	6.974	6.265	5.668	5.162	4.730	3.887
17	15.562	14.292	13.166	12.166	11.274	10.477	9.763	9.122	8.544	8.022	7.549	7.120	6.373	5.749	5.222	4.775	3.910
18	16.398	14.992	13.754	12.659	11.690	10.828	10.059	9.372	8.756	8.201	7.702	7.250	6.467	5.818	5.273	4.812	3.928
19	17.226	15.678	14.324	13.134	12.085	11.158	10.336	9.604	8.950	8.365	7.839	7.366	6.550	5.877	5.316	4.843	3.942
20	18.046	16.351	14.877	13.590	12.462	11.470	10.594	9.818	9.129	8.514	7.963	7.469	6.623	5.929	5.353	4.870	3.954
25	22.023	19.523	17.413	15.622	14.094	12.783	11.654	10.675	9.823	9.077	8.422	7.843	6.873	6.097	5.467	4.948	3.985
30	25.808	22.396	19.600	17.292	15.372	13.765	12.409	11.258	10.274	9.427	8.694	8.055	7.003	6.177	5.517	4.979	3.995
35	29.409	24.999	21.487	18.665	16.374	14.498	12.948	11.655	10.567	9.644	8.855	8.176	7.070	6.215	5.539	4.992	3.998
40	32.835	27.355	23.115	19.793	17.159	15.046	13.332	11.925	10.757	9.779	8.951	8.244	7.105	6.233	5.548	4.997	3.999
45	36.095	29.490	24.519	20.720	17.774	15.456	13.606	12.108	10.881	9.863	9.008	8.283	7.123	6.242	5.552	4.999	4.000
50	39.196	31.424	25.730	21.482	18.256	15.762	13.801	12.233	10.962	9.915	9.042	8.304	7.133	6.246	5.554	4.999	4.000
60	44.955	34.761	27.676	22.623	18.929	16.161	14.039	12.377	11.048	9.967	9.074	8.324	7.140	6.249	5.555	5.000	4.000

APPENDIX A4
Future Value of an Annuity of $1 Per Period for n Periods

$$FVIFA = \frac{[(1+k)^n - 1]}{k}$$

Period	1%	2%	3%	4%	5%	6%	7%	8%	9%	10%	11%	12%	14%	16%	18%	20%	25%
1	1.000	1.000	1.000	1.000	1.000	1.000	1.000	1.000	1.000	1.000	1.000	1.000	1.000	1.000	1.000	1.000	1.000
2	2.010	2.020	2.030	2.040	2.050	2.060	2.070	2.080	2.090	2.100	2.110	2.120	2.140	2.160	2.180	2.200	2.250
3	3.030	3.060	3.091	3.122	3.152	3.184	3.215	3.246	3.278	3.310	3.342	3.374	3.440	3.506	3.572	3.640	3.813
4	4.060	4.122	4.184	4.246	4.310	4.375	4.440	4.506	4.573	4.641	4.710	4.779	4.921	5.066	5.215	5.368	5.766
5	5.101	5.204	5.309	5.416	5.526	5.637	5.751	5.867	5.985	6.105	6.228	6.353	6.610	6.877	7.154	7.442	8.207
6	6.152	6.308	6.468	6.633	6.802	6.975	7.153	7.336	7.523	7.716	7.913	8.115	8.536	8.977	9.442	9.930	11.260
7	7.214	7.434	7.662	7.898	8.142	8.394	8.654	8.923	9.200	9.487	9.783	10.090	10.730	11.410	12.140	12.920	15.070
8	8.286	8.583	8.892	9.214	9.549	9.897	10.260	10.640	11.030	11.440	11.860	12.300	13.230	14.240	15.330	16.500	19.840
9	9.369	9.755	10.160	10.580	11.030	11.490	11.980	12.490	13.020	13.580	14.160	14.780	16.090	17.520	19.090	20.800	25.800
10	10.460	10.950	11.460	12.010	12.580	13.180	13.820	14.490	15.190	15.940	16.720	17.550	19.340	21.320	23.520	25.960	33.250
11	11.570	12.170	12.810	13.490	14.210	14.970	15.780	16.650	17.560	18.530	19.560	20.650	23.040	25.730	28.760	32.150	42.570
12	12.680	13.410	14.190	15.030	15.920	16.870	17.890	18.980	20.140	21.380	22.710	24.130	27.270	30.850	34.930	39.580	54.210
13	13.810	14.680	15.620	16.630	17.710	18.880	20.140	21.500	22.950	24.520	26.210	28.030	32.090	36.790	42.220	48.500	68.760
14	14.950	15.970	17.090	18.290	19.600	21.020	22.550	24.210	26.020	27.970	30.090	32.390	37.580	43.670	50.820	59.200	86.950
15	16.100	17.290	18.600	20.020	21.580	23.280	25.130	27.150	29.360	31.770	34.410	37.280	43.840	51.660	60.970	72.040	109.700
16	17.260	18.640	20.160	21.820	23.660	25.670	27.890	30.320	33.000	35.950	39.190	42.750	50.980	60.930	72.940	87.440	138.100
17	18.430	20.010	21.760	23.700	25.840	28.210	30.840	33.750	36.970	40.540	44.500	48.880	59.120	71.670	87.070	105.900	173.600
18	19.610	21.410	23.410	25.650	28.130	30.910	34.000	37.450	41.300	45.600	50.400	55.750	68.390	84.140	103.700	128.100	218.000
19	20.810	22.840	25.120	27.670	30.540	33.760	37.380	41.450	46.020	51.160	56.940	63.440	78.970	98.600	123.400	154.700	273.600
20	22.020	24.300	26.870	29.780	33.070	36.790	41.000	45.760	51.160	57.270	64.200	72.050	91.020	115.400	146.600	186.700	342.900
25	28.240	32.030	36.460	41.650	47.730	54.860	63.250	73.110	84.700	98.350	114.400	133.300	181.900	249.200	342.600	472.000	1055
30	34.780	40.570	47.580	56.080	66.440	79.060	94.460	113.300	136.300	164.500	199.000	241.300	356.800	530.300	790.900	1182	3227
35	41.660	49.990	60.460	73.650	90.320	111.400	138.200	172.300	215.700	271.000	341.600	431.700	693.600	1121	1817	2948	9857
40	48.890	60.400	75.400	95.030	120.800	154.800	199.600	259.100	337.900	442.600	581.800	767.100	1342	2361	4163	7344	30089
45	56.480	71.890	92.720	121.000	159.700	212.700	285.700	386.500	525.900	718.900	986.600	1358.2	2591	4965	9532	18281	91831
50	64.460	84.580	112.800	152.700	209.300	290.300	406.500	573.800	815.100	1164	1669	2400	4995	10436	21813	45497	280256
60	81.670	114.100	163.100	238.000	353.600	533.100	813.500	1253	1945	3035	4755	7472	18535	46058	114190	281733	2610118

APPENDIX B
Standard Mortality Tables

The tables provide the number of deaths expected during any year of life for a hypothetical cohort of 100,000 Canadians.

The first column, Age, is the starting age for the given year. Thus, the first line covers the year from birth to immediately before the first birthday.

The second column, Alive at Start of Year, shows how many of the cohort were alive at the start of the year of the age shown in column 1. For example, looking at Appendix B1 for Canadian females, we see that on their fifth birthday, 99,306 of the original cohort were expected to be living.

The third column, Deaths During Year, records the number of deaths expected to occur during the year starting on the birthday in Column 1. Thus, again looking at Appendix B1 for Canadian females in the year starting with their fifth birthday, we see that on average, 14 of the 99,306 alive on their fifth birthday are expected to die before their sixth birthday. The entry for Column 2, Alive at Start of Year, Age 6, is equal to Column 2 minus Column 3 from the previous line, Age 5.

Column 4, Probability of Survival, is calculated as (Column 2 − Column 3) ÷ Column 2, rounded to four decimal places. Thus, a five-year old girl has a .0001 (or 1/100%) probability of dying before her sixth birthday.

Column 5, Probability of Death, is calculated as Column 3 ÷ Column 2, rounded to four decimal places.

APPENDIX B1
Standard Mortality Table — Canadian Females

Age	Alive at Start of Year	Deaths During Year	Probability of Survival	Probability of Death
0	100000	577	0.9942	0.0058
1	99423	45	0.9995	0.0005
2	99378	30	0.9997	0.0003
3	99348	24	0.9998	0.0002
4	99324	18	0.9998	0.0002
5	99306	14	0.9999	0.0001
6	99292	13	0.9999	0.0001
7	99279	12	0.9999	0.0001
8	99267	11	0.9999	0.0001
9	99256	11	0.9999	0.0001
10	99245	13	0.9999	0.0001
11	99232	11	0.9999	0.0001
12	99221	16	0.9998	0.0002
13	99205	19	0.9998	0.0002
14	99186	23	0.9998	0.0002
15	99163	27	0.9997	0.0003
16	99136	32	0.9997	0.0003
17	99104	36	0.9996	0.0004
18	99068	36	0.9996	0.0004
19	99032	36	0.9996	0.0004
20	98996	36	0.9996	0.0004
21	98960	36	0.9996	0.0004
22	98924	36	0.9996	0.0004
23	98888	36	0.9996	0.0004
24	98852	38	0.9996	0.0004
25	98814	38	0.9996	0.0004
26	98776	40	0.9996	0.0004
27	98736	41	0.9996	0.0004
28	98695	42	0.9996	0.0004
29	98653	45	0.9995	0.0005
30	98608	46	0.9995	0.0005
31	98562	48	0.9995	0.0005
32	98514	53	0.9995	0.0005
33	98461	56	0.9994	0.0006
34	98405	61	0.9994	0.0006
35	98344	67	0.9993	0.0007
36	98277	73	0.9993	0.0007
37	98204	79	0.9992	0.0008
38	98125	85	0.9991	0.0009
39	98040	91	0.9991	0.0009
40	97949	98	0.9990	0.0010
41	97851	105	0.9989	0.0011
42	97746	116	0.9988	0.0012
43	97630	129	0.9987	0.0013
44	97501	145	0.9985	0.0015
45	97356	161	0.9983	0.0017
46	97195	180	0.9981	0.0019
47	97015	200	0.9979	0.0021
48	96815	219	0.9977	0.0023
49	96596	240	0.9975	0.0025
50	96356	263	0.9973	0.0027
51	96093	286	0.9970	0.0030
52	95807	315	0.9967	0.0033
53	95492	344	0.9964	0.0036

APPENDIX B1
Standard Mortality Table — Canadian Females (continued)

Age	Alive at Start of Year	Deaths During Year	Probability of Survival	Probability of Death
54	95148	375	0.9961	0.0039
55	94773	410	0.9957	0.0043
56	94363	447	0.9953	0.0047
57	93916	488	0.9948	0.0052
58	93428	532	0.9943	0.0057
59	92896	578	0.9938	0.0062
60	92318	627	0.9932	0.0068
61	91691	681	0.9926	0.0074
62	91010	740	0.9919	0.0081
63	90270	804	0.9911	0.0089
64	89466	870	0.9903	0.0097
65	88596	940	0.9894	0.0106
66	87656	1019	0.9884	0.0116
67	86637	1106	0.9872	0.0128
68	85531	1197	0.9860	0.0140
69	84334	1289	0.9847	0.0153
70	83045	1391	0.9833	0.0167
71	81654	1504	0.9816	0.0184
72	80150	1635	0.9796	0.0204
73	78515	1778	0.9774	0.0226
74	76737	1924	0.9749	0.0251
75	74813	2079	0.9722	0.0278
76	72734	2247	0.9691	0.0309
77	70487	2428	0.9656	0.0344
78	68059	2613	0.9616	0.0384
79	65446	2791	0.9574	0.0426
80	62655	2967	0.9526	0.0474
81	59688	3142	0.9474	0.0526
82	56546	3317	0.9413	0.0587
83	53229	3475	0.9347	0.0653
84	49754	3605	0.9275	0.0725
85	46149	3706	0.9197	0.0803
86	42443	3775	0.9111	0.0889
87	38668	3810	0.9015	0.0985
88	34858	3798	0.8910	0.1090
89	31060	3732	0.8798	0.1202
90	27328	3613	0.8678	0.1322
91	23715	3447	0.8546	0.1454
92	20268	3235	0.8404	0.1596
93	17033	2980	0.8250	0.1750
94	14053	2688	0.8087	0.1913
95	11365	2372	0.7913	0.2087
96	8993	2044	0.7727	0.2273
97	6949	1720	0.7525	0.2475
98	5229	1405	0.7313	0.2687
99	3824	1114	0.7087	0.2913
100	2710	854	0.6849	0.3151
101	1856	632	0.6595	0.3405
102	1224	450	0.6324	0.3676
103	774	306	0.6047	0.3953
104	468	200	0.5726	0.4274
105	268	122	0.5448	0.4552
106	146	146	0.0000	1.0000

APPENDIX B2
Standard Mortality Table — Canadian Males

Age	Alive at Start of Year	Deaths During Year	Probability of Survival	Probability of Death
0	100000	709	0.9929	0.0071
1	99291	51	0.9995	0.0005
2	99240	41	0.9996	0.0004
3	99199	34	0.9997	0.0003
4	99165	25	0.9997	0.0003
5	99140	19	0.9998	0.0002
6	99121	16	0.9998	0.0002
7	99105	15	0.9998	0.0002
8	99090	13	0.9999	0.0001
9	99077	13	0.9999	0.0001
10	99064	14	0.9999	0.0001
11	99050	16	0.9998	0.0002
12	99034	23	0.9998	0.0002
13	99011	33	0.9997	0.0003
14	98978	48	0.9995	0.0005
15	98930	64	0.9994	0.0006
16	98866	79	0.9992	0.0008
17	98787	90	0.9991	0.0009
18	98697	98	0.9990	0.0010
19	98599	103	0.9990	0.0010
20	98496	107	0.9989	0.0011
21	98389	110	0.9989	0.0011
22	98279	112	0.9989	0.0011
23	98167	113	0.9988	0.0012
24	98054	113	0.9988	0.0012
25	97941	112	0.9989	0.0011
26	97829	111	0.9989	0.0011
27	97718	112	0.9989	0.0011
28	97606	113	0.9988	0.0012
29	97493	116	0.9988	0.0012
30	97377	120	0.9988	0.0012
31	97257	122	0.9987	0.0013
32	97135	128	0.9987	0.0013
33	97007	132	0.9986	0.0014
34	96875	138	0.9986	0.0014
35	96737	144	0.9985	0.0015
36	96593	151	0.9984	0.0016
37	96442	158	0.9984	0.0016
38	96284	165	0.9983	0.0017
39	96119	171	0.9982	0.0018
40	95948	178	0.9981	0.0019
41	95770	187	0.9980	0.0020
42	95583	201	0.9979	0.0021
43	95382	218	0.9977	0.0023
44	95164	239	0.9975	0.0025
45	94925	262	0.9972	0.0028
46	94663	288	0.9970	0.0030
47	94375	318	0.9966	0.0034
48	94057	349	0.9963	0.0037
49	93708	383	0.9959	0.0041
50	93325	419	0.9955	0.0045
51	92906	461	0.9950	0.0050
52	92445	509	0.9945	0.0055
53	91936	562	0.9939	0.0061

APPENDIX B2
Standard Mortality Table — Canadian Males (continued)

Age	Alive at Start of Year	Deaths During Year	Probability of Survival	Probability of Death
54	91374	619	0.9932	0.0068
55	90755	683	0.9925	0.0075
56	90072	751	0.9917	0.0083
57	89321	830	0.9907	0.0093
58	88491	915	0.9897	0.0103
59	87576	1007	0.9885	0.0115
60	86569	1104	0.9872	0.0128
61	85465	1206	0.9859	0.0141
62	84259	1311	0.9844	0.0156
63	82948	1418	0.9829	0.0171
64	81530	1523	0.9813	0.0187
65	80007	1632	0.9796	0.0204
66	78375	1748	0.9777	0.0223
67	76627	1873	0.9756	0.0244
68	74754	2002	0.9732	0.0268
69	72752	2129	0.9707	0.0293
70	70623	2259	0.9680	0.0320
71	68364	2395	0.9650	0.0350
72	65969	2535	0.9616	0.0384
73	63434	2676	0.9578	0.0422
74	60758	2807	0.9538	0.0462
75	57951	2931	0.9494	0.0506
76	55020	3049	0.9446	0.0554
77	51971	3160	0.9392	0.0608
78	48811	3256	0.9333	0.0667
79	45555	3328	0.9269	0.0731
80	42227	3374	0.9201	0.0799
81	38853	3393	0.9127	0.0873
82	35460	3381	0.9047	0.0953
83	32079	3334	0.8961	0.1039
84	28745	3251	0.8869	0.1131
85	25494	3131	0.8772	0.1228
86	22363	2979	0.8668	0.1332
87	19384	2796	0.8558	0.1442
88	16588	2588	0.8440	0.1560
89	14000	2358	0.8316	0.1684
90	11642	2112	0.8186	0.1814
91	9530	1861	0.8047	0.1953
92	7669	1609	0.7902	0.2098
93	6060	1364	0.7749	0.2251
94	4696	1133	0.7587	0.2413
95	3563	919	0.7421	0.2579
96	2644	729	0.7243	0.2757
97	1915	563	0.7060	0.2940
98	1352	424	0.6864	0.3136
99	928	310	0.6659	0.3341
100	618	219	0.6456	0.3544
101	399	150	0.6241	0.3759
102	249	100	0.5984	0.4016
103	149	63	0.5772	0.4228
104	86	39	0.5465	0.4535
105	47	22	0.5319	0.4681
106	25	25	0.0000	1.0000

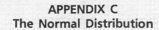

APPENDIX C
The Normal Distribution

$$Z = \frac{X - \mu}{\sigma} \quad \text{(standardized normal)}$$

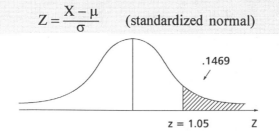

.1469

z = 1.05   Z

z	.00	.01	.02	.03	.04	.05	.06	.07	.08	.09
0.0	.5000	.4960	.4920	.4880	.4840	.4801	.4761	.4721	.4681	.4641
0.1	.4602	.4562	.4522	.4483	.4443	.4404	.4364	.4325	.4286	.4247
0.2	.4207	.4168	.4129	.4090	.4052	.4013	.3974	.3936	.3897	.3859
0.3	.3821	.3783	.3745	.3707	.3669	.3632	.3594	.3557	.3520	.3483
0.4	.3446	.3409	.3372	.3336	.3300	.3264	.3228	.3192	.3156	.3121
0.5	.3085	.3050	.3015	.2981	.2946	.2912	.2877	.2843	.2810	.2776
0.6	.2743	.2709	.2676	.2643	.2611	.2578	.2546	.2514	.2483	.2451
0.7	.2420	.2389	.2358	.2327	.2296	.2266	.2236	.2206	.2177	.2148
0.8	.2119	.2090	.2061	.2033	.2005	.1977	.1949	.1922	.1894	.1867
0.9	.1841	.1814	.1788	.1762	.1736	.1711	.1685	.1660	.1635	.1611
1.0	.1587	.1562	.1539	.1515	.1492	.1469	.1446	.1423	.1401	.1379
1.1	.1357	.1335	.1314	.1292	.1271	.1251	.1230	.1210	.1190	.1170
1.2	.1151	.1131	.1112	.1093	.1075	.1056	.1038	.1020	.1003	.0985
1.3	.0968	.0951	.0934	.0918	.0901	.0885	.0869	.0853	.0838	.0823
1.4	.0808	.0793	.0778	.0764	.0749	.0735	.0721	.0708	.0694	.0681
1.5	.0668	.0655	.0643	.0630	.0618	.0606	.0594	.0582	.0571	.0559
1.6	.0548	.0537	.0526	.0516	.0505	.0495	.0485	.0475	.0465	.0455
1.7	.0446	.0436	.0427	.0418	.0409	.0401	.0392	.0384	.0375	.0367
1.8	.0359	.0351	.0344	.0336	.0329	.0322	.0314	.0307	.0301	.0294
1.9	.0287	.0281	.0274	.0268	.0262	.0256	.0250	.0244	.0239	.0233
2.0	.0228	.0222	.0217	.0212	.0207	.0202	.0197	.0192	.0188	.0183
2.1	.0179	.0174	.0170	.0166	.0162	.0158	.0154	.0150	.0146	.0143
2.2	.0139	.0136	.0132	.0129	.0125	.0122	.0119	.0116	.0113	.0110
2.3	.0107	.0104	.0102	.0099	.0096	.0094	.0091	.0089	.0087	.0084
2.4	.0082	.0080	.0078	.0075	.0073	.0071	.0069	.0068	.0066	.0064
2.5	.0062	.0060	.0059	.0057	.0055	.0054	.0052	.0051	.0049	.0048
2.6	.0047	.0045	.0044	.0043	.0041	.0040	.0039	.0038	.0037	.0036
2.7	.0035	.0034	.0033	.0032	.0031	.0030	.0029	.0028	.0027	.0026
2.8	.0026	.0025	.0024	.0023	.0023	.0022	.0021	.0021	.0020	.0019
2.9	.0019	.0018	.0018	.0017	.0016	.0016	.0015	.0015	.0014	.0014
3.0	.0013	.0013	.0013	.0012	.0012	.0011	.0011	.0011	.0010	.0010

Note: The table plots the cumulative probability Z ≥ z.

APPENDIX D
Nominal Returns of Asset Classes, 1950–95 (in %)

Year	CPI	T-Bill	Bonds	TSE	S&P	World	OilGold
1950	2.93	0.55	1.74	27.91	24.06		
1951	10.55	0.79	−7.89	25.50	17.71		
1952	2.42	1.06	5.01	1.17	7.25		
1953	−0.89	1.71	5.00	−8.28	0.57		
1954	0.60	1.43	12.23	43.61	49.49		
1955	0.15	1.62	0.13	24.11	29.37		
1956	1.48	2.92	−8.87	8.81	4.16		
1957	3.21	3.76	7.94	−20.64	−8.97		
1958	2.69	2.25	1.92	30.67	42.91		
1959	1.10	4.81	−5.07	2.28	11.51		
1960	1.23	3.20	12.19	1.49	4.17		
1961	0.09	2.81	9.16	34.09	35.25		
1962	1.20	4.05	9.03	−7.56	−7.08		
1963	1.71	3.56	4.58	14.18	21.80		
1964	1.81	3.75	6.16	24.69	15.88		
1965	2.42	3.98	0.05	5.75	14.19		
1966	3.73	4.99	−1.05	−5.24	−8.23		
1967	3.59	4.64	−9.48	20.29	26.48		
1968	4.05	6.27	2.14	23.55	12.01		
1969	4.56	7.19	−2.86	−1.32	−9.72		
1970	3.29	5.99	15.39	−2.65	−4.07	−1.92	
1971	2.88	3.56	14.84	11.27	13.79	18.93	
1972	4.80	3.56	8.11	30.16	17.34	23.11	
1973	7.54	5.47	1.97	−3.72	−16.67	−14.64	
1974	10.91	7.82	−4.53	−27.02	−27.58	−23.94	
1975	10.80	7.40	8.02	22.18	41.24	35.87	
1976	4.93	8.87	23.64	11.72	26.86	14.26	
1977	7.48	7.33	9.04	15.45	2.48	2.16	
1978	10.14	8.69	4.10	29.36	15.41	19.55	20.79
1979	10.47	11.69	−2.83	50.56	20.86	13.00	96.14
1980	11.44	12.79	2.18	28.05	35.76	27.67	48.84
1981	13.20	17.72	−2.09	−10.89	−5.12	−3.39	−25.72
1982	9.33	13.63	45.82	4.07	26.48	11.60	11.27
1983	5.45	9.31	9.61	36.04	23.99	23.24	16.03
1984	4.72	11.06	16.90	0.37	12.01	6.07	−20.64
1985	3.86	9.43	26.68	24.79	38.69	44.06	31.59
1986	3.31	8.97	17.21	12.19	15.58	43.52	8.90
1987	4.10	8.15	1.78	−0.28	−4.27	16.00	26.03
1988	3.55	9.48	11.30	11.10	−2.63	22.24	−7.35
1989	4.36	12.05	15.70	21.40	27.66	16.54	30.39
1990	4.00	12.81	4.32	−15.00	−6.10	−16.28	−14.43
1991	5.60	8.76	25.30	12.00	20.57	18.63	−15.13
1992	1.90	6.50	11.60	−1.43	10.15	−4.92	6.64
1993	1.80	5.50	18.10	32.60	20.38	24.68	68.50
1994	−0.10	5.30	−4.30	−0.20	1.30	5.91	−5.50
1995	2.10	7.57	20.67	14.50	37.60	21.41	9.40
Geometric Mean	4.30	6.34	6.91	10.68	12.25	13.21	13.37
Arithmetic Mean	4.36	6.41	7.40	11.99	13.58	16.74	16.98
Standard Dev.	3.52	3.89	10.65	17.10	17.25	11.90	30.23

CPI   Change in Canadian Consumer Price Index
T-Bill   Government of Canada 91 day Treasury Bills
Bonds   Scotia McLeod Bond Index (long-term Government of Canada Bonds)
TSE 300   Toronto Stock Exchange 300 Index — Canadian equity
S&P   Standard and Poor's Index of 500 shares — US equity — in Canadian $
World Morgan and Stanley World Index — International equity — in Canadian $
OilGold   50% TSE Oil Subindex + 50% TSE Gold Subindex

Source of annual returns: PlanPlus Inc.

APPENDIX E
Real Returns of Asset Classes, 1950–95 (%)

Year	T-Bill	Bonds	TSE	S&P	World	OilGold
1950	−2.31	−1.16	24.27	20.53		
1951	−8.83	−16.68	13.52	6.48		
1952	−1.33	2.53	−1.22	4.72		
1953	2.62	5.94	−7.46	1.47		
1954	0.83	11.56	42.75	48.60		
1955	1.47	−0.02	23.92	29.18		
1956	1.42	−10.20	7.22	2.64		
1957	0.53	4.58	−23.11	−11.80		
1958	−0.43	−0.75	27.25	39.17		
1959	3.67	−6.10	1.17	10.30		
1960	1.95	10.83	0.26	2.90		
1961	2.72	9.06	33.97	35.13		
1962	2.82	7.74	−8.66	−8.18		
1963	1.82	2.82	12.26	19.75		
1964	1.91	4.27	22.47	13.82		
1965	1.52	−2.31	3.25	11.49		
1966	1.21	−4.61	−8.65	−11.53		
1967	1.01	−12.62	16.12	22.10		
1968	2.13	−1.84	18.74	7.65		
1969	2.52	−7.10	−5.62	−13.66		
1970	2.61	11.71	−5.75	−7.13	−5.05	
1971	0.66	11.63	8.16	10.60	15.60	
1972	−1.18	3.16	24.20	11.97	17.47	
1973	−1.92	−5.18	−10.47	−22.51	−20.62	
1974	−2.79	−13.92	−34.20	−34.70	−31.42	
1975	−3.07	−2.51	10.27	27.47	22.63	
1976	3.75	17.83	6.47	20.90	8.89	
1977	−0.14	1.45	7.42	−4.65	−4.95	
1978	−1.32	−5.48	17.45	4.78	8.55	9.67
1979	1.10	−12.04	36.29	9.41	2.29	77.55
1980	1.21	−8.31	14.90	21.82	14.57	33.56
1981	3.99	−13.51	−21.28	−16.18	−14.66	−34.38
1982	3.93	33.38	−4.81	15.69	2.08	1.77
1983	3.66	3.94	29.01	17.58	16.87	10.03
1984	6.05	11.63	−4.15	6.96	1.29	−24.22
1985	5.36	21.97	20.15	33.54	38.71	26.70
1986	5.48	13.45	8.60	11.88	38.92	5.41
1987	3.89	−2.23	−4.21	−8.04	11.43	21.07
1988	5.73	7.48	7.29	−5.97	18.04	−10.53
1989	7.37	10.87	16.33	22.33	11.67	24.94
1990	8.47	0.31	−18.27	−9.71	−19.50	−17.72
1991	2.99	18.66	6.06	14.18	12.33	−19.63
1992	4.51	9.52	−3.27	8.10	−6.69	4.65
1993	3.63	16.01	30.26	18.25	22.47	65.52
1994	5.41	−4.20	−0.10	1.40	6.02	−5.41
1995	5.36	18.19	12.14	34.77	18.91	7.15
Geometric Mean	1.95	2.50	6.12	7.62	7.15	7.07
Arithmetic Mean	2.00	3.04	7.41	8.99	16.58	10.47
Standard Dev.	3.10	10.67	16.50	17.07	5.78	28.06

$$real\ return = \frac{(1 + nominal\ return)}{(1 + CPI)} - 1$$

T-Bill	Government of Canada 91 day Treasury Bills
Bonds	Scotia McLeod Bond Index (long-term Government of Canada Bonds)
TSE 300	Toronto Stock Exchange 300 Index — Canadian equity
S&P	Standard and Poor's Index of 500 shares — US equity — in Canadian $
World	Morgan and Stanley World Index — International equity — in Canadian $
OilGold	50% TSE Oil Subindex + 50% TSE Gold Subindex

Source of nominal annual returns: PlanPlus Inc.

Index

ABOUT THE AUTHORS

KWOK HO is Associate Professor of Finance, Department of Administrative Studies, Atkinson College, York University. He teaches personal and corporate finance. He received his Ph.D. in finance at the University of Toronto in 1982, and his Certified Management Accountant designation in 1985. Prior to his academic career, he gained extensive business experience in Hong Kong, China, Japan and Canada. His current research interests include personal finance, dividend policy and capital structure.

CHRIS ROBINSON is Associate Professor, Schulich School of Business, York University, where he teaches personal finance, financial statement analysis, corporate finance and environmental management. He articled with Thorne Riddell in Toronto and received his Chartered Accountant designation in 1977. He received his Ph.D. in finance at the University of Toronto in 1985. During the 1980s he was a Contributing Editor of *The Financial Post*, and he wrote many articles for publication in Canada and internationally. His current research interests include personal finance, alternative and critical perspectives on finance and accounting, environmental management, deep ecology and corporate governance.

The authors have worked with MOSHE ARYE MILEVSKY, Assistant Professor of finance, Schulich School of Business, York University, to develop more rigorous models of personal financial planning. Their personal finance papers have won awards in 1993, 1994 and 1995 at the Academy of Financial Services conferences, and have appeared in *Financial Services Review*, *Review of Quantitative Finance and Accounting*, *Canadian Investment Review* and *Canadian Shareowner*. Their models of probabilistic financial planning form the basis for Chapter 19, which develops for the first time a sound basis for assessing the probability of success or failure of a financial plan, including how to allocate investment assets to avoid shortfall.